[*Bassano.*

EARL HAIG.

THE K.O.S.B. IN THE GREAT WAR

BY

CAPTAIN STAIR GILLON

(LATE KING'S OWN SCOTTISH BORDERERS)

WITH ILLUSTRATIONS

THOMAS NELSON AND SONS, LIMITED

LONDON, EDINBURGH, NEW YORK, TORONTO, AND PARIS

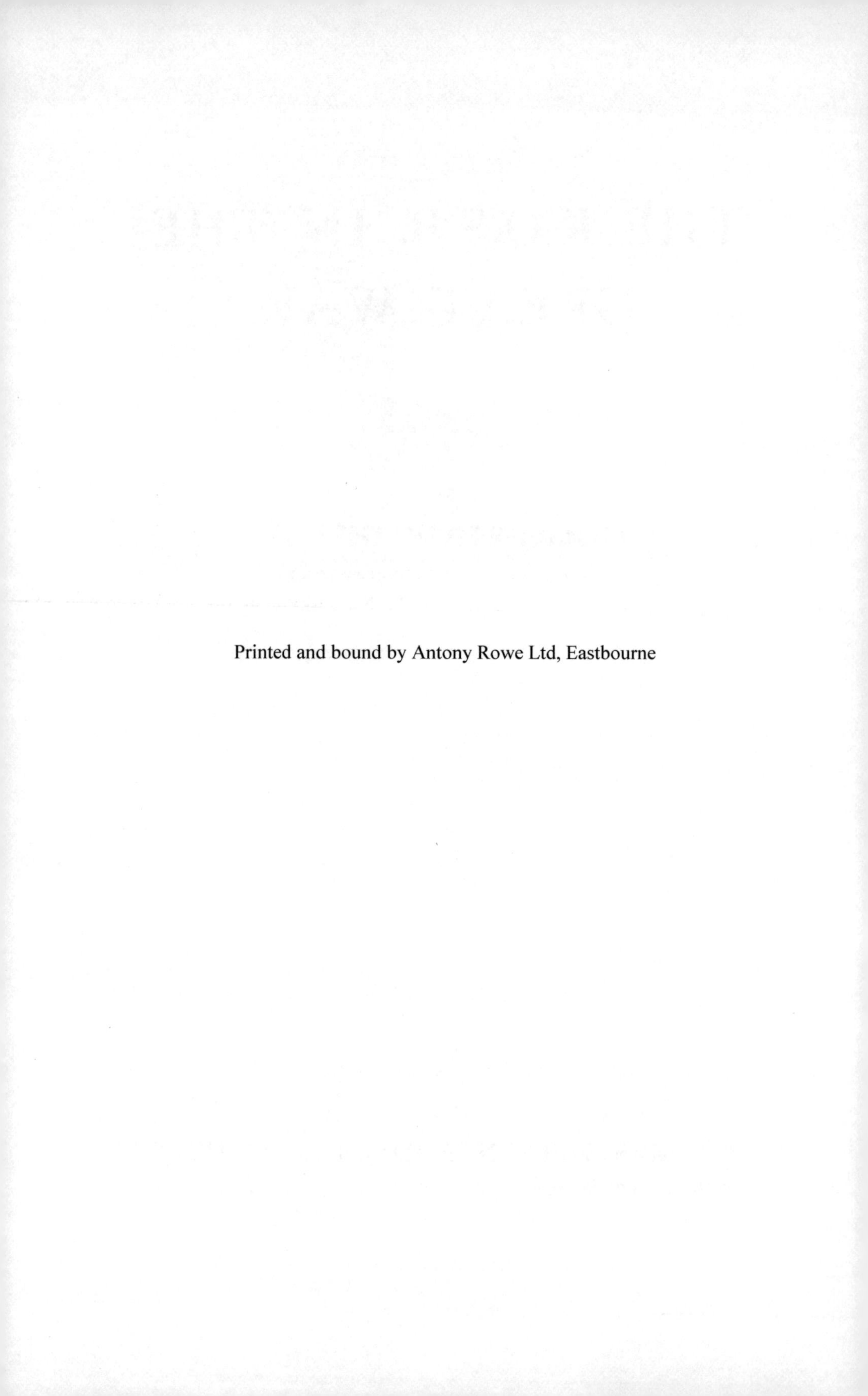

Printed and bound by Antony Rowe Ltd, Eastbourne

DEDICATION

DEDICATED TO THE MEMORY OF THOSE GALLANT MEN OF ALL RANKS BELONGING TO OR SERVING IN THE KING'S OWN SCOTTISH BORDERERS IN THE GREAT WAR WHO, ANIMATED BY THE SPIRIT OF DUTY AND DEVOTION, GAVE THEIR LIVES FOR THEIR COUNTRY

"Their name liveth for evermore"

PREFACE

MANY unforeseen difficulties have delayed the production of the War History of the King's Own Scottish Borderers, but there is the less reason to regret the delay as we read the very moving histories of the various battalions which Captain Stair Gillon has compiled, and can appreciate our good fortune in having secured the services of such a competent author.

It has been the privilege of the Committee to see the typed proofs of these histories, and they feel sure that every reader will experience the absorbing interest that they have felt in the vivid accounts which the author has written of the stirring events and the gallant actions of units and individuals.

At the close of the War the Colonel of the Regiment, Lieut.-General Sir Charles Woollcombe, endeavoured to make a beginning, but owing to various circumstances nothing could be done at that time, and he told his successor in the colonelcy, Field-Marshal Earl Haig, that nothing had as yet been done. The Field-Marshal was insistent that the War History of the Regiment should be undertaken without delay, and efforts were made by him and by Brig.-General Arthur Blair to find a suitable author. Again many hindrances were encountered, but eventually the Association of Lowland Scots offered to take the History in hand, and began the work of collecting the necessary material.

Once more financial and other difficulties intervened, and finally a committee of the Regimental Association was formed, the services of Captain Stair Gillon as author were secured, and adequate financial arrangements were made. The Association of Lowland Scots handed over the mass of material which they had collected, and the History, which is now before us, was begun.

The author's arrangement of the work will no doubt commend itself to the reader: a brief but interesting account of the early history of the Regiment in an introductory chapter leads to the consecutive history of each battalion in the order in which they entered into the Great War; and Captain Stair Gillon is to be congratulated on the success with which he has completed his task.

The Committee are greatly indebted to the Association of Lowland Scots for the generous support which they have given throughout, and for the collection of the material necessary for the compilation of the History.

The Committee also wish to thank all those, too numerous to mention individually, who have assisted by suggestions and advice, and by the loan of diaries, maps, letters, and other material.

D. A. MACFARLANE, *Brigadier-General,*
Chairman Regimental History Committee.

May 1930.

INTRODUCTION

ONLY those who have faced the task know how difficult it is to write a regimental history. To satisfy everybody is impossible, for while some are hoping to find facts recorded and vouched, which would save original research, others are looking for mention of relatives or even of themselves; some appreciate illustrations, others a terse narrative either in military terms or in popular phraseology; some revel in detail, and would rather suffer three volumes than chafe at omissions; others, again, desire a compact book at a moderate price, giving the essentials of truth, clarity, and regimental spirit.

So far as the writer is concerned the task is definitely set him, and his difficulties and responsibilities lie in the manner in which that task is carried out. The task is to compress the war story of The King's Own Scottish Borderers into one volume.

In some respects the K.O.S.B. story is not so difficult to tell as others. The battalions do not invade the teens and twenties. The principal theatre of war is the Western. In the East we shall be concerned only with the Gallipoli tragedy and the Egypt-Sinai-Palestine campaigns. There will be a little about the home front, but nothing about India or Macedonia, Africa, Russia, or Mesopotamia. Borderers were distinguishing themselves in all relevant parts of the globe, but the fighting battalions, the 1st and 2nd, 4th and 5th (Territorials), the 6th, 7th, and 8th (Service) Battalions, and the short-lived 10th Battalion, were confined to the areas given above.

In the next place, the units stuck very faithfully to the commands in which they started the war. The 1st Battalion joined and never left the 87th Brigade of the 29th Division. The 2nd Battalion at the outbreak of war was in the 13th Brigade of the 5th Division, and with a brother unit, the 1st Battalion the Royal West Kent Regiment, served throughout the whole war in the same brigade and division. The 4th and 5th Battalions were not separated till the end of June 1918, on the introduction of the three-battalion system for brigades. In the 155th Brigade of the 52nd (Lowland) Division they bore the sorrows of the 12th July 1915 and "second Gaza" in April 1917, and shared in the eventual capture of Gaza in November of that year, finishing with a brilliant crossing of the river Auja in December and in the advance on the Holy City. The 6th Battalion was a typical "Jock" unit of "K1," being in the 28th or 27th Brigade of the 9th (Scottish) Division from embodiment in 1914 till the crossing of the Rhine on Friday, 13th December 1918. The 7th and 8th—so soon to be, perforce, amalgamated—never leave the 15th (Scottish) Division. In result, the framework of the regimental war story consists in the doings of the 5th, 9th, 15th, 29th, 34th, and 52nd Divisions, all of which have printed histories. Moreover, there exist already in print histories of the 3rd, 4th, 5th, and 7/8th Battalions of great interest and merit in their various ways, and quarries of information for the regimental historian. And then there are the war diaries of the eight overseas battalions, the official records of Audit House and Isleworth, the private diaries, letters, notes, maps, and drawings placed at the editor's disposal, newspaper cuttings—*et id genus omne.*

But all of these advantages only make the task more anxious. With competent editing and adequate research and a sense of proportion the material should be capable of being moulded into some sort of representation of the Borderers' prowess and *esprit de corps.*

It is for this reason that a *résumé* of the earlier history of the regiment has been considered essential. An Englishman and a Scotsman may preserve their national characteristics and diversities to the grave. But put them together in the K.O.S.B. for a spell —and it doesn't take long—and both develop a second characteristic to be shared in common, namely, that of being Borderers. In that capacity the best of their fighting and enduring qualities are brought out and developed. The spirit is one very difficult to define. It is distinctly but unaggressively Scottish, and distinctly and possibly a little more unmistakably military. In short, it is just the child of the British Army, but a child with a very definite personality, which passes on from generation to generation and is absorbed by drafts and recruits with surprising rapidity.

I have tried in the text to express my gratitude to previous labourers in the field. The full and acknowledged use made of such books as the divisional histories mentioned above is in itself the best proof of that. Without the four volumes of the official history for the Western Front with their wonderful maps, appendices, and indices, the story from the concentration down to and including the battle of Loos would have entailed vastly greater labour and anxiety regarding accuracy. I may here append my thanks to Gen. Edmunds and his staff for the uniformly friendly reception and ready help invariably extended at Audit House. To Mr. E. A. Dixon I am specially indebted. Without the freshness and personal touches of Maj.-Gen. Lord E. Gleichen's *Doings of the 15th Infantry Brigade* and of Capt. R. V. Dolbey's *A Regimental Surgeon in War and Prison*, the narrative of the retreat from Mons and the arrival in Flanders would never have shaped itself in the form in which, rightly or wrongly, it is depicted. Without the stories of kindred regiments like the Royal West Kents (" Invicta "), the Royal Scots Fusiliers, and the H.L.I. many sidelights would have been missed. The three battalion histories of the Scottish Borderers in the war—the 4th, 5th, and 7/8th—place me under a very special debt of gratitude. They could not absolve from the duty of probing as many of the same sources as were available, but they afforded a running commentary and almost invariably a clear pointer. Capt. G. Scott Elliot kindly gave me permission to make the fullest use of his War History of the 5th Battalion, so I just assumed the same favour from the other authors.

Apart from footnotes and references to and citations from books, etc., I desire to express my thanks to the following: First and foremost to Major J. K. B. Campbell, who succeeded the helpful and energetic Major Crake just as the book was shaping into form, and has taken unwearying trouble in enabling author and regimental committee to collaborate and in regard to publication; to Lt.-Col. A. J. Welch, Lt.-Col. W. T. Wilkinson, Capt. C. S. Stirling-Cookson, Capt. Agar, and Capt. D. C. Bullen-Smith in connection with the 1st Battalion; to Brig.-Gen. Coke, Lt.-Col. Connell, Lt.-Col. A. E. D. Anderson, Major Furber, Major Pennyman (whose Diary was invaluable), Major G. W. Smith, and Sir Hew Hamilton-Dalrymple of North Berwick for lending his brother's short but vivid jottings of 1914, in connection with the 2nd Battalion; to Lt.-Col. Ker, Major Keith, Capt. Hobbs, and Lieut. Staple in connection with the 6th Battalion; and to Capt. Newbigging, who was kind enough to read the part relating to the 7/8th Battalion. To my friend Mr. A. L. Cordiner I am under a special debt of gratitude for revising the whole of the page proofs. The fact that the Committee have read the proofs and given much valued help does not detract from the author's responsibility for any inaccuracies: I merely desire to record my gratitude.

Among the material submitted originally to that pattern of war historians—Major John Ewing—there was much of the highest value to the story. I have profited thus by the zeal and energy, particularly, of Col. P. A. V. Stewart, Col. A. E. Haig (one of the Committee), Capt. R. Joynson, Capt. James Oliphant of New Zealand, Mrs. L. F. Machin (especially in connection with Y Beach), Mrs. Gillespie, who lent her son's valuable Diary, and Lt.-Col. W. D. Young-Herries, who lent a typescript of his son's letters home, covering a period from the Aisne to the Somme, of which good use has been made. To others who by sending short accounts of actions or by lending maps or official reports helped on the good work, I owe my best thanks. Many references will be found to the Diary of Capt. A. M. Shaw in the Gallipoli story. That Diary, the gift of his brother, is a treasured possession of the regiment, and is preserved at the depot. Finally, I owe a hearty vote of thanks to Mr. A. Maitland Smith, C.A., of the Scottish Lowland Association for acting as an ideal intermediary between author and War Office, and passing on the War Diaries and other material for the book.

The question of arrangement has given me anxious thought. The readability of Major-General Wauchope's *History of the Black Watch* in the end convinced me that each battalion's tale must be told right through, and that the chronological method must be discarded.

If the war were treated, as Colonel Buchan has done in his thrilling *Scots Fusiliers*, as only one of many campaigns, one could slip from scene to scene under the spell of the march of the narrative. But where more detail is the aim for a war history, it makes very restless reading to leap from unit to unit just as interest is being roused in the one left—though, no doubt, " to be continued in our next."

In the interests of compression it has been necessary to resort to a sort of shorthand : " K.O.S.B." is the most frequent example, and has the sanction of long usage. " G.O.C." and " C.O." are also common, but I have ventured to add the simple and unadorned letters A, B, C, and D for the various companies where the context shows that a company is referred to. A brigadier-general is " B.G.," and his command is the " 10th I.B." (*i.e.* infantry brigade). Arabic figures are used for units up to and including divisions. Army corps are numbered with Roman figures, *e.g.* " VIII." Corps, and armies have the numbers written in words thus, " Fourth Army." All of these abbreviations are used without inverted commas.

S. A. G.

CONTENTS

BOOK III—THE TERRITORIAL BATTALIONS, 1915-18

BOOK IV—THE SIXTH BATTALION

BOOK V—THE SEVENTH AND EIGHTH BATTALIONS AND THE SEVENTH/EIGHTH BATTALION

BOOK VI—" THEY ALSO SERVED "

LIST OF ILLUSTRATIONS

Note.—Those marked with * are Imperial War Museum Photographs, of which the Copyright is reserved.

MAPS

I HAVE thought it best not to attempt to delineate the elaborate trench systems that grew up in all theatres. The student will soon have complete official maps available. For the purpose of the ordinary reader it has been thought sufficient to have in a pocket at the end of the book a general map and certain sectional maps of the Western Front, as well as one each for the Gallipoli and Sinai-Palestine campaigns. The endeavour has been to include as many places as possible out of those mentioned in the text, including the rest areas and lines of advance and retreat. Major John Bartholomew's interest and help have been invaluable. The tactical sketches will, it is hoped, clear up the various engagements outlined. As I drew them they would have been uninviting and unintelligible, but, thanks to my wife, I put them forward as conveying my meaning for what it is worth.

S. A. G.

THE K.O.S.B. IN THE GREAT WAR

INTRODUCTORY CHAPTER

THE King's Own Scottish Borderers did not fight their first fight on the 23rd August 1914. However much we may yearn and strive for the abolition of war, few of us can believe that the regiment closed its fighting career with the Armistice on 11th November, 1918. It is one of the institutions of our land, and those who served in it in the Great War were the inheritors of long and honourable traditions whether they were conscious or unconscious of the fact. Without the key of history the spirit of the regiment would only partially be understood if a plunge were made into the story of the great and latest war. This is the more true because the name " Scottish Borderers " and the existing and let us hope permanent association of the regiment with the south of Scotland are apt to mislead and confuse the unwary.

The traditions of the Borders of Scotland are noble and inspiring, but they were not linked with those of our regiment until a quite recent date. The late Mr Andrew Ross, in *The Lowland Scots Regiments*, at page 329 wrote as follows: " Justice remains to be done to the recruiting capacity of the Lowlands of Scotland. It is too late in the day to suggest the establishment of new units. Each of the four great Lowland regiments ought to be allowed to form additional battalions—the King's Own Scottish Borderers being withdrawn in the course of the process from the half-way house, where they at present halt, to the City of Edinburgh, where the regiment sprang into existence on the 18th March 1689."

No doubt the allusion in the words " half-way house " is to the presence of the regimental depot at Berwick-on-Tweed, which is not in Scotland and in any event is suitable only for a limited district of the Border regimental area. Sir Herbert Maxwell in an editorial note deprecates the return to Edinburgh. "After the land, from Roxburghshire * on the east to Galloway on the west, has been drained of the flower of its manhood to fill the ranks of the old and new battalions of the K.O.S.B., we should justly resent the severing of a bond which the Great War has surely made historic." The purpose of this introduction is, accepting Sir Herbert's judgment as conclusive, to sketch briefly the regimental tradition, which forced so learned an historian and so patriotic a Scot as the late Mr. Ross to plead for things to be put back as they were in the beginning. The regiment, which now is called The King's Own Scottish Borderers, has had a continuous existence for 240 years. For close on 220 years it has ranked 25th of the Line, ever since it was placed on the English pay establishment to date from 20th June 1689, the date on which commissions were issued to officers. With the years the Scottish connection slowly but steadily weakened. At one time it was numbered among English territorial regiments. In spite of the Royal gift of the title "The King's Own Borderers" the ties with Scotland were fitful and feeble until 1881, when, as the result of vehement protests, it was virtually restored to Scotland, and received thereby a new lease of life.

It is the custom at the present time to bewail the seventeenth century as the epoch of ferocious wars of religion. Certainly Scotland was not a happy country. But out of these troublous times were born four famous Scottish regiments which still flourish. The Royal Scots, The Royal Scots Fusiliers, The King's Own Scottish Borderers, and The Cameronians. If the Fusiliers had their origin in the Royal measures to quell the Covenanters, the King's Own Scottish Borderers equally with the Cameronians, though less truculently, represent the determination of the Presbyterians to defend *vi et armis* their beliefs and liberties. The rank and file represented a solid mass of thinking Scots who despaired of the Stuart Kings and looked for salvation to William of Orange who had just landed in England. It is, therefore, the very incarnation of the Revolution Settlement. Its officers were the younger noblemen and gentlemen of the large band of exiles who for Presbyterian views or opposition to so-called methods of government had fled to or been banished to Holland. Among these returned natives in attendance on William was David Melville, third but oldest surviving son of George, 1st Earl of Melville, by his wife Catherine, daughter of Alexander, Lord Balgonie, eldest son of "the little crooked soldier," Alexander Leslie, 1st Earl of Leven, a famous

* He might have added Berwickshire.

general of the civil war, which ended in establishment of the Protectorate. 1689. By 1688 David Melville, who had succeeded to the earldom of Leven in 1681 on the death, without a second son, of the notorious John Duke of Rothes, ranked higher than his own father among the peers of Scotland. The information in Sir William Fraser's massive memoir of the Melvilles and Levens does not disclose a specially military education.

He was born in Fife on 5th May 1660, was at Kiel in 1685, Hamburg in 1686 and Berlin in 1687. Through the influence of the Electress Sophia of Hanover, who was proud of her Scottish descent and, unlike her son, was ever a true friend to Leven, he obtained a colonelcy in the army of the Elector of Brandenburg.

The birth of Leven's Regiment,* in March 1689, was sudden and dramatic. Indeed Mr. Ross is justified in describing the swiftness with which it sprang into being as "unparalleled in our military annals." Leven had held a commission to raise a regiment from King William III. since 1688, and, according to the invaluable Captain R. T. Higgins in his book ***The Records of The King's Own Borderers, or the Old Edinburgh Regiment*** (1873), had brought his officers from Holland *via* England. But not an officer started for Scotland till 7th March 1689 when Leven obtained a pass for Scotland, and not a man was enlisted till, on the escape of Graham of Claverhouse, Viscount Dundee, from Edinburgh, the Castle of which still held out for King James under the Duke of Gordon, the full peril of the new monarchy was realized. "The flight of Dundee from Edinburgh on his errand of insurrection warned the city to take speedy measures for its defence. Lord Leven caused the drums to beat, and within two hours, it is said, raised 800 men ; but the work of these two hours has lasted for centuries, for the regiment thus hastily enlisted is still alive as the twenty-fifth of the Line." †

A careful modern commentator on the records puts the complete recruitment at 1,000 men in four hours.‡ It is a well-known fact that none of the ultra-Covenanting men from the west of Scotland joined Leven's. In the opinion of Major-General Mackay, Commanding in Scotland, Leven's recruits were as good as any in Scotland, and that at a time when the cream of the country was eager to join the

* In 1898 authority was given for officers to wear as the tartan for their trews the Leslie tartan. At the close of the Boer War this privilege was extended to the rank and file, so that from 1903 the regimental tartan has been that of the Leslies, although Leven was not himself a Leslie by male descent. His mother and her mother (a sister of the Duke of Rothes) were, however, both Leslies. Of course, no such tartan existed in 1689.

† The Hon. Sir J. W. Fortescue, *A History of the British Army*, 1910, vol. i. p. 340.

‡ *Lowland Scots Regiments*, p. 256.

1689. army. This great day in the history of Scotland and the British Army was the 19th of March 1689.

The new regiment was soon to be put to its ordeal. Dundee had been north raising the clans of Lochaber, Moidart, Skye, and other regions of the north-west. In July he was making for Atholl, hoping further to increase his host and make a bold bid for King James by a descent on the Lowlands. To frustrate this temptation to the warlike Stewarts and other septs of Atholl, Mackay hurried north and narrowly escaped the Caudine Forks of the gorge of Killiecrankie and complete annihilation, only to find himself forced to give battle in a thoroughly unfavourable position to the Highlanders who had manœuvred so as to gain their favourite " cothrom a' bhruthaich " or advantage of higher ground. He was completely defeated, and only saved from destruction, along, probably, with the whole cause, by the death of Dundee.*

In these pages our concern is solely with Leven's. How did they do ? Mr. Fortescue says at page 341 of the *History* cited already : " The Twenty-fifth broke like the other Scottish regiments, as was pardonable in such young soldiers, though they made some effort to rally." In support of this verdict no evidence is given. There is a considerable body of evidence the other way. For instance, Mr. Ross says they faced Dundee at Killiecrankie in a way which " repeatedly called forth the General's commendation," and gives reference to the memoirs of that general in support. The *London Gazette* of the time claimed that the regiment " with extraordinary Bravery and Resolution " retired by Mackay's orders.†

Mackay wrote, soon after the battle, to Lord Melville : " My Lord, your son hath behaved himself with all his officers and soulders [*sic*] extraordinary well, as did also Colonel Hastings with his."

But the best proof of the stoutness of heart of Leven's is the spontaneous conferment by the Provost and Magistrates of Edinburgh upon the regiment of the exclusive privilege of beating up at all times within the city without asking permission of the Lord Provost.‡ § This privilege pertains unto this day.

Two valuable lessons were learnt by the regiment, namely, the deadly effect of flanking fire, the Cameron clansmen in particular losing 120 men owing to well-directed flanking fire of the regiment,||

* See *A Military History of Perthshire*, 1908, by the present Duchess of Atholl, pp. 253–273.

† Higgins, *Records of the K.O.B.*, p. 2.

‡ Captain Scott Elliot's conclusion regarding Leven's Regiment at Killiecrankie is the same as my own. See p. 4 of the *History of the 5th Batt. K.O.S.B.*, Dumfries 1928.

§ Higgins, *op. cit.*

|| Duchess of Atholl, *op. cit.*, p. 267.

and the utter uselessness of a bayonet that has to be pushed into the musket barrel instead of being clamped round it.* 1689.

Few people are indispensable, but for the Scottish counter-revolution Dundee was indispensable. The Jacobites were defeated and rendered incapable of military insurrection till 1715. Leven's Edinburgh Regiment did garrison duty in Scotland until, in the spring of 1691, it proceeded to Ireland, still under Leven, in the army of the general who had commanded at Killiecrankie, Hugh Mackay of Scourie. It would be out of place in this work to enter into the campaign against the Raparees, the captures of Ballymore, Athlone, which won de Ginkell his earldom, of Galway and Limerick. Suffice it to say that, in this their first visit to a country in which many long tours of duty were to be served, Leven's suffered severe casualties. General Mackay won back his laurels, but his hour was approaching.

Two years later Leven sent his regiment at full strength to Flanders and joined it himself after the battle of Steenkirke. The fact is, he found it very difficult to combine being colonel of a regiment on active service abroad with being governor of Edinburgh Castle, a post which he had held since 14th June 1689.†

He was well out of Steenkirke, which has made the name of Count Solmes stink in British nostrils, which saw cruel carnage among the deserted British troops, and cost Scotland Mackay and the promising young Earl of Angus. It was a rough introduction to continental warfare. And there were worse and worse trials in store. William III. was brave, but he was no match for Luxembourg, especially with numerically inferior forces. In the bloody but gallant defeat at Landen the 25th took their share, but the knock-out blow came two years later when they were under Maitland at Namur and an explosion killed more than half the remaining strength of the regiment, besides giving "my uncle Toby" his wound in the groin.‡ It was a skeleton that left for Scotland after the Peace of Ryswick.§

Leven, meantime, had been losing favour with the King, which he attributed to Tory influences. He bitterly felt the loss of the regiment of which he was so justly proud. In writing to Count Bothmer in 1717 he speaks of the loss of his regiment "still commanded by the Lord Shannon," and he is confident that Princess Sophia knows how well he and his men did at "Gillycranky." It

* For a different version of the change in the bayonet see *The Lowland Scottish Regiments*, pp. 192–193.

† *Dict. Nat. Biog.*, *s.v.* Melville, David.

‡ See *Tristram Shandy*, by Rev. L. Sterne.

§ Higgins, p. 20.

1715. may have been intrigue or it may have been his absenteeism, but his personal contact with the regiment he had made ended on 19th March 1694, when he was succeeded by Colonel—afterwards Lieut.-General—James Maitland, of whom a brief notice may not be out of place. Leven's name, however, will for all time be associated with our regiment, and his name be recalled with gratitude and respect.

Maitland was a younger son of a certain Robert Maitland "of the Bass," a member of an ancient Aberdeenshire branch of the house of Thirlestane, who owed his chances in life, and in particular his deputy-governorship of the fortress and prison of the Bass Rock, to the favour of his remote kinsman John, Duke of Lauderdale, so long the all-powerful minister of Charles II.. It is therefore a little surprising to find him colonel of a Whiggish corps so soon after the expulsion of the Stuarts. Possibly his friendship for the celebrated and influential Principal Carstairs—a friendship disclosed in his will—may have mellowed his political views and helped to commend him to the King. Suffice it to say that Maitland's regiment figures in the public records until he resigned in 1711, after having commanded for seventeen years in the Low Countries, notably at Namur, and in Scotland chiefly at Fort William and Fort Augustus.

It does not appear that the regiment took part in Marlborough's campaigns, and it was not until 1715 that it was called upon to take the field in the battle of Sheriffmuir fought on 13th November. It was then commanded by Richard (Boyle) Viscount Shannon, and formed part of Major-General Wightman's victorious force in the centre of Argyll's army. The regiment, since 25th February 1712,* when it was commanded by Brigadier William Breton, who followed Maitland, officially recognized as the 25th of the Line, "did admirably well" † in the uncongenial business of civil war, and contributed to the unsensational but substantial defeat of Mar's plans, which left Scotland in peace for thirty years.

This period was one of uneventful duty for the 25th. A tour on the Isle of Wight and a demonstration at the Bay of Vigo led to a long stay in Ireland, which was followed by ten weary years on the Rock of Gibraltar.

On 17th June 1721 Shannon was succeeded by John Middleton, who held command for eleven years, when he was succeeded on 29th May 1732 by John, 10th Earl of Rothes, who had the mortifying experience four years later of seeing the whole of the private soldiers

* *The Lowland Scottish Regiments*, p. 240.

† *A Military History of Perthshire*, p. 282, footnote.

of the regiment drafted off to join General Oglethorp's regiment in Georgia. The regiment was then sent to Ireland to recondition, presumably recruiting from the Protestant Irish. Thus the first blow was dealt at the Scottish character of the regiment. Even in 1739 the census of officers shows that out of 29 officers only 5 names were not distinctively Scottish. Barring the decade which included the colonelcies of William Breton (four years) and Lord Shannon, the command had been entrusted to Scotsmen. And as Rothes was succeeded in April 1745 by Hew, Lord Sempill; Sempill, on Christmas Day 1746, by the Earl of Crawford; Crawford, a year later, by William, Earl of Panmure; and Panmure by William, 8th Earl of Home, in 1752,* in which year a clear majority of Scottish names appear on the Nominal Roll of Officers, the command was from the start to all intents in Scottish hands. The 25th had less to complain of than many of the defunct or absorbed Scottish regiments chronicled by Ross. They had not been disbanded like Sir William Douglas's two regiments, they had acquired the permanency of a number, they had retained in 1736 a cadre or framework for speedy reconstruction, and the spirit had been fostered and conserved by the representative Scottish character of the command. 1745.

We left the regiment in Ireland. It was destined, though not at full strength, to participate in the aftermath of the Dettingen campaign in 1743 and, after one winter at Bruges and another at Ghent, fought the bloody fight at Fontenoy on 11th May 1745, which brought more renown to the British privates and their leaders than to Cumberland. The 25th lost 9 officers and 143 non-commissioned officers and men, and worse was to follow. Along with certain Dutch troops it was employed to defend the town of Ath, and, owing to the treachery of the Dutch, was compelled to surrender. It was then only 400 strong, but the most favourable terms were obtained, and it marched out with all the honours of war.

Once more the regiment faced the Scottish Jacobites. Recalled in haste, it landed in Essex in November 1745, marched *via* Derby, Kendal, and Newcastle to Edinburgh, which was reached on 17th January 1746, just too late for the battle of Falkirk, and occupied Edinburgh Castle. Culloden won it a mention in despatches, but the paltry casualties of 1 soldier killed and 13 wounded shows the one-sided nature of the saddest of battles.

After the battle, the regiment was sent back to the Continent to Williamstadt and later on to Bois-le-Duc, where it wintered. In 1745 the capture of two stands of colours at the battle of Laffeldt

* Higgins, p. 85.

1759. — showed the offensive vigour of the 25th, but no efforts or sacrifice availed to defend Bergen-op-Zoom, and the regiment was withdrawn and wintered in Breda.

Once more, after delays through storms, Ireland, in the shape of Cork and Cashel, saw the regiment, until in 1755 it was transferred to Scotland where it recruited up to 70 men per company and, after a short sojourn at Fort William, marched to Buckinghamshire early in 1756 and, after the abortive expeditions to Oléron and St. Malo, joined that excellent soldier, Prince Ferdinand of Brunswick, in Germany.

Minden, one of the regiment's proudest battle honours, was fought on 1st August 1759, and cost the regiment dear. It was no longer thought impolite to take aim with the firelock, and the casualties amounted to 190 of all ranks killed, 154 wounded, and 9 missing. It was brilliantly led by Lieut.-Col. Henry Pleydell (Dawnay), Viscount Downe, who, alas, died of wounds received at Campen on 15th October 1760 when only thirty-three years of age.* We may pass over two years in Germany and note the return to England *via* Holland early in 1763. The colonel then was a famous name in the regimental story, Lord George Lennox. Lord Home had died in 1761 and his successor, Sir Henry Erskine, had resigned in 1762.

The tattered colours in use since 1743 were buried in St. Nicholas Church at Newcastle-on-Tyne with military honours.

The 25th once again saw Scotland, being stationed there from 1764 to 1768, when twelve years of the Mediterranean followed. In 1780 Scotland again—this time Edinburgh—was visited for two years, when a march was made to the south. It was received by its colonel, now a major-general.

It was then, at the moment when the Scottish spirit had gained by two terms of duty and recruitment, that it pleased those in authority to take away the historic title "The Edinburgh Regiment" and substitute therefor "The Sussex Regiment," to the glorification of the Duke of Richmond, but to the dismay of his brother, the colonel, and of his regiment. The misnomer clung for more than twenty years, viz. from 31st August 1782 till 7th May 1805. The Sussex Regiment served under Lord Heathfield,† a Scotsman and a native of the Borders, at Gibraltar.

In 1792 a strange thing happened. To meet the exigencies of

* *Complete Peerage*, *s.v.* "Downe," vol. iv. p. 45.

† The late Lieut.-Col. the Hon. W. F. Elliot used to maintain that Heathfield was one of the most consummate masters of the military art produced by Scotland.

the French War the regiment was broken up into Marine parties, which acquitted themselves well, but the arrangement was not conducive to regimental life. 1799. —

Meanwhile a 2nd Battalion (the first of three, the last of which exists still and of which more anon) was formed on 25th February 1794. It existed only for a short time. It soon merged in the 25th which, so far as existing and thus strengthened, left early in the following year for what must have been the most trying form of military service endured by patient Britons in the eighteenth century—service in the West Indies. The long and perilous voyages on slow and overcrowded convoyed transports, exposed to the danger of isolation and capture by hostile privateers, the miseries, agonies, and deaths by the hundred from yellow jack, the horror of unchivalrous brigand foes, and a type of French soldier or sailor very different from those met in "the good old days" of continental warfare, the heat, discomfort, lack of supplies, and, above all, the slack grip of things exhibited by the home authorities, make Captain Higgins' records sad reading. The gallantry of Major Wright at Grenada in March 1795, and on numerous subsequent occasions, won him the public thanks of the anxious civilians on that island. A curious feature of the period was the impressment of captured foreigners into our army, and the 25th did not escape these undesirables. The rank and file may safely be put down as a mixed lot, when the weedy wrecks from the tropics landed at Mullion Cove in 1796. The regiment was allowed to send a recruiting party to Scotland, but Chatham supplied the bulk of the recruits, and they were mostly neither English, Scotch, nor Irish. Beyond helping to put down mutinies in the Navy, the regiment had a quiet time.

But we shall find Wright, in 1799, lieutenant-colonel, doing good service at the head of the Sussex Regiment at Egmont-op-Zee in Holland in the campaign which Sir Ralph Abercromby was powerless to prevent miscarrying under the direction of H.R.H. the Duke of York.

The regiment acted as advanced-guard of a brigade commanded by another famous Scottish soldier, Brig.-Gen. John Moore,* and forced the enemy to evacuate the Helder. When the evacuation on terms was completed the regiment returned to England, and did not engage in active service until 1801, when it was sent out after the battle of Aboukir to reinforce the British army in Egypt, and was present at the capture of Alexandria.

In 1804 we find it back again in Ireland, and in December

* Sir John Moore of Coruña fame.

1805. of that year a new colonel was appointed in the person of the Honourable Charles Fitzroy. He proved to be a worthy successor of Lennox, so long the father of the regiment. Lennox had had no hand in the conversion of the Edinburgh Regiment to the Sussex Regiment, and it is said that he "never permitted the Scotch beats to be discontinued." *

Fitzroy's first step was to agitate for a fresh name for his regiment now that the shadowy connection with Sussex was severed, and, thanks to his efforts and the personal interest of King George III., the 25th was given blue facings instead of yellow to mark its new status of a Royal regiment to be styled The King's Own Borderers. The motto, *In veritate religionis confido,* was specially directed by His Majesty to be placed on the colours as part of the insignia. Recognition of the Edinburgh connection was to come twenty-seven years later.

The year that saw the end of "The Sussex Regiment" as a title saw the birth of another 2nd Battalion of the 25th. If it had a longer life than the preceding one it did not survive 1816, being disbanded in Cork in that year. It was raised at Penrith out of supernumeraries from the 35th Regiment and volunteers from "The Army of Reserve and Militia." An Irish contingent yielded 129—40 out of 169 having deserted.

The K.O.B. took no part in the Peninsular War. In 1808 the regiment was sent to the West Indies, and was largely instrumental in the capture of Martinique in February 1809 and of Guadeloupe in 1810. Chief credit seems to have been due to Lieut.-Col. James Alexander Farquharson, who was the recipient of a most flattering message, dated 12th June 1817, from the Governor of Barbados, Lord Combermere, one of the best judges of troops then alive. The regiment did not see England till July and August 1817, and in 1826 had to do yet one more decade in the West Indies. It was during that period that Col. Farquharson was promoted Major-General by brevet on 22nd July 1830, and was followed by another tower of strength to the regiment—Lieut.-Col. Courtnay Chambers, a name to be held in honour by all Borderers, for he commanded them for eighteen years, in cloud and sunshine, in the West Indies, the British Isles, the Cape of Good Hope, and the Madras Presidency.

He took pride in "The Royal Borderers," a corps to which he was "sincerely and devotedly attached," † and only left them for higher responsibilities and, alas, an early grave.

It was during the colonelcy of Sir Henry Campbell, K.C.B.,

* Higgins, p. 149. † Higgins, p. 285.

Fitzroy's * successor, that King William IV. caused intimation to be sent from the Horse Guards, on 12th March 1832, that he had been graciously pleased to "permit the 25th Regiment or The King's Own Borderers, which on its formation in the year 1689 was called 'The Edinburgh Regiment' † (it having been raised in the short space of a few hours for the purpose of guarding the City of Edinburgh), to bear on its colours and appointments the arms of Edinburgh with the motto *Nisi Dominus frustra*, also to retain the motto *In veritate religionis confido*, which was authorised by his late Majesty, King George III., in reference to the badge and motto above specified. This motto is to be placed under the crown, surmounted by a lion, in two corners of the Regimental Colour." 1832.

More was to follow. In October of the same year the *Gazette* announced: "In addition to the distinctions formerly granted to the 25th Foot, H.M. has been pleased to permit the regiment to bear the White Horse ‡ and the motto *Nec aspera terrent* in the fourth corner of the Regimental Colour." The connection with Edinburgh had been revived in 1829 by the energy of Major Chambers when in command of a "depot company" in Edinburgh Castle.

The right to beat up for recruits had not been exercised since 1762, but the Lord Provost was no sooner approached on the subject than he gladly assented, and in the name of the Magistrates and Council of the City expressed the hope that the regiment would soon be restored to its primitive name and honours. Nor had recruiting parties neglected Scotland; four depot companies had never left England for the West Indies. Out of these recruiting parties visited Aberdeen, Dumfries, Edinburgh, Glasgow, Montrose, and Berwick-on-Tweed. For some time detachments occupied such remote and romantic fortresses as the castles of Braemar and Corgarff.§ Indeed the depot seems to have been in Scotland or at Berwick for six years, and only in October 1833 was it transferred to Ireland. In 1836, when reincorporated with the regiment in Ireland after a ten years' separation and the drain of many drafts, it had grown so as to number 269 rank and file.

On Christmas Day, 1839 the K.O.B., with 33 women and 52 children on the strength, set sail for the Cape, where two and a half uneventful years were spent, save for the part played in 1842 by Major D'Urban's detachment in the expedition under Lieut.-Col.

* Gen. Fitzroy died on 18th October 1831.

† *Gazette*, 28th March 1689.

‡ *I.e.* of Hanover.

§ On the Don. See *Proceedings of the Society of Antiquaries of Scotland*, vol. lxi. p. 48.

1859. — Cloete against the Dutch rebels in Natal. The K.O.B. assisted in the capture of Port Natal, and won warm praise from Sir George Napier, as did the smartness, discipline, and good conduct of the regiment during its stay in South Africa.

Of India and Arcot, Bangalore, Arnee, and Fort St. George little need be said. On the regiment's return to England in 1856 new colours were presented by Lady Smith, wife of Sir Harry Smith. In less than two years the K.O.B. were sent to Gibraltar to the recorded sorrow of the people of Dover, where they then were quartered. In April news came out that the three pipers, permission for whom was "lost in time," were authorised by H.R.H. the Duke of Cambridge to be continued as bandsmen, not as drummers, but their clothing was not to be an expense on the public.

1859 was an eventful year, for its close saw the formation at Preston, Lancashire, of that 2nd Battalion whose doings will bulk so largely in the ensuing pages. In three months its establishment was complete, in two more months it had won golden opinions for efficiency; it served in Edinburgh in 1862–63, received colours there in April of 1863, and in July was sent to Ceylon (five years) and India (seven years).

Meanwhile the 1st Battalion was ordered to Canada in 1864 to cope with the guerilla bands of American Fenians disbanded from the Federal Army of the United States. Almost on arrival at Montreal the K.O.B. took the field, but did more marching than fighting. Eventually the Government of the United States took the matter in hand and the Fenians were compelled to desist.

In 1867 the regiment left Canada and sailed direct to Scotland, with H.Q. at Glasgow and depot companies at Stirling, Paisley, and Ayr, whence they were moved in the following year to Aldershot, where they earned encomia from His Royal Highness the Commander-in-Chief for smartness in 1869 and for good musketry in 1871.

Since 1864 the regiment had been allowed to resume the Kilmarnock forage cap with dicebox border, and in 1869 a new pattern shako-plate was allotted—

> Edinburgh Castle encircled by a laurel wreath and surmounted with a crown with mottoes *Nisi Dominus frustra* and *Honi soit qui mal y pense*.

There is little calling for mention in the 2nd Battalion's thirteen years in the East, or in the 1st Battalion's laborious campaigns (*a*) in the Peshawar Field Force against the Afghans under Gen. F. C. Maude, V.C., C.B., in 1878, (*b*) in the punitive expedition against the Zakka Khels in 1879, or (*c*) in the Cabul Field Force under Gen. Doran against the Mohmands in 1880. A crisis was approaching in the life of the army and that of our regiment. In 1881 all the infantry of the line, at that time divided into brigades, to which recruiting areas were allotted, were territorialized and had in most cases militia battalions affiliated to them. The 25th, the old Edinburgh Regiment, now the K.O.B., was in the 6th Brigade in England, but expected to get a Scottish depot. To its amazement it was sent to York with four depot companies. A gem of a name was selected—" The York Regiment, King's Own Borderers." Both the 2nd and 5th West York Militia were affiliated and donned the glengarry with diced border.

1881–1903.

The whole of Scotland was up in arms. The heather was on fire. Deputations assailed Mr. Childers, the Minister of War, who eventually saw that the York business would not do. What probably weighed more with the Minister than popular clamour or national sentiment, considerations which War and other departments and corporate bodies have been known to disregard, was the advocacy of Col. David Milne Home of Wedderburn, M.P. for Berwick, briefed with the splendid material supplied by Major C. E. Hope of the 2nd Battalion, a perfervid Scot learned in the lore of the regiment. Anyhow, the right cause prevailed.

That is how the K.O.B. came to have a depot at Berwick-on-Tweed but was without a militia battalion for six years. That situation more accurately deserves Mr. Ross's term " Half-way house " than the present situation, when the regiment has the magnificent district of the Border counties and Galloway. But better was to follow. In 1882 Lowland dress, doublet, trews, and claymore, with the M'Childers or standard tartan was granted, and in the Jubilee year came that magic word " Scottish " between Own and Borderers, with the affiliation of one of the finest militia regiments in the United Kingdom—the Scottish Borderers Militia (of which a brief notice will follow in the body of this work as the 3rd Battalion K.O.S.B.). For this happy affiliation much credit is once more due to C. E. Hope, then a Lt.-Col. and commanding at Dublin. The writer has seen a copy of the pithy letter which he addressed in January 1886 to the Secretary for War, pointing out that the Scottish Borderers Militia was the natural militia battalion for the King's Own Borderers, and that it had only been styled the 3rd Battalion Royal Scots Fusiliers since 1881.

The preliminaries are drawing to a close. A brief notice of the doings of the two regular battalions will lead straight to the opening of hostilities in the Great War.

To continue the story of the 1st Battalion, it remained in India

1895. — during the 'eighties, had seven months campaigning in Burma, and returned home in 1890. In 1896 there was a beat up for recruits in Edinburgh with bayonets fixed and colours flying. In 1898 there was a march through the Borders and Dumfriesshire. A term in Ireland filled up the time till 1900, when the battalion joined Tucker's 7th Division in South Africa, was engaged at Waterval Drift on 15th February, and witnessed the surrender at Paardeberg in the same month. March saw the K.O.S.B. at Poplar Grove, Bloemfontein, and at Karee, at which last place they materially contributed to the dislodgment of the Boers from a strong position.

The 1st Volunteer Service Company joined the 1st Battalion in May, and in the following month they reached Pretoria together. The task was far from finished. Much hard work lay ahead. De Wet was harassing the lines of communication. There was the affair of Zilicats Nek, and later on the Magaliesberg hills were the scene of many exploits. But even the aftermath of the South African War was harvested, and the battalion departed in 1903 for Ireland. The stay there was not for long. Colchester was reached in 1905, and in November 1906 the battalion was ordered to Cairo.

Meanwhile, on 4th October, in the presence of that ardent volunteer Sir Robert Cranston, Lord Provost, the Borderers' Memorial which adorns the North Bridge of Edinburgh was unveiled by the G.O.C., Scottish Command, Sir E. P. Leach. The 1st Battalion supplied a guard of honour consisting of 4 officers and 100 other ranks. Veterans, the Volunteers, and the Militia were all represented. The memorial reminds the representatives of the Edinburgh Regiment and the rest of Scotland and the Empire that K.O.S.B. between 1879 and 1902 have fought and fallen in Afghanistan, India, Burma, Egypt, and South Africa.

In 1911 a move was made from Egypt to India. Ranikhet, Bareilly, and the final station of Lucknow were always cropping up in conversation in 1915 and 1916. It was evident the battalion worked hard and played hard, and was as well led, well officered, well non-commissioned officered, and well found in rank and file as any infantry unit that entered the war.

Meanwhile the 2nd Battalion had passed six years, from 1880 to 1886, in Ireland. After a short stay in Gibraltar and Aldershot respectively it was sent to Egypt on short notice in 1888, and fought under Grenfell against the Dervishes at Gemaizah in December, just missing Toski in 1889.

The 2nd Battalion left Egypt, and on 2nd January 1890 came on the Indian establishment. Between 1895 and 1898 it came in for continuous heavy fighting, being twenty-three times in action.

Chitral, Malakand Pass, the Tirah Campaign may seem very far-off names, and Dargai means for the ordinary Britisher a piper playing the "Cock o' the North"; but they mean a lot to the veterans who took part in these exacting campaigns against brave and crafty enemies. In the *Lowland Scots Regiments,* so largely drawn on for the later history of the K.O.S.B., Brig.-Gen. Wilkinson has recorded the appreciation expressed by Brig.-Gen. Westmacott in bidding farewell to the time-expired men at the close of the Tirah campaign. He said, "We have been together long enough for me to find out for myself . . . that the Borderers are one of the finest regiments in the service. You have been tried very highly in constant rearguard actions, marching through ice-cold water and then going up to the highest hills on picquet duty and fighting all night without either food or blankets, and I have never heard a murmur or an unsoldierlike word. It is men like you who have made the name of the Fourth Brigade famous throughout the civilized world." The battalion was then commanded by Col. Henry Dixon, who later on, in the South African War, commanded Dixon's column, one of the units of which was the 1st Battalion K.O.S.B.. 1914. —

The next war for the 2nd Battalion was to be the Great War. India was left in 1903, Burma in 1905, Aden in 1906. Three years at Glasgow followed. In January 1910 the 2nd K.O.S.B. were transferred to Ireland and served there continuously till the outbreak of war. Their first station was Holywood, Belfast, where they stayed nearly two years. In November 1912 they moved to Dublin. On 17th October 1912 the old colours of the 2nd Battalion were sent to Edinburgh and impressively deposited in St. Giles Cathedral.

"On 26th July 1914 a daring and successful attempt was made to land guns and ammunition for the Irish Volunteers at Howth, where over 1,000 men took possession of them. A party of constabulary and 100 men of the K.O.S.B. were sent from Dublin to prevent the removal of the arms. Shots were fired from revolvers, and only about twenty rifles were captured. On the return march the party of 100 Borderers was reinforced by about 200 more from barracks, but was met and stoned by a very hostile crowd near O'Connell Bridge. Although no order appears ever to have been given, shots were fired and two or three of the crowd were killed and several injured, a number of the soldiers also being injured."

This incident is recalled here because of the effect its consequences had in impeding the work of mobilization. Not only was it unsafe for officers or men to leave barracks in uniform unless in parties strong enough to overawe the assassin, but senior officers were called off their duty of supervising mobilization to waste hours over

1914. military courts, civilian inquests, and a commission with Lord Shaw as chairman, in which the insoluble problem was laboured *ad nauseam*: What can the soldier do or not do in the face of a riotous mob when he is reluctantly complying with the behest of the civil power to maintain the King's peace?

Of the same stuff as the parent battalion but as a home service unit with the handicap of a certain number of young recruits and the potential softness of the recalled reservists, it showed from the beginning to the end of the war a toughness and an evenness of good work to which the following chapters pay an inadequate tribute.

BOOK I

THE SECOND BATTALION

CHAPTER I

MONS *

AS a concession to chronology our tale opens with the 2nd Battalion K.O.S.B.. No doubt the thunderbolt of war found them in much that frame of mind in which all or most of us have remained ever since—namely, that we were fighting in the most righteous of causes, for right as against might, for democracy as against tyranny, and for the life of the British Empire. There was no hatred of the Germans either pre-existing or springing full-grown into life on the invasion of Belgium. But there was an intense, deep-seated distrust of the powers that were in Germany, and a conviction that in their plots, plans, and preparations responsibility for the war was chiefly to be found. Later on, the acts of the German soldiers in the countries they invaded superadded a disgust and aversion which, in spite of incidents like the Christmas fraternization in 1914 (in which Borderers took no part), grew and expressed themselves in the terms Hun and Boche, which in unofficial sources, and frequently in official diaries, are used as a suitable synonym for German. The terms were compatible with appreciation of bravery, skill, and industry. They implied no sense of superiority on the part of the Allies in matters æsthetic or moral. They implied a readiness to do systematically and under orders as well as from natural depravity things unmentionable and unjustifiable. No doubt the whole has been made to suffer for the part. There were hundreds of thousands of Germans of the noblest character and the most chivalrous instincts. And for that reason no opprobrious terms will be used except in quoting exact wording. The object of a regimental history is to record the gallant deeds of its sons, not to perpetuate animosities. Still, it admits of no doubt that the defiled châteaux and dwellings of France, the callousness towards prisoners, and the doings in Belgium and France under the military occupation created something like detestation of Germany and Germans in the minds of Britons, combatant and civilian alike. That was to develop later. At first, the *cause* was everything. Aug. 1914.

* See Map 1 in pocket.

Aug. 1914. — It was therefore with a whole heart that the K.O.S.B., like the rest of the British Army, prepared for the ordeal by battle. " You would be proud if you could see how our men are *longing* to have a go at the Germans." * The 2nd Battalion was stationed at Dublin. Its depot was at Berwick-on-Tweed, and there were something like 700 Reservists to be collected there and sent in parties to Dublin to bring the unit up to full strength. The task, however, was accomplished in four days, and the reservists turned up to a man. Whether they or the recruits could be classed as " the most expert army in the world " (as the " Old Contemptibles " have been styled) is doubtful. But they would soon work into the very fine machine, and, as will be seen, the general standard of endurance and efficiency was high. None the less these home battalions could not boast of the flawless efficiency of the foreign-service units ; the dilution was too great, and some of the younger men were only nineteen years old.

Mobilization orders arrived at 6 p.m. on the 4th of August, and during the next nine days the officers, non-commissioned officers, and men were working from morning to night. Preparations included a parade at full war strength on 10th August in the Phœnix Park, and a modest route march on the following day indicated very fair physical condition.

Embarkation began on 13th August 1914, at 8 a.m., and was completed by 12 noon ; the companies had paraded hours beforehand. The Bibby liner S.S. *Gloucestershire* was overcrowded to an insanitary degree. Besides the K.O.S.B. there were on board the H.Q. of the 13th Infantry Brigade, henceforth " 13th I.B.," in which the K.O.S.B. were serving, the 2nd Duke of Wellington's (West Riding) Regiment, henceforth " D. of W.," and the 1st Queen's Own (The Royal West Kent Regiment), henceforth " R.W.K.".

It may be interpolated here that the remaining infantry battalion of the brigade was the 2nd, The King's Own Yorkshire Light Infantry, henceforth " K.O.Y.L.I.," which sailed on the *Buteshire*, and that the 13th I.B. was under command of Brig.-Gen. G. J. Cuthbert, C.B., of the Scots Guards, and with the 14th I.B. (Brig.-Gen. S. P. Rolt, C.B.) and 15th I.B. (Brig.-Gen. Count (now Major-Gen. Lord Edward) Gleichen, C.B., C.M.G., D.S.O., etc., etc.) formed the infantry of the 5th Division, commanded by Major-Gen. Sir Charles Fergusson, C.B., D.S.O. .† Further, that the association with the R.W.K. lasted throughout the war in the same brigade on terms of close friendship

* Private letter written by Major Coke on Friday, probably 7th August 1914.

† Sir Charles became K.C.B. in 1915 and G.C.M.G. in 1924, in which year he was appointed Governor-General of New Zealand.

and mutual confidence. A charming tribute to our battalion can be read on p. 237 of Major C. B. Maloney's *Invicta*, of which the writer has made frequent use. No Borderer can read that thrilling story of the Royal West Kent Regiment without realizing that the standard set by the 1st R.W.K. was a stimulus to the 2nd K.O.S.B.. To mention one exploit only, the defence of Neuve Chapelle in the last days of October 1914 was one of the most glorious actions fought in the whole war.

Aug. 1914.

But we are very nearly all aboard by now ; not only between three and four thousand infantrymen, but some 220 horses, 80 wagons, equipment, food and clothing, and, let us not forget, ammunition. To the public, mysteriously and as if by magic, to those engaged by eager systematic toil, the Expeditionary Force, including the K.O.S.B., left the British Isles, and after a voyage of thirty-six hours landed intact on the Continent. The trip on the *Gloucestershire* began at 1 a.m. on the 14th of August, and Le Havre, the sealed port of destination, was reached between 3 and 5 p.m. on the 15th in a torrent of rain. The night was spent in a wharf in the docks in quite good sheds. On the 16th it was still raining, but a move was made to a rest camp. The *Gloucestershire* was not the only transport in the harbour by any means, and the excitement of feeling that something big was really under weigh was intense. And this was augmented by the eager welcome of the crowds. "No. 3" Camp was at Tréville about six miles from the harbour, and after the rain was muddy and cheerless, though well arranged. Here also were the civilian visitors. Next day the battalion paraded at dawn, marched back to Le Havre, and entrained at the Gare Maritime for the front. Thanks to the efficiency of Lieutenant R. Joynson and the willingness of the somewhat untrained reservists of the transport, horses were boxed and wagons entrained in two hours. The whole battalion was ready to start in three and a half hours. Some of the men travelled in third-class compartments, others in cattle trucks. The day was fine, but hot, when the train started about 10.30 a.m.. But no amount of heat could repress the spirits of the Borderers. Fêted all along the line in this new and beautiful country, loaded with fruit and flowers and benedictions they rolled along towards the unknown in the intoxication of excitement. Like a lot of other people, who should have known better, they imagined that the war might be over before they got their chance of getting at Fritz : they peopled the front with vast imaginary French armies, and sad were the supernumeraries who were left at home or at the base. Thus went the leaders of that weary stream of comers and goers along the well-known track between F. & F.

Aug. 1914. (France and Flanders) and Blighty (home). How familiar they became—Rouen of the churches and Jeanne d'Arc, and Amiens of the mighty cathedral and the familiar railway station !

On went the train over the fateful fields past Villers-Bretonneux, St. Quentin, and Le Cateau, till at 2.30 a.m. on the 18th of August it pulled up at Landrecies in the valley of the Sambre near the south end of the great forest of Mormal, and some 16 miles S.W. of the fortress of Maubeuge, of which so much was erroneously expected as a barrier against the invader.

The K.O.S.B. detrained and marched 4½ miles to the village of Maroilles, in or near which they were billeted comfortably and treated hospitably. The whole of the next two days was spent resting and training.

On the 20th, at 3.30 p.m., Sir Charles Fergusson delivered a stirring address. He reminded his hearers that they would be in the thick of battle in a matter of hours rather than days. Unlike a unit of the 15th Brigade,* the K.O.S.B. emitted no sound of " 'ear! 'ear!" There was the silence of riveted attention and realization of war. By this time the heat was intense. Dublin district was nothing to it ; and when the march towards Mons began on the morning of the 21st it was not long before the new boots and the soft feet of the reservists "fell out," and in a few cases the wearers followed suit. However, the K.O.S.B. were not the worst marchers on the road that day, and in the end only two stragglers were missed at Houdain after a march of 17 miles. Houdain lies just N. of Bavai, and the forest of Mormal, containing about 36 square miles of fine trees, and within 10 miles of the Mons-Condé Canal on the N. Once more there were good quarters for the weary and dainties for the hungry. Houdain swarmed with British troops, and it was plain that the whole of the 5th Division was concentrated in the district. Nobody had the slightest idea what was happening elsewhere or where they were going. As Gen. Gleichen says, it was understood that the other division of the II. Corps—the 3rd Division—was "somewhere on the right" and that some French cavalry were "somewhere on the left." Otherwise the fog of war reigned, and there was nothing to be done but to trust the higher command and be ready. On the 21st the 13th Brigade were on the right of the 5th Division and the remaining brigades were on the line St. Vaast—Gommegnies.†

On the 22nd the 13th Brigade received orders to march due

* Major-Gen. Lord Edward Gleichen's *Doings of the 15th Infantry Brigade*, p. 9 (Blackwood, 1917).

† *Official History*, vol. i. p. 50.

N., to hold the canal already mentioned. The K.O.S.B. and R.W.K. formed the advanced-guard. Off soon after 5 a.m., the Belgian frontier was crossed after 3 miles, and the reception at Athis and subsequent villages and towns showed that the Belgians did not lag behind the French in hospitality and goodwill.

Another frontier was also crossed on this day—that between the pleasant fields, downs, and woodlands of rural France and the black country of the Belgian Borinage coalfield in Hainaut. From Dour, 2½ miles N. of the frontier, to Boussu on the Valenciennes-Mons road is one continuous street more than 2 miles long. Towards Mons for 6 miles stretches a densely populated and hideous tract of spoilt country dotted over with slag heaps and cut up with railways and smelling of coal smoke. It was a poor battlefield. There was no field of fire. Besides the intersecting railways there were tracks, ditches, casual roads with dead ends, etc., but there were no suitable roads for artillery. If a mound were ascended, it would be found to have the view in every vital direction obstructed by higher or equally high rivals in the bing line.

However, this story is not concerned with the shortcomings of the Mons district but with the one feature of tactical importance for the K.O.S.B., the Mons-Condé Canal.

After a halt at Boussu the K.O.S.B. continued to march northwards to Haine, and to the extent of three companies to Les Herbières at the road bridge and lock (hereafter called Lock 4) on the Mons-Condé Canal. The march was much like its predecessors. It was hot and sultry. Boots seemed if anything to be tighter and feet more puffy. There was a tendency, not diminished by offers of drinks and tobacco from the friendly Belgians, to fall out.

Nothing eventful happened, but it was learned by midday from cyclists that contact with the enemy had been made and at Haine that Uhlans (to the uninitiated all German cavalry are Uhlans) had been there the day before. The screen of the advancing hostile host was therefore thrown out! It was time for action. Under Majors Coke and Chandos Leigh trench-digging began into the bank on which the towpath rested.

In an E. direction from Condé the canal extends in a straight line to the outskirts of Mons, round which it forms a pronounced salient. In this salient, quite apart from the fortune of war farther E., lay the danger. The S. bank of the canal at Lock 4 yielded little field of fire except here and there from the roofs of houses or obliquely at a few distant spots. But it was a formidable obstacle in the hands of brave and skilled users of the rifle. The canal itself is fully 20 and the basin at Lock 4 fully 50 yards wide.

Aug. 1914. All along the sector held by the Borderers a 10–15 foot wide and deep watercourse runs at the foot of the northern bank of the canal. Off the roads the country is flat, marshy fields, mostly under grass. There are plenty big trees about of the poplar, willow type. At the lock on the N. side there is a short row of houses, and not quite opposite to them there are few houses S. of the S. bank. Of one of these, a white house, Lieut. Pennyman made admirable use with his machine-guns (henceforth "M.G."), firing from the top story. N. of the road bridge the road proceeds straight as a die to a bifurcation 400 yards away; the road to the right leading to Tertre, in German hands. About 200 yards W. of the road bridge a railway crosses the canal by a bridge and continues N. to Petit Villerot, whence it bends to the W.. This bridge and railway bridge and embankment being about 20 feet high marked the eastern limit of the sector in the hands of the 1st Battalion of the East Surrey Regiment of the 14th I.B., to the exclusion of the Borderers, who also did not extend E. as far as St. Ghislain, which with Lock 3 was held by the R.W.K.. The K.O.Y.L.I. and the D. of W. were in reserve a little N. of Boussu. The M.G. of the K.O.Y.L.I. were between the K.O.S.B. and R.W.K..

At this moment when houses are being knocked unceremoniously about for defensive purposes, when breastworks and trenches are being dug and a barricade thrown across the straight bit of road at a distance suitable for a good field of fire, as *der Tag* approaches, it may be convenient to take stock of our battalion.

The officers who were at Les Herbières and Boussu on the morning of the 23rd August 1914 were as follows: Lieut.-Col. C. M. Stephenson was C.O., Major A. E. Haig was Senior Major and Second-in-Command. The Company commanders were Major E. S. D'Ewes Coke, O.C. B Company; * Major Chandos Leigh, O.C. D Company; Captain L. D. Spencer, O.C. A Company; Captain E. W. Macdonald, O.C. C Company. Besides Captains C. F. Kennedy (D), H. Cobden (C), and G. W. Smith (B), there were Captain R. C. Y. Dering, the Adjutant, and Hon. Captain A. Murray, the Quartermaster. The senior subaltern, Lieut. J. B. W. Pennyman, was Machine-gun Officer. The remaining officers were Lieuts. G. H. M. Lindsay (A), J. R. Hamilton-Dalrymple (D), R. P. M. Bell (C), R. Joynson (Transport Officer), R. H. P. Holme (D), and 2nd Lieuts. E. G. Miles (B), H. J. Harvey (C), G. P. Hammond (D), W. A. O. Rutherfurd (B), W. G. M. Shewen (B), G. B. Bayley (B), and G. S. Amos (D).. Attached from the supplementary reserve were 2nd Lieuts. A. L. Y. Dering (A) and T. F. P. B. J. Teeling

* The company signs will be in future A, B, C, and D.

(C). The Regimental Sergeant-major was Norman Macwhinnie, a herculean Borderer from Dumfriesshire, and the R.A.M.C. were represented by Captain Gibbon. Aug. 1914.

Before passing to the tale of Lock 4 mention must be made of one of the last incidents of the calm before the storm. Major Coke and several other officers found the occupants of a small isolated cottage N. of the canal and close to the lock, and therefore of considerable tactical importance, so far from resenting the liberties taken with their home, friendly in the extreme. Much was made of the officers of Coke's company by the father, the mother and the daughter of the household. Coffee and omelettes were forthcoming, and as other similar visitors turned up there seemed always to be plenty for them. When the work of fortification was finished, the strain ended and a really social evening was enjoyed. Little did the guests think of the impression they were making; one that he was tall, another that he would not, or could not, talk French, and so on. At last the lady of the house suggested that all the visitors should write their names on a tablecloth as a souvenir, and this happy idea was duly put into execution.

More than four years afterwards, in November 1918, it occurred to Coke, then in command of the 169th I.B., stationed only 7 miles from the spot where the war began for him, that he might hunt up Lock 4 and find how the kind friends of 22nd August 1914 had fared. A car and two legs took him to the scene. In his own words, "How well I recognised every spot—where C Company's trenches were; the window from which our M.G. fired, etc.. Arrived at the lock, I at first failed to recognise our little house, for it is now only a shell, and not a complete one at that. . . . However, I went down some steps into the back garden, and while exploring I heard voices, and out of the cellar appeared our two good women! I explained that I was one of the Scottish regiment that was there in 1914, and their pleasure was too touching for words." In a few moments they were all drinking coffee together as in 1914 and talking of old days. "How was Capt. Smith and Capt. Spencer? and the tall officer, and the young one who couldn't speak French? Major Leigh, they knew, had died of his wounds." And then, wonder of wonders, they produced from another house THE TABLECLOTH! There were the names embroidered! Coke had to write his once more and then say farewell, his only regret being not to have shaken hands with the man of the house, who was, however, alive and well in spite of four years of German occupation. The "Mons tablecloth" is now and will always be one of the most cherished treasures of the 2nd Battalion K.O.S.B., in whose ante-room it hangs framed.

23 Aug. 1914. So much for the lull before the storm. An attack was expected and everybody stood-to at dawn on 23rd August 1914, but nothing happened till after 11 a.m., and when the first German gun gave tongue at 12.40 p.m.* the general situation was much like this—

Battle was substantially joined on the Western Front and everywhere the French offensive-defensive had got the worst of it. They had expected the brunt of attack, not from the Brussels plain, but from farther E.. They were entirely ignorant of the masses of men under the command of General von Kluck, who for the last fortnight had been pouring into and through Belgium and were now starting the famous "wheel" southwards † on Paris. They were embarrassed by the collapse of Namur on the 22nd and the reverse which the Fifth French Army had received at Charleroi. It looked as though Maubeuge would share the fate of Liége and Namur, and that retreat was the only method of averting disaster.

The danger to the British Army between Binche, 11 miles E. of Mons and 12 W. of Charleroi, and Condé, 15 miles W. of Mons, was that of being isolated from the French, enveloped on both flanks, its line of communications cut, and forced to surrender, *e.g.* by being herded or rather hurled into Maubeuge, if still holding out. Two Army Corps and one Cavalry Division, and what help could be got from French territorials and cavalry not yet at hand were inadequate to stem the onrush of five Army Corps, two Cavalry Divisions, and at least treble the amount of artillery. The II. German Corps on the 23rd was actually setting about the capture of Tournai. There was some excuse for the pro-German Swedish Jew, Sven Hedin, comparing the swarming armies to the race migrations of early ages. That the migration lasted only four years is due in very substantial measure to the valour of the "Old Contemptibles" of 1914, and on this peaceful Sunday of 23rd August to the 3rd and 5th Divisions of the II. Corps.

Of the seriousness of the situation the British Higher Command was entirely ignorant; but they never at any time contemplated a stand on the line of the canal. The field of fire was inadequate. There was no time to blow up houses and fell trees to improve it. Round Mons, a most undesirable bull's-eye for a target, the canal threw a pronounced salient at Nimy, and the dense civilian population would form a screen. The intended line of defence lay behind among the pits. The 15th I.B. were actually engaged in preparing the 5th Divisional sector behind the 14th (L.) and 13th (R.) on the canal when the attack was launched. The story of the K.O.S.B. is

* Gleichen, *op. cit.*, p. 21.

† Points of the compass will be lettered E., W., N., and S..

that of a stout and skilful holding action, ended by order, after a repulse of the adversary, and followed by thirteen days of retreat to escape from the perils of the general situation. Apart from the drawbacks attaching to the Mons salient and the fact that a number of Germans had crossed the canal at Jemappes (which belong to the story of the heroic 3rd Division) the black country was hopelessly untenable. In the battle of Mons six German infantry divisions opposed two British which held an outpost line of 13 miles in a chain of small groups.*

23 Aug. 1914.

It is strange to think that both the 1st and 2nd Battalions of the K.O.S.B. fought their first fight in the war on a Sunday. If the 23rd August was less lovely at dawn, it became as hot and sunny at 1 p.m., when the fight began for the 2nd Battalion, as that even more famous 25th April in the Ægean next spring.

The dispositions to be given have the authority of Colonel—then Major—Haig, Second-in-Command. In addition to the barricades N. and S. of the road-bridge and the lock-house, the houses farther E. were also fortified and a small length of the bank E. of them. Of course if artillery spotted the houses, it would be all up with anyone who stayed on, and as the canal and lock were behind, the only defence would be to advance.

Away out half a mile from the lock Major Coke with B covered the cavalry and cyclists. The defence of the bridge and N. bank was entrusted to D under Major Leigh. A and C on the R. nearest to the R.W.K., and co-operating with 2nd Lieuts. Pepys' (K.O.Y.L.I.) M.G., lined the S. bank.

The battle began at Mons about 9 a.m.. It took a long time spreading W.. At noon, their task accomplished, B came back into reserve without having been in action. It was not till the pleasant sunny afternoon about 1 p.m. that the horror of war smote the unhappy people of Les Herbières and the strung-up K.O.S.B..

The first Germans were seen by Major Haig from " M.G.-house O.P. " moving diagonally S.W. along the road from Tertre. They were fairly well under cover, but their leader, an officer, was throughout conspicuous on account of a white " bandage " round his head. It is now known that the attackers were the Brandenburg Grenadiers of the III. Corps. Advancing in skirmishing order by alternate bursts over the marshy meadows, occasionally using their nippers to cut wire fencing, they were subjected to rapid fire and suffered heavily. But, nevertheless, enough came on to make it necessary to reinforce the troops on the far bank, especially as those on the near bank had such a poor field of fire. By this time the German

* *Official History*, vol. i. p. 66.

23 Aug. 1914. artillery had got the range, established fire superiority over the single and unsuitably placed F.A. battery in support of the 13th I.B., and hit the front barricade twice with shrapnel. The hospitable lock-house fared worse. Capt. Smith saw a direct hit which must have caused many casualties to the garrison and brought the owners in haste from the cellars. They disappeared with a canary in a cage and little else. But, as we know, they did not forget their would-be defenders.

The new dispositions were to send part of A under Capt. Spencer to join D, and to send Capt. Kennedy and the centre of D to get clear of the threatened houses. Major Leigh was on the R. * of the houses, and probably he found it necessary to advance from the actual banks—a nasty operation considering the deep and wide ditch that flows along the bottom of the canal bank. This really amounted to a counter-attack, and according to the account given that evening to Lieut. Joynson by the late Lieuts. Dalrymple and Holme it was a trying affair. The former, as senior officer left, handled D in such a way as to earn a recommendation for his coolness and gallantry. The K.O.S.B. were not having it all their own way. Major Haig had a poor opinion of the German rifle shooting; but the counter-attack was shelled at 600 yards range and peppered by M.G. at close range, and in a very short time Kennedy was wounded in the arm, and a little later Spencer too. And worse news was to come in: Major Leigh was missed when the general retirement was accomplished. Spencer had hunted for him in vain between 3 and 4 p.m.. Even now it is uncertain how he came to be wounded, but his wounds were so bad that he only survived six days.† Just forty years of age and with the ripe experience of service in the Egyptian Army and in the South African War, in the course of which he won the D.S.O., Chandos Leigh was a heavy loss to the regiment. But his gallant and skilful defence of the bridge on which the safety of B depended—to say nothing of checking the German advance—was worthy of an ancestry which combined nobility and brains.

Capt. Gibbon, R.A.M.C., was hit in the foot and had to be evacuated. He was much missed. A little later his place was taken, during the very period when a scribe was of most value to the K.O.S.B.—the days of stress and storm from Le Cateau to La Bassée—by Capt. Robert V. Dolbey, M.B. (Lond.), F.R.C.S. (Eng.), R.A.M.C., whose book, *A Regimental Surgeon in War and Prison*,‡

* Right " R." and Left " L." in future.

† Official Record of Officers who died in the War.

‡ London, John Murray, 1917.

is a gold mine of information and acute observation. All Borderers, at least all of the 2nd Battalion, should read and re-read that book if they wish to live in the thrills and anguish of that tremendous ordeal. 23 Aug. 1914.

For some time Lieut. Pennyman and his M.G. did much execution searching the woodlands and firing bursts on all who showed themselves in the open; it seems clear from a German account * that the white house in which the guns were was identified as the cause of much loss to the attackers. At any rate it became too hot for its occupants, and the guns were removed to a less "kenspeckle" position. Later on Major Haig was able once again to use it as an O.P.. The value of sticking it out materialized at the end of the day with the failing light. The Germans made their final effort. They had a battalion concentrated for storming in a copse, but it was located by the left platoon of Leigh's company. Rapid fire so intense as to sound like M.G. fire was opened, and the assailants melted away, and the first round in the four-year contest was over, with the honours to the Borderers and the 1st Battalion the East Surreys, on their left. Farther E. young Pepys had been killed, but his guns still found targets, and the R.W.K. held the St. Ghislain sector intact.

The enemy had thrown away splendid troops in hundreds in his haste to force a formidable natural obstacle. "The battalion is battered to pieces, my fine, proud battalion." * The Germans had underestimated the musketry of the British, at whose military efforts they were accustomed to laugh.

But the remorseless logic of big facts dislodged the victors from the outpost line.

Orders issued from D.H.Q. at 7.30 p.m. came at sundown for the K.O.S.B. to retire upon Wasmes. This was carried out without difficulty and hardly a casualty. The passage of the canal was covered on the west side of the lock up to the railway bridge, 200 yards away, by two companies of K.O.Y.L.I., who also acted as rearguard, and in a short time the battalion was in column of route with the blown-up bridge behind it, marching towards Haine.

On the whole the casualties were slight. B and C were never seriously engaged. Besides the officers mentioned, something between 40 and 100 O.R.† were killed, wounded, or missing,‡ including C.S.M. Wilson (d. 24th) and Sergt. Adair. Sergt. A.

* English translation of Walter Bloem's *Vormarsch*.

† O.R. will invariably be used for N.C.O.s and men.

‡ Exact figures are unobtainable: Lieut. R. Joynson puts the total at 45, Major Smith at 100.

23–24 Aug. 1914. Murray, afterwards killed in the Somme on 30th July 1916, was hit but would not report sick, and lasted out the long march. Corp. Fields was shot through the forehead and given up as dead; he made a miraculous recovery after months in a German hospital, and was seen by Major Haig in Holland in 1918. Some loss was suffered among the horses of the transport. Four horses had to be shot, but enough were left to pull the loads. Headed by the transport and guarded by B, the battalion marched S. through Boussu, and then by devious roads S.E. to Wasmes, and then S.W. to Petit Wasmes. When they finally came to rest in a field behind the outpost line held by the 15th I.B. between 1 a.m. and a few hours before dawn the men were too tired to eat. They were yet to learn that there was a tiredness compared with which their then condition was freshness. Confusing as it is to read about this trying midnight march in the dark, it was infinitely more confusing to pick out the route. But the adjutant and transport officer managed to puzzle it out successfully. B seems to have marched by a more direct route through Dour.

All were astir before dawn on the 24th, no matter how little sleep was had. On that day, as well as on the 23rd, the K.O.S.B. fared better than the troops of the brigade to the E.. The D. of W., in particular, suffered severe casualties. German shells were bursting around the bivouac, and the transport was got under weigh for Athis and Houdain after some confused but not costly fighting in a rearguard action near Wasmes at Champ des Sarts. The bulk of the regiment, however, marched, after Blaugies, by the eastern parallel road southwards, and did not halt till a point near Bavai was reached. Here a block ensued, for this was the crossing point of the two divisions of the II. Corps. The 3rd was marching S.W. from Mons towards Le Quesnoi; the 5th took the Roman road on the W. edge of Mormal Forest to the outskirts of Le Cateau. The I. Corps (Sir D. Haig) was retiring from Binche by the E. side of the forest, which there widely divided the British forces into two.* A German division was rumoured to be somewhere to the W., and it was feared the transport might have been lost, as nothing was heard of it at the battalion bivouac between Bavai and St. Vaast-la-Vallée, though both bivouacs were near one another. However, all was well. On the 25th the K.O.S.B. were still farther removed from the enemy, as the 14th I.B. took over the duties of rearguard. It was therefore a day spent in toiling along the dusty, straight pavé † road mile after mile for close on

* On 26th they were 8 miles apart.—Smith-Dorrien, *op. cit.*

† General Smith-Dorrien, *Forty-eight Years*, p. 395.

MONS LOCK IV
AUGUST 23RD 1914

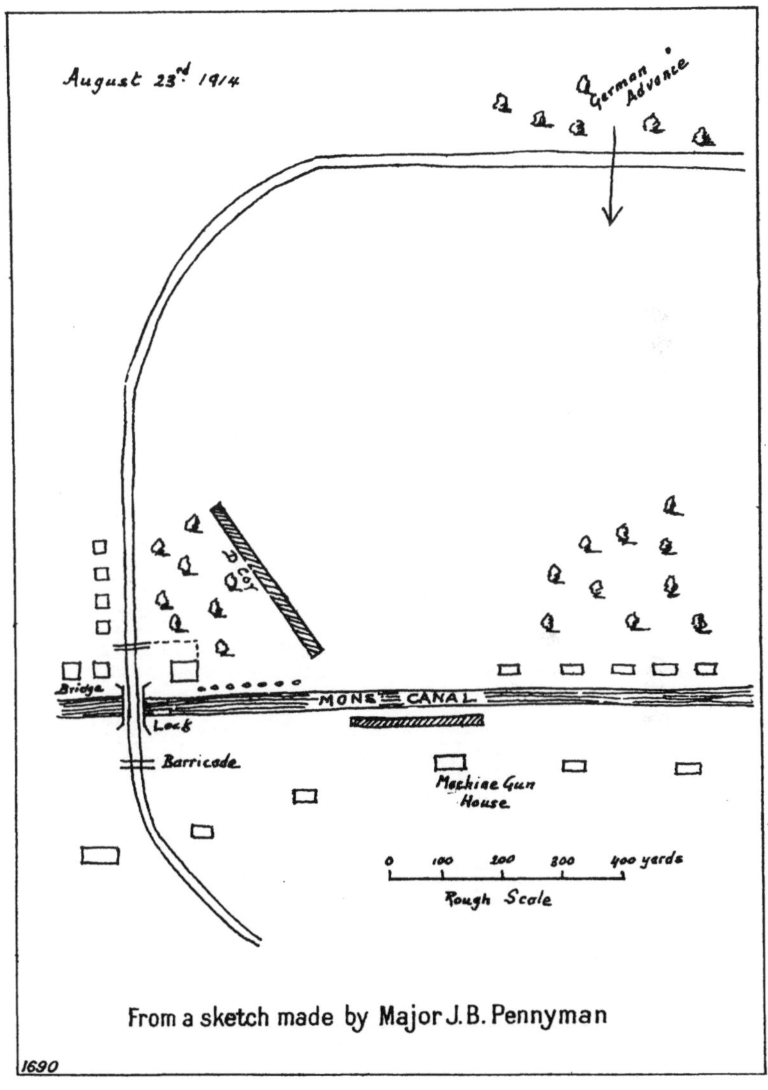

From a sketch made by Major J.B. Pennyman

To face Page 30

22 miles (for the lucky minority) in the sweltering heat : packs had begun to disappear when the retreat began. As the physical strain told, discarding became frequent. Packs, including greatcoats, were natural sacrifice ; entrenching-tools or "grubbers" occasionally, but rarely, shared the same fate. Boots chafed ; rough trousers rubbed to the point of bleeding ; thirsty, sweaty, straggling, puzzled, pursued, yet not downhearted, the columns retreated and retreated. They had looped the loop of the huge forest in the inside of a week, and had fought a battle as well. They were now to fight a stiffer action and have a narrower escape from capture or annihilation. 25 Aug. 1914.

The unlucky majority of the battalion had an extra 3 miles, as they were detailed for flankguard to some wagons and had to march 1½ miles back to find them, but at last they had the joy of seeing the first-line transport go by, and of having no contact with the pursuers. More asleep than awake, footsore and leg-weary, the battalion halted a mile W.N.W. of Le Cateau, a small manufacturing and market town nestling in a hollow in the rolling downs, at an altitude varying from 400 to 480 feet. One tree-lined road, after a couple of twists, the better to climb out of the hollow, ran, French fashion, on the crest of the open, unenclosed downs through Inchy, 4 miles off, 15 miles to Cambrai. The Roman road knew not of Le Cateau. It continues undeviating from Montay (due N. of Le Cateau) where it crosses the Selle, and climbs the high ground, nearly a mile W. of Le Cateau, for 4 miles to Reumont.

The K.O.S.B., halted at Montay, picked up their stragglers, continued their march, crossed the aforesaid Le Cateau—Cambrai road, and bivouacked * in rain on the high ground a mile to the S. of it, W. of Le Cateau, 2 miles E. of Troisvilles. Rain was not unwelcome, but it outstayed its welcome. Drowsiness made the men uncritical of this form of discomfort, but deep sleep was impossible. Such as it was, the K.O.S.B. had as much as any unit in the brigade.

* Dalrymple, Hammond, and Amos shared a hencoop.

CHAPTER II

THE BATTLE OF LE CATEAU AND THE LONG TREK *

26 Aug. 1914. THE 26th of August 1346 † meant less to England than the 26th of August 1914 to the British Empire. The situation was critical in the extreme. The anxieties of Sir Horace Smith-Dorrien and his lieutenants, Generals Hubert Hamilton of the 3rd and Sir Charles Fergusson of the 5th Divisions, were great. The II. Corps was faced with the alternative of either joining a battle that must eventually be broken off (always a difficult operation) or continuing to retreat with the risk of being squeezed away from Sir Douglas Haig's I. Corps. For the enemy were advancing through the forest past the very Landrecies and Maroilles of that hot and happy day one week ago, and on the W. there was the risk of being engulfed by the mobile forces of Von Kluck before French help could arrive.

The Commander-in-Chief was well aware of the dangers of a continued retirement. Equally, he felt that if the line from Ribemont on the Oise, in front of St. Quentin on the Upper Somme, to Vermand on the Omignon a tributary of the Somme could be gained, a defensive position and contact with the retiring French would be ample reward for extracting the last grains of marching stamina from the tired troops. He urged retirement, but on a report from the Corps Commander that battle must be accepted if the Corps was to evade pursuit as the Germans were too near, he trusted the man on the spot and placed the available additional troops at his disposal. There were—(1) the newly-arrived 4th Division under Major-General T. D'O. (afterwards Sir Thomas) Snow, (2) two of Sir E. Allenby's cavalry brigades, and (3) the 19th I.B., one hastily formed on 25th August out of units on the line of communications under Major-General L. G. Drummond, C.B.. It had already taken part in Mons and the retreat and was, therefore, as tired as the 5th Division. Its formation was responsible for all later divisions having the number of their middle brigade divisible by 3.

* See Map 1 in pocket.

† See *Official History of the War*, vol. i. p. 141, "Anniversary of Crécy."

The high ground south of the Le Cateau—Cambrai road had been prepared for defence by civilians under French military direction. Opinion seemed to vary according to locality as to whether the trenches were well sited. K.O.S.B. opinion is that the trench lengths, *i.e.* about 20 yards each, were too short and the trenches too shallow. From long before dawn the battalion had marched by companies into its allotted sector S. of "140" on the sketch map. It was the W. unit of the 13th I.B., between the K.O.Y.L.I. (R.) and the Bedfordshire Regiment of the 15th I.B. (Gleichen's). Beyond the K.O.Y.L.I. was the 14th I.B. (Rolt) with an exposed flank and on the other flank were the 9th, 8th and 7th I.B. of the 3rd Division, and beyond them again and slightly refused the incompletely mobilised 4th Division (Snow) which had detrained at Le Cateau and marched north-west to Solesmes on the 25th, only to be recalled more than 10 miles to the battle position. Divisional H.Q. were at Reumont; II. Corps were at Bertry. **26 Aug. 1914.**

There is nothing intricate about the battle. It was an unequal artillery duel and was an object-lesson in the volume and accuracy of the German fire, which was for so long to damage and put at a disadvantage the B.E.F.. At no time was there a serious infantry attack opposite the 13th I.B.. But a worse way of spending a fine warm August day than crouching in shallow trenches during a rain of shells hour after hour from 8 a.m. to 3 p.m. can hardly be imagined. The British gunners, rightly no doubt, preferred the magnificent massed infantry targets to counter-battery work, and left the Germans the freer to bombard their own and their infantry comrades' position. The real danger lay in the casualties through gun fire and in infiltration through Le Cateau, the valley of the Selle, and the slopes east of the valley.

Appreciating this danger the Corps Commander gave orders between midday and 1 p.m. to break off the battle. He had achieved his aim, checked the enemy, and compelled him to deploy, given his own men a kind of rest, and enabled much of his impedimenta to clear away. But breaking off an engagement rarely happens by the clock. Orders reach one unit and not its neighbour, or reach one company of a unit and not the others, or fail to reach one particular company or platoon.

The K.O.S.B. have to be fitted into this picture. The final decision to stand and fight only reached battalion H.Q. *via* Major Haig as dispositions were being made for taking up the duties of the rearguard of the division together with the K.O.Y.L.I. on the R.. The necessary changes had the effect of putting C under Capt. Macdonald in trenches across the centre of the flat salient marked on the

26 Aug. 1914. sketch map with the figure "140," from 300 to 400 yards S. of the Le Cateau—Cambrai road. On the R. was A (Lieut. Lindsay) extending to where the down slope towards the town began but not so far as the Roman road and, unfortunately, not within sight of the K.O.Y.L.I.. D (Lieut. Dalrymple) was in support in dead ground, without a view, in two half-companies, and B (Major Coke), originally intended for the firing-line farther W., found itself once more in reserve in a gap between the 15th and 13th I.B., where there were no trenches. Fortunately few men had been guilty of the unpardonable crime of throwing away their "grubbers" and quite fair shelters were made as the result of feverish digging with these. This sector was not so heavily shelled as others, but the reserve company saw a battery of our artillery literally "blown to pieces" * and the one surviving officer most gallantly brought in by Col. Stephenson and an orderly in full view of the enemy. About 11.30 a.m. a tendency to retire was observed on the R., but before the cause was ascertained to be due to orders failing to reach the particular body, the G.O.C. himself was seen to gallop forward and turn the troops back to the original positions. There they were joined by D's reserve under Major Haig, who found a fair field of fire and a view to the R. as well. But beyond the Le Cateau—Cambrai road there were folds by which the enemy could be dribbled up out of sight. It was soon evident that the brunt of the attack was nearer Le Cateau and against the K.O.Y.L.I. and the 14th I.B., and also on the other flank against the 15th I.B. covering Troisvilles. But about 2.30 p.m. artillery from a new position opened on the K.O.S.B.. Some of these trenches were conspicuous on account of newly-turned earth, and casualties began to occur so that the trenches had to be evacuated and open ground R. and L. occupied.

For the first time masses of Germans in column were observed about two miles off on the other side of the Selle, apparently past the British position. Major Haig was then wounded in the shoulder but managed to report the situation to the C.O. before painfully walking to Reumont dressing-station. As bad luck would have it the station was overrun by the Germans, and Major Haig awoke from an opiate next morning to find himself a prisoner. The order to retire reached the C.O. soon after 3 p.m. and was passed on. But one of the difficulties of war is to get orders through to everybody. On this occasion C were the sufferers. One platoon under Lieut. Harvey, nearest D, did retire in sympathy, but the remaining three platoons were out of sight, and having orders to hold their ground to the last, did so till completely surrounded and outnumbered.

* Major Smith.

Thus ceased the participation of nearly three-fourths of what had been a practically intact company. Meanwhile A had occasionally had long-range targets of infantry and had had wonderfully few casualties considering the way shells fell all round. Soon after 3.30 p.m. they also retired in a S.W. direction dictated by the German thrust on the R. until the point " tree," where a stand was made for nearly an hour, while the men fired at and checked the enemy at about 900 yards range. Then came a further retreat on Maurois on the Roman road. Intense shelling caused casualties, among them the C.O., Col. Stephenson. A horseless * ambulance was found and the C.O. and six other wounded were hauled by hand as far as Bois de Gatigny, where it was left by order, as its retention would have merely led to the capture of the team. Thus by the hard fate of war the 2nd K.O.S.B. lost its two senior officers, and they in turn were robbed of further opportunity of leading in war those whom they had so ably trained and so gallantly introduced to war. As it was, pursuit was so close that Lieut. Joynson while trying to rescue a wounded man of another regiment was charged by cavalry, hit on the head and made prisoner. Another prisoner was Lieut. Shewen of B.. He was made delirious and unconscious by the close passage of a shell. On coming round, a confused idea that a medical armlet might help him to escape induced him to put one on. This might have earned him a bullet, but the Germans evidently took the sensible view that he was not in his sound senses; besides these, Lieut. G. P. Hammond † had fallen and Lieut. Bayley was wounded but declined to report sick. Capt. Cobden, along with 2nd Lieut. Bell and Teeling, all of C, were missing. Thus ended the battle of Le Cateau in general, hurried retreat, with a loss of about 8000 men. It was the last battle for many a long day when a Divisional Commander would be seen personally directing the front troops from horseback. Sir Charles Fergusson seemed to lead a charmed life as he galloped up and down the line throwing in a cheery word now and then.‡ A K.O.S.B. officer carried away a picture of the complete *sang froid* of Gen. Gleichen, who might have been at manœuvres. A good deal of mixing up and confusion resulted, although the Army never became a mob. The K.O.S.B. had fared better than their neighbours the K.O.Y.L.I., who never received any order to retire, but

26 Aug. 1914.

* Civilians were accused of unyoking the horses while the driver was attending to the wounded (Gleichen, *op. cit.*, p. 54). That general saw men of the K.O.S.B. harness themselves to the wagons.

† Erroneously marked " K. in a., 10–9–14," in Official List. Major Pennyman's Diary.

‡ See Lord E. Hamilton's ***The First Seven Divisions*** (Hurst & Blackett, 1919), p. 64.

26–27 Aug. 1914. continued to stand their ground and take heavy toll of the enemy until their flanks were turned, and despite the efforts of Major Yate and his gallant men the line was rolled up, with the result that only 8 officers and 320 O.R. escaped.* Their resistance did, however, enable the bulk of the 5th Division to get at least an hour's start of their pursuers. It was as Dalrymple noted in his diary, "a wonderful escape" from dire peril.

For some unexplained reason the German advance W. of the Selle stopped at Honnechy, 4 miles from Le Cateau, and thanks to the operations of Generals d'Amade and Sordet, whose forced march from Avesnes had begun to bear timely fruit, immediate peril was averted from the W. flank. Batches of men, therefore, as best they could, made their way across country eventually to join the long trail on the Roman road. These groups often believed themselves to be the sole survivors of their battalion.† Scottish troops tended to herd under officers with glengarries. The instinct for formation was present even though the scene was an orderly crowd, and in the inside of three days the 13th and 14th I.B. were sorted out into their proper commands. The 15th I.B. had never been so much broken up as the others. By the time the march had reached Noyon, near the Oise, the 5th Division was itself again. But of the ordeal let Dr. Dolbey speak : ‡ "In a dream we marched, unconscious of the towns we passed, the villages we slept in ; fatigued almost beyond endurance ; dropping to sleep at the five-minute halt that was the reward of each four miles covered. All companies, dozing as they marched, fell forward drunkenly on each other at the halts ; sleeping men lay, as they had halted, in the roads and were kicked uncomplainingly into wakefulness again. . . . Once more forward with feet that hurt like a hundred knives. None but a Regular Army could have done it, and after the war we shall worship the gods of spit and polish and barrack-square again."

The pursuit was not pressed. The day was oppressively hot. From the British cavalry point of view the enemy gave no trouble at all after Le Cateau.

The night of the 26/27th was passed anyhow and anywhere about 7 miles from the battlefield ; that of 27/28th at Ollézy, 3½ miles E. of Ham on the Somme ; that of the 28/29th at La Pommeraye in the woods 4 miles S.E. of Noyon and of the Oise. But on this occasion twenty-five hours' halt was allowed, for it was known that the peril of the pursuit was now over. On went the same old tramp, tramp, but S. of the Oise lies the Aisne and over it the B.E.F.

* *Official History*, 1914, p. 166.
† Dolbey, *op. cit.*, p. 8. ‡ *Ibid.*, p. 10.

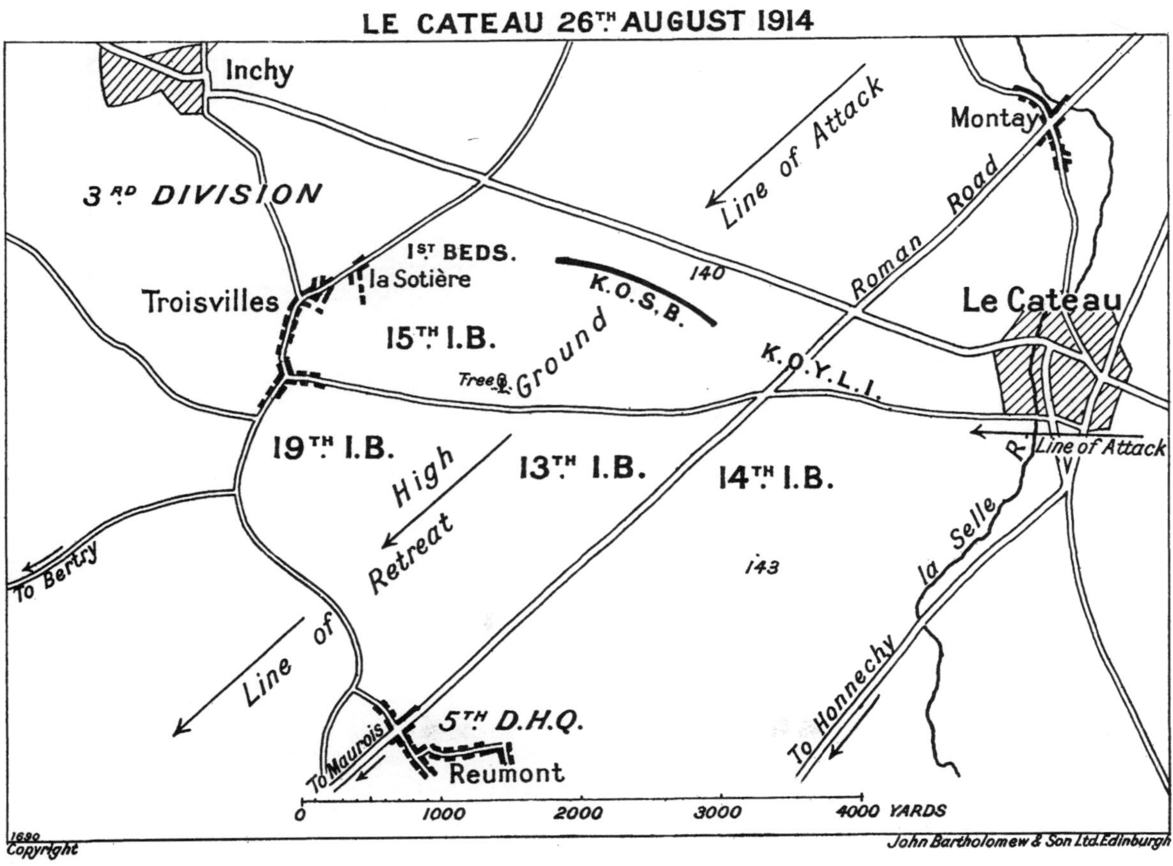

To face Page 36

retreated. The K.O.S.B. crossed at Atichy and passed the night at Jaulzy on the S. bank. But there was one more river to cross, the most famous in Britanno-French history—the Marne. On the last day of August a march of about 17 miles took them south of the enormous and lovely forest of Compiègne to Crépy-en-Valois. At this point Bayley's pluck availed him no longer, and he was evacuated wounded. The War Diary does not disclose the fact that he returned to the battalion only to be killed at Richebourg during the battle of La Bassée, deeply regretted by all.* 1 Sept. 1914.

CRÉPY-EN-VALOIS

Crépy is interesting as the first point at which the I. and II. Corps resume contact. But a stirring little affair, to all intents and purposes, and, so far as this story is concerned entirely, an infantry action, in which the K.O.S.B. took part, began early in the morning of the 1st of September. The R.W.K. were on outpost duty N. of Crépy and the K.O.S.B. were enjoying a few hours snatched repose, when, before 7 a.m., they were called up to stand-to and reinforce the firing-line in turnip fields astride the main road to Compiègne, and eventually to cover the retreat of the outposts. Contact was soon established and the vigorous attack as vigorously met. The real danger lay in the possibility of the hostile artillery opening on the retreating columns streaming S. towards Silly-le-Long. The K.O.S.B. were quite enjoying the fight and annoyed at having to retire about 10 a.m., but they had the satisfaction of keeping up a rearguard action all day and finding that contact had died away before the comfortable billets of Silly were reached. The brigadier was never uneasy and the retirement went like clockwork. Paris was now less than 40 miles away and still the fine hot 2nd of September saw the British retiring in the small hours upon Cuisy about 5 miles N. of Meaux-sur-Marne. The Diary mentions Coulommes as "next stop," but does not tell us that the march—one of the hottest and weariest and apparently most pointless of the lot—involved the passage of the Marne at Esbly with the traverse of the Forêt de Crécy still to be made. And even then the cup of bitterness had not yet been drunk. By 5th September the neighbourhood of Presles was reached and Paris lay only 20 miles to the N.W..

* Officers' Casualty Roll: George Baird Bayley, 2/Lt., k. in a. 26–10–14.

CHAPTER III

THE MIRACLE OF THE MARNE *

The Aisne

Sept. 1914. WITH characteristic stolidity the British troops welcomed but did not speculate as to the cause for the order to advance. It is no part of a regimental history to discuss the miscarriage of the German "great wheel" in its latest phase of an extra hook or whip-tail eastwards across the front of the British force. It happened, and that is enough. The pursued became the pursuers, and the next week's news did much to hearten the home front even if it raised false hopes of warfare open till victory. The K.O.S.B. C.O. got the news from Sir Charles himself in the afternoon, while the following admirable little "beat" of a covert suspected (unjustly) of harbouring Uhlans was being carried out. Good shots were posted at points where the game were likely to break covert and it was part of the joke that one of the "guns" was a noted poacher in private life. The covert was in fact drawn blank, but every one was amused. But the G.O.C.'s news drove all other thoughts away. All were elated. That very day Captain "Charlie" Connell joined up after a weary hunt for the battalion with the first reinforcements.† The K.O.S.B. did not march back on their tracks when they started at 4 a.m. on 6th September. The route lay more to the E. by Coulommiers, Saacy on the Marne, Chouy N. of the Ourcq and W. of Oulchy-le-Château, across the battlefield round Hartennes, where so many Borderers fell in 1918, and down into the trough of the Aisne below its junction with the Vesle 6 miles E. of Soissons, and across to the stone wall of the Aisne heights.

They were not heavily engaged in the momentous combats from the 6th—a Sunday as usual—to the 9th of September, which compelled the Germans to hasten by forced marches to the N. bank of the Aisne, and are properly styled the Battle of the Marne. In fact

* See Map 1.

† Lieut. Dalrymple records that only 13 officers were left, and that on 5th September he and Amos were the only ones in D. He also notes that among the casualties on the 8th was C.S.M. Spraggon (w.).

Sept. 1914.

the British forces merely had brushes with the enemy. But they shared in the pursuit and in the uplift of spirit which pervaded the whole division, and in their turn as advanced-guard of the leading brigade were often on the very heels of the cavalry, and eye-witnesses of the evidence of the flight and defeat of their opponents in dead and dying men and horses, abandoned guns, M.G., transport, dirty bivouacs, fired houses, and rifled estaminets. Chaos and wanton damage marked the path of the plunderers. A few "miserable Uhlans" * were picked up at Courtry on the 6th. The march through the quaint old town of Coulommiers, knocked about by the retiring Germans, on the Grand Morin, to bivouacs near Boissy 3 miles farther E. was without incident. On the 8th the weather broke. On the road by 6 a.m. the K.O.S.B. found contact with an enemy rearguard N.E. of Doue about 9 a.m.. Thereafter there was a running fight all the way down to the Petit Morin, the brush at Mauroy terminating in the capture of St. Cyr close to St. Ouen. In this action the battalion as advanced-guard and in support of the K.O.Y.L.I. played its part. Capt. Connell describes the action as of a "stereotyped pattern." The cavalry and R.H.A. were first to come into action and then they cleared to the flanks. The K.O.S.B. (then about 600 strong) thereupon deployed with two companies in front and two respectively in support and reserve and took up the tale. Skirmishing sometimes in rushes at the double over high and exposed ground the battalion reached the shelter of down-sloping woods with only 12 casualties * and reformed in a railway cutting at the bottom of the slope. "Battle raging ahead: Division at Doue," is the terse note in 2nd Lieut. T. C. Gillespie's diary. He was close at hand bringing the third reinforcements, and had found them an unruly crowd to handle on the journey from the Verne, Portland, *via* St. Nazaire, Tours, and Villeneuve near Crécy Forest. The second lot were also at hand under Lieut. J. M. Ferguson, an ex-K.O.S.B., who had hurried back from the Malay States to rejoin, and, in fact, both drafts reached the battalion on the 9th but, officially, were handed over on the 10th. The action on the 8th was a hot enough affair and Dering, the adjutant, had his horse shot from under him. The Grand Morin crossed, the battalion bivouacked on the heights to the N. and moved off on the 9th at 11 a.m. in cold rain. On this day the K.O.S.B. were the rear unit of the division, and in due course crossed the Marne by the intact bridge at Saacy 4 miles E. of La Ferté-sous-Jouarre, where the Petit Morin joins the Marne, and bivouacked in a wood. It was bitterly cold and raining heavily.

* Major Pennyman's Diary.

Sept. 1914. They had witnessed the superb spectacle of the forcing of the Marne, and they took up positions won by the gallantry and sacrifice of their comrades of the 14th and 15th Brigades. The morning of the 10th was wet, and the battalion, once more in the front, passed through the human, equine, and material wreckage of yesterday's battle over country intended to be tranquilly rural. The pursuit was not pressed past Chézy-en-Orxois, a bleak spot for a chilly night. The 11th was no better. Rain fell, carcasses smelt, German litter was lying about everywhere, and Hartennes, 10 miles S. of the Aisne, was overcrowded. 2nd Lieut. Gillespie's nice quarters had been looted. Dalrymple also slept in a ransacked house, commenting that it was luck to find any shelter at all. The German retreat was a more hurried, disorderly performance than that of the Allies. But there was evidence of systematic sacking and of strange conduct on the part of the pioneers of Pan-Germanic Kultur. "In nearly every house these men had left filthy evidence of their bestial habits behind them." * Wanton destruction met the eye everywhere in the shape of burnt houses and looted estaminets. The K.O.S.B., however, paid more attention to groups of real prisoners and to roadside litter as signs of headlong flight. Their enemy was evidently not invincible. The march was *via* St. Quentin, Chouy, St. Rémy-Blanzy, and the 13th I.B. were well ahead.† As the rain still poured on the 12th the roads were in a bad state, and the growing congestion caused delay. The K.O.S.B. thought their rest was won when they reached Serches, in a deep chine 2 miles from the Aisne. But they were marched off E., across the Vesle, to support the cavalry at Chassemy, only to find that they were not needed, and, like the Duke of York's men, must march down again. Oddly enough, a wood near Chassemy is called Bois-du-Temps Perdu. The night's rest at Serches was brief. The battalion had to be up betimes to support the R.W.K. in an attempt to cross the Aisne and continue the pursuit. The march was over the upland north, through Ciry towards Sermoise down in the valley. But further progress could not be made. The greater part of the fine sunny day they sheltered in fields behind haystacks and other cover, or later on in the cellars of Sermoise, listening to the artillery duel or working off arrears of sleep, and oblivious of the fact that one stray shell had "found" the transport behind and had killed two invaluable warriors, Q.M. Murray and R.S.M. Macwhinnie.

* Dolbey, *op. cit.*, p. 17, corroborated with emphasis by Brig.-Gen. Coke. Lieut. Pennyman saw fewer evidences of misconduct, and nothing that amounted to atrocities; it is comforting to know that the nasty, prevalent racial blemish was not universal.

† Six miles (13th I.B., W.D.).

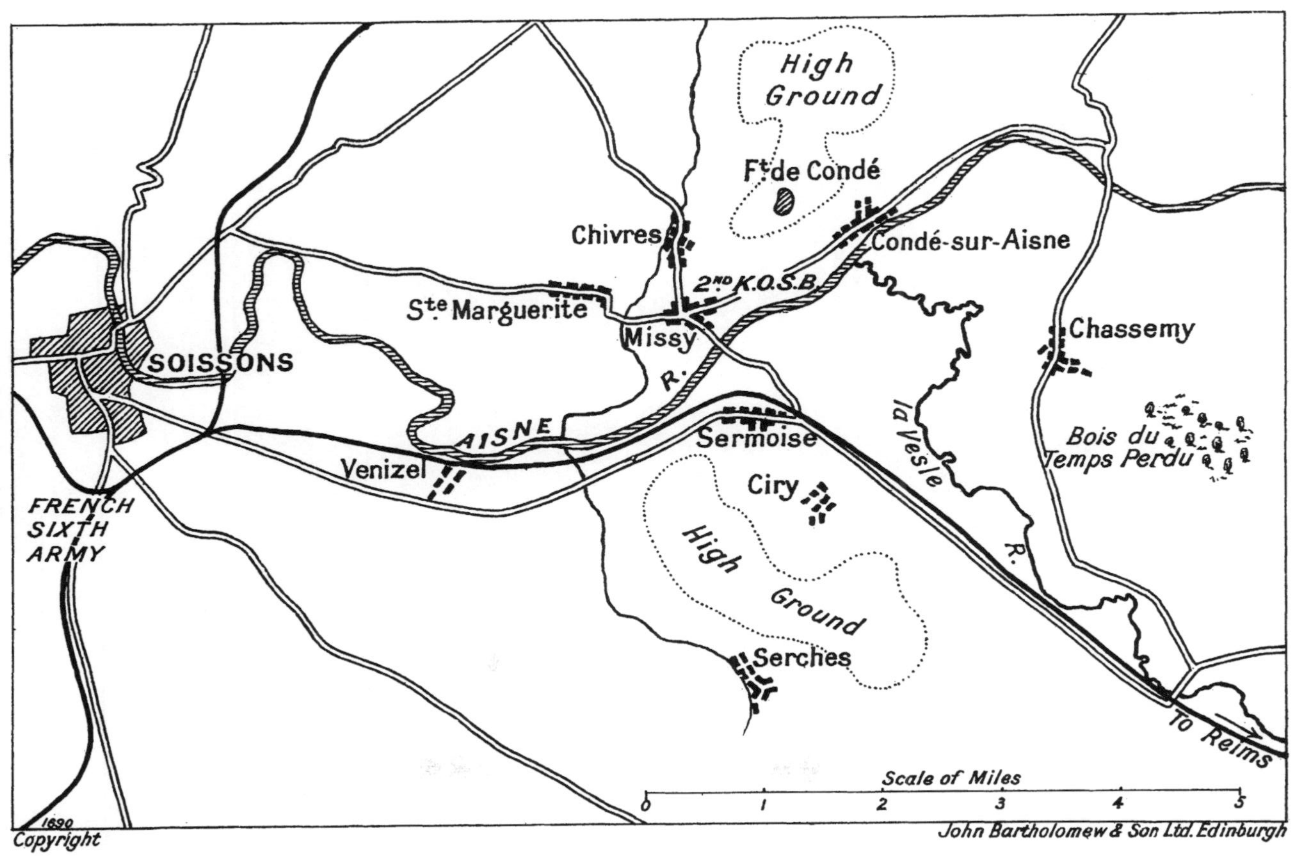

To face Page 40

The transport had halted near the crest of the road to Sermoise to let the cavalry ambulances pass. As bad luck would have it, the spot was visible to the enemy gunners (in the opinion of Capt. Dolbey and of Brig.-Gen. Gleichen), or it was a chance hit. "There were 6 feet 5 inches of Macwhinnie, and every inch was good," says Dolbey, and with justice. He was a native of Caerlaverock, and a notice of him appeared in the Dumfries local war souvenir of November 1914. He was killed outright. Capt. Murray died the same day. He had been R.S.M. of the 2nd Battalion in India, and had been appointed Q.M. of the 1st Battalion in 1903 at Belfast. He exchanged to the 2nd Battalion as Q.M. in 1911. Quiet, competent, and efficient, he was a serious loss.

Sept. 1914.

The general situation on the 13th was that the wings of the British army were across the Aisne, and that the centre was setting about crossing with varying success. The French Sixth Army were across at Soissons, and the British III. Corps at Venizel, 3 miles to the E.. The heights N. of the Aisne strike the eye of the greenest greenhorn as a terrific military obstacle. Standing at Sermoise one looks E. and W. along immense and apparently unending "haughs" of dead-flat rich land, mostly water-meadows, watered by the Aisne and the Vesle. Behind the former rise the natural ramparts. The valley is never less than a mile wide, and the Aisne is deep and from 24 to 50 yards wide. The heights consist of a plateau over 600 feet above sea-level, for the greater part narrow, like most of the famous "Chemin-des-Dames" (assaulted by Haig and his men), and fairly broad towards Allemant, N. of Soissons.

But *the* feature is the way in which the plateau is trenched and scarred by lateral, narrow, gorge-like valleys, each sending its small affluent to the Aisne. Opposite Sermoise is the snout of Chivres, crowned by the Fort de Condé, which commands the upper and lower Aisne and looks up the Vesle for miles. The slopes of this spur, whether on the face towards Condé or Chivres, or on the ridge towards Missy, where it projects on to the plain, are densely wooded. Our greenhorn can at once see that those who had to deal with the crossing at Missy and any advance beyond that village had the most formidable task of any troops engaged. Apart from the chances of its being too lightly held owing to a gap in the German line, or of success elsewhere by a turning movement forcing the Germans to evacuate, the Chivres *massif* was literally impregnable. Towards evening the K.O.S.B., in single file through crops and odd banks, dribbled out in parties towards Missy bridge in the wake of the R.W.K.. Another topic for speculation is why the Germans allowed the Aisne to be crossed without molestation (by means of rafts

Sept. 1914. hurriedly constructed by the R.E.) by the whole of the R.W.K. and K.O.S.B.. Perhaps it was intentional. Certainly the next fortnight was not a bed of roses for the 13th I.B. with the 12-feet deep river at their backs and the snipers at their front, and the lie of the ground against them. It was, to put it mildly, an unconventional military position. Backwards and forwards, and unmolested, about 50 to 100 yards above the bridge, went the little basket rafts with hay, taking four men at a time (and wetting them up to their knees and occasionally half-drowning them).* At dawn on the 14th the Germans in the woods on the slopes offered a target. The K.O.S.B. M.G. opened fire on them, and a regular rifle battle began as the troops were deployed with a view to attacking the ridge. But it was all they could do to hang on to their ground. "Evidently they could see us though they were invisible." † Casualties came swiftly and had to be placed behind a house a few yards E. of the road leading to Missy and quite near the river. The bullets rained like a hailstorm, but the ordinary German was not a marksman, and as he was shooting downhill, most of the bullets swept overhead into the river. But things were bad enough. Later on the front was usually held too thinly. At the Aisne it was too densely held. "The K.O.S.B. were not allotted sufficient frontage for a battalion; they were squeezed between the West Kents and the river, and (apart from a little dead ground under the lee of the road)" [to Missy] "they had to be content with a small area of boggy ground covered with trees." ‡ Major Pennyman has a neat sketch of the ground, and it is reproduced with his permission. An attempt was made to extend E., but fire from somewhere or other stopped each effort.§ There was an enfilading M.G. concealed on the R..|| "We were told that another brigade was coming from our left front to drive the Germans out of their position." ¶

This was true. The brigade in question was the 15th I.B.. The order was to advance from Ste. Marguerite, *i.e.* from the W. upon Missy, and clear the Chivres spur and push on to Condé. Gen. Gleichen calls this "a large order," and so it was.** Much depended in the first instance on what the 14th I.B. could do to clear Missy and Chivres and enable the 15th I.B. to pass behind them and attack the spur from the S. E..†† Space forbids an account of the

* "It had a nasty trick of sinking" (Major Pennyman).

† 2nd Lieut. T. C. Gillespie's Diary. ‡ Information from General Coke.

§ There was a gap of 3 miles between the K.O.S.B. and the 3rd Division (*Official History*, vol. i. p. 335).

|| Dolbey, *op. cit.*, p. 56. ¶ Major Pennyman. ** Gleichen, *op. cit.*, p. 114.

†† *Official History*, vol. i. p. 354. These brigades had crossed by rafts at Moulin des Roches, the site of a former mill, a little above Venizel (Gleichen, *op. cit.*, p. 112).

gallant attempts made by these brigades to accomplish the impossible. In the end of the day the K.O.S.B. were still pinned to their original holding and the story is simply how brave men met wounds and death. This was the beginning of that steady toll of casualties which rapidly changed the personnel of the entire B.E.F. and made the conservation of trained regular officers, including juniors, a matter of vital importance. 2nd Lieut. G. S. Amos, the son of a Borderer, the late Major M'Leod (Peter) Amos, a famous cricketer, fell in the square projection of the boggy woods shown on the sketch. He was guarding that bit of the front against surprise with a platoon. At first he was at the edge, but he reported 5 men casualties by rifle fire and was withdrawn by order more into the middle. But still the fire poured into the salient and the end came soon. He was hit in the heart and died almost at once, and was buried on the field of battle with 19 others the same day. He was a most promising young officer, and had proved his sterling worth at Mons, bringing in a wounded man under fire.* Lieut. Pennyman was the next officer to become a casualty. He felt what seemed like a cricket ball on the chest. He had been struck by a bullet on the left hand below the little finger. The bullet emerged by the thumb bone and passed sideways into the left lung, where it remains. He made a wonderful recovery, and we shall meet him again in the story of the 1st Battalion from 1916 onwards. But the historian is henceforth minus his diary, and the poorer for the want. The experiences of the M.O. give a vivid picture of the wider aspects of the battle. While the rifles of the men at close grips rattled unceasing at the river, the artilleries of both armies were exchanging compliments. The shelling in the flat turned back the Maltese cart with the surgical and medical appliances, but Dolbey with his surgical haversack and the stretcher-bearers were not, like the cart, restricted to the road, and " in very open order " reached the river after running the gauntlet of a rain of bullets across plough and meadow and ditches. A breather at the bank and then a worse lap of 50 yards along the towpath past nasty white stones and British corpses to the broken-down bridge, which was sheltered. And here comes a link with the heroic Capt. W. H. Johnston, V.C., R.E.,† who worked the sodden canvas raft by a guy rope across the stream and fetched Dolbey and a bearer across as coolly as if the Aisne were one of the canals at Aldershot. He kept on that work all day. Once there the M.O. did splendid work

Sept. 1914.

* Dolbey, *op. cit.*

† Capt. W. H. Johnston, R.E., won the V.C. for his direction of the crossing. Alas, he was sniped as Bde.-Major of the 15th I.B., on 8th June 1915, near Zwarteleen.

Sept. 1914. among the wounded K.O.S.B., and he tells in sinister phrase that his morphia and chloroform never gave out. In the long stick-it-out the C.O., the Adjutant, and all the officers set a splendid example which was followed by all ranks.

After 6 p.m. the firing died down, sites for trenches were selected and digging begun. The wounded were accommodated in a farm-house, those from the wood being often hard to find. The rain poured down in buckets and the search went on till 3 a.m. on the 15th. But a veil can be drawn over scenes inseparable from war. Thus ended the 14th, a black day in the annals of the K.O.S.B. .*

The 15th of September brought little change, except that the rifle fire never approached the intensity of the day before ; neither they nor the R.W.K. were able to join in equally unsuccessful forest fighting which the sister brigades were once more called upon to try. That detested Chivres spur, garnished with new trenches, defied all efforts. The day was spent in improving the trenches and shelters. Away behind, Sermoise was tumbling into ruins. Open warfare was drawing to a close and the static underground existence of trench warfare was taking its place. On the 16th, after a pelting night of rain, congestion was relieved by the loan of Connell and two companies to the 14th I.B. at Missy. That evening the arrival of 7 officers of the 3rd Battalion marked the change from professional soldiers to a nation in arms with a leaven of regulars. They were Major W. S. C. Allan, Capts. C. E. Bland,† I. B. Hopkins † and A. J. H. Caird, Lieuts. G. H. Cox and A. D. Young-Herries, and 2nd Lieut. I. A. MacRae. With them came 2nd Lieut. C. S. Woollcombe, son of Sir C. L. Woollcombe, K.C.B., the colonel of the regiment. Of these eight only two survived the war. On the 23rd a draft of 177 arrived under charge of Lieuts. Dixon and Robertson. Unless the K.O.S.B. were in a peculiar position, the draft probably represented the same change in the character of O.R. as has been noted in regard to officers. In most units the regular reservists were soon exhausted and special reservists, *i.e. alias* for militiamen, took their places.

Soon the raw recruits hurriedly made into soldiers in the intensive incubators at the Verne, Edinburgh, and Duddingston, would represent the citizen army. Herries' letters to his father, the Second-in-Command of the 3rd Battalion, are strikingly different from the jottings of a regular officer. They exhibit the naïf interest of a

* "It was the longest and most awful day of my life" (Lieut. Gillespie). "Most awful day of my life: an eternity! 52 men in my company were casualties" (Lieut. Dalrymple).

† Both regulars.

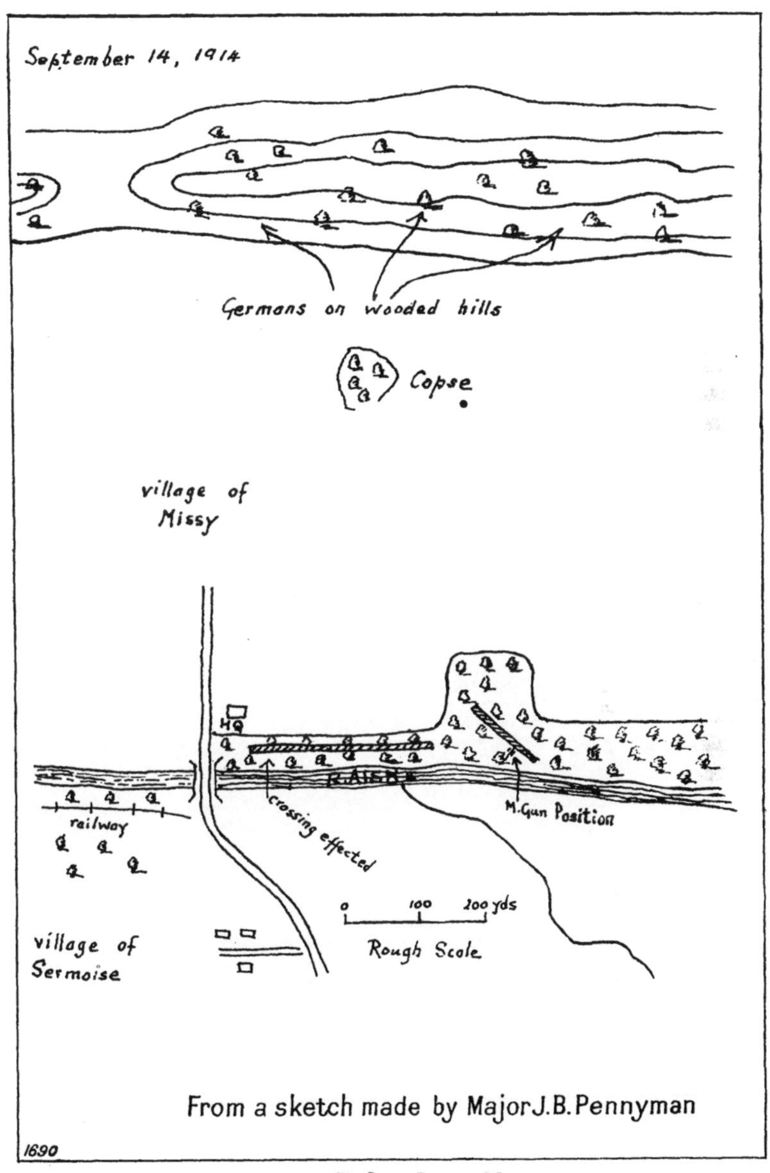

From a sketch made by Major J.B. Pennyman

To face Page 44

serious, purposeful lad in the new life, with the old interests—*e.g.* in entomology and books and home life—still absorbing attention. From him one gets a clear idea of the life during the stagnation of the Aisne. He has plenty of time to watch the artillery duel, the feeble attempt of the pom-poms to hit hostile aircraft. He lives in a hole in the bank, of which the roof is apt to fall in, grows a beard, keeps a careful note of the rations, and is almost exasperatingly discreet about officers' names and information. Letters take twelve days from England. Here is a day: "Roused at dawn and wait about or look-out till breakfast at 7 a.m., bacon, bread, jam, and tea. Bask in the sun or hide in hole from rain and lyddite shells. Write, read any papers sent out. Lunch (bully-beef, bread, cheese, tea) at 12 noon. Tea at 4.30, bread and jam. Get out sentries, etc., at dusk. Supper at 7—a hot stew, tea, and sometimes rum, ugh! Bed (*i.e.* flea-bag), either in the hole in bank or, if on duty, out in trench at 8. But two hours of the night on patrol. It . . . has been the same every day since we got here a fortnight ago."

Sept. 1914.

Up to the last moment he has no suspicion of the move that was the prelude to active warfare sufficient to tax his energies and his comrades' to breaking-point. Such news as reached the trenches was of vague French successes. The current *on dit* was that the war would be over in a few months or weeks. Even in November at the Verne the same illusion prevailed, though the Dumfries local War Souvenir of November 1914 shows that the Duke of Buccleuch gave the most solemn warning of the desperate nature and probably long duration of the conflict.

As the weather improved, from the 20th onwards feelers were put out towards the R., and a large brand-new villa about a mile to the E. of the K.O.S.B. was visited by them and by the K.O.Y.L.I. —and by the Germans—in turn, for foraging.* This rather indicates that the deadly rifle fire on the 14th was more from the slope to the N. and less from the exposed flank than was supposed at the time, and this is confirmed by the fact that Sergt. Quick was shot through both ankles from L. to R.. The German shelling was very persistent and disquieting, but except on the 18th, when 1 man was killed and 15 wounded, was not destructive. What was fatiguing was the outpost duty in the wet and the inadequacy of the shelter of the excavations. "Slept with Smith in a pigsty; spent quite a comfortable night," is an illuminating entry.† The nights were apt to be cold, but the health of the troops was excellent and impressed the M.O..

* Gillespie's Diary.

† Gillespie's Diary. Major Smith.

CHAPTER IV

THE RACE TO THE SEA

The Salient *

Oct. 1914. — SOME facts have been pointed out so often and so clearly that they are common property. The breach of the treaty with Belgium had doubled the French frontier and made it 320 miles instead of 160. By the time the eastern portion from Switzerland, which even the Germans did not violate, to the Aisne had settled down to siege warfare, a turning movement could only be made on the W.. Would the French succeed in rolling up Von Kluck's flank and snap his communications, or would the Germans reach the Channel ports and the Béthune coalfields? Both wings were ill protected, and it is no disparagement of our Ally to say that the coastal wing constituted the greater peril. Sir John French persuaded Gen. Joffre that his true base was not St. Nazaire, but Le Havre and Boulogne, and in consequence of one of the most momentous decisions of the war the British were withdrawn from the Aisne and transferred to the N.. Confining ourselves to the K.O.S.B., we find that orders reached them at 6.30 on Thursday, 1st October, to hand over to the 2nd Lancashire Fusiliers of the 12th I.B., of the 4th Division. Curiously enough the 1st Battalions of the Lancashire Fusiliers, the Royal Inniskilling Fusiliers and the Essex Regiment (three out of the four regiments represented in the 12th I.B.) were afterwards in the 29th Division, in which the 1st K.O.S.B. served throughout the war. The Engineers had done wonders in the way of bridging, and the German guns had not destroyed the bridges. The relief was carried out at night without incident, and the next day spent at Ciry, just S. of Sermoise, in hiding from aeroplanes. A short night march took the battalion to Violaine, where the 3rd of October was similarly passed. Another still shorter march to Hartennes was the precursor of a 15-mile trek by night W. to Largny, beyond Villers-Cotterets on the road from Paris to Soissons. It was a bit of a strain for men who had been standing in mud for a fortnight and unable to get their boots off, but the stragglers were not too

* See Maps 1 and 2 in pocket.

numerous.* The 5th was a blessed day of rest, except for a short march of 6 miles to ideal quarters at Fresnoy.†

On the 6th, after a march of much the same length, which crossed the line of the retreat 3 miles N. of Crépy-en-Valois,‡ the K.O.S.B. entrained at Pont- St. Maxence, 39 miles N. of Paris, for Abbeville on the Somme. Nearly four years would elapse before Borderers would detrain at Pont-St. Maxence to win fame at Buzancy and Rozoy. But the 2nd Battalion saw the Oise for the last time. The night was spent at Noyelles on the Somme estuary, and the troops rested there all the 8th. On the 9th they marched to Gueschart and halted till late at night, when they started again and marched 6 miles across the Authie to Haravesnes, where they halted and bivouacked till they were picked up by French buses in the afternoon of the 10th and driven through St. Pol (soon to be a familiar name) to (5 miles) Valhuon. On the 11th they marched about 16 miles to Verquin, just S.E. of Béthune, and were rewarded by admirable billets. The officers were sumptuously entertained at the château by ladies, whose charm and hospitality will never be forgotten by the survivors.

But the ugly flat country and the smoke and slag heaps recalled Belgium. On the 12th the K.O.S.B. took over a bit of the " front " from the Norfolks of the 15th I.B., and as they are entering on a spell of almost unbroken, desperate fighting, we may once more take stock of the battalion and the situation. The drafts brought by Connell, Gillespie, Ferguson, and Dixon brought up the regiment practically to full strength. Major Coke was C.O., Dering still Adjutant, Connell was Second-in-Command, Major Allan commanded A, Smith B, Bland C, and Dalrymple D. There were 24 officers. They had one of the finest M.O.s in the service, and were sufficiently rested and re-equipped to be in fighting form. The Aisne had taught them the value of pick and shovel and grubber. The 13th I.B. had lost Brig.-Gen. Cuthbert on 1st October, and Brig.-Gen. W. B. Hickie (afterwards Major-General and G.O.C. Irish Division, and Sir W. B. Hickie, K.C.B.), who replaced him, went sick on the 13th, when Col. A. Martyn of the R.W.K. took over the duties of Brigade Commander. The R.W.K. had lost heavily by the end of the Aisne, viz. 15 officers and close on 400 O.R., Missy accounting for 127.§ The D. of W. and, still more, the K.O.Y.L.I. had been badly mauled, the former near Mons, the latter at Le Cateau, but the nucleus was there and the reinforcements well absorbed.

* Either on this march or the next, one K.O.S.B. was shuffling along without boots and with puttees wrapped round his feet (*Invicta*, p. 53).

† Dalrymple.

‡ See p. 37.

§ *Invicta*, p. 48.

Oct. 1914. It was a puzzling situation that presented itself to Major Coke in the difficult region of high hedges, small fields, suburbs, *corons* or miners' rows, canals, railways, and slag heaps.

The place-names are household words. Eight miles E. of Béthune, reached by canal or road *via* Annequin (half-way), lay La Bassée, 7½ N. of Lens and 9 miles S. of Estaires on the Lys. The plain extended W. towards Aire and the forest of Nieppe, and N. to the "ranges" of Cassell, Mont-des-Cats, and Kemmel, which by contrast to the monotony of the plain seem like the Delectable Mountains. Four miles N. of La Bassée is Neuve Chapelle. Eleven miles N.N.E. of La Bassée is Armentières. At Annequin the K.O.S.B. were only 10 miles N.W. of Lens, and there they entered into the fog of war once more. They knew the French were on their R. and were supposed to hold a line more or less continuous S. by Arras, the Somme heights to the Aisne, and that the III. Corps (Pulteney) and the I. (Haig) would probably be found to extend to the N.. "Nobody seemed to know anything except that we should probably soon be fighting again." * "The idea was that we were to push forward to Festubert (3 miles N. of Annequin) and act as a pivot, with our R. near the canal at Rue de l'Épinette, to the 3rd Division, and the remainder of the corps, which were swinging slowly round so as eventually to face S.E. and take La Bassée." †

But the planned offensive soon felt "the strong rebuff of some tumultuous cloud, instinct with fire and nitre." Falkenhayn's ‡ masses were striking for the W., and the La Bassée area was one region where the weight of his blows was felt. On the 12th the bad news came that the French had lost Vermelles, 2 miles S. of Annequin. The language problem had already started, when the K.O.S.B. were relieved by the arrival of the other battalions of the 13th I.B., and were ordered forthwith, *i.e.* at 4 p.m., to attack Cuinchy between the road (S.) and the canal (N.) towards La Bassée. Beyond the canal were the Dorsets slightly in advance of the K.O.S.B.; on their R. were the D. of W.. The attack did not last long. D on the L. met with heavy fire which killed Major Allan (from whom Captain Caird took over) and 2nd Lieut. Woollcombe, a true son of the regiment. Dalrymple was wounded, and there were 10 other casualties. A were also opposed strongly, but the C.O. was able to reinforce before 5 p.m. and, before 6 p.m., to intimate consolidation on the ground then won. The importance of touch with the 15th I.B., for which purpose

* Gleichen, *op. cit.*, p. 156. † Gleichen, *op. cit.*, p. 158.

‡ Falkenhayn had superseded Moltke since 14th September as Chief-of-Staff of the German Field Armies.

Lieut. Rutherfurd and a platoon of B were sent, and of guarding against surprise was impressed on the O.C. firing line, Capt. Connell. Next day it was hoped with the aid of a field-gun to press forward, and a start ordered for 5.30, as part of a larger operation in which the 3rd Division were taking part. The K.O.S.B. still pointed towards Cuinchy and the D. of W. faced Auchy. It was for a brilliant bit of patrol leading that Sergt. J. Skinner won his first honour in the Great War—the D.C.M.. A/C.S.M. H. Pike was similarly honoured. Oct. 1914.

On the 13th, once more the Dorsets N. of the canal were ahead, and by 10 a.m. had halted E. of Givenchy and offered help by oblique fire. But an advance of a furlong was the utmost the K.O.S.B. could achieve, and it was reported that the D. of W. were simply consolidating. So there they also consolidated. As is well known, the Dorsets came in for a terrible shelling, 13 officers were killed and more than half the battalion were killed, wounded, or missing. They were withdrawn to Pont Fixe. Our battalion had 60 casualties (k. and w.), besides losing 2nd Lieut. MacRae, who died on 14th, and Capt. Smith, who could ill be spared, and Caird, both wounded. The 13th was therefore another sombre day for the Borderers. On the 14th Coke was in suspense all day. No messenger could pass the barrage from Connell, and it was only realized, after relief by the 256th Inf. Regt. of the French, that the K.O.S.B. had smothered what might have developed into an attack *en masse*, by steadiness and good musketry. 2nd Lieut. H. J. Harvey was wounded. The French took over speedily and silently about 2 a.m. on 15th, and the K.O.S.B. marched back in the small hours 2 miles to Beuvry utterly exhausted. Early on 16th October a move was made to Le Touret, 4 miles to the N., and rest continued until evening when the battalion marched to Richebourg l'Avoué nearer Neuve Chapelle as reserve of the 14th I.B.. On Sunday, 18th October, the K.O.S.B. were sent to Beau Puits, more than half-way to La Bassée, which they were ordered to storm—in the opinion of Coke an impossible operation in the circumstances. Close on 60 casualties due to gun and M.G. fire demonstrated the futility of an unsupported infantry advance in full view of the enemy. The attack cost the battalion young Gillespie, who had behaved with great gallantry at the head of C in rushing the churchyard in front of Annequin on the 13th and was a most promising officer. His diary reveals a mature mind with pronounced military aptitude. Captain I. B. Hopkins was badly wounded. There was nothing to be done but to consolidate the 300 yards or so of gained ground. On the 18th the 5th Division lost their G.O.C.,

Oct. 1914. — promoted Lieutenant-General. He was much missed by the only Scottish battalion. Almost the last note in Gillespie's diary is that Sir Charles had congratulated the Borderers on their three days' fight. He was succeeded by Major-Gen. (Sir T. L. N.) Morland, afterwards a Corps Commander like Sir Charles, under whom Borderers would often serve.

This is what Sir Charles Fergusson wrote :—

"15*th October* 1914.

"MY DEAR COKE,—Will you please tell your battalion that their work during the last three days has been spoken of in the highest terms by General Hickie, and the Corps Commander directs that you and your men should be informed of his great admiration and appreciation of their pluck and grit.

"I can't say how proud I am of them, and the fact that we are all Scotsmen * adds to the pleasure. I will take the first opportunity of coming to see you, but shall not bother you till you've had a rest and sleep, of which you must all be in need.

"With many thanks to you and the battalion.—Yours sincerely,

(Signed) CHARLES FERGUSSON."

The situation was anxious in the extreme. In these days it was a question of stopping gaps. If the British had been disappointed of a wide gap to lead to Lille, the enemy might be successful in finding one which would separate the Allied Armies and roll the British up against the Flanders coast. Staff work in these early days had not been elaborated as it was in the later stages. C.O.s acted on their initiative, and all careful ones never rested, till they had found touch with neighbours R. or L. or found out how large a gap separated them. After the action on the 18th had died down and positions had been taken up in the tobacco fields confronting Le Bizet, it was found necessary for Capt. Connell personally to reconnoitre in the dusk to the L. of the Borderers. As he only found 1 sergeant and 1 man he reported to the C.O., who satisfied himself that his flank really was in the air for several hundred yards, and that the nearest officers and men were at a farm near Lorgies Church. These were pushed forward to link up with the L. of the K.O.S.B.. Another prudent act is to patrol the front. On this occasion it was reported that the Germans were preparing to come on. Forewarned is forearmed, and the attack was beaten off. But suppose it had been directed against the empty bit of line ? The

* Borderers not Scotsmen by blood are so by adoption, "Scots *ad hoc*" as a lawyer would put it. This was a puzzle to the Germans. See Dolbey, *op. cit.*, p. 222.

consequences might have been serious indeed! It seems also on one occasion to have been the case that with the sway of the battle line some of the enemy on one flank of the K.O.S.B. were level with the firing-line. Either could therefore have turned sideways and seen who was best at enfilade fire. Both combatants were so engrossed with their respective fronts that the lateral proximity remained unexploited. Yet the gap was only 50 yards wide.*

The impregnability of La Bassée, with its famous sugar factory and railway triangle, was realized at last, and the 14th Brigade found it necessary slightly to recoil. The K.O.S.B. in executing a skilful and silent retirement on Richebourg had the misfortune to lose the M.O. and Sergt. Thompson, his right-hand man, who were rushed by Germans at night in the forward clearing station. The last day and night of the M.O. with the K.O.S.B. are vividly related in *A Regimental Surgeon in War and in Prison*, while his subsequent pages reveal something dreadfully amiss in *Kultur*, and something that shows up the Germans of the 1871 *Reich* as unfit for the *Weltmacht* they coveted and all but won. The pages also reveal a gallant and charming character.

Six days' continuous fighting was rewarded by something of a rest at Richebourg, or rather behind it, in bivouacs to avoid shells. On the 24th Capts. Fullerton and A. F. Anderson (the latter an old cavalryman who had rejoined for the war) of the 3rd Cameronians reported along with 2nd Lieut. C. K. Scott-Moncrieff † of the 3rd Battalion, in charge of a draft of 83 men, for whom there was only too much room. At the end of the month the strength was little above 600. If the long share in the battle of La Bassée (10th October to 2nd November) borne by the K.O.S.B. lacks something of the dramatic *tour de force* of the R.W.K. at Neuve Chapelle, it rivals it in the exhibition of military instinct and of tenacity under sound leadership.

The K.O.S.B. did not return to their original brigade when on 31st October they bussed from Merville in the plain near the Forêt de Nieppe and about 7 miles N.W. of Richebourg. For a time they were every man or any man or no man's child; on this occasion they were driven *via* Wytschaete (still in our hands) to Wulverghem, and placed under the orders of a future G.O.C. Division of the 1st Battalion, Major-General B. de Lisle, G.O.C. 1st Cavalry Division, with a view to the recapture of Messines.

A word about the lie of the land at this point. Mont Kemmel

* Information from Gen. Coke and Col. Connell.

† Afterwards M.C.. His early death, cutting short a brilliant literary career, was announced in the Press on 3rd March 1930.

Oct. 1914. with a height of 500 feet above sea-level does not stick out of the plain on the E. side like a pyramid or North Berwick Law. N. and E. of the Douve the ground rises to Messines (2 miles E. of Wulverghem) some 215 feet above sea-level, and N.E. to (3 miles) Wytschaete, a most commanding and imposing situation 260 feet high, and connected by a mildly concave saddle with the Kemmel *massif*, by which in turn it is dominated. For the purpose of the ensuing actions this description may be extended by the reminder that the Wytschaete ridge, though never again so high, continues N.E. (cut by the canal and railway from Comines on the Lys to Ypres on the Yser by deep cuttings), by Klein-Zillebeke (in 1914 the centre of quite an attractive woodland country) to Zonnebeke, and thence N. to Passchendaele and Vestrosebeke, to drop into the wood of Houthulst. The ridge thus encircled Ypres, to which the ground rolled down on the inner slopes, and formed the watershed with the usual commanding views between the maritime plain and the industrial plain of Flanders. It was the fate of that ridge to be the scene of recurring epidemics of furious battlings. *Si monumentum quæris, circumspice.* The ubiquitous cemeteries chill the most frivolous to awe at the terrors of war even at this date.

Once again there was no question of initiative. The enemy were more numerous and had attained a lodgment on the coveted Messines ridge. The K.O.S.B. entered the final phase of the three weeks' battle of Messines as counter-attackers and stop-gaps. On the 31st October, that supremely critical day of the whole war, while the fight raged E. of Ypres and the issue hung by a hair, a detachment of cavalry—the 5th Dragoon Guards—were hanging on, also by a hair, to the village of Messines. They were on one side of the main street and the Germans on the other. It was the task of the K.O.S.B., in co-operation with the K.O.Y.L.I. on the N., to pass through the cavalry, clear the S.E. half of the village, and push on E. in the open country to the S., as well as beyond the village. Major Coke commanded these infantry reinforcements, who were less than 800 strong. Their advance began at 1 p.m., and was so far satisfactory that not only was the line held by the cavalry extended to the E. edge of Messines by C, but A gained a short distance in advance on the R., until checked by heavy rifle and M.G. fire. It was desperate, close fighting. Sometimes only 50 yards or less separated the foes. House-to-house fighting is as difficult to describe as it is to conduct. 2nd Lieut. Dering's M.G. found a site for a perfect enfilade at point-blank range on a populous target. The wretched gun chose that moment to fail. The chance was gone. In that most nerve-stretching, surprising type of warfare, when death may threaten from above, below, at the side, and even from behind, the K.O.S.B. took the convent and cleaned out the houses near the church. But though the enemy was seen hurrying back to his prepared positions by the brickfields E. of Messines, once he got there, by covering fire from reserves, he was able to hold the K.O.S.B. within the E. edge. Our troops were not displeased with the day's work, and consequently not expecting an order to retire the next morning. The salient could not be retained indefinitely by troops so inferior in numbers without reinforcements, and the descent behind the Steenebeek (a tributary of the Douve from the Wytschaete ridge) was the price for shortening the line. Moreover, on the northern half things had not gone so well. The Germans still had their footing in the village, and the K.O.S.B. had to send two platoons of D to make a defensive flank between the cavalry and the K.O.Y.L.I.. Orders to retire were sent forward at 8 a.m., but the seniors on the spot—the O.C. troops and Major Coke—sent back a message that the withdrawal was premature and the situation, if stationary, was well in hand. Nov. 1914.

The message must have miscarried, for the German bombardment was soon supplemented by a vigorous British rival, and the garrison of Messines beat a hasty retreat with heavy loss. Not a vestige of blame attaches to the R.A., for not a British soldier was in sight. Their heroism at Le Cateau, their superb shooting at the La Bassée sugar factory, and the ever-improving liaison kept the infantry from even theorising on the basis of carelessness on their part. It was just one of the prices of the fog of war—a mishap.

All the troops then retired to a line of trenches E. of Wulverghem. The enemy left them unmolested, content with the "croon o' the caus'ey." Better was to follow for him, for Wytschaete fell to the Bavarians on the same day.* This points to the inevitability of the loss of Messines at that time. Nearly three years to wait for Plumer's masterpiece, and "wisdom at one entrance quite shut out," for Hill 60's importance was small by comparison! With Messines went a most commanding view, and we had to be content to be seen and not see. The K.O.S.B., besides 139 O.R. casualties, lost Lieut. G. H. Cox of the 3rd Battalion, to whose superb bravery and cultured charm Dolbey pays tribute.† But perhaps the most serious loss was Lieut. Holme, an experienced regular, trusted and tried. He died of wounds about a fortnight later.‡ Lieut. B. C. Lake of the 1st Battalion (now Major B. C. Lake, D.S.O.),

* Buchan's *History of the War*, vol. i. p. 363.
† Dolbey, *op. cit.*, p. 110 (with note of assent by Coke in pencil).
‡ Official Death Roll ("d. of w., 9-11-1914").

Nov. 1914. whose arrival on 27th October at Richebourg with a draft is not mentioned in the War Diary but is chronicled by the faithful Herries with the letter "L," was wounded and had to be evacuated. It seemed that fate forbade the reassembly of "the old lot."

The next few days were spent resting, absorbing a small draft and 3 junior officers, and in speculating as to what higher unit the battalion belonged. Count Gleichen thought they were in his brigade, and they *were* for part of one day. The 5th Division staff were stranded troopless at this period; * but "Q" saw to it that rations reached the K.O.S.B. without fail. The immediate solution was an order to join the 9th I.B. at Ypres, and accordingly the battalion marched off early on the 6th of November for Locre, 5 miles to the N.W., lying snugly in the heart of the "mountains" W. of Mount Kemmel, crossed the "col," and descended by Dickebusch into the famous city of the plain—Ypres. They were in the northern cockpit and would take some time to get out of it. That night they marched out by the Ménin Gate and took over from the Northants trenches in the triangular fir wood known as "Nonne Bosschen," nearly a mile E. of Hooge, 3 miles E. of Ypres, on the road to Ménin. There they were subjected to severe, at times almost continuous, shelling, not only by guns but by Minenwerfer, *i.e.* trench mortars, for thirteen days. They were the anvil not the hammer. A quarter of the strength, which at Neuve Eglise had been round about 600, was kept in a line of support trenches, the rest were needed for the firing-line. Rifle fire was still lively at that early stage of the war at all hours, and it must have been a revelation to a draft of 70 who turned up on the 8th. The 10th inaugurated a period of intensive shelling which was very trying to *moral* and saw 13 casualties. It so happened that C, which the reader will remember bore the brunt of that sinister game of hide-and-seek and shoot at Messines and was shelled at finally by both sides, found itself attacked by infantry on the 11th. This straightforward human business acted like a tonic, and the enemy were repulsed (some reached our wire) with heavy losses, and at a cost of only 10 casualties. Sixty of the enemy were counted dead. It is the helplessness of passivity which undermines *moral*, and the 12th, with nine hours' shelling, was a dire strain, not least upon H.Q., which narrowly escaped direct hits. On the 13th Capt. H. V. C. Turnbull fell.† His arrival is unrecorded in the Diary, but, thanks to Herries, we know that "T" brought the draft on the 8th. He was a regular captain of the 2nd Battalion, and that is enough to indicate the extent of his loss. The rest of the time in the line

* Gleichen, *op. cit.*, p. 204. † Official Death Roll. See Book IV. p. 317.

Capt. Connell commanded, the C.O. having supervisory command over the K.O.S.B. and another unit. One day was much like another. It was getting colder and the strain was telling, as the steady drain on the strength with wounded and sick made reliefs less frequent and shorter. On the 17th the enemy again launched an infantry attack, which just reached the flank company—once again C. The attack was beaten off, thanks to excellent musketry. One of a group of stalwarts who made it a point of honour to occupy a wet bit of the line, shot 6 Germans who had actually entered his trench. It was on the 18th that the first " Minnie " commenced operations. At any time the pompous parabola of the big sphere, followed by the *déchirant*, rending crash of impact and appalling destructive effect was alarming. In the early days, without " funk-holes " or hope of swift revenge by S.O.S. calls to the gunners, the men in the trenches dreaded them almost worse than the guns. On this occasion C adopted the French method of retiring a few yards until the fell work was done, and returning to what was left of the trench. That night a new section of trench had to be dug with the aid of the R.E.. There were 20 casualties, killed and wounded. Relief came at last on the 19th after another experience of Minenwerfer on the same sector. Besides 17 casualties, 1 M.G. was destroyed. Major Coke resumed command, and that night the battalion was relieved by the D. of W. and some Royal Fusiliers, and fell back on Hooge for one night—still well within shell range. At 9 p.m. on the 20th the K.O.S.B. retraced their steps to Locre in bitter cold weather. The tour had cost them 1 officer killed, 1 wounded (Lieut. C. R. Millar accidentally), and of O.R., 18 killed, 297 wounded. A/C.S.M. K. P. Kirkwood showed a splendid example throughout this prolonged ordeal as he had done from Le Cateau onwards, and well deserved his D.C.M..

Nov. 1914.

On the 24th the five survivors of Mons—Coke, R. Dering, Lindsay, Rutherfurd, and A. Dering—went for short leave. On the 26th 2nd Lieut. Sandison of the 3rd Battalion brought a draft of 50. On the 27th Sir John French addressed them and others. On the 28th they descended the hill to Neuve Église in the Slough of Despond at the foot of Hill Difficulty, and a day later took sasine of the Wulverghem sector as the L. Battalion of the 13th I.B.. Thus ended the first round of the four years and more of the fight. There were strenuous days ahead. Hill 60 and Pilckem, High Wood and Falfemont, Vimy Ridge, Polderhoek, Forêt de Nieppe, the Hindenburg Line! But somehow the thrill of thrills for this particular battalion was the continuous strain of combat and movement from Maroilles to Nonne Bosschen, extending over more than three months and levying heavy toll on the trained officers and men. When it comes to Hill 60 it will be seen that it was practically a new battalion —yet very much its old self. The part played by the 2nd K.O.S.B. at Mons, Le Cateau, Crépy, the Morin, the Aisne, La Bassée, and Messines was appreciated by the mentions and honours conferred as the result of the C.in-C.'s despatch of 26th November 1914. Major Coke was awarded the C.M.G., Capt. Bland the D.S.O., Capt. Caird the M.C.. Besides Sergt. Skinner, C.S.M.s J. J. Stewart, and J. Main, A/C.S.M.s H. P. Kirkwood and H. Pike, Corps. A. Brown and H. Wheeler, and Pte. G. Turner were awarded the D.C.M.. In addition the following were mentioned: Capts. Dering (Adjutant) and Connell, and Lieut. R. Gibson, along with R.S.M. Macwhinnie, C.S.M.s P. Welsh and R. Fuller, C.Q.M.S. T. Geggie, Sergts. T. Lawrie and S. Ramsden, Corp. J. Deal, L.-Corps. K. Maxwell and W. Connell, and Pte. R. Rennie.

CHAPTER V*

LINDENHOEK
HILL 60
GRAVENSTAFEL
ST JULIEN

A FEW words now about their place of sojourn for two and a half months. Novel readers are apt to skip descriptions of scenery; but in a regimental history topography is of the essence, and never more so in the annals of the K.O.S.B. than in December 1914 and January and half of February 1915, the darkest, wettest, and coldest months of the year. Six miles behind the firing-line, just beyond the Ravelsberg, lay Bailleul, with its Grand-Place and its estaminets, so near and yet so far. By contrast with trench life it was a soldier's haven of bliss; for the Jocks, as a rule, did not share Herries' aversion to rum or to any form of stimulant. Half-way to the front was Neuve Église—a brigade H.Q. and reserve area. Three miles N.E. of Neuve Église was Dranoutre, the other brigade H.Q. and reserve area, and on the road from Neuve Église to Ypres *via* Kemmel was Lindenhoek, a mile E. of which can be read on the map "75" (indicating that the ground thus marked was just under 250 feet above sea-level).† This figure marked by way of exclusion the N. limit of the divisional sector. As the Douve at Wulverghem is only 85 feet above sea-level, it is evident that the brigade front sloped northwards and upwards from R. to L.. The hostile trenches were widest apart where they cut the Wulverghem-Messines road, viz. about 800 yards; ‡ but in places as near to one another as 30 yards. The divisional front was 3,500 yards long. It might be thought that as the imposing figure "75" was approached the trenches might improve, but such was not the case. The War Diary reads like the Book of Lamentations, but I find the clearest

1914–1915.

* See Map. 2.

† The simplest way of turning metres into feet is to add an o and divide by 3. The error is trifling, as in a mile (1,609 metres) 5,280 feet would be misstated as 5,364 feet.

‡ Hussey and Ingram's *5th Division in the Great War* (London, 1921), p. 51.

1914–1915. picture in a work which, alas, is too soon to close.* The ground consisted of greasy, slippery, Flanders mud—stoneless clay. "Whether you are moving across plough or grass fields or along lanes you are perpetually skating about and slipping-up on the firmer bits and held fast by the ankles in the softer ones. . . . However much you dig, you . . . come across . . . nothing but sticky mud, which clings to your shovel and refuses to be parted from it—mud that has to be scraped off at almost every stroke, that absorbs water like a sponge, yet refuses to give it up again." Owing to the danger of high breastwork and the fact that water was retained in the trenches and could not be drained away, the men stood in water up to the ankles or knees. The usual trench equipment was non-existent. Draining was lost labour, for parapets fell in after the porridge had been ejected. Existence was, in Hobbes' phrase, "brutish, nasty." Good rations may account for the absence of lung and throat ailments, but trench feet were a phenomenon only too common, and costly in man power. In thirteen days there were about 130 evacuations from the battalion, including Lieut. G. H. M. Lindsay.† How many of us there are who, while still at home in 1914–15, remember meeting or hearing of those, in whom our interest centred, lamed for months by this malign affliction. Behind the firing-line it was no better. Those vital passages for ration and stretcher parties and walking cases, to say nothing of reliefs and visitors—the communication trenches—were fearful sloughs. The divisional horse lines were fields in which horses and mules stood up to their hocks in mud.‡ In such a terrain any offensive was out of the question. Moreover, in rifle and hand-grenades we were inferior by 6 to 1.§

Any detailed day-to-day account of the K.O.S.B. for the two and a half months would be a waste of space. Its revolting and dangerous monotony and physical discomfort do not invite analysis. Reliefs were frequent and stays were short, behind or in front. Wulverghem (A Sector), Neuve Église, Dranoutre, Lindenhoek ("75"), Lindenhoek (A Sector), Dranoutre, St. Jans Cappel, back to Neuve Église, Wulverghem (D Sector), succeed one another at a rate both boring and bewildering. The fact that the divisional sector ceased to be held as a two-brigade sector with triangular reliefs, and was, *quoad* a smaller sector, held permanently by the 14th I.B., and for the rest by the 13th and 15th turn about, asks for no amplification.

* Gleichen, *op. cit.*, pp. 256 *et seq.*
† W.D. ‡ Hussey and Ingram, *op. cit.*, p. 54.
§ Gleichen, *op. cit.*, p. 260; Hussey and Ingram, *op. cit.*

On the 14th, 15th, and 16th December attempts at a demonstration to distract the Germans from a feeble and abortive Franco-British attack elsewhere resulted in 5 killed and 27 wounded. Lieut. L. M. Sandison was severely wounded. On the 20th Herries went sick and Capt. Wade and Lieut. George Lewis Sparrow were wounded—the latter fatally. His death on the 23rd robbed the K.O.S.B. of a valuable loan and the S.W.B. of an officer on their reserve. He had volunteered from Africa, and was a tower of strength to *moral.* Dec. 1914.

The casualties for thirteen days exceeded 230, and the response of the 3rd Battalion to the call for more men may be gauged from the total ration strength being 812 on the famous Christmas Day, so creditable to human nature, so unsuited to serious war, and consequently so obnoxious to higher authority. The same potentate also suggested with a certain asperity that harder work would mean better security, and ordered a more vigorous use of the spade. The K.O.S.B., as a matter of fact, were at St. Jans Cappel, and did not fraternize with the Bavarians. The New Year was brought in at Neuve Église and the K.O.S.B. faced the New Year bathed, reclothed, and in its right mind, cheered by the tangible evidences of the personal interest taken in them by the King on his throne, his Consort, his daughter, and those at home to whom the regiment was all in all. Extra wraps, grub, and 'baccy! What more could a soldier want, except—perhaps in theory only—a "cushy, Blighty" wound?

1915

Neuve Église was more often shelled than Dranoutre.* One shell prevented three new arrivals from even reaching the firing-line. Bailleul's temptations resulted in a heavy crime sheet on the occasion of the first visit, but a second decorous visit at the end of the month indicated that the best way of keeping men out of the "pubs" (*pace* Lord Birkenhead) is to occupy their time with work, play, and entertainment.

As the battalion is soon to be in action the arrival of Brig.-Gen. R. Wanless O'Gowan on the 9th of February calls for record. He inspected the K.O.S.B. on the 16th at a camp at the Ravelsberg, from which, on the 19th, a move was made to Ouderdom, 5 miles due N. of Dranoutre on the N. side of the "mountains," about the same distance W.S.W. from Ypres and 6½ miles due W. of Hill 60, which will figure so much in the ensuing pages. Probably the bulk of the battalion little knew the debt they owed to the cavalry,

* Hussey and Ingram, *op. cit.*

Feb. 1915. — the III. Corps, and possibly to a mere temporary embarrassment of the Germans for the priceless possession of the Mont-des-Cats-Kemmel massif, with its commanding views and secret recesses.

The K.O.S.B. were once more in the Ypres salient proper S.S.E. of Ypres, for on the 20th they relieved the York & Lancs. Regt. in a sector called " C " near Verbranden Molen,* between which and Hill 60 lies the deep cutting of the Ypres-Comines railway.

Their task for the next six days was to improve the poor trenches, and into the work they plunged with zeal. The soil was dry and repaid toil, but the line was too thinly held, and much had to be done to secure signal communication with R.A. and R.E. and to clean up battalion H.Q.—a filthy farm. Daylight movement was here possible, and the supports had woods as cover. The work was done honestly, and the K.O.Y.L.I. co-operated, with the result that when the Army Corps, 28th Divisional, and 13th I.B. Commanders paid a visit at Vlamertinghe on 13th March the first named, *i.e.* Sir H. Smith-Dorrien, congratulated the battalion in words which showed that the battalion had taken to heart Sir Charles Fergusson's call for more spade work at Messines, and done something to better even that unresponsive swamp.

The rest of March, so far as spent in the line, was spent in Sector A, nearer St. Eloi, either at Ypres or Vlamertinghe when at rest, or at Rosendaal or Kruisstraat when in brigade reserve. On 31st March Lieut.-Col. D. R. Sladen, D.S.O., arrived and took over command from Major Coke.

HILL 60

It is somewhat of an enigma that Hill 60 was considered worth 100 officers and 3,000 O.R. of the 5th Division. Its loss on 5th May, after being an undesirable British possession in which to be quartered for three weeks, had no appreciable effect on the Western Theatre. Its possession meant more to the Germans, as the widest and comprehensive views were towards Ypres. It was to be expected that the enemy would make the fullest use of his superiority in armament to recover it if lost. No attempt is made in the *Official History* to link the episode on to some strategic scheme. It is treated just as a record of events, a soldier's battle. Mr. Buchan thinks that Hollebeke would have been untenable if we had retained Hill 60. Be it so. The regimental historian attempts no solution, and confines the story to the doings of his own unit. Hill 60 is the debris dug out to make a cutting for the Ypres-Comines-Lille railway through the crest of the encircling ridge described on p. 52, and

* The mill is once more in use (*S.A.G.*, 1928).

PANORAMIC VIEW HILL 60, NEAR YPRES, 1915.

deposited on the ground E. of the railway. It is about 300 yards long parallel to the line, and 100 yards wide. About 300 yards to the N.E. of it on the opposite side of the railway is a similar, smaller, rounder mound, nicknamed the Dump. On the same side as the mound, farther S.E., was yet a third excrescence with the self-explanatory name of the Caterpillar. The Dump was in our hands, the Caterpillar and Hill 60 in German hands—the latter having been captured from the French on 10th December 1914.* It remains to this day a monument of the chaos caused by mines and shells of H.E., just as the hardly less famous Butte de Warlencourt, also artificial,† emphasizes the resisting power of spoil of Picardy chalk to engines of destruction.

April 1915.

The plan was a microscopic anticipation of the Battle of Messines in 1917—namely, to mine the hill in three places, rush it by assault with storm troops and a working party, and consolidate the position when won. The R.W.K. were to conduct the assault and the K.O.S.B. to supply the consolidators and relieving troops along with a contingent of R.E.. During April the K.O.S.B. occupied Sector C in the line and Ypres as a resting-place. On the 10th they withdrew to Vlamertinghe and practised the attack precisely as it was eventually delivered. On the 14th Major Coke left the battalion which he had so splendidly led for more than six months of hard fighting to become C.O. of the 5th Notts and Derby Regiment. His loss on this occasion was only temporary. On the 16th at 10 p.m. the battalion left Vlamertinghe and passed through the bottle-neck of Ypres to the jumping-off place in Sector D.

Dering, the adjutant, and his brother Anthony, Hamilton-Dalrymple, and Rutherfurd represented the men of Mons. The greater bulk of the officers and men came from the Special Reserve. Capt. T. P. Wingate was a Regular Borderer, and had acted as adjutant of the 3rd Battalion prior to coming out. Besides the K.O.S.B. there were Capt. A. F. Anderson and Lieut. W. S. Scott of the 3rd Cameronians, and 2nd Lieut. E. Cattley of the 4th North Staffs.. B and C formed the pioneers. A and D were held in reserve in the shelter of a wood called Larch. At 7 p.m. on the 17th of April seven mines in all, dug by Welsh miners, exploded, and under cover of French and British guns the R.W.K., to the sound of bugles, stormed the hill and cleared it of some 50 German survivors.‡ Strictly speaking, B and C of the K.O.S.B.

* *Official History*, p. 167.

† See p. 338 *post*.

‡ In case anyone has access to trench maps of the period, the jumping-off place was numbered 39 and 40, and consisted of two new trenches (13th Brigade Report of Action).

April 1915. were there to dig, but the R.W.K. historian tells us * that "needless to say the 'Jocks' were not going to allow their mutual friends to do an attack without taking a greater part than consolidating their position. When the hill was taken many were using their shovels and picks quite freely on the heads of the Bosche." The top of Hill 60 was blown clean off, and the enormous craters were difficult to consolidate. Work was begun at once. A fair firing trench was made out of the German one, and the German "boyau" was eventually found and blocked. It was the transforming of the craters near the railway into safe trenches that gave most difficulty. They were never properly garrisoned. The capture was the prelude to a real fight, beginning about 1 a.m., and the brunt fell on the K.O.S.B.. The enemy soon realized the position, and some 50 batteries † concentrated on the narrow target and treated the garrison to a stunning and terrific bombardment. Tasks endure according to local difficulties or facilities. B did theirs and withdrew according to plan at midnight. C's at 2.30 a.m. was not completed, when A and D relieved the R.W.K. in the firing-line on the L. of the hill. These three companies were involved in sanguinary hand-to-hand combats with Germans able to crawl up unseen to the crater lips and bomb. These "bombing scraps" continued all night, and when the D. of W. relieved the K.O.S.B. at 11.30 a.m. on the 18th they found them sore smitten. A wonderfully stimulating and steadying influence in that time was exercised throughout by Capt. (afterwards Major) G. Hilton (afterwards wounded at the Somme on 1st July 1916), whose conduct was described to the writer as "simply splendid." The genial and capable Wingate was dead, and so were Lieuts. M'Diarmid, who had won a mention in the supplement to the despatch of 5th April 1915, and Malet, a Borderer of the Reserve of Officers. Malet was killed from behind in one of the "railway" craters, such was the angle of fire available to the enemy. Capt. Dering, the adjutant, was mortally wounded ; he also had won a mention for the October–November campaign. His experience, which covered the whole campaign, was an invaluable asset. His battalion mourned a tried friend when he passed away on the 19th April. Capt. R. C. C. Campbell, who had only joined on the 4th, also died of wounds on the 19th.‡ Capts. Burnett and C. R. Dudgeon and Lieuts. Lewis, Paterson, and Hammond were all wounded, and the newly arrived C.O., Colonel Sladen. To these 10 officer casualties correspond O.R. casualties of 201. Though the seconds must have often dragged on like hours, the whole affair was over by 5.30 p.m. on the 18th, when

* *Invicta*, p. 109. † *Invicta*, p. 110. ‡ Official Death Roll.

the battalion was relieved and returned to Vlamertinghe. The greater part of the day of the 18th was spent in reserve in the shelter of the railway cutting. While they are reorganizing as best they can and while fortune is swaying, as the struggle for Hill 60 continues with fresh troops, we may perhaps introduce the next act in the K.O.S.B. drama.

April 1915.

Gravenstafel

The Second Battle of Ypres, which broke out on 22nd April, will for ever be associated with the surprise use of chlorine gas by the Germans, who added insult to injury by fabricating a false charge against the Allies of preparations to commit the same abomination. It was one of the dispensations of Providence that the Germans confined this first experiment to a comparatively small area, and only moved a limited number of troops to a limited objective, where they dug themselves in.

What would have happened had they poured in masses into the gap cut into the Allies' line and developed a pursuit, one shudders to think. Chlorine acts as an irritant to the breathing organs, the eye, and the mucous membrane. The effects are intensified when, under the stimulus of exertion, breathing is deeper or sharper. The heart and the lungs suffer immediate injury. Whether asphyxiation results or not is a question of time and degree. The gas is most potent near the ground, and was therefore an added horror for the wounded.

The Battle of Gravenstafel Ridge began on the 22nd April at 5 p.m. with a preliminary bombardment by howitzers. It was a fine day, and the phenomenon of a bluish, yellowish, whitish mist * was soon noted stealing along, propelled by the steady N.E. wind from the region of Langemarck, 5 miles N.N.E. of Ypres. It was the chlorine gas released from long cylinders on its deadly mission. What followed can be read in general histories. Two inferior French divisions bolted, leaving only those incapacitated by gas or shell. A gap was formed of 8,000 yards between the British L. on the St. Julien–Poelcapelle road and the French troops, who held their ground towards Steenstraate on the canal 5 miles N. of Ypres. The direction of the attack was practically due S., straight towards Ypres, and behind the British forces covering that town was a flattish salient through Zonnebeke to Hill 60. The canal seaward was exposed, and troops had to be hurried from anywhere to stop the gap. A Canadian counter-attack, the first of the splendid services rendered by overseas non-regular troops to the cause, led off the

* *Official History*, p. 177.

April 1915. defensive measures which by the morning of the 23rd extended 10 weak battalions in a patchy and precarious line across the new front. It was on the evening of the 22nd that the K.O.S.B. received their sudden and for too many last call to duty. They spent the night in the open near Ypres, and next morning moved N. and lay W. of the canal in readiness to recover Pilckem and a hamlet with the sinister name of Mauser 3 miles N. of Ypres on a low but tactically commanding ridge, along which a road runs from the outskirts of Ypres to Pilckem.

In those days marked deference was paid to the French theory of defence by immediate counter-offensive. Accordingly, without proper liaison, sufficiently elaborated plan, or artillery support the K.O.S.B. entered upon a hopeless task under the orders of the G.O.C., 1st Canadian Division.* With the R.W.K. on their left they were the leading troops of the 13th I.B. (O'Gowan), once more torn from the 5th Division (Morland) and attached to the V. Corps (Plumer). At 2 p.m. they moved to the canal, crossed it by a pontoon bridge E. of Brielen, and advanced under rifle and M.G. fire to the cross-roads, where a service road cuts the Ypres–Pilckem road 2 miles N. of Ypres. They then turned N., so that their R. rested on the road and advanced at 4.15 p.m. in four lines. The only French movement visible was that of some Zouaves impeding the advance of the R.W.K. by crowding in from the canal. This was a blessing in disguise to the R.W.K., whose losses were only half those of the K.O.S.B.†. The latter, tired after Hill 60 but with stout hearts, managed with heavy losses to advance some 700 yards to the relief of Canadians in a *quondam* reserve trench. Further advance against Mauser Ridge—now some 300 yards away—was out of the question. With great gallantry Capt. Bland of C led a small party to a trench 100 yards farther on, but, on attempting a further advance, he fell, and his party was wiped out. Bland was killed while trying to drag a wounded man to shelter. It was a noble end to a promising career early marked with the D.S.O.. The battalion stayed on in the trench till relieved by the 4th Rifle Brigade at 2 a.m. on the 24th, and withdrew behind the canal. Only four junior subalterns—R. Gillespie, W. R. Gaskell, E. Cattley, and A. E. Moreton—emerged unscathed. Besides Bland, Capt. A. F. Anderson was killed, and on the assumption that he had come to stay, his was a real loss to the

* The sentence in which this massacre is disposed of in Sir John French's despatch (No. 2, p. 251) is couched in euphemistic terms : "The loss of the [French] guns on the night of the 22nd . . . much aggravated the situation. Our positions were, however, well maintained by the vigorous counter-attacks made by the V. Corps" (Plumer).

† *Invicta*, p. 114.

K.O.S.B.. Besides his experience, his soldierly bearing and his witty remarks were assets. Real soldiers were becoming rarer every day. Hamilton-Dalrymple also fell. He had been everything to D since the opening of the campaign, and his mentions in despatches show that his services were appreciated. Lieut. J. R. Caird of the 3rd Battalion and 2nd Lieut. W. S. Scott were also killed. The wounded included Lieuts. A. G. Dobbie and Rutherfurd (the last of the old gang), and 2nd Lieuts. E. Robertson and F. C. Royce. To a unit and army without large reserves of trained officers and N.C.O.s this was an appalling blow. Casualties among O.R. exceeded 240. In the afternoon of the 24th the battalion advanced and dug itself in on the E. bank of the canal near the pontoon bridge E. of Brielen on a front of 500 yards. It was under command of Major P. M. Robinson, C.B., along with the R.W.K.*. Lieut. Gibson rejoined along with 5 new subalterns from the 3rd Battalion and took over the duties of adjutant, and on Gallipoli Day (Sunday, the 25th) Capt. L. D. Spencer rejoined with 3 more subalterns and took over command for a brief season. It will be remembered that he was wounded at Mons. The next time the 13th I.B. came under Canadian orders it was a very different story. If the reader has patience he will find the events on 9th April 1917 more cheering.

April 1915.

THE BATTLE OF ST. JULIEN.

The second gas attack struck the Canadians on the morning of the 24th at the N. apex of the salient. In effect, a serious dent was made in the line N. and E. of St. Julien, and St. Julien itself fell. With the aid of wet handkerchiefs dipped, if possible, in a solution of bi-carbonate of soda and their stout hearts the Canadians yielded but did not break, except in one place. There was the usual hand-to-mouth collection of reserves, and on the 25th what is known as Brig.-Gen. C. P. A. Hull's attack was launched with the 10th Brigade and an extra battalion to attempt the impossible.† It was the story of the 23rd over again—inadequate artillery support, advance in the open, exposure to M.G. and rifle fire.

In the small hours of the 26th the K.O.S.B. and R.W.K. were called upon to advance E. over a mile and occupy some trenches in the valley fronting Mauser Ridge in support between the French and the Lahore Division. Here they suffered from gas shells and shelling of an ordinary type, but took no active part in the battle, and were withdrawn to a wood near Vlamertinghe on the 30th after relief by

* *Invicta*, p. 115.

† *Official History*, p. 240 *et seq.*

5 May 1915. 12th I.B.,* where they passed an uncomfortable sojourn, being marched backwards and forwards between the canal and Vlamertinghe. During this period 19 officers joined or rejoined, and of these only 7 were Borderers—among them Herries. Twelve were from the H.L.I., including Capt. Mayne, D.S.O., and Lieut. D. Kindersley, of whom more anon.

Meanwhile Hill 60 had been faithfully held by the 15th Brigade under Brig.-Gen. Northey, who succeeded Count Gleichen on the latter's promotion to be a Major-General. But luck favoured the wicked. On the morning of 5th May the direction of the wind was such as to enable the Germans to release gas, so to speak, in enfilade of the British trenches.

Those long-suffering D. of W. of the 13th I.B., attached to 15th I.B., were once more victims. Their position with such feeble prophylactics as they had became untenable. Those who stayed died. The Germans assaulted the Hill after a short pause, gained a lodgment in the sector vacated, and a close bombing fight began and lasted all day, exhausting the reserves of the 15th I.B.. Call came to the remnant of the 13th I.B., " which had taken part in the original capture of the Hill and retrieved so many desperate situations," † to retake the portion of the Hill still in German hands. In the afternoon they found themselves in the wood from which A and D had advanced to relieve the R.W.K. on the 17th of April. Their orders were to attack at 10 p.m.. Capt. Mayne's dispositions were for C and D to assault and A and B to support and consolidate. After twenty minutes' bombardment, which warned without cowing the enemy, the K.O.S.B. left the shelter of trenches opposite the Hill. On their L. were the R.W.K.,‡ with Zwarteleen for their objective. C's attack was crushed instantaneously by heavy fire. D reached their objective, but were exposed to enfilade fire from the Caterpillar, and were also bombed from close range. Both companies had to retire and occupy the trenches from which they had started. Two platoons under Lieut. J. M. Challinor stuck it out until only three men were left besides the officer. In the end the party only retired because their neighbours on the flanks were doing so under orders. All were decorated for their gallantry except Sergt. J. Holmes, who was killed in June 1915 before the awards were made. Pte. R. Scott received the D.C.M., Pte. A. Batten the M.M., and Lieut. Challinor, the leader, the M.C.. Capts. Mayne and Spencer were wounded, the latter for the second time. Capt. I. D. Dalrymple, a regular of the H.L.I.,

* 13th I.B.W.D. † *Official History* (1915), vol. iii. p. 306.
‡ *Invicta*, p. 120.

May 1915.

Lieut. R. Gibson, and 2nd Lieuts. R. F. A. Edgell and J. M. G. Brown were killed. 2nd Lieuts. Ferguson and Hood were wounded, as were Smith, Judd, Chambers, and Strethill of the H.L.I.. Casualties amongst O.R. amounted to 130. The R.W.K. were equally unsuccessful. Hill 60 remained German, and no further attempt was made to retake it. Yet we did not thereby lose the war. The men were either tired out or raw, and the dash of the April attack was absent.* An attack on the Hill without taking in the whole Zwarteleen salient was doomed to failure, and the ground was too much broken up for night attacks.†

Thus ended the first phase. By the time the battalion is again seriously engaged it will have been transformed in personnel and training and tactics, as just one among many units of a homogeneous force. Nothing but the unchangeable Borderer spirit will be exactly as before. Hardly a man will be left who fought at Mons and Le Cateau. It is easy to be wise after the event, but somehow or other the conviction comes to readers of the events of 1914–15 that highly trained officers and men were hurriedly and prodigally sacrificed for insufficient military ends. We must console ourselves with General Edmonds' encomium. "Pinned as they were in the narrow salient and on Hill 60, shelled day and night from three sides, the conduct of the troops was magnificent. Seldom have there been finer displays of courage than the fighting of the 13th, 14th, and 15th Brigades of the 5th Division; the advance in daylight of . . . [among others] the 13th Brigade."‡ The 2nd K.O.S.B. can place "Second Ypres" among their proudest achievements. "No battalion has done finer work than this," said their future colonel, Sir D. Haig, when, as C.-in-C., he visited the 2nd K.O.S.B. at Agnez, near Arras, on 30th March 1916.

Relieved by the Cheshires and under command of Capt. Herries, with a novice—but a very capable one—as adjutant, namely, Lieut. J. M. Challinor of the 3rd Battalion, the K.O.S.B. retired to dugouts on the S.W. outskirts of Ypres, now a smouldering ruin, having been still the resemblance of a town in April. During the rest of May the scene changed from dugouts on the railway embankment to huts at Ouderdom and trenches in front of the embankment in the St. Éloi area. Life was quiet and casualties were light. Life was also monotonous. Accepting the option of being relieved every four days from within itself, the battalion held a two-company sector with two companies in close support on the canal bank for fifty-six days on end in the midst of lice and croaking frogs. But there

* 13th I.B.W.D. † *Official History, sup. cit., ibid.*

‡ *Official History* (1915), p. 299.

May–June 1915.

was better music "indoors" when Lieut. Harvey discoursed on the chanter, and the ingenuity of Capt. Mackenzie in setting "Hun-traps" out in No Man's Land was a source of interest and expectation. But it was a period of stagnation rather than rest, and no progress could be made in rifle-shooting or training. There was no cohesion within the battalion or the companies. It was positional warfare at its most numbing, and the muddy water was useless for bathing purposes. However, this hideous abomination served as a contrasting background for the Somme attractions to be recorded in our next. Hard work was done in the trenches. Amateurish trench mortars were sparingly used.

Major Coke returned on 21st and took over from Capt. A. E. D. Anderson of the 3rd Battalion, C.O. since 14th. Capt. Anderson served with distinction in the Great War, and rose to be Lieut.-Col. On several occasions he commanded the 2nd Battalion. He became, later on, Brigade Major of 13th I.B., until he became G.S.O.2 in the 61st Division. He was one of the first of the non-regular officers to reach the front, serving with the 2nd H.L.I. (the old 74th) from 2nd December 1914. On joining up wtih his own regiment he found himself in command. Eleven officers, 10 of them Borderers, arrived in the course of the month, but the battalion was considerably under strength. On 9th June 2nd Lieut. H. S. F. Robinson died of wounds received on 6th, otherwise the War Diary is uncommunicative.

CHAPTER VI *

THE SOMME, 1915
ARRAS, 1915

FRESH woods and pastures new opened to the 5th Division when it was withdrawn towards the end of July and transferred to a sector between the River Somme and Carnoy. The 2nd K.O.S.B. said good-bye to the salient without regret on relief by 2nd R.I.F., and marched by night some 7 miles to Zeveten. Up early, they marched in rain 10 miles to Steenvoorde, over the frontier, where the battalion was billeted for a week. On the 30th they entrained at Steenvoorde in the evening, and found themselves at Corbie-sur-Somme at 9 next morning. We can roll up the Flanders map and concentrate on the country between the Somme and the Ancre, which run side by side with one another just below Corbie, with its massive church. The K.O.S.B. marched quietly to Ribemont on the Ancre and settled down in billets. It was a glorious change from the cramped, crowded monotony of the N. to the spacious, somewhat English, downlands so often well wooded, and the whole 13th I.B. were new men when they were inspected on the 3rd August by the 3rd Army Commander, General Sir Charles Monro,† the man whose advice decided the evacuation of the Gallipoli Peninsula. The Brigade Diary actually notes the pleasure the change gave the men. The country reminded the Brigadier of Salisbury Plain. On the night of 4–5th the K.O.S.B. relieved the 302nd I.B. of the French N. of Carnoy on the ridge overlooking Mametz. On the R. of the 13th I.B. were the 14th I.B., and on the L. of the 13th, the 15th. Beyond them, and as yet unknown to fame, were the 51st Highland (T.) Division. The 14th's R. rested on the Somme, and beyond were the French. The 5th Division, now commanded by Major-Gen. C. T. McM. Kavanagh, was in the X. Corps commanded by General Morland along with the 51st, and (a little later) the 18th, Territorial and New Army Divisions respectively. Divisional H.Q. was at Étinehem, and brigade H.Q.

July 1915.

* See Maps 1, 3, and 4 in pocket.

† Gen. Monro died in December 1929.

July 1915. were at Sailly (13th), Morlancourt (14th), and Chipilly (15th). Bronfay Farm and Billon Wood, 3 miles N.E. of Bray, were K.O.S.B. battalion H.Q. when they were not in the front line. The next year was a complete contrast to that which was nearing completion. Eight months of fighting and three of close proximity to an over-crowded battlefield were succeeded by almost twelve months of garrison duty in trenches, the elaborate structure of which was far in advance of any field fortifications hitherto seen by our battalion. Chalk has its defects, as the winter showed, especially if blended with clay. It is soluble and sticky, with a grip more tenacious than Flanders mud at its most prehensile mixture of soil and water. But as visitors to the Champagne *caves* at Rheims or Épernay or to the underworld preserved on the Vimy Ridge as a tribute to the skill of the Canadian engineers and the valour of their infantry, can testify, chalk slices under dry conditions into the shape desired, and retains it. In the Carnoy sector the trenches were mostly above the chalk, in soil so perfect in dry weather that a certain C.-S.-M. is said to have run a man in for throwing an extinguished match on the "floor." But it was another story in wet weather. Given the right admixture of water, and the result was —a caramel, immeasurable, inedible ! * Freedom from active operations of war did not mean a lazy life. Constant work on the maintenance and improvement of trenches (and there were long communication trenches making daylight traffic feasible) ; hard work on the new technique, bombs, catapults, and mortars—and gas-masks ; instruction, received from experts, or imparted by example and precept to the "K" novices, *e.g.* by our battalion to an attached party of the 9th Gloucesters of the 18th Division ; finally, the steady, if somewhat pin-pricking, hostilities essential to secure a peaceful and respected existence. All these kept the 5th Division troops from Capuan sloth. Such a life, with its monotonous vigilance, its rests, drillings, inspections, and marches, its reliefs and fatigues, demands summary treatment during the period when the Gallipoli campaign and the Loos experiment absorb all our attention. The reader can find an excellent picture of the line and the life in the sector in *The 5th Division*,† and also from the point of view of a battalion in *Invicta*.‡ But the rats ! One knows that these deadly foes of man were everywhere in France, but Carnoy was famous for its rats and its rat hunts. The first night the M.O. slept in

* Lieut.-Col. A. E. D. Anderson.

† Hussey and Ingram. See Chapter V.

‡ The war history of the 1st R.W.K., *i.e.* a battalion, not a regimental history.

the trenches he awoke to find a rat shaking him by the nose! * Henceforth rats are banished from these pages, but they did not vanish from the lives of the K.O.S.B. or B.E.F. any more than those graver horrors on which it is useless to dwell.

Autumn 1915.

On the 21st of August Brig.-Gen. W. O'Gowan departed on promotion to command 31st Division, and ultimately, in the beginning of November, the comparatively young Brig.-Gen. L. O. W. Jones took command of the 13th I.B.. He stayed there till 1918, and so saw the Somme, Arras, and Third Ypres, Italy, and the Lys with the 13th I.B.. While not in temporary command at brigade H.Q., Coke, now a Lieut-Col., was C.O. during the rest of the year. In February 1916 he became a B.G. in command of the 169th I.B. of a distinguished London Division—the 56th. The mutual interest of the regiment and battalion in him and his in the K.O.S.B. remained the same. The past pages give a poor tribute to the distinguished services he rendered to the 2nd K.O.S.B.. Connell, now a major, had rejoined in May, and acted for a time as adjutant. But he was shifted to command the 7th Battalion after Loos, and later on to the 6th. So we shall meet him again. In Coke's absences Major A. E. D. Anderson of the 3rd Battalion, a future C.O., took command. About the New Year 1916 the 13th I.B. was reconstituted. It lost its two Yorkshire battalions—the 2nd Duke of Wellington's West Riding Regiment, and the 2nd K.O. Yorkshire Light Infantry—and received in their place the 14th and 15th (Birmingham) Battalions of the Royal Warwickshire Regiment (" R.W.R.") and New Army.

The River Somme seems to have been " dissociable," for there is no mention of the French on the other bank in the War Diary after taking over. The Carnoy sector is not associated with K.O.S.B. fighting, but it had the interest of overlooking Montauban, the Pommiers Ridge, and Mametz—the gate to the shambles of 1916.

The advent of November foreshadowed the atrocious condition of ground and trenches to be experienced a hundredfold in the following winter. But all things considered, the most unpleasant experience was the " Retreat from Moscow," as one stage of the march to the Arras area was called by some wag in the 5th Division.†

The trenches were at their worst about the beginning of 1916. Reliefs often took place over the top. Short-legged men walked

* Lieut.-Col. A. E. D. Anderson.

† Gen. Hussey and Major Ingram, *op. cit.*, chap. v. The former was C.R.A. of the 5th Division at this time.

1916. waist-deep in liquid. Gum boots, now a ration, frequently failed. The K.O.S.B., however, were at the end of their toil and suffering. On the 3/4th of January they were relieved for the last time by the D. of W., and marched back all the way to Bray. A night and day there was succeeded by an evening march of 9 miles to Vaux-sur-Somme, just E. of Corbie. On the 7th a short move to La Neuville, a western suburb of Corbie, brought the K.O.S.B. to rest. There the remainder of the month was devoted to military training, and picks and shovels were dumped.

On the 6th of February the K.O.S.B. started for the delightful region of Cavillon, W. of Amiens. It was a leisurely trek, for a week was spent at Rainneville, 6 miles N. of Amiens, before crossing the Somme below Amiens, and settling down in Saisseval after an impeded march of 15 miles. Here two wounded officers—Lieuts. Sandison, who was transferred to the 6th before the Somme battles, and Rutherfurd—rejoined, and here Col. Sladen conducted ten days' training. Their departure seems to have been due to pressure on the French at Verdun. The 5th Division was to take over at Arras. The K.O.S.B.'s first day's march over the Somme to Vaux-en-Amienois was uneventful. But on the 25th the 18 miles' daylight march to Doullens in the teeth of a blizzard was physical torture. The roads were covered with ice and snow. All sorts of traffic blocked them. Horses and men fell about, and transport stuck on the hills. Much of the long straight road crosses uplands, and the cold was intense.

It is satisfactory, therefore, to find that in the C.O.'s opinion the men marched well. Three whole days were spent in that charming old-fashioned Picardy town of immortal fame,* indissolubly associated with our late beloved colonel. Humbler associations cluster about its streets and the old fortress for many of us, when we remember the delight to eye and stomach, be it confessed, of a visit to Doullens from the Somme battlefields. A short afternoon's march to Warluzel on the 29th was followed by one of 15 miles to the capital of Artois, where billets in cellars and houses received the K.O.S.B. on their first visit.

ARRAS

The next four months passed pleasantly enough. The peculiarity of this part of the front was the proximity of the trenches to the damaged but far from demolished city, with its cellars and sewers,

* The famous meeting which resulted in Unity of Command of French and British forces, under Foch, took place at Doullens on 26th March 1918.

civilians and comforts. It was one of the quietest parts of the line. Arras was seldom subjected to more than gusts of shrapnel, and neither side indulged in any but the most minor operations of war. Raiding was in its infancy. The 5th Division occupied the sector from the N. bank of the Scarpe to the Labyrinth near Roclincourt. Further N. was the 51st Division (XVII. Corps), and S. of the Scarpe the 14th. The 5th and 14th formed the VI. Corps under Lieut.-Gen. Sir J. L. Keir. The 5th occupied the front with two brigades, and the 13th being on the R. and the K.O.S.B. being the R. battalion, their R. rested on the Scarpe. In fact, there was an isolated Lewis-gun post (the Lewis light M.G. was a recent and invaluable arm) on an " island " in the inundation usual to a French river. As can well be imagined, it was troublesome to relieve. The sector was over half a mile long, and the trenches taken over after dark on the 2nd from the 209th I.R. of the French were similar to those left on the Somme, but, thanks to drier weather, in better condition. At one point the German trenches were only 10 yards from a sap, but as the Diary only records two officers sniped dead (2nd Lieut. A. J. Morley-Brown on 29th April and 2nd Lieut. R. A. Cook on 30th June), and some twenty casualties to O.R. in four months, the danger resulting therefrom cannot have been great. The line was held by three companies in the fire trenches and one platoon of the fourth in close support. The remainder of the supporting company lay with Battalion H.Q. at the *huilerie* in the suburb of St. Laurent. Added to which the battalion due for the next tour supplied two companies to man a line of support trenches, and similarly the relieved battalion left two companies. In each case the extra troops were under the orders of the C.O. holding the line. The German high-velocity gun, which, if it did nothing else to make us grateful, supplied the name of the famous 5th Divisional entertainment troupe, the " Whizzbangs," played freely as a welcome on the 3rd, but innocuously. The next three days were very wintry; and on relief by the 1st Cheshires of the 15th I.B., the companies for complete relief were glad to return to the warmth of the deep cellars of Arras, even if heavy fatigues were part of the price. After three days the whole battalion marched to Wanquetin, 7 miles W. from Arras, and occupied good huts. There arrived several subalterns, but Col. Sladen was indisposed and was evacuated, Major A. E. D. Anderson taking his place as C.O.. After six days the battalion returned to a different sector further N., viz. E. of Roclincourt. On this occasion they made the acquaintance of Granatenwerfer, pear-shaped and -sized projectiles fired with a stalk with considerable rapidity. But *the* sensation

Spring 1916.

Summer 1916. was the Stokes gun, which arrived on the scene about the middle of the month, with its effective and rapid bursts of fire. But the enemy was inclined to be placid here and declined to be teased into serious artillery retaliation.

On this sector the redoubt line was in the suburb of St. Nicholas. Advantage of the fine weather was taken, and those not actually in the firing-line were kept busy at reconstruction and repairs. When this was ended on the 27th the battalion rested in Agnez-lez-Duisans, 5 miles W. of Arras. And so on passed the time. The third tour was in the river sector, and rest was at Agnez. The fourth at Roclincourt and back to Duisans (near Agnez). Both sides were indulging in mining activity, and in June there appeared three large craters just in front of our front line; three were sufficiently outstanding to be named "Cuthbert," "Clarence," and "Claud." * They took a bit of watching, and the enemy was constantly suspected of occupying the far lips. An officer, Lieut. Giles, was deputed to keep an eye on them, and was known as "O.C. Craters."

On the outbreak of the Somme battle, so fatal to the 1st Battalion, the 2nd K.O.S.B. were at Agnez training hard for a projected attack in the Wailly area (4 miles S.W. of Arras), and, as it was suddenly sent to the Somme on the 13th, a glance at the personnel may be in place. Major A. E. D. Anderson had handed over to Capt. (T./Major) P. Stevenson on 4th June. He had been decorated with the M.C. and had been in temporary command of the 15th R.W.R., but was back as an extra major by 24th June. Col. Sladen was once more in command; the Second-in-Command was Major P. Stevenson. Captains Herries (returned from the 6th Battalion on 2nd April), W. A. O. Rutherfurd (fresh from Third Army School), D. Mackenzie, and Kindersley (H.L.I.), were all officers of considerable war experience. The 2nd Battalion was rested, well up to strength in subalterns, N.C.O.s and men, and keen to give a good account of itself. It was well schooled in the latest devices, impetuous bayonet fighting, gas-mask drill, revolver shooting for officers, a smattering of German tags to force surrender or effect a *ruse de guerre*. Their legs needed bracing, and this was secured by the march Somme-wards.† They were still in the 13th I.B. (Jones) and 5th Division now commanded by Maj.-Gen. R. B. Stephens since 1st April, when Gen. Kavanagh got command of the Cavalry

* *5th Division*, p. 103.

† Luckily the C.O. had managed to increase the strength of their pipe band while at Agnez-lez-Duisans. The pipes made all the difference to marching, and affected *moral*.

Corps. The route was in the form of a horseshoe—no doubt to avoid heavy traffic—right round Doullens *via* Houvin-Houvigneul, a trying trek of 17 miles by night, Heuzecourt and Hérissart and Franvillers (on Sunday, 16th), where the troops rested. Next day, at Méaulte, the K.O.S.B. struck the hurly-burly and congestion of the field of a battle in full swing.

July 1916.

CHAPTER VII *

THE BATTLE OF THE SOMME

July 1916. —

THE Battle of the Somme has such a hold over the memories of those likely to read this story that few words of introduction are required. The casualty list affected millions at home and overseas. The initial success and the persistent push awakened hopes. The battle was followed with unflagging interest. Otherwise obscure villages won instant immortality. and the situation maps attracted every eye. It was Britain's first real offensive on the Western Front, and the country had the fullest confidence in the Commander-in-Chief and the now homogeneous Old Army, Territorial and New Army divisions. There were seventy divisions on the Western Front ; ample reserves were behind them and a plan to hand. Much, though far from all, had been done in the matter of training. The actual date of the infantry assault —the 1st of July—was the result of the general situation. The pressure in front of Verdun required easing, and the Germans had to be prevented from reinforcing the Eastern Front, where Russia was taking a splendid and last offensive under Brussiloff. The battle of Albert resulted in a breach of the strong German trench system on a sufficiently wide scale to invite exploitation. N. of Albert the gains were trifling, and beyond Thiépval the 1st of July is a tragedy. But Fricourt was doomed, Mametz had fallen, Montauban was brilliantly stormed ; and our Allies, who encountered less resistance, advanced to a varying but never unsubstantial extent in touch with the British and astride the River Somme. The whole breach was 14 miles in extent. The next day saw the fall of Fricourt. But the possession of La Boiselle and Contalmaison were essential to the exploitation of the success won. The titanic struggle ended in the capture of La Boiselle, Ovillers, and Contalmaison by the 16th, thereby putting the British astride the Albert-Bapaume road behind the German first line fortifications. But the principal advance had lain more to the E. . Mametz Wood, E. of Contalmaison, Bernafay Wood, which cost the 6th K.O.S.B. dearly,

* See Map 3.

July 1916.

as we shall see, with the Briqueterie near Montauban, were ours, and the strongly held Trônes Wood, E. of Bernafay Wood, was more ours than the enemy's by the 14th. On that date the assault upon the German second system of defence began. The sector selected lay from Longueval to Bazentin-le-Petit Wood, and its capture involved that of Bazentin-le-Grand, Bazentin-le-Petit, and the Wood. So successful was the attack, that all these objectives were taken and an advance made N., which won temporarily all but the N. end of High Wood. Longueval, however, had not yet fallen, and was to be the scene of fiercely contested fighting on the 15th, and, though Waterlot Farm was taken, Delville Wood was still the scene of fierce struggles and the sway of battle. The enemy still held the crest of the dominating ridge in the historic triangle Albert-Bapaume-Péronne, High Wood, part of Longueval, most of Delville Wood, and the culminating fort of Ginchy and the woods towards Combles. A visit to the Butte de Warlencourt and a glance S., S.E., and E. will best explain the intensity of the fighting and the slowness of progress. For High Wood, now scrub, and the South African memorial and Ginchy rebuilt dominate the horizon. From Guillemont the line bent sharply S. and joined the French at Maltz Horn Farm. Combles and Morval were still German. The British thrust had therefore developed a vulnerable salient, the only cure for which was to keep hammering on on the R. in co-operation with our Allies. " In addition, it was desirable further to secure our hold on the main edge W. of Delville Wood by gaining more ground to our front in that direction." *

High Wood

At last we come to the 5th Division and the 2nd K.O.S.B. . It may be said in advance that the battalion only stayed two and a half months in the Somme, and that the scene of its activities extended only from High Wood to Morval. The horrors of winter in the Somme were avoided. But while it lasted the fighting made call on skill, courage, endurance, and discipline to the limits of human capacity.

On the 19th of July the 2nd K.O.S.B., led by Major Anderson (in the absence of the C.O. on reconnaissance and of the Second-in-Command left behind), marched in all the panoply of modern war—steel helmet and gas-mask included,—past Fricourt and Mametz, and across country, freely shelled, towards High Wood. After dark the battalion was guided to the old German second line between

* Sir D. Haig's despatch, in vol. vii. p. 17.

July 1916. — Bazentin-le-Grand and Guillemont, and took up position, relief being completed at 2.30 a.m. in consequence of the guides being six hours late.* Horne's XV. Corps, to which they belonged, between the 3rd Division on R. and the 7th on L., had a line extending from N. of Bazentin-le-Petit to the S. end of High Wood, whence it bent in front of a track leading S.E. thence to Longueval. About 400 yards N.E. of this latter portion of line, and roughly parallel to it, was a sunk road called Wood Lane, lying invisible 50 yards down the reverse slope of the crest. Thus there were 350 yards gently uphill and 50 down to reach Wood Lane, the first objective.

But if that task were accomplished greater difficulties lay ahead. The ultimate objective, the German third line, "Switch Trench," ran not S.E. but E. from the N. of High Wood, where it formed part of the German firing-line, so that its distance from the attacking force increased the more Longueval was approached. This would involve a change of front of a quarter-circle, and the K.O.S.B. did not relish the prospect of executing this manœuvre in darkness over unknown ground. The attack was on a three divisional front, the 5th being in the middle. The attack had two stages. The first was the acquisition of the track as a jumping-off place. This task was entrusted to the Borderers. Lieut.-Col. Sladen rejoined just in time to direct the attack. After artillery preparation of some hours and intensity, A and D went over the top at 3.30 a.m. on the 20th of August and took their objective and dug in. They held it all day, and handed over to the 14th R.W.R. at night. They then returned to the rest of the battalion and awaited further orders. Three subalterns—Bignell, Brown, and Oldfield—were wounded, and there were 124 O.R casualties (15 k. and 6 m.). In consequence of the death of the Brigade Major of the 13th I.B., Major Anderson left the battalion on succeeding him.† The whole of that day and the next were spent in sheltering from shells, but the bulk of these were for the communication approach to Bazentin-le-Grand from Fricourt direction.

At noon on the 22nd orders came for the capture of Wood Lane by the R.W.K. and for the 2nd K.O.S.B. to pass through them and swing N. upon the 500 yards of Switch Trench nearest to High Wood. The 51st (Highland) Division were to be on the L. of the K.O.S.B. and the 1st D.C.L.I. of the 5th Division (95th I.B.) were to be on their R.. The story is brief and tragic. It will be found in the pages of *Invicta*. The bombardment was ineffective, as so often happens in an improvised attack. The 33rd Division had not

* 13th I.B.W.D.

† Captain W. T. Wyllie was killed by shrapnel at Brigade H.Q..

eradicated the strong M.G. posts in High Wood which mowed down the R.W.K. in platoons. Meanwhile a strong counter-barrage from gunners who knew their ground met the assailants, and from the ridge came M.G. fire from a sunken road, which the enemy only occupied at night. Only two small detachments joined forces in a small portion of Wood Lane. Thus it came about that at 10.45 p.m. the K.O.S.B. were called upon to support the initial attack and not to develop a success. A and D were again the attackers and B and C in support. But only one platoon of D could make any headway. They seem to have been the K.O.S.B. referred to as joining the R.W.K. in Wood Lane.* At any rate the whole of the 5th Divisional troops were back whence they started. The 51st fared no better in High Wood. The R.W.K. lost 14 officers and over 400 O.R.. The K.O.S.B. lost 2 officers killed and 3 wounded, and the O.R. casualties were 110 (13 k. and 29 m. †). Thus the engagement cost the battalion 8 officers and 234 O.R.. The C.O. was again wounded at his advanced H.Q. in the "track" trench. It is with great regret that the death of Capt. A. D. Young-Herries ("younger of Spottes," to drop into our Scottish thought and phrase) is recorded. We may shortly expect a better informed "appreciation" of his short life and its work.‡ No one ever was prouder of being a Borderer and no one shouldered responsibility with more serious purpose. His letters reveal an interest in the welfare of the men and their comforts and a cheerfulness of spirit and sense of duty that prove that in him a good and promising officer was lost.

July 1916.

At 9 p.m. on the 23rd the 1st Norfolks of the 15th I.B. relieved the K.O.S.B., who retired to Pommiers Redoubt, called after some long defunct apple-trees familiar to the 5th Division gunners in the Carnoy days. There they bivouacked and absorbed a draft of 71 O.R., and there the G.O.C. thanked them (along with R.W.K.) in person on the 24th for steadiness in the face of withering fire.

On the evening of the 29th the K.O.S.B. left Pommiers and relieved the 95th I.B. in N. Longueval on the W. side of Delville Wood. On their R. were the 2nd Division and on their L. the 14th R.W.R.. It was a perilous post, spattered all day with gun and M.G. fire, and casualties came thick and fast. Our barrage (partly divisional and partly contributed by 51st and 33rd Divisional batteries) lifted at 6.12 p.m., and an attack was made on an orchard

* *Invicta*, p. 143.

† In these battles "missing" meant that in the vast majority of cases nothing was ever again heard of the soldier.

‡ It has since appeared, written by the Rev. Dr. D. Frew of Urr, and published by Wm. Blackwood & Sons (1928).

July 1916. to an objective beyond it. Short of leadership the troops struggled through on the L., and, though unable to hold the objective, dug in some 30 yards short, with their R. refused, so as to form a defensive flank. They managed to kill some Germans. There was not much to show for the cost in valuable lives, but all that could have been accomplished was done. After a long-drawn-out, difficult relief by the 15th I.B. the battered K.O.S.B. "crawled back" in small parties, in the small hours of the 31st, to Pommiers Redoubt. 244 O.R. were casualties, but the chief loss was in officers. Capt. W. P. Paterson, the very *beau ideal* of the new order—young, strong, cheerful, adaptable—heads the list of the killed. Had he been spared he would have gone far. His fate was shared by 2nd Lieuts. Saxton, Petrie, Robertson, Macdonald, and Yarrow. Lieuts. Giles, Church, and Thorburn-Brown, and 2nd Lieuts. M'Neill, Grant, Smith, Collier, Stewart, and Price were wounded. It was a terrible experience for Major P. Stevenson, who with H.Q. actually in the village of Longueval with A Company and the R.W.K., who were having a second dose, in support, was experiencing his first command of the battalion in action. In their first phase of the Somme the Brigade suffered casualties to the extent of 82 officers and 1,932 O.R.. Of these the K.O.S.B. had 23 officers and 469 O.R.. (The R.W.K. 18 officers and no less than 569 O.R..)

After two days' camp at Dernancourt the battalion entrained on 4th August for Airaines, S.E. of Abbeville, and marched *via* Metigny (one night) to Heucourt, where, in pleasant country, recuperation, absorption, refitting, and training were the order of the day for seventeen days. Five subalterns of the H.L.I. joined, and by the 20th reinforcements had dribbled in to the tune of more than 360.

A return was made on 24th for the last tour in the Somme till the grand finale, 1918. An early march and a day in the crawling train saw the 2nd K.O.S.B. marching into Dernancourt Camp from Méricourt station. Next day aroused memories in the survivors of 1915, for the daylight march was to Happy Valley, W. of the very farm of Bronfay, where the battalion H.Q. used to be, when the Somme was quiet. Next afternoon trenches near Maricourt received them, and suggested operations on the R. of the British front next the French, who had taken Hardecourt and Maurepas and now faced Combles.

The battle for the central ridge had raged all August. Longueval and Delville Wood were still German, and Guillemont was mostly so. A glance at the map will show that Combles lies in a valley and that the high ground to the W. of it is a wedge pointing S.W. and that at the lip is a farm marked Falfemont Farm, S.E. of Guillemont. It was immensely strongly fortified and impregnable without the aid of a destructive bombardment, and even then better entered by the back than the front door. 3 Sept. 1916.

Falfemont

The K.O.S.B. remained in reserve from 26th to 29th August before occupying trenches opposite Falfemont Farm. For theirs was to be the honour of assaulting the fort. The day did not come till the famous 3rd of September, and when it did the honours were with the K.O.S.B., but the ground remained with the enemy. It is idle to inquire why the French failed to fulfil the promised bombardment, and why their infantry made no move forward on the R.. The place had not been touched. Yet the men, led with superb gallantry by inexperienced officers, crossed the parapet of the trenches N. of Angle Wood as one man and advanced in broad daylight to certain death consciously yet without flinching.* It was magnificent, but it was not war. Only 2 officers remained unhit. The attacking force was wiped out; Lieuts. Addis, H. F. Miles, A. N. Sulley, H. E. Wheeler, R. W. Lees, E. C. Rex, R. S. Ross, and T. M. Scott were killed. Addis had joined up at Carnoy in 1915. He had a cheery disposition, a happy flow of talk, and as he was a gallant and kindly soul he was beloved by all ranks. He lay there in front of his men, and they and he all pointed the right way. It is as if they had been mown down on parade. Giles, it will be recalled, had been "O.C. Craters" at Arras, and was a good officer lost. But it is no place to pile up mentions; the facts show that everyone fought like heroes.

Capt. W. A. O. Rutherfurd (a veteran of Mons) and 2nd Lieuts. Strachan and A. M. Little were wounded. O.R. casualties were 283, of whom 91 were killed and 55 were missing (a synonym for killed in an attack of this kind). The rest were wounded. The dispositions of the companies are not given in the War Diary, but they are without interest. There is the tragedy and the heroism for the actors, and for us the sorrow and pride. The scene was witnessed from battalion H.Q. of the R.W.K.. "It was the old story of the murderous efficiency of the German M.G.. The 15th R.W.R. were sent in to assist the K.O.S.B., but also failed to reach the farm." † There was actually an officer who directed the sniping of the runners to and from the front, and to the chagrin of the onlooking R.W.K. none escaped.† It is recorded that Lieut.-Gen.

* Letter of 2nd Lieut. A. M. Little, 2nd K.O.S.B., quoted at length in the War Diary.

† *Invicta*, pp. 154–155.

Sept. 1916. Stephens' assurance at Citadel Camp on the 6th that the 13th Brigade were not to blame for the failure cheered up the men of the 2nd K.O.S.B.. On the 10th the K.O.S.B. returned to the scene of disaster and faced Falfemont once more. But on the 13th they were relieved by troops of Brig.-Gen. Coke's 169th Brigade. They were out of the line on "tank-day" (the 15th of September), which saw the capture of High Wood, Flers, Martinpuich,* and Courcelette, and the threat against Morval, Lesbœufs, and Gueudecourt. It may be mentioned that if the 13th Brigade did not storm Falfemont, their brother brigade the 15th I.B., to which the R.W.R. were attached, *did*—on 5th September—and by the back door too and after a proper preparation.† Ginchy had fallen on the 9th.

MORVAL

The K.O.S.B. were to find their true consolation in an attack on Morval, though when it came as a surprise—the call to replace the 1st D.C.L.I. in the 95th I.B.—it cannot have been particularly welcome. It involved remaining in trenches, the preparation of fire trenches for going over the top, and holding the line. Lieut.-Col. P. Stevenson had hardly an officer of experience. Kindersley was Second-in-Command and in reserve, and he and the Adjutant (Lieut. L. F. Machin) alone had experience. The news came to the C.O. when in the "Quadrilateral," for a time a thorn in the flesh, even after the capture of Ginchy, which seemed to open up such possibilities. It had at last fallen on the 18th. The K.O.S.B. were in for a set piece with 4 lifts of barrage and waves of troops. On the 24th the batteries opened and the whole untaken third line strong points were bombarded from Thiépval to Saillisel opposite the French. The guns were still thundering on the 25th when the final burst in full volume at 12.35 signalled to the infantry to advance. The 95th I.B.'s objective, Morval, was the key to complete success. Without it the French would not be able to "pinch" Combles by the simple process of passing it on the heights and taking Frégicourt. Morval was a formidable stronghold.‡ The K.O.S.B. were to follow and pass through the 1st Devons and secure the village. Their flank on the R. was in the safe hands of the 56th (London) Division, in which Coke was a B.G.. That division had come through very stiff fighting in the attacks on the German third line.

The whole thing went like clockwork. The K.O.S.B. gained their

* By the 7/8th K.O.S.B.. See Book V, Ch. iv.
† *Invicta*, p. 156; *5th Division*, pp. 121–122.
‡ Buchan's *History of the War*, vol. iii. p. 199.

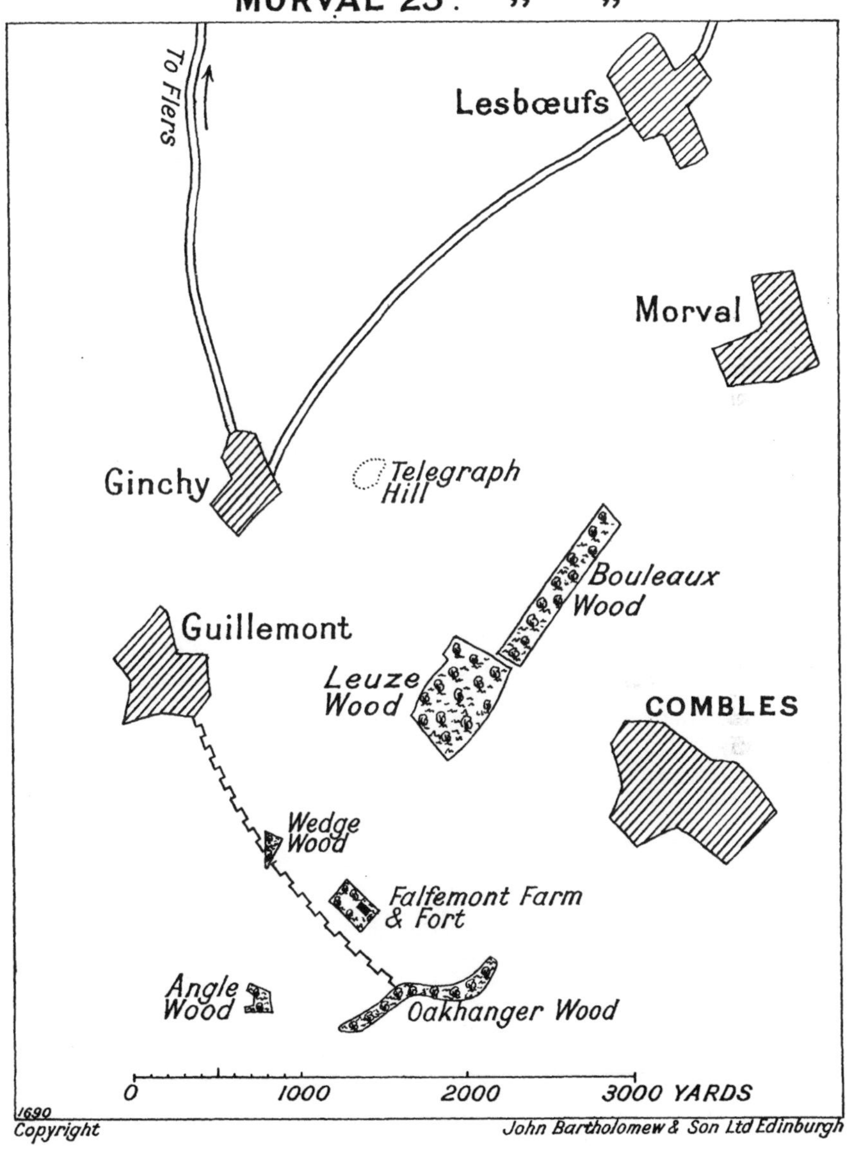
FALFEMONT 3RD SEPT. 1916
MORVAL 25TH " "
To Flers
Lesbœufs
Morval
Ginchy
Telegraph Hill
Bouleaux Wood
Guillemont
Leuze Wood
COMBLES
Wedge Wood
Falfemont Farm & Fort
Angle Wood
Oakhanger Wood
0
1000
2000
3000 YARDS
1690
Copyright
John Bartholomew & Son Ltd Edinburgh

To face Page 82

objective at 4 p.m., leaning against the barrage, in four dashing bounds. They took the bulk of the 700 somewhat demoralized prisoners and 5 M.G.. "Nearly every man secured a trophy." * In accordance with orders, they did not continue the pursuit but lay on the outskirts of the captured village taking "pot shots" at the Germans retiring from Combles. But patrols established that on this sector a real break through had been made. "Morval is ours, Combles will be ours to-night." † Next day the French took Frégicourt and thus Combles fell as the direct result of a combined operation of French and British troops. Congratulations rained in on Col. Stevenson from the B.G.C. 95th Brigade, from 5th Division, XIV. Corps and Fourth Army. Three subalterns fell, R. M. Rogers, J. Anderson, and E. A. Knipe. The last died of wounds next day. One subaltern, 2nd Lieut. G. Thomson, was wounded. Capt. J. L. Grant was hit but able to remain at duty. O.R. casualties were 165. Among these was the imperturbable R.S.M. Geggie, whose services from Hill 60 onwards were invaluable. He was wounded in the leg. In all the Somme cost the 2nd Battalion 19 officers killed and 23 wounded; 136 O.R. killed; 708 wounded; 266 missing.‡ And so farewell to the Somme. Next time the 2nd K.O.S.B. visited that grizzly cemetery of the brave they would move faster and their foes perforce faster still.§

Sept.–Oct. 1916.

A REST CURE NEAR LA BASSÉE

The battered infantry of the 5th Division found its way by the ordinary stages of march and rail from the Somme battlefield to the outskirts of Abbeville. On the 1st of October an early start enabled them to reach Lillers in the afternoon by rail from Abbeville. Thence the K.O.S.B., now in the XI. Corps (Haking), marched 8 miles S.E. to Vendin, a suburb of Béthune, and after a short stay at Le Hamel and Le Touret, N.E. of Béthune, moved into front trenches or rather posts in the Prince's Island sector of the Givenchy-Festubert front. Hardly a shot was fired. It was a change from the hectic days exactly two years ago. The Diary for October discloses no casualties. Brigade reserve was at Gorre, midway between Festubert and Béthune. Col. Sladen rejoined the brigade on 25th October, but commanded it and not the battalion until the second week of November, when Col. Stevenson relinquished to him the trust he had so faithfully kept since the dark days of 22nd July.

* War Diary.

† Translation of a French airman's appreciative account of the battle quoted in *5th Division*, pp. 126–127.

‡ Brigade War Diary.

§ See chap. xii, *post*.

1917. Subalterns had been dribbling in since the Battle of Morval, 2nd Lieut. P. Cameron joining on the 26th, the day after Morval, at Maricourt. Nothing is said about drafts except that a particularly promising batch from the Fife and Forfar Horse commenced serious training at Gorre in the middle of December, nor about the weather, and the natural inference is that the B.E.F. had little to learn in the way of draining, flooring with duckboards, revetting inconspicuous breastworks, and generally making the best of a waterlogged site. What one notices is that in January part of the division training in reserve (at Béthune in Feuillard Barracks) consisted of range practices.

It is well known that the paramount need for weapons of siege warfare displaced attention to rifle fire for a time. Bombs, Lewis-guns, mortars of all sizes, bayonets and revolvers occupied men's minds. But the aimed rifle shot was never out of the C.-in-C.'s training scheme. Musketry had saved us in 1914; it would help to repel the last onslaught and bring victory in 1918.

January was rather livelier with tear shells and a few casualties resulted. One announcement in the *Gazette* delighted all ranks. Their severely tried but never failing Q.M., Hon. Lieut. Sam. Brocklehurst, was awarded the M.C. for gallant service dating from the beginning of the war. February was marked by mutual mine blowing and by a huge and amazingly successful raid by the R.W.K.*. March was ushered in by a successful raid carried out by 2nd Lieut. J. J. M'E. Aucott, of the 4th Cameronians, who had joined the 2nd K.O.S.B. on 16th October, and 24 O.R.. The purpose of the raid was to secure identification and incidentally do as much harm and kill as many of the garrison as possible. The party divided into three, and the leading one was in position ready to rush a saphead the moment the barrage opened at 4.50 a.m. All this happened according to plan and to the entire surprise of the enemy, who were isolated by the "box" character of the barrage which poured on the support trenches and "boyaux de communication." Nine prisoners were taken—a fair field for the wily inquisitors of Corps and Army, 5 dug-outs were bombed, and there were probably a good number killed and wounded one way and another. It is a bad plan to prolong one's pleasures. The gallant leader wisely withdrew his party. He and two of his men were wounded. Otherwise all returned unscathed in triumph. Aucott won the M.C.,† and 5 awards were given to 3 N.C.O.s and 2 privates. No retaliation seems to have followed,

* *5th Division*, p. 144.

† "Jimmy" Aucott's daring and skilful raiding were greatly prized by his various C.O.s.

and the battalion gave place to the R.W.K. and went to close support. The C.O. had recognized in 2nd Lieut. J. S. Hogarth of the 4th K.O.S.B. an officer of promise. He had completed four months at the front and been one of the party sent to reconnoitre the ground at Mont St. Eloi for the coming "push," when a chance shell killed him on 25th March. The battalion was not then in the line but at Auchel, 7 miles W.S.W. of Béthune in the Canadian Corps area. "He was much regretted by all ranks." * March 1917.

* War Diary (Lieut.-Col. Sladen, C.M.G.).

CHAPTER VIII *

VIMY RIDGE

April 1917. — THE ceaseless pressure of the Fourth Army (Rawlinson) and the Fifth Army (Gough), by which the Germans were thrust off the main heights between the Ancre and the Tortille † and his original line was pared down to a pronounced salient with the S. point at Grandcourt, the apex at Gommecourt, and the N. termination at Arras corresponding to the S. termination close to Péronne, was baulked of its reward by the state of the ground (to be explained in connection with the 1st Battalion). But in spite of the winter such a strain was put upon the Germans that in March 1917 they abandoned the front and retired to the Hindenburg or Siegfried Line, a vast engineering work of enormous strength, pushed on with forced Russian and other labour during the progress of the Somme battle. This line from near Arras cut the Bapaume-Cambrai road not quite half-way to the latter and covered St. Quentin more than 40 miles to the S.E..

This retirement caused a modification in Sir Douglas Haig's plans, but that need not concern us because the capture of the Vimy Ridge, with which we are about to be concerned, always formed part of the plan of campaign of any battle of Arras contemplated by him, and it is with Vimy that we have to do. The traveller from La Bassée towards Lens becomes sensible in clear weather of a bold barrier on the S. of the uninviting coalfield of the Béthune-Lens area, the bluff of Notre Dame de Lorette, 541 feet above sea-level. It is by far the most imposing physical feature N. of Champagne on the Western theatre, forming the E. end of a ten-mile-long "falaise" from Houdain to Souchez, which often attains a height of 600 feet. As he bends his gaze to the left across a gap (the Souchez River) he sees a resumption of height in an almost equally lofty ridge, the Vimy Ridge, slanting S.E. and declining towards low ground, which he knows must be the valley of the Scarpe as it trails away from

* See Map 4.

† The tributary of the Somme which enclosed the E. battlefield, *e.g.* Sailly Saillisel and St. Pierre Vaast Wood.

Arras towards the Scheldt. By the time he has cleared the purlieus of Lens he will see the country rising gently, cleanly, and wooded in places, *e.g.* near Givenchy-en-Gohelle, to what seems to promise a precipitous ascent. Certainly the old straight road across the ridge would serve for a hill-climbing test, and even the well-engineered curve of the Lille-Arras " route national " demands a change down —or two—as within the space of a kilometre it negotiates the climb through a glen or indent into the ridge. Down on the L. lies Vimy village, the last of the coal country. As the crest is reached at about 400 feet it reveals an immense prospect W. and S. and E.. The road rolls down a broad plateau 5 miles to St. Nicholas with Thélus to the L. nearest to the ridge, and, on the R., Neuville St. Vaast. Behind it is Mont St. Eloi, and away beyond a vista opens towards St. Pol. The true line of the ridge is seen pointing S.E. towards Farbus (close) and Bailleul. But the N.W. continuation is higher than the road summit. In less than a mile W. the true top, " Point 147," can be reached, and then something of the military importance of the Vimy Ridge comes home to the least military of minds. N. to Mont Kemmel and E. to Douai, a nodal point in the railway net, and beyond and across the Scarpe to Monchy and beyond on either side along the " Hindenburg Line " the country is spread out like a map. Notre Dame de Lorette, with monument and shrine, is seen as an escarpment to the N.W.. At its foot lies Souchez, and on the tilt, N. of the Vimy Ridge about a mile E. of Souchez, lies Givenchy-en-Gohelle, prominent on the R. on the way from Lens. Between these villages ran the opposing lines in a generally S.E. by S. line just N. of Roclincourt to Blangy, names associated to the 2nd K.O.S.B. with peaceful times in 1916. And all the way the Germans had the " cothrom a' bhruthaich," * for the whole of the high ground was theirs.

April 1917.

Before the 2nd K.O.S.B. could fight on the flat or downhill they would have to toil uphill in their weighty fighting kit. Meanwhile, before descending to the plain, as we stand at the junction of the old and new roads on the crest, we notice that the N.E. face is steep, that the W. is gentler and steepest near the top, and that in 1917 a wood (Goulot Wood) must have clothed the N.E. slope just beneath us, and that there were trees on the left of the glen we came up (Bonval Wood). We can imagine our battalion working its way up from N. of Neuville St. Vaast through the mazes of wire, and smashed trenches and shell-holes, and the E. wind and the sleety drizzle, with its L. marching on us. We can almost see it cross the road to Arras and descend the steep drop to Goulot Wood.

* See Introductory Chapter, p. 4.

April 1917. The story of Vimy Ridge belongs to the Canadians. Theirs is the glory, and the 13th I.B. may mildly add *pars parva fuimus.* For they were loaned to give extra weight to the R. centre division, the 2nd, of the four divisions composing the Canadian Corps, which had planned and mined and prepared for months.* The 2nd K.O.S.B. were on the L. of the R.W.K., on whose R. were the 6th (Canadian) I.B.. The 3rd (Canadian) Division on their L. was to supplement the initial burst of 1,500 yards of the 5th (Canadian) I.B. by passing through them, as they consolidated on the second objective—the red line—and by reaching in turn the blue and the brown or final objective. The 14th R.W.R. were to be in support and the 15th R.W.R. in reserve.

We left the 2nd K.O.S.B. at Auchel. They trained in the Bois des Dames, and on one occasion were watched by the Third Army Commander, Sir J. Byng, while at work practising on model trenches. The scheme of attack was long since fixed and there was no "secrecy" nonsense. On the 2nd of April the 13th I.B. marched towards the battlefield, and halted for five days in the great Wood of Olhain on the "Lorette" ridge, 8 miles N.W. of Neuville in bell tents without boards, a chilly refuge, in the bleak April of 1917, at an altitude higher than any part of the Vimy Ridge. Mud, lost kits, colds, aches, sore feet, and unchangingly vile weather were unpropitious preludes to an ordeal of life and death.

Consequently it says worlds for the men that Brig.-Gen. Jones was pleased with the combined practice of the two battalions of assault over ground taped out and selected to resemble the actual ground of the attack. Time was of the essence of the business, and as the weather would not improve the British Commander had to fix the day. The choice fell on Easter Monday the 9th of April, Ludendorff's birthday.† Accordingly we find the 2nd K.O.S.B. on the 8th making an early start from their tents near Verdrel to draw their equipment at Villers-au-Bois under cover of woods. There they bivouacked till guided after 9.30 p.m. to the trenches of assembly N. of Neuville, under direction of Major C. T. Furber, a Borderer of the 1st Battalion with Indian experience (including first class polo), of whom we shall hear much as O.C. 2nd K.O.S.B.. He had reconnoitred the trenches with a party of Officers and N.C.O.s. The bivouac was only half-way to assembly point and there were still 5 miles to go. At 9.30 p.m. the zero hour, viz. 5.30 a.m., was imparted and a start made for the place of assembly. The 8th of April was fine, and it helped enormously. The late Col. Sladen's

* The Canadians always referred to them as the 13th *Imperial* Brigade.

† See Ludendorff's *Meine Kriegserinnerungen*, p. 334.

account of the action on the 9th is the main source of the narrative that follows.* 9 April 1917.

The 5th Divisional artillery were in support but too near to co-operate until the second phase opened. The advancing troops were not much shelled and they were in position by 2.30 a.m..

Punctually at zero the Canadians launched their attack, but the K.O.S.B. stayed where they were, as according to a time-table they were not to move till 7.20. Shells of heavy calibre came in large numbers on the belt of No Man's Land, and some hundreds of yards on either side of it, but the 2nd K.O.S.B. were off by scheduled time by companies one after the other in alphabetical order. The C.O. and H.Q. followed, but as usual the "dumped personnel," as the Second-in-Command and his small reserve of officers and N.C.O.s and men were termed, were left behind. It was on resumption of the advance, after a halt in the next or forward position of assembly, that casualties occurred soon after 8.30. The leading company was then advancing beyond the former German support line, and the others continued to follow, all in "artillery formation," a phrase so meaningless to the recruit but to the military mind conjuring up little columns or sections in fours not too close to one another to risk being "browned," and not too far apart to lead to loss of formation and control. It suggests troops engaged but not yet deployed for attack. For the reasons already given the going was vile, and there was a steady drizzle. Direction was hard to keep. It was daylight, yet the aid of the compass had to be invoked, but the men were in their places in time to pass through the Canadians in open order at the place of deployment—the Red Line—just short of the Arras–Lens road. At scheduled time, 9.30, A and B abreast were advancing on Thélus trench, followed by C and D. That trench ran from the front of Thélus village towards Vimy parallel to the Lens road half a mile or so to the E. of it. The capture of Thélus trench was no plain-sailing business. When A crossed the highroad they were at the glen head already described, and the point of Bonval Wood confronted them. To skirt the S. or top edge of the wood, *i.e.* to leave it on the L., it was necessary to move by file of sections before reforming for the final assault. It was here that enemy snipers, shooting across the glen from dugouts yet untaken, caused considerable casualties. The Canadians on the L. had suffered a temporary check; in fact, they continued to be held up long after the K.O.S.B. had stormed Thélus trench without much opposition and had done some mopping-up. If touch was

* As given in the W.D..

9 April 1917. — to be recovered with the 3rd (Canadian) Division, the snipers must be silenced. The C.O. accordingly sent two platoons of D to reinforce A, whose most capable and reliable commander, A/Capt. G. T. Pringle (awarded the M.C.), then detached a bombing and Lewis-gun team, who dealt faithfully with the nest, taking 3 officers and 33 O.R. prisoners.* By this time it was about 4 p.m. and the objectives were all reached. Meanwhile the main body had been potting at the stream of Germans retreating down into Vimy village, and no doubt the " range practices " proved their value. They were also able to bomb along Thélus trench and to advance to what were known as the " Quarry Dugouts." These were either cleared or well bombed by A and B alike. The enemy artillery response appeared to be feeble and misdirected, with the result that telephone wires were less frequently cut than usual. Meanwhile B had made more rapid progress on the R.. Hugging a perfect barrage they dropped into their allotted bit of Thélus trench where it skirts the N. end of an isolated copse called Count's Wood. This was their southern boundary. They were in two parties. The L. bombed down towards A, and sent a party forward to the Quarries by a " boyau " called Fling Trench, and assisted A in cleaning up the dugouts there.

The R. pushed on through empty gun-pits to a network of trenches, the Gridiron. A certain adjustment of frontiers had to be made with the R.W.K.. Both battalions had had to squeeze through the space, about 300 yards wide, between Count's Wood and Bonval Wood. They had then to fan out, the K.O.S.B. going more or less straight ahead N.E. and the R.W.K. more to the R. to face their several objectives. The reason for the manœuvre was that a thick belt of wire ran S.E. along the line of the ridge from Count's Wood (420 feet), forming the second or inner defence of the Farbus line. It had not been continued N. of Count's Wood, and thanks to our airmen and the Canadian Corps staff it was turned intentionally—probably with economy to wire-cutting artillery. The R.W.K. did not deflect enough at first, but the slight over-crowding in the gun-pits beyond the Gridiron, which was C's final objective, was soon remedied.

Considering the late hour at which the snipers in the defile were silenced, it is remarkable that all the K.O.S.B. objectives were gained by 11 a.m.. The K.O.S.B. pushed patrols into the village of Vimy and once more reports came back that we were " through," and once again, as at Bonval, it was proved to be true. The Germans

* This company accounted for more than 150 German prisoners before the day was over (Report by Col. Sladen).

had no troops available on the spot ; * but with the Pimple farther N. still in hostile hands advance at Vimy was impracticable. Later on in the day snow fell and continued to fall till the ground was white, and moving figures stood out and invited the sniper. The final position was on or immediately short of the narrow track from the W. edge of Vimy village towards Farbus, at an average level, to judge from Map 3 of *Sir D. Haig's Despatches*,† of from 250 to 300 feet. Two platoons of D were with A on the L.. Then came B, then C, then the R.W.K.. The remaining two platoons were higher up the hill in a sunk road between the S.W. corner of Bonval Wood and Cramer Haus, a dugout which H.Q. of the K.O.S.B. shared with three other battalion H.Q.—viz. 1st R.W.K., 15th R.W.R., and 25th (Canadian) I.R., another 100 yards or so farther S. on the plateau about 440 feet high. 9 April 1917.

All the objectives having been taken and contact established with the R.W.K. on R. and 3rd (Canadian) Division on L., the K.O.S.B. settled down to the work of consolidation. The carrying parties, two reserve platoons of D, from behind had brought an adequate store of implements and ammunition. The night brought one alarm but no change, and the 10th, except for occasional bursts of gun fire and persistent sniping from Vimy village, was uneventful. Snow lay on the ground, and visibility for either side was good.

Observation Line, the line of support, speaks for itself. It lay along the N.E. edge of the ridge, and commanded a bird's-eye view of the hinterland N. and E. and S..

The outpost line was beyond Goulot Wood, but high enough up to look into Vimy and a bit beyond. That night after dark the 2nd K.O.S.B. were relieved by the 24th (Canadian) I.R., and retired by companies to the monastery at Mont St. Éloi, 5 miles W. of the new front. They could look back with gratitude and satisfaction to the fighting on the 9th. It was a more dramatic and brilliant Morval. To them had been allotted the task of storming the crest and working down to a defensible outpost position through the woods of Bonval and Goulot. That they had done their work economically and thoroughly is shown by the capture of somewhere about 250 prisoners ‡ (lion's share being A's), two 8-in. howitzers,§ and one M.G. (by A), 3 M.G. (by B), and, in the glen after the

* Information from Lieut.-Col. Anderson, D.S.O., then Brigade Major, 13th Brigade.

† Edition edited by Colonel Boraston (London : Dents, Ltd.).

‡ W.D.'s conservative estimate.

§ These were used with effect until the enemy realized what was "los" and put a stop to the insult. See *5th Division*, p. 156.

9 April 1917. capture of the snipers' nest, a wireless installation, a motor bicycle, and 6 ordinary bicycles adapted for wireless purposes. The cost must be counted.

One subaltern, 2nd Lieut. R. Gallon, whose name does not appear in the "Officers died in the Great War, 1914–19," and may therefore have been lent by the Canadians, was killed, another was (accidentally) wounded, while of the O.R. 21 were returned killed, 1 wounded and missing, 1 missing, and 137 wounded. The signalling under 2nd Lieut. Forster was excellent, and any wires severed were mended with promptitude. A tribute is due to Capt. A. Dick, R.A.M.C., who, despite the discomfort of an open trench exposed to snow and shells for his regimental aid-post, most ably carried out the duties of M.O.. He was awarded the M.C.. Capt. D. Kindersley had once more proved his sterling worth as adjutant, and richly deserved the D.S.O. conferred on him on 3rd June 1917 for dash and courage in clearing up the enemy trenches at the point of the bayonet. Sergt. F. W. Walls received the D.C.M., and no fewer than 14 M.M.s were bestowed on N.C.O.s and men, and two 2nd Lieuts., G. Watson and G. M. Rennie, were awarded the M.C. for good work at the head of bombers. As for the gunners, they made the attack possible. They were the indispensables, and the 5th Division artillery did wonderful execution among retiring groups of Germans. But the most credit of all is due to the team work. The men kept their heads in spite of six and a half hours bombardment, and responded to the leadership of company and platoon officers, who showed marked initiative. The value of practice was strikingly vindicated. But the infantry were loud in praise of the most important liaison of all—with the gunners. Only a perfect barrage can be "hugged," and that is what the K.O.S.B. and R.W.K. were treated to. The carrying parties were of immense value, always well forward and willing.

Brig.-Gen. Jones received a shower of congratulations, and the two battalions of assault may fairly appropriate a share. Nothing could exceed the warmth of the G.O.C.'s (2nd Canadian Division) letter of thanks for the 13th's contribution to the glorious victory.* Perhaps those from the sister brigades touched them most. "Magnificent success," said the 15th I.B.. "Nothing better done in the war," said the 95th I.B.. The Army Commander (Sir H. Horne) said the 13th had maintained its high reputation of 1916.† The writer ventures to add 1915 and 1914 to 1916.

The movements of the battalion in reserve, while they mended roads and waited for the clouds to roll by, call for little comment.

* Given in extenso in *Invicta*, pp. 173–174. † *5th Division*, p. 154.

A satisfactory draft brought the Batt. nearly back to its pre-battle strength, and in the second battle of the Scarpe it had a merciful escape from the calamitous losses which befell the sister brigades at La Coulotte in front of Avion near Lens on the 23rd of April. For a time it was in reserve trenches half a mile W. of the Arras–Lens road, *i.e.* on the lower slope of the Vimy Ridge between Vimy and Givenchy. But on the 24th, as the attack was not pressed, it was recalled and handed over to the 4th (Canadian) Division troops, retiring by an interesting traverse of the famous ridge including the Tottenham Tunnel to La Maison Blanche, just over a mile S. of Neuville St. Vaast. There the men furnished huge working parties for the roads. From this camp a move was made to Camblain-l'Abbé, *i.e.* quite close to their former station at Villers-au-Bois.

April–May 1917.

The night of the 2nd of May saw the 2nd K.O.S.B. heading for the line once more. This time they relieved 2nd (British) Division troops in a support line behind the railway embankment near Bailleul. Mention has already been made of the wide view from the Vimy Ridge, and of Farbus nestling under it to the E.. Beyond Farbus one picks out Arleux and Fresnoy, with its small square wood tacked on to the S. end, and as one shifts one's gaze to the R., Bailleul, 3 miles to the S.E., and across the Scarpe the prominent height of Monchy * comes into view. N.E. and S.E. respectively of Bailleul,† in either case about 2 miles, lie Oppy and Gavrelle.

The Third Battle of the Scarpe loses all but a personal and domestic interest after the failure of the Nivelle offensive on the Aisne on the 16th April. As the Germans recovered from the impetus of the British onslaught and brought up reinforcements from the Eastern front, Somme-like features in the fighting began to re-emerge. Counter-attacks were frequent, and artillery positions and likely points of assembly were plastered with shells on a scale indicating no shortage of ammunition.

The Third Battle of the Scarpe opened on 3rd May on a 14-mile front, extending from about a mile N. of Fresnoy to the far bank of the Sensée at Bullecourt on the Hindenburg Line. The part with which we are now concerned is the sector in the XIII. Corps (Congreve, V.C.), between Fresnoy Wood and Oppy.

The two Warwickshire battalions were holding the line during the attack on the 3rd, which brought heavy shelling on the support line. On the 7th the K.O.S.B. took over from the 15th R.W.R. just S. of Fresnoy Wood. They had not long to wait for trouble.

* See Book II, chap. iii.

† Not to be confused with Bailleul in Flanders.

May 1917. In a few hours the enemy opened a bombardment which lasted for three and a half hours from 2 a.m., and killed and wounded and rendered *hors de combat* by shock and by burying a large number. Three Lewis guns were knocked out of action in the L. sector held by B (Capt. J. L. Grant). The front was not itself attacked, but immediately to the N. Fresnoy had been enveloped and taken with disastrous results once more to the 95th I.B.. Capt. Grant, having his flank in the air, with great presence of mind used his company, both the remnant left in the line and his reserve, to form a defensive flank in a sunk wood in touch with 95th troops. An adjustment by the remaining companies and by the 15th R.W.R. and 1st R.W.K. to conform was effective, and the positions held all day in spite of steady and costly shelling. The last-named unit reinforced the K.O.S.B. with two platoons with a view to an improvised counter-attack on Fresnoy Wood at 2 a.m. on the 9th. The darkness, the hostile barrage, the unsuitable place of assembly, ignorance of the objective's features, and the physical condition of the attackers resulted in total failure, but brought out many instances of pluck in trying circumstances. Sergt. S. E. Hall's bearing, on the top of a long, creditable record, won him the D.C.M.. Nor had the units on the L. any better success.*

The two days cost the K.O.S.B. one 2nd Lieut. (C. Watt) killed, one wounded, and 158 O.R. casualties (20 k.). They were relieved by the 1st R.W.K., and retired to support early on 10th, only to return to a less strenuous tour in a sector near Oppy on 12th, where they lost 2nd Lieut. W. J. S. Forsyth, killed, and suffered 29 O.R. casualties.

The next stay in the support lines (near and forward) was marked on the 19th by a chance shell from a long-range gun which killed a veteran of Gallipoli, Capt. J. A. Ainslie of the 1st Battalion, who had come through the battle of Y Beach in 1915 and another battle nearly opposite Y Ravine on 1st July 1916,† and a typical Borderer in the making in the shape of Lieut. W. W. Laurie, of the famous Dumfriesshire house of Maxwelton. It was a sad and weary unit that embussed on the 25th for Diéval near St. Pol (20 miles W.N.W. of Arras). But rest and musketry did wonders in a week that passed too quickly.

The first fortnight of June, *i.e.* the period of the final preparations for and the brilliant execution of the attack on the Messines Ridge, was spent at Écurie just W. of Roclincourt, and was dedicated to trench-digging, to link up the Vimy Ridge with the trench system on the Lens–Arras railway, training, and Brigade Horse Show and

* *5th Division*, pp. 162–163.

† See later, p. 181.

Sports (in which the battalion did brilliantly), before relieving a battalion of the 2nd Division on the Arleux-Oppy front on the 13th. It is interesting to note that the Germans were expected to repeat their previous tactics and retire to the Drocourt-Quéant Switch.* The stay was short, for the 15th I.B. took their places on the 16th, and they returned to Écurie, to " put up quite a good show " at the 5th Divisional Horse Show and Sports, and to hear the news of the decorations bestowed in reward for the exploit at Vimy Ridge. June 1917.

The next tour of front duty brought a heavy loss. On 22nd Capt. D. Kindersley was killed. His invaluable services had been recognized by the recent award of the D.S.O., and the French had bestowed the Croix-de-Guerre. He was so much a part of the battalion that it was forgotten that he was but a sojourner. Quiet in manner, he had a rich vein of dry humour, and was a general favourite.

The only part played by the K.O.S.B. in the capture of Oppy Wood by the XIII. Corps on 28th June was to relieve, on the 30th, the 1st Norfolks, 1st Cheshires, and 1st Bedfords of the 15th I.B. in the new front, which they had just captured. In the usual rain of shells after an engagement a recent arrival, 2nd Lieut. J. M. Lawson, was killed. The weather was brutally unseasonable for midsummer in France, complicating the relief and hampering the urgent work of joining up the posts in the front line and digging communication trenches. B, under Capt. Grant, worked like beavers, and undoubtedly saved many lives by so doing. But a bright moon on the night of 4/5th July was even more trying for relievers and relieved. At 4.30 a.m. Lieut. Rennie, M.C., reported the last parties as having handed over to the Hawke Battalion of the 63rd (once Royal Naval) Division. Thus K.O.S.B. and R.N.D. troops who had first met at Cape Helles met once more in France.

At Écurie bathing was a welcome adjunct. From 9th July to the 2nd of September the 5th Division engaged in no major operations. The enemy was unenterprising, and there is little to recount. The most important event was the departure of Col. Sladen on 24th July to command the 46th I.B. of the 15th (Scottish) Division, in which were the 7/8th K.O.S.B.. An officer of his standing and record could not be expected to remain long a battalion C.O.. It was satisfactory that Major Furber was there to take his place, and had been long enough with the battalion to secure continuity.

* War Diary. This supplementary work to the more famous Siegfried Line branched off the main line at Quéant, 10 miles due W. of Cambrai, ran N. to Drocourt, 7 miles N.W. of Douai, which was devoid of natural defences. It was hardly complete in 1917, but was never seriously threatened. It was about 18 miles long. The Germans called it the *Wotan Stellung*.

Aug. 1917.

Capt. B. C. Lake arrived on 30th July and Lieut. A. E. Moreton on 8th August, signs that the authorities were still trying to officer the 2nd Battalion with regular Borderers whenever it was feasible.

The bad weather, intense heat varied by drenching thunderstorms, is the constant comment of the War Diary. Trench strength was usually round about 600, and subalterns were every now and then reporting for duty.

On 2nd August Major A. E. D. Anderson, K.O.S.B., was appointed G.S.O.2 to the 61st Division, and was succeeded by Major G. A. H. Bower as Brigade Major, 13th I.B.

CHAPTER IX

THE THIRD BATTLE OF YPRES *

Polderhoek

ON the 2nd of September the 2nd K.O.S.B. said good-bye for good to the Vimy front and moved to the Lucheux area N.E. of Doullens by easy marches suitable to troops stationary for five months. From Écurie the route was Anzin, Écoivres near Mont St. Eloi, Acq on the St. Pol–Arras railway, thence, on the 5th, across the Arras–St. Pol road to Maizières *via* Hermaville and Izel-lez-Hameau. At Maizières three days' training preceded the march on the 9th to the high-lying but commodious Ivergny just N. of the fine Forêt de Lucheux. The infant waters of the Canche were twice crossed at Magnicourt and Etrée-Wamin respectively. The ground was ideal for training and ranges, and the countryside for peace and rest. So the next fortnight flew like a schoolboy's summer holidays. Against a background of football and Highland games, intensive training and musketry were the order of each day. Every day that passed in Flanders revealed the need for such attention to detail in the *minutiæ* of the tactical tasks confided to the platoon, or it might be section, that something of the instinctive and automatic character of drill required to be attained. Gen. Stephens presented a cup for the best attack to be carried out by a platoon of the Division on a prepared " enemy " stronghold, each battalion to select its representatives by competition. 2nd Lieut. Rennie's platoon won the right to represent the K.O.S.B. and was placed sixth in the contest proper. They could console themselves that they fought a hard fight in the football final, losing to the 1/6th A. & S.H. by one goal to *nil*. Furber, now a Lieut.-Col., notes the improvement brought about by the training. The musketry of the drafts needed all the teaching and practice that could be spared from gas-drill, marching by compass, and set tactical schemes.

Sept. 1917.

A short march N. to Petit Houvin station on the evening of the 24th of September was followed by a detrainment at Wizernes, a mildly industrial town close to St. Omer on the road to Boulogne.

* See Map 4.

Sept. 1917.

After a rest, another train journey took the K.O.S.B. to Vlamertinghe and the stereotyped camp life of the Ypres hinterland. It was not till the 28th that the 5th Division was definitely allotted to the X. Corps (Morland, formerly G.O.C. 5th Division) of the Second Army, then immersed in the battle of Polygon Wood. This is not the place for a discussion of the aims of the Flanders offensive, or whether it hastened or retarded the end of the war. Both sides concur in the view that the Third Battle of Ypres was the sorest trial of nerves and discipline that soldiers had hitherto been called upon to face. To the terrific bombardments of the British artillery the enemy responded by a defence in depth pivoting on strong points made of reinforced concrete and known as "pill-boxes." These were held by picked men of resolution and skill in the use of M.G.. Direct hits would bounce off these hard and solid forts, and the only way of entry was by the "back-door." Unless demolished by a shell of largest calibre, pill-boxes constituted an absolute barrier to infantry unless they filtered through on either side and took the garrison from the rear. The weather had broken from the outset on 31st July 1917. The soil was the same as that described in connection with the Lindenhoek front in 1914. But it was in a vastly more advanced state of decomposition and was one miry swamp in which water-holding shell-holes touched and overlapped one another. It is one of the blessings of this stoneless soil, that at this day, thanks to the patient toil of the Flanders peasant, there are, broadly speaking, few traces of battle to be seen apart from the scrub-like successors of the fine old woods of 1914. But stonelessness was far from a blessing to the men of Third Ypres. The Somme had taught the value of duckboard tracks, and in the salient progress could, more often than not, only be made by means of definite tracks liable to be swept by shrapnel. Progress had been slow. What could be expected when the standard speed was one mile or less per hour?

What the situation map attached to Col. Boraston's *Sir D. Haig's Despatches* shows is that by 20th September, thanks to an improvement in the weather, a considerable advance in a N.E. direction towards Langemarck, Poelcapelle, and Zonnebeke had been made. As a sort of Achi Baba, the Passchendaele Ridge drew and seemed to mock every observant eye, and the Belgian coast seemed to be a hundred miles away.

To come to our setting, the battles of Pilckem (31st July–2nd August), Langemarck (16th–18th August), and the Ménin road (20th–25th September) were over, and that of Polygon Wood had been raging since the 26th on something a little less than a six-mile front from St. Julien across the Ménin road 600 yards or so to Tower Hamlets. The attack resulted in the Australians taking the wood and British troops gaining strong point objectives astride the Wieltje–Gravenstafel road. In the southern sector progress was slower, but by the night of the 27th the objectives there too were won, and the following days saw the ground held in the face of determined counter-attacks. Sept.–Oct. 1917.

The line taken over by the 5th Division from the 23rd Division rested on the Ménin road half a mile short of Gheluvelt and extended N. to Polygon Wood. It was held by two brigades with one in reserve. The 13th I.B. were on the R., the 95th on the L., and the 15th in reserve near Dickebusch. On the R. of the 13th were the 1st R.W.K. and on the L. the K.O.S.B., who confronted and had as objective the remains of the château of Polderhoek, a place of sombre memories. The impassable Reutelbeek formed their L. and the Scherriabeek their R. boundary, the château and its woods occupying a ridge between the two.

Our battalion at full strength left billets round Berthen on the S. slope of the Mont-des-Cats bit of the "mountains" on the 1st October, presumably *via* Bailleul and Locre, for Dickebusch. There they fitted out elaborately and weightily with extra rations, bombs, tools, etc., and marched across the Comines Canal and Messines Road to Bedford House, just beyond the latter and exactly 1,500 yards S. of Ypres ramparts. After a halt of four hours the relief of the support line troops of the 70th I.B. in the Stirling Castle area, a long mile W. of Polderhoek, was accomplished at 1 a.m. on the 2nd. Here they were vigorously shelled all day, and that night relieved the 8th Y. & L. on a two-company front in trenches that were still worse shelled. They were now under their own G.O.C., and their own division artillery on historic Hill 60 were behind them.

As an attack on a big scale had been planned for 6 a.m. on the 4th, it was in keeping with the "thrawnness" of things in Third Ypres that the weather broke on the 3rd and that rain soused our troops, swelled the "beeks," and put shell-holes into good drowning condition. At zero it was a "dark and tempestuous morning." * Yet there was a heavy ground mist which greatly impeded progress. Care had been taken to send officers to reconnoitre the ground and have its lie pointed out by the Y. & L.. The 13th I.B. were not to advance from the line held on 3rd but from an advanced position in No Man's Land, to be taped out at right angles to the line of advance so that each man could march to his front towards the objective.

* *5th Division*, p. 177.

4 Oct. 1917. The late Lieut. T. J. Carlyle superintended this delicate task to the entire satisfaction of his C.O. on the night of the 3rd. C and D then took up their positions and dug in. Both battalions of the 13th I.B. owed their capacity to attack to this precaution, for at 4.45 a.m. the utter physical and mental misery of toiling to convert a morass into a fort in the dark and wet was increased by a crashing hostile barrage. The battle of Broodseinde, as this engagement is termed, anticipated a massed German attack by the 19th Reserve Division of the German X. Corps (Hanover) by ten minutes,* so that there happened here what more than once, *e.g.* at Monchy† and at La Bassée,‡ happened in a continuing battle—both sides attacked on the same day much about the same time. The bulk of the shells passed over the heads of the firing-line,§ but the K.O.S.B. fared worse than the R.W.K. and suffered severe casualties and resulting disorganization. It speaks volumes for the *moral* that the first line, with B in support and A in reserve, stood ready and steady waiting for our barrage and the tardy dawn. At 6 a.m. a superb creeping barrage heralded the advance, and the Borderers directed their "uneasy steps" over the slimy inferno against the strong place. "Going should be extremely good on the high ground, and though the low ground is wet in places it should not be difficult to make headway." And there were to be no formidable obstacles. O sanguine staffs that write such stuff! || From that moment an obscurity in harmony with the conditions settled down on the battalion. Col. Furber had to call on his reserve in half an hour, as he saw men moving backwards and Germans advancing. Working in co-operation with the support companies' timely flanking fire, A advanced to a position on the ridge by which the L. of the position was covered and the enemy brought to a halt. But C and D had vanished into what was certainly not the blue. At 10 a.m. a request was sent by Col. Furber for reinforcements. These arrived at 5 p.m. and helped to consolidate the new position. They were composed of men of both the Warwickshire Battalions. The delay in response was due to difficulty in communicating with Brigade H.Q.. It is common ground with the R.W.K. and K.O.S.B. that pigeons were actually the most reliable means of communication. Lamps needed a clearer atmosphere, and the Verey Light signal for "Objective Won" proved to be equivocal.

Col. Furber thinks, and this view was adopted at Brigade H.Q.,

* *Official Despatches*, vol. viii. p. 40.

† See *The Story of the 29th Division* (Edinburgh, 1925), p. 112.

‡ See chap. iv., *ante*, p. 48.

§ *Invicta*, p. 185.

|| From an Appendix in 13th I.B.W.D..

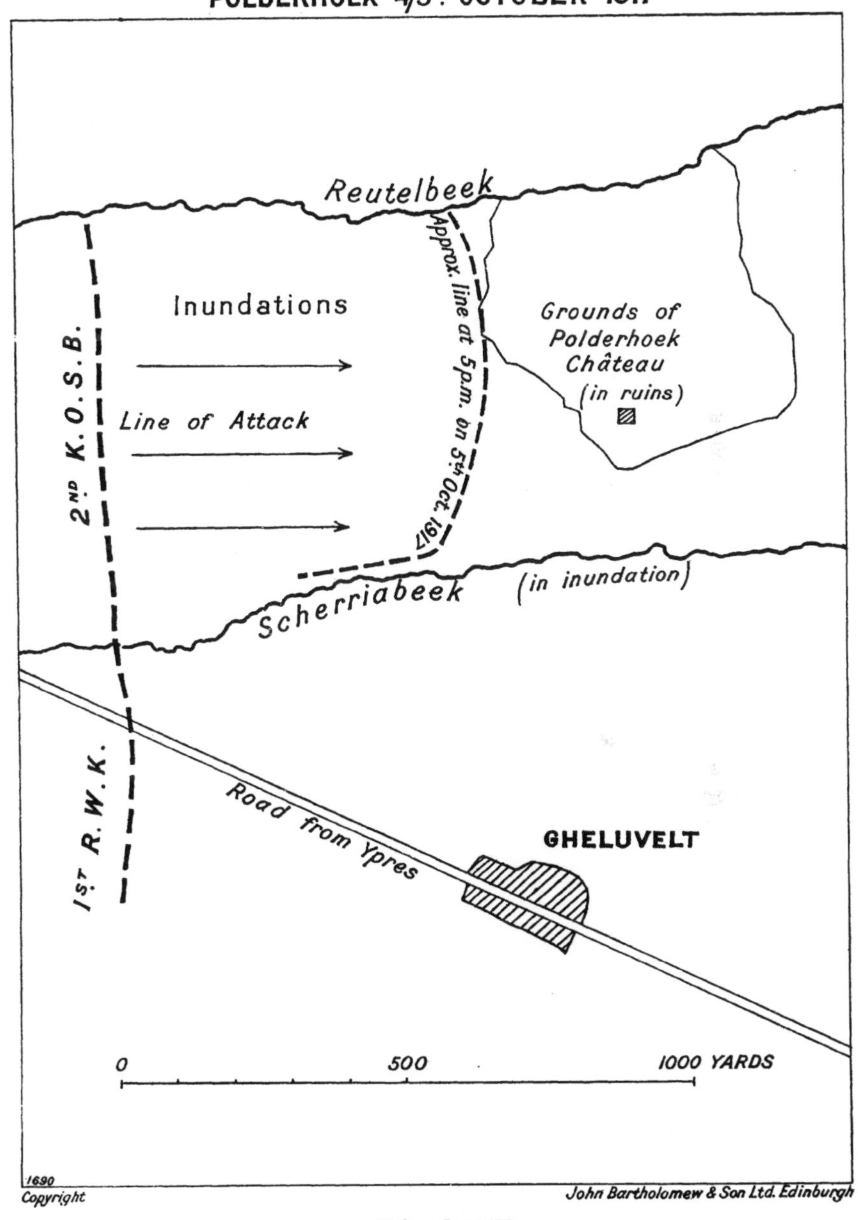

 John Bartholomew & Son Ltd. Edinburgh

To face Page 100

that the two companies in front, owing probably to a swamp intervening at the outset, lost touch with the barrage and were counter-attacked and overwhelmed by troops spared by the barrage. After all, a barrage cannot hit everybody. A significant fact is that no N.C.O. returned who was not wounded early, and the same is true of the officers, among whom casualties occurred from the very start, *e.g.* 3 of D and 2 of C. It was clear on the 5th that as there was no chance of further progress the time had come to call in the barrage. There being no likelihood of further news of C and D, request to that effect was made and acted on. The barrage receded and left no space for counter-attackers, if many such had survived the punishment already meted out. The K.O.S.B. were able to hand over a line of sorts to the 1st Norfolks on relief on the night of the 5/6th October. The exact position is not clear from the War Diary. The official despatch includes the 2nd K.O.S.B. among those who carried their objectives. This is putting it too high as regards final objectives; we know that B never advanced against the actual château, which was its main objective. But a substantial advance was made which the 5th Division historian places at a line in the "policies" of Polderhoek just short of that "veritable fortress." * What does redound to the credit of these Borderers (the 1st Battalion were distinguishing themselves at Langemarck on the same day) was the way they stood punishment since the 2nd, advanced over bad ground and beat off numerous counter-attacks in the course of that long 4th of October. They had nothing to be ashamed of when, some 90 strong, a little remnant crawled into Bedford House 4 miles behind and wolfed their breakfasts. Three days later they received congratulations from the Corps Commander, and honours were liberally awarded. Lieut.-Col. Furber received the D.S.O. and a mention in despatches; Capt. L. F. Machin, whose services in clearing up the situation by daring reconnaissances and in rallying the men at the flanks (where the enemy was pressing forward) were invaluable, received the M.C.; Capt. Aucott won a Bar; and 2nd Lieuts. J. F. Clarkson, E. A. Paterson, and R. A. H. Kappey the M.C..

4 Oct. 1917.

It is interesting to compare the K.O.S.B. losses with those of their stout-hearted comrades on the R.. The R.W.K. lost 10 officers and 368 O.R.†. The K.O.S.B. lost 11 officers and 438 O.R.. These fell more severely on B, C, and D than on A, the reserve company. A/Capt. James E. Ford of the 1st Battalion, Lieut. R. P. Kirkwood ‡ (erroneously stated to have been killed while attached to "1/G.B.

* *5th Division*, p. 178. † *Invicta*, p. 186.

‡ Official War Deaths, as corrected by comparison with the W.D..

4–5 Oct. 1917. North Staffs Regiment"), Lieut. T. J. Carlyle and A. Y. P. Johnston,* both of the 5th Battalion, and 2nd Lieut. J. S. Dunn, O.C. party to storm the château, *i.e.* a platoon of B, were all killed. Lieut. Rennie, M.C., with Capt. C. J. D. Church, Lieut. J. T. Wilkie, and 2nd Lieuts. C. Duigan (O.C. "Moppers"), D. A. M'Leod, and R. J. M'Donald were wounded. Even with the dumped personnel the battalion had to submit to a drastic reorganization to correspond to the heavy casualties.

The next few days were spent at Ridge View Camp near Dickebusch. It was a bad mauling, but in Third Ypres two bad maulings at least was the usual ration. A unit had to be literally knocked out; the orange had to be squeezed dry. Thus it came about that after a comfortless fortnight at La Clytte at the N. foot of Mont Kemmel in country useless for training and with imperfectly absorbed drafts of other Lowland regiments and H.L.I.—some of whom had everything to learn, having only joined up a little over three months—on the 24th of October the battalion neared Bedford House once more and dumped the last batch of the Johnnie Raws and the usual percentage. It is possible that higher authority concurred in the C.O.'s view that more bombs, more Lewis guns, more lights, etc., were required. Anyhow, what with greatcoats, 220 rounds of S.A.A., two days' rations, the usual "iron" ration, entrenching tools, etc., etc., the men had as much as they could bear. Of Lewis guns, however, they were one short, for the simple reason that not enough men could fire them.

This time they were in reserve, B.H.Q. being in a pill-box (opening the wrong way of course) 1,500 yards due W. of Polderhoek and just N. of the Ménin road. Fighting had been almost continuous. It must not be forgotten that the action of the 4th looked at as a whole was a substantial success, resulting as it did in the capture of 5,000 Germans. It was followed up on the 9th by the battle of Poelcapelle, by which British forces on the N. of the salient added 2,000 more prisoners to the bag, and finally on the 12th the first Battle of Passchendaele was launched with 8 divisions of the Second Army and 4 of the Fifth. But the pressure had been N.E. towards Houthulst Forest or E. towards Passchendaele and Polderhoek, and Gheluvelt—a commanding site, as anyone can go and see for himself—still defied the British. A determined attempt was therefore to be made by the 5th Division to take Polderhoek and by the 7th Division to take Gheluvelt. Both were admirable divisions in the well-staffed X. Corps, and yet the difficulties were such that the

* His name does not occur in Scott Elliot's Roll of Officers (an Appendix to his *5th K.O.S B.*), but is recorded in the Official Death Roll on p. 224.

Oct. 1917.

Second Battle of Passchendaele, which began on 26th October and dragged on till 10th November, showed no advance in the S. flank, but developed into a marked salient with the apex on the dear-bought ridge. These difficulties were hostile barrages, pill-boxes, inundations, and mud. The tale is soon told. The K.O.S.B. had D under brigade orders. C was Col. Furber's reserve. A and B were in close support to the attacking force, consisting of 1st R.W.K., on the R. on their old line of advance, next them the 15th R.W.R., and beyond them the 14th. Under a tornado of shells and extra M.G. fire the assault at 5.20 a.m. progressed so far that the 15th R.W.R. stormed the château and took 100 prisoners. Things looked well at this point, but the soldiers' nightmare—a rifle that isn't loaded or can't be fired—obtruded itself everywhere. The rifles were choked with Flanders mud and became useless as firearms. The 15th R.W.R. were not supported, as the 14th were held up by the swollen Reutelbeek, and the R.W.K. were hampered by having to retake the original British front-trench,* and after capture of their objective through flanking fire from Gheluvelt and from choked rifles and M.G.. The 15th had so few rifles in action that it was decided to withdraw. The Germans reoccupied the château and park, organised counter-attacks, and by the end of the day the attacking divisions were in their original place. The K.O.S.B. received their first call for reinforcements at 8.30 a.m.. This request could not be complied with till after 11 a.m., when A went to the 14th and B to the 15th R.W.R.. It took more than two hours to reach the 14th's starting-point. The O.C. the latter company sent back word about the retirement and the choked rifles. In the afternoon C was sent and was very welcome to the R.W.K.†. D was retained till nightfall at Brigade H.Q., but eventually joined the R.W.K.. The 15th I.B.'s arrival eased the situation, the 1st Cheshires and 1st Norfolks relieving the N. and S. sectors respectively under heavy fire. The K.O.S.B. took the first opportunity to reorganize on the 27th. No company was more than 60 strong. The order to retire to Bedford House was more than welcome. On the 28th Ridge Wood was once more occupied and the K.O.S.B. counted the cost. It was nothing like that of the 4th. Best of all, the newcomers had shown pluck. They were of the right stuff and their officers were well pleased. One officer was wounded, Lieut. W. H. F. Hunter-Arundel. One was gassed, Lieut. J. R. Kellie, the intelligence officer. Of O.R. 14 were killed, 90 wounded, and 7 were missing. Some were known to have been drowned—quite a common horror of the salient. An award of 17 Military Medals

* *Invicta*, p. 187.

† W.D., and *Invicta*, p. 188.

Nov. 1917. was the next sign that the work of the 2nd K.O.S.B. on 4/6th October had been valued in high places.

On the 2nd of November the corps commander conferred the D.S.O. on Col. Furber and the M.C. on those noted on page 101. There were also 5 D.C.M.s awarded.

The survivors of the last two visits to the front zone must have felt their hearts sink as they heard of the move ordered for the 5th of November. Yet another attack was to be made by the 5th Division, this time by the 95th I.B. on the impregnable "Polderhoek." The K.O.S.B. were once more in reserve, and when the attack on the 6th failed in spite of the best efforts of the 1st Devons (the heroes of "Devon" trench near Fresnoy in April 1917), and of the 1st D.C.L.I. and the East Surreys, they relieved a sector covering two companies of the Devons and two of the East Surreys and were excused further movement. The condition of the ground beggars description and accounts for the check to the impetus of the attack. Mud was often well over men's knees. Some of the 95th men had to be got out with ropes after a wait of 36 hours.* (One man of the 1st Devons was submerged to the neck, and it took 48 hours to get him out.)† As for repairing trenches it was once more Lindenhoek. After herculean toil the semblance of a parapet and a firestep would be erected and then the usual deluge would treat it as the incoming tide treats a child's castle on the sands. Sides fell in and soon all was afloat. The state of the ground to the rear led to doubt if anybody could ever relieve the huddled occupants of the muddy patches not yet submerged. Exposed to view on the slightest sign of movement by day, the 2nd K.O.S.B. touched bottom in the way of misery. All hung on whether a duckboard track could be laid by the 14th R.W.R., aided by a platoon of D. They did not fail, and relief by the 39th Division on the night of 11/12th November was relief indeed. There were 90 cases of their old enemy—trench feet. In time the whole battalion would have succumbed. To add to their troubles the M.O., Captain W. A. Murphy, was wounded by a shell that was all but a direct hit. About 65 O.R. were wounded, apart from the 90 cases of trench feet. The men were utterly done when they reached Scottish Wood at 4 p.m. on the 12th, and glad to stay there all the 13th. They would never again be nearer the accursed spot than the Forêt de Nieppe. In the space of little over a month they had had concentrated on them the full gamut of evil which that cockpit had to offer—cold, wet, intense shelling, pill-box receptions, fatigue,

* Recorded in W.D..

† Information furnished by Col. Furber.

discomfort, sleeplessness, and stenches in the midst of a featureless and apparently endless morass. Nov. 1917.

Col. Furber (now a Major in the Tank Corps) has furnished me with his impressions, still vivid after eleven years.

" I never want to go through another phase of war worse than that. It was horrible all through. The men were literally standing to their knees in water from the time they went into the line till they came out. As fast as we laid duckboard tracks for the incoming unit, the Bosche destroyed them. We were laying boards till midnight on the night we were relieved. On that (final) tour I lost 180 men. The whole thing to me was a nightmare. The men were simply magnificent ; how they stick some of the situations beats me, and they were so cheery through it all."

If a reader asks why the battle was prolonged into the autumn and why it was not begun earlier, he can only be referred to the big general surrounding circumstances : the trouble of the French, the trouble of Italy, but chief of all the defection of Russia.*

* For a criticism of the Higher Command one can only refer to such works as Churchill's *World Crisis*, Boraston and Dewar's *Sir D. Haig's Command*, Buchan's *History of the Great War*, and Charteris' *Life of Lord Haig*.

CHAPTER X

ITALY

1917–18. THE defection of Russia in 1917 had been of great service to the enemy. It left him free to devote troops to the other theatres. It necessitated constant and costly pressure by the British on the Flanders front, while the "Von Armin" system of "defence in depth," aided by the state of the ground, economised the German man-power. It undermined the *moral* of the Italian nation and the Italian army, with the result that Caporetto is a name like Cannæ, synonymous with disgrace and disaster, and the month of November 1917 is one of the gloomiest of the whole war.

This is not the place for the story of the retreat from the Isonzo to the Piave or the steps taken by the Allies to come to the aid of Italy or the magnificent recovery of the stricken nation, the great heart of which was all along sound.

From the point of view of the 2nd K.O.S.B. their three and three-quarter months in Italy were a pleasant interlude in the grim succession of operations on the Western Front. The change of scene, of air, and life all helped to fit the battalion for the strain of the Lys and (final) Somme. Two slight wounds only find mention in the Diary. Except for energetic patrolling of the Piave front, involving a certain amount of chilly wading, operations were *nil.* Hard work marching on roads or mending them, or improving defences, with drill and athletics, kept sloth at bay. The 5th Division did not reach Italy until the invasion had been checked. They had been greeted with smiles, but were seen off with scowls when the imperative call to return came at the beginning of April 1918.

A few words will tell the tale. There are two routes from France to Italy, one by the coast and the other through the Alps. The K.O.S.B. sampled both. We left them at Scottish Wood on 12th November. By stages the St. Omer area was reached and was their training-ground for ten days, until exchanged for Hernicourt in the St. Pol area on 27th November. The move to Italy was the talk of the time, but not until the 11th December did the battalion entrain with a ration strength of 850 O.R.,* " complete in horses (31), transport, and equipment." † 1917-18.

The Mont Cenis party were stuck for five days W. of Turin owing to an accident on the railway, so the coasters were the first to reach Milan and proceed towards the Asiago front. In due course the battalion was reunited in the village of San Giorgio in Bosco, still in the plain of Venetia but near the rampart whence the Brenta flows. Here it remained, carrying on the training schemes begun on leaving Flanders as best might be, considering the enclosed and unsuitable country in which they were billeted. There were compensations. Poultry was procurable at reasonable prices, the Christmas dinners were a record. One incident must be mentioned, when the division was inspected by a French general (de Mestre), commanding the Tenth Army on Italian soil, after which a British general (Haking) presented the medals so nobly won in Flanders. The 5 D.C.M.s were Sergts. Currie, Miller, and Thomson (the last named killed in action on 18th April 1918) and Ptes. Cunliffe and Sizer.

The New Year was brought in in Scottish fashion and the month of January saw the K.O.S.B. defeat the R.W.K. at football pretty easily, but only draw with the 15th (Birmingham) R.W.R. .

Although parties of officers and N.C.O.s had reconnoitred the passes of the Asiago front, it was to Villorba and the Piave that the 5th Division found its way in the last week of January. The move was effected by two marches of 15 and 18 miles each. On the front the enemy was unenterprising, and the most interesting event was the successful trip of 23 pipers and drummers under the Second-in-Command, Major Dudgeon, to Rome. The week there from 22nd to 29th March passed quickly, what with massed band performances at the big athletic meeting of the Allies and sight-seeing in the Eternal City.

It was getting warmer, and preparations were being made for a return to the mountain front when rumours of a return to France reached the battalion. In due course the summons came and found a battalion strong in numbers, physique, and training ready to face what might come.

* War Diary. † *Ibid.*

CHAPTER XI

THE BATTLE OF THE LYS

The Defence of the Forêt de Nieppe

April 1918. THE quasi-débâcle on the Western Front, when the Fifth Army was overwhelmed by weight of numbers, so far as pertinent belongs to the story of the 6th Battalion of the K.O.S.B., and the thrust to Mont Kemmel and Hazebrouck primarily to that of the 1st and 6th Battalions. The rock-like defence of Arras is bound up with the 7/8th K.O.S.B.. As far as the 2nd Battalion is concerned, it helped to stop a gap just E. of the great Forest of Nieppe, which is the only military feature in the flat land between Merville and the vital nodal point on the Allies' railway system—Hazebrouck. If Hazebrouck fell, God help the channel ports! Even if the enemy got within shelling distance of the railway line Ypres would have been untenable. Fortunately for the 2nd K.O.S.B. the enemy had pretty well shot his bolt on this sector, and his driving power was concentrated on Bailleul and those " mountains " which find such frequent mention in these pages. In point of fact, although other divisional units were heavily engaged farther N.* and won the highest praise, our battalion took part in no major operation till the 28th of June, a great date for Borderers, whether in 1915 or 1918.

On the 3rd of April the 2nd K.O.S.B. entrained at their then station, Campo d'Oro, for France. The maritime route was taken, and late on the 7th the long railway journey ended at our old friends Petit Houvin and Frévent between Doullens and St. Pol. To skirt Paris was a commonplace of all travel from the Mediterranean, but the gravity of the situation came home to these Borderers when Amiens also was " turned " on the W. side, and even then some trains did not escape German shells. At that time the enemy was within 10 miles of Amiens and our backs were indeed to the wall.

The subsequent movements illustrate the hand to mouth use of available troops by the now unified command of Foch. At first the 5th Division were in the VI. Corps and destined for the front S. of

* "The 5th Division saved Hazebrouck" (see *The 5th Division in the Great War*, pp. 214–215; and *Sir D. Haig's Despatches* (Boraston, p. 227).

Arras. But suddenly on 11th April the 13th I.B. were ordered to entrain at Mondicourt (on the Doullens–Arras railway) in " tactical trains " for the XI. Corps (Haking). Our battalion was off by 8 p.m., and next morning at 9 a.m. found itself ordered to fall-in at Thiennes, just outside the W. edge of the Nieppe forest astride the Tannay-Merville road. The Corps orders were to attack with a view to the recapture of Merville at the junction of the Bourre and Lys, a town of some size * a couple of miles E. of the S. end of the forest where it is called Bois Moyen. The Portuguese had been but were no longer there, though no doubt they were somewhere in France. The whole situation was rather fluid. The weary 61st Division,† which had just been rushed up from the Somme, was holding its own with difficulty near Le Sart, just N. of the Lys Canal. The K.O.S.B., being in support, followed astride the road from Tannay to Merville in the wake of the 15th R.W.R., and extended the refused R. flank of that battalion with one company to the river and dug-in in close support with the remainder. By this time it was dark and the K.O.S.B., after a 7-mile march in fighting equipment after thirteen hours in the train, were glad that the night passed off quietly. The 13th also was quiet. Artillery were gathering in the rear and dealing faithfully with any signs of aggression. The divisional artillery were ready for action that evening. The night of the 14/15th was marked by the advance of the R. of the line and the relief of the 15th R.W.R.. Contact with the enemy was obtained by a bold dash of Capt. Pringle, the officer who had silenced the snipers on the Vimy Ridge, as he rushed an enemy post and killed 5 men, aided by Lieut. T. J. A. Kellie.

It was a life of tenterhooks. Heavy shelling seemed to indicate hostilities, but they came to nothing on the K.O.S.B. front, and the most poignant memory of the time which stands out is the pervading smell of gas. All sorts, but principally the dreaded mustard variety, were lavishly sprayed over the forest, and lingered in its thickets for hours, *inter alia* rendering that rare luxury—wild strawberries in plenty—" unfit for human food." Lucky was it for the 5th Division that the G.O.C. (Stephens) carried his point with Corps, and held the line *outside* the forest and not inside. Any idea of retaking Merville ‡ was abandoned on the 12th, and the task

* About 3,000 inhabitants.

† *Sir D. Haig's Despatches* (Boraston), p. 226.

‡ It seems to be generally accepted that there was a " psychological moment " when Merville might have been recovered. More potent spirits (of the kind to be found in B.E.F. canteens) than those of Mons chained Fritz to the spot and diverted his thoughts from war. But the chance had gone by the time the 5th Division addressed itself to the task.

May 1918. was to stand fast. The K.O.S.B. were relieved on the 21st, and had a quiet time in the W. section of the forest known as Bois d'Amont.

During this somewhat amorphous but perilous period of fifteen days the casualties totalled 5 officers, of whom 2nd Lieut. A. R. S. Millar died of wounds on the 27th,* and 152 O.R.. It was unsensational, but it was war.

The next tour was in the sector immediately to the N.. Next the K.O.S.B. were the 14th R.W.R., and beyond them were the 29th Division, in which the 1st Battalion K.O.S.B. were serving. The 29th and the 87th Brigades had just come through a severe trial of rearguard actions in the country between Steenwerck and Estaires, and the 1st K.O.S.B. had had a terrible mauling.† During the campaign in the open, flat country the rule was—not a movement all day, and work like beavers all night (not without casualties from the copious indirect M.G. fire).

On the 9th of May the two regular battalions met. The 1st Battalion were then at Morbecque, a few miles N.W. of the forest. and, stranger still, the 4th and 5th Battalions, back with the 52nd (Lowland) Division from their triumphs in Palestine, were at Aire within easy reach. No description of these meetings has reached the editor, and it must just be left to our imaginations to picture the excitement which they would create. When not in the line the battalion worked under the R.E. making a camp, which was named "Villorba," after one of the Italian stations of the 5th Division.

On the 29th the 2nd Battalion went into divisional reserve at Pecqueur, and had an easier time, with baths in plenty and brigade training. On the next tour in the L. sub-sector of the L. sector of the 5th Division the 2nd K.O.S.B. found themselves next their own 1st Battalion. Although such situations were not unknown,‡ they were rare enough to be historic, and on this occasion a joint raid was contemplated, to celebrate such a wonderful reunion of two regular battalions of the same regiment in a vast citizen host. Fate said nay, for No Man's Land was too wide, and a workmanlike scheme could not be devised. At the end of the tour, at 2 a.m. on 11/12th June, a 2nd Battalion raid secured two prisoners, but at the cost of 2nd Lieut. R. Heygate (of that battalion), killed (originally reported missing), and 5 wounded O.R..

On the following night the 14th R.W.R. relieved them in the

* Official Death Roll.

† See Book II. chap. vi.

‡ *E.g.* on 9th October 1917, at the battle of Poelcapelle, the 1st and 2nd Battalions of the Lancashire Fusiliers fought side by side. (See *Story of the 29th Division*, p. 138).

front, and they occupied the support trenches. As we are on the subject of the 29th Division, it may be noted that the same influenza, or P.U.O., which afflicted the bodies and souls of so many in the British * and German † armies, was rife in the 5th Division, 13th I.B. and 2nd K.O.S.B.. In the month of June 132 men went sick in the battalion.

However, by the time the great day came any lassitude and want of enterprise were things of the past, and in any event the K.O.S.B. were not so heavily affected as to retard the preparations. On the 19th they were relieved by 15th I.B. troops, and went for a week to divisional reserve, bathed, practised the attack, listened to the ever-popular "Whizzbangs," ‡ and studied the plan of the ground they were to attack. On the night of the 27th the battalion advanced to the jumping-off place for an attack on the Plate Becque, a tributary of the Lys, which they were not to cross, but the foot-bridge over which they were to destroy.

THE 28TH OF JUNE

The battalion had the honour of sharing in the first sign of a resumption of the offensive in the N.. It had been realized that the position E. of the Forêt de Nieppe would be improved if a thrust forward were made in the Arrewage area to the line of the Plate Becque, not far from its confluence with the Bourre, a tributary of the Lys. The original date was the 20th of June, but the enterprise, one with strictly limited objectives, gained rather than suffered by being postponed till the 28th, a Friday. The delay enabled a model of the objective trenches to be studied at Plaine Haute, just W. of the forest, and a week's practice in a divisional reserve to be put in, which ultimately bore fruit. On the 27th the 2nd K.O.S.B. moved forward through the forest due E., and took up a position opposite their objective, which was a front running almost due E. and W., the W. boundary being about 500 yards S.E. of Arrewage. The plan of attack was one frequently successful, an advance simultaneously to and leaning on a barrage lifting at intervals. On the present occasion the barrage was perfection. This operation demands a cool nerve and a determination not to be in a hurry. C under Lieut. H. C. Fraser on the R. and D under Lieut. Macfarlane

* *Story of the 29th Division*, p. 197.

† Ludendorff, *op. cit.*, p. 514. The outbreak was specially severe in Prince Rupprecht's group of armies.

‡ The name of the 5th Division's entertainment troupe, one of the earliest and best, on a par with the "Bow Bells" of the 56th (London) Division and the "Diamond Troupe" of the 29th. See *ante*, p. 73.

28 June 1918. on the L., went over the top at zero, *i.e.* 6 a.m.. The latter company profited by the co-operation of Stokes mortars (Lieut S. Cossar, afterwards M.C., doing great work) and Lewis gunners, and were able to reach and overpower two hostile M.G. firing from the direction of Arrewage, with the result that within a few minutes the front line of the enemy was captured by both companies, and the barrage followed towards the hostile support line. A piece of good luck, to make up for the Messines jamb in 1914, was that an active enemy M.G. failed at a critical moment when C was held up in front of the wire. As it was, A (on the R.) and B (on the L.) were able to leapfrog according to schedule and advance towards the final objective, and thanks to the co-operation of the D.C.L.I. on the L. of the K.O.S.B., and to a skilful use of his reserves by Lieut. R. D. Peat * of B (on L.), the objective was taken and consolidated with the aid of a platoon of C. Apart from M.G. fire, casualties were due to impetuosity on occasions and to a loss of direction on the part of some men of C sent by the C.O. as a reinforcement. In little over half an hour the action was over, and B.H.Q. advanced to the S. outskirts of Arrewage in the old German front line. On this occasion the Germans actually stood to the bayonet and died by it. The objectives were taken and more ground besides, but the losses were severe. No officer was killed, but 9 out of 20 were wounded, and 200 O.R. casualties constituted a severe drain on a unit low in strength.† Ten M.G. taken, and the conviction that heavy loss had been inflicted on the enemy added to the satisfaction of having risen to the occasion. On that day our Jocks got home with the bayonet, as a good heap of slain testified.‡ A/Sergt. B. H. Cunniffe and Corp. T. Rooney greatly distinguished themselves in the hand-to-hand fighting and rushing of M.G.. The battalion was evidently thought to have distinguished itself. Lieuts. R. D. Peat and J. Macfarlane were awarded the M.C., and no less than 17 decorations reached O.R..

Feverish work was done in the brief hours of darkness to improve the shelter and finish the work of clearing the battlefield of wounded. Stretcher-bearer A. Weir set a magnificent example and not a man was left behind. But the German gunners had the range and more casualties were the result. Our airmen had had the best of it, but some German flyers may have spotted the line by the stream, or their gunners may have used their local knowledge, and the information that most if not all of the bridges were destroyed. Touch had been maintained with the R.W.K. on the R., and altogether it

* An efficient transport officer as well.

† The battalion went into action about 500 strong in O.R..

‡ Lieut.-Col. A. E. D. Anderson.

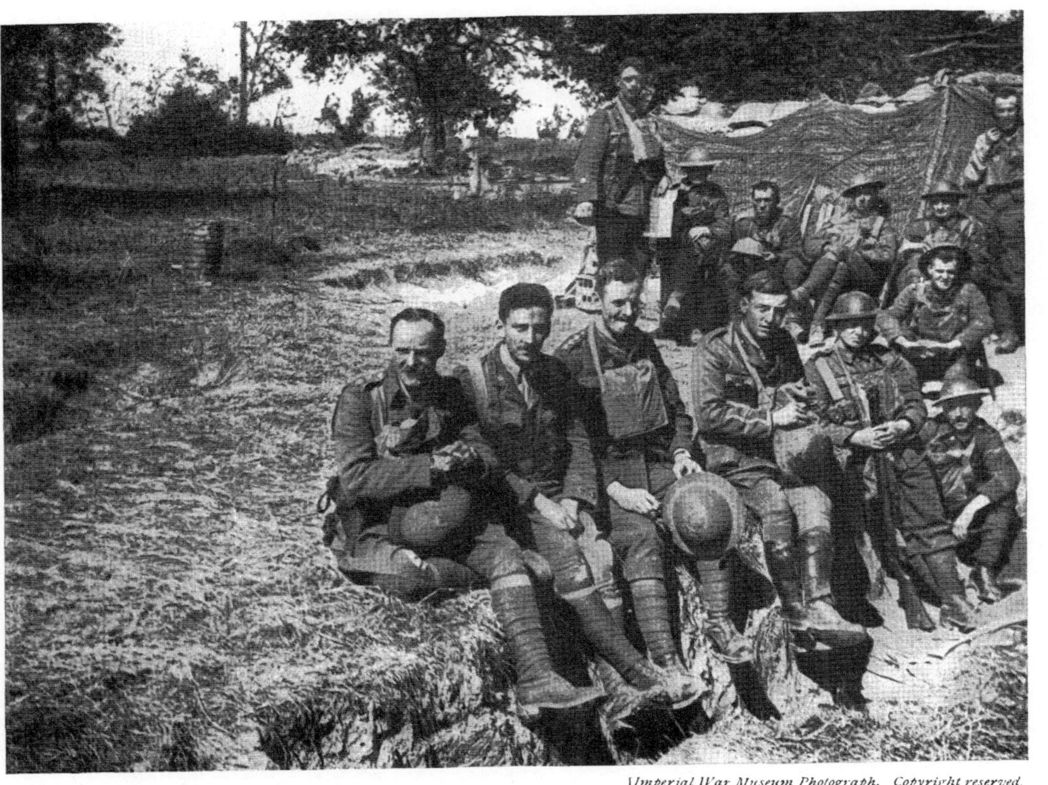

[*Imperial War Museum Photograph. Copyright reserved.*

HEADQUARTERS AND STAFF OF THE 2ND K.O.S.B.
NEAR ARREWAGE, 4TH JULY 1918.

was what soldiers like to call "a good show." Gen. R. Haking congratulated Gens. Stephens and Jones in no uncertain terms. Brig.-Gen. Hussey's guns were as usual the backbone of the enterprise. The two divisions engaged (5th and 31st) took 500 prisoners, 3 field-guns, 5 T.M., and 50 M.G.. Two hundred German dead were counted on the battlefield. July 1918.

On Sunday night, after two motionless days, the K.O.S.B. were relieved by the East Surreys, and began July in close support. On the 3rd they returned and did some useful retrieving, *e.g.* a field-gun and a couple of T.M., before being relieved by the R.W.K.. It was a quiet time, and nothing but hard work to mark it. Divisional reserve at La Lacque, near Aire, on the canal from and after 11th July gave opportunities for resting, cleaning up, and musketry. The finale to the stay in this district was not quite so successful. On 30th July, at 1 a.m., Lieut. J. MacDougall and 17 O.R. of B attempted to raid the German trenches, but met with a hot reception in No Man's Land. The leader had a narrow escape, being saved by the devotion of Pte. Walker. No identifications were secured, and the raid, costing as it did 1 officer and 9 O.R. casualties, was a failure. To the Germans all credit for boldly cheating the barrage of its prey by holding posts in front of the line proper, and in handling their bombs skilfully. But more was to follow. During relief on 30/31st July the enemy put down a heavy gas barrage, which made 7 O.R. casualties, and caused discomfort, not to say misery, to every one as they trudged back. But the Borderers were not downhearted. Foch had struck on the 18th, and a feeling was abroad that at last the Allies were going to turn the tables on the haughty invader and call the tune, and make him conform to their will.

CHAPTER XII

THE FINAL EFFORT

Aug. 1918. THE situation had so far improved that for the last time during the Great War the 2nd K.O.S.B. celebrated the battle of Minden * at Tannay in good spirits. Farewell was soon to be said to Flanders, for on the 4th buses whirled the battalion off to the country just S. of St. Omer, where they trained on the uplands, and were distributed in billeting parties in the villages of Heuringhem, Le Ronz, Coubronne, and Islinghem. While there they heard the glad tidings that their comrades in the Fourth Army had dealt a wound that might, as it did, prove mortal to the foe, and the young officers read their Field Service Regulations with a practical interest that made it seem a different book. Divisional training was back to open warfare manœuvres.

The call to the 5th Division came soon. On the 13th the 2nd K.O.S.B. entrained at St. Omer, and next morning marched from Bouquemaison *via* their old friend Frévent on the Canche 6 or 7 miles, some to Ligny and some to Nuncq. On the 18th they returned to Neuvillette, close to Bouquemaison, whence on the 20th buses conveyed them to Marieux, once the H.Q. of the VIII. Corps in the 1916 Somme battle. The very next evening the battalion were in the line in brigade reserve in trenches W. of Bucquoy, and either that night or the following morning brought casualties.† Lieut. J. A. Garvie, M.C., and 6 O.R. were killed by a chance shell. That officer had done very good work at Polderhoek, and recently distinguished himself in the Lys fighting, and his M.C. was only awarded on June 8th. His death was a blow to the battalion.

The 5th Division, now commanded by Major-Gen. John Ponsonby of the Coldstream Guards, in the place of their beloved Gen. Stephens, promoted to command X. Corps, now found itself in the IV. Corps under Lieut.-Gen. Sir G. M. Harper, who had done so much to "make" the 51st Highland Division. The IV. Corps were in Sir Julian Byng's Third Army, which had just opened the battle of

* See Introductory Chapter, p. 8.

† The W.D. gives the 22nd as the date; the Official Death Roll of Officers gives the 21st.

Albert on the 21st by an advance E. through that once conspicuous landmark, the "Bois de Logeast," and by taking Achiet-le-Petit, 2 miles S.. The general line of advance pointed E. towards Bapaume, *via* such classic spots as Grévillers and Loupart Wood. Farther S. Albert had been taken by the III. Corps (Butler), and Miraumont and Irles were threatened. But the real effort was begun on the 23rd when there began "a series of strong assaults on practically the whole front of thirty-three miles from our junction with the French" (3 miles S. of the road from Amiens to Péronne),* "to Mercatel, in which neighbourhood the Hindenburg Line . . . joined the old Arras–Vimy defence line of 1916." † The 22nd had been a day of consolidation and mopping up. In the two days some 850 prisoners had been taken. On the 23rd the division attacked on a two-brigade front, the 95th I.B. being on the R. and the 15th on the L.. The 13th I.B. were in reserve, and the 2nd K.O.S.B., under Major Dudgeon in the absence of Col. Furber (on leave), was its R. reserve battalion supporting the 14th R.W.R.. Participation did not begin till the evening, when, despite the resistance at Irles, the situation warranted an advance on Loupart Wood. The account in the War Diary is far from clear as to what happened. We are not told what resistance was met with by the R.W.R., or to what extent the main body of the K.O.S.B. were involved. But what must have happened is that the New Zealand Division leapfrogged them, and went on ahead to the edge of Loupart Wood. In the small hours of the 24th Lieut. K. A. T. McLennan, with a platoon of C., and 2nd Lieut. G. Howat (Cameronians), with a patrol, did good work in clearing the wood of a M.G. nest, taking 14 M.G. and 47 prisoners. Unfortunately the gallant young Howat was killed, but L.-Sergt. J. M'Leod took charge of the little band of 87 men. He divided them into two parties, which proceeded by different trenches to various M.G. posts, pinching them out and killing all who would not surrender. Eight M.G. were taken, and all the teams were killed or captured. "A very fine feat." ‡ Keenness at this time was marked. This support from the R. rear must have materially improved the position of the New Zealanders. The result of the day and night was that Irles and Loupart Wood were ours, and that on the three days' fighting the division had advanced 2 miles and more, and had captured 2,768 prisoners, 25 guns, over 350 M.G., etc., at a casualty cost of 70 officers and 1,600 O.R.§.

Aug. 1918.

The rest of the 24th was spent in preparing the ground gained for defence, as Miraumont on the R. had not yet fallen. But the

* Editor. † Official Despatch.
‡ 13th I.B.W.D.. § *The 5th Division*, p. 234.

Aug. 1918. possession of the high ground E. and S. of Irles by the 12th Gloucesters and the 1st R.W.K. made its abandonment by the Germans a matter of hours. Next day the advance of the IV. Corps enabled the K.O.S.B. to march in column to an assembly point W. of Grévillers, with a view to pass through 37th Division troops and support the New Zealanders' L. flank by a movement in the direction of Beugnâtre, 1¾ miles N.E. of Bapaume. The auspices for what turned out a fine feat of arms were none too favourable. Casualties at assembly point were caused by shelling, and when the orders came at 11 p.m. to advance to the jumping-off place the absence of guides made progress slow. When the unit in front was relieved E. of Favreuil, about 4 a.m. on the 26th, word came that the attack would be launched at 6.30 without a barrage.* The village of Beugnâtre, with the usual M.G. nests half a mile to the E,† confronted them with the dawn, but, "undaunted by . . . difficulties," ‡ the K.O.S.B., supported by the 14th R.W.R., slowly but steadily moved forward in the face of heavy M.G. fire from the village.

They are described as gaining their objectives; but the rate of progress cannot have been rapid, for it was 6 p.m. before the actual assault of Beugnâtre was begun. At 10 a.m., Major Dudgeon, the C.O., was wounded. It was greatly to his credit and that of the battalion that they had found their way to and through the confusion which always marks troops at the end of a battle such as the 37th Division had come through.§ Luckily, Major B. C. Lake, who had been Bde.-Major 13th I.B. since October 1917, was available, and took command at 3 p.m., in time to direct and play a gallant part in the attack, which went off splendidly.

The gunners, now level with Bapaume, rained shells on Beugnâtre; and under the protection of the creeping barrage the Borderers stormed the village, took 48 prisoners,‖ and consolidated a line 200 yards to the E. of it, firing rapidly at bunches of retreating Germans. The actual village was cleared by B under Lieut. R. D. Peat, a recent recipient of the M.C., with the aid of two platoons of C under Lieut. K. A. T. McLennan (awarded the M.C.), who had done such useful work at Loupart Wood. On the L. of B were D under Lieut. W. Robertson, on whose L. again was D company of

* War Diary.

† The War Diary speaks of an advance of 1,500 yards, which must be an exaggeration if the *5th Division* (p. 234) is correct in placing the 111th Brigade E. of Favreuil.

‡ *Ibid.*, p. 234.

§ The relief of the 111th I.B. by the 2nd K.O.S.B. was a "brilliant" bit of work. Major-Gen. Ponsonby (13th I.B.W.D.), was struck by the initiative and go of the fighting on 26th August.

‖ 13th I.B.W.D..

the M.G. Battalion, who proved most helpful. On the R. of B were some of C under Lieut. H. C. Fraser (afterwards M.C.) and A led to the assault by the C.O. in person, as all its officers were *hors de combat*. Major Lake was twice badly wounded, but refused to be carried off the field till he knew all was secure on his flanks. It was a most gallant exit from the Great War. A D.S.O. followed as of course. All agree that touch was maintained internally, thanks largely to the intrepid and unwearied "running" of Pte. J. S. F. Pattullo (awarded the M.M.), and also with the invaluable loan troops of the 14th R.W.R., as well as with the equally successful New Zealanders on the R.. Naturally there was mixing up of companies and regiments when Lieut.-Col. W. Wilberforce, O.C. 14th R.W.R., took charge of both battalions, but the sorting out and re-allotting of sections was soon managed. The artillery beat off a threatened counter-attack that night, and on the night of 27/28th the K.O.S.B. handed over their sector of the ground won intact to the 15th R.W.R., and retired to trenches near Bihucourt, close to Achiet le Grand. It was then under command of Major J. Kay, D.S.O., of the 1st R.W.K., who had taken over at 8 a.m. on 27th. Aug. 1918.

For some reason the War Diary omits to mention the casualties, but a careful scrutiny of the list of officers who died in the Great War fails to disclose any officer of the K.O.S.B. killed or died of wounds in that long and brilliant action, except Lieut. G. S. Johnstone of the 3rd Battalion, who was then attached. The action ranks with Morval and Vimy and 28th June 1918 as an example of what the battalion could do in the way of offensive fighting, given a fair chance and similar neighbours. Too often the 2nd K.O.S.B. had rougher fortune, and, as the sequel will show, a bad day was in store ere a month would elapse.

Throughout the Loupart–Beugnâtre action, as on 29th June, the care of the wounded was beyond criticism. Capt. O. E. Finch, R.A.M.C., braved shell and M.G. for hour after hour on end in devoted attention to the wounded, and was awarded the M.C. Pte. W. Veitch vied with the energy and zeal of Weir on the Lys on 28th June, and his M.M. represented not only his own but his comrades' devotion to duty.

Meanwhile the IV. Corps (Harper) continued the advance to the Scheldt. At first the line was towards Cambrai, *via* Frémicourt, Beugny, and Lebucquière (Bapaume had been engulfed on the 29th of August), but when the K.O.S.B. returned to the line in the middle of September, once more under Lieut.-Col. Furber, the line of advance pointed more to the S., and the R. of the 6th Division rested on the E. edge of Gouzeaucourt Wood, which is a freakish

Sept. 1918. plantation like a bit out of a jig-saw puzzle, and extended N. along the Trescault spur.

One more parting! Brig.-Gen. L. O. W. Jones, D.S.O., fell sick and was evacuated on 8th September 1918. It was a sad parting, for he and his brigade loved one another.

The French and the Fourth Army and part of the Third were engaged in what proved to be a most successful operation on the 18th of September. It was the task of the K.O.S.B. to form a defensive flank by advancing some 400 yards and capturing a trench called African Trench. The battalion relieved New Zealand troops on a front of 1,000 yards with troops of the 31st Division on their R. and the 15th R.W.R. on the L.. At 5.20 a.m. C and D attacked from a position in front of the trenches occupied by the battalion, but were met, in spite of the barrage, with withering M.G. fire, some of it enfilade, and lost all their officers, and the only parties who reached the objective were bombed out. D found that the trench gained exposed them to enfilade fire. The support and reserve companies were not employed. The unit on the R. was no more successful. African Trench was a real barrier. The account of a similar failure by the R.W.K. on the 27th shows the same features—fire from in front and flanks, severe bombing of any who entered any section of the trench. But, as so often happened, it was what took place elsewhere that cleared the brave garrison out. They melted away in the night and the R.W.K. entered on the 28th unmolested.

Our battalion suffered heavily in proportion to the numbers engaged, especially in officers. Another M.C. was killed in the person of Capt. G. P. Randall of the 3rd. Lieut. L. T. O'Hanlon was wounded and missing. Five subalterns were wounded, of whom 2nd Lieuts. W. R. Cox and J. Trow had only just arrived. Relieved by the R.W.K., the battalion withdrew 10 miles W. to Villers-au-Flos, just N. of Le Transloy, where five days were spent resting and training. A draft of 25 signalized the first reinforcements since 20th August.

On the 27th the K.O.S.B. played a modest part by acting as reinforcements to the troops in the front, viz. two companies to R.W.K. and one to the 14th R.W.R., and, as two platoons were needed as stretcher-bearers, Col. Furber found himself "O.C. H.Q. and two platoons." The loaned companies were heavily involved, and the casualties amounted to 12 O.R.. At last, on the 30th September, the 5th Division were relieved by the 37th Division, and the K.O.S.B., now reduced to a fighting strength of 13 officers and 285 O.R., recuperated at Bus near Ytres (D.H.Q.), a few miles

W. of the great wood of Havrincourt. When they returned to the charge a great change had taken place. On the 9th of October on the march forward they ate their dinners E. of Gonnelieu, which had stubbornly held out for days. They were far past La Vacquerie (famed in the battle of Cambrai, 1917, as we shall see), and as they marched on to the Esnes-Haucourt area, and even farther to Caudry, they met with no military opposition but, instead, a kindly civilian reception. They saw their first undamaged French town; the Scheldt was past; Cambrai behind their L. shoulder. Straight ahead lay the Le Cateau battlefield, the River Selle, the weary Forêt de Mormal. Maps were issued, including Mons and Maubeuge. There was a move on in very fact. Exactly one month before Armistice day the 2nd K.O.S.B. billeted in Inchy, within a mile or two of their trenches of 25th August 1914. Within a few days they would cross the Selle, then the Roman road cut due E. across the Forest, across their "Aufmarsch" Mons-ward in '14 at Pont-sur-Sambre, and pick up their last prisoner beyond the road from Maubeuge to Avesnes. Their last serious engagement took place in the small hours of the 20th of October 1918. On the 12th the 5th Division with the 13th I.B., since 21st September under Brig.-Gen. A. T. Beckwith, D.S.O. (formerly O.C. 2nd Battalion, the Hampshire Regiment, and a veteran of the 29th Division), in front, took over the line on the Selle between Neuville and Briastre, just N. of Inchy. The K.O.S.B. passed straight into the front line overlooking the Selle Valley, with the road and railway beyond. These were their objectives for the pending attack, and, thanks to the view obtained and to the character of the ground behind, they were able to get an idea of the task and practise it for the three days immediately preceding the attack, which was—to use a famous expression of Gen. Harper—a "full-dress affair." *

Oct. 1918.

Col. Furber considers this circumstance to have helped enormously to the success of the last engagement of the 2nd K.O.S.B. Anyhow, in the mist and rain, at 2 a.m. on the 20th October, to the tune of a mass of gun and T.M. fire, B and D under Capts. Paterson and Kappey swept down the bank, crossed by bridges put up by the R.E. for the attack,† and took their objectives,‡ serious opposition being encountered only E. of the railway.

* *5th Division*, p. 248. † *Ibid.*, p. 248.

‡ Owing to paucity of men, the battalion had been reorganized on a two-company basis. It is of interest that this is the only engagement in which the K.O.S.B. formed part of a three-battalion brigade. The reduction which was universal seems to have come to the 5th Division later than almost any other. On 20th October the 13th I.B. consisted of the 2nd K.O.S.B., the 1st R.W.K., and 16th R.W.R..

Armistice, 11 Nov. 1918. — It was the 95th I.B., owing to the glacis-like slopes beyond the Selle and towards Beaurain, who had the " heavy end of the stick." But 6 killed and 49 wounded is severe enough out of a strength of 309. The last officer to be killed with the 2nd Battalion fell in this engagement. Lieut. R. Logan * of the 4th Battalion had only joined on the 29th of September. Relieved, along with the 16th R.W.R., by the 1st D.C.L.I., who were to support the advancing East Surreys, the K.O.S.B. withdrew to Béthencourt, N.W. of Inchy, and on the 21st to Caudry. On the 28th the Corps Commander presented medal, ribbons, and battle honours to companies.

The final advance began on the 3rd of November. The first night was spent at Briastre and the 5th at Jolimetz, near the great wood of Mormal, now a vast clearing with bunches of uncut timber here and there and dense undergrowth. After a rest of a day the battalion proceeded to cross the forest due E..

The first night was spent in the forest at La Porquerie.

By dinner-time on the 8th the Mormal Forest was left far behind, and by the 10th patrols were on and beyond the road from Maubeuge to Avesnes. One prisoner was taken, and the advance was continued until pursuit had to be abandoned to cyclists and cavalrymen and an outpost line established, which was the farthest point reached by the battalion in the Great War. It was on the march back to Le Carnoy, on the W. of the forest, that the Great News came. The battle was over, the Great War won, and a New Era begun.

One word and this part of the story is over. Earlier in this book will be found mention of the siege of Namur in connection with Leven's Regiment. It so happened that towards the end of December the 2nd Battalion K.O.S.B., one of the lineal descendants of Leven's was marching close to Namur. Now, in the same division, were the lineal descendants of the old 16th Regiment of Foot, namely, the 1st Bedfordshires, which also had taken part in the famous siege. Both battalions' colour-parties were ordered to Namur, and there there was a trooping of their respective colours, much to the local interest. The War Diarist was evidently not interested, as the only entry thereanent (for which Scotticism I make no apology) says, " Colour Party returned with the Regimental Colours " without a word, as the almost too popular war-time song had it—as to " where had they been ? what had they seen ? " Lest we forget, let it be recorded that the battalion on 16th December marched past their former commander, Brig.-Gen. E. S. D'Ewes Coke. After a stay in Belgium, the 2nd K.O.S.B. passed over from Antwerp to England, and the tale is over.

* Official Death Roll.

[*Imperial War Museum Photograph. Copyright reserved.*

GROUP OF 50 K.O.S.B., WEARING THE RIBBON OF 1914 STAR; BN. H.Q., BETWEEN MONS AND LE CATEAU, 1918.

BOOK II

THE FIRST BATTALION

PART I—GALLIPOLI

CHAPTER I

THE 29TH DIVISION

THE 1st Battalion served throughout the war in the 29th Division. Everybody knows that that division was the beginning and the middle and the end of the Gallipoli campaign, and its backbone. Fewer are aware of the sterling service done on the Western Front from 1916 onwards. The Somme battle opened with a tragic note. Magnificent soldiers in the making and made were shot down by machine-gunners coolly and comfortably as they left the shelter of the fire trenches. The losses were excessive and the disappointment acute. Yet, later on in the gloom of the Somme winter, excellent work was put in, and at the Battle of Arras an arduous rough-and-tumble fight on the Monchy Plateau was sturdily and successfully waged in the latter half of April and in May 1917. The Third Battle of Ypres gave an opportunity for the precise tactics, the individual initiative, and the tenacity which marked the 29th Division, and made it a formidable formation. But the capture of scheduled objectives in scheduled time pales in interest before the thrills of Cambrai. The part played in the second phase of that battle—*i.e.* from 30th November onwards—by the K.O.S.B. will ever be a source of pride to all Borderers. Nor did the way in which they took the hammering on the Lys in April 1918 diminish their glory. Their part in the final attack and pursuit was worthy of the uphill years preceding. Their lot was no easy one. From the famous Sunday, 25th April 1915, to the almost as famous Monday, 11th November 1918, the 1st K.O.S.B. were seldom far from shot and shell in the following battlefields: Gallipoli, Somme, Arras, Flanders, Cambrai, Lys, and Flanders. The wastage was enormous, and the personnel among officers and men was constantly changing. Yet the unit always preserved its individual character—the 25th Regiment of Foot in the twentieth century—all through.

1914. —

1914. When war was declared this battalion was stationed at Lucknow, and it will be remembered that in addition to three years of India it had behind it five years of Egypt. It was therefore in a high state of efficiency,* and in the swing of the mastered routine young officers and recruits absorbed military A B C and regimental spirit with unconscious ease.

Naturally all were pining for the front. Without doubt even the best informed would be under the spell of the strange notion that the war would be over by Christmas, and that they might miss it. On 11th September came the news that, along with certain Indian regiments, they were to be employed in Europe as part of a line of communication brigade. At once mobilization began. The detachments at Landour and Kailana and minor out-stations required more time than the main body at the station, but in ten days the battalion was in readiness to embark. On the 29th of October the 1st K.O.S.B., consisting of 24 officers and 898 O.R., began to board S.S. *Sardinia*, and embarkation was so swiftly carried out that the transport left dock and anchored in the harbour the same day. The depot skeleton stayed behind at Lucknow under the command of the disconsolate Lieut. C. S. Renny. Capt. C. T. Furber was then employed extra-regimentally in India. His war service in Europe, as we have seen, was with the 2nd Battalion. Capt., now Major, R. H. Crake, D.S.O., was also adjutant to a volunteer battalion in Lucknow, and his distinguished war service was entirely extra-regimental, mostly in Mesopotamia. The C.O., Lieut.-Col. A. S. Koe, happened to be in England on sick leave, as was Major McAlester on ordinary leave. The War Diary has preserved the list of officers who sailed on Transport 109, escorted by the *Swiftsure* and the *Dufferin*, on the 2nd of November 1914. Major D. R. Sladen, D.S.O., was in command, but his service, as we have seen, was with the 2nd Battalion, and later with the 46th I.B., in which were the 7/8th Battalion. Second in command was Major A. J. Welch, of whom more anon. Capt. E. A. Marrow was adjutant. Besides him there were Captains R. D. Whigham, C. A. Antrobus, A. S. Cooper, J. B. Hartley, and M. A. N. Becher; ten lieutenants—A. J. Sanderson, G. M. H. Ogilvy, P. N. Sanderson (signalling officer), C. A. G. O. Murray (transport officer) (who commanded at Cambrai in 1917), A. G. Paterson (M.G. officer), C. S. Stirling-Cookson (afterwards adjutant), W. J. N. Cheatle, J. A. Ainslie,† J. C. Grogan, transport officer at

* Four N.C.O.s received commissions in English regiments and returned to India from Egypt in November 1914 (W.D.).

† Killed when with 2nd Battalion in 1917.

the landing, and W. Simpson, the quartermaster, who served longer and more continuously than any other officer of the battalion; 2nd Lieutenants R. M. Shorter, E. W. T. Agar, and T. A. G. Miller. The chaplain was the Rev. (Capt.) G. E. Dodd, and the M.O. was Capt. T. E. Eves, R.A.M.C.. 1914.

British sea-power was much in evidence as the immense convoy of 26 transports left Bombay at 10 a.m.. The convoy was still further increased by joining up with the Karachi contingent under the wing of the *Duke of Edinburgh*. By the 9th Aden was reached, and on the 16th Suez. The K.O.S.B. were not one of the three battalions which drove the Turks out of the Sheikh Sa'ad Peninsula at the W. corner of Arabia on the 10th,* but were detailed as part of the reserve in readiness to land.

The 22nd Brigade, as it was numbered, was grouped in and around Ismailia as part of the general reserve of Sir A. Wilson's Suez Canal Defence Force, but the stay of the K.O.S.B. at Moascar Camp from 17th November to 14th December was short. Orders had come summoning them to England. Even the depot was under orders to leave Lucknow. Two trains sufficed for the journey to Alexandria, destined to be travelled in the opposite direction in little over a year. Much was to happen to the Allies and the K.O.S.B. in the interval. At Alexandria the first sight was obtained of those unconventional but consummate soldiers, the Australians, who had just left S.S. *Geelong* to enliven Egypt with "high jinks" (as Sir Ian Hamilton has phrased it). It was the *Geelong* on which the K.O.S.B. embarked the same day, and early on the 15th she sailed. There were no horse boxes, and the 13 animals had to be taken on S.S. *Wiltshire*. The journey was uneventful, except that room was found on the *Wiltshire* for 660 German prisoners, and that Major Welch with two officers and two platoons took charge of them as far as Plymouth and by rail to Southampton, and that the *Geelong's* passengers had a nasty time cruising around in a storm waiting for their turn to enter the haven. The *Geelong* anchored in the harbour of Plymouth at 10 p.m. on the 28th of December 1914.

The first sojourn was at Warley, in Essex, and there the eventful New Year was brought in. In little over a fortnight the scene shifted to Rugby, where the newly formed 29th Division was assembling. The 1st K.O.S.B. were ordered to join the 87th Brigade, composed, besides the K.O.S.B., of a Welsh battalion (the 24th), the 2nd South Wales Borderers (henceforth S.W.B.), an Irish battalion (the 27th), the 1st Royal Inniskilling Fusiliers (henceforth

* *Official History* (Egypt and Palestine), p. 222.

1915. R.I.F., as the Royal Irish Fusiliers do not happen to cross the path of our regiment), and an English battalion (the 34th), the 1st Border Regiment (henceforth "Borders," as distinguished from Borderers). The "Union Brigade" was fortunate in its B.-G., W. R. Marshall, afterwards Sir William R. Marshall, G.C.M.G., K.C.B., K.C.S.I., and its B.M., Capt. C. H. T. Lucas of the Berkshire Regiment, destined to play a great part in the life of our battalion.

It is essential to know the remaining infantry units of the 29th. The 86th Brigade was composed of the 2nd Royal Fusiliers (henceforth R.F.), the 1st Lancashire Fusiliers (henceforth L.F.), the 1st Royal Munster Fusiliers (henceforth R.M.F.), and the 1st Royal Dublin Fusiliers (henceforth R.D.F.). The 88th Brigade was composed of the 4th Worcestershire Regiment (henceforth the Worcesters), the 2nd Hampshire Regiment (henceforth Hants), the 1st Essex, and the territorial unit of a Scottish Lowland Regiment, the 5th Royal Scots (R.S.). Major-Gen. F. C. Shaw, C.B., formerly commanding the 9th I.B. in France, and wounded at Nonne Bosschen on 11th November,* was G.O.C., but he did not accompany the 29th to the Dardanelles.

The district was not well adapted for divisional or brigade training. Possibly the post-landing attacks in April and May might have gained in drive from previous practice. But the time was well spent in the pleasant homeland. After all, the 29th, barring one battalion, were all seasoned units, and health and nerve and go were greater assets than a final manœuvre polish, which might have no resemblance to the task awaiting them.

Early in March the great secret was out. The 29th were for the Dardanelles. It was a more stimulating task than to join the exhausted B.E.F. in Flanders. There was something about this modern crusade that fired the imagination. To turn the German front by forcing the back door of her ally might save rivers of blood. The irritating episode of the *Goeben's* flight to sanctuary in Turkish waters would be punished fittingly by the fall of Constantinople, and the corridor of the Mediterranean opened to Russia.

Some soldiers shook their heads and wondered if the Government would go whole-heartedly into the expedition, or whether it would share the fate of previous British enterprises of the nature of side-shows. It was a great conception, but from the start it was mismanaged.

Col. Koe passed fit, more's the pity, for he wasn't, and took over command on 12th March, the day on which His Majesty King

* *Official History* (France and Belgium, 1914), vol. ii. p. 430.

George V. reviewed the division on the Holyhead Road, near Dunchurch,* where it crosses the Roman Fosse Way. March 1915.

His Majesty's message to the 29th after the review ran thus :

"I was much struck with the steadiness under arms and marching powers of the splendid body of men composing the 29th Division. The combination of so many experienced officers and seasoned soldiers whom I particularly noticed on parade will, I feel confident, prove of inestimable value on the field of battle.

"That the 29th Division, wherever employed, will uphold the high reputation already won by my army in France and Belgium I have no doubt.

"Rest assured that your movements and welfare will ever be in my thoughts."

On the 15th Major-Gen. Aylmer Hunter-Weston, C.B., of the R.E., a distinguished veteran of the South African War, whose handling of the 11th I.B. notably at Ligny in the Battle of Le Cateau and at the crossing of the Aisne at Venizel in the early hours of the 13th of September had won him the right to head a division destined for a hazardous adventure, took over command of the 29th. He was and is a true friend of the battalions that fought on Gallipoli, as many a gathering during the war in France and Belgium, and, since the war, at home can testify.

* A description of the Review, which is really an abstract of one by Colonel Wolley-Dod, the G.S.O.1, will be found in *The Story of the 29th Division* (Nelson, 1925).

CHAPTER II *

EASTWARD BOUND

March 1915. On the 17th of March the K.O.S.B. entrained at Rugby for Avonmouth. The transport under Lieut. Grogan, 90 horses, 90 men, and 24 carts, embarked on S.S. *Marquette.* The H.Q., with the full strength of 26 officers and 998 O.R., were on the *Dongola* and sailed at 8 p.m. on the 18th. The list of officers has been preserved and varies slightly but interestingly from that of those who left India. There were Lieut.-Col. Koe in command, Majors Sladen,† McAlester, Second-in-Command at the landing, and Welch ; Capts. Whigham, Antrobus, Cooper, Marrow, Hartley, Becher, A. J. Sanderson, Ogilvy, and P. N. Sanderson (the three last having been promoted) ; Lieuts. Paterson, Stirling-Cookson, Cheatle, Grogan, Ainslie, Renny,‡ Deighton, Shorter, and Miller, and 2nd Lieut. Agar. 2nd Lieut. J. T. Redpath is a new name in the list of officers but an old and valued one as a N.C.O. in the regiment. He was granted his commission just before sailing. There were attached 2nd Lieuts. J. R. Keltie and F. A. Williamson, both of the 4th (Special Reserve) Battalion of the Cameronians (Scottish Rifles). Lieut. W. Simpson was still Quartermaster and Capt. " Peter " Marrow was Adjutant. Capt. Murray was attached to the Cyclist Company of the 29th Division. The M.O. was Lieut. W. N. Rishworth, and his services were to prove invaluable. The Rev. D. A. Cameron Reid, D.D. (afterwards M.C.), § was chaplain and was present at the landing.

The voyage to Alexandria was uneventful. The Mediterranean was not then so infested with submarines as it afterwards became. The K.O.S.B. left the *Dongola* at 5 p.m. on 30th March and marched to Mex Camp. On the 9th of April, according to the Diary, 7 men and 14 officers' chargers embarked. Poor beasts ! Few survived the landing long. Gallipoli was no equine paradise.

The main body on the S.S. *Southland* had the honour on 16th

* See Map 5 in pocket.
† Summoned back from Malta to join 2nd Battalion on promotion.
‡ He had followed the battalion with the depot to England.
§ Dr. Reid is in 1929 minister of St. George's, Glasgow.

April of receiving General D'Amade, commanding the "Corps Expeditionnaire Français d'Orient," a body of French and African Colonial troops under the supreme command of Sir Ian Hamilton. March 1915.

No one could fail to be struck with the soldierly bearing and look of distinction of that comrade of the Great War. He was received on the quay by a guard of honour from B * under Capt. Cooper and Lieut. Agar.

General Hunter-Weston had spared neither himself nor his staff on the voyage out in the tremendous task of framing his scheme of invasion. The significance of the stay in Alexandria was that the troops had to be reshuffled so as to be ready to hand, fully equipped as a striking force with their supplies and reinforcements echeloned behind them. Fatigues and not manœuvres were the order of the day. There were to be got on board engineering materials, lavish supplies of water in ships' tanks, *fanatis*,† skins, and petrol tins; horses and carts, on or off their wheels, with poles and other detachables marked for identification and reassembling. Clothing, medical stores, spare ammunition, and a hundred other minutiæ had to be attended to.

The famous inspection by the Commander-in-Chief, General Sir Ian Hamilton, described so vividly in the fifth volume of the *Times History of the War*, was the one spectacular incident. He was impressed by the 29th, and he knew good from bad troops as well as any man alive. We are entitled to hope that his eye did not dwell least appreciatively on his fellow-countrymen, the Borderers.

This is of course not the place for a general discussion of the Gallipoli campaign. The rôle of a battalion is to go where it is sent and do what it is told. But the reader may be reminded that in March the Government had taken the responsibility of trying to force the Dardanelles with the Navy alone. The engagement of 18th March marked the victory of forts *versus* ships, and, besides, the British aims were exposed. The Turks and their German advisers took the hint and fortified the peninsula. They procured Skoda (Austrian) guns and German aeroplanes. They kept an ear open for news from Egyptian and other sources. Their own attack on the Canal‡ had been a feeble affair and had been repulsed. They could therefore without distraction other than the Russian and Greek

* In a compressed tale a certain amount of shorthand must be forgiven. Unless the context points otherwise, B is short for B company, and so on with the other letters.

† Thanks to the *Official History* (Egypt and Palestine), p. 193, I am able to give the correct plural for *fantasse*, a small metal tank for camel transport of water.

‡ A brief sketch will follow in the next part. See *Official History* (Egypt and Palestine), vol. i.

March 1915. frontiers concentrate on the problem of defending their capital and their *mare clausum,* which sundered Russia from her allies. Every day's delay meant one stage in the advance of the vulnerable parts of the Gallipoli Peninsula towards impregnability. By the 25th of April our enemies thought they had achieved their goal. They had openly boasted so. Sir Ian Hamilton had witnessed part of the naval action on the 18th March. He was convinced and said so that only with military aid could the straits be forced. He never underestimated the enormous difficulties of the task set him by the Government—to direct that military aid to a fresh naval effort to a successful conclusion. He was in the unfortunate position of having to improvise his line of action from the very beginning without even a hint from Lord Kitchener (or anyone else) as to how he should set about it. Sir Ian hit upon the plan of a triple landing; one intended to be a temporary feint by D'Amade at Kum Kale on the Asiatic coast at the entrance to the Dardanelles, another intended to be permanent at "Anzac" cove 15 miles up the Ægean coast by Birdwood with his Antipodeans, and the main effort against the end of the Gallipoli Peninsula by Hunter-Weston with the 29th Division and the R.N.D.*.

Kum Kale and Anzac are outside this tale. They both attained their object of a "draw" and a lodgment respectively.

But the Helles area calls for some words to explain the operation at Y, which constitutes perhaps the most dramatic episode in any K.O.S.B. unit's career.

"On account of its concavity the southern end of the peninsula of Gallipoli has been compared to a spoon and to a saucer with a bit out of the left-hand side looking towards the tip. On the W. there are a line of high bluffs falling steeply to the sea. At the very tip above and due E. of Cape Tekke there is quite an eminence. The British military name given to it was Hill 114. From Cape Tekke the coast takes a right-angle turn S.E., and the character of the coast here is a beach for a quarter of a mile, followed by more cliffs all the way to Cape Helles, above which stood a lighthouse. N. of the lighthouse is the highest ground at the tip, and it was named Hill 138. The coast turns E. at Cape Helles, and for three furlongs consists of cliffs, but thereafter comes the best of the beaches at and around the tip of the peninsula. It curves S. towards the southernmost point of the peninsula, Sedd-el-Bahr, upon which was an old

* It was the opinion of the late Gen. Callwell (see his *Dardanelles*) and many others that the C.-in-C.'s scheme was about the best that could be devised. Its inception has been lucidly and cogently explained by its author. It holds the field.

castle backed by what was known as Hill 141. This high ground, the principal heights of which are Hills 114, 138, and 141, overlooks all the country between the western bluffs, the Achi Baba range and Morto Bay on the straits, which was the name of the ' bit out of the saucer.' It was obvious that the Turks from Achi Baba had ideal observation of every movement of troops N.E. of the hills at the tip, for Achi Baba stood 709 feet above sea-level. At the eastern end of Morto Bay cliffs succeed, and at Eski Hissarlik—in future called Eski—was an old battery known as ' de Tott's.'

March 1915.

" All the beaches were given military names. That at de Tott's Battery was lettered S. Morto Bay can be ignored. The beach between Sedd-el-Bahr and Cape Helles was lettered V; that immediately S. of Cape Tekke, W. N. of the corner and facing the Ægean there was a feasible landing lettered X. Finally, more than 2 miles to the N. of X, and nearly a mile N. of the opening of a long and sinuous ravine (called Zighin or Zaghir Dere, and named by the invaders Gully Ravine) on to a sort of beach called Gully Beach, came Y Beach at the foot of a steep but scalable line of cliffs. It may be added that W Beach is also known as Lancashire Landing and X as Implacable Landing, for reasons which the sequel will show. The assault of this veritable fortress had been planned as follows: A large covering force was to make five separate landings. The 1st K.O.S.B. and one company of the 2nd S.W.B., along with the Plymouth battalion of the R.N.D., were to land at Y and scale the cliffs, with the object, *inter alia*, of getting into touch with those landing at X. Right opposite Y the remainder of the S.W.B. were to land at S, *alias* Eski. Two flank positions, one on the Ægean and one on the straits would thus be secured. The most perilous task fell to the principal covering force, namely, the whole of the 86th Brigade, who were to land at X, W, and V, and push up to join hands with the forces at Y and S in the course of the day, and the final objective included Achi Baba." *

* From *The Story of the 29th Division*, p. 14.

CHAPTER III *

THE LANDING

April 1915. — On the 16th of April the *Southland*, full of "brass hats" and Borderers, sailed from Alexandria for Mudros Bay in the island of Lemnos and two days later the K.O.S.B. were staring at that noble harbour and its contents from the *Queen Elizabeth* to the smallest row-boat, and hearing of the escape of the *Manitou* † and a Divisional Artillery Brigade. The island of Lemnos was at its best, but the K.O.S.B. were too busy practising their part to take much notice of scenery. Disembarkation by means of small boats is not a manœuvre for improvization. There was many a rehearsal in Mudros Bay in the use of rope ladders. " Every man was an expert." ‡ It was then that the K.O.S.B. made the acquaintance of Lieut.-Com. Adrian Keyes, for he superintended the boat practice.

Let us for a moment consider what was the great adventure on which the old 25th were embarked when they left harbour on the afternoon of Saturday, 24th April 1915, with 28 officers and more than 900 O.R., true to type and at unity among themselves, one of the few remaining specimens of a British Regular Infantry Battalion. Their's was to be an isolated operation—in simple words, a side-show, but a serious affair pregnant with possibilities. They were part of Gen. Hunter-Weston's covering force under Brig.-Gen. (afterwards Sir Stuart) Hare, but as soon as they parted from the rest of that force which was to assail the tip of the Peninsula and 3 miles of unknown ground came between them, they were independent, and their commander had to use his discretion until orders came from the Higher Command. The troops allotted to this pivotal point consisted, besides the K.O.S.B., of one company (A) of 2nd S.W.B. and nearly but not quite all of the Plymouth Battalion R.M.L.I. of the Royal Naval Division,§ which had had such an unceremonious introduction to soldiering and to real war

* See Map 5. † See *The Story of the 29th Division*, pp. 12 and 13.

‡ Lieut.-Col. A. J. Welch.

§ For this enterprise through Naval Division spectacles, see D. Jerrold's *Royal Naval Division*.

24 April 1915.

at Antwerp in October 1914.* It was almost entirely composed of men specially enlisted for the war.† The whole force was something over 2,000 strong and was under command of the senior officer, Lieut.-Col. G. E. Matthews of the Royal Marines.‡ There was a smaller side-show on the other side, where the remaining three companies of the 2nd S.W.B. were to land at Eski Hissarlik; but the main effort, which must succeed if anything was to result at all, was directed against and round the tip.

Before a foot of the Y force could step on shore three moves had to be made. The trooper had to be exchanged for two war vessels, these in turn for four trawlers, these in turn for twenty cutters.§

Sir Ian has told us that his scheme could never have been adopted had the climate been British. Fine weather was to be expected, and when the wind dropped on the 23rd, after a bout of some days, the 25th (a Sunday) was chosen for the assault, and the K.O.S.B. started to move at 4 p.m. on the 24th.

"The battalion transhipped from the S.S. *Southland* to H.M.S. Cruisers *Amethyst* and *Sapphire*—A and B into the former, C and D with H.Q. and M.G. section into the latter. At 7 p.m., amidst the cheers of the crews of the 'Modern Armada,' we left the crowded harbour,|| rounded the headland, and pointed to our destination. Our first great adventure of the war had begun.

"About 2.30 a.m.¶ the battalion transhipped again, and with A Company S.W.B. were 'sardined' on to four trawlers, each with a tow of boats. These trawlers, manned by fishermen, were to ground, bows on, at intervals of 100 yards on the open shore at Y.

"The night was calm but it was dark, and some of us wondered how a task of such nicety was to be executed. But if there was one thing which was impressive in those forty-eight hours, from start to evacuation, it was the masterly handling of those trawlers. Round and round we circled once we were all aboard, each boat out of sight of the other, gradually working towards the shore with a feeling that the boat on which we were was going to be the only one to land a load, when at 4.45 a.m. on Sunday, 25th April, we hit the

* How well they had done will be found in the 2nd 1914 vol. of *The Official War History*, at p. 63.

† *Ibid.*, p. 202. G.H.Q. were unaware of this (*ibid.*, p. 203).

‡ See Royal Commission's Report (Cmd. 371), p. 20. Sir I. Hamilton's despatch of 5th May is wrong in saying that Lieut.-Col. Koe was in command, although he himself was for a time under that impression (see *Official History*, p. 202).

§ G.H.Q. Order of 19th April 1915.

|| The sight has been described for all time by John Masefield in *Gallipoli*, pp. 33–36.

¶ Transhipment took place about 4 miles W. of Y. (*Official History*, p. 203).

Sunday, 25 April 1915.

shore. Visibility had by then reached 100 yards, and there was every trawler in its exact position." *

Each trawler had boats "tied on to their sides" † manned by bluejackets. "As soon as the trawlers pulled up we all got into the boats, rowed ashore, and jumped on to the beach." †

Almost immediately Major Welch with A and Capt. Cooper with B landed, to find that a complete surprise had been effected. Sir Ian's foresight in steering clear of Gully Beach, a tempting cove 1,000 yards in the direction of X, was amply rewarded. Gully Beach was held by Turks.‡ A more inhospitable shore could hardly have greeted the adventurers. The dim light of dawn showed a line of bluffs about 200 feet high.§

"The so-called beach was a bouldery, pot-holey foreshore, and many men landed far wetter than they expected.|| From the narrow strip of foreshore the cliff rose steep, but not unclimbable, to a height of about 150 feet. Running N.W. from the beach was a steep stony nullah,¶ which gave the best approach to the top. On the N. side of the top of the nullah was a distinct bluff, higher than the surrounding ground. It commanded a fair field of fire, *e.g.* to N. about 1,200 yards. In fact, the site would have made an admirable base for further operations had it not been for the unexpected and unwelcome natural feature, afterwards known as Gully Ravine, which presented itself not more than 300 yards from the top of the bluff.

"Parallel more or less to the coast-line from between Krithia ($1\frac{3}{4}$ miles E.N.E.) and the Ægean was a deep, dry nullah, terminating at Gully Beach already mentioned. The official maps had misplaced it too far inland. The W. or seaside commanded the E. side. It was to court disaster to put the nullah between the troops and their communications. The ground between the cliff edge and the nullah edge was therefore the only defensive position, cramped as it was and committing the force to a rigid mode of defence. Worst of all, this sunk corridor was a natural communication trench for the Turks right up to the firing-line, and an ideal place for deployment. Vegetation was rife. The cliffs were covered with scrub. On the top a view opened up of occasional

* Lieut.-Col. A. J. Welch.

† Letter written by Lieut. C. S. Stirling-Cookson, dated 11th May 1915.

‡ The force, according to the *Official History*, was only two platoons strong (see Map opposite p. 159 in that work).

§ The official height is about 150 feet (p. 201).

|| "Some men jumped into the sea and waded up to the breast in water." Information from the late Major McAlester. See *The Story of the 29th Division*, p. 19.

¶ Dry or wet water channel.

"Y" BEACH AND THE COAST-LINE, SHOWING CAPE HELLES IN THE DISTANCE; GALLIPOLI CAMPAIGN.

clumps of trees, many low bushes, and the ground was carpeted with wild flowers." * 25 April 1915.

The sabbatical calm of a lovely spring day in pleasant common-like country, ringed round by noble mountains in Imbros and Samothrace on one side and the Troad on the Asiatic side, was broken by the bombardment at 5 a.m. at Cape Helles.

As X was less than 3 miles S. of the Borderers, the salvoes of H.M.S. *Implacable* were audible reminders that their nearest neighbours, the 2nd R.F., were probably in the thick of it—as indeed they were.† Under the capable supervision of Major McAlester, the Military Landing Officer, and his assistant, Capt. Ogilvy, things went with a swing. The next tow brought the three remaining companies of regulars, and the Plymouth followed in due course.‡ All on shore had packs, but none had spades or picks. There was much hard work dragging up ammunition, food, and, above all, water. The only casualties were two men killed by a naval " short." With the force was the naval liaison officer, Lieut.-Com. Adrian Keyes, and there will be occasion to refer to his testimony. The whole episode to be told was over and done with in thirty-four hours, but as eighteen of these were occupied with incessant fighting and nearly all the men § engaged had had their last good sleep on the night 23/24th, it seemed like a hundred years.

THE BRITISH FEELERS

Major Welch took his company A up N. along the top of the cliff, and his patrols found the enemy entrenched in strength 1,200 yards N. of Y. The enemy, however, showed no aggressive spirit, although his position barred any further advance on the part of A. Capt. Cooper, with B, went straight inland and across the big nullah far enough to enable his party to see Morto Bay and the ships firing off Sedd-el-Bahr. This party was recalled by order without having encountered any of the enemy.|| Things were equally quiet towards Krithia.¶ The situation as regards finding touch with Brigade H.Q. at X is somewhat obscure, but it is certain that it was never got. Sometime after noon the O.C. Force decided to draw his advanced parties to the defensive zone and await developments elsewhere, *i.e.* the expected advance of the rest of

* Lieut.-Col. Welch.

† See *The Royal Fusiliers in the Great War*. (O'Neill.)

‡ According to G.H.Q. Order of 19th April they were to disembark first, but in point of fact they did not.

§ Some support troops enjoyed naps in the bluff in the earlier part of the 25th.

|| Capt. E. W. T. Agar, who was present. ¶ *Official History*, p. 205.

25 April 1915. the 87th I.B.. It was plain from the continued bombardment farther S. that things were not going rapidly with the invasion in that quarter. The troops were all withdrawn intact, and we can direct our attention to their position on the cliff and their dispositions.

The first offensive is recorded by Major Welch. At 11 a.m. the Turks opened with field-guns, and considerable bodies of the enemy showed to N. and N.E.. This also was a factor in bringing about a purely defensive attitude. But the real hostilities opened after 4 p.m..

A LONG, GRIM, DEFENSIVE STRUGGLE

Following the British military custom of starting at the R. and working L. we begin our count. Three companies of the Plymouth Battalion were on the R., some being in local support. Next them came the S.W.B. followed by Borderers—B, C, and A in order, the last covering the bluff—then the K.O.S.B., M.G. section (Vickers guns under Lieut. Paterson), and finally the remaining company of the Plymouth up to the cliff edge. D, under Capt. Whigham, were in reserve. Close support is in one sense more exact, for they were just behind the crest of the nullah running from the bluff to the shore, but as there were no other troops ever on the scene they were in fact the reserve.

" The line was formed by the men's packs * and with entrenching tools. It never reached what could be called a trench, and was constructed under a most harassing and ever-increasing rifle fire.†

" Although never a serious menace,‡ bursts of gunfire, *e.g.* at 11.30 a.m.,§ sniping, and threats had accompanied the construction of the frail fort. Rifle fire was heavy at 11.30 a.m. and again at 1 p.m.. Between 2.30 and 4.30 it is common ground that ' a series of spasmodic attacks were begun against the L. of our position from the Turkish trenches located by A and from the big nullah.'§ These persisted until dusk (about 7 p.m.), when the Turks withdrew—

* This disposes of the statement on p. 210 of the *Official History* that practically every man's kit was abandoned on the beach. Nor do any K.O.S.B. sources of information admit knowledge that there were " heavy entrenching tools " on the beach. As Major McAlester wrote to the writer, they would have given anything for them. The kits were an improvised necessary breastwork, and after the battle they were not worth salving; but they must have saved many lives.

† Col. Welch.

‡ Major McAlester dated vigorous hostilities from 4 p.m., and Lieut. Cookson of D in a letter dated 11th May puts it at 4.30. He was in support and never saw a Turk all day.

§ War Diary.

25–26 April 1915.

for a season. They had drawn nearly all our available supports into the firing-line. The lull lasted thirty minutes, and then the storm broke, this time all along the line from Gully Ravine. On the R. and centre the attacks retained the spasmodic character of those earlier in the day, but the garrison were kept on tenterhooks and a disquieting number of casualties occurred mysteriously, until it was realized that the bullets were 'overs,' aimed at their comrades farther N., and that it was a case of missing a pigeon and killing a crow. But it was round the bluff that the heaviest attack was launched. Loss of the bluff would have split the force in two and cut off the centre and R. from the beach while overwhelming the L. into the sea or capitulation. The situation became critical. The line was pierced in several places. Hand-to-hand fighting had occurred in places. D, under Capt. Whigham, were all absorbed. I had to apply to Col. Matthews for more men, and was allotted an R.N.D. company from the R., which had to traverse the position to the point where D had originally stood in support.* These not proving sufficient, some platoons of the S.W.B. were also diverted to strengthen this vital post. They were just in time. From now on a desperate battle raged in the dark.† Attacks were pressed more savagely. The last supports were absorbed by 2.30 a.m. without sign of a cessation. Just a thin khaki line, and then the cliff—and the wounded. No 'Very' lights were there to expose bombers—and we hadn't a bomb with which to reply. In places the line was pierced, and Turks fired into the reserve of our men at the head of the nullah. Stirling Cookson was detailed to clear the bluff of these unwanted guests. Whether it was then or not, he certainly had a bullet through his glengarry and another which grazed his puttee. Almost unbelievable is the encounter of Lieut. Miller with a party with a M.G. on a pack pony. They had turned the position of the L. of the K.O.S.B. and were coming calmly along behind our position. He dealt with them with his revolver—each officer had twenty-four rounds.‡ Sergt. Bidgood held a section at the apex of the salient formed by the bluff single-handed until reinforced.§ For this he won the D.C.M. . In fact, the rough and tumble defies orderly description and is merely a collection of authentic but disconnected incidents." Before recounting these we had better follow Major Welch in the final phase.

* Lieut.-Col. Welch speaks with special authority, as he was O.C., Northern Section of defence.

† War Diary and *Official History*, p. 207, both mention showers of rain at this time.

‡ Col. Koe's Orders, dated when O.C. troops on S.S. *Southland*.

§ Col. Welch.

26 April 1915.

"Just before dawn the Turks eased their attacks, but not for long. At 6 a.m. they launched a massed attack against the whole line, pouring in waves out of the great gully. At that very moment one of our guardian angels, H.M.S. *Goliath*, for once sent a short shell. It fell in the middle of our line. It was more than flesh and blood could bear. One section of the Borderers wavered, broke, and were back at the edge. If they had gone over who could have blamed them ? For they had been shelled, but were without artillery, other than the handicapped and unsuitable naval guns, bombed without bombs, outnumbered, exhausted, disheartened, deserted (as it seemed). But they did NOT. They rallied and returned to the old line with a cheer, led by their C.O. Col. Koe, a sick man and a hero. He received his death wound, but he saved the situation. Young Miller charged across our line, and fell in stopping a last Turkish rush." * Honours lay with the defence.

Then an uncanny calm fell with suddenness on the scene and the battle was over. "Stick it out" had triumphed. In *The Story of the 29th Division* the time when firing stopped is placed too early. Major McAlester put it at 4.30 a.m., but the allusions to break of dawn in other accounts, and the very fact that the *Goliath* could see to fire point to a later hour. Col. Welch puts it at 6 a.m., *i.e.* in broad daylight. But certainly by 7.30 it was all over.

The character of this gruesome example of night fighting, perhaps the fiercest in the whole war, is striking. Rifle-fire was incessant. The Turks were noisy with voice and bugle. Everything was confused and at close quarters. English-speaking officers invited surrender. One, said to be a German, called out, "You English, surrender! We ten to one." But an engine was ready to "Smite once and smite no more," for a soldier smashed his head with his entrenching tool.† Another linguist ejaculated a guttural "Retire," but Major Welch "told him off" suitably. Ammunition was a source of anxiety. K.O.S.B. opinion is that an epidemic of jambing was due to the ammunition for the long rifles of the Plymouth having got mixed with that for the short rifle of the regulars. Undoubtedly there was a shortage, and Col. Matthews had to signal for reinforcements and more ammunition. Possibly the dusty soil may have increased the tendency to jamb, and the battalion had not yet adopted the bone-dry treatment of the bolt and mechanism

* He was a fine Rugby full-back. The debt of the allied cause to that noble game is incalculable. It seems to breed dash and leadership.

† Various eye-witnesses.

that so disconcerted later arrivals fresh from home. The following incidents point the moral. Lieut. Cheatle stood with a bleeding head cheering on the men until he was killed. Pte. J. Sweeney, an Iro-Scot from Gorebridge, dashed into a group of Turks, bayoneted two, lost his rifle, and emulated the famous Sir Ewan Cameron of Lochiel by fastening his teeth in a Turk's throat, receiving a wound that eventually proved mortal. Capt. Antrobus, the "Sir Galahad" of the battalion, as Col. Welch styles him, shook hands with his comrades, and led them in the final recapture of the line, to fall when he reached it.

26 April 1915.

Then came the great summons to Capt. Marrow, the adjutant. It came in the form of a bullet through the head as he was going to speak to the C.O., Major McAlester. His head was shattered, and he fell dead over the C.O.. All good officers leave a blank, but at this juncture Marrow was irreplaceable. He knew his work from A to Z. He had served under Sladen and Koe as adjutant to the satisfaction of both, and was respected and adored by all ranks. To his brother officers he was a prince of good fellows. Adrian Keyes wrote of the skill with which he organized and directed the boat practice and the supply of food and ammunition from the beach to the front. During the black chaos of that awful night he seemed to be ubiquitous and always in the right place. Thanks to the daring and determination of his comrade and admirer, R.S.M. Douglass, his body was found on the "return journey," and he eventually was buried by Padre Reid beside his friend Antrobus. Modesty, Lethe, the flight of time, distraction, and death all combine to restrict the number of brave deeds recorded. But without the valour of the unrecorded heroes we could have no rolls of honour. Information and space are alike lacking for an account of the doings of the S.W.B., but every Scottish Borderer knows that if the Welsh Borderers had not been as gallant as themselves there would have been disaster. The R.N.D.'s part can be read in the graphic pages of Jerrold.

"That any of us got away was due to the gallantry and heroism of the K.O.S.B.. They were magnificent, and I can safely say that no other battalion has done anything finer in a day when nearly every man in the division earned the V.C.". Such was the deliberate opinion of Lieut.-Com. Keyes. "It was quite the most gallant part of the landing the way the K.O.S.B. held on for these two days, and their final bayonet charges, though very little will ever be said about it, as they had to re-embark." These words were penned by one who had studied the battalion since mobilization, and was incapable of flattery.

26 April 1915.

"And so on down the whole line feats of gallantry unrecorded by all ranks for the honour of the regiment." * And every word that fits the K.O.S.B. applies to the S.W.B. and the R.N.D. force, allowing for the inexperience of the last named.

The question arises, How did the Y force come to evacuate after they had repulsed the Turks? The answer is easy. Col. Matthews unquestionably gave the order,† reluctantly, but with a full sense of responsibility. He was, at first, on the 26th, in favour of a sally towards X. In fact, he issued an order to that effect *while the final battle was still raging*. On receipt of that order, *in writing*, just after things had quietened down, Major Welch, then Second-in-Command, sought his then C.O., Major McAlester, and both these officers then approached Col. Matthews, and a consultation took place, at which Lieut. Paterson was also present, and it was pointed out to him that it was impracticable for the tired-out force to fight its way to X, and that in any event all the wounded would have to be evacuated before a start was made, and that that very essential preliminary would take a long time. It was therefore a question of carrying on as they were or clearing out. The immediate result of the consultation was that Col. Matthews rescinded his first order,‡ which consequently never was sent, and directed Major Welch to send a message from the signal station to the effect that if another attack took place the position could not be held without reinforcements and ammunition, and requesting that if a Turkish attack were made and our men were observed coming down the cliffs, to turn the guns on to the top and send in boats.§

But the K.O.S.B. were not the only unit of the force, and it is very significant that at this very time Lieut. Paterson (M.G. officer) reported to Major Welch that the Plymouth company on the extreme L. had withdrawn to the beach. The companies of the same unit in the R. sector did likewise, and left the Regulars with an attenuated line. It is not reasonable to suppose that a K.O.S.B. officer *only* received the order to retire. Col. Matthews was with his own battalion throughout the battle, and the impression left on the K.O.S.B. officers was that the Plymouth were retiring to the beach in obedience to the order to "try to withdraw towards X landing." This was not an unreasonable interpretation. The

* Col. Welch to the writer.

† Cmd. 371, p. 20.

‡ The writer has seen the original, which is in Col. Welch's hands. It is written on p. 112 of a Field Service pocket-book. The *ipsissima verba* run as follows: "As soon as fire slackens ~~Ip~~ we will try to withdraw from the R. towards X landing.—(Signed) G. E. M."

§ This is to be inferred from Cmd. 371, p. 20; and indeed the *Official History*, at p. 210, quotes *ad longum* the message sent through Major Welch.

alternatives to feeling along the shore under cover of the naval guns were to force a passage along the cliff top or down the corridor of Gully Ravine, the one a desperate venture, the other sheer lunacy. Another mode of "withdrawing" to X would be by sea, and just at that moment it so happened that boats were seen coming in to shore. It seems that some unwounded men did embark, possibly through misinterpreting the curious order. The explanation given on page 210 of the *Official History* that Col. Matthews was unaware of the withdrawal, and that the withdrawal was due to panic, and that the panic infected a large proportion of the force is not understood. Panic is an ugly word, connoting the madness of the god Pan—irrationality, craven, headlong flight. No account has in the last fourteen years ever come to light of incidents suggestive of panic as the word is used with regard paid to precision. None are now disclosed, but panic is inferred from the tone of certain anxious and irresponsible signallers' messages,* despatched at the very critical moment of a fierce fight. That evidence is insufficient to support the charge of general panic and is quite irrelevant to the definite orders to embark. The wounded were all got away, and the embarkation was orderly and methodical. 26 April 1915.

At 9.30 a.m. the definite order was given for all troops to embark. It was in consequence of that order that the 1st Battalion of the King's Own Scottish Borderers vacated their position at Y, and for no other reason. The O.C. K.O.S.B. told off a company skilled in scrub warfare to act as rearguard.† Assisted by barefooted bluejackets all the wounded were safely embarked, and the troops and rearguard followed. The last to leave were McAlester (awarded the D.S.O. for his services on these two days) and Keyes. The former's memory must have played a trick. It was not at 11 a.m. but as late as 3 p.m. that he said good-bye to Y.‡ (It was not, alas, *au revoir* for "Jock" McAlester.) And all that time not a Turk in sight; not a shot fired! That is one surprise. But there is another. There was not a wire nor a word *pro* or *con*, nor indeed

* A K.O.S.B. message asking for help as "we are cut off and have no ammunition and also a number of wounded" is attributed to a "young officer." That in itself does not amount to more than a proper solicitude for the wounded and continuing the fight. It does not suggest "please take us off." The sting is in an ambiguous sentence that the navy "at once sent in boats and the party was re-embarked." This implies that the "young officer" was evacuated. But in point of fact no K.O.S.B. officer re-embarked except under orders. Who the "party" were is obscure. Presumably they were wounded.

† See information in *Story of the 29th Division*, p. 31, supplied to the Editor by Major McAlester himself.

‡ Colonel Welch and other K.O.S.B. officers present. The *Official History* (p. 210) puts the time at 11.30 a.m., but without reference to authority.

25–26 April 1915. a sign of life from G.H.Q.. If the evacuation had been a dreadful mistake, if help was at hand, if all that was needed was to dig deeper and man the trenches, a message could have been sent by the higher command, as was done at Anzac.

The Report of the Commission makes it clear that Matthews' two messages—(1) that he had landed unopposed, (2) that he must withdraw unless he had more ammunition — were never answered.*

Meanwhile as we picture the Borderers steaming round to pastures new on their old friends the *Amethyst* and *Sapphire*, and also the *Goliath* and *Dublin*, we can see at what cost they had repulsed the apparently numerically superior, fresher, and better armed Turks.†

Besides those mentioned, the following gallant officers were killed or died of wounds: Capts. Cooper, Becher, and both Sandersons, and 2nd Lieut. J. T. Redpath. The last named was killed almost immediately after he regained the lost trench by a bold and inspiring charge, having done honour to his recent commission and his old regiment. Lieuts. Shorter, Agar, and Renny were wounded. 2nd Lieut. F. A. Williamson of the 3rd S.R. (attached) was wounded at this landing, and died on 4th June in consequence. The heavy casualties among senior officers was a terrible blow, and the next few weeks practically made a finish of the cheery *Southland* party. The casualties were heavy for the type of fighting—296 killed and wounded.‡ These figures are dwarfed by the holocausts near another Y, Y Ravine on the Ancre in 1916, at Loos in 1915, and on Gallipoli are exceeded by those of the 12th of July. There were no mines nor mortars nor heavy artillery. But a full strength battalion was reduced by almost half its battle strength. Certain facts speak for themselves. The deaths were high in comparison with the wounded who recovered. The Turks got no prisoners.

The effort and sacrifice were not in vain. A large proportion of the available Turkish force was held at bay all through the 25th and the earlier part of the 26th April. These otherwise would have been used against those of the 29th, who had such a precarious grip on the tip of the Peninsula,§ and such a grim struggle to reach the Eski line.

* It is clear from the *Official History* recently published that Y was insufficiently remembered.

† Turkish sources put the force at only 1½ battalions (*Official History*, pp. 207, 208).

‡ The S.W.B. Company suffered in proportion, but the Plymouth Battalion fared even worse.

§ Official Despatch of 5th May 1915; *Story of the 29th Division*; Buchan's *History of the War*.

Suppose the surprise had been adequately supported and exploited? However, this is idle speculation.* 25–26 April 1915.

Perhaps Stoney's † summing up is the safest: "Unfortunately the force which landed there" (*i.e.* at Y) "was not strong enough to hold on, so had to be withdrawn. The actual withdrawal was not very difficult nor was the original landing. It was that night from the Turkish counter-attack that we suffered so heavily. There is only one officer with us now (*i.e.* 7th August 1915) who was in the battalion when I joined it" (*i.e.* May 1915). I conclude the account with the weighty words of the senior surviving officer of those who took part in this operation. "If the history of the first brief fighting in which the 1st K.O.S.B. took part is given at such length, it is because the Gallipoli campaign, so conceived that it might have had momentous results in shortening the war by bringing victory to the Allies, was yet so mismanaged that it was predestined to failure. Nevertheless, by the gallantry and tenacity of the fighting troops engaged, it came to within measurable distance of glorious success between 25th April and the early days of May. Future generations will only extract this truth by not resting content with general war histories but by studying the details of the

* The "finding in fact" (to use a lawyer's phrase) by the *Official History* that the Turkish force opposed to the 29th Division and attached troops was a tiny fraction of what it had hitherto been believed to have been has naturally given scope to the critics. The Y Force is an obvious mark. One light-hearted article writer has written of the chance missed by the K.O.S.B., as though neither Marines nor S.W.B. had formed part of the force. As a rule, however, criticism is directed to the alleged inactivity of, and lack of initiative shown by the O.C. Force. But the writer has yet to find a ruling as to precisely what Col. Matthews ought to have done by the "bold advance"[1] which it is said he ought to have made. Sometimes it seems as if his omission to seize and hold Krithia was the offence, sometimes as though he ought to have joined hands with the S Force, and with them, or with his own troops alone, have attacked the Turks at Helles from their rear. These plans are mutually exclusive. That of an advance on Krithia is open to the objection that it was counter to the orders to act as a pivot at Y, and that to increase the distance between himself and the main body was to court disaster, for the weight of Turkish reinforcement lay N. of Krithia, and, as A had found out, there was an entrenched force on the Ægean flank.

As to the move to free the southern beaches,[1] it would have been a gamble, which at the time offered little hope of success. Col. Matthews was well aware that things were going badly at Helles. The X Force were long overdue to join him where he was and proceed to Krithia and Achi Baba. He had no idea that the Turks at Helles were—according to post-war Turkish information accepted as accurate—a mere handful, and without a proper base or any artillery support, and with that deadly gully between the troops and Y Beach neither he nor any responsible officer on the spot thought of the solution, which seems so simple to the critics of 1929. The pinching of the Turks at Helles was essentially a measure to be directed and controlled by the Higher Command. They had their hands full and the chance was missed.

[1] *Official History*, p. 215.

† Major G. B. Stoney, D.S.O., of whom later.

25-26 April 1915. — fighting, unit by unit. Then they will realize that in little more than a week's desperate fighting success was withheld only through causes far beyond the influence of human valour."

Nearly two thousand years ago Horace struck a warning note when he wrote the lines :

Vixere fortes ante Agamemnona
Multi : sed omnes illacrimabiles
Urgentur ignotique longa
Nocte, carent quia vate sacro— *

that the story of gallant deeds should be told before it is too late. No events in the regimental story are worthier of commemoration than those connected with the Landing on Gallipoli.

* " Before Atrides men were brave
But ah : oblivion, dark and long
Has locked them in a tearless grave
For lack of consecrating song.
Odes, Bk. IV., No. 9 (Conington's Translation).

CHAPTER IV

SO NEAR AND YET SO FAR

IN the meantime what General Hunter-Weston described as the impossible had been achieved. The fortified, strongly garrisoned tip of the Gallipoli Peninsula was stormed on the 25th of April 1915. This exploit has immortalized the 29th Division. It was a soldier's battle.* The gallantry of regimental officers and men wrought the miracle. Through thickets of barbed wire, which extended along the shore and even into the waters of the sea, through a hail of fire from pom-poms, M.G., and rifles, across prepared trenches, that astonishing infantry won its way to the crest of the shore hills from X to Cape Helles. The 1st L.F. landing at W is the most striking combination of daring, difficulties overcome, and ultimate success in the whole day. And this without minimizing the dash and valour of the 2nd R.F. at and after Implacable Landing at X, or the determined rush with which Col. Casson and 3 companies of 2nd S.W.B., aided by Capt. A. P. Davidson, R.N., and some blue-jackets made good a landing at Eski Hissarlik on the straits side and took de Tott's Battery at a cost of something round about 60 casualties † there to hang on unmolested till the general advance caught them up on the 27th. Still less is one unmindful of the tragedy of V. Had it not been for the fact that the sand in the bay between Sedd-el-Bahr and Cape Helles shelves steeply at the very water's edge and creates a scanty cover, not a man would have survived. The valour was there right enough, but by the time the fight was broken off in that sector, it was represented by a few crouching figures on shore or drifting often in whole boat-loads in the blood-red water. The chief sufferers were the Irish Fusilier regiments of the 86th (or covering force) Brigade. The Dublins and the Munsters suffered fearful casualties and, in addition, a piece of bad luck involved part of the main body, who might have landed scatheless at X like the bulk of the 87th

25 April 1915.

* The tale has been told again and again but by no one more movingly and brilliantly than by Sir Ian Hamilton in his despatch of 20th May 1915.

† *Official History*, p. 237.

25 April 1915. I.B.. Brig.-Gen. Napier of the 88th I.B., his Brigade Major, Capt. Costeker and a large number of the Hants were involved in the V landing and killed. Not to put too fine a point on it, it was a bloody repulse, which might easily have wrecked the expedition had the *River Clyde* been struck by bursting shells. She was struck several times but the fuses failed to act. What her contents—some 2,000 and more officers and men, some of them grievously wounded—must have suffered all that long, broiling day can hardly be imagined.

But with darkness came quiet and an unmolested landing was effected there also, and the entire force was on shore.

The next day saw the grip on the western position tightened and the capture of the village and fort of Sedd-el-Bahr, thanks to the covering fire of the navy, including that of the *Queen Elizabeth*, and of the height, Hill 141, just N.W. of it. The attack on Sedd-el-Bahr—a very difficult feat, especially after the strain of the preceding day—owed much to the inspiring leadership of Col. Doughty-Wylie, V.C. Borderers can take pride in the fact that Major George Butler Stoney, loaned from the Egyptian Army, a Borderer and the son of a Borderer, did magnificent service both on 25th and 26th April, which my informants told me well merited the V.C.. The battalion soon came under his able leadership, but his end came all too soon as the sequel will show.

It will be remembered that the French were to make a diversion at Kum Kale in Asia by means of a landing in force. General D'Amade executed his task to perfection, withdrew his force and landed at V on the morning of the 27th, when it was observed that the Turks were beginning to retire. Eager preparations for the advance were made, for speed was of the essence of the capture of Achi Baba. The Franco-British attack did not, however, materialize until the afternoon. There was no opposition, and by 9 p.m. a line was reached from de Tott's Battery to Gully Beach, now evacuated by the Turks. Orders were issued that the advance was to be resumed on the 28th at 8 a.m. with such exiguous artillery support as there was available.

We can now return to the K.O.S.B., whom we left embarking as the result of orders to evacuate Y.

"We were most kindly received on board H.M.S. *Goliath*, *Amethyst*, and *Sapphire*, and during the evening we transhipped to the transport *Ansonia*. Early next morning our large-hearted padre, Dr. Cameron Reid, held a memorial service on board. His indefatigable attention to the wounded (repeated on many subsequent occasions) will always be remembered by the survivors of Y.

"Early on the 28th the K.O.S.B. landed at 'Lancashire Landing'

(W) and refitted. The packs, it will be remembered, had been used as revetting material and had not been salved. 28 April 1915.

" With new equipment and packs the battalion received orders about 11.30 a.m. to rejoin their own proper brigade, the 87th I.B., which was attacking on the L. sector of the Allies with the 88th on their R., the battered 86th in reserve, and the French on the R. of the 88th and resting on the straits." * In the course of the advance Major McAlester was badly wounded and had to be evacuated. He eventually lost his leg and became an invalid, a cruel fate for one so active in body and mind.† The news cast a shadow over the Verne,‡ which he had recently left. But the gloom was greater on Gallipoli. Everywhere officers of experience—priceless assets—were dead or *hors de combat*. As we have seen, the K.O.S.B. could ill afford to lose such a fine soldier as Jock McAlester, and it was with a heavy heart that Major Welch took over the command.

It was a curious day—the 28th. The 29th Division were dog tired and one-third under strength. The artillery support was incomplete. The country was unreconnoitred. Units were somewhat mixed. No one was in his expected place. General Marshall was not with his brigade but was O.C. British troops. For part of the day he was *minus* a staff. The brigades were commanded by battalion commanders, as Brig.-Gen. Napier was dead and Brig.-Gen. Hare had been wounded at the landing. Hardly a battalion had its original C.O. to lead it. And yet the most competent judges are of opinion that, with just a little more drive in the shape of reserves, Krithia and Achi Baba might have been ours.§

" During this advance (*i.e.* on Krithia) we passed on our L. a battalion of the R.N.D.,‖ who were retiring to the beach for dinners, and on the R. some French Colonials, who were lucky not to be shot by being mistaken for advancing Turks, retired through us, also rearward bound. Soon after we came on General Marshall, who told us to push on, stimulate the front troops and press on to Krithia." ¶ If there is one thing that emerges from the meagre data so far available (apart from the records of the separate units) it is that there was confusion and mixing of units throughout the

* Col. Welch.

† He passed away in 1928.

‡ The 3rd (Reserve) Battalion was quartered at the Verne Citadel, Portland, at this time.

§ Buchan's *History of the War*, vol. ii. p. 207. Official Despatch. Col. Wolley-Dod, Chief Staff Officer of Landing Force, quoted in *The Story of the 29th Division*, at p. 34.

‖ Possibly the *Drake*, who are mentioned in the despatch as attached to 87th I.B. during the absence of the K.O.S.B. and S.W.B..

¶ Col. Welch.

28 April 1915. advance. The experience of the K.O.S.B. was no exception. "By the time the remnants of the battalion reached a point about 900 yards from Krithia and could actually see into the village,—not then occupied by hostile troops and therefore to be had for the asking—the fighting troops lacked officers; in other words, leadership. They consisted of K.O.S.B. and almost every unit of the 87th and 88th I.B., and were one and all in fine fighting form. 'Thank God! here's an officer. What can we do now, Sir,' said one corporal of another unit to me. He had not seen an officer since early morning, *i.e.* soon after 8 a.m. It was a strange situation that met our eyes. Apparently on the R. the French were in full retreat. Away on the L. on the Ægean side of Gully Ravine the Borders were being held up by M.G. fire. And there were we in the L. centre, opposite the open door, but without reserves other than our own depleted D, then busy digging in, to protect our R. flank. If *one fresh brigade* had been available, far-reaching results might have been gained.* General Marshall reluctantly ordered us back in line with D and we retired there unmolested, a distance of about 1,700 yards, and dug in for the night. Fortunately the Turks were inactive, as our R. flank remained exposed till far on in the night, until reinforcements arrived from the direction of Helles. Even in the morning a reconnaissance by Com. Keyes, R.N.† discovered no Turks in front of us and a general and staff officers rode along the front unmolested." ‡

Thus the 28th was a bitter disappointment in spite of the fact that the C.-in-C. could claim quite an appreciable push forward.§ It wasn't yards or even furlongs or miles that were wanted. It was a decisive thrust at a momentarily beaten and discouraged enemy. The day had been broiling. Let us hope the K.O.S.B. were not of those who flung away their new packs. For with the night came rain and cold.|| One thing was driven home to all Borderers and many others that day, namely, that General Marshall, their brigadier, was a wonder of energy, courage, coolness, and sagacity. All accounts of the 29th April indicate a quiet day. A lateral movement of no import and one casualty is the diarist's contribution. In the small hours of the 30th the K.O.S.B. were relieved by the S.W.B. and withdrew to Gully Beach, where without shelter or sleep the remaining hours of darkness were passed. Padre Reid would probably admit that *medio tutissimus* applies to the sharing of *one* waterproof-sheet by three persons. (The C.O. and Cookson were the outsides.) Another quiet day followed, though on the 1st of May,

* This tallies with the opinion of Col. Wolley-Dod already quoted.
† The bold inquirer was nearly shot by our men on returning.
‡ Colonel Welch. § Official Despatch. || W.D..

when the battalion relieved the Borders on the L. sector about 1,000 yards on the Helles side of Y, a few bursts of shrapnel indicated that the Turks might be ranging. At any rate, about 10 or 11 p.m. the whole front was heavily shelled and the first of the famous night attacks at Helles (reminiscent to K.O.S.B. of that awful night at Y), so bravely pressed and so bravely repulsed, was launched. It was not such a touch and go business on the K.O.S.B. front as in the centre.* The line held, and when dawn rose " we could see the Turks in full retreat, in one place forming a splendid target, but the difficulties of adjusting the range for the naval guns and the absence of available land guns enabled some 3,000 Turks to escape unhurt." † 29 April 1915.

" Another revelation of the dawn was an isolated party of Turks left high and dry in a trench opposite our R. neighbours, the R.I.F.. Lieut. Paterson stole out to a point, from which his M.G. could enfilade the trench, and 132 prisoners surrendered to the R.I.F.. The line was then pushed forward 500 yards by B and a patrol even reached the Y position. Things seemed propitious when the order to advance was received at 11 a.m. and D started to leap-frog B and give a turn to the key that would unlock Achi Baba. It is stated in the War Diary that the movement was checked by M.G. fire. That, however, is not the case. On our front and on our immediate R. there was not sufficient opposition to withstand a resolute attack and the men had the *moral* for the task.

" The recall of D and, ultimately, of B (who, being well ahead and therefore more exposed, incurred casualties, including Lieut. Keltie (wounded), in the process of retiring) was the result of a counter-order to retire. It seemed to me and still seems that a chance was missed. It was when I was on my way to Brigade H.Q. to report the situation at noon that a shell burst, rendering me a casualty and my participation in the Dardanelles campaign ended." ‡

Thus in the space of a week's fighting the K.O.S.B. lost 3 C.O.s, and Capt. R. D. Whigham found himself in command.

The result of the day's fighting was—" as you were," and Achi Baba was no nearer in prospect. The night brought a less vigorous Turkish attack which was easily repulsed, and the three succeeding days passed quietly.

On the night of 5/6th May relief by the 6th L.F. of the 42nd (East Lancs.) Division announced the arrival of reinforcements and the new era. The K.O.S.B. retired to Gully Beach and stayed there till the 7th in reserve, resting.

Meanwhile the Territorials, who relieved them, had a swift intro-

* See *The Story of the 29th Division*, pp. 36 and 37.

† Col. Welch. ‡ *Ibid.*

6–8 May 1915. duction to the grim realities of war, for on the 6th began that three days' scrappy fighting, in which Australians and New Zealanders also took a gallant part, the main object of which was to lodge the French on the ridge overlooking the Kereves Dere. The success attained was modest, 600 yards in some parts and 400 yards in others, and, as no offensive on any scale was resumed till 4th June, it may be termed a rebuff. The Turks had made good use of their time and things had reached the stage when artillery preparation was necessary to enable infantry to advance in face of fire from strong points, undetectable tree-posts, bushes, and often barbed wire and entrenchments. The K.O.S.B. found progress on the 7th up the somewhat straight Gully Ravine to be impossible in face of a sweep of bullets, after they had gone some distance from the beach. They suffered 9 casualties in O.R. and halted. At about 5 p.m. the battalion side-slipped along a trench to the very edge of the bluffs with a view to turning the Turkish position at dawn on the 8th. In the end, possibly because on the 8th the battle had more of a set-piece air about it, they were withdrawn through the S.W.B. and placed in support in trenches previously occupied by themselves.

The next day, the 8th, was a comparatively light day for the K.O.S.B., still in support. At about 6 p.m. they participated in the final effort, of which such a spirited account is given by Sir Ian Hamilton in the despatch of 26th August 1915. The K.O.S.B. moved astride Gully Ravine, A and B in the wake of the R.I.F. on the landward side and C and D behind the S.W.B. on the sea side. The latter unit, despite most gallant efforts, could make no progress and had heavy casualties. On relief by the K.O.S.B. at dusk they withdrew into reserve. The former were more successful, gaining 200 yards. During the night a new trench was hurriedly dug, the extension seawards from A and B being effected by the remaining companies under cover of darkness and the protection of a party in front.

Siting a trench in the dark may easily turn out a failure, but daylight showed that the position was tenable and 400 yards in front of their old trench. After a day of comparative quiet the battalion was relieved by Ghurkas and retired to reserve trenches exposed to shell fire from Asia as well as the Peninsula in the low ground S. of Pink Farm. They had lost Lieut. Ainslie (wounded on the 8th) and 12 O.R..

For the first time Sir Ian felt his hold of the point of the Peninsula was secure, and at last the 29th were taken out of the line as far and for as long as possible. By the 12th May the whole division was at rest. The constant strain had lasted for close on three weeks. Sir Ian Hamilton issued the following Special Order :— May 1915.

"SPECIAL ORDER

"For the first time for eighteen days and nights it has been possible to withdraw the 29th Division from the fire-line. During the whole period of unprecedented strain the Division has held ground or gained it against the bullets and bayonets of the constantly reinforced forces of the foe. During the whole of the period they have been illuminating the pages of military history with their blood. The losses have been terrible ; but mingling with the deep sorrow for fallen comrades arises a feeling of pride in the invincible spirit which has enabled the survivors to triumph where ordinary troops must inevitably have failed. I tender to Major-Gen. Hunter-Weston and to his division at the same time my profound sympathy with their losses and my warmest congratulations on their achievements."

The G.O.C. addressed a remnant of 90 officers and 4,810 O.R. out of an original total of 312 officers and 12,000 O.R.. Half the force had been put out of action at the landing and on the succeeding day.

More than three weeks were spent in the back area. Resting, bathing, fatigues for the R.E. mostly to W Beach, and later on communication trenches for the 88th I.B. were the routine. It was no place for the unduly nervous. On the 11th a shell buried 5 men, 1 of whom died, through a trench falling in. The beach came in for attention, but the only casualties recorded beyond one wounded man were 8 transport horses. The first draft mentioned in the War Diary is one of 45, which arrived on the 16th. Two days later Major G. B. Stoney took over from Capt. Whigham. He was just in time, for yet another of the original landers disappeared from a bereaved battalion, when Whigham was wounded on the 25th. A month was a long term of service in Gallipoli in these days.

Gallipoli in April and May and from October to the end of the year is quite a good climate suitable for a health resort. When the K.O.S.B. had their back spell it was still very pleasant. Rain fell on the 11th and 12th and there was a cloudburst on the 25th. The country was not yet dried up, and though considerably "hacked up" did not present the dusty brown aspect which repelled later arrivals. "It was quite fair to look upon," says Col. Wolley-Dod, and proceeds to catalogue a floral, arboreal, and cereal claim to colour and variety.* The pleasantest bits in Allied hands lay

* *The Story of the 29th Division*, p. 40.

June 1915. between Fir Tree Wood and Sedd-el-Bahr ; and between Kereves Dere and the lower slopes of Hunter-Weston Hill. But the June sun put an end to all that. Soil turned to dust under the wheels of the Indian mule carts, the hooves of horses, and the foot of man. With the dust Beelzebub and his tens of thousands of legions of flies lorded it over unhappy humanity, and brought wasting plagues that would have had direr effects had not energetic measures been taken by means of strict attention to sanitation, inoculations, and water sterilization to curb the onslaught of disease. And for that discipline is necessary. Gen. de Lisle, so long G.O.C. 29th Division, impressed on the writer the significance of the fact that nearly 99 per cent. of the men of the division followed his example in submitting to a second inoculation against enteric.

To return to the flies, they were at their worst at eating times. Capt. Shaw, to whom we shall frequently refer, simply could not face food in the middle of the day. Some held and waved the "jammy piece" in one hand, beat off the flies with a handkerchief held in the other, and quickly bit the morsel. But no satisfactory solution was found to the problem of eating—or drinking—before dark.

After such drastic losses the battalion altered in outward character. The drafts were supplied from the 3rd Battalion, then at the Verne, Portland, but the officers were mostly not Borderers. Capt. A. C. Hamilton and Lieut. B. Rooney, both of the 9th Battalion K.O.S.B., were the first officers to leave Dorchester for the front and among the first, if not the first, Borderer officers to take a draft of the 3rd Battalion from the Verne to Gallipoli. Their career was lamentably short, but as they typify the men who were the backbone of the M.E.F. and played a distinguished part on the Western Front, it may be said that they were of ripe years (between 30 and 35), in good positions in business in Burma and India respectively, and trained volunteers. As soon as they appeared at Dorchester it became evident to all in the 9th Battalion that they "knew the business" and had the requisite self-confidence and habit of discipline—whether to obey or enforce. In civil life they were men of action and masters of one or more oriental languages. Of like kind was Alexander Mackintosh Shaw, of the 13th K.R.R. by commission but a Borderer by adoption and, one is tempted to hope, predilection, for he served all his foreign service with us, and when he left for France for the last time in 1916 he was dressed as, and was, a K.O.S.B.. His diary, from July 1915 to the close of June 1916, was presented by his brother Mr Norman Shaw to the 1st Battalion K.O.S.B.. Shaw had held an important post in China for years, and it is interesting to see how many similar officers he meets at

Gallipoli. Here are a few: "Jimmy Stewart of Tsientsin (mutual astonishment)," "Chater of Hong-kong (a Cameronian serving with 1st K.O.S.B.)," "Walker of the S.W.B. . . . I hope to have a chat with him about Peking." "Met J. A. Robertson of Peking, who is in the 2nd S.W.B.". Not an 87th man who had known him could ever forget Lieut. A. W. Fraser, D.S.O., of the Borders, an African administrator, who was prepared to leave his dignified post and serve and die on 1st July 1916 as a 2nd Lieut.. Such men rendered very valuable service when the supply of trained regular officers gave out.

4 June 1915.

While we are thus discursive, the 4th of June is drawing near. As will be read in the next Book, great things were expected of the 4th of June among the talkers of Mudros.

A general attack was planned from sea to sea. It had, perforce, to be frontal. The French were on the R.; next them came the R.N.D.; and then the 42nd (E. Lancs.) Division. The 29th were on the extreme L., and were flanked by the Ægean. Artillery preparation was necessary. At 8 a.m. the bombardment began. Such heavy artillery as were available poured a steady, deliberate rain of shells on the Turkish positions. H.M.S. *Swiftsure* and *Vengeance's* shooting was a wonderful sight. At 11.20 a.m. an abrupt stop was made, as a feint for ten minutes, during which the men ostentatiously fixed bayonets and cheered. Firing was then resumed, *i.e.* at 11.30, and became intenser until "on the stroke of noon the artillery increased their range and along the whole line the infantry fixed bayonets and advanced." *

The parlous state of the 29th will be gathered from the composition of the assaulting troops. They belonged mainly to the 88th I.B. under Brig.-Gen. W. Doran, C.B.. But there were troops on loan from the other brigades. The 86th was temporarily broken up. The Irish Fusilier battalions went to the 87th I.B.. The English (Royal and Lancs.) were attached to the 85th. Thus, when the K.O.S.B. was ordered to assist the 88th and formed up in trenches in Fir-Tree Copse, they found themselves with the R.F. on their R. and the 4th Worcesters on their L., and they knew that beyond, on the extreme L., were the 5th Ghurkas and 14th Sikhs of the 29th (Indian) I.B..

When the moment came—at noon—for going over the top, A and B were greeted with a withering fire and suffered badly. No Turkish trench was reached at this stage. The most advanced men reached the shelter of a small nullah, which was still 100 yards from a hostile trench. In spite of the work in May in sapping †

* Official Despatch.

† *Ibid.*

4 June 1915. with a view to come within rushing distance of the front trenches, No Man's Land was too wide. The fire seemed to be oblique, particularly from the L., where there was a redoubt. The advance of the Indian troops eased the situation soon after 12.30 p.m.. The welcome sight of a Sikh's turban in the redoubt was followed by an advance of the Worcesters, and then it was that Capt. Ogilvy, O.C. C and D on this occasion, seized his chance, cleared No Man's Land by a series of platoon rushes, and, after crossing a network of trenches, including one we may call H11, reached H12 (one beyond), and began to consolidate, touch being got with the Worcesters on the L. and the R.F. on the R.. The Borderers sent back 60 prisoners and a M.G. (Hotchkiss).

Later on in the day some of D were actually in the communication trench leading back into yet another Turkish line. They charged with the bayonet, and claimed some 60 victims from among the Turks massed there. A company of the Essex Regiment, who had already done yeoman service to the K.O.S.B. and R.F. in consolidating under fire, held this communication trench for some hours, but in the end the line which it was decided to hold at all cost was H12. But it was not to be! The position seemed fairly secure, although the L. flank was somewhat in the air when day came on the 5th. Gen. Doran visited the K.O.S.B. in the afternoon about 3 p.m., and before nightfall A and D relieved C. It was in the small hours of the 6th that Turks, without being fired on, but through a pure misunderstanding, were able to turn the flank of the K.O.S.B. detachment, then under Capt. Cunningham, and hurl them on to H11, in which C was. There they rallied, and eventually made good the line. We draw a veil over the toils and perils of the next few days of the defensive.

The net gains of the battle of the 4th June were paltry all along the 4,000 yards of British front, and the 29th were hampered by uncut wire. But if the K.O.S.B. had only the nearest Turkish trench to their credit in the end of the day, they had fought so as to earn a message from Gen. Hunter-Weston for their good work by a gallant advance and tenacious hold.* The casualty list shows the havoc among officers since the campaign began. One reads with a pang of another captain lost to the battalion, this time Capt. J. B. Hartley. The C.O.'s report on the 5th is silent as regards Lieut. Grogan, but the official list of dead officers states that that valuable transport officer also fell.†

* Sir William Marshall's warm tribute to the K.O.S.B. in this battle will be found on p. 81 of his *On Four Fronts*, 1929. He says they "put up a brilliant show."

† On 4/6/15. Official Death Roll.

CHAPTER V

THE BATTLE OF GULLY RAVINE

SEVEN weeks of almost incessant fighting had impaired the vitality of the 29th Division. If the 87th I.B. had met with less crushing disasters than the other two brigades, it had suffered such depletion in officers and particularly senior officers, that it required nursing into offensive efficiency. Fortunately the right men were at hand. Under the supervision of Brig.-Gen. Marshall and Major Lucas recovery would in any event have been a certainty, granted the requisite repose. But in the last days of the battle of the 4th of June there appeared a new G.O.C. for the 29th in the shape of Major-Gen. Beauvoir de Lisle, C.B., D.S.O., who had commanded the 1st Cavalry Division in France in the touch-and-go days of the October 1914–April 1915 campaigning, and in that capacity had had under his command for a few momentous days or hours at Messines the 2nd K.O.S.B.. He took a grip of things at Helles from the day when he took over, and the K.O.S.B., like others, found themselves the mark of unsparing criticism and insatiable demands. But without knowing it they were profiting all the time. The trenches left much to be desired. They were shallow, and had no proper communications to the rear—disadvantages that told the more in the close fighting that followed the set-back of the Turks, fighting in which the British were at the additional handicap of having a few poor amateur bombs with which to compete against ample supplies of very efficient Turkish bombs. It actually cost the division more casualties to hold the conquered territory between the 28th of June and the 5th of July than to win it on the 28th. It was a stirring and strenuous time under worsening climatic conditions. The corpses gave out a terrible smell, which seemed to cleave to the very dust, and one of the duties of the infantry was the nightly burial parade and hunt for equipment. The War Diary discloses a visit of the G.O.C. to K.O.S.B. trenches as early as the 10th of June, and the period between that day and the 28th contains an entry of hard work on front and support line and back

June 1915.

28 June 1915. areas, *e.g.* beach fatigues and terracing into the cliffs for shelters, the only relaxations being bathing and church parades, which were held on three successive Sundays, somewhat of a variety in those times. From the 12th to the 17th and from the 23rd to the 27th (Sunday) the battalion was in bivouac on the beach. Otherwise they were in the front or support lines. Capt. C. A. G. O. Murray returned to the battalion from Divisional Cyclists on the 15th. On the 19th, while in support, the K.O.S.B. suffered those wasting casualties, so typical of Gallipoli, from Turkish gun-fire, viz. 12 O.R. (4 k. and 8 w.). They stood to, but the S.W.B. beat off daylight Turkish attacks, and the Borderers were never called on to join the fray.

The last major operation of the 29th at Helles was tactical rather than strategic. It marked the definite recognition of siege warfare rather than the inception of new aims there or elsewhere. In its purpose it was more precise than the subsequent holding battle of 12th July, which was the Gallipoli Swan Song of Gen. Hunter-Weston. To the regret of all, the commander of the VIII. Corps received a sunstroke which placed him *hors de combat* until the following spring. He was evacuated sick on 24th July. He dearly loved the 29th, and not least the K.O.S.B., for whom there was always a kindly corner in his heart. The inception and execution of the Battle of Gully Ravine are enough to explain the warmth of the tribute paid to him by the C.-in-C. in his despatch of 26th August 1915.

As the result of the early June fighting "the front was now in the form of a semicircle with the horns flung well back, and our business was to straighten it." * Owing to M.E.F. deficiency in artillery, it was necessary that the straightening should be set about in two definite phases—French and British—to enable the latter to draw on the more generous gun and ammunition resources of their Ally. On the 21st the French, under the famous Gen. Gouraud (Gen. d'Amade's successor), won about 600 yards † of the Kereves Ravine. The improvement on the R. was sufficient to justify the British operation a week later. For one thing, observation was gained for the French artillery. The sector involved ran from the Krithia road (*i.e.* to Sedd-el-Bahr, the only "road" there was) to the sea astride that Gully Ravine, which had played such a sinister part in the history of our battalion, but the idea was to confine the attack to the sea zone and both sides of the Ravine, and pivot from a definite point about a mile inland. This meant an advance of 1,000 yards along the bluffs into the fifth of five lines

* Buchan, vol. ii. p. 215. † *Ibid.*

of Turkish trenches. Towards the R. the distance naturally decreased. This, however, did not seriously complicate matters, as the Turkish trench system lacked depth opposite the R.. Two lines were all that had to be taken there. The Turks had dreaded the turning of Krithia from the sea rather than a frontal assault; hence the concentration of work on the former sector. Besides the 29th Division and the 29th (Indian) Brigade, the 156th I.B. of the 52nd (Lowland) Division were engaged on the R.. The bombardment represented the maximum of which the Allies were capable, but was not of long duration. From 9 a.m. until 10.20 a.m. the "Heavies" played on the first three lines of trenches. (As was appropriate to an amphibious force, the naval guns did great execution. H.M.S. *Talbot*, along with T.B. *Scorpion* and *Wolverine*, stood in close to the shore and made admirable shooting. The first named had 12-inch guns, and fired ounce shrapnel bullets in enfilade over the area of dispersion per shell of 12,000 square yards. There was also a systematic, indirect M.G. barrage—a commonplace in the Western fighting. Small ammunition was not so scarce, and the front Turkish system was literally sown or plastered with bullets from ranges on both sides of 2,000 yards.) The F.A. then opened on the wire protecting the first two lines and fired for twenty minutes. At 10.40 the Heavies resumed for twenty minutes, and at 11 a.m. the infantry, except one unit, which had already pounced on a special part, went over the top, conspicuous to observers through having triangular bits of biscuit tins tied on to their packs, which flashed in the brilliant sunshine.

Coming to the K.O.S.B., they were (along with the R.I.F. on their L.) in support of the S.W.B. on the L. or sea side of the gully. On the other side of the gully the Borders were dedicated to the capture of a fort known as the Boomerang, and their assault preceded those elsewhere by a quarter of an hour. They literally engulfed it on three sides, and were ready for a further advance in the afternoon. It is disappointing that no account dealing intimately with the battalion's adventures has come to hand. We know that, the S.W.B. having duly taken two lines of trenches, the K.O.S.B. passed through them and captured a third and made it good as a fire trench, that the operation was carried out quickly, and that seven hours or ten later they side-slipped so as to be partly on one side and partly on the other of the nullah. The casualties are stated to be eight officers and 223 O.R.. The Brigade Report, however, sheds a ray of light. The objective trench was mostly roofed. Now, one may dash across a fire zone and plunge out of sight with comparatively small loss. Dash was the teaching Sir Ian was constantly inculcating. The R.I.F.

28 June 1915. on the L. had few casualties; but the dash of the K.O.S.B. was wasted when the expected shelter was amissing. The search for entrances was the very time for officers' casualties, and none but three escaped unscathed. The following regimental officers are included in the Official Death Roll of Officers—Capt. A. C. Hamilton and Lieut. B. M. Rooney, both of the 9th K.O.S.B., both deeply regretted. The other fatal casualties must have belonged to other regiments. But perhaps a fuller account is more appropriate to a battalion history. The main facts stand out. The K.O.S.B. did their bit in one of the most striking successes of the campaign, for when the 87th I.B. had taken its objective, the 86th passed through them and advanced, supported by the Indians, to the celebrated Fusilier Bluff, the farthest objective. Moreover, the ground thus won was held until the final evacuation against the most violent, repeated, and persistent attacks of the Turks during the next few days. As soon as consolidation began the Turks started a lively M.G. fire, which, in the K.O.S.B. sector, wounded an R.E. officer and 4 men. All of these were rescued one after the other by L.-Corp. Thomas Ardie under fire all the time. Prior to this war he would have won the V.C.; bravery can go no farther. A previous attempt had already been made and had failed when he volunteered. The limited objectives only serve to whet the appetite for what might have been had there been another division in reserve. Once again at a very vital point the fixed Turkish defences were pierced and the open lay beyond, but to no purpose. This was the action that extorted the adjective "incomparable" from the C.-in-C. for the 29th Division. "In my nine years of war," wrote Gen. de Lisle, "I have seen many thrilling sights, but not one compared to the 28th June. Its success was well-nigh complete, and the troops appeared to move with the assurance of victory. I could see every company, and even every man, as the tins shone like heliographs." * It was a great day, but it has its dark side. For some reason the artillery support was confined to the 29th sector and part of the 156th I.B. were starved. As Col. Thompson has pointed out, corpses cannot advance, and masses of the Royal Scots and Cameronians were corpses and never reached the hostile trenches in their sector, which lay between the Boomerang and that plain N. of Fir Tree Wood known as Worcester Flat. All 29th accounts pay tribute to the valour of the 156th, particularly the Royal Scots, who were nearest them. The K.O.S.B. seem to have had a less trying time in the counter-battles than, say, the R.I.F. from the 29th June to the 7th July inclusive. The gully was sufficiently concealed from the Turks to enable salvage

* *The Story of the 29th Division*, p. 49.

July 1915.

work and corpse burning to be carried on. Otherwise the K.O.S.B. were toiling at new saps day and night. Wastage in man-power was less severe than it was seawards. On 7th July the K.O.S.B. withdrew to the beach, and at last embarked for a true rest on Lemnos on the 11th. They took with them seven new officers—all New Army—when they embarked at V Beach for Mudros in trawlers, and reached Lemnos without mishap. One of the newcomers was Capt. A. M. Shaw, who commanded B, except for a short interval, until his death on 1st July 1916.

CHAPTER VI *

SUVLA

Aug. 1915. — WHILE the 4th and 5th K.O.S.B. were being grimly introduced to real war on 12th July, the 1st were camping and changing camps, marching, drilling, bathing, participating in brigade sports with distinction, and holding a concert. Stoney was relieved of the command by Lieut.-Col. Quentin Agnew, D.S.O., of the R.S.F., on the 17th, but returned to it when the latter held a short time command of the 87th I.B..

On the afternoon of the 21st sweepers took the K.O.S.B. back to the battlefield. In the small hours of the 22nd they landed at Lancashire Landing and became cave-dwellers in the bluffs S. of Gully Beach. After six days' road-making the battalion found itself in the same sector as before—namely, W. of Gully Ravine. It is clear from the War Diary that the battalion was unaffected by the demonstration in force on 6th August on the 88th's front, by which the three regular battalions of that brigade lost 60 per cent. of very valuable effectives of 2,500. Indeed the only "incident" of July and half of August was the mine explosion on the 18th of August, laid and fired with a view to pushing forward the barricades in Gully Ravine. The mine had been laid by the R.E. opposite the sector held by B (Capt. Shaw). Very short notice was given, and at one time Capt. Worsley (C) was warned that his company might also be required. In the end B alone was engaged. The explosion was to take place at 11.30 p.m., and when things had subsided the crater was to be rushed, made defensible, and from it the front Turkish trench (called H13C) was to be bombed and stormed. In the darkness a sap was to be dug from the British front line to the crater and on to the new acquisition. "The mine went off terrifically at 11.30 and a wonderful scene followed. It was not far enough away and shook us up. I had one man's leg broken by falling rocks and many injured. Short and his men have never been seen since, nor any of the men who followed. The whole front was swept by a terrific fire from M.G., so after sticking it for a bit I got the remnant of two fine

* See Map 5.

platoons out of action, losing 1 officer, 2 N.C.O.s, and 35 O.R. killed or missing." * The officer was 2nd Lieut. W. J. Short. The two trenches were only 30 yards apart, and as the mine was out of place and only injured our parapet and not the enemy's, the assault was foredoomed to failure. In addition, another subaltern, 2nd Lieut. Saxton, hit slightly on the head, developed septic poisoning with abnormal swelling. One of Worsley's officers, Capt. I .F. S. Grainger of the Black Watch, who had accompanied Shaw from England, was hit through the lung by a bullet and died on 12th August. "I had many chats with him ; he was a good fellow " † is his epitaph. Aug. 1915.

On the 16th sudden orders came to sail for Suvla. Not that the 29th were bound for any inspiring quest. They were to stiffen the backs of the shaken novices whose somewhat clumsy and ill-guided attempt at a break through had ended in definite failure. About a week's ineffective fighting has had dedicated to it as much despatch and report writing as the whole of the preceding three months' fighting and the policy that led to it. Here it will suffice to say that Suvla Bay lies some 16 miles up the Ægean from Tekke Burnu, the W. cape of the Peninsula, in a direct line and about 7 miles N. of Anzac Cove, and that Sir Ian's plan was to drive S. 8 miles to a dominating hill 4 miles E. of Anzac, and from there "grip the waist of the Peninsula " ‡ where it is less than 8 miles wide and *inside* the Narrows close to Maidos. The force employed included 3 divisions of the New Army and two territorial divisions, which we shall meet in the next Book, the 53rd (Welsh) and the 54th (East Anglian) then doing great things. But on the Peninsula they shared the fate of the 42nd and 52nd and got more knocks than their efforts merited.

Into this depressed and depressing area the 29th Division arrived under command of Gen. Marshall. Gen. de Lisle had just taken over command of the entire Suvla force, *i.e.* the IX. Corps, and the only operation of importance in which the division took part was that on the 21st of August. The 87th I.B., under its former Brigade Major, Capt. Lucas, landed at Suvla Bay early on the 17th. It was a superior harbour to any other on the Peninsula but exposed to S.W. winds. Another advantage was the temporary absence of flies.§ The immediate hinterland was flat and suggested open warfare, and down the coast the Anzac Ridge was visible. The 18th and 19th were quiet days for the K.O.S.B., and Shaw noticed that quite close to the dried-up salt lake by the seaside, sweet drinkable water could be obtained by digging in the sand (which, incidentally, was un-

* Capt. Shaw's Diary. The W.D. statistics of loss are 2nd Lieut. Short and 8 O.R. missing, 20 wounded, 9 killed.

† *Ibid.* ‡ Official Despatch. § Capt. Shaw's Diary.

Aug. 1915. suitable material for trenches). He also witnessed the landing of the fine Mounted Division, dismounted on this occasion, commanded by Sir William Peyton * on the 18th. The 86th I.B. arrived on the 19th and the 88th on the 20th. By no possibility could much be expected of the latter after their terrible losses on the 6th. A small eminence near the bay yielded the following view E.S.E.. The lumpish, scrubby "Chocolate Hill," an isolated projection of the Anafarta Hills 3 miles from the sea, behind the dry lake, rose 170 feet above the plain. To the L. of it, something over 1,000 yards E.N.E. of it, *i.e.* farther off, was Hill 70, *alias* Scimitar Hill (about 230 feet high), S. of which and behind Chocolate Hill the ground rose to Hills 112 and 100 before dropping steeply to the plain to the S..

The operation was intended to improve the defensive position of the IX. Corps by the capture of Hill 100 (the back part of which was called Ismail Ogla Tepe, and was over 400 feet above sea-level) and the dominating heights between it and Scimitar Hill, as well as that eminence too. Chocolate Hill afforded the only natural cover for forming up. It was therefore fortunate for the 87th I.B. that they had time to dig some sort of shelter trenches behind the single fire trench on the night of the 19th. At 7.45 p.m. on the 20th the K.O.S.B. left their trenches in sand dunes along the bay and headed the brigade in the advance to the front line. They were followed by the R.I.F., the S.W.B., and the Borders in that order. The K.O.S.B. relieved some Sherwoods and Buffs of the 54th Division, who "looked a fine lot but lacked leadership." The remaining battalions dug in behind the R.I.F., the first to advance on the morrow, in two lines in support, and the others in reserve behind the R.I.F. in greater depth but the same width. The 86th were not forward in time to dig in, and such natural protection as the reverse slopes gave was all they had to rely on when the counter-bombardment fell.

The battle of the 21st was a complete failure, except as a proof that the British race is not yet played out, and the K.O.S.B. were fortunate in not having to attack. The plan was this: After a short bombardment the 87th I.B. were to advance from the N. half of Chocolate Hill, straight for Scimitar Hill, and the 86th were to skirt the southern slopes of Scimitar Hill and head straight for Hill 112. Beyond them the 11th Division were to march from trenches S. of Chocolate Hill, so as to turn Hill 100 from the S.. It is difficult to say which was the most formidable task. Bad luck continued to dog the M.E.F.. The 21st of August was hazy and visibility was bad. As the bulk of the gun support came from the navy this was a serious drawback. The bombardment, such as it

* G.O.C. Scottish Command in 1929.

Aug. 1915.

was, lasted only half an hour before the 11th Division went over the top at 3 p.m.. The K.O.S.B. poured their maximum fire output on to trenches between Scimitar Hill and Hill 112. The 86th and 87th did not attack till 3.30, although the assaulting battalion of the 87th, the R.I.F., advanced at 3.5 400 yards under the protection of the barrage, and lay ready to storm. When the time came they went like stags; but as their gallantry brought them to the skyline they were swept off by fire from all directions and of all kinds, and this was repeated until they were past further effort, and came down under cover of the slopes. The Borders, the supporting battalion, were no more successful soon after 4 p.m., although equally gallant. A third attempt by the S.W.B. about 5.30 also failed, and it implies no want of regimental faith to feel convinced that, had the K.O.S.B. made a fourth attempt, they too would have shared the same fate. But they were not called on, nor were the 88th after an equally decisive failure on the part of the 86th I.B., owing to the scrub on Chocolate Hill going on fire and to a terrific counter-bombardment.

"We are reserves, so I got up near the M.G., and had a perfect view of the whole fight. Casualties very heavy, but men splendid. A feature was the advance of the Yeomanry Division across the open.* A fine lot. Glorious well set-up youth of England marching straight for the enemy under heavy fire quite undismayed—for the first time too." † The K.O.S.B. lost one officer, Capt. C. C. H. Hamilton ‡ of the Cameronians, killed, and of O.R. had 25 casualties.

The night was spent in getting in as many of the wounded as possible—a heartrending experience. By the time morning broke the attackers on the slopes of Scimitar Hill had withdrawn through the K.O.S.B., and the positions were as before the attack.

The next important military event in the history of the M.E.F. was the evacuation of Suvla and Anzac. From a human point of view the most impressive event of Suvla was the great storm of November, which caused more suffering than any work of man during the war. In neither of these had the K.O.S.B. any part. As we shall see, the blizzard was bad enough at Helles in all conscience, but it was nothing to what was endured further N.. The five weeks at Suvla that followed the battle of Scimitar Hill admit of curt treatment. They were spent in work on the trenches, and, as the soil was rocky, the work-parties were largely under the R.E. and

* This took place at 5.50 p.m., and is world famous.

† Capt. Shaw's Diary.

‡ Henderson-Hamilton was a famous Oxford athlete on the running track. Sadly enough, his only brother, James, of the Black Watch, was killed at Loos within six weeks.

Aug.–Sept. 1915.

were frequently employed in blasting. Neither Gen. de Lisle nor his G.S.O.1, Lieut.-Col. C. G. Fuller, R.E., were satisfied with anything short of the best; and as the idea of improving the situation by an offensive-defensive was abandoned, trench improvement was the sole guarantee of security.

On the 24th August Lieut.-Gen. Sir J. Byng took over command of the IX. Corps, and Gen. de Lisle returned to the 29th Division. On the promotion of Gen. Marshall to a division he was succeeded by his former Brigade Major, who enjoyed the temporary rank of Brig.-Gen., C. H. T. Lucas. It was during this period that officers began to appear from the 9th (Reserve) Battalion. It did not follow that those who were first to leave Stobs, to which the 9th moved from Dorchester in June, were first at the front. Officers were apt to be marooned in Lemnos, bereft of their drafts (frequently taken from them by officers of other units), and summoned to the 1st Battalion when least expecting it. No attempt is made at a catalogue, but it may bring back memories to some Borderers to recall the arrival at Suvla of many subalterns, including B. Mellon, who was one of the first two officers to leave after Hamilton and Rooney; E. J. Long, a brawny Canadian from Ontario, who did splendid work in France as a transport officer; Victor Gordon, whose recent death came as a shock to his friends here and in Newfoundland, of which he was Agent General; D. C. Cayley, one of the original members of the 9th, so to speak; W. Dickie—afterwards killed on 1st July 1916—who was duty personified; and G. M. Jenkins, also one of the 9th's earliest subalterns. The 3rd Battalion was represented by Rowley and two Muirs. N. Macleod was fresh from four months of Sandhurst. A. N. Lewis, a veteran of the 2nd Battalion, was a survivor of Hill 60, and had come through much and had worse to go through. And then Shaw's diary mentions James Oliphant, the Scoto-New Zealander, who was afterwards 87th I.B. intelligence officer. What with drafts and good officer material, the K.O.S.B. were in a fair way to take their turn in the next offensive. The health of the troops was not satisfactory. Flies began to come at Suvla also, and Shaw mentions large bluebottles with a note of disgust. Stomachic troubles were rife, and energy seemed to leave those attacked, and not the best will in the world could stand up against the lassitude and collapse. For instance, out of 126 casualties in the first nineteen days of September, 101 O.R. were admitted sick to hospital. Out of four killed, one—2nd Lieut. J. H. Brameld—was shot through the head on 19th September while out in front with a working party (a calamity less often recorded than one might suppose, considering that the constant cracking of bullets was one of the distinguishing marks of a Gallipoli as opposed to a Western night). He was reverently buried by Capt. Shaw. Aug.–Sept. 1915.

An all too short visit to the attractive island of Imbros from the 24th to the end of September came as a pleasant break in the monotony. As an instance of the strange uses to which vessels were put, as compared with their pre-war use, may be mentioned the use of a pilgrim ship for Mohammedans, called the *Prince Abbas*, as a ferry-transport from Suvla to Mudros. One of the steamers —a paddle-boat—that took some of the 29th from Imbros to Mudros on 9th January 1916 was a Bristol Channel pleasure cruiser. But their war services all pale before that of the *River Clyde*.

While at Imbros, the G.H.Q. of the M.E.F., the 1st K.O.S.B. had the honour of being inspected by the C.-in-C..

CHAPTER VII

THE EVACUATION OF CAPE HELLES

Sept.–Oct. 1915.

Just as the 29th had been sent to stimulate the Kitchener and Territorial troops at Suvla, so the 87th afterwards passed under command of Major-Gen. the Hon. Herbert Lawrence, afterwards Gen. Sir Herbert Lawrence, Chief of the General Staff from the Doullens Conference at the end of March 1918 to the end of the war, to give the depleted and poorly reinforced sufferers of the 52nd Division the numerical semblance of a division and provide a training school for the instruction of young officers. Even before the 87th left Suvla mention is made of the new cricket-ball bomb with a time fuse, which was a vast improvement on the jam-pots, if less ideal than the Mills which superseded it. Trench discipline, sanitation, conduct of patrols, F.G. courts-martial, as well as bombing and sniping were branches of military knowledge in which the 87th and the 1st K.O.S.B. had something to impart of value. Writing of bombs brings one naturally to a future C.O. of the 1st Battalion, Lieut.-Col. J. Sherwood Kelly, afterwards V.C., of the 10th Norfolks, who had fought in the South African War. In Shaw's diary for 23rd July this entry occurs: "A new major has joined us." The new major was a Herculean giant of Irish-South African origin, with quite a remarkable disregard for danger and a gift for bombing, as for all branches of hand-to-hand combat. But more than that, his interest in ballistics extended to catapults, to obtain greater range. Such things would have been out of date on the Western Front, but on the Peninsula the catapult came into its own. There the aerial pig, *alias* "crapaud volant," *alias* "demoiselle" of the French, and a smaller Japanese mortar were rarities, and the only rivals to the catapult were the Garland grenade and the stove-pipe mortar, which, by the force of a cartridge exploded by means of a hand trigger on a rifle butt, propelled a cylinder (rather like a half-pound tin of tobacco) and lit a fuse about 4 inches long. The range of this ingenious but only fairly reliable weapon rarely exceeded 120 yards. The bold major won the soubriquet of "Bomb"

Sept.–Oct. 1915.

Kelly, and excelled in " stunts," on occasions alarming his own side. For a time he was requisitioned to command a bombing school. He chafed at that, but Gen. de Lisle knew a fighting man, and his day was bound to come. It may be added that he was what is called in Scotland a " character," and possessed a strikingly vigorous if not specially wealthy vocabulary. The old routine had hardly commenced when a dreadful calamity befel the K.O.S.B.. Their C.O. and the orderly officer for the day, 2nd Lieut. J. D. Mill, were killed on 15th October by the direct explosion of a shell from Asia. Capt. Shaw had been half-buried hard by one minute before and he describes the gruesome sight that met his eyes. The writer well remembers the stunning effect of the news. The following characterisation will show what a loss the battalion suffered. " He lived for the regiment, which was his sole thought ; a strict martinet and very severe at times. Yet all respected him and most feared him too. Stoney was so tremendously energetic and strong, though a small, delicate-featured, bronzed man, that we miss him exceedingly." * It may be added that he was a professional soldier, and a master of his profession. It was not only the hero of the landing and the disciplinarian, the calm, dignified, spick and span British officer, it was the man who knew the army machine in and out, who would see justice done to his officers, and who had the gift of clear exposition that was most missed. If the Egyptian Army could have spared him his war career was assured, had he lived. But Egypt kept a tight grip, as Capt. Worsley found when he had to return in September after two months' service with the battalion. Capt. Cookson as C.O. carried on until word came that Major Kelly was to be C.O..

The change in manner and method affected more the officers than the men. For the latter the regimental system, " the machine," and the fact that they were brought in contact with officers and N.C.O.s of the platoon or the company only, except on occasions, made life run on much the same. The former, having adjusted their lives to one type of C.O., had to settle down to work in with and serve a very different type. It was soon accomplished, and the K.O.S.B. maintained their reputation throughout the Kelly interregnum.

To revert to the battalion story, reinforcements continued to arrive. 2nd Lieuts. C. A. Moreton of the 1st and R. N. C. Marsh (afterwards M.G. Officer and killed at Englebelmer early in July 1916), K. S. Robertson, D. B. Dempster, J. S. Bell, J. D. Mill, R. H. Pringle (afterwards a Staff Officer), and J. D. Davidson, all of the

* Capt. Shaw's Diary.

Oct.–Nov. 1915.

3rd, were added by the 9th, and on the latter day a draft of 400 O.R. also were of the party. A draft of 150 and the writer also turned up late on the 9th. The weather was still warm enough for bathing and garments were still light, and rain, though tropical in force when it did fall, was the exception rather than the rule. The supply of flies was still ample. The newcomers were initiated to the front by attachment to the Borders, then in the line in the sector nearest to the French, which contained the Horseshoe and the Couronne. The comparatively uneventful last three months of the Dardanelles campaign, passed over by Mr. Masefield in a few pages of his masterpiece, seem to warrant a broad touch and a drop into the first person singular. It is difficult to feel how long ago it all was, so vivid is the impression of that weird *angulus terrarum* and the life we lived on it. I was for most of the time 52nd Divisional Trench Mortar Officer, but saw something of the life of the battalion at work, on fatigues, and in the line. It was not in the least a disagreeable life, and there was a camaraderie—the fruit of a sense of common peril—which was not so conspicuous in France. The staff of the 52nd Division seemed to be able to extract the needful amount of work with the minimum of friction. General Lawrence inspired confidence and affection. The Corps Commander, a future G.O.C. Scottish Command, was the deservedly popular Sir Francis Davies. The 87th Brigade functioned with a flawless efficiency, but there was often time for a rubber of bridge. The K.O.S.B. might have had a quiet time in the trenches, but Col. Kelly was in his element nursing the fighting spirit, and entries in the War Diary show that on the 9th and 10th of November continuous catapult bombing day and night seriously damaged the parapet of a Turkish trench. Hardly had the great storm passed when the bombers were at it again despite intense frost. In December in the Worcester Barricade sector more than 750 bombs or Garland grenades were expended on making life uncomfortable for " Johnnie." When the battalion was in Corps Reserve on 16th November, 2nd Lieut. Bell and eight bombers were lent to Lieut.-Col. Peebles of the 7th Royal Scots and materially helped them to retain the trenches won on the 15th in W. Krithia Nullah. The return of Lieut. and Q.M. Simpson on the 24th October, and the arrival of Capt. A. Pollock of the 1st R.S.F., considerably strengthened the battalion. The former was adjutant throughout the remainder of the campaign and Cookson was second in command, while Capt. Pollock took over B, Shaw having been evacuated sick on 24th November. It so happened on the 12th of November that when I was buying wine at the " Intendance " at Sedd-el-Bahr, I saw a small group of

French and British officers of distinction saluting a tall man who had just embarked in a boat. That's very like Kitchener, I thought, and dismissed the subject from my mind. Sure enough it was Kitchener, and his visit had momentous consequences. But I doubt if more than a very few thought of evacuation. Rather the thought was that Kitchener would see to it that more guns and more men were sent, and that in the spring a push would be made. Nov.–Dec. 1915.

"And now the storm-blast came and he was tyrannous and strong." Such rain as there had been in October and November came in plumps and was followed by spells of sunshine. Occasionally storms of violence occurred. One wrecked the pier at Lancashire Landing, in the rebuilding of which Lieut. B. Mellon, a mining engineer, and a gang of K.O.S.B. assisted. Another held up the landing of a draft for more than twelve hours, while they bumped about in the *Ermine*. But they were nothing to the blizzard. It began with rain on the 26th. I recall thankfully that I had only just fastened a fragile but efficient waterproof sheet on the roof of my dugout when the huge deluge began to fall. By the next morning the rain had turned to snow. The wind blew with terrific velocity at a piercingly cold temperature. All day long on the 27th the snow fell, and on the 28th we all woke to a white world and a cold that rivalled the top of Ben Nevis in a winter storm. The battalion escaped comparatively lightly in the way of frost-bite casualties, as there were less than 20 cases. But it must have been a chilly business relieving the R.I.F. on the 28th, and no doubt the best way to get warm was to make it hot for the Turks. An appropriate message reached the 1st K.O.S.B. from their comrades in the battle of Gully Ravine, the 156th I.B., on St. Andrew's Day—"Lang may your lum reek." Another welcome St. Andrew's Day greeting was from the VIII. Corps Commander to all ranks of the 52nd Division. He knew his Scotland in and out and had found a wife there.

The news of the evacuation of Suvla and Anzac on 18/19th December took our breath away, but it did not suggest to the simple-minded that a like attempt would be made at Helles. The return of the 86th and 88th I.B. to Helles and of the 87th I.B. to the 29th Division conveyed rather the idea of stiffening the line, and there was an announcement that the VIII. Corps was going to be relieved by the IX. and that the 29th were to get quit of the Peninsula altogether. It came therefore rather as a shock to be told that we were to try and bring off successfully the trick so successfully practised at Suvla and Anzac. It seemed so unlikely that a second escape could succeed after the first. The weather had been

Jan. 1916. — favourable on the first occasion, but it broke immediately thereafter and remained broken. The alternative of hanging on was unattractive. Since the advent of Bulgaria into the war on the German side shelling had been considerably severer, and the amount of attention lavished on the beaches indicated that the Turks had suspicions—it might be of an impending evacuation or reinforcement. Hostile aeroplanes were very active in reconnaissance and bomb-dropping. Raids too were frequent all along the front. Christmas Day was the end of the cheerful period. After the capture of GIIA* on the 30th, when there was time to look about one the emptiness of the place had something uncanny about it.

On the 1st and 2nd of January 1916 our trench mortars were conveyed to the beach, the unused few rounds of hoarded ammunition were flung into a slimy hole and we all returned to our various units. The 1st K.O.S.B. were taking the situation very calmly, and work and life in the trenches, if alert, was much as usual but for one striking change. Mention has been made more than once of the rattle of musketry that went on all night and night after night. Orders were given to reduce the volume of rounds, until for a week before zero day there were long spells when not a shot would be fired. The Turks at first kept up their fire, but gradually fell in with our ways and the long nights would be still but for an occasional crack from a rifle. It was this standard of fire and of flares that was initiated on the last night by a mechanical device. A rifle or flare pistol was wired in a fixed position. A tin was filled with sand and hung by a loop of string from the trigger of the rifle or pistol. The sand weighed six pounds. Above the tin was suspended another tin containing water. Through a carefully bored hole in the water-tin water dripped at the rate of 1 lb. weight in fifteen minutes. The "pull" was seven pounds. Therefore each rifle with six pounds of sand would go off in a quarter of an hour. By using less sand more time would be taken.

The work was also different. It consisted of blocking up all trenches unnecessary for the evacuation. There was such a ramified network of trenches that it would be easy to go astray. Columns of single file are prone to break up into disconnected fragments, and, if possible, the path to the ships had to be made fool-proof.

On the afternoon of the 7th the Turks laid down a heavy barrage on the 53rd Division sector on the L. of the 29th sector, which was round about Worcester Barricade. It looked like business and we all stood to, when the cheery voice of a Lancastrian sung out: "They

* See Book III. chap. i.

ain't a coomin' over. They're a poopin' off their roifles in the air." It was a feeler to see whether we were still holding the place in force. The battalion suffered only one casualty, one man wounded. It was the last sign of aggression on the part of the Turks. Jan. 1916.

The actual evacuation was carried out on 8/9th January (the night of Saturday–Sunday) in seven parties. Capt. Ainslie took the first party, 200 men of A, out of the Eski line at 5 p.m. The last parties, composed of picked men of B under Capt. Pollock and D under Capt. Malcolm of the 11th Black Watch, were to rendezvous at a particular spot and leave the fire trench at 11.45. Watches were carefully synchronized. The M.G. were withdrawn at 5 and 7.35 p.m. respectively under Lieut. Lewis and Capt. Chater. In minor details the withdrawal to the beach of the 1st K.O.S.B. did not take place exactly as planned. The marching was atrocious and the B party split into two, the rear portion of which being leaderless came to a halt. It was near a control post, and when the officer at the tail of the column squeezed his way to the front he had only a few more steps to go to find Lieut.-Col. Pierce, O.C. R.I.F., and the most charming of gentlemen, who directed them to the beach. They did not, as some others did, have to find their way over the top across country.

The arrangements were a miracle of organization. As the last men left the fire trench, a party of R.E. blocked the communication trench with festoons of wire. Booby traps had been prepared and placed in tempting positions in dugouts.

Policemen were posted at corners where there was a possibility of going wrong. Our very feet were tied up in sacking to avoid making a sound. All's well that ends well. We passed through the entrenched line held by a picked body of the Borders to whom Lieut. Miller of the K.O.S.B. had been lent, and then found ourselves part of a dense crowd. In the stillness the explosion of a shell on Hunter-Weston Hill was a reminder that if the Turk took it into his head to shell the beaches we were in for a pretty bad time. Then the mind shifted off at the familiar tap-tap of rifle fire. One learnt that the horses that couldn't be evacuated were being shot, and that the sound could not possibly penetrate to the Turkish lines three miles away. The weather had given the Navy an anxious time and hung up the work of evacuating animals and material.

At last a slow movement was felt. One step at a time, a *queue* formed and began moving forward, and it could dimly be seen that it was Lancashire Landing we were heading for and that there was a fair sea on, even in harbour.

Sunday, 9 Jan. 1916. —

Patience, and one trod a gangway. A heave and a hoist on to the deck and a pleasant invitation to come downstairs. One had seen one's last of Gallipoli. One last excitement—a terrific explosion followed by a thunderous shock above our heads. It was the big dump being destroyed. Soon after, nautical noises and rattling chains were followed by the soothing shudder of the screw and the unmistakable roll of the sea. Perhaps the Turk thought we couldn't get away that night and was reserving his shells for a more likely occasion.

Every K.O.S.B. got away that night just as every man in the M.E.F. did. Great is the debt we owe to Sir Charles Monro who ordered the evacuation, to Gens. Davies and Lawrence (in personal charge of the arrangements), to Gen. de Lisle and the 87th's Brigadier and Staff.

The 1st K.O.S.B. had suffered severe casualties during the Dardanelles campaign. On the theory of averages the figures of the 29th Division may be applied to our unit. The wastage has been calculated at 100 per cent. every two months out of the eight spent—with two short respites at Lemnos and Mudros—on the Gallipoli peninsula. *

* See *The Story of the 29th Division*, p. 71.

PART II—THE WESTERN FRONT

CHAPTER I

RECUPERATION

THE seas were running pretty high on the morning of the 9th January 1916. We were all transhipped at Imbros from the destroyers and battleships that had rescued us on to minor transports, which took us round the N. side of Lemnos into Mudros Bay. There we transhipped straightaway into big transports, and after one of those forked lightning courses, adopted to evade submarines, reached Alexandria on 14th January. The same day the battalion entrained for Suez, where it remained for two months, training and guarding the Suez Canal. The climate was well-nigh perfect. Cool, starry nights were followed by warm, sunny days. The men were in tents and the officers in curious loosebox-like huts. I acted as adjutant throughout the period, which brought me in contact with R.S.M., afterwards Lieut. Dale, M.C., and Sergt., afterwards 2nd Lieut. J. J. Gracie, the orderly-room clerk, two of the best men one could find in the whole of the IX. Corps. The first named saw to the pitching and striking of tents, guards, orderly rooms, and other parades, and was a tower of strength and dignity. We wouldn't have swopped him even for R.S.M. Framlingham of the R.I.F., one of the noblest figures of a soldier in the division. Much time had to be spent in the orderly room, and Gracie's company was equal to his efficiency. He was entirely wrapped up in the regiment and in the military life, and was looking forward to more combative duties than totting up strengths, filling in returns, and instructing the adjutant. Although we were always yarning away, he was so modest that I never found out that he was a real "star" sprinter. What with his education and intelligence and experience, to say nothing of his moral and social merits, a commission was bound to come. When it did come, it was right well held till death. His favourite topic of conversation was the officers of the regiment,

Jan. 1916.

Jan.–March 1916.

not the flotsam and jetsam of the war, but those who trained it in India or landed at Y, and what wonderful men they were and what a wonderful regiment the 1st K.O.S.B. was. In short, he personified *esprit de corps*.

Officers came thick and fast. Some had succumbed to Gallipoli sickness. Others were new arrivals. I see from the far-from-model war diary which I wrote up that Lieuts. A. Kennedy and V. Gordon, and 2nd Lieuts. N. MacLeod, F. H. Christison, and J. Oliphant rejoined in the course of the month, and 2nd Lieuts. Graham-Clarke (a very promising lad from the 9th Battalion), M'Nab, Gaskell of the 3rd Battalion, Stewart, M'Nicol (afterwards a divisional road-maker in the Somme), Hay, Patterson, Elliot, King and Dennis. Lieut. E. J. Long brought the transport from Alexandria towards the end of February.

The training was not conducted with the drive that afterwards prevailed in France, and rightly, for we needed rest. Not that the time was passed slackly. There was squad drill and handling of arms for junior officers and men. There were route marches, which will ever be associated with Willie Mackenzie and his splendid pipers, ringing the changes on all the classic quick-steps. There was musketry and signalling, of which latter Christison was a *virtuoso*, just as he was at goal-keeping. Most of us got our first sight of our G.O.C. in Egypt, when he would look on and help us by good tips to instructors. There was a ceremonial brigade parade, in which, thanks to the N.C.O.s' work as markers, the battalion made quite a good appearance. Boxing and football were the sports. A few of the officers managed to play lawn-tennis. The great event was the final of the divisional football competition. Sir Francis Davies, the Corps Commander, witnessed the match, which was between the Lancashire Fusiliers and the K.O.S.B.. The latter won by one goal to nothing, thanks largely to Christison, and it was an even and thrilling game. The cup for this competition has not yet reached the 1st Battalion!

A week was spent on the far bank of the canal at the end of February. A defence line was being constructed, and while a certain number of outposts had to be found the bulk of the men were employed as navvies.

Before the 3rd of March it was known that the 29th Division were to sail to France. By this time Stirling-Cookson had gone to the 87th Brigade as Staff-Captain, and the return of Captain Shaw, completely recovered, was very welcome. On that day the first-line transport entrained for Port Said, and by the morning of the 11th not a Borderer was to be found in Suez. Some of us embarked at Suez on the *Wandilla*; others entrained there and embarked at Port Said on the *Megantic*. The strength of the battalion was 34 officers and 963 men. March 1916.

The *Megantic* sailed on the 11th and the *Wandilla* on the 12th. Both transports passed unscathed through the submarines, and the 1st K.O.S.B.'s first contact with France was Marseilles on the 17th and 18th. The French railway arrangements were excellent. Starting in the evening, long trains proceeded steadily if not at breakneck speed *via* the Rhone Valley, Lyon, Beaune (a thrill for some of us), and the outskirts of Paris. Darkness had long fallen when Pont Rémy on the Somme, 5 miles S.E. of Abbeville, was reached, and the 11 miles march to Domart-en-Ponthieu began.

Ten days were spent in that snug little village, and on most days there were route marches through the rolling Picardy country not far from the famous field of Crécy. Those of us who went on leave envied the sheepskin coats, the enormous boots, and British warms of those who were evidently far from strangers to France. The weather was decidedly chilly, and the 1st K.O.S.B. had just come from Egypt.

On 30th March the battalion started for the front and passed the night and following two days at Amplier, E. of Doullens. By this time temporary Capt. F. H. Christison was Adjutant, until Lieut. A. W. B. Miller (a regular) took over early in April.

CHAPTER II *

THE BATTLE OF THE SOMME

First Phase

April 1916. — WHEN the 1st K.O.S.B. had left Amplier for the trenches and were some 3 miles on the road they received warning to march to attention and salute their Corps Commander, whose H.Q. were in the handsome château of Marieux. This was no less than Lieut.-Gen. Sir Aylmer Hunter-Weston, K.C.B., who had commanded the division at the landing and was now in command of the VIII. Corps, consisting of the 4th, 29th, and 31st Divisions. The VIII. Corps along with the III. (Pulteney), X. (Morland), XIII. (Congreve), and XV. (Horne), formed part of the Fourth Army (Gen. Sir Henry, afterwards Lord, Rawlinson). The marching was all right past Louvencourt (excellent B.H.Q., when the 87th were out of the line), and Acheux (D.H.Q.), with its Sucrerie-chimney and big wood, reminiscent of horse and mule lines and church services. But the next stage from Forceville, 10 miles from Amplier, into Mailly-Maillet was marked by straggling. However, the Corps Commander didn't see that! The men were not yet acclimatized and properly hardened. Lifeless, pointless, practice marches never have the tonic quality of the real thing, the trek.

Mailly-Maillet was not much damaged, and never was shelled till the great bombardment began. Auchonvillers, often pronounced Auction Villas or, by the Jocks, Ochenvullers, was the last village in British territory. Beyond it the ground was flat and then dropped and rose again slightly through Beaumont-Hamel and continued to rise beyond.

The sector taken over from the 15th West Yorkshire Regiment on 3rd and 4th April was on the Hawthorn Ridge between Auchonvillers and Beaumont-Hamel and was quiet. There was little rifle fire, and apart from sniping the danger came from sudden gun-fire at point-blank range. As early as the 6th the newly joined 2nd Lieut. J. M'Nab was killed in this way. But that night the 1st K.O.S.B. experienced German shelling for the first time, fortunately

* See Map 3.

April 1916.

for them concentrated in the form of a box barrage upon the sector held by the S.W.B. at Mary Redan, S. of where the K.O.S.B. were. A trained body of German specialist raiders brought off a very successful raid, which not only cost the S.W.B. losses in killed, wounded, and prisoners, but led to the death of the gallant Capt. E. H. W. Byrne in a retaliatory raid a little later.

Quiet reigned once more, and the time was taken up with trench improvement.

On the 13th the battalion was withdrawn to Louvencourt and trained for the "push," which it was known was going to be made "on the Somme." Major Campbell of the Gordons gave his famous lecture on and demonstration of bayonet fighting, and such novelties as co-operation between aeroplanes and troops were practised. The Lewis gun and Stokes mortar were mechanical novelties. The 25th was naturally a day of proud remembrance. The Corps Commander inspected the officers, N.C.O.s, and men who had landed at Y exactly one year before, and spoke eloquently to them. Alas, there were only two officers and 120 O.R.. Ainslie and Simpson were the officers and, of course, there was Cookson at B.H.Q.. There was also a rally at Battalion H.Q., when officers and N.C.O.s met and talked of the landing.*

On the 28th the battalion relieved the 16th Middlesex—once the Sportsman's Battalion—which had replaced the Munsters in the 86th I.B., in the Hawthorn sector and almost immediately felt the effects of the S.W.B. counter-raid, which failed. The Germans responded to our guns with a vigorous barrage on our front system, and two subalterns and five O.R. were killed and 44 O.R. were wounded. The officers were 2nd Lieut. H. S. F. Hunter and 2nd Lieut. A. P. Hay. Considerable material damage was done. This incident was succeeded by a calm, and marked the end of the 1st Battalion's association with Beaumont-Hamel.

The 87th's subsequent sector lay further S. opposite—once more a letter Y—Y Ravine. Brigade H.Q. were at Englebelmer, a smelly, flea-bitten but picturesquely straggling village with a good church, having a fine view towards Bapaume, Irles, and Bois de Logeast, as well as towards Bois d'Aveluy (near Albert) and Thiépval on the other side of the Ancre. The natural objective in the event of an advance was the low-lying Beaucourt-sur-Ancre, but the key to its capture and retention was the Beaumont-Hamel ridge.

The Somme battle will, no doubt, be a matter of controversy for many years, That it cost us dearly in man-power is beyond doubt. But no one who has conversed with German prisoners fresh from the

* Capt. Shaw's Diary.

May–June 1916. — battlefield can forget what an indelible effect " die Sommeschlacht " was having on the *moral* of the German rank and file. The opinion was universal that the Eastern Front was a picnic compared to the Somme. Its date was fixed by the pressure on Verdun and the magnificent effort of Brussilov in Galicia. Its purpose was fixed by the lessons of the past and by the still defective training of the junior officers and N.C.O.s. The course of the battle would depend on how things moved, after an attack had been opened on a much wider front than at Festubert or Loos. No advances were to be attempted without drastic artillery preparation, or beyond definite limited objectives. The path towards Germany had literally to be blasted out with explosive. The immense amount of ammunition and stores necessary made the back regions hum with ceaseless activity day and night. The roads were often blocked with traffic, but the British are at their best in a crowd and good sense and good nature invariably untied the knots so that the stream flowed freely once more. The administrative branches and their technical advisers seemed to have made provision for everything. The rations were superb, and the canteens, incentives to extravagance, catered for every possible taste. Baths, dentists and dentures, gas-masks, steel helmets, waterproof sheets, concerts, troupes of entertainers were there for the health, safety, comfort, and amusement of the men. And all this in spite of persistently unsettled squally weather. The sleek horses and mules were a treat to behold. In short the " choregia " for the play was perfect, the soldiers were fresh and in good heart, and the one problem was whether the bombardment could cope with the counter-bombardment and also destroy the very remarkable system of entrenchments which confronted the assailants along the whole battle front, and was particularly strong in the sector opposite the 29th Division. There was only one way to prevent wastage from German guns, and that was to take a leaf out of the German book and dig deep. Admirable work was done by the 29th in the construction of these refuges in the three months before the battle. But in the end they were a paltry affair compared with what the enemy had found time to make in nearly two years. But these " funk holes " might prove the bane of their occupants. They could be overrun and bombed to death—much the most terrible of all deaths. It is interesting to know that in addition to " Tankschrecken " some Germans suffered from " Unterstandsangst." * What really mattered was the strength of the above-ground fortifications. " Some 10,000 yards north of Fricourt the [German] trenches crossed the River Ancre, a tributary of the Somme, and still running

* Tank-funk and dugout dread.

northwards passed over the summit of the watershed about Hébuterne and Gommecourt." * As a matter of fact, the highest ground of the watershed between the Ancre and the Douai plain lies between Courcelette on the Albert-Bapaume road and Combles, the line being marked by High Wood, Longueval, and Delville Wood, Ginchy (the highest of all points), Guillemont, and Leuze and Bouleaux Woods.

Our concern is with the fortifications just N. of the Ancre, and the following language of the despatch applies to them as if each word were written in enormous capitals. "The first and second systems each consisted of several lines of deep trenches, well provided with bombproof shelters and with numerous communication trenches connecting them. The front of the trenches in each system was protected by wire entanglements, many of them in two belts forty yards broad, built of iron stakes, interlaced with barbed wire often almost as thick as a man's finger." †

Seen from the air the German system was like a Vauban masterpiece, compared with which the British system looked like a sketchy improvisation. When it is added that No Man's Land was 500 yards wide, except at Mary Redan, it will be realised that anybody's thoughts, capable of being directed to the prospects of the coming day, were taken up with speculating how the bombardment was getting on. Would the men over the top be greeted with a barrage? Would the M.G. emplacements have been knocked out? Would the wire be cut?

On 19th May Lieut.-Col. A. J. Welch, just a year and seventeen days since his wound, resumed command, and when Major G. Hilton arrived and relieved Malcolm of the duties of Second-in-Command, and by the time Capt. J. K. B. Campbell had got comfortably in the saddle as Adjutant, the battalion was itself. Gallipoli and the landing were represented by Padre Cameron Reid.‡ Padre Ritchie, who had seen the battalion through Egypt and the start in France, where his fluent French was most useful, had exchanged into another unit about the middle of June. Lieut.-Col. Kelly was given another command in the division but was soon severely wounded, but made a wonderful recovery and won the V.C. at Cambrai on 20th November 1917.

The battalion presented a noble spectacle as it marched up from Acheux Wood on the night of the 30th of June. The bombardment

* Haig's despatch.

† Same despatch.

‡ His brother, the Rev. H. S. Reid, was then chaplain to the 2/S.W.B., and was a frequent and welcome visitor to the Borderers' lines. He is now (1930) Bishop of Edinburgh (Epis. Church in Scotland).

1 July 1916. had been going on since the 24th and there were some bad corners and cross-roads to pass. The C.O. and the Chaplain were at the head of the column on foot. The marching was steady and slow, reminding me of the purposeful step of a mountain guide. The men had coats and all sorts of weighty equipment. There was a note of solemnity, something processional about these grave men on their way to victory or disaster. The battalion had been praised for its good discipline by the G.O.C., who was not easily pleased or deceived.*

The way to the front lay along a long *boyau de communication*—Gabion Avenue—which began soon after Englebelmer, and the battalion got into position in the trenches N. of Mary Redan, in the support line, known as Buckingham Palace Road, St. James's Street, Piccadilly, and Brook Street facing Beaucourt Station, in a direction parallel to Y Ravine behind the R.I.F., who were to lead the attack. On the R. of the R.I.F. were the 36th (Ulster) Division. On the L. were the S.W.B., whose L. aimed at and included Y Ravine, supported by the Borders. Further to the L. were the 86th I.B., with Beaumont-Hamel and Beaucourt Redoubt as immediate objectives. No casualties were incurred *en route*, but during the shuffling into position 2nd Lieut. Gow was killed.

As has been told many times, the attack of the 29th was a total and complete failure. When the big mine at Hawthorn Redoubt gave warning at 7.20 a.m. to the German machine-gunners to be up and doing, they lost no time in setting to work, and they had ten minutes to spare for preparation.† Confining ourselves to the R. half of the 87th front, we find that when the R.I.F. went over the top at 7.30 a.m. on 1st July 1916 they were greeted with terrific bursts of M.G. fire, and those behind them felt the lash of the barrage. If the G.O.C. could have flown or rather hovered over the scene for ten seconds the attack would have been countermanded. The carnage that so swiftly destroyed the 87th was perfectly useless. Dummies could have done as well. The German Ancre garrison could not have been hurried off at a moment's notice to stop the leak astride the Somme. But the terrible thing about war is that an attack once launched can rarely be broken off. Those in control don't and can't know what is going on in front. So although the answers presented themselves to the three questions figured above ran: (1) Counter-barrage? Yes; enough to annihilate a division! (2) M.G.? Yes;

* One of the last entries in Capt. Shaw's Diary.

† "The advertisement of the attack on our front was absurd. Paths were cut and marked through our wire days before. Bridges over our trenches for the 2nd and 3rd waves to cross by were put up days in advance. Small wonder the M.G. fire was directed with such fatal precision."—An officer present.

enough to sweep every cubic foot of air. (3) Wire? Well, time enough, if you ever get there, to solve that problem! 1 July 1916.

The men on the spot had no alternative but to go on and be killed or wounded, or find cover. After the R.I.F. failed and after the lapse of half an hour the battered K.O.S.B. tried what they could do. But, without any discredit, they did not succeed in even reaching the few Fusiliers who were lying out in No Man's Land. In their waiting positions in and behind the front line they had been heavily shelled by the counter-barrage. By an unfortunate coincidence the Germans put up the precise signal—a white flare—selected by us to mark capture of the 1st objective, just at the place and time which made it seem imperative to launch, in accordance with divisional orders, the K.O.S.B. in the wake of the Inniskillings. But Borderers can console themselves with the thought that they were never out of the thoughts of those whose duty it was to apprise those in authority of the likelihood of useless sacrifice, and that the situation as it appeared to those in front was made known. Fate was against the Borderers. The fog of war was outspread and they had to dree their weird. They were well aware of this. They knew the first wave had broken to atoms, yet they never hesitated to start or wavered when off until cut down in swathes. One company had 202 casualties out of a strength of 219. The officers' disguises as private soldiers made no difference in such a browning hail of M.G. bullets. Major Hilton's reserve of about 80 was thrown in to hold the front trenches, and the Borderers handed over the impossible task to the 88th. Newfoundland Park * calls to mind a superb effort on the part of the N.F.L.D. Regiment, which, except as an example to future fighters, made no more impression on the Battle of Albert than the butt of a Weddell seal against a rorqual. The Essex on the R., who leapfrogged the K.O.S.B. at 8.45 a.m., found them, so to speak, weltering in their gore, the trenches blocked and damaged so that it was not till nearly 11 a.m. that a new attack was pushed half-way (in parts) across No Man's Land.†

The K.O.S.B. remained in the front trenches till 4 p.m., when they were withdrawn to Fort Jackson, a defensive redoubt in rear of the support line, and passed a quiet night. A party of 20 were left behind to dig graves for the dead.

The casualties were heartrending. Capt. Ainslie was the only company C.O. who was untouched. He saved many casualties by working many back into the point of Mary Redan, where No Man's Land was narrowest. Capt. Shaw (B), respected and loved as a wise comrade, a good officer, and a sincere Christian, was killed. Ten,

* See *post*, pp. 186 and 187. † Burrows, *Essex Regiment History*, p. 100.

1 July 1916. little more than lads, all second lieutenants, had shared the same fate. R. Reid (an aspirant for the ministry), J. L. Gow, R. Stewart, I. A. S. Scott, S. H. Glennie, W. Dickie (another divinity student), F. Paterson, H. F. B. Cooper, P. T. Bent, and J. A. S. Graham-Clarke. Major Hilton, Capts. Malcolm (O.C.D),* Lieut. A. Kennedy (O.C.C, a Cameronian who had done much good work in the battalion), 2nd Lieuts. Howey, Dixon, Dempster, Moreton, and M'Laren were wounded—in all 20 officer casualties. Eighty-three O.R. were killed, 406 were wounded, 59 were missing—making a total of 548. Providentially H.Q. did not go forward beyond battle H.Q., and the framework for a reconstruction was left. Losses were invariably borne bravely by the bereaved at home during the Great War, but one compliment, paid after the battle of 1st July, may be mentioned as a great honour to the regiment. The father of one lad, killed on 1st July 1916, wrote that he was the last of three sons killed, and that his only regret was that he had not three more to give to the regiment.

On the 2nd the battalion side-slipped S. to trenches in front of Hamel on the Ancre and remained there for a week, mending the battered parapets, burying the Ulster dead, and watching the fighting round Thiépval.

It was at this time that Englebelmer came in for some attention from howitzers, notably on the 3rd, when 2nd Lieut. R. N. C. Marsh, the untiring, promising M.G. officer, was instantaneously killed, though hardly touched, in the courtyard of the farm in which B.H.Q. had been, by a shell which deroofed an office and wrecked everything except a file of court-martial papers. But the Germans soon lost interest in Englebelmer, and in 1928 the village was looking very much its old self.

On the 8th the 1st K.O.S.B. returned to Acheux. On the 10th they were inspected by the Corps Commander. Their last tour of duty was opposite Y Ravine. On the 24th they left the melancholy scene. The whole division was thankful to be quit of a place that was associated with a black, inexplicable, and undeserved disaster.

Second Phase

The 29th Division could not be spared for a rest outside the front system. On the 27th of July the battalion left Doullens by train at 3.34 p.m. and reached Proven *via* Hazebrouck the same night. The journey took seven hours. The remainder of the month was spent in camps near Poperinghe, with exception of the 31st at Ypres,

* He seems to have reached a point nearer the German line than anyone.

ATTACK OF THE 87TH BRIGADE ON THE ANCRE ON 1ST JULY 1916

NORTHERN DIVISIONAL BOUNDARY
New Beaumont Road
Old Beaumont Road
Mine
Beaumont Hamel
Hawthorn Redoubt
Mine
Hawthorn Ridge
German Front Line
British Front Line
86TH BRIGADE
1st Royal Dublin Fusiliers
2nd Royal Fusiliers
Auchonvillers
Station Rd.
Ravine
88TH BRIGADE IN RESERVE
BRIGADE BOUNDARY
Auction Road
Newfoundland Regiment
88TH BRIGADE
3RD WAVE
1st Border Regiment
2ND WAVE
2nd S.W. Borderers
1ST WAVE
87TH BRIGADE
BATTALION BDY
1st Avenue
1st R. Inniskilling Fus.
1ST WAVE
1st K.O.S.B.
2ND WAVE
Mary Redan
To Hamel & Ancre Valley
4th Worcestershire Regiment
2nd The Hampshire Regiment
(did not attack on 1st July)
Gabion
To Englebelmer
1st Essex Regiment
3RD WAVE
To Mesnil
DIVISIONAL BDY.
0
500
1000 Yards
1690 Copyright
John Bartholomew & Son, Ltd. Edinburgh.
Fort Jackson

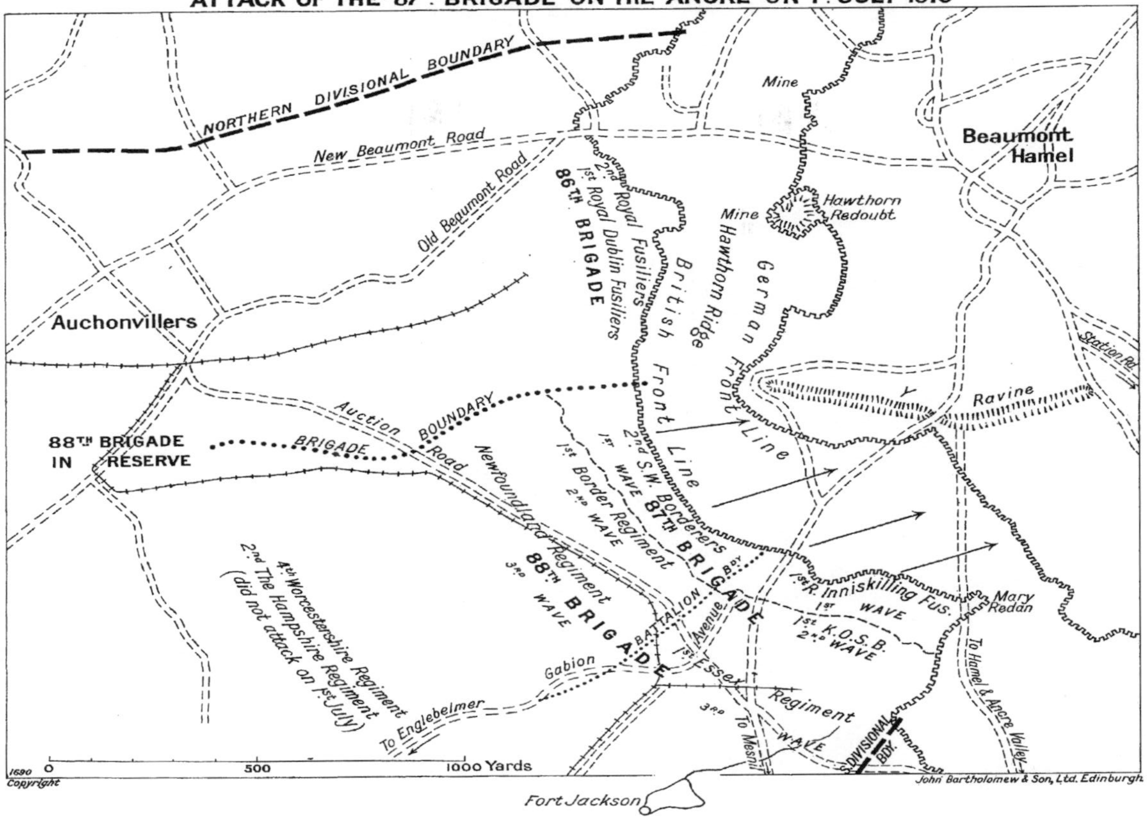

To face Page 182

and on 1st August the 1st K.O.S.B. found themselves once more in the line, having relieved the 1st Leicesters of the 6th Division.

Aug.-Sept. 1916.

The next two months were the quietest of the war on the Western Front for the 1st K.O.S.B.. The sector held was on either side of a line from Potijze (" Pottage ") Château (often Battalion H.Q.) to Verlorenhoek on the German side of the line, *i.e.* N.E. of Ypres and only 1¾ miles from the Ménin Gate. The condition of the trenches was deplorable in places. They were quite useless for protection against small-arm fire. In many places water and mud came over the ankles. The battalion was soon at work making breastworks, fitting in frames and duckboards and wiring. It was the old, old story of Flanders mud. The ground was waterlogged, and it was no use digging down below 2 feet except to fix in a wooden frame like a capital A upside down and protect it by breastworks. Minenwerfer were particularly active, but thanks, no doubt, to the drastic and efficient covering of the front by the 20th Division Artillery, and to the vigour in retaliatory fire of the 87th I.B. T.M. battery casualties were negligible. Nor can the salient have been unhealthy. The sick returns for August and September 1916 are remarkably small. The most serious incident during the stay in Flanders was the gas attack by the enemy on the night of 8th August, which would have affected the battalion if they had not just been relieved by the R.I.F.. In fact, the K.O.S.B. were about to start by train from Ypres for Brandhoek Camp, about 2 miles E. of Poperinghe, a little N. of the Ypres road, when the gas was discharged. The gas started as the Borderers left the jail, and no time was lost entraining on reserve line in Ypres. The R.I.F. had some 300 casualties in the Potijze sector evacuated on the 6th by the K.O.S.B., and lost all their transport horses.*

During the time spent in Brigade Reserve (Brigade H.Q. being in the snug but rather dark ramparts of Ypres) Battalion H.Q. were in the famous prison and the men worked on the back defences. When they were at Brandhoek they trained, marched, and bathed. And thus time passed. They were in the line from 1st to 6th August inclusive, at Ypres till the 8th, Brandhoek till 18th, and then back to the Front till 29th, when relieved by R.I.F.. September passed in like manner, and it may be mentioned that on 28th September the King of the Belgians visited the front line and various H.Q., including those of the K.O.S.B., and expressed his appreciation of the officers and men of the 29th. The Army Commander (Gen. Plumer), the Corps Commander (their old friend Lieut.-Gen. Sir A. Hunter-Weston), and even the G.O.C. were pleased with the work

* Most of the horses of the K.O.S.B. transport also died next day.

Sept. 1916. — put in on such almost forgotten trenches and redoubts as Warwick Farm, Congreve Avenue, Fleet Street, Strand, Wieltje, etc. But possibly another visitor aroused more interest. His visit, too, was informal and incognito, but was without invitation or welcome.

Early one morning the C.O. had just seen the divisional and brigade generals off on their round after a short conference in a front bay, when he heard the bursts of bombs and rifle shots coming from the opposite direction and evidently quite near. He had only to enter the next bay to be informed of the cause of this sudden fusillade. A subaltern on entering it found a man just finishing changing his trousers. He must have been within a few yards of where the conference took place. The man was a German, and he at once hurled a stick bomb which hit the officer on the head, but fortunately did not explode. The latter was unarmed, and bolted round the traverse to get aid. Returning with a small party he found that the wily spy had got over the parapet and was making his way along a ditch or drain in No Man's Land. Bombs were flung and shots were fired, but the plucky fellow got away. He was no thief. There in the bay was his disguise—a pair of ordinary British khaki trousers and a private's greatcoat. Strange, but true!

At the end of September Lieut.-Col. Welch (then on leave, but returned by the time the Somme was reached) was still C.O.; Major J. B. Pennyman, formerly with the 2nd Battalion, was Second-in-Command; Capt. J. K. B. Campbell was Adjutant; and T. Prentice was A/R.S.M.. The last named was awarded the M.C. on 24th August along with Capt. G. E. Malcolm and C.S.M. J. J. Gracie for good work on 1st July. The M.M. had already been awarded to Ptes. A. Humphrey and I. F. Cope. Prentice fell as a C.S.M. near Monchy on 16th April 1917, and Humphrey was killed in the salient on the day after the battle of Langemarck, fought on 16th August 1917.

When word came that the 1st K.O.S.B. were to return to the Somme it found them recovered. If soldiers brooded over their fallen comrades they could not carry on, much less win wars. If they had spent their time picturing the very real horrors of the past and the future, conjuring up scenes like those drawn by the author of *Im Westen Nichts Neues*,* they could not have discharged their patriotic duty as they did. Quite a "cheery crowd," on 7th October, left Hopoutre near Poperinghe for Longueau near Amiens. One peaceful Sabbath (the 8th) was spent at Cardonette near Allonville (B.H.Q.), N.E. of and near Amiens, and the advance forward began *via* Buire-sur-Ancre, Fricourt, Montauban, Bernafay, Longueval, and Delville Woods, towards Gueudecourt. The development of

* By E. M. Remarque, translated as *All Quiet on the Western Front.*

the wearing-out battle can be followed in the stories of the 2nd, 9th, and 7/8th K.O.S.B.. At tremendous cost the heights had been stormed, and Sir D. Haig was forcing his way down the hill towards Bapaume. The 88th I.B. had just improved the capture of Gueudecourt, 3 miles S. of Bapaume, by two boldly executed attacks. The well-named Grease Trench was part of the captured territory and was the destination of the K.O.S.B. in the wake of the S.W.B.. Oct. 1916.

The march was an eye-opener. The train journey had concealed the vast volume of traffic which circulated under elaborate route regulations in the back areas between St. Pol and Amiens. But as soon as Méaulte was passed, the appalling congestion of traffic on roads hopelessly inadequate to bear it made itself felt. In spite of the preference given to marching troops, progress was dead slow, and there was all the more time to take in the dolorous desolation of a modern battlefield after subjection to three months' pitiless shelling, and, latterly, to buckets of rain. The region had ceased to be country. From the dismal, wind-swept heights above Fricourt, the eye could see nothing but destruction. Vile as they were, the roads were the only safe ways. Off the roads was a mass of shell craters—not, it is true, quite one on the top of the other as in the salient, but thickly enough strewn and with slimy ground in between and remains of barbed-wire obstacles. On the roads was deep, sticky mud, churned day and night incessantly by wheels and hooves and endless chains of caterpillars. On the dreary heights of Montauban were D.H.Q.. B.H.Q. were tunnelled into a bank just E. of Flers.

On a pouring wet, chilly night on 20th October the K.O.S.B. relieved the Essex * in the support line, and the next day relieved the S.W.B. in the front, the relief taking seven hours to complete. In the morning three men of the S.W.B. were found stuck fast. They had been bogged for twelve hours. When they were extracted after an hour's strenuous digging, the poor fellows were nearly dead. If the Somme has to give the palm to the Salient, it was a remarkably close second. The first frost of winter had come, not yet hard enough to bind into a rock, but sufficient to chill the soaked soldiers to the bone. The tour in Grease Trench was marked by general beastliness and steady casualties. There was neither attack nor counter-attack, but when Fricourt was reached on 30th October the battalion had had over 90 O.R. casualties (chiefly wounded), and the following officers wounded—2nd Lieuts. W. M. Clark, D. L. Keir,

* See *The Story of the 29th Division*, pp. 87–89; *1st Essex Regiment*, pp. 104–105.

Nov. 1916. A. L. Aitchison,* Broadway (slightly), and C. B. Anderson. The terrain was awful to move over and the return to the support line after relief at 2 a.m. on the 26th was a painful proceeding. One man just off the track was told to hurry on, but he said he had just lost one boot in the mud and didn't intend to leave the other behind. By the following evening they were back in Bernafay Wood, relieved by N.F.L.D. and earmarked for a push. The push was spared them, and after two days of draughty Fricourt, where 3 subalterns and a draft of 78 O.R. joined up, the 1st K.O.S.B. marched to Albert and took train on 3rd November for Airaines, a pretty little interesting town about 18 miles W. of Amiens in what is usually called the Cavillon area, from the fact that D.H.Q. were there.

In ten days they were back at Fricourt and in the line between Lesbœufs and Le Transloy (still German). The line faced N.E. at that point, and was the extreme R. of the British zone, the French 152nd Division touching the K.O.S.B. at this point. The Borderers took over from the 2nd Lincs. of the 8th Division. They had hitherto been in the XV. Corps (Sir H. Horne).† Now for the first, but not last, time they were in the XIV. (Lord Cavan). It is a curious thing about the 29th Division that in the Somme it always took over a sector to the R. of where it had previously been—after Lesbœufs, Morval; and after Morval, Sailly Saillisel. The three weeks passed in this sector, with Carnoy Camp as a background, call for little comment.

A glance at the despatches shows that the impetus of attack had been transferred N. to Gen. Gough's Fifth Army and that the Fourth was more or less marking time. The line on either side of the Albert-Bapaume road was now N. of Le Sars, and Eaucourt l'Abbaye a mile to the E.. The Butte de Warlencourt barred further progress. As the gains about Gueudecourt were maintained and the capture of Thiépval and Schwaben Redoubt afforded fine positions for enfilading the stronghold, the German salient between Arras and the Ancre was none too secure.

When the K.O.S.B. were usefully spending their last day at Airaines the storm broke. In the five-day battle of the Ancre the Fifth Army took Beaumont-Hamel and the ground behind it, Beaucourt ridge, and Beaucourt-sur-Ancre. The 51st (Highland) Division's capture of the first-named fortress is commemorated by

* He died of these wounds on 3rd November (W.D. and Official Death Roll).

† This distinguished general, better known as the Commander of the First Army, died in August 1929.

the superb figure of the Highland soldier in Newfoundland Park on the very battlefield.*

Dec. 1916– Jan. 1917. —

To return to the 1st K.O.S.B., they bussed on the 14th to Buire-sur-Ancre and marched to Lesbœufs to find comparative quiet and less vile weather than in October. On the 20th they were encamped at Carnoy, Capt. A. E. Burnett of the 2nd Battalion being evacuated shell-shocked to hospital. The wet 24th and 25th were spent at a camp at Guillemont, and then another spell of three days at the front followed by two at Carnoy finished the month.

On 4th December the battalion went to the Morval sector of the firing-line. Major S. Campbell-Johnston, who had come out from the 3rd Battalion on the 8th, had charge of advanced H.Q. a little N.E. of Morval and due E. of Lesbœufs, round which shells rained day and night. St. Andrew's Night cannot have been a specially cheery one.

On 7th December 1916 the 1st K.O.S.B. left the front line for more than a month *via* Carnoy, Méricourt (near Corbie), Corbie, Hangest, for Le Mèzge in the Cavillon area. It was at Méricourt that Capt. J. K. B. Campbell and the battalion parted with mutual reluctance. His special knowledge of West Africa could no longer be dispensed with. It was a very serene, competent combination —Welch and Campbell. Fortunately Lieut. A. N. Lewis, a veteran and a regular, was available, having survived the dangers and privations of both tours as a company commander. He took over as adjutant, and retained the post until the middle of August 1917.

It is evident from the records that the month out of the line was well spent. With Soues (B.H.Q.) a few yards away, and Cavillon little over a mile, the K.O.S.B. had every incentive to play up to the new brigadier—Brig.-Gen. R. N. Bray, D.S.O.—and satisfy that expert in training, Gen. de Lisle. In particular, the 87th I.B. practised for the two-battalion raid, which effected such a surprise on the Kaiser's birthday—the 27th January 1917—and resulted in the capture of close on 400 Germans (9 officers), and much glory to the R.I.F. and Borders. Neither the supports (S.W.B.) nor reserve (K.O.S.B.) were called upon, but they would have been ready. Specialists visited various schools for instruction. A feature of the Somme period was the number of N.C.O.s who obtained temporary commissions at home or permanent ones at the front. Sergt. W. E. Aitchison obtained one of the latter in

* The battlefield has been left alone, and more than any other spot on the Western Front, except the Chemin des Dames, recalls the awesome happenings from 1914 to 1918. It well repays a visit.

Feb. 1917. the Hants. C.S.M. J. J. Gracie was gazetted to his own battalion as 2nd lieutenant on 17th January 1917.

By 23rd January 1917 the battalion was back in the sector opposite Le Transloy. The iron frost had set in. Zero was often passed, and boiled eggs turned to solid ice. Digging was wellnigh impossible, except for the Monmouth pioneers, who were expert miners. But no longer was it possible for a man to stick up to his neck in the mud and have to be dragged out of his boots, as had happened when the weather was " saft."

The principal incidents on this occasion were the losses—50 O.R. casualties in two days caused by shell fire, when the K.O.S.B. relieved the victors of the 27th; the capture of Capt. N. Macleod and 2nd Lieut. Haining and 8 O.R., who lost their way in the mist (a thing only too easily done); and, thirdly, the capture of a German officer and 21 O.R. through precisely the same mistake as Macleod's —loss of direction. The actual surrender was brought about by the gallantry of C.S.M. Battle and L.-Corp. F. O'Neill at the head of a party of four volunteers, who, appreciating the situation, slipped round behind and bombed them into giving themselves up. In honour of the platoon commander, Lieut. R. D. Peat, the captives were dubbed " Peat's Prussians."

Casualties still mounted up, and the item of 28 sick looks as though the best efforts with whale oil and special exercises (" foot-warming drill ") had not altogether succeeded in driving away that scourge.* When the battalion marched back to Carnoy on the 30th it was ready for the warm meal provided, and let us hope warm beds.

The month of February was spent partly in the line and partly at Méaulte. 2nd Lieut. J. Routledge was out with the patrols of A on successive nights, on the second of which—the 26th—the hostile line was penetrated and bombs thrown into the trench.

By the end of the month they were back at Bronfay, once familiar to the 2nd Battalion, and in March spent nineteen days, mostly at La Neuville-lez-Bray, before returning to Le Mèzge on the 19th for a ten days' stay. During the whole of this period the battalion trained steadily and continuously, and all the way to Arras, often when on the march, continued to train. For Gen. de Lisle's views on training I must refer to *The Story of the 29th Division*.†

* During the winter of 1916–17 the Essex claim to have had not one single case of trench feet. Is it a case of some system ? or some feet ? (*Essex History* (*cit.*), p. 109.) Perhaps a touch of luck in regard to length of tours and weather conditions may have helped.

† Pages 99–101.

CHAPTER III

ARRAS *

SPACE forbids a discussion of the *raison d'être* of the Battle of Arras. So far as that is germane to a regimental history, it will precede the part dealing with the 6th and 7/8th Battalions. Nor are the marches of a length to warrant description. The Somme was crossed at Picquigny. Flessels, Hem (a suburb of Doullens), Lucheux (three days), Grand Rullecourt, Liencourt, and Monchiet were places of sojourn. All lie between Doullens and Arras in country pleasantly typical of Artois. April 1917.

On the 12th of April 1917 the 1st Battalion paid its first visit to Arras, then in all the commotion of the fourth day of the battle, dined there, and passed without casualties on to the Brown or third line of trenches captured in the advance of Allenby's Third Army.

On the 14th the battalion took over the front line between La Bergère and Marlière, opposite Guémappe, and S. of the Route Nationale from Arras to Cambrai, and S. of Monchy-le-Preux, in and near which the 29th Division passed two strenuous and costly months while accounts were being settled up in the Battle of Arras. As the 1st K.O.S.B. never fought at Guémappe, in the valley of the Cojeul, but on the Monchy plateau, a few words regarding that sinister village may be of use. It is perched on the summit of a ridge running S.E. from Beaurains, just S. of Arras, between the Cojeul on the S. and the Scarpe on the N.. It lies about 5 miles from Arras, and is about 200 feet above the Scarpe. N., W., and S. wide views extend in clear weather. Westwards the ground undulates towards Beaurains and Arras, *e.g.* at Telegraph Hill and Ridge, and at Orange Hill and Observation Ridge, 3,000 yards E. of Arras station. But it is with the country immediately to the E. of Monchy that we are concerned. As one emerges from the village the fields lie as a flattish plateau on a front of 1,000 yards or more in width. Due E. there is a dip, and then there is a rise to a point nearly a mile off, known as Infantry Hill, not quite so

* See Map 4.

April 1917. high as Monchy itself. E.N.E. lie some small plantations, the largest and farthest off of which is the Bois du Sart. S.E. of Infantry Hill is the Bois du Vert, three-quarters of a mile W. of which, at a cross road, stood (in April 1917) all that was left of a windmill.

On either flank the Monchy plateau falls away in exposed slopes that make the two woods mentioned valuable posts on which to pivot a defence. They served as M.G. nests and as points of assembly, and as long as they were held, progress on the flanks must be (and invariably was) retarded, and in consequence they acted as a brake on the troops advancing across the plateau. The ground on the plateau, as elsewhere, is possessed of water-bearing strata (artesian wells, in other words), and the occupants of the trenches had to contend with waterlogged trenches in the inclement spring weather.

From a defensive point of view Monchy was the key to the position of the VI. Corps (Sir A. Haldane), and the VI. Corps was the key corps of the Third Army (Allenby). This was quickly made known to the K.O.S.B., for, on the very day they took over, the Germans made a fierce attack on Monchy, which happened to coincide in time with a vigorous thrust by the 88th I.B.. Monchy was saved, but the Essex and N.F.L.D. were all but annihilated.*

The battalion was in for rather a trying time. Unless when actually working (under risky conditions) at a new firing trench nearly 600 yards in front of the one hitherto occupied or patrolling, they felt the cold in the absence of greatcoats and blankets. But the work was arduous and warming. After three nights' digging and two days' occupation and improvement, the battalion found itself in possession of a trench fully a mile long. The work and covering parties suffered casualties. Three second lieutenants were killed—D. H. Robertson and P. S. Mackay on 14th, and J. Routledge on 16th. So was A/R.S.M. Prentice, M.C.. O.R. casualties were continuous: 8 on 13/14th, 15 on 14th, 7 on 15th, 8 on 16th, 5 on 17th, 7 on 18th, and 8 on 19th April. 2nd Lieut. R. D. Peat had been wounded on the way up from the Brown Line. To finish up, the relief was complicated in the extreme, no less than five battalions and two divisions occupying the sector.

But the real test was at hand. After three days at Arras resting and preparing, the battalion returned to the line in a sector which extended about 500 yards from the E. outskirts of the centre of Monchy † to a point opposite the N. edge of the Bois du Vert.

* *The Story of the 29th Division*, pp. 111–114. *Essex Units in the War*, pp. 110–113.

† The sights and smells of Monchy, with its dead horses and men, beggar description.

They therefore faced Infantry Hill. On their L. were the S.W.B. facing the Bois du Sart and intervening plantations. On their R., but echeloned back 1,000 yards, were the Worcesters. The 29th were attacking Infantry Hill with limited objectives as part of an advance by the Third and First Armies on a 9-mile front, intended to include the capture of the two troublesome woods. The 87th I.B. had less than half a mile to go to gain their first objective. What happened afterwards would depend on how fortune favoured the flanks. Fortune did not favour the flanking divisions, as we shall find when we study the story of the 7/8th K.O.S.B., and the main interest in the share taken by the 1st K.O.S.B. consists in the carefulness of the plans, the boldness of the advance behind the barrage, and the exemplary energy with which an entirely new trench was sited, dug, and fire-stepped on the site chosen by the Higher Command.

April 1917.

At 4.45 a.m. on 23rd April the barrage dropped on the German trenches, and the infantry, including the 1st K.O.S.B., went over the top. Each man had a flare and a bomb in his pocket. Each man was victualled for three days, had enough to drink, if sparing, and carried a pack. Moreover, each man carried two sandbags. From the word " go " the adventure went well. D on the R. and A on the L., without loss of direction, moved in four lines and two waves, *i.e.* two lines advancing simultaneously. In close support went C in one similar wave, with special bombers to secure the flanks, special " moppers up," and a roving commission to reinforce either flank of the leading companies. The reserve company (B) followed C at double the interval, viz. at 100 yards, and had Lewis gunners on the flanks instead of bombers. Communication from the front was uninterrupted. More than twenty messages passed back to Battalion H.Q., and were sent on to Brigade H.Q. by 6.45, *i.e.* in two hours. The R.I.F. occupied the trenches vacated by the 1st K.O.S.B., both original and acquired, and later on dug a trench behind the " blue line " in readiness for the second stage, which never eventuated.

The advance was marred only by a few casualties, thought to be due to " shorts," and the Worcesters, whose advance was wonderfully rapid, seem to have had the same complaint. Division seem to have thought that casualties were caused through impetuosity in going beyond the " blue line " (the objective). It would have been little short of a miracle if long lines of men groping in the dark or dusky mists of morning behind a belt of bursting shrapnel shells fired at long range had escaped unscathed. Nor on these occasions is it easy to know when to stop. The " blue line " was not marked

April 1917. blue on the ground. In one hour consolidation was begun on the "blue line," and casualties had been so far slight. The enemy seemed to be preoccupied elsewhere. Their "heavies" passed over the heads of the 1st K.O.S.B., directed against the trenches originally left, those first taken, and Monchy behind both. Meanwhile a party of Germans massing in the Bois du Vert were spotted by 2nd Lieut. J. Watt, M.C., O.C. A, and on the transmission of the news backwards by Col. Welch the front line troops soon had the satisfaction of seeing them scattered in all directions. In any case the systematic bombardment with M.G. at long range must have made the Bois du Vert a dangerous spot unless it was lavishly provided with cover.

In consequence of the check to the 15th Division the 87th I.B. were not called on for a further effort, and the K.O.S.B. made good their tenure. In the course of stabilizing a defensive flank Lieut. N. G. Willock * accounted for many Germans with a couple of Lewis guns. Their new trench was well sited. By next morning they had posts out in front of each company, and A and D could hand over to the L.F. and R.F. of the 86th I.B. with a clear conscience and occupy trenches in support. B and C remained in the line till 8.30 p.m. on the 24th, but by 3 a.m. on the 25th—Gallipoli Day—the whole battalion were in the cellars of Arras.

The battalion had gone into action with 21 officers and 500 O.R.. The casualties submitted by the G.O.C. in his report show that 3 officers were killed and 7 wounded, and that 20 O.R. were killed and 133 wounded, 19 being missing. 2nd Lieuts. L. Solomon and B. H. Roberts were killed on the 23rd, and 2nd Lieut. S. Farish on the 24th, the last named was one of the dwindling band who had formed the nucleus of the 9th Battalion. In Farish a promising and trustworthy subaltern was lost, as well as a charming companion.

These were two days of which a C.O. might well be proud, and Col. Welch told his men so on the 29th. He was satisfied with the *moral*.

On 25th the K.O.S.B. exchanged salutations with the *Amethyst* and *Sapphire* and Gen. Hunter-Weston. They were then at Duisans, but a couple of easy marches to Lattre-St. Quentin, about 9 miles west of Arras, landed them at St. Amand on 26th April, about 13 miles S.W. of Arras, where they enjoyed a thorough rest. It was then that Capt. Ainslie said farewell for ever to the 1st Battalion on transference to the 2nd. He had landed at Y in 1915, had survived the 1st of July 1916, where he did excellent work pulling things together after the disaster, and the winter and spring campaigns on the Somme and in Artois. But in less than

* He fell at Marcoing. See p. 207, *post*.

three weeks of leaving the 1st he was killed in action, as we have seen, in the aftermath of the Vimy fighting. May 1917.

It was not until the 14th of May that the 1st K.O.S.B. re-entered the line on the Monchy plateau, relieving troops of the 3rd Division. They had in the interim been at Arras in the Cathedral cellars or at Duisans, and had absorbed drafts and some new subalterns—Wylie, M'Gregor, Howie, and A. H. Malcolm. The last named was killed the very next day.

By this time things had shaken down to positional warfare with its daily roll of casualties and incessant toil with pick and shovel. Monchy was Battalion H.Q., and I have always been informed would have been untenable but for deep German-dug Unterstände,* as whenever the Germans felt punitive or nervous they gave it hot to Monchy. When in the Brown Line, the battalion were behind Observation Hill.

On the 21st they retired to Arras for eight days and trained. There seems to have been some epidemic in May, for the sick returns are higher than at any time except in the worst of the Somme.

On the 28th Lieut. R. M. Shorter, a Gallipoli veteran, rejoined, and on the 30th the battalion returned to the Brown Line and finished the month in the firing-line. But it was soon over. The division was needed elsewhere. It was taken right out of the line, handing over to the 3rd at 10 a.m. on 3rd June. Late on the 2nd June the 1st K.O.S.B. had said a final farewell to the Arras front and lay in Arras two days. On the 3rd Major Pennyman, an old hand at the Maxim in the 1914 fights, left them to join the Small Arms School at G.H.Q.†.

The 29th Division were out of the line for twenty-six days. Most of these were spent in the Bernaville area, S.W. of Doullens. The 1st K.O.S.B., who had arrived at Candas by rail from Arras, had only three miles to march to find their excellent billets at Autheux on the 5th of June. Their first sojourn in France, Domart, was only 8 miles off.

The reader now knows exactly how the British troops put in their time on such occasions. The features of the June spent by the 1st Battalion K.O.S.B. in Picardy were the fineness of the weather, the variety and interest of the work done, the functions, such as sports and horse shows, and the excitement of entertaining their gallant and distinguished colonel, Lieut.-Gen. Sir Charles Woollcombe, K.C.B., then commanding the IV. Corps. In spite of the paramount claims of training on the time available, time was found for a thorough " dress rehearsal." On the 23rd the Colonel arrived

* Dugouts.

† War Diary.

May 1917. and inspected his regiment, first in line and then marching past. He then addressed them, spoke of the past and the future, and wished them success. The G.O.C. and the Brigadier were of the party and joined Sir Charles at the lunch given by the C.O. and officers of the battalion. It was a fine day, and the battalion sports in the afternoon were a great success. Altogether it was a stimulating and memorable occasion. Another feature of the interlude was that the 29th had the whole place to themselves. No questions as to priority in connection with field-ranges or baths or manœuvre ground! The very absence of crowding made the inhabitants friendly, and of the jolly, accommodating lads of the 29th those of the Scottish battalion were not the least kindly.

[*Swaine*.

LIEUTENANT-GENERAL SIR CHARLES L. WOOLLCOMBE, K.C.B., K.C.M.G., COLONEL OF THE KING'S OWN SCOTTISH BORDERERS, AT THE TIME OF AND DURING PERIOD OF THE GREAT WAR.

CHAPTER IV

YPRES

June–July 1917.

We have yet to be told the meaning of the three and a half months' battle which began on the 31st July 1917. We know that the Joffre-Haig plans of the end of 1916 had suffered such modifications as to be no longer attractive to one of their authors, at any rate, when called for. The British effort had included an attack on the Vimy Ridge, restricted operations E. of Arras, the capture of the Messines Ridge, and the maximum effort against the Passchendaele Ridge and beyond in early summer when dry weather was likely. But when each "came off", it seemed to be out of proportion and of its proper setting in time. In particular, the Flanders campaign opened too late. The weather had saved the Germans in September 1916, and it served them well in the Ypres salient in 1917. There was no element of surprise. It was evident it was in Flanders or nowhere that the Allies would attack. The French had gambled and lost.* The British were strung out on the Somme, had been fought to a standstill at Arras, and had blown up and rushed and were holding the Messines Ridge (a wonderful tactical masterpiece in itself). There was nowhere left for further operations but the salient, and the year was only half over. The Germans carefully planned a scheme of defence and were waiting. But something had to be done. Russia was virtually out of the war. British arms had suffered reverses in the East. Allenby had not yet struck. The result was positional warfare at its slowest and at its nastiest. The theatre was cramped and was sewn with fortlets or blockhouses, known as pill-boxes, from which a few stout, skilled men with M.G. could hold up a whole battalion. Not a yard could be gained without a lavish use of H.E., and pill-boxes needed the direct hit of the greatest calibres to silence them. Their only vulnerable spot was the entrance at the back and the slit through which they fired

* How Pétain quelled the mutiny which broke out after the Champagne disaster on 16th April 1917 and restored the *moral* of the French Army is well told in the last number of *L'Illustration* for June 1929.

Aug. 1917. — to the front and flanks. The result was that the condition precedent to every advance meant the enhancement of the difficulties of the next stage. The whole area became a shifting, quaggy bog, traversable only by means of narrow, often shelled, duckboard tracks. Along these generals, even princes of the blood, had to take their chance like privates or subalterns.

On ground in such a state objectives become more limited and the task of putting the line won into defensible condition is more Sisyphean than ever. Moreover, the elastic German method of defence in depth led to sudden checks in the advance calling for individual initiative in every man. A strong point would be encountered. How was it to be turned? It was to all sorts of situations of that kind that the two last spells of training had been directed. But if the right leadership and quickness of decision and disregard of personal danger were not forthcoming, the training would have been thrown away. The Battles of Langemarck, Broodseinde, and Poelcapelle, in which the 29th suffered in battle casualties alone 206 officers and 4,530 O.R., afforded constant opportunities for all ranks to display their quality. Four V.C.s were won for the division in the course of the campaign, two of them by N.C.O.s of the 1st K.O.S.B..

A word about the course of the battle and then we return to the Borderers.

One of the results of the attack of the Second (Plumer) and Fifth (Gough) Armies on 31st July had been that in the N., in the Boesinghe sector, Pilckem Ridge, so fatal to the 2nd Battalion in 1915, had been taken and the XIV. Corps (Lord Cavan) had progressed to the Steenbeek. We are indebted to the Guards and 38th Divisions for the advance. Thereafter things had slowed up in consequence of the unexampled torrential downpour for four days on end, but when the K.O.S.B. came into the line it was time to make a further advance N.E., beginning with the crossing of the Steenbeek, a Stygian ditch swollen into a treacherous inundation.

On 26th June the 1st K.O.S.B. took train at Doullens and reached Hopoutre,* near Proven, in the small hours of the 27th. A march of about 2 miles N.E. landed them in a camp near Crombeke. On the evening of the 28th they marched about 10 miles *via* Elverdinghe and Dawson's Corner to the support line in the canal bank 2 miles N. of Ypres. And then began a strenuous time for the 87th I.B., the L. extremity of the sector of which (on the R. of the Boesinghe sector of the Guards) rested on the E. bank of the canal but slanted

* I unfortunately miswrote it as Hopoutie in *The Story of the 29th Division*. See p. 124.

away from it towards Wieltje. Two miles of new trenches had to be dug in addition to the improvement of these existing. Enormous loads in connection with the coming " push " had to be carried to the front. Life was lived under the strain of constant aeroplane observation and consequent shelling.* The K.O.S.B. worked on the front line and supplied no fewer than three patrols, all under Lieut. T. C. Noel, before relief on the 6/7th July. The last, viz. on 6th July, was planned as an identification raid and artillery support was employed. But the enemy was on the alert, an entry could not be forced, and the party retired. How many of the seven wounded on that day were raiders is not stated. 16 Aug. 1917.

Relieved by the Hants, the battalion toiled through the night to Caribou,† where five days were spent.

From the 12th to the 26th they were delivered over to the R.E. and were quartered mostly at Caribou camp. Though not in the line, the battalion supplied a party for an abortive raid on the 19th. Our own guns and Stokes mortars are blamed for the 17 casualties. From the 26th July to the 12th August the battalion was in the Proven–Elverdinghe area in cheerless camps with meaningless names.

THE BATTLE OF LANGEMARCK

When the 29th Division took over the front on 8th August it relieved the Guards Division in the Boesinghe sector, now more fitly termed the Wijdendreft, from the hamlet that confronted the division on the opposite bank of the Steenbeek, a mile N.W. of Langemarck. The Ypres–Staden railway-track in ruins was the R. boundary, and the 29th's neighbours were on that side the 20th Division. The division sector was about 1,600 yards wide, and on the L. to the N. was the 2nd French Division. The 29th were to attack on a two-brigade front, the 88th on the R. and the 87th on the L.. In the *Story of the 29th Division* the positions of the K.O.S.B. and the S.W.B. were erroneously reversed. In point of fact the K.O.S.B. were on the R. and the S.W.B. next the French on the L.. On the R. of the K.O.S.B. were the N.F.L.D. and beyond them the Hants. The 86th I.B. lay in reserve just N. of what had once been Pilckem.

The task of the 29th was to cross the Steenbeek, overwhelm Wijdendreft and consolidate a line in front of the next beek—the Broembeek. The line of advance was almost exactly N.E. and was parallel to the railway. The distance to be traversed amounted to

* One shell disposed of ten men, 4 killed and 6 wounded (War Diary).

† One of the numerous camps dotted about the back regions.

16 Aug. 1917. 1,700 yards on the R. and 1,100 yards on the L.. But none of the units opening the attack were to go beyond the second objective nearly 1,000 yards off. The final objectives were to be taken by the Essex (R.) and Worcesters (L.) in the 88th's sector, and by the Borders in the 87th's. When we think of the K.O.S.B. we must think of two jumps forward, the second being the more eventful.

By the time the 1st K.O.S.B. were in the support line, the first step had already been taken. On the night of 10/11th August the 86th I.B. crossed the Steenbeek and by the capture of " Passerelle Farm " on the following night established a bridgehead. Wooden bridges were brought up and laid across the beek. In result the K.O.S.B. were " on the tape " across the Steenbeek and ready to assault in the small hours of the 16th. As can be imagined, it was an awful time between the 12th and the 16th. Shelling with mustard gas * was a new horror for the 29th. On the 13th A had twenty casualties when in support. On the 14th in the line the battalion had 28. On the 15th it was worse, 47 O.R. casualties and one officer wounded. But the enemy was not having a rosy time. The War Diary records five direct hits by our " heavies " on the Wijdendreft Redoubt. For a fortnight every trench-length, pill-box, or occupied crater had been subjected to a severe bombardment by heavy guns. The final burst lasted from 10 p.m. until 4.30 a.m. on the 16th. The actual barrage during the battle would take too long to detail.†

Zero was at 4.45 a.m. on the 16th August 1917. D was on the L., B on the R. of a front about 400 yards wide. A was 10 yards behind D, and C behind B. The leading companies reached the first objective and started consolidation. Then A and C passed through them to the second objective. That it ever was won was due to the astonishing gallantry of two N.C.O.s—A/C.S.M. J. Skinner of A and C.Q.M.S. W. Grimbaldeston of B. The latter took a blockhouse on his L. front and 36 prisoners by resource and intrepidity. He directed the fire of a small party of rifle grenadiers, and with the aid of one rifleman forced past the blockhouse under fire until he gained the back door and menaced the garrison with bombs. Six M.G. and one T.M. went with the entire garrison into captivity. He had saved the situation. The advance was resumed.

Skinner's feat, however, on this day has always been regarded as the most wonderful achieved, single-handed, by any Borderer in the great or probably in any other war. As the *Gazette* puts it, when M.G. fire from the L. was holding up the attack, he " collected six men, and

* See earlier, p. 109.

† It will be found in the *1st Battalion the Essex Regiment* (Burrows), at pp. 119 and 120.

C.S.M. SKINNER, V.C.

C.Q.M.S. GRIMBALDESTON, V.C.

SERGT. M^C GUFFIE, V.C.

PIPER LAIDLAW, V.C.

with great courage and determination worked round the left flank of three blockhouses from which the machine-gun fire was coming, and succeeded in bombing and taking the first blockhouse single-handed; then leading his six men towards the other two blockhouses he skilfully cleared them, taking 60 prisoners, 3 M.G., and 2 T.M.. The dash and gallantry displayed by this warrant officer enabled the objective to be reached and consolidated." 16 Aug. 1917.

This was no flash in the pan. We have already seen what he could do at Le Cateau and at Cuinchy in 1914. He was hit on 1st July 1916, after magnificent work, cheering on the R.I.F. from the parapet. Skinner was ever the bravest of the brave, and, if he had been the wisest of the wise, the balance of nature would have been awry. Capt. Currie, whose account is given *ad longum* in *The Story of the 29th Division,* says that Skinner had to crawl seventy yards alone, in order to come to grips with the first blockhouse. It took ten minutes! That gives a man time for reflection. And further, Currie tells us that in dealing with the second blockhouse Skinner placed bombs in the loopholes from which the guns were firing, *i.e.* got them in at the front door. He must have had the nerve of a Blondin. It was not the place for a shaky hand.

One word more. Both these men were wounded at the time when they started on their exploits. In fact, Skinner had only returned from a position as instructor. It would be indiscreet to say how he managed it. But there he was when needed. Needless to say, both were awarded the Victoria Cross.

The 29th's Red Letter Day Calendar of Capt. Maurice Healy for 16th August 1917 has this: "The division successfully attained all its objectives." In reaching and consolidating their position on what was called the "green line," the 1st K.O.S.B. executed their allotted task.

How successful the Borderers were on this momentous day in the history of the regiment can be gauged from the following extracts from a letter written to Col. Welch on 25th August 1917 by Sir Beauvoir de Lisle.

After describing the attack as "the most successful we ever had," the letter goes on: "The regiment did very fine work, and I have recommended two for V.C.s.—Grimbaldeston * and Skinner. But for the fine spirit shown by your fellows, the S.W.B. would not have been able to get on. No doubt you heard we got up to the whole of our line in scheduled time and held it—the only division that did so in both armies."

* Grimbaldeston attended the famous V.C. dinner in 1929 over which H.R.H. the Prince of Wales presided.

16 Aug. 1917. The fight was over and the work of consolidation begun by 8 a.m.. The C.O. sent Capt. J. Watt to the nearest gun-pit to transmit the glad news to Brigade H.Q., which was fortunate for that excellent officer. Hardly had he gone when Battalion H.Q. received a direct hit. Coming to the casualties, 2nd Lieut. J. Murray (of the 5th Battalion) was the only officer killed, but 25 O.R. fell. Five officers and 71 O.R. were wounded, including the whole H.Q. personnel, Lieut.-Col. A. J. Welch (badly burned) A/Capt. A. N. Lewis, the Adjutant, and 2nd Lieut. W. C. Douglas of the 3rd Battalion, who died the next day, the promising intelligence officer of the battalion. It is interesting to recall how he came to hold that post. 2nd Lieut. Oliphant had been I.O. since the institution of the office in the spring of 1916, and he and Sergt. Guy Boothby were as well known to the battalion as the C.O.. "Me an' Oliphant" formed a strong combination, and as we shall see, Oliphant became 87th Brigade I.O.. But on this occasion he had obtained leave to return to his platoon and go over the top. Douglas was the obvious man to succeed him, and it was his fate to be killed in the position which at first sight anyone would pronounce the less dangerous of the two.

The C.O.'s wound was very painful, and he never returned to his battalion during the war, though he was able to do fine service in the 51st Division in the following year. But he could reflect as he lay in the hospital at Étaples that the plans he had elaborated with his trusty subordinates had succeeded brilliantly, thanks to the gallantry of the troops he had trained, without which all schemes must gang agley. Major C. A. G. O. Murray was well able to carry on, but unquestionably Lieut.-Col. A. J. Welch was a great loss to the battalion, brigade, and division.

The battalion was relieved by the R.I.F., and passed back to the Elverdinghe area, and during the week out of the line worked on the all-important tracks. Five days in the line brought sporadic shelling but no hostile operations. They were passed in the sector captured by the Essex and Worcesters on the 16th. On the 29th the battalion went out of the line with only one casualty, marched to Elverdinghe and trained to Bandaghem,* camping at Paddock Wood, near Proven, and 6 miles from the division training-ground at Herzeele.

The Corps Commander, Lord Cavan, had already sent appreciative messages for the good work on the 16th. He had evidently received a good report from Gen. de Lisle, and passed it on to the army, for on the 3rd September there was an "Honours Parade," at

* The inventor of "Bandaghem" for a casualty clearing station deserves full marks.

THE BATTLE OF LANGEMARCK 16TH AUGUST 1917

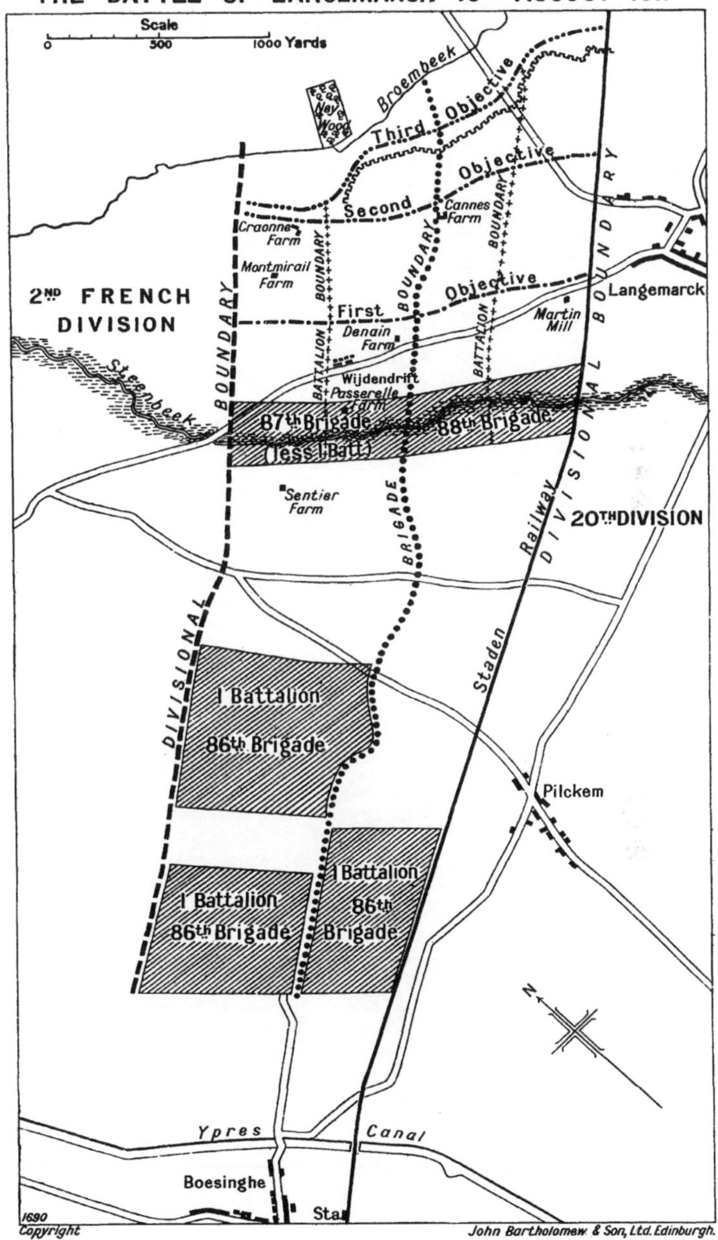

To face Page 200

which the G.O.C. presented the following medals: to Capt. Watt, M.C., a bar; to Lieut. T. C. Noel, 2nd Lieut. J. Oliphant, and Capt. T. J. L. Thomson, the M.O. of the battalion, the M.C.. Sergts. M'Connon (B) and Graham (D) received the D.C.M.. Sept. 1917.

The following 10 O.R. received the M.M.—Sergt. H. Smith (A), Corps. Atkin (A), Wallace (C), and Margrave (with T.M.B.), L.-Corp. M'Taggart (B), and Pts. Bracewell (B, killed in action 11th April 1918), Johnstone (B), Quinn (formerly H.L.I.) of A, killed in action 18th August 1918), M'Millan (C), and Watson (C). The 29th were out of the line from 29th August to 22nd September, and the time was spent training and absorbing drafts. In a brigade boxing tournament the battalion won 3 out of 4 finals. In the band competition they were third out of all the XIV. Corps entries. This was on 18th September when Gén. La Capelle presented the Croix de Guerre at the close of a brilliant ceremonial parade of the whole division to the two V.C. heroes and Sergt. Graham, D.C.M..

On 30th September the battalion returned to an Elverdinghe camp, and on 2nd October relieved the R.I.F. with unexpected ease. It was well for them that they did not have to move up on the night of 3rd/4th October. As we have seen, the 2nd Battalion had the awful experience of a storm of lashing, drenching, continuous rain, before getting "taped" for the first assault on Polderhoek. It was also well for the 1st that they were on the outskirts and not in the thick of the battle on October 4th. The 3rd brought 14 casualties—the result of shelling. A fight of magnitude was impending and the guns were searching the back areas. The gallant Q.M.S. W. Crombie was hit while bringing up supplies, and died of his wounds. He was one of the best men in the whole regiment—a regiment that contained men of the quality of Mackenzie the Pipe-Major, C.S.M.s R. H. Smith, Michie, and H. B. Turnbull. No battalion in the division was better off for N.C.O.s than the 1st K.O.S.B.. Capt. and Q.-M. W. Simpson, the very prince of quartermasters, whose efficiency was never so conspicuous as when lack of supplies seemed inevitable, and whose long and splendid service had won him an outstanding position not only in the battalion but in the brigade and division (who won the M.C. for gallantry in this battle), assured me it was one of the most terrific bombardments he ever witnessed. But the German guns would have been better employed had they been concentrated on the area between Langemarck and the Broembeek on either side of the railway. For the Dublin Fusiliers were making ready for battle on the S. side of the track and the K.O.S.B. similarly employed on the N. side.

It may seem strange that two battalions out of different brigades

4 Oct. 1917. should have been the only troops of a whole famous division to be employed, and only two platoons of one of the two battalions. The explanation is that all operations have got to have a flank somewhere. The thrust was being driven E. in the form of a salient, and that salient had to be joined to the stationary bit of the line. The K.O.S.B. were on the extreme L. of the battle, and their neighbours on the L., the Borders, did not move at all. The farthest objective of the K.O.S.B. on the R. was not as much as 400 yards off, and the Dublins' farthest point only 1,000 yards.

In the ordinary course it would have been an 87th I.B. show, but the Dublins (86th I.B.) wished to give a parting gift to Gen. de Lisle before exchanging the 29th for the 16th (Irish) Division. The "Dubs," therefore, had the long end of the stick. How successful they were has been told in *The Story of the 29th Division*. Let us fix our attention on A, the K.O.S.B. company of assault. Starting at zero, 6 a.m., two platoons advanced by rushes from their trench 1,000 yards N. of Langemarck, with a view to protecting the Dublins' flank by the formation of three strong posts. Two hostile strong-points on the railway-track were still unsilenced. It had been a splendid barrage, but something was bound to escape somewhere, and these points threatened trouble. In fact, the Dublins on the R. were being held back. Two corporals came to the rescue—M'Knight and Chittenden. Employing the Skinner tactics they worked round the L., and, when they reached the back door, the garrison of 12 surrendered and 2 M.G. were taken. For this gallant *coup de main* they were awarded the D.C.M.. The occupants of the other pill-box had lost heart at being attacked on both flanks and had decamped. The War Diary is entitled to describe the operation as an unqualified success, for the work of consolidation was promptly carried out, and the garrison were in a position to repel counter-attacks in the afternoon. The cost was not heavy. 2nd Lieut. E. B. Wilson was wounded, but insisted on superintending consolidation. He was awarded the M.C. for his services on the 4th. There were 49 O.R. casualties. The heavy shelling, which so often followed a hostile set-back, on the 5th accounted for 2 more subalterns *hors de combat*, G. M. L. Smith and J. L. Gibson, and 11 O.R. became casualties. It was fortunate battalion H.Q. were shellproof, as they received direct hits several times. They were situated at the stump of a mill (Martin Mill), on the wrecks of the road from Langemarck to Bixschoote, about a mile from the farthest off of the new strong points. After relief on 5th October by Guards and S.W.B. (no doubt explained by a readjustment of the line), the battalion retired to Elverdinghe camps; and on 9th October, when the 29th were fighting their last engagement in the Third Battle of Ypres in the Battle of Poelcapelle, the Borderers were moving farther back to a muddy (" Pitchcott ") camp in the Proven area. On the 15th they entrained at Peselhoek, just N. of Poperinghe (the 29th having handed over to the 17th Division on the 11th), alighted at Saulty on the Arras-Doullens Road, and marched 4 miles N.E. to Bailleulval, cheek by jowl with Divisional H.Q. at Basseux, in country ideal for training. Bad as was the experience of the 1st K.O.S.B. in the salient they were certainly less mauled than many other units, including other Borderers. There had been no calamity of magnitude. It may be claimed that they owed a certain immunity to their own resourcefulness and energy. Besides those mentioned already as recipients of decorations, Sergt. Parkinson (D), Corp. Falconer (A), and Ptes. Robbins (A) and Syme (D) were awarded the M.M.. They certainly appreciated the flank support of their comrades of the S.W.B. and 88th I.B. on 16th August, and of the Dublins on 4th October, and the barrages of the guns and T.M.B.. Gen. de Lisle's verdict that the 29th left the salient with enhanced *moral* holds good of the K.O.S.B., who with the rest of the division shared the praises of Gen. Gough and Lord Cavan. Given a brush up, plenty sleep and food, and a " spot of leave," the 1st K.O.S.B. could be reckoned on to give a good account of themselves.

Oct. 1917.

CHAPTER V *

CAMBRAI

First Phase

Nov. 1917. THIS enigmatical finale to the long drawn-out Allied offensive of 1917 brought to the Germans that rest of which in their exhaustion they stood in such pressing need.† Its relation to the British war strategy is obscure. What exactly was expected of it has not yet come to light. Informed criticism has accounted for the petering out of the offensive by the familiar *cliché* " want of weight behind the spear." But if forces were not available to exploit the pursuit or roll past the flanks of an obstruction and engulf it, it is difficult to see why an experiment pregnant with such vast possibilities was put into operation at that point of time when we too were exhausted. Early in November the Third Battle of Ypres had literally stuck in the mud. Passchendaele was a word like a nightmare. It stood for the exhaustion and depletion of scores of splendid formations.

Hindenburg credits our Higher Command with a " higher operative spirit," and admits the surprise of the onslaught. He attributes to subordinate leaders the failure to exploit the initial victory—a charge difficult to substantiate.‡ Ludendorff simply says that the Army Commander (Sir J. Byng) did not make use of his initial success. He attributes much to the opportune arrival of the fresh 107th Infantry Division from Russia in the very nick of time.§ But still the question arises: Suppose the 107th had not been at hand, suppose the Germans had not fought so well at Flesquières, Bourlon, and, generally, on the N. flank of the new salient, what were the British going to do? Where were they going to stop in the process of rolling up the line towards Douai? How was the new territory to be garrisoned and made defensible? No! The episode was unlike what had gone before and unlike what was to follow in the victorious advance of the 100 days.||

* See Map 1. † Ludendorff's *Kriegserinnerungen*, p. 397.
‡ *Aus Meinem Leben*, p. 266. § Ludendorff, *op. cit.*, p. 396.
|| The despatch of 4/3/1918, in the *General Review* (see vol. viii. of the Naval and Military Despatches, p. 77) sounds a note of uncertainty foreign to

But *in itself* this battle is one of the real thrills of the war. As a tactical feat, the 20th November is without a rival, and in its later stages the battle gave scope for the steadfastness and grit of the British fighting man. It is with this aspect of it that we are concerned. In the history of the K.O.S.B. the Battle of Cambrai is an event of the first magnitude. Nov. 1917.

The 1st K.O.S.B. remained at Bailleulval for more than a month and trained hard in preparation for a divisional field-day held on 15th November, when, in the presence of Sir Douglas Haig, the C.-in-C., and Sir L. E. Kiggell, Haig's Chief of Staff, the battalion acted as advanced-guard to the 87th I.B. in a village attack. There were also present Lieut.-Gen. Sir Wm. Pulteney, commander of the III. Corps., to which the 29th were to be transferred, and Brig.-Gen. C. G. Fuller, his B.G., G.S. or Chief Staff Officer, formerly Gen. de Lisle's G.S.O.1 from June 1915 to 11th October 1917. The entries show that everything possible was done to harden and equip the troops for open warfare. There were marches always with some tactical purpose and usually over the open fields in full battle order with packs. There was a brigade field-day on the 12th. There was bayonet fighting, range practices, gas-chamber practice, outposts, siting and spitlocking earthworks. Above all, attention was paid to fire and movement.

The repaired railway from Arras to Albert and Péronne had a station, Boisleux, 7 miles S. of Arras. Thither the 1st K.O.S.B. repaired by march in the afternoon of 17th November, and there they entrained for Péronne at 7.30 p.m., and in the dark rumbled past Beaucourt Station—their objective on 1st July 1916—past Albert and Corbie to the outskirts of Amiens, and thence past Villers-Bretonneux to the ruins of historic Péronne. It was still dark when they marched about 3 miles N. to Haut-Allaines past famous Mont St. Quentin. They waited till next night. Secrecy was all in all. They lay at Fins a little farther N. beyond Nurlu on the 18th and in tents in Dessart Wood on the 19th, preparing for the fight. On the same day D.H.Q. moved into Quentin Mill, near Gouzeaucourt, and about 3 miles E. of Dessart Wood. Due N. of Dessart lay the great wood of Havrincourt. Both woods were crammed with troops and camouflaged tanks. The wet, chilly November weather had been a help to General Byng, for visibility was poor. The plan was to attack on a 6-mile front with tanks equipped with fascines to facilitate trench-crossings in advance

the usual cogently reasoned confidence associated with Lord Haig's despatches, *e.g.* " Whatever may be the final decision on this point (*i.e.* to go on after 21st November), as well as on the original decision to undertake the enterprise at all with the forces available."

20 Nov. 1917. of six divisions. The direction was N.E. towards Cambrai. The path was barred by the Siegfried or, as we call it, the Hindenburg Line, backed by the admirably sited and broadly and massively wired support line. Both of these were deemed to be impregnable, and were lightly held. Without tanks they were safe from assault, until blown to bits by siege guns. With tanks it was hoped they could be breached without a preliminary bombardment. The III. Corps had four divisions at its disposal. The 12th (Scott), 20th (D. Smith), and the 6th (Marden) were to capture the Hindenburg and Hindenburg support lines. The 4th Division, the 29th, was to pass through on a three-brigade front as a division of pursuit, capture Marcoing and Masnières, secure the Scheldt and its canal, and finally seize the last German stronghold, the partially made Beaurevoir line, beyond which lay Cambrai and openness. Their place of assembly near Gouzeaucourt had been selected and taped, and all the units had to do was to shoulder their heavy fighting equipment and follow their guides. The 87th led the way, the first unit leaving Dessart Wood at 1 a.m. on 20th November. The only audible sound was the chug-chugging of the tanks,* and the staff work had been so comprehensive and exact that not a hitch took place anywhere. All the troops were ready in their places long before the hour of zero.

The tanks led off the attack at 6.10 a.m.. Ten minutes later there followed a terrific bombardment, the registering of which had been one of the most difficult problems in the preservation of secrecy. The rear areas and gun positions were plastered with H.E. and smoke. The assaulting troops moved with the barrage, and the 29th moved quietly up in rear to their various destinations in the old British front line. When the time to move forward came soon after 10 a.m., the 87th I.B. were in the centre, the 88th were on the R., and the 86th on the L.. The K.O.S.B. threw out an advanced guard, and made straight for Villers-Plouich and Marcoing preceded by a tank. The diarist says nothing about the crossing of the German trenches, but it must have been a strange sight. There was no counter-shelling and very little opposition till Marcoing was reached. The brigade did not adopt the diamond formation of those on the flank, but advanced as a square. But the battalions did, and represented the divisional sign, half a diamond with the point uppermost. The K.O.S.B. were the L.-hand corner and the S.W.B. the R.. Behind the K.O.S.B. were the Borders, and behind the S.W.B. the R.I.F.. With the clearing of Marcoing (50 prisoners) and the formation of a bridgehead on the far side of the Scheldt

* Note by Lieut. J. Oliphant, M.C., K.O.S.B..

canal (it was a touch-and-go affair to save the bridge from destruction) the K.O.S.B.'s work on the first day ended. They did not join in the unsuccessful hammering at the now strongly manned German defences in which the Borders and R.I.F. took part. It was the 107th Division that barred the path. 30 Nov. 1917.

Casualties were light but A/Capt. Willock was fatally wounded,* and there were 26 O.R. casualties. The next day's attempt to force the Masnières-Beaurevoir line was unsuccessful despite the efforts of 16 tanks. There was no artillery support forthcoming. Two lieutenants, Currie and Howie, were wounded, and there were 57 O.R. casualties. The S.W.B. fared worse and had hardly any officers left by the end of this day. The 22nd and 23rd were spent in improving the defences, the 25th and 26th were spent in the Masnières sector. On the 27th the battalion returned to the Marcoing sector and remained there till the storm broke on the 30th.

Second Phase

The Battle of St. Andrew's Day

Early in the morning of that day the Germans broke through the 20th Division on the Crèvecœur-Banteux-Honnecourt flank of the huge British salient. Masses of Germans poured across the Bonavis Ridge, along which runs the great road from Péronne to Cambrai, overran Villers-Guislain and Quentin Mill, capturing the C.R.A., but missing the G.O.C., and finally penetrating most of Gouzeaucourt, where a brisk fight started. A glance at the map will show that Masnières and Marcoing bade fair to be cut off at first from supplies (which hitherto reached the front by the Couillet Valley Railway), and then from all succour. The first thing, therefore, that Gen. de Lisle did was to get forward and organize the defences of his brigades.

At that time the 86th I.B. (Brig.-Gen. Cheape) were in the Masnières or R. sector in a semicircle enclosing that village down to the R. bank of the Scheldt and also on the L. bank in the suburb of Masnières known as Les Rues Vertes, henceforth L.R.V.. The 87th I.B., with the exception of our battalion, covered the bend of the river from the Cambrai road on the N. outskirts of Masnières and most of Marcoing (about 600 yards behind the front line at that point). Beyond in the Nine Wood–Noyelles sector were the 6th Division.

* He died much regretted on 22nd November (Official Death Roll). His *sang-froid* was a great asset.

30 Nov. 1917. The 88th I.B. and the 1st K.O.S.B. were in reserve in the cellars of Marcoing sheltering from the vehemence of the bombardment.

The general drive of the German attack on the morning of 30th November 1917 was from E. to W. astride Crèvecœur, and on both sides of the river and canal. It is obvious that the 86th I.B. would be —as they were—the first to be involved—in the Masnières salient and at L.R.V.. But it is equally clear that the enemy troops S. of L.R.V. on "Welsh Ridge" (see Map) would pass clear of that village, and once they cleared the copse called Marcoing Copse would be in a fair way to envelop Marcoing (2 miles W. of Masnières) from the rear and thus cut off most, if not all, of the 29th Division. Further, if Masnières and L.R.V. fell, Marcoing was doomed, for there was no room for deployment of the troops trapped in the river bend, and which would have first to come through the bottle-neck of Marcoing before coming into action.

The splendid fight of the 86th in defence of Masnières and the recovery of L.R.V., largely due to the matchless bravery and dash of Captain Robert Gee, V.C. (surely his was the most important feat in the divisional story), are not for these pages.*

The Fight

About 9 a.m. news came to the K.O.S.B. from B.H.Q. that the enemy were advancing down from Welsh Ridge in extended order right for Marcoing. It was touch and go whether the village would be overwhelmed before the garrison could turn out. From the 23rd, when they registered, the German guns had poured almost continuous shell-fire into Marcoing and Masnières. It was thanks to German catacombs that casualties were so light. The bombardment increased in its intensity on the 29th, continued all night, and stopped suddenly at 9 a.m. on the 30th. 87th and 88th H.Q. personnel rushed to the nearest sunk road and poured volley after volley into the Germans, some of whom were hurrying up M.G., then skirmished forward to another coign of vantage taking 8 prisoners *en route* and enabling the 88th troops and *in primis* the K.O.S.B. to deploy. A vigorous fire from N. of the canal was directed against the Germans by the S.W.B., in whose sector Capt. James Oliphant, the brigade intelligence officer, happened to be at the time. †

The 1st K.O.S.B. at first made for the canal bend on the E. edge of the village, but finding further progress barred were directed by

* For an account of this fighting reference may be made to *The Story of the 29th Division* and to *The Royal Fusiliers in the Great War* (O'Neill).

† Account by Capt. J. Oliphant, M.C., kindly furnished.

Lieut.-Col. C. A. G. O. Murray, their C.O., to hasten S. down the cover of one of several sunk roads leading towards La Vacquerie until a point was reached at which an attack could be organized to the E. on a two company front (A and B). It was then about 11 a.m. when, for the first time since the early fighting in Gallipoli, the 1st K.O.S.B. "did the attack" in grim earnest. Capt. Oliphant thus describes the situation as he found it on running to 87th H.Q. in Marcoing. "The K.O.S.B. were attacking and had relieved the situation." Until then "the 87th Brigade H.Q. had been out and fighting for their lives." On their L. were the 88th I.B., and the whole force advanced just as their G.O.C. would have had them do. "All units working independently by platoons advanced to the east instinctively, acting in accordance with the careful training they had received in 'Fire and Movement.' The outskirts of the town were at once cleared and the advancing Germans driven back 2,000 yards beyond the right flank of the 29th at L.R.V.. These five battalions then linked up the 5,000 yards gap between this village and the left of the 20th Division, which had fallen back to the Hindenburg support line. This performance was the more creditable in that platoons and companies were mixed, and that all units worked *without any orders* and *without control*." * On the R. of the line the K.O.S.B., flanked on the L. by the Hants, Worcesters, Essex, and N.F.L.D., advanced fully 1,000 yards, fighting all the way, in short bounds using covering fire. Everywhere the expenditure of small-arm ammunition was heavy, but supplies were ample. By noon the K.O.S.B. reached a defensible position about a mile due S. of the bend. With the aid of two companies of the Worcesters, they were able to link up about 2.30 p.m. with some *disjecta membra* of the 20th Division and to hold and eventually, after dark, to consolidate the position. Nearer the canal in the lower ground the 88th had advanced somewhat farther, past L.R.V., and the 29th held an unbroken front facing S.E.. "General de Lisle has given it as his considered opinion that this counter-stroke was the most effective work the 88th did during the whole war." † The same remark may be applied to their comrades, the K.O.S.B., who on that day proved themselves worthy successors of the men of 25/26th April 1915. It was a tactical masterpiece, and one cannot help hoping that some day one of the surviving participants will tell the story in full detail.

The casualties were not excessive—8 officers and 130 O.R.. As not infrequently happens in manœuvre action there were more missing (often really killed) than usual. Lieuts. D. Grant and

* Gen. de Lisle, quoted from *The Story of the 29th Division*, p. 166.

† *History of the Essex Regiment*, at p. 132.

Dec. 1917. W. R. D. Meikle and 2nd Lieuts. F. G. Carson and P. Milroy were killed; Capts. J. Watt, M.C. (the A/Adjutant), and E. Giles and Lieut. R. Macdonald, along with 2nd Lieut. G. V. Mackay, were wounded. Of O.R. 11 were killed, 79 were wounded, and 40 were missing.

It looked as if the Germans had had enough of it in this quarter. While the battle raged round Marcoing, Masnières, and L.R.V. on 1st, 2nd, and notably 3rd December, and the other troops of the 87th Brigade and the 86th were performing prodigies of valour, the K.O.S.B. have nothing to record.* Such is the fortune of war. But it rarely happened in the war that any unit got off scot free. The 1st K.O.S.B. paid dearly in the Lys in its very next combat in April. In the meantime they reaped the fruits of their alertness, their dash, and their shooting and digging in the shape of a quiet finish—almost an anti-climax.

They were shelled, of course, and sniped, but 40 O.R. casualties on the fringe of a battle were light. But the long strain was telling, and they were glad when the 2nd R.I.R. relieved them on 5/6th December. The 1st K.O.S.B. marched out—one cannot say to a man—but in good force under their successful C.O., Col. C. A. Murray, 16 miles to Étricourt *via* Ribécourt and Fins, over or near ground destined to fame through the valour of the 6th K.O.S.B. and their comrades in the 9th Division in a few months.

The train took them to the familiar rest area N. of Doullens, to Beaudricourt, just N. of Lucheux big wood. Ceremonial drill on the 10th must have been a chilly proceeding. On the 14th the A/G.O.C., Brig.-Gen. C. H. T. Lucas,† inspected the battalion and spoke highly of their work in the recent battle.

It is very doubtful if the 29th have yet received the universal recognition which their services in defending the nose of that jutting salient merit. But those who knew—that is to say, Generals Haig, Byng, Pulteney, and de Lisle—voiced their "warm congratulations on a splendid fight worthy of the best traditions of the British Army" and their "sincere," "deep," and "high" appreciation respectively.

On 17th December the K.O.S.B. began the march to Flanders. The prospect was unattractive, the reality if possible worse, as the snow did not tend to make the march easy. However, they struck the Canche, and covered 14½ miles down it to Fillièvres. Next day they crossed the river and the fine Forêt d'Hesdin, and billeted in Wambercourt-Cavron-St. Martin. The snow was deeper here, and

* Perhaps I may refer to my *Story of the 29th Division* and the chapter entitled "The Battle of Cambrai."

† Now a major-general (1929).

THE BATTLE OF CAMBRAI - THE 29TH IN THE COUNTER ATTACK NOV. 30TH DEC. 5TH 1917

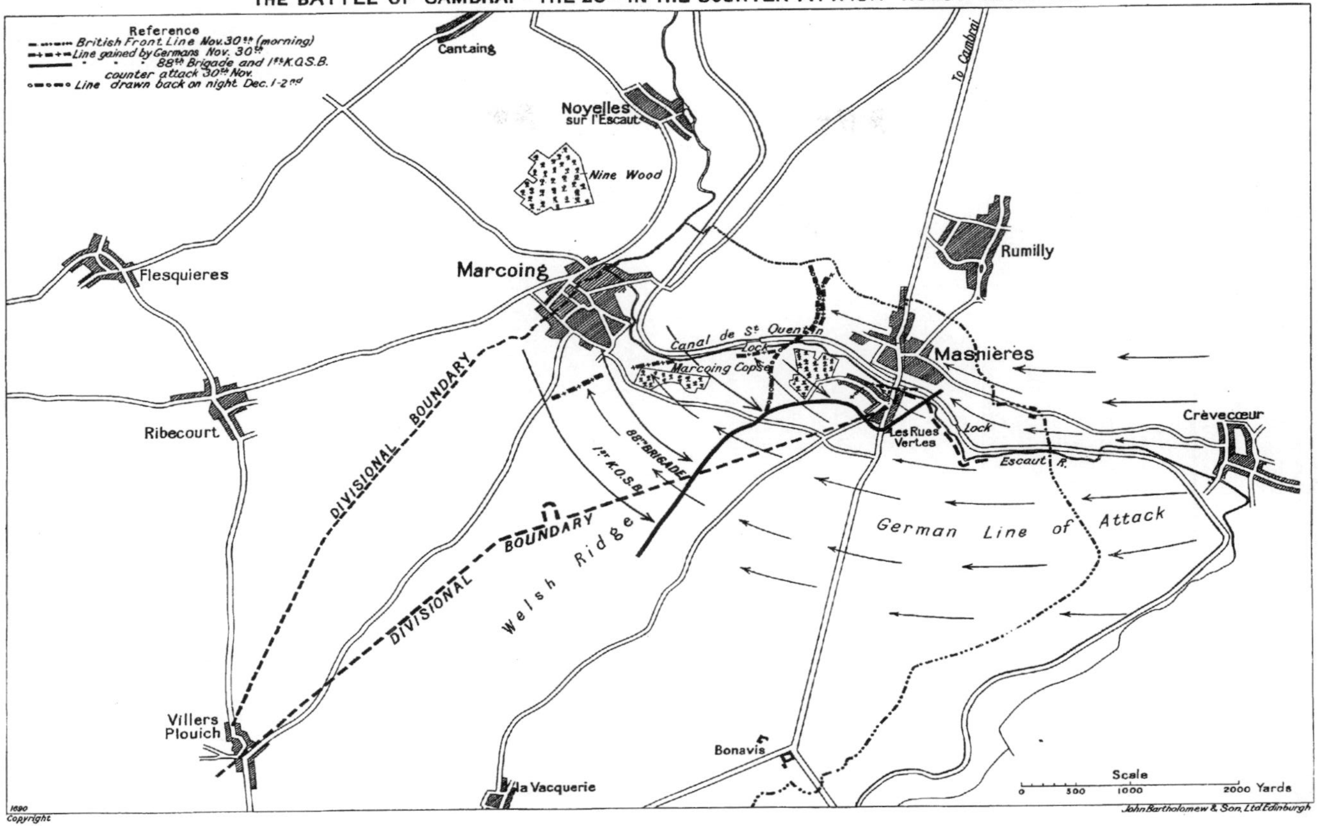

Reference
British Front Line Nov. 30th (morning)
Line gained by Germans Nov. 30th
" " " 88th Brigade and 1st K.O.S.B. counter attack 30th Nov.
Line drawn back on night Dec. 1-2nd

Cantaing
Noyelles sur l'Escaut
Nine Wood
Flesquieres
Marcoing
Rumilly
To Cambrai
Canal de St Quentin
Lock
Marcoing Copse
Masnières
Ribecourt
DIVISIONAL BOUNDARY
88th BRIGADE
1st K.O.S.B.
Les Rues Vertes
Lock
Escaut R.
Crèvecœur
German Line of Attack
DIVISIONAL BOUNDARY
Welsh Ridge
Villers Plouich
Bonavis
La Vacquerie
Scale
0 500 1000 2000 Yards

1690 Copyright

John Bartholomew & Son, Ltd Edinburgh

To face Page 210

drifts in places made the roads almost impassable. The 11¾ miles seemed like 30. Next day finished the first stage of the trek, and was the worst march of all, though it was only 10½ miles long. The country between Hesdin and Boulogne is distinctly hilly and is broken into ridges and valleys. To get to Herly the K.O.S.B. marched on small country roads like switchbacks, and the drifts in places were awful. They remained here till the 31st.

Dec. 1917.

After cleaning up, the de Lisle curriculum started as of yore, and there were 114 newcomers to be initiated. A large batch of officers joined. Christmas Day brought good cheer, voluntary church services, and Sir A. Hunter-Weston. A parade was hurriedly called, and the original G.O.C. 29th gave them a rousing speech and afterwards exchanged greetings with old friends of all ranks, and was fêted with a boisterous enthusiasm which was not excelled by any other unit of the division. On the last day of 1917 the K.O.S.B. marched down the Aa to Assinghem near Lumbres. They were in before dark and settled down to such Hogmanay fare and fun as were available. 1917 was a dreadful year for Britain and the Allies. It was a great year for the 29th Division and the old 25th of Foot, and I believe they would face the New Year cheerfully.

CHAPTER VI

THE LYS AND AFTER

Jan.– April 1918.

THE last year of the war divides into four periods for the purposes of this part of the story. There is winter in and behind the very tip of the Passchendaele salient. Then follows the " back to the wall " defensive period, in the latter part of which things brighten. With the capture of Outtersteene Ridge on 18th August, a great day for the 1st and 6th K.O.S.B., a third phase opens. The Germans then began to withdraw from Flanders. Finally, there is the fourth period, that of the last of the Ypres battles, ending in the expulsion of the Germans and the occupation of the Rhine bridgehead. In this last fighting the 1st K.O.S.B. took part in two pitched battles, that of the 28th September and the action of 22nd October near Ooteghem.

The first period was one of toil, in which the valuable lessons learned at Beaudricourt and Herly tended to be forgotten and the braced up leg muscles to relax. Three months of Passchendaele was bad for mobility and hard on the health. But on New Year's Day 1918 the 15 miles march to Le Nieppe was a trifle. After stays of a night at Rietveld (N. of Cassel, which was skirted on the W. side) and two nights at " Privett " Camp, near Proven, the 1st K.O.S.B. proceeded, some by train and some by road, to Boesinghe and the canal banks (still within range of shells) N. of Ypres. Here the men worked like navvies at hut construction and carried masses of material. On the 18th they marched back to Brandhoek, near " Pop.," and trained as best they could for a week before moving into the front zone. Intimations of Cambrai honours kept coming in the while. Capts. H. S. Harvey, E. Giles, and H. R. Collier, and Lieuts. F. Dale and W. Barnard were awarded the M.C. . A/C.S.M. P. Stevenson and Ptes. Waite and Bowers were awarded the D.C.M. . Nine M.M. were allotted to the 1st K.O.S.B., and L.-Corp. J. F. Cope received a bar to his. It was strange to find Wieltje ruins provided with a railway station. To take the train to Wieltje from Proven was unthinkable in 1916. At first the battalion worked on the division defence line near Wieltje, and only on 3rd February did it relieve the 4th Worcesters in two sides of an angle, the sides being a series of disconnected posts. The front was insecure, it was short of the road from Passchendaele to Westroosebeke and was overlooked by the enemy. It was not water- but wet filth-logged. Corpses lay around unburied. The approaches to it were confined to duckboard tracks unusable by day and dangerous by night. The task of improving such outposts called for superhuman exertions, inexhaustible patience, and faith. They were only tested by two or three raids (not on K.O.S.B.), and each of these was driven off. The War Diary describes the work thus: "Deepening trench and laying duckboards." A tour in the front line lasted six days. At the end of the February tour when the Division was relieved by the 8th Division on the 12th, the K.O.S.B. found themselves at Watou, W. of "Pop.," for the rest of the month, pulling themselves together. At the end of the month they returned to the forward zone. The value of the railway can now be appreciated. Men could sleep at "Pop.," rail forward to Wieltje, do a hard day's "darg" and return to comparative peace. But work on the "Army" line near "Pop." was more convenient as well as safer.

Jan.–April 1918.

The 1st K.O.S.B. were one of the first battalions to take over from 8th Division units on 6th March. With them were half of the S.W.B., and the work of linking up posts so as to form a continuous trench was continued. A good deal of wiring was being done and things began to look a bit more shipshape. An incentive to effort was the certain knowledge, allowed to reach all ranks, who hadn't the perspicacity to see it for themselves, of the approaching German offensive. The tour only lasted three days, and was followed by three days at St. Jean, so familiar to the 29th in 1916. The next tour was marked by an outstanding calamity. C.S.M. Skinner, V.C., D.C.M., was sniped on 17th March. He was given a great funeral on the 19th at Vlamertinghe with six V.C. pall-bearers. He had been wounded eight times in his career and seemed incapable of considering his personal safety, or of understanding how anyone could enjoy a fight less than he did. He was certainly one of the most remarkable men in the British Army. The very next night the battalion was relieved locally, and on 22nd returned to Brandhoek until the end of the month, when they re-entered the line, relieving troops of the 86th I.B., and got to work "improving trench system." *

The news of the reverse on the Somme on and after 21st March created a natural expectation that the 29th would be sent there. But it fell out differently, although at one time Tinques was named

* War Diary.

April 1918. on good authority as the first stage southwards. They were rapidly relieved on 8th April from the front line. By nightfall they were in camp at St. Jans-ter-Biezen, and the following night (the 9th) as the result of the more immediate peril on the Lys they were bussed to Neuf Berquin to the XV. Corps (du Cane). They reached Neuf Berquin, 3 miles E. of the Forêt de Nieppe and only 2 miles N.E. of Merville, on the morning of 10th April. They had left behind with the usual 10 per cent. dumped personnel Lieut.-Col. C. A. G. O. Murray and Capts. H. R. Collier, M.C. (C), and Higgins (D). They arrived early and the bitterly cold, raw, misty morning was a better friend than at first appeared. German aeroplanes were active, and the detrained, bunched battalion would have been an ideal target on a fine day. As it was, they were marched 3 miles N. to Vieux Berquin, where they shed their *impedimenta* and lay quiet in "battle order" until 5 p.m.. At one time in the afternoon hostile aeroplanes showed an inquisitive interest in the village. One of these was actually brought down by K.O.S.B. Lewis gun-fire, and the pilot and observer were captured and taken to Brigade H.Q.. That evening about 5 p.m., and just in time to avoid heavy shelling, they moved E. towards the line of the impending attack, *i.e.* in the direction of Steenwerck, near the Franco-Belgian frontier. In short, they were slightly N.E. of the scene of the 2nd Battalion's activities two days later. The country was dead flat. It was enclosed and cultivated, and the numerous roads were tree-lined. The roads were cumbered with the carts of peasants, who were trying to carry away something out of this late and unexpected wreckage of their lives. The whole atmosphere was one of tension, confusion, and the fog of war. The 29th were only two brigades strong, the 88th being still unrelieved at Passchendaele, and *minus* the divisional artillery. Brig.-Gen. G. H. Jackson commanded the 87th I.B., and Brig.-Gen. Cheape the 86th. The K.O.S.B. were on the R. of the S.W.B., with A, B, and C in the front line and D in reserve. Touch was difficult to keep owing to the enclosed nature of the country and darkness, and at one time A in its efforts to keep touch with the S.W.B. lost contact with B. The advance continued till the Germans were located by patrols in concealed entrenchments. This put an end to further advance. D was brought into the gap between A and B, and the former was eventually brought back to Battalion Reserve early on the 11th.

On the morning of 11th April the K.O.S.B. were ready, with A now in reserve and the remaining three companies in the line N. of Doulieu. And sure enough about 8 a.m. the Germans came on in overwhelming force, supported by intense M.G. fire. They got a warm reception from the 29th everywhere, but nowhere were they more sturdily resisted than on the front of the three K.O.S.B. companies, who mowed down attack after attack, until the enemy poured through a gap on the L. of B and began to engage A, the company in reserve. It was then 5.30 p.m., and A, unable to advance in the face of M.G. fire, fell back slightly to the bank of a small stream, until the general retreat was effected under cover of night. By this time Major Muir was missing and Capt. Crawshaw was wounded, and Capt. Thwaites, the Signal Officer, was senior and in command of the battalion. As the 86th I.B. on the N. had failed to find contact with British troops near La Crèche, and the 87th, on whose R. the K.O.S.B. were, soon found that their neighbours in the S. had gone, the two brigades had either to fall back or be surrounded. The crossings of the Lys, both at Estaires, after which this battle is named, and Merville, were by now in hostile hands, and the onrush was so rapid that the three companies were, to use the words of the War Diary, "practically surrounded." It would seem, to judge from the large numbers of wounded, viz. 207 O.R. and 7 officers, including Major Muir of the 17th Lancers, then second in command and in command on this occasion, and 5 subalterns, that the action had been contested for some time before the inevitable collapse, which is indicated, to a considerable extent, by the 243 missing. The remnants of these companies, along with A and some miscellaneous items, continued the fight until nightfall, when the whole force under Gen. Cayley's command retreated westwards. On the 12th, despite the lack of adequate artillery support and in face of extra heavy hostile M.G. fire but comparatively little shelling, position after position was contested and reluctantly yielded until a definite stand was made on the line Vieux Berquin-Merris. The fighting was of the hand to mouth kind, in which men without maps or overhead direction make what stand they can to cover a continuous retrograde movement. Officers and N.C.O.s are inevitably exposed and general casualties run high. The 12th April was no exception. Lieut. Stewart, the battalion Intelligence Officer, had to be evacuated suffering from shell-shock early in the day. Lieut. Campbell (one of the surviving officers of C) was wounded, as was Capt. Thwaites. Heavy toll was taken of stretcher-bearers, who upheld the finest traditions of the British Army.

11–12 April 1918.

On the Merris line at a point about half a mile S. of that village the remnants of K.O.S.B. came under Brig.-Gen. Cheape's orders, and were sent to reinforce the 86th I.B.'s front between the 2nd R.F. and the 1st L.F., and the time was spent digging in and resting.

13-14 April 1918. — At this time A/Capt. D. C. Bullen-Smith reckons that he had only about 80 men of the whole battalion under his command. On the 13th no further hostile attacks were delivered, but owing to the shallowness of the trenches casualties due to shell-fire persisted. The 80 had dwindled to 37,* and the balance who made up the 150 at roll-call on 14th were men who had got lost and done their fighting in other units and now returned to their proper battalion. The Diary does not say who relieved the handful of Borderers left on the 13th/14th, but it was probably Australians of the 1st Division, who certainly relieved the 1st Border Regiment that day.† On the 14th the war-worn remnant were welcomed by the pipers and marched to Sylvestre Cappel (between Cassel and the mountains). When the roll was called, Capt. D. C. Bullen-Smith (O.C. A and A/O.C. in the field) and 150 O.R. were all who answered. Col. Murray, who now resumed command, found himself without an adjutant. Capt. Crawshaw, M.C., was wounded ‡ some time on the 11th, on which day the following officers were killed along with 17 O.R.: Lieut. H. C. Rooke (of the 3rd), 2nd Lieuts. N. E. N. Henderson, and G. G. Doughty. 2nd Lieut. E. C. I. Crofts died of wounds, a prisoner of war, on the 28th of the same month. Three officers were missing. All these were casualties on the 11th.

The fortune of war had turned against the 1st K.O.S.B. to some tune. But they had done all that was possible in the adverse circumstances—helped to delay the Germans, till those behind them had dug a line that held for the rest of the war. On 15th April, owing to 87th Brigade casualties, Lieut.-Col. Murray was given a mixed command of the three battalions, S.W.B., K.O.S.B., and Borders.

It is regrettable that more detail is not yet available, but in a situation so constantly fluctuating much must have passed into oblivion for good and all. But one fact stands out—that the K.O.S.B. put up a great fight in a losing battle.§ Not that the battle was yet over. On the 17th the composite battalion || (which, of course, now contained the 10 per cent. dumped personnel) moved

* Information supplied by Capt. Bullen-Smith, M.C..

† This fighting was the opportunity for Col. Forbes Robertson, who later on commanded the 155th I.B. at Hénin Hill, to render signal services, which won him the V.C..

‡ He was able to return to duty on 20th April.

§ The following decorations were awarded: To Sergt. W. Graham the D.C.M.; to Pte. O. Reilly a bar to his M.M.; to Sergt. W. Wilson, Corp. J. Brown, and Ptes. Ditchburn, J. E. Ward, and W. Dunlop, the M.M. A/Capt. D. C. Bullen-Smith, Lieut. G. G. Thwaites (wounded on 12th), and A. F. Campbell (wounded on 12th) all received the M.C..

|| Composed of K.O.S.B., S.W.B., and Borders, and forming part of a composite brigade (87th and 88th remnants) under Brig.-Gen. Jackson (*87th I.B. War Diary*).

May 1918.

to the support of the 1st Australian Division, and came in for a terrific bombardment, which went on for four hours, and in the course of which A/Capt. H. R. Collier, M.C., was killed, and Lieut. Bullen-Smith was wounded, 13 O.R. being casualties, and (C.S.M.) A/R.S.M. A. Muirhead (of Castle Douglas), D.C.M., one of the Gallipoli veterans, being killed, to the grief of all in his battalion. It was another piece of bad luck following swiftly on the main disaster. But it is consolatory to know that no attacks followed the box barrage and that the wounded were all removed to the casualty clearing-station 2 miles behind the line. The crisis was also over.* "Its dogged as does it." The German force for a second time was spent.

After a breather from the 18th to the evening of the 27th, the battalion relieved the 11th E. Yorks just S. of Strazeele railway station, and spent a busy but otherwise normal tour there until relieved by 88th I.B. troops on 5th May and retired to Le Grand Hasard, near Hazebrouck, on the road to Aire. On the 6th, 10 subalterns joined from the 3rd Battalion, and on the 9th Lieut.-Col. G. E. Beaty-Pownall, D.S.O.,† replaced Lieut.-Col. C. A. G. O. Murray, D.S.O.,‡ who received a home appointment.

The 1st K.O.S.B. remained on in the XV. Corps, now commanded by their old friend Gen. de Lisle since Gen. du Cane's appointment as liaison officer at G.Q.G. between Haig and Foch.§ Hard work was done to improve the front line and the reserve line at Petit Sec Bois. The strength was gradually being built up, and a raid was ordered by Brig.-Gen. Jackson. This outstanding event of the month came off in the small hours of the 27th. It reflects the greatest credit on 2nd Lieut. J. Cunningham Howie, O.C. raid (one of the recent arrivals from Duddingston), and 2nd Lieut. R. S. Slade (another), as well as on Sergt. J. Wilson and 32 O.R. of A, and deserves a fuller treatment than it can receive in a regimental story. The whole thing occupied only twenty-five minutes.

Two hostile M.G., a northern and a southern, on the road a trifle N. of Vieux Berquin had been troublesome, and it was decided that they must be silenced. Airmen took careful photographs. Howie and his team studied them well. A box barrage was prescribed for 2.15 a.m.. Howie had divided his team into three—two for assault and one to cover. But owing to the change in the position of one of the two objective M.G., which made its capture impossible, and the fact that one of the three parties was a covering Lewis gun

* Churchill, *World Crisis*, 1918, vol. ii. p. 435.

† Of the Border Regiment.

‡ Awarded as one of the Birthday Honours, and noted in the War Diary for 3rd June 1918.

§ Churchill, *op. cit.*, p. 436.

June–July 1918. party (which never was needed and came back at its convenience when things had quieted down) the ultimate assault was directed against the southern of the two M.G. by one party only.

Under Lieut. Slade that party crawled S. down a ditch parallel to the road and about 150 yards from the objective, got ready in good time and as the barrage lifted for the second target, rushed the position, took the gun (a light one), shot two Germans, and took 3 prisoners of the 132nd Inf. Regt. of the 39th Division. Three of the raiders were wounded while waiting for the barrage to lift. But these accidents will occur. It marked the resumption of the aggressive, offensive spirit. Retaliation fell behind or into intentionally empty trenches. It had all been well thought out and may be described as a " good show," and congratulations poured in. On 28th/29th May the battalion were relieved by the Dublins (back once more in the 86th Brigade) and had a week of Hazebrouck—a pleasant change.

June was an uneventful month either in the line or in Hazebrouck or Morbecque on the Aire road, and nearly all July was spent out of the line altogether—at Racquinghem and Blaringhem and St. Marie Cappel—except a short spell of work with the Australians, which reminds me irresistibly of the retort given by the justly celebrated sanitary expert of the 1st K.O.S.B. to an " Aussie " at an earlier stage of the war, who asked, " Who (etc.) are the K.O.S.B.? " " Never haird o' the Kayusbee ? We dug your baully peninsula for ye ! " *or words to that effect.*

The third phase, that of Outtersteene and the obliteration of the Hazebrouck salient, was heralded by stirring deeds elsewhere. The 18th of July saw Foch's first blow on the Aisne. Before the end of the month the 5th and 7/8th K.O.S.B. were heavily involved and doing grand work in the common cause with Scotland's auld ally. On 8th August events quite outside K.O.S.B. country marked the change to the offensive of the British Army as such. But further to the N. the situation was still unchanged. It was then that Gen. de Lisle, G.O.C. XV. Corps, planned the capture of the Méteren Ridge, using the 9th (Scottish) and 29th Divisions, and as it happens both the 1st and the 6th K.O.S.B. side by side as tactical mates. The possession of the ridge would be a priceless boon, as it would transfer from German to British eyes a wide range of observation. The ridge is fronted by the Méteren Becque, lies S. of Méteren (British since a dashing affair carried out by the Highland Brigade of the 9th), and is bounded by the Hazebrouck railway in the flat on the S. and E.. To the N.E. it falls gently down towards Bailleul.

The 29th were in the Merris sector. The 9th to the N. occupied the Méteren sector. The C.C.'s plan was for the 9th Division (using the Lowland Brigade) to attack *southwards* and capture Hoegenacker Mill, exactly one mile S. of Méteren. The 29th by an *eastward* movement were then to develop the situation on the ridge S. of the mill, and, if the omens were favourable, to assault Outtersteene, about 2,000 yards S.W. of the mill and just E. of the Méteren Becque.

Aug. 1918.

Gen. Cayley has called Hoegenacker Mill the key of the position, and has described its capture by the 9th as brilliant.* As the 6th K.O.S.B. doings are written elsewhere we can confine ourselves to the 1st K.O.S.B., keeping, however, in view the fact that they had lent one company (A) to follow in rear and support of the 6th and come under Lieut.-Col. G. Smyth's orders.

But before we launch our Borderers into the fight let it be mentioned that every effort had been made since the close of the Lys battle to make good those defects in manœuvring power which three months in the salient had brought about. Let it be frankly admitted, the Germans in 1918 showed a standard of open warfare tactics superior to anything we could show at the outset of the Allied offensive.

Minden was celebrated on 31st July under the erroneous idea that there was to be a move on 1st August. When August opened the 1st K.O.S.B. were still at St. Marie Cappel. On the 3rd they camped near Hazebrouck. On the 6th they drew up by the roadside at La Bréarde to receive at the salute H.M. King George V., who rode past them on the road.

It was not till the 15th that they moved into the line, relieving the 2nd Leinsters of the 88th I.B. in the L. (*i.e.* outside) sector of the brigade front, and to the extent of one company (B), taking over a bit of the 6th K.O.S.B.'s front.

In the early hours of the 16th there were bombardments and counter-bombardments. It was a wild night, and the Germans were apparently nervous and inclined to surrender. 2nd Lieut. A. L. Cranston of the 5th Battalion, along with one man, Pte. Stewart, when on patrol secured 9 prisoners of the 4th Division. Unfortunately Cranston was mortally wounded and his short career ended. Apparently Stewart brought the prisoners in, as Cranston was lying outside and was only got in through the devotion of the M.O., Capt. H. B. Sherlock, M.C..

Coming to the attack, Lieut.-Col. G. T. Raikes, D.S.O., was acting Brig.-Gen. of 87th I.B., and Brig.-Gen. W. D. Croft, D.S.O., directed the 27th I.B. on the L..

* See *The Story of the 29th Division*, pp. 200 and 202–204.

18 Aug. 1918. There was no preliminary bombardment on the 18th. Fire consisted of smoke and H.E. at zero, which was at the surprising hour of 11 a.m.. But its volume and accuracy left nothing to be desired. The battalion is said to have gone over the top as one man, and to have had an easy passage to the ridge S. of Hoegenacker Mill, which was taken in forty minutes, and then the 2nd S.W.B. carried on the good work by passing through them, storming the village, and even patrolling beyond. That night a line was consolidated, which included every inch of ground desired. The attack was a complete surprise, and the 1st K.O.S.B. took 300 prisoners out of a divisional total of 347, and no fewer than 60 M.G.. 2nd Lieuts. A. Maclean and H. J. Forbes were killed and 3 subalterns were wounded. There were 15 O.R. killed, 105 wounded, and 6 missing.

The 19th was a disturbed day, but at no time was a serious effort made to recover the ridge. That night they were relieved by the Borders, and withdrew to Hazebrouck. Whether it was *post hoc* or *propter hoc* is unknown; but the Germans did begin to withdraw on the 29th, and soon the whole division and corps were threading their way through booby traps, such as the 29th had left for the Turks at the Helles evacuation, past Bailleul towards Armentières. The 1st K.O.S.B., fresh from rest, got well past Bailleul by the 31st.

Continuing the advance on 3rd September, contact was found 1,000 yards W. of Nieppe, near Armentières, and the battalion dug in, and handed over to the 11th E. Yorks., relief by the 31st Division having begun. It was a sad day, for they lost their valiant M.O., Capt. Sherlock, who was evacuated, wounded. The 1st K.O.S.B. had no share in the brilliant capture of Hill 63 and Ploegsteert Wood by the 29th Division.*

Neither the Hazebrouck (Nevada Farm) nor Wallon Cappel spells of service call for comment. On 16th September the 1st parted from Gen. de Lisle, though not for good, and marched to the II. Corps (Sir C. W. Jacob) area at St. Jans-ter-Biezen, between Poperinghe and Watou.

The final and last period was about to dawn. On the 20th September the 29th took over from the 14th Division the front from Zillebeke Lake to the Ménin road, between the 35th (XIX. Corps) on the R. and the 9th on the L.. The K.O.S.B. were in by the 19th, and started vigorous patrolling round the ruins of the *tulerie*. On the 24th they were back at St. Jans-ter-Biezen. The 25th was a day of rest. On the 26th the battalion marched quietly to "Pop.," and on the following day (partly by light rail) to Ypres.

* See *The Story of the 29th Division*, pp. 200 and 202–204.

The last Battle of Ypres and the final period began at 5.30 a.m. on Saturday, 28th September 1918. The Germans had thinned out their garrison in the salient to some five divisions. The bombardment, which started at zero, was of terrific intensity. The boundary between the Belgians on the N. and the British was roughly a line from Ypres due E. to Bécelaere. The Belgians, therefore, had to do with the 1st Battalion's scene of action in 1917, *i.e.* Poelcapelle and Houthulst way, and the 1st K.O.S.B., farther S. than even Potijze and S. of the Ménin road, were in quite new territory. Both Belgians and British achieved a brilliant success. The entire saucer was cleared of the invaders, and by no unit more thoroughly than the 29th Division. Nothing prevented drastic exploitation of the gains on the 28th except the appalling transport difficulties, accentuated by a steady downpour. The main Ménin road was impassable for vehicles. Pack animals brought up food and ammunition. Some guns were ultimately brought up along a parallel corduroy road track, but something of the nature of a lull occurred from the 2nd until the middle of October. 28 Sept. 1918.

But nothing amounting to a set-back was experienced, and the Battle of Courtrai with its 6,000 of prisoners taken between the 14th and 19th October testified to the wonderful engineering capacity and power of organization of the British army.

The 1st K.O.S.B. took a prominent part in the first battle, played a more modest part in the second, and figured finally in the advance on the Scheldt near Ooteghem.

In the battle of the 28th the battalion, under Major Crawshaw, M.C., were in reserve at Caravan Trench, just S. of the railway, about 1,000 yards E. of Hellfire Corner. There was a preliminary bombardment of five minutes' duration, which merged suddenly and unmistakably into the real barrage at 5.30 a.m.. The 87th I.B. (Jackson) were on the R. and the 86th (Cheape) on the L., the 88th (Freyberg) being in reserve.

The 87th advanced on a one-battalion front, the S.W.B. in front of the Borders, and the K.O.S.B. third, in reserve. It was anticipated that resistance would be met on the Stirling Castle–Clapham Junction Ridge, and the K.O.S.B. were dedicated to its capture. But if things went well, as in fact they did, then the K.O.S.B. were to take Tower Hamlets and Veldhoek on the Ménin road. The 88th were then to pass through and take Ghéluvelt, a strong place on the Ménin road, with wide views towards the Lys plain, and the French industrial towns Tourcoing, Roubaix, and Lille.

The barrage was perfect; the S.W.B. and Borders made good

28 Sept. 1918. progress, the latter reaching Stirling Castle just after 7.30 a.m. The K.O.S.B., not at zero but twenty-five minutes later, moved forward—at first in artillery formation, then extended—and passed through to the assault of their prescribed objectives. A on the R. directed, and there were clear orders as to the route forward, a compass bearing (102° mag.) being used after the last easy landmark.

The objectives were captured soon after 9.30 a.m., and the Borderers pressed on and took a battery of guns near levelled Ghéluvelt. Pill-boxes were no longer a novelty, and the practised methods of co-operative advance proved effective silencers. In spite of the rain a cheery spirit prevailed, which was intensified as the gallant Freyberg and his 88th Brigade passed through, having followed hard after the leading brigades, and, so to speak, champing at the bit for the barrage to bound forward. All that there was above or below ground of Ghéluvelt fell to British arms for the first time since November 1914.

By this time the afternoon was wearing on, and the reorganized Borderers were utilized—(1) A and B to man Tower Hamlets-Veldhoek Ridge, and (2) C and D to form a defensive flank on the R. of the 88th between them and the 35th Division, who had found Zandvoorde on its isolated mound a hard nut to crack.

No Borderer officer fell that day, and only one man was killed. But Capt. A .H. Aiton of the 5th H.L.I.* (not 7th, as stated in the War Diary), an attached officer, was killed, and cast a gloom over a day on which only one officer (Capt. C. C. Robertson, Highland Cyclists Battalion) and 16 O.R. were wounded and none were missing.

The captures included 250 prisoners, 10 guns, 12 M.G., 2 T.M., and 4 anti-tank guns.

Next day, Sunday, while the 88th had a stiffish fight in pushing on towards Ménin, the K.O.S.B. were fully occupied in relieving one another for the next two days on the flank facing the Kruiseecke Ridge, the Germans having reinforced the line here and apparently trying to break through between the 35th and 29th Divisions. This task, which was far from being a sinecure, the Borderers succeeded in doing with the aid of the S.W.B..

On the night 29/30th September the Borders relieved the S.W.B., and on 30th advanced a little in sympathy with the 88th, who were moving on Gheluwé. This advance made the task of the K.O.S.B. more anxious as the breach was widened, but no change in the dispositions is recorded, and only 10 O.R. casualties occurred. It was on the 30th that Lieut.-Col. Beaty-Pownall returned off leave, and on 1st October he joined A and B, who were the companies

* Official Death Roll.

then in the flank firing-line, and was followed by the remaining companies the next day, who relieved men of the Hants, showing that the 29th were getting to be somewhat worn in every sense. In fact, a relief was overdue. On 3rd October the K.O.S.B. were relieved by troops of the 41st Division, and retired to miserable camps in the most comfortless of regions—Veldhoek. They were shelled *en route*, and 2nd Lieut. J. A. P. Renwick was wounded and there were 17 O.R. casualties. Oct. 1918.

After two days in Westhoek (due E. of Ypres) the battalion marched to Ypres, still unfortunately within range. On the 8th the transport lines were hit, and on 10th the C.O. was killed. Col. Beaty-Pownall was a great loss. The very next day Major Crawshaw led the 1st K.O.S.B. to Westhoek, and on the 12th they were back in the firing-line watching gas being projected and carrying and digging. On the 13th they were withdrawn in readiness for the attack on Lédeghem, for which they were in reserve, and during the counter-preparation shelling 2nd Lieut. J. K. Dron of 6th H.L.I. was killed.

Lédeghem, as General Cayley has phrased it, was a tough-looking proposition. Its capture was the first stage in the Battle of Courtrai. It presented one new difficulty, the fact that it was inhabited by its rightful owners as well as by its frightful trespassers. Such a town could not be shelled except with the greatest care, and preferably with smoke. It could not be treated like Méteren and Ghéluvelt or the Somme villages and levelled to the ground. Indiscriminate (German) shelling was reserved for it after the Germans had left and the inhabitants were still there. On the other hand, there were no more pill-boxes. Fog, smoke, and British dash wrenched Lédeghem from the Germans on the morning of the 14th, when the 86th and 88th I.B. attacked with the 87th in reserve.

The K.O.S.B. moved off after a hot meal at 7.30 a.m., zero having been at 5.35, and " marched " through Lédeghem, halting from 9.30 till 3 p.m. E. of the town. Thereafter in diamond formation, *i.e.* not only companies " diamonded," but with each platoon diamonded in each company, they proceeded 1¾ miles and billeted for the night. Think of it! real houses, if rather humble cabins. On this occasion 2nd Lieut. Slade, M.C., who had rushed the M.G. so gallantly at Vieux Berquin, and as O.C. Scouts was directing the march with a flag, was wounded.

On the 15th the K.O.S.B. passed through a heavy barrage and troops of the 86th I.B. soon after 9 a.m.. The 87th were continuing the pursuit of the enemy, now in full retreat, down the Heulebeek valley towards the Lys, and the K.O.S.B. were the reserve battalion to the Borders (R.) and S.W.B. (L.). Good progress was made

22 Oct. 1918. up to Heule, and the S.W.B. were able to do a good turn to the 9th Division on their L. and themselves by attacking the wood to the N. of Salines (taken by the Borders) from the N.W. and S. and turning the position.* The whole line then progressed. It was real open skirmishing, and such opposition as there was came from well-handled and posted M.G.. The line of the railway from Courtrai to Roulers was reached (the first objective), and at 3 p.m. the K.O.S.B. took up the running, and the three leading companies, A, B, and D, pushed E. and S. over the Heulebeek between Watermolen and Cuerne, A capturing two M.G.. That night posts were established on the banks of the Lys, but that formidable obstacle barred further progress meanwhile. It was a great day. Six miles in fighting formation and a real brush to finish up with. Major Crawshaw had much reason to be proud of his men and they of him with the 28th September and 14th and 15th October to look back on. Only 2 men fell, but 18 were wounded and 2nd Lieut. Jamieson of the 4th Battalion. The 88th relieved the 87th after a nasty day of sniping and shelling on the 16/17th. Thus it did not fall to the 1st K.O.S.B., but to their relievers, the Hants, to take a part in the relief on the 17th of the 6th K.O.S.B. from the Harlebeke bridgehead, which will be found in the story of that unit.

While the K.O.S.B. were resting and cleaning up at Heule, the R.E. and 88th were hard at work preparing for the crossing. On the night 19th October the 88th crossed by stealth and began to advance towards the Scheldt at 6 a.m.. Word was passed back to the other brigades, and at half an hour's notice Lieut.-Col. W. T. Wilkinson, D.S.O., who had only just arrived to take command, and the 1st K.O.S.B. were following on and crossing the Lys peaceably by a pontoon bridge S.E. of Cuerne. They billeted in uncomfortable quarters round the scattered "township" rather than village of Steenbrugge near and N. of Staceghem. In spite of nasty shelling there were no casualties on the 21st—spent resting.

For their last fight the 1st K.O.S.B. were up betimes. The C.O. cannot have gone to bed at all, because oral orders only reached him of the plan of operation at 2 a.m.. These orders were explained by Gen. Jackson to battalion C.O.s and had at once to be put into effect. The K.O.S.B. were to advance on the L. and the Borders on the R., the S.W.B. being in reserve. The troops started at 5 a.m. and assembled on the up-slope of a well-defined ridge—Banhout Bossch—praying for mist to usher in the dawn. Each battalion had a frontage of about 700 yards, and the K.O.S.B. dispositions were A

* There is an account of this splendid bit of applied tactics in *The Story of the 29th Division*, at p. 214.

on the R. next the Borders and C on the L. next the 9th Division. Behind A was B, and behind C was D. But there was no mist, and no advance was possible without a barrage, which was directed too far ahead, it being assumed that the infantry would work forward as soon as they were properly organized at the point of assembly. The action was fought virtually without artillery support. The outpost line was on the far side of the hill and was held by the 86th. At 9 a.m. the barrage fell and the K.O.S.B. cleared the crest in order to pass through the 86th, only to come under heavy M.G. fire from various nasty nests in small farms. But they managed to keep in touch with the 9th Division and to make full use of ditches and hedges. Thus, in one farm A rounded up 6 M.G. and 49 prisoners. This sudden cessation of hostile fire enabled C on the L. to turn another important farm, inflict heavy losses, and eventually a platoon took a farm 200 yards ahead of the whole line where 50 prisoners and 4 M.G. were taken. 22 Oct. 1918.

The Borders had suffered cruel fire from their front and R. flank, and on the L. towards the end of the day the 9th Division and the K.O.S.B. diverged from one another. Towards dusk Gen. Jackson decided to rest content with the general line then held, and the S.W.B. moved forward at 5.30 to relieve the K.O.S.B. and Borders. But it could not be done just in a minute, and it was close on midnight that the K.O.S.B. reached Kappaart (a few miles W.), and balanced gains and losses. Just as the 6th failed to take Ingoyhjem, so the parent battalion could not name the neighbouring Ooteghem as the prey of its bayonet. But the 1st K.O.S.B. can boast that the ground taken by them was the farthest advance in that battle made by the 29th, who were relieved on 23/24th October by the 41st Division, and retired to the Harlebeke–Cuerne area. At the cost of 2nd Lieuts. J. H. Maxwell and T. W. L. Birrell wounded, and 8 O.R. killed, 1 missing, and 58 wounded, the 1st K.O.S.B. took 178 prisoners and 28 out of the 33 M.G. captured by the brigade. It was a fine finish to the Flanders fighting, and the War Diary, with its appendices in the shape of orders and brigade reports, kept by the Adjutant, A/Capt. F. Dale, M.C., contains much matter of interest outwith this story, of contact with aeroplanes, of pigeons, dogs, avoidance of disease to man and beast, wonderful forethought for conveyance and treatment of wounded. The writer cannot help hoping that some day some Borderer or syndicate of Borderers will publish a detailed account of the whole campaign from Outtersteene to the Scheldt heights, stressing the military lessons which it exemplified or taught. Honours poured thick and fast. Major Crawshaw was awarded

11 Nov. 1918. a bar to his M.C. and soon after left the battalion for a tour of home duty. Capt. A. W. Wylie received the M.C., as did Capt. R. D. Smith and 2nd Lieut. G. F. M'Vean (just before being evacuated sick). Those pillars of the battalion C.S.M. H. B. Turnbull and C.S.M. R. H. Smith were again distinguished, the former by a bar to his D.C.M. and the latter by one to his M.M.. L.-Corp. C. Bell received a bar to the M.M. and later on the D.C.M.. It would demand too much space to set out the 18 awards of the M.M. notified on 26th October, but it is interesting to note that Pte. D. Little had a bar added to his, notified on 6th November. The battalion was obviously well manned and well led.

All unconscious that their dangers were over, but cheered by news of victories on all parts of the front and intrigued (to use a war word once very common) by rumours of peace, the 1st K.O.S.B. had a very pleasant time at St. André on the N.W. outskirts of Lille, until the 29th's turn for a resumption of the offensive came round. The Borderers reached Celles, when Brig.-Gen. Freyberg at the head and front of his brigade, the 88th, saved the bridges over the River Dendre from destruction a few minutes before 11 a.m. on Monday, 11th November 1918,* at Lessines 15 miles ahead. When the news of the Armistice reached the K.O.S.B. they had paraded in full fighting order ready for the march to the fray, and had actually moved off. The going was heavy; the men were tired; the officers were tired. A staff officer, who seemed to ride almost too close to and too fast past the ranks, was approaching the C.O., Col. Wilkinson, from the rear of the column. A short, possibly sharp, question elicited the following: "I'm from H.Q. and am to tell you that manœuvres (*sic*) are over." That was all. One oldish man found relief from his pent-up feelings by taking off his pack, sitting on it, and letting the tears flow. Otherwise no emotion was shown either of joy or thankfulness.† But the latter feeling was there all right, unexpressed perhaps. The war was over. The entry that follows is characteristic of the most matter of fact of units, to which fuss and panic and elation (except at a football match) were equally foreign. "Orders for move cancelled and battalion instructed to work on the improvement of the roads in the vicinity of the village."

* *The Story of the 29th Division*, p. 219.

† The diarist has recorded the news as coming while parade was *still* being held. Col. Wilkinson has been good enough to record the incident exactly as it occurred, *i.e. just after*.

EPILOGUE

The 25th of Foot now proceeded as part of the Army of Occupation across the cockpit of Europe to Cologne. In their passage from Celles *via* St. Sauveur and Lessines to Soignies they just missed Ath, of honourable but sorrowful memory. Their route lay between Quatre Bras and Waterloo. Skirting the field of Ramillies they crossed the Meuse at Huy midway between Liége and Namur, an early glory. On the 27th November a party took part in the 29th's parade before King Albert at Brussels, on that monarch's historic entry into his capital, under Brig.-Gen. Freyberg, V.C., with his 8 wound stripes, and shared in the ecstatic welcome. But the welcomes were not confined to Brussels. Everywhere it was the same. It was at first sight like the welcome accorded a little farther S. to the 2nd Battalion in 1914, but it was soon seen to be the mark of a deeper and more understanding gratitude than that blend of gush and curiosity, that so soon died a natural death in 1914. Passing on through Spa, for long German G.H.Q., the K.O.S.B., then under Major Pennyman,* entered what was then Germany near Francorpchamp (half a mile on the Belgian side). This historic event took place on 4th December 1918. Continuing the march *via* Malmédy (now part of Belgium), Montjoie, and Gladbach, they reached the outskirts of Cologne on the 9th and settled down in the suburb of Kriel to prepare for the triumphal state march across the Hohenzollern Bridge on the 13th and leave the Holy City † in the safe hands of a Scottish governor and a British garrison. Dec. 1918.

The rainy mornıng of the 13th was a terrible disappointment to the spectators—Germans included. But to those with the understanding and not merely with the gazing eye the sight of the victorious 29th Division passing Lord Plumer at the Bridge underneath figures of vast imperial pretension was one of splendour. To one pair of eyes the supreme moment came when Willie Mackenzie came into view behind the S.W.B., and behind him and the swinging kilts of his pipers the long column of hard, weather-beaten, somewhat dour-looking Borderers,‡ with their waterproof sheets hanging, dripping, over their shoulders, tramped steadily on to watch the Rhine at Burg.

* W.D..

† Heine, in his Lyric Intermezzo, writes of "Das grosse, heilige Köln."

‡ They were one short, alas! Capt. (A/Major) H. C. V. Crichton-Browne, M.C., son of the C.O. of the 3rd Battalion, died that very day near Mons. Besides excellent service with the 2nd Battalion early in the war, he had joined the 1st Battalion in June 1918, and was for a short time A/Adjutant, and second in command from 30th October. He was granted a posthumous award of the M.C..

1919. The rest seems to belong to another book and another world. It is enough to say that the Borderers conducted themselves, just as we know they would, without insolence, without undue familiarity, quite naturally at home in their new environment. Gradually officers and men dropped out. Demobilization was proceeding steadily if slowly. Before the end of March the war service elements had been shed and the cadre of professional soldiers made ready for Home Service. They had then been 10 days at Mülheim, when on 29th March they entrained at Cologne through Namur and Merris on the Lys—to select two stations with associations ancient and modern—to Dunkirk. On 2nd April they crossed to Dover in S.S. *Antrim* and proceeded forthwith to Aldershot, where they were welcomed by Sir Archibald Murray, whom we shall meet later on in this story, the general in command there. Col. Wilkinson was still C.O., Major Pennyman had been second in command when not A/C.O. ever since November and was still with the battalion. Lieut. A. A. West, D.C.M., was Quartermaster, C. A. Moreton, who had fought in Gallipoli and seen much service in the Western Front, was a captain. Capt. F. Dale, M.C., who had had long service in Gallipoli and almost unbroken service in France, except when attending instructional courses in England, was Adjutant. Lieut. D. T. Holmes, M.M., and 2nd Lieut. J. Simpson were in charge of the symbol of all that the regiment had striven to do and had done—the Regimental Colours.

SCHLOSS BERG, GERMANY, 1918.

BOOK III

THE TERRITORIAL BATTALIONS, 1915–1918

GALLIPOLI SINAI PALESTINE

WESTERN FRONT, 1918

FOURTH BATTALION. HINDENBURG LINE

FIFTH BATTALION. BEUGNEUX FLANDERS

PRELIMINARY

THE 52nd (Lowland) Division fought stoutly on the Gallipoli Peninsula in 1915 and in the spiky mazes of the Siegfried fortress in 1918. The 103rd Brigade of the 34th Division earned the praise of General Mangin when fighting shoulder to shoulder with the French for the recovery of the Aisne in 1918 as a prelude to the " 100 days " * that won the war. But Borderers and other readers will perhaps share the writer's feeling that the three weeks' effort in Palestine in December 1917 was the supreme achievement of our Lowland Territorials. During that campaign the 4th and 5th K.O.S.B. were side by side or one just in front of the other from the " march past " Gaza, on, *via* the mountains of Judea, to the N. bank of the Nahr-el-Auja River, in the Jaffa Plain. There is a note of novelty from the moment good-bye is said to the Suez Canal in 1916. From a Gallipoli point of view the crippling frontal attack of the 12th July 1915 and the consequent garrison life of Cape Helles are drab as compared with the experience of the 1st Battalion at the landing, in the subsequent day and night attacks, on the 28th June, at Scimitar Hill or the evacuation. What the 4th Battalion went through in 1918 during the thrust from Arras to Cambrai was very much what the 2nd Battalion experienced between the Ancre and the Forêt de Mormal. What the 5th faced at Beugneux was very like what the 7/8th Battalion had to face at Buzancy, and when they settled down to the smash through in Flanders they were almost in contact with the 1st Battalion. Almost up to the last the war in France and Flanders was a siege war that had gone on since November 1914. Except for a few days, the same holds good of the Gallipoli campaign.

But the Sinai and Palestine campaigns open up a new side of military life—a life of marches and bivouacs, of periodic and sometimes continuous changes of scene, in which the canteen played a small part and a roof was a rarity. The battalions engaged suffered extremes of heat and cold. The Khamsin or desert wind scorched, and the nights were often a torture of cold to thinly clad men. " From beds of raging fire to starve in ice their soft ethereal

* See Major-Gen. A. Montgomery's *History of One Hundred Days.*

warmth" can serve as a pardonable exaggeration of a very real contrast. Life in France was monotonous in all conscience. It was nothing to the dullness of the desert or of the fringe "betwixt the desert and the sown" on the edge of the Promised Land, when the long, hot days without a drop of rain for month after month glared down on troops toiling or training after the Gaza repulse in April 1917. Never a drop of fresh water like those rare treasured draughts at Romano's Well in the Peninsula! Besides, water was always scarce. Men were trained to subsist on a quart a day. Yet there was little grumbling, for it was felt that Allenby meant business, and in the fullness of time the blow fell at a distance from where the K.O.S.B. were and on a scale that brought home to them that they were pawns in a huge thought-out game. When the call came it found them ready, hard and eager. They hustled the Turk from pillar to post over the sands, out of rocky forts, up sterile gorges, and across a swollen river, until Jaffa was out of range of his Austrian guns and a safe way lay for sea-borne supplies to "Jerusalem Delivered." The men frequently had no boots or the kind of boot that "one sees washed up on the shore," * but the battalions of the 52nd left no stragglers on the march. No Scottish force in history ever carried on a sustained offensive with greater success. Nor could one brigade pride itself on its achievements at the expense of either of the others. Royal Scots, R.S. Fusiliers, Borderers, Cameronians, H.L.I., and A. & S.H., and the battalions of these regiments *inter se,* each shouldered the burden in turn and gave a good account. It was a national effort and a national triumph, in which our two battalions upheld the traditions of the Borders, the West Marches, and Galloway.

There are therefore elements in this part of the regimental story which are quite unique and supply the dramatic element, so conspicuous in the entries of the 2nd and 1st Battalions into the Great War and so inconspicuous at other times. The problem of space would be more difficult if the broad outlines of the Gallipoli campaign were not so generally known, and if there were not such an admirable divisional history as Lieut.-Col. Thompson's and such well-written and compiled battalion histories as those of Capt. Sorley Brown (4th) and Capt. G. F. Scott Elliot (5th).

An immense amount of domestic detail in the day-to-day life, in lists of personnel, in minor operations that had no general effect on events can be omitted and the story reduced to its purely military side. That again admits of compression. The doings of the 1st Battalion have already caused allusion to be made to the purpose of

* *Story of the 5th H.L.I.*.

the Dardanelles Expedition, its execution, its wavering fortunes, the case for evacuation, and the ultimate failure. Terrain, climate, ailments, and military shortages have been mentioned. The time is not yet ripe for a controversial handling of the operations of the 12th of July 1915—that black day for the Borderers and especially for the 4th. The Official History is in course of preparation, but has not yet reached the operations in which the 52nd Division were engaged. The tale of the minor fighting in the Krithia Nullah has been well told again and again, and for those who are not satisfied with a brief account there are references to books and despatches, in which they may find what they want.

CHAPTER I

GALLIPOLI

1914. THE response to the call to arms was immediate in the south of Scotland as elsewhere. Whithorn and Kirkconnel have claims to have sent forth the largest number of volunteers in proportion to population in Britain.* And this from a district that since the "Covenanting" times had never been remarkable for enthusiasm for service in the regular army.

There is a well-known story connected with Selkirk, from which had come batch after batch of recruits. Towards the end of August a batch of Selkirk men entered the recruiting office at Galashiels, and the sergeant in charge felt moved to say, "I'm wonderin' if there's ony folk left in Selkirk at a'"! The answer was simple, "Aye, there a few, but they're comin' on wi' the next train."

Of course they were not all, or even an excessive proportion, joining the 4th or 5th K.O.S.B., or trekking for the depot. The glamour of the kilt drew many far afield. But the first entry in the (model) War Diary of the 5th Battalion tells us that mobilization began at Dumfries on the 5th of August 1914, and that on the 11th they were off to a place more inspiring in association than commodious in billets—Bannockburn. The 4th Battalion was hard by, at Cambusbarron, and there both battalions with their veterans and recruits set to work to fit themselves to fight Germans or any other of the King's enemies. It is matter of controversy whether Lord Kitchener made as full use of the expansive possibilities of the Territorial Force as he might, instead of directing the volunteering spirit into the new armies and service battalions, which were so lamentably short of equipment and had to begin with improvised headquarters and a haphazard collection of officers. Be that as it may, thanks to the prescience of that great army reformer, the late Lord Haldane, the old volunteers had been for more than six years transformed into territorials, organized on much the same lines as the regular army, provided with reserve battalions for the supply of reinforcements, and

* Scott Elliot, *5th Battalion K.O.S.B.*.

accustomed to the notion of being brigaded in a division. The 4th K.O.S.B. represented the old Border Rifles and Berwickshire Volunteers; the 5th K.O.S.B. the Dumfries Volunteers and the Galloway Rifles. At the outset of the war, along with the 4th and 5th R.S.F., they formed the Southern Scottish Brigade of the 2nd Lowland Division of the T.F.. Associated with them was a solid block of Glasgow and adjacent elements, whose volunteer originals awake memories of famous footballers and marksmen at Wimbledon and Bisley. By affiliation to the 26th and 71st regimental traditions there was an entire Scottish Rifle brigade and an entire H.L.I. brigade.* The division was scattered over the Fife shores of the Forth on coast defence during the autumn and winter. Owing to the splendid readiness to volunteer for foreign service, the division was soon labelled "1/2nd" Lowland Division, and men anxiously wondered when they would go, and how they would go (*e.g.* would they go as a division?) and whither? The last question was acutely raised by the fact that by April there were several rival theatres of activity and the 1/2nd Lowland Division were by then definitely selected for foreign service. Even as late as the 11th of May, when the 52nd (Lowland) Division received the number and name that never will be forgotten in the annals of the British Empire, or very shortly before that date, the G.O.C. was under the impression that the destination was France—Flanders.† 1914.

The time that had slipped so swiftly by had not been unprofitable. Such training as had been feasible, owing to the difficulty of units having to supply so many guards, had been on open warfare lines. Bombs, so important on the Peninsula, had been conspicuous by their absence. There is little to chronicle except, perhaps, the observation that on the whole, by remaining all the time at Cambusbarron, a sort of S.W. suburb of Stirling, and having better ground for training, the 4th Battalion fared better than the 5th, which watched the Forth and its bridge from W. of Rosyth to North Queensferry.

As already stated, the K.O.S.B. were in the newly named 52nd Lowland Division. The G.O.C. was Major-Gen. G. G. A. Egerton, C.B., formerly of the Seaforth Highlanders, the 72nd Regiment of Foot.

The constituents of the South Scottish Brigade were unchanged. Along with the K.O.S.B. were the 4th and 5th R.S.F. and the brigade was now the 155th, and remained as constituted till, as

* These brigade names lingered on some time after the renaming and numbering of the division and its brigades, as entries in the 4th K.O.S.B. War Diary show.

† *The 5th H.L.I.*, p. 2.

1915. stated, the 5th K.O.S.B. had to be transferred in 1918. It was commanded by Brig.-Gen. F. Erskine of the Scots Guards.

The Clyde basin brigades had suffered some modification, and at the date of embarkation the 7th and 8th Cameronians (original members) and the 4th and 7th Royal Scots formed the 156th I.B.. Only one change had taken place in the H.L.I. Brigade, henceforth the 157th I.B.. It now consisted of the 5th, 6th, and 7th H.L.I. and the 5th Argyll and Sutherland Highlanders. Armed with the long rifle the battalions were all afloat by the 1st of June. All those who sailed on 24th May on the *Empress of Britain* felt the shadow of the awful Gretna disaster which had wellnigh wiped out half of the 7th Royal Scots.*

The *Maurelania* took the 155th H.Q., the R.S.F., and the 5th K.O.S B.. The *Empress of Britain* took D.H.Q. and, along with others, the 4th K.O.S.B.. The first named sailed straight into Mudros harbour, the latter only reached Alexandria on the 4th. The 5th K.O.S.B. were first on the Peninsula, viz. on the 6/7th June 1915. The 4th Battalion followed from Egypt on the 14th. The voyage was hot, but uneventful. The spectacle in Mudros harbour on the island of Lemnos was a tribute to the wealth of the British Empire and the magnitude of the effort. But great ocean steamers shrunk when the *Mauretania* or the *Aquitania* anchored and dwarfed all other craft. The 5th K.O.S.B. had arrived to find excitement rife as to the likely success of the impending "push," † but when the 4th K.O.S.B. arrived the effort had failed and trench warfare was the order of the day. The introduction of both battalions to Gallipoli on their different dates was much what most reinforcements experienced—the 60-mile trip in a crowded trawler or destroyer and the long file through the hull of the *River Clyde* in the darkness. Then a forming up, the quicker done for want of tools and equipment (which were sent separately), under a usually reliable but occasionally fallible guide to some part of the hollow saucer with roofless holes cut in it, known as a rest camp. In fact, the place was like a heavily bunkered, unplayable, inland golf-course with sea views. There was always plenty digging to be done behind, and also to add to the complicated and apparently unnecessarily confused network of trenches shown on the map. These, however, really tell the true tale of the campaign, of its ebb and flow, of the close hand-to-hand fighting, of sapping and bombing, of night attack and set piece with artillery support of a modest kind.‡ The very

* Lieut.-Col. R. R. Thompson, M.C., *The 52nd (Lowland) Division*.

† For an account of the 4th of June, see earlier pages.

‡ The *locus classicus* for a description of Gallipoli fighting is John Masefield's *Gallipoli*.

names have their associations, as, for example," Backhouse Post," which tells of the days when the N.D. named the captured trenches after their officers, while the visit of some Australians in the early May fighting was commemorated by the " Australian Lines." June 1915.

The 5th K.O.S.B. landed on the night of the 6/7th May, and by the 10th were pushed into the line in reserve, relieving troops of the 88th I.B. of the 29th Division in urgent need of relief in the recent cock-pit of Twelve or Fir Tree Copse. They were then under command of Lieut.-Col. P. Murray Kerr, with the future C.O., Major W. J. Millar, as Second-in-Command, and were about 900 strong, with 28 officers.

When the 4th Battalion landed, Lieut.-Col. John M'Neile of Kippilaw, Roxburghshire, late of the Coldstream Guards and a South African veteran, a tough Ulsterman of fifty-two years, was C.O., and Major W. E. A. Cochrane was Second-in-Command, the strength being much about the same as that of the 5th.

Shrapnel, rifle bullets, and sickness soon began to levy toll on the battalions. The 5th K.O.S.B. actually lost their C.O. through sickness before the end of June. Dust and flies and contaminated food and stenches and heat undermined the stoutest constitutions. The young and the too-mature seemed to suffer most, and the exacting fatigues and constant strain owing to inability to avoid observation and fire except under the ground level accentuated the evil. But the strengths were not seriously impaired when the Borderers went into action for the first time. They took no part in the battle of Gully Ravine, which hit the 156th Brigade so hard on the 28th of June, depriving them of Brig-Gen. W. Scott-Moncrieff (killed), and of 72 officers and 1,281 O.R. .*

Where the artillery was mostly directed and had most effect, namely, out on the L., an important advance was made by the 29th Division, which accounts for the projection of the line up the coast at Fusilier Bluff, almost outflanking Krithia. Unfortunately there was no artillery in fact dedicated to the sector on the R. to be stormed by the 156th Brigade, and the result was an unsupported advance across the open in the face of a hail of gun, M.G., and rifle fire, at the terrible cost mentioned. The objectives were only partially gained, but prodigies of inevitably ineffective valour were performed. The 52nd's baptism was bloody but glorious. It was to be hoped† that the fate of the other brigades would be kinder, for their turn was bound to come. In the interval the 157th I.B. arrived on 2nd July. The

* Thompson, *op. cit.*, p. 67.

† Col. M'Neile of the 4th Battalion expressed such a hope, but like many hopes it did not come to fruition.

12 July 1915. G.O.C. had only landed on the 21st with his staff and the 156th Brigade had been under the command of Major-Gen. de Lisle, G.O.C., 29th Division, for the operations of the 28th June. There was at one time an order issued to the 155th I.B. to prepare for a renewal of the attack on the 30th, but no attack was made and life reverted to the normal (Gallipoli normal), until by the 4th of July it was known the brigade was to attack on the British R..

Sir Ian Hamilton has explained the genesis of the operations of the 12th and 13th July in his despatch dated 11th December 1915.

By some date in June and after the stalemate of the 4th June he had decided on the Suvla adventure by landing fresh troops 17 miles N. of Cape Helles on the Ægean coast of the Peninsula. That is outside the story of the 4th and 5th K.O.S.B.. The date for Suvla landing having been fixed for the second week in August, he felt it incumbent to fill in the interval with as much fighting as his small stock of H.E. would permit. Hence (presumably) the brilliant affair of 28th June with its aftermath of bombing, sniping, and mining. He goes on: "The action of the 12th and 13th of July was meant to be a sequel to the action of the 28th June. That advance had driven back the Turkish R. on to their main second system just S. of Krithia. But on my centre and R. the enemy still held their forward system of trenches, and it was my intention on the 12th July to seize the remaining trenches of this foremost system, from the sea at the mouth of the Kereves Dere to the main Sedd-el-Bahr–Krithia road, along a front of some 2,000 yards."

The French were to operate on the R., the 52nd on the L., the 29th Division were to demonstrate. It was hoped that the enemy's attention would be distracted from Suvla and Anzac. When an enemy's attention has to be distracted, and his nose, so to speak, put off the scent, it is done by a diversion, which may be anything from a demonstration to a demonstration-in-force, and so on, to a holding battle. The 6th of August was to witness a demonstration-in-force very costly to the 88th I.B.; the 12th of July was one of these real holding battles which vary in degree according to the weight of artillery available.

On Gallipoli the shortage of heavy artillery with high angle fire and H.E. was such that it was decided that the attacks of the two brigades of the 52nd concerned could not take place simultaneously.* According to Sir C. E. Callwell,† the artillery preparations for this battle meant nothing in the slightest degree approaching to the

* Despatch of 11th December (Official Despatches, vol. iv.). See Thompson, *op. cit.*, pp. 82 and 83.

† Callwell, *op. cit.*, p. 164.

volume of that at Neuve Chapelle (*i.e.* in March 1915), much less Loos. It was almost entirely field-guns that bombarded the enemy's trench system, but as they were mainly 75s, handled by French gunners, they did the maximum damage of their calibre in the shortest possible time. But the bombardment could not silence the enemy's guns or avert casualties to our men from the very start. 12 July 1915.

Again, it is part and parcel of a holding battle that it should have a limited objective. There was a limited objective ordered for this battle, namely, three lines of trenches in a 1,000 yards front to be taken by two brigades. Unfortunately for the Borderers, and particularly for the 4th K.O.S.B., there was no third line for them to take in their sector, and the consequences were disastrous. Curiously enough, the R.N.D., who had been so terribly cut up in this very sector on the 4th of June, were once more to pay toll; this time, like the 4th K.O.S.B., to the imaginary trench.

The assaulting troops were back in the line—which they had only left on the 10th—by the 11th, in good heart but possibly not quite clear on all points regarding the enemy land. Only the front objective trench was visible to the K.O.S.B.; what was behind was hidden; there were no maps; and though they had rehearsed the preliminaries on the 4th of July, on the 11th fresh orders had a tendency to arrive piecemeal, too late to be written out.* On the R., where the ground dropped into the Kereves gorge, the French and Turks were close to one another, and the trenches were ramified. On their L. the 4th R.S.F. had also a short distance to cover to reach their objectives, but it was complicated by a difficult R. wheel.† One battalion was deemed enough for this section of the 155th's front, and the 5th R.S.F. were in brigade reserve. On the L., on both sides of the Achi Baba Nullah, the 157th had the longest journey, but as we shall see they were able to travel it in the afternoon and after a fresh bombardment. In the centre, with which we are concerned, No Man's Land varied in width from 40 yards on the R.‡ to some 200 yards opposite Parson's Road, the jumping-off place. Three battalions were to be used here, and the Borderers and the 4th R.S.F. were to advance in four waves. The 4th K.O.S.B. in two waves were to lead the attack past two lines of Turkish trenches and capture and consolidate a third. The 5th Battalion were to advance from behind our front line, cross it in the wake of the second wave, and occupy the farther of the Turkish front trenches with the fourth wave and the original Turkish front trench, E10, with the third. The fourth would therefore leapfrog the third.

* 5th Battalion W.D..
† Buchan, *Royal Scots Fusiliers* (Nelson), p. 332.
‡ 5th Battalion, K.O.S.B.W.D..

12 July 1915. The 4th R.S.F. supplied four waves for their (narrower) sector, and the 5th R.S.F. were in brigade reserve.

Early in July there had been heavy rain, entailing fatigues to drain the trenches, but by the 12th things had dried up and a glorious morning developed into an intensely hot day, productive of thirst, dust, and decomposition. About 4.30 a.m. the artillery opened, and at 7.35 a.m. the infantry cleared the parapet and started to cross the bullet-swept zone.

There is only one voice of testimony touching the manner of that advance whether on the R. or in the centre. It was magnificently steady. Col. M'Neile must have indeed been proud of his men as these Borderers, in both senses of the word, without one glance behind, briskly took E10 and passed on the second trench, E11, a loop trench like the bow to a section of E10, the string, and then proceeded towards "E12." Alas, it was a wild-goose chase. There was no E12 in the Borderers' line of advance. There were scratches of what might have been the embryo of a future trench or an intentional dummy * trench, though that is a *ruse de guerre* somewhat premature for the pre-camouflage period of the war. In any event it was not a ready-made, dug trench that merely needed to have its features reversed, and its living or dead occupants suitably disposed of, to become a British fire trench capable of resisting counter-attacks, if stoutly manned.

Major Cochrane, the Second-in-Command, was up with the charge. He consulted with the C.O. and the Adjutant as to the proper course to take, seeing that both the waves were obviously far ahead of any objective ever thought of, for they were in the zone of our own barrage. He survived the day (indeed he and Lieut. A. Galloway were the only officers of the 4th K.O.S.B. who came out of the charge unscathed) and wrote up the Diary. His statement is confirmed by what happened to the Portsmouth battalion of the R.N.D. on the following day, and has been accepted by every historian who has investigated the happenings of the 12th of July in the light of the 52nd Divisional testimony, *e.g.* Thompson, Sorley Brown, Ewing, Scott Elliot, and the unnamed but most reliable and instructive author or authors of the *5th H.L.I.*. † The maps were wrong. The 4th K.O.S.B. were in the void, and as they could not by themselves take Achi Baba, they were rightly ordered to fall back on the loop trench, where the 5th K.O.S.B. were feverishly at work bombing

* Scott Elliot, p. 32. At least one survivor of the attack is of the same opinion.

† Quite one of the most readable battalion stories of the Great War in print.

and digging. Up till then their casualties had not been unduly heavy, but as those retired who had not, in the joy of battle and adventure, got out of sight and control on the bushy slopes of Achi Baba, they received the hostile barrage and flanking fire from rifles and M.G., and suffered terrible losses. 12 July 1915.

How the gallant M'Neile came by his end is not known, but it is certain his end was, as his leadership all through, noble. The details of this harrowing episode will be found in Capt. Sorley Brown's pages. Capt. J. C. Lang,* the adjutant, found a length of ditch two feet deep and occupied it with a handful. He was found there later in the day by Capt. Coventon of the 5th Battalion, but in the end was killed with Lieut. J. B. Patrick, and all his post except a few who were made prisoners. We must pass on to the doings of the 5th K.O.S.B., and take stock of their situation as the men of the 4th came dribbling back upon them.

Fortunately for the writer, the Diary of the 5th K.O.S.B. has been studied by Capt. Scott Elliot, who has had the zealous co-operation of Col. Millar, the writer of that bit of it, and through him of eyewitnesses, and the following account is essentially a reduction to regimental scale of what is a most careful attempt to give a true account from a battalion point of view.

Lieut.-Col. W. J. Millar † had his men in readiness in a trench nearly 300 yards behind the 4th K.O.S.B. first wave. British artillery opened on the enemy at 6.55, and the effect of the combined Franco-British bombardment on Turkish territory was soon visible in spurts of earth. British naval fire was always a delight to watch, and it attended to the back regions, but of course was of less immediate use than on the 28th of June. Clouds of dust obscured the scene and embarrassed the M.G. officers.

The battalion, close on 700 strong after withdrawal of the disappointed and submerged 10th (the "dumped personnel" of France), had not been long enough out to have lost their native vigour. At zero they rose and strode across the rough, scrubby moor, over Trotman Road (support) and Parson's Road (jumping-off trench), across No Man's Land, and into a horrible hole, once a trench, full of corpses and wounded, and, curiously enough, with a certain number of unwounded and still armed men in occupation. It was only about 8 a.m. when the bolt of the attack was shot, and the rest of the day is a confused and confusing mêlée of defensive fighting against an enemy fresh keyed-up for the fight, with safe *boyaux*

* Capt. Lang was very highly thought of among his comrades. He was a regular officer of the K.O.S.B..

† His promotion from major came a day or two after the battle.

12 July 1915. — to and from the battlefield, and directed by leaders with commanding observation of our every move. The Turkish *moral* was undoubtedly good. Many withstood the British charge, and preferred the bayonet to surrender, which shows wonderful nerve after the awful treatment meted out by the 75s. Cool riflemen were sniping to their heart's content at our officers and N.C.O.s, directing and superintending the reconstruction of the captured trenches, and so inevitably exposing themselves. Besides these marksmen, machine-guns and shrapnel from the unsilenced Turkish guns swept the field, and the numbers of the K.O.S.B. garrison dwindled. Danger was imminent. According to 5th K.O.S.B. evidence, what has been called the loop trench—the arc of the bow—was not joined on to E10 at the N. end. There was a considerable gap which had to be barricaded at both ends until hands were joined with the H.L.I. much later in the day.

At this deadly spot many Borderers fell, including Capts. Tom Welsh and J. J. Dykes. As for those in the loop itself, their lot too was precarious. Not only were they cut off on their L., and, of course, during daylight, from behind, but on their R., in the loop itself, there was an unoccupied stretch of trench, which at any moment might be filled with Turks, who might then drive a wedge between the Fusiliers and Borderers.

In E11, the bowstring where Col. Millar, Capt. A. H. M'Neill and others were in charge, it was almost as unpleasant. The attack had been planned to be made in two stages (a marked peculiarity), and the 157th were not nearly yet due to move. Therefore there were bound to be exposed flanks both at E10 and any remoter trench captured. There was a clamant call for bombs. But here again quantity and quality were on the side of the enemy. One wonders whether Col. Millar ever got the 400 to 600 bombs of the jam-pot type he so eagerly craved. The handy, sure, and effective Mills No. 5 bomb, which helped us to win the war if it did not bring a fortune or much more than renown and litigation to the ingenious inventor, never was on the Peninsula. The excellent cricket-ball bomb did not reach Gallipoli till the autumn.* The Turks had a cricket-ball type of bomb, the fuse of which delayed sufficiently to enable the dangerous game to be played of throwing him back his own bombs.†

Capt. Coventon (of the 5th), unable to squeeze into Lang's

* Its welcome issue in September to the M.E.F. has already been noted by Captain A. M. Shaw.

† Two instances of this, quite independent of one another, are given by Col. Thompson, *op. cit.*, pp. 107 and 108.

advanced post, had wriggled his way back to the loop, where Lieut. Robert Douglas was doing magnificent work in inspiring the men to their strenuous task. The R.E. parties seem to have suffered something like annihilation, and the infantryman had to rely on his grubber. Reinforcements and bombs were urgently needed. Fortunately Col. Pollok-M'Call made a most judicious use of his reserve. Soon Lieuts. Brotherton and J. G. Hamilton-Grierson with two platoons crossed the open space between E10 and the loop and joined the defenders. Unfortunately the gallant Grierson was shot dead while stemming a Turkish rush on the L. barricade of the loop within a few minutes of his arrival. But it so happened that as the crowded Turks were halted on the top of the barricade they were wiped out and ignited, so that their bodies smouldered for hours, and acted as a deterrent at a nasty spot.* 12 July 1915.

Meanwhile at the other end succour came in the shape of 7th Royal Scots out of divisional reserve under Lieut. David Lyell (an advocate of the Scottish Bar), who fell almost immediately, to the regret of many outside as well as inside his regiment. But just as Brotherton carried on when Grierson fell, so 2nd Lieut. M'Lelland (R.S.) proved invaluable to the K.O.S.B. when Lyell fell. These and other timely reinforcements of R.S. and Cameronians made good the position on the R., while that on the L. was secured by the brilliant attack of the H.L.I. and 5th A. & S.H. astride the Achi Baba nullah. They "splendidly carried the whole of the enemy trenches allotted to their objective." † It was while co-operating with the H.L.I. that the gallant Douglas received a wound that proved mortal.

As the shades of night fell the situation was that our line opposite the 157th I.B.'s original point "had advanced some 400 yards, while the 155th Brigade and the 2nd French Division had advanced between 200 and 300 yards." ‡

The next few days saw the gains consolidated into a permanent front line, which was only evacuated on the 8th of January 1916.

The 13th opened with Turkish counter-attacks. Our story is not concerned with the misunderstandings that involved the R.N.D., in what to 52nd eyes was an unaccountable and costly adventure, but with the dour grit with which the weary garrison in the loop and in E10 faced repeated counter-attacks. The K.O.S.B. contact with the R.N.D. was confined to supporting with covering fire some men of the *Hawke* in an unsuccessful attempt to capture a point in advance of the N. end of the loop.§ They knew not of the surprise

* Scott Elliot, p. 40.
† Despatch cited of 11th December 1915.
‡ *Ibid.*
§ Scott Elliot, p. 48.

13 July 1915. visit over the open into H.L.I. trenches, or of the fruitless search of the Portsmouth battalion for the missing trench, which *must* have been there, or how, otherwise, could it have got on to the map?* The strain of the 12th had been cruel. The sights, the smells, the fog of dust, the noise, the confusion, and the heat had all combined to exhaust brain and nerve and sinew. Ration parties from the base in the Eski line with incredible difficulty, *via* narrow trenches often crowded with wounded, had reached parts of the firing line, and their leaders, such as Capt. "Wattie" Forrest, often found themselves switched on to the more immediate need of taking charge of the fighting forces. Water—tepid, insipid, and unpalatable, as it would have tasted at other times—was worth a ransom. The wounded never cried for it in vain if a whole comrade was at hand. The call for sacrifice and resignation met with a noble response. So things dragged on over the 13th and the 14th, and only in the afternoon of the 15th were the K.O.S.B. blend relieved by scarcely less weary men of the R.N.D.. Caked with dust, sweaty, filthy, unshaven, all but asleep, they shambled down to the bogus rest camp. But a voice inside told them that they had fought the good fight, and that their labours had not altogether been in vain.†

The battle of the 12th July 1915 was the only major engagement in which the 52nd took part in this campaign, and it demonstrated the difficulties which hampered the C.-in-C. from the moment that the thankless task was flung at him of forcing the Dardanelles without adequate troops or siege guns. The 52nd had much useful work to do, and nobody whose privilege it was to be in daily touch with its units and staff during the last three months of the campaign could fail to see that those men's spirit was unbroken and that there was a future before the division. In other words, their *moral* was unimpaired, possibly enhanced, by the stern lesson of real warfare. But the blow still saddens many a Scottish home. "The losses . . . had been such that for the . . . Lowlands it was a second Flodden. In large areas between Tweed and Forth scarcely a household but mourned a son." ‡

Col. Thompson gives the figures for the 155th I.B. and the K.O.S.B. for the actual battle. The brigade had a total casualty list of 1,268. The 4th K.O.S.B. had 12 officers killed or died of

* "How could I have got Daniel on my notes, unless you told me so, Sir?" *per* Starley J. in Bardell *v.* Pickwick, *Pickwick Papers*, Centenary Edition, Chapman & Hall, vol. ii. p. 87.

† It was his leadership on the 12th and following days that won for Col. Millar his D.S.O., intimated 30th April 1916.

‡ Buchan, *Royal Scots Fusiliers*, p. 334.

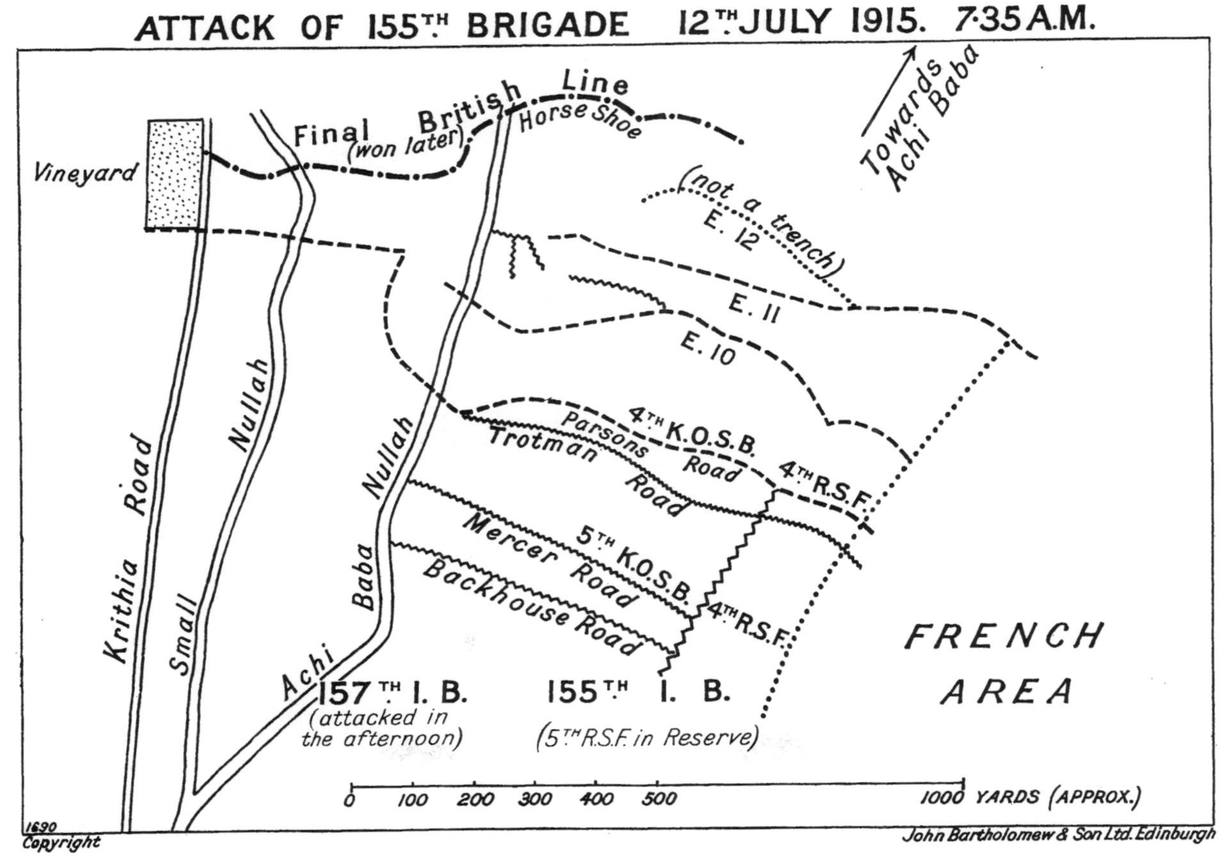
ATTACK OF 155TH BRIGADE 12TH JULY 1915. 7·35 A.M.
Towards Achi Baba
Vineyard
Final British Line
(won later)
Horse Shoe
(not a trench)
E. 12
E. 11
E. 10
4TH K.O.S.B.
Parsons Road
Trotman Road
4TH R.S.F.
5TH K.O.S.B.
Mercer Road
Backhouse Road
4TH R.S.F.
FRENCH AREA
Krithia Road
Small Nullah
Achi Baba Nullah
157TH I. B.
(attacked in the afternoon)
155TH I. B.
(5TH R.S.F. in Reserve)
0 100 200 300 400 500 1000 YARDS (APPROX.)
1690 Copyright
John Bartholomew & Son Ltd. Edinburgh

To face Page 244

wounds, 6 officers wounded, and of O.R. 319 killed, 203 wounded, and 13 taken prisoners. The 5th Battalion lost 6 officers killed and 5 wounded, and 76 O.R. killed and 183 wounded. 12–13 July 1915.

The 4th K.O.S.B. lost their C.O., Lieut.-Col. M'Neile, their adjutant, Capt. Lang, the M.O., Surgeon-Major D. R. Taylor, Major J. Herbertson, Capts. H. Sanderson and A. Wallace, Lieuts. T. M. Alexander, J. B. Innes, and A. Bulman, and 2nd Lieuts. A. H. M. Henderson—almost the first to fall, as Parson's Road was left at 7.35 a.m.—P. Woodhead, and J. B. Patrick. Capt. Wallace, after receiving his mortal wound, cheered on his men till he died, and Innes had the *sang-froid* after losing his arm to smoke a cigarette and urge on the charge.*

The wounded officers were Capts. Jobson and Macdonald, Lieut. J. Harrison, and 2nd Lieuts. J. Elder, R. P. Smith, and the M.G. officer, W. K. Innes (cousin of " J. B."). Major Cochrane took command of all that was left until he handed over to Major Maclean of D.H.Q. and the A. & S.H., and eventually to Lieut.-Col. G. T. B. Wilson, also of the A. & S.H., on 22nd September.

In addition to Capts. Welsh and Dykes and Lieut. R. Douglas, the 5th K.O.S.B. lost Lieut. E. Smith and 2nd Lieuts. R. Carlyle and W. B. Macfarlane. Major E. J. Bell and Capt. W. F. Crombie and Lieuts. Coventon, R. J. Sinclair, and D. Macrae were wounded. The 52nd's subsequent experiences differed only from those of the 1st Battalion in that in connection with the evacuations they were called upon to demonstrate by operations directed against and really intended to blunt the Turkish salient in the Krithia nullah. Otherwise they went through the daily round of that picturesquely situated lazar house. The territorial K.O.S.B. had their fair share of the dysentery and jaundice and the general fall-off in physical fitness that marked life on the Peninsula just in the same degree as the 1st Battalion. They felt the cruel cold of the November blizzard. They did the unceasing fatigues and the recurring outpost and scavenging work of the front line. They watched the " brass hats " perambulate the firing-line, and eyed the trench mortars with ill-concealed disapproval but with less open contempt than their brethren of the 1st Battalion. Dwindling in numbers, as the steady drain of sickness and casualties went on, and with the weight of the losses of the 12th of July, they were not called on to take more than a minor part in the three definite operations in which the 156th, 157th, and finally the 155th Brigades took part—namely, on 15th November and 18th and 29th December, which in the end won "GIIA"—a trench running from the W. Krithia nullah to the E.K.N. for the British

* Sorley Brown, p. 34.

Autumn 1915.

for the short space of ten days. These actions are admirably told by Col. Thompson (*op. cit.*), and in the 5*th H.L.I.*, and can be shortly dealt with here.

In September, Gen. Egerton, whose health had suffered from close on three months of Gallipoli at its worst, who had seen, as it were, his own family (for he had known them from peace trainings, and superintended their mobilization and war-training) melt away before his eyes, in schemes not of his own making, was called away to Alexandria to command the Base troops of the M.E.F., and was succeeded by Major-Gen. Lawrence, as already noted. Col. Pollok-M'Call was promoted to command the 155th I.B. *vice* Brig.-Gen. F. Erskine, invalided; Brig.-Gen. J. C. Koe, a brother of the late C.O. of the 1st Battalion, commanded the 156th, and Brig.-Gen. H. B. Casson of the 2nd S.W.B. and 29th Division the 157th. Brig.-Gen. Pollok-M'Call reigned long over the 155th, and was precisely the right man for the job, for he had a manner that was not ultra-military and a power of speaking and writing simply and unambiguously, due to clear thinking. He was, forby, an Ayrshire man who, besides Cunningham, Kyle and Carrick—and the 5th R.S.F., which he had commanded for three years—knew his Galloway and Borders and how to couch the appeal for an effort.

On 15th November Brig.-Gen. Koe initiated the Krithia Nullah Campaign by a well-planned and immediately successful raid on both nullahs. While the Royal Scots under Col. Peebles stormed a trench H11A on the bluff of the western fork, the Cameronians (Col. Bridge) invaded a trench G11 in the low ground of the eastern fork. There was no preliminary bombardment, and it certainly looked like a surprise. Three mines and a burst of artillery, which included the jam-pot artillery (strictly rationed), a spirited rush, and the thing was over—for the time.

The Royal Scots and some Ayrshire Yeomen, sons of Anak, and the Cameronians and some Lanarkshire Yeomen, also on the large side, had a strenuous, savage night defending the gains. The Turks were assertive on the 21st, but the situation remained unchanged until long after the storm, most potent of pacifiers, had rolled by, leaving a not disagreeable climate, if inclined to be boisterous and chilly at times.

The time had come for the Suvla-Anzac evacuation. On the 18th December a diversion was made by the 157th I.B.—this time on G11A. It was to be pinched from both ends, as it ran across the spit of land enclosed by the confluence of the E. and W. nullahs. It was partly head covered, and at the E. end was outside hand-bomb range but within short "jam-pot" artillery range. At its W. end it almost touched H11A (now called Rosebery Street), and tunnelling was the proposed mode of forcing an entry. End of 1915.

The scheme was well planned and gallantly put in action, but the Turks seemed prepared and responded to the explosions, which preluded a simultaneous assault of G11A from the W. and certain parts of G12 on the E., with a vigour which contrasted with the comparative passivity with which the offensive of 15th November had been received. In the writer's experience it was the heaviest fire put up by the Turks in the last three months of the campaign. The 5th K.O.S.B. War Diary describes the fire on both sides as very heavy. The result was that half of G11A was taken from the W. and barricaded, and that the eastern attack was successful. The casualties of the 5th H.L.I. were severe, and only justified on the assumption that they aided the Suvla-Anzac evacuation and deceived the Turks as to our intention at Helles.

The K.O.S.B. occupied the original fire trenches, and supplied a hot meal to the shock troops, besides sniping and bombing and carrying bombs and materials and food and drink.

On the 23rd Col. Millar received a warm letter of appreciation from Col. Morrison of the 5th H.L.I., which he finished by saying that the 5th H.L.I. would not readily forget the 5th K.O.S.B.. We may add the 4th too, for 30 stout Borderers of that battalion took part in the fray.

Comforts were forthcoming for Christmas Day. There was a cheerful spirit manifest from 155th B.H.Q. downwards, although none knew the great secret, and the enemy guns were busy in the morning. On Wednesday the 29th the last offensive was carried out by Brig.-Gen. Pollok-M'Call with the 5th R.S.F. in the firing-line and the K.O.S.B. with the 4th R.S.F. in support. It was a pure *ruse de guerre*, and the objective was limited in such a way as to leave no scope for doubt.

The uncaptured half of G11A was to be taken with the aid of a couple of mines. The debris was given ten seconds to settle, and the R.S.F. were to rush the trench and link up with the now advanced British line in the eastern nullah. Col. A. H. Leggett, afterwards B.G.C. 156th I.B., was an admirable leader. His men, nothing daunted by a chance Turkish *Straaf* * a quarter of an hour before zero (1 p.m.), and by quite a stubborn show of resistance, took their objectives and held them. The K.O.S.B. played the same rôle as before, and played it well. 2nd Lieut. J. A. G. Cairns (of the 4th)

* Phonetic spelling of a war word of general use derived from the German *strafe* (fine or punishment).

1916. was killed while wiring, and was the last K.O.S.B. officer to fall in Gallipoli.

The story of the evacuation has been already told. Suffice it here to record that the 4th K.O.S.B. evacuated from W beach in two parties. One of 80 * left on the night 2/3rd January 1916. The rest, numbering only 147 all told, with some Scottish Yeomanry included, followed on the 7/8th. The 5th K.O.S.B. main body left, as they came, *via* the *R. Clyde,* on the 7/8th, and a working party of 100 under 3 officers saw it out to the bitter end. It is strange to think that the battered old tramp was reconditioned after the end of the war, and is believed to be still afloat and in use. On the 22nd November 1928 an article appeared in the *Glasgow Herald* suggesting that some generous person with a touch of romance might rescue the old ship, whose Port-Glasgow rivets had held so well, from the perils of the sea, and paint out the name *Angela,* and restore that under which she rivalled the Wooden Horse of Troy.

* Sorley Brown, pp. 49 and 51.

CHAPTER II

EGYPT AND PALESTINE *

CONTROL of the Suez Canal and its uninterrupted use by vessels of war and commerce were essential to the victory of the Allies. The flight of the *Goeben* and the *Breslau* into the Dardanelles pointed to probable danger to peaceful possession of the canal from Turkish territory. The danger became certain when the Turks declared war on 5th November 1914, and imminent when aerial reconnaissance revealed hostile forces advancing across Sinai in the beginning of 1915. In point of fact, the menace turned out something of a bogey. Egypt, well handled by the experienced Major-Gen. Sir John G. Maxwell,† remained quiet. "So far as was possible the Egyptian people as a whole strictly disinterested themselves from the war." ‡ The Arabs and Syrians wasted no love on the Turk, and the danger was not political but purely military. The invasion was directed against the stretch of canal at Tussum, between Lake Timsah and Great Bitter Lake, about 9 miles S.S.E. of the important junction of Ismailia, where, moreover, the sweet water canal from Cairo meets the Suez Canal. It was beaten off decisively by Major-Gen. Sir Alexander Wilson's Indian troops, and the story can be read in the report which he forwarded to Sir J. Maxwell,§ and in Lieut.-Gen. Sir George Macmunn's (official) *Military Operations, Egypt and Palestine.* The Turks retired unpursued to Beersheba, and the threat ceased to be imminent. If there had been any chance of a further attack before the hot weather of 1915, the Dardanelles campaign put an end to that idea. That undoubted result has been one of the justifications for that much-criticized venture. We can therefore pass on to the moment when the ex-Gallipoli forces were landing in Egypt in January and February 1916 and consider the situation as it then was. The blow to Turkish prestige caused by their defeat at the canal and the invasion of their European and

1916.
—

* See Map 6 in pocket. † He died in February 1929.

‡ Col. A. P. Wavell's *The Palestine Campaigns* (London: Constable, 1928), p. 13.

§ Naval and Military Despatches.

1916. Asiatic territory had been discounted by the British failure in Gallipoli and the Kut disaster to an entire British division in Mesopotamia.* The Grand Duke Nicholas had not yet taken Erzerum † and Trebizond. It looked as if the Turks would launch a formidable force against the canal, and various schemes were considered, including defence by attack, *e.g.* by a landing at Alexandretta in the N.E. angle of the Eastern Mediterranean. But in the end the problem of canal defence narrowed itself down to two alternatives. The canal itself was definitely discarded as the first line of defence for many excellent reasons, based on the experience of the previous year.

The choice lay between having a line of posts some 12,000 yards E. of the canal or of crossing the desert of Sinai and confining the Turk to Palestine.

As a matter of fact the general responsible for the defence adopted the first alternative, elaborated his field fortifications, and then as opportunity arose pushed E. his railway track and pipe line, which were necessary for a crossing of or even an appreciable advance into the Sinai desert. Sir Archibald Murray, who had been Chief of the Imperial General Staff, succeeded Sir C. C. Monro as Commander of the M.E.F. on 9th January 1916. Had he been master of the situation he would have preferred the bolder, more aggressive, and man-saving method of an advance E. to a place of which we shall hear much—El Arish. But, as already observed, he contented himself with pressing on with the preparations for a protecting line, already in hand, when he took over.

And now a few jottings about the Suez Canal and what lay E. of it. It is about 100 miles long, from 65 to 100 yards wide, and 34 feet deep. By land to Aleppo, near Alexandretta, is about 500 miles. Its immediate neighbour is the dry, sandy, and in the southern parts mountainous desert of Sinai, 120 miles wide in the only part with which we are concerned, namely, the extreme N. near the coast. The large oasis of Qatiya lies 26 miles E. of the canal and just under 10 miles from the sea. The nearest railhead was Qantara on the canal, connected by rail with Port Said (30 miles), Ismailia (20 miles S.), and Cairo (110 miles, *via* Zagazig 60 miles).

Although Ismailia is about half-way from Port Said to Suez, the military division fell naturally into three sections. In the S. Byng's IX. A.C., in which the 29th Division and 1st K.O.S.B. spent three pleasant months in the best of climates before embarking for France,

* The garrison did not surrender till 19th April 1916, but was closely invested early in December 1915.

† Erzerum fell on 15th February 1916.

extended from the Red Sea to Kabrit on the Great Bitter Lake. 1916. From Kabrit N. as far as Ferdan, N. of Ismailia were the Anzac Corps under Gen. Birdwood, and from Ferdan to the sea the remaining 40 miles were allotted to Sir Francis Davies' VIII. A.C., part of which was the 52nd Division and, consequently, the 4th and 5th K.O.S.B..

The S. section, the most unlikely point of attack, consisted of a few isolated posts in the desert. The middle section was the most elaborate, there being continuous trenches for many miles from the Great Bitter Lake to a new railway under construction from Qantara to Romani.* But we are not concerned with the never-to-be-tested works near the waterway, nor with the vast inundations of the Plain of Tina, nor with the life at Tell-el-Kebir, Cairo, or Qantara, but with the advance of the railway towards the Holy Land, with the organization of an enormous Egyptian labour corps and the collection of vast masses of camels for what turned out to be the real crusade. As truly as Murray built on the work of Maxwell, so did Allenby's triumphs rest on the work of Murray and his coadjutors, military and civilian—such as Sir Murdoch Macdonald, Under-Secretary for Public Works, and Mr. E. M. Dowson, the head of the Survey Department, so vital for maps—alike.

On 9th January Gen. Murray took over from Gen. Monro, who returned to England, command of the M.E.F. with the special charge of the Suez Canal defences. But neither at this time nor after he superseded Sir J. Maxwell was he independent of military control from home.

By this time the office of Chief of the Imperial General Staff had been created,† and there were daily communications sent by the C.-in-C., M.E.F., and later E.E.F. (*i.e.* Egyptian Expeditionary Force), to Sir William Robertson, C.I.G.S..‡ This control powerfully affected the number of troops allotted to the E.E.F..

Nevertheless, Murray was locally master of the situation from his arrival, and it may be stated in advance that the new command was created on 10th March. It made no difference to the life of our Borderers, to whom we must shortly return.

By 27th February Gen. Murray had obtained assent to an advance to the Qatiya Oasis, with its water and sheltering palms. Soon the railway was doubled between Zagazig and Ismailia (from which there was a direct line to Qantara) and a new line extended from

* Three miles N.W. of Qatiya.

† For Mr. Asquith's share in this work of reorganization, see an article by Sir F. M. Maurice in the *Edinburgh Review* for January 1929.

‡ *Egypt and Palestine*, vol. i. pp. 100 and 157.

1916. El Salhiah to Qantara, supplying an even more direct line between Zagazig and Qantara. The next step was to push the railway across the canal at Qantara out into the desert N.E. towards Romani. Water, transport, training were the clamant needs. The first was to be supplied by a pipe track from the sweet water canal from the Nile, which reaches Qantara *via* Ismailia. At one time there was a shortage of piping, but the world's resources were called in, thanks to Britain's sea-power, and eventually thirsty Britons drank the filtered waters of the Nile in the Holy Land. The pipe track kept company and pace with the new railway. Necessarily so, for the Egyptian can only work if unstinted water can be swallowed.

The wire road, so useful to marching troops and Ford cars, did not come into use till the middle of November. In any case, horses' hooves cut it, and it was out of bounds for them. The camel was the stand-by, especially for mobile columns. The proper desert-bred type was not so easily come by, but was gradually forthcoming to the number of 35,000. The sand was so soft that 15 miles was a long march for infantry and 25 for cavalry.

As for training, and no troops stood more in need of it than the tired trench men from Gallipoli, there was the great imperial training centre at Zeitun,* and one chiefly frequented by Anzacs at Tell-el-Kebir. There was a M.G. school at Ismailia.

The weather turned to heat about the middle of April. Nine a.m. was the worst time, before the sea breeze blew. But the arch enemy was the S. wind from the desert, a scorching tormentor—the Khamsin.

The Turks were known to be meditating a renewed offensive. Their numbers were exaggerated by the men on the spot, and even the modest 100,000, which the C.I.G.S. regarded as the maximum, never were forthcoming. They were known to be frugal and easily supported, rapid and tough marchers, enured to the climate, and, only too well, to be brave and in their own way skilful. The moving spirit, though hampered by Turkish interference, was a Bavarian colonel named Kress von Kressenstein, who gave numerous proofs of his ability and alertness. An attack was expected before the hot weather, and would have to be beaten off if Napoleon's route to Acre were to be followed. We can therefore place the K.O.S.B. in historic setting, with the Serbonian bog † (of Tina)

* In eighteen months, from January 1916 to end of June 1917, more than 20,000 officers and N.C.O.s passed through this "college."

† "Betwixt Damiata[1] and Mount Casius[2] old
Where armies[3] whole have sunk."
Milton, *Paradise Lost*, bk. ii.

[1] Now Damietta. [2] Mons Casius, now El Kas.
[3] One is said to have been an army of Darius II.

on the L. and the much-traversed route to the E. by the sea in front of them, destined to a long and weary pilgrimage. Spring 1916.

No one who has been through the evacuation from Helles can fail to recall the rebound of spirits which lasted some days and was succeeded by a conviction that the great thing to do was—as little as possible. Whereas the 29th Division sailed almost immediately to Alexandria, the 52nd remained for some time in Lemnos.

The weather was delightful on the whole. The drills were not overdone. For officers there were possibilities of excursions to Thermopegæ (hot springs), where velvety water at an ideal temperature banished dirt and fatigue. In favourable weather the top of the pass from Mudros W. to the baths yielded one of the world's noblest sights—Mount Atlas like an obelisk, three-fourths under gleaming white snow, rising out of the wine-dark sea. In time the healing hand of nature revived the troops, and boredom, such as oppressed the solitary Philoctetes, was revealed as the chief product of the classic isle.

The 4th K.O.S.B. were the first to escape. An advance-party left in the *Nestor* on the 27th and reached Alexandria on the 31st, to be followed by the main body (still with the Glasgow Yeomanry attached), which left on the 31st. How small a remnant were left will be realized when a count at Heliopolis showed that there were only 433 O.R., inclusive of a draft of 92 men. Officers were disproportionately plentiful. As many as 31 were at the disposal of Col. Wilson when he moved to Port Said on the 17th and to Qantara on the 27th. The Glasgow Yeomanry then left the K.O.S.B. and went back as cavalry of the 52nd Division.

The 5th Battalion sailed on the *Ionian* on the 1st of February, reached Alexandria on the 4th, absorbed a draft of 2 officers and 69 O.R., and settled down at Abbassia (also near Cairo) to refit.

The 5th were numerically stronger, and their physique won a compliment from Gen. Horne when he inspected them at Port Said on the 21st. The stay at Cairo had included a visit to the Pyramids,* and elementary squad and platoon drill relaid the foundations of a sound discipline. Camp was left on the 16th, and after ten days at Port Said, Qantara was reached—uncomfortably. An advance-party, 41 O.R. under 2 officers, had been at Ballah, since one of the bridgeheads on the canal 5 miles S. of Qantara, and rejoined on the 28th.

* The temptation to digress caused by the associations of this historic land is going to be sternly repressed and the theme confined to *bella, horrida bella!* Col. Thompson and Capt. Scott Elliot have done the fullest and most scholarly justice to the Biblical and other historical associations that crowd into this chapter in the life of the battalions.

Summer 1916.

From now onward for a whole year and more the K.O.S.B. sojourned in the wilderness. The period is marked by only two incidents: the brilliant surprise towards the end of April by a large raiding party directed by Kress, which resulted in the death or capture of three and a half squadrons of yeomanry at Oghratina and Qatiya respectively (see Map); and the smashing defeat but somewhat feeble pursuit of some 18,000 Turks by the E.E.F. under the local direction of Gen. Lawrence (formerly G.O.C. 52nd Division) at Romani.

In the former engagement, the sole military result of which was to delay the progress of the trans-Sinai railway in its thrust towards Romani, the 155th I.B. were engaged at Dueidar, half-way between Qatiya and Qantara. But the successful defence of that isolated post belongs to the story of the R.S.F.; * and the K.O.S.B., though ready, were never in contact with the enemy.

In the really important battle of Romani the principal rôle was played by mounted troops on the southern flank. But the part played by the 52nd Division in manning the prepared defences from the sea some 6 to 7 miles S. to the sandy knoll of Katib Gannit,† taking their shelling with steadiness and repelling any attempts at hostile attacks, was by no means negligible. The K.O.S.B. were under fire all day, and lost their signalling officer, Lieut. H. E. Pollard, and 1 O.R. killed, and had 10 O.R. wounded. What will linger in K.O.S.B. survivors' memories is the 7-mile march in the awful sweltering heat of the 5th of August to Er Rabah, near the caravan route to El Arish and Palestine.‡ The mobile Turk "had the legs of them," and the solitary scrap on the 4th was the only contact which the K.O.S.B. had until April 1917.

The early part of the "desert" year had been taken up with outpost routine on the fixed defences of the canal and heavy fatigues in the Qantara area. Spit Post, Hill 40, Hill 58, Hill 70, Ballybunion are names without a thrill, but may call up starry nights strangely spent by kindly Scots. Training went steadily on. Officers went to and returned from Zeitun and Ismailia. O.R. got lessons in cookery, and let us hope profited by them. All ranks popped in and out of hospital, and leave—to Egypt—was granted regularly.

* See Buchan, *Royal Scots Fusiliers*; and Gen. Murray's Despatch, dated 25th September 1916.

† There were 18 redoubts capable of accommodating 100 rifles each. (Wavell, *op. cit.*)

‡ Besides the interesting personal experiences of Scott Elliot in the 5th Battalion *History*, in Sorley Brown's 4th Battalion *History*, and Thompson's *52nd Division*, reference may be made to Lieut.-Gen. Sir Geo. MacMunn's *Egypt and Palestine* volume (official), Wavell's *Palestine Campaigns*, and above all to the vivid despatch of General Murray, dated 1/12/1916.

The weather behaved according to schedule. Hardly has May opened before the diaries contain entries referring to intense heat. But in this connection it is to be noticed that sunstroke was rare and that the nights were cool and often cold. Altogether, it cannot be extracted from the authorities that the roasting which these Northerners received in the rainless summer and autumn of 1916 had any bad effect on the general health of the troops. In the despatches the health of the troops is invariably matter of favourable comment.

Sept. 1916.

Col. G. T. B. Wilson, D.S.O., of the A. & S.H., still commanded the 4th K.O.S.B.. In fact, at Romani he was for a time in charge of both battalions. Col. Millar's years did not admit of a longer spell of foreign service, and, to his own and his officers' and men's regret, he departed home in May 1916, to continue the good work of training more Borderers. He wore the D.S.O., won on 12th July 1915. He was succeeded for a season by Capt. W. T. Forrest of the 4th K.O.S.B., and then by Major J. R. Simson of the H.L.I., who took over on 17th June, and remained C.O. till his death at Gaza in April 1917.

In September 1916 Lieut.-Col. Wilson was summoned home, and after a short tenure by Major Jobson and Capt. Forrest, Lieut.-Col. J. M. B. Sanders of the Leinster Regiment became C.O., and remained such until September of the year following.

During the whole period in the desert the K.O.S.B. gained not only in quality but in quantity. Part of the merit of the 5th Battalion Diary is the way in which strength returns and moves of officers, N.C.O.s, and men are regularly recorded. The battalion had less than 500 when Dueidar was fought, more than 700 when Romani was fought—a strength maintained at the end of the year in spite of many days of 110° Fahr. in the so-called shade, and when the Gaza battle opened an effective strength of something like 35 officers and 800 O.R..

Another feature of value was an accession of senior officers. Besides Major W. F. Crombie of the 3/5th K.O.S.B., who rejoined in June, there was Major John C. Kennedy of the Ayrshire Yeomanry, who had served in Gallipoli, and joined the 5th K.O.S.B. on the 11th March 1917.

A short account of events must precede the tale of the second major engagement in which K.O.S.B. participated in the eastern theatre.

From the moment when the Turks were repulsed at Romani the Suez Canal was safe from anything except sporadic bombs from the air. The works which cost so much toil have never yet been put to use.

1916. The time had come to carry out Gen. Murray's plan in its entirety—namely, push the railway and the sweet water-pipe line all the way to El Arish, and fortify a line between that town and El Kossaima. El Arish lies 62 miles or so E. of Romani, and El Kossaima nearly 50 miles S.E. of El Arish, which is practically on the sea.

The advance went on remorselessly, methodically, and peacefully. The picture of the cavalry screen out in front, the faithful "foot sloggers" (with the 52nd nearly always at the front) dogging their steps, while alert and experienced minds played the deep game of Arabian politics and peacefully penetrated the back regions of Turkish territory; the quaint and picturesque columns of camels, never quainter than when controlled in the Scots Doric; * the ponderous heavy guns creaking along on their "ped-railed" tyres, hauled by teams of 16 horses; the chattering, drouthy, but indefatigable Labour Corps delivering the goods in laid lines of sleepers, is one that rouses the imagination in a way that no picture of events on the Western Front can rival, with its monotonous series of positional warfare, in which machines predominate and man is literally cannon fodder. If this story of the K.O.S.B. leads others to investigate the Palestine campaigns and read the works of the other Lawrence "of the Arabians," it will be the source of interest in and admiration for All-British brains and grit.

In August the C.-in-C. found the political situation such that he made Cairo his H.Q. and handed over Ismailia and the new-named E.F. (*i.e.* Eastern Force) to Major-Gen. Sir Charles M. Dobell, K.C.B., C.M.G., D.S.O., as his principal subordinate. Omitting the 42nd (East Lancashire) Division, which had done so well in Gallipoli from the early days and left for France in February 1917, there were, besides the 52nd, two Territorial Divisions in the E.F., namely, the 53rd (Welsh) under Major-Gen. A. G. Dallas, C.B., and the 54th (East Anglian) under Major-Gen. (afterwards Sir Stuart) Hare, a Scotsman, who had led the 86th I.B. on to the rocks W. of W Beach on 25th April 1915, and been wounded there. There was also a division, composed of dismounted Yeomanry, numbered 74th, under Major-Gen. E. S. Girdwood, an old 52nd Divisional Staff Officer, one of the most helpful mentors and inspiring leaders in the campaign. These are the comrades who keep flitting across the path of the K.O.S.B..

Then come those whose doings have so largely to be excluded—

* "The men took charge of the (regimental transport) camels as if they had been born in Sinai instead of in Scotland." Thompson, p. 269; Scott Elliot, pp. 93 and 94.

the newly baptized "Desert Column," commanded by Lieut.-Gen. Sir Philip Chetwode (Baronet), C.B., commanding among other troops two mounted divisions, which for sheer audacity and enterprise it would be difficult to surpass, the Anzac M.D. commanded by Major-Gen. Sir H. G. Chauvel and the Imperial M.D. commanded by Major-Gen. H. W. Hodgson. The latter contained 2 Australian Light Brigades and 2 Brigades of English Yeomanry. General Chauvel was an Australian soldier by birth, breeding, and training, just as Brig.-Gen. Chaytor was a New Zealander. In the Palestine campaign Chetwode, Chauvel, and Chaytor were a most distinguished triumvirate.

Winter 1916.

By 21st October the leading division was within 40 miles of El Arish, and Gen. Murray determined to eject the enemy and use El Arish as a base for his defensive line and for occasional offensive operations against S. Palestine. The Home Government had not yet captured Jerusalem on paper. The defence of Egypt was still the governing aim of all military action. There was no sign of reinforcements. Things pointed rather in the direction of depletion than augmentation of the forces.

So the systematic march was resumed and the 52nd, nearly always at the head of the infantry column, reached El Arish on the 22nd of December.* They marched hot and heavily laden, with wonderfully few falls out, in the wake of the Anzacs. It was like a creeping barrage. A creeping barrage marks time, gives a bound, and marks time. So it was with the desert trek. So far; then fatigues in connection with security and water; then, as rails and pipes and wire came forward, another bound; and so on as it seemed *ad infinitum*. Unmolested; but heavy loads and heavy roads (the wire road was not for the vanguard) and vigilance taxed their energies.†

El Arish, reached bloodlessly, opened the way for better going and more rapid progress, and for sea transport despite surf and currents.‡

The very next day a brilliant exploit of Chauvel's division up country in surrounding a Turkish post at Magdhaba resulted in the capture of a regimental commander and close on 1,300 other prisoners at a cost of under 150 British casualties, and paved the way for a further advance towards Rafah on the frontier between Egypt and Turkey and Africa and Asia. It lay 117 miles E. of Qantara on the

* By this time Brig.-Gen. Casson had left the 157th I.B. and been succeeded by Brig.-Gen. C. D. Hamilton-Moore.

† Col. Thompson gives the 52nd's Itinerary on p. 301.

‡ To the K.O.S.B., as to other units, this meant heavy beach fatigues, a very frequent entry in both diaries.

17

1917. Suez Canal, now a considerable port receiving cargoes direct from the U.S.A. and elsewhere, and about 26 miles from El Arish. The usual pause, which happened to include Christmas and New Year, and a second cutting-out "operation" on a larger scale equally successful and equally due to the resource of "the man on the spot" at the critical moment yielded a "bag" of over 1,600 prisoners and a quantity of material. Gens. Chetwode and Chauvel surrounded the enemy at El Magruntein on 9th January 1917.*

Gaza was now only 20 miles off, but the K.O.S.B. were not involved for some time.

Both battalions stayed at El Arish from the 24th of December 1916 to the 27th of February in what Scott Elliot describes as quite pleasant surroundings. Garrison life was as before; working, drilling, training, marching, playing. The weather was now broken, but an entry of a case of drowning while bathing indicates that sometimes the sea might tempt.

During January and February drafts were arriving. The 4th Battalion received 91 O.R. in January and in February 97. Three more subalterns joined, W. Robertson, J. J. S. Thomson, and J. Elder. The 5th's strength rose from about 700 to 800 in the first quarter of 1917. The new drafts were worked in by intensive platoon training. It may safely be claimed that both battalions were fitter for war than they had ever been. Better men than those lost could not be found, but the 1916–17 drafts were of the same stuff, and much time in marches, odd jobs, bivouacking, night operations, ceremonials, football, and bayonet practice had produced for Gen. Dobell an instrument of keen temper and considerable mobility.

The test was near at hand. The capture of Gaza would round off the Egyptian defence campaign. There would be water in abundance and satisfactory enough touch with the sea. We are told that the War Cabinet approved of the C.-in-C.'s design, that it fitted in with that livening up of things all round in the spring of 1917, which had such a ghastly outcome everywhere. On the Palestine front the first clash of arms resulted merely in failure. The First Battle of Gaza was no disaster. It was hailed at first as a victory, and the claim was based on the C.-in-C.s own words in reporting its results. But it paved the way for Second Gaza, which was simply a calamity. For the element of surprise was gone for ever after the first battle. There is a sort of parallelism in the course pursued in March and April 1917 with that in March and April 1915. Substitute for the futile dash of the navies of Britain and France into the

* See *Egypt and Palestine*, chaps. xiv and xv; and Wavell, *Palestine Campaigns*, pp. 65 and 66.

Dardanelles the encircling rush of the mounted troops on Gaza, and the head-on infantry landing at Helles on 25th April 1915 finds its counterpart in the destructive frontal attacks in which the K.O.S.B., and especially the 5th, suffered so severely on 17th April 1917. April 1917.

The First Battle of Gaza must receive short treatment here, inasmuch as the 52nd Division took no part in it. Gen. Dobell's ("G.O.C., E.F.") plan was that while the 54th Division guarded the landward flank, the Desert Column should repeat on battle scale the tactics so successfully adopted in the minor engagements already recounted. The principal infantry part was a straightforward advance by the 53rd Division. Four miles S.W. of Gaza was the nearest point of the Wadi el Ghazze on its northward but twisting course from the S. Judean hills to the Mediterranean. Wide, deep, and at this time full of spate water, this canyon-like watercourse was a tremendous military obstacle. Its sides were steep and here and there cleft by narrow sheltering nullahs. The substance was firm mud.* Once across the Wadi the 53rd were to advance parallel to the ancient road straight on the ancient city, over some intervening undulations which we shall soon study more carefully. Meanwhile the mounted troops, with a more roving commission in various columns, were to cross the road from Gaza to Beersheba and wheel L. and cut off Gaza from the N.. The day chosen was the 26th of March. Much turned on the weather and the working of the arrangements for supplying water. The importance of a water supply cannot be exaggerated. A few hours without water, and no hope of it coming, could turn a victory into a defeat.

Long before dawn on the 26th all the troops were across the undefended Wadi, but soon thereafter a dense and unseasonable † fog played havoc with the time table, and only started to lift at 7 a.m.. The mounted troops did wonders in finding their way through the mist, so that by 10.30 a.m. some of them were actually N.E. of Gaza. Nor did the 53rd Division fail General Dobell. With a very modest amount of artillery support they covered 5 miles of undulating sandy country and forced the front-line trenches on the summit of the famous ridge of Ali el Muntar, the southern key to Gaza. But through no fault of theirs they only reached their goal as night fell, black and swift. No one knew in time that von Tiller, the commander of the local garrison, was in desperation, that he was surrounded except on the sea side, that he had reported to Kress that he must surrender. While the Desert Column, including the 53rd Division (which was attached to it for the action), felt all the sensations of victory and eagerly awaited the morrow and a triumphant

* *Official History*, p. 282. † *Official History*, p. 290.

17 April 1917. entry into Gaza, its commander, Gen. Chetwode, and Gen. Dobell, the commander of the whole force, were anxiously discussing the water problem and the inevitable arrival of Turkish reinforcements. To the astonishment of all, the mounted troops were recalled. This involved the abandonment of the captured and improved trenches on Ali el Muntar and the withdrawal of the 53rd to the L. bank of the Wadi. It is easy to be wise after the event, but it is terrible to think that in reality Gaza was ours. Scott Elliot records the disgust of some Australians as the order to evacuate reached them. These men had actually been in the town. And there was the 52nd keyed up and ready for the fray at In Seirat. " Few actions of the late war have been the subject of greater differences of opinion," says the *Official History*, to which as well as to Col. Wavell those interested in the problem are referred. The losses were trifling. The horses and camels came back and drank their Egyptian water. Wells were sunk in the trough of the Wadi, but the great work had all to be done again. For on 30th March the C.-in-C. received orders from the War Cabinet to take Jerusalem, and the way lay through Gaza. Hence the Second Battle of Gaza.*

We left the K.O.S.B. at El Arish. They moved thence on 27th February to El Burj and a week later to Sheikh Zowaaid, more than half-way to Rafah, in brigade reserve until on 25th March, as part of the main body of the E.F., they went forward to Khan Yunis, and on the following day listened to the battle at In Seirat, 7 miles from Gaza. After the retirement to the Wadi el Ghazze they were either on outpost duty or in brigade reserve near El Burj. The only incident prior to the actual battle was a skilful withdrawal by Capt. A. K. Clark Kennedy of a company unscathed from an observation post called the Red House, beyond the R. bank of the river, when attacked by a battalion of Turks.† No better description of Gaza can be found than Col. Thompson's.‡

"Gaza lies in a shallow fertile valley, which is about 2 miles wide, and runs parallel with the sea between a belt of coastal sand-hills and an extensive table-land. The belt of dunes is almost 2 miles wide. The table-land rises gradually, and in the distance can be seen the blue Judean hills. On its coastal and southern sides, this table-land is fringed by ridges and hills. The southern are referred to as the ridges of Mansura and Sheikh Abbas. On the side over-looking Gaza there rises up the great rock of Ali el Muntar, 272 feet

* Scott Elliot is wrong in saying that " this brilliant little victory was so described that it read as a defeat." On the contrary, so *couleur de rose* was the tone of the C.-in-C.'s report that it materially influenced the War Cabinet.

† Scott Elliot, *War Diary*, pp. 127–128.

‡ At pp. 309 and 310 of his *52nd Division*.

in height, just south-east of the city, the gates of which are said to have been carried up this hill by Samson. It is a commanding height, overtopping everything within several miles to the south. This is the key-position. From Muntar there runs southward, for nearly 5 miles, the ridge of El Sire, terminating at the Wadi Ghuzze. Parallel to it, from the southern edge of the table-land, two other ridges run down to this great Wadi, the centre one of the three being called El Burjaliye after a small garden. These ridges are separated by a labyrinthine tangle of nullahs, from 10 to 20 feet deep, which twist and turn in every direction.

17 April 1917.

"Gaza is the usual white-walled Eastern town, with red roofs and minarets showing here and there. It is embosomed in palm trees, and all around it is a belt, to the southward almost 3 miles deep, of small fields and gardens, each surrounded by high cactus hedges. These cactus hedges grow out of mud banks, are from 6 to 12 feet high, and about a yard or more deep. They form natural barbed entanglements, and give perfect cover from view. Shrapnel does little more than pierce their leaves. Direct-hits from H.E. shells will blow holes in them, and, after much labour, gaps can be cut in them with hedging tools and sickles, but such expedients could have little effect, since they ran for miles. The Turks made use of these hedges by digging their machine-gun emplacements, fire-trenches, and snipers' posts below them. Tanks alone can cope with them effectively."

Gen. Dobell's formidable task necessitated the maximum use of artillery and other mechanical devices available. He could not fling a wide net like Allenby because of the water difficulty and insufficient superiority in numbers. To prepare for a full dress affair on Western lines, time was necessary. The 53rd and the Desert Column needed rest. The railway must be hurried as far forward as possible. The Turks naturally enough made good use of their time and turned Gaza into a veritable fortress pivoting on Ali el Muntar. Gen. Dobell applied for reinforcements. These were refused. It was a case of using all troops available and making the attack in two stages. There had to be a jumping-off place won within gun-range of the objective. Gaza could never be stormed in the stride of an 8-mile march. There must be a halt of at least a day. How long the delay lasted would not be material, because surprise was out of the question. The enemy was vigilant and alert, and had to be blown or poisoned or bombed or shot out of his entrenchments or be bayoneted in them. The real battle would open with a full barrage, under the support of which infantry would assault the fortress. The field had a front of 7 miles from the sea

17 April 1917. to Sheik Abbas. The 2 miles of sand-dunes from the sea to the road to Egypt were the territory of the 53rd Division. Much was not expected of them. The brunt was to be borne by the 54th Division on the extreme R. of the front and by the 52nd in the centre. The 155th I.B. faced Ali el Muntar * and its foreworks, the warren and the labyrinth, its cornfields, cactus hedges, and the formidable Outpost Hill, a good mile S. of the fort. This "Eastern attack" was under the 52nd's own G.O.C., Major-Gen. W. E. B. Smith. The 54th were under Major-Gen. Hare. Brig.-Gen. Pollok-M'Call commanded the 155th I.B.. The 4th K.O.S.B. were under Lieut.-Col. M. B. Sanders and the 5th under Lieut.-Col. J. R. Simson, D.S.O., of the H.L.I..

After dark on the 16th the Wadi was crossed and by a flawless night march the objectives were reached. The 155th marched along the El Sire ridge as far as Kurd Hill, exactly a mile from Outpost Hill and 2 miles from Ali el Muntar. There they entrenched. Their objective was Ali el Muntar. The intervening country has been described by Col. Thompson: † "From Kurd Hill to the N.E., the El Sire ridge for 2½ miles rises at regular intervals into a series of elevations known as Queen's, Lee's, Outpost, Middlesex, and Green Hills, gradually increasing in height, the last being overtopped by the precipitous sides of Muntar with its mosque and single tree. Innumerable nullahs have been bitten deeply into the ridge on both sides almost to the crest-line. . . . Unless men climb in and out of these nullahs every few yards, it is only possible to advance along the ridge by following the narrow crest-line," ‡ called elsewhere the "spine." §

The 18th was spent by both sides in hectic activity. Ammunition and water, *e.g.* 100,000 gallons in *fanatis* alone, were brought forward.

The regimental aspect of the Second Battle of Gaza is almost entirely taken up with the desperate attempts made by Borderers of both battalions to reach Ali el Muntar, attempts which never succeeded farther than the temporary hold of the semicircular redoubt or lunette on the summit of Outpost Hill. An explicable loss of direction through the magnetic attraction of flanking fire

* The strength of Muntar and the amount of work spent on it is well described by Scott Elliot at p. 130.

† Thompson, *op cit.*, p. 317.

‡ Those familiar with the Scottish Highlands will recall many an intended traverse frustrated by similar parallel dry watercourses vertically scarring the mountain side. The *Official History* tells us of a tank that did a nose-dive on the advance on the 19th into one of these nullahs, and took no further part in the battle.

§ *Official History*, p. 340.

concentrated almost the entire 5th K.O.S.B on the lunette. Of those dedicated to Middlesex Hill farther to the R. only No. 2 Platoon under Lieut. Turner kept direction and touch with the 4th R.S.F.. On the L. the 53rd Division took Sheikh Ajlin on the coast and the prominent dune—Samson's Ridge—2 miles S.W. of Gaza, but were unable to progress. 17 April 1917.

Beyond the R.S.F. the 156th I.B., with open ground to cross, could only struggle to the slopes of Middlesex Hill. Beyond them the 54th Division faced a task, the stark impossibility of which pinned them down while well short of their objectives. Their casualties were all but 1,000 greater than those of our division, being no less than 2,870.* The experiences of the Mounted Screen are outwith the purview of this survey of a small portion of a hopeless head-on attack on a natural and improved fortress. The hopelessness was due to insufficiency of guns and ammunition. At no point did the battle present any other feature than costly failure. The French *Requin* and two Monitors firing from the sea did little structural damage. The counter-battery work was negligible, and the 68 † guns of the Turks (all but 12 were field-guns) were unlocated and mischievous. Where our artillery shone was in crushing Turkish counter-attacks.

The battle opened at 5.30 a.m. with a heavy-gun bombardment, which continued till 7.20, at which hour the 53rd left their trenches and the R.F.A. poured gas shells on Ali el Muntar and neighbourhood. At 7.30 the two E.A. Divisions, from whom the greatest effort was expected, launched their attacks. The 157th I.B. was in reserve. The 156th were R. of and echeloned behind the 155th, which had the " croon o' the caus'ey " or spine of the El Sire ridge for its main road. The ridge is scarred on E. and W. by nullahs cutting the slopes and making bad going, in and out and up and down. The brigade therefore advanced along the top over Queen's Hill and on to Lee's Hill in artillery formation. At 8.15 a.m. the serious business began for the battalions which thus deployed for the attack. On the R. were the 4th R.S.F., destined for Middlesex Hill. On the L. were the 5th K.O.S.B., partly for the W. end of Middlesex Hill and partly for Outpost Hill. Echeloned on their L. rear were the 5th R.S.F., whose task was to protect the flank and gain contact with the 53rd. Gen. Pollok-M'Call, with H.Q. on Kurd Hill, held the 4th K.O.S.B. in hand as reserve.

As the 5th K.O.S.B. cleared the shelter of Lee's Hill they were met with a withering fire from Outpost Hill and from the wooded ground seamed with cactus hedges to the W. of Outpost Hill. In

* *Official History*, p. 348. † *Official History*, p. 349.

17 April 1917. eight noble waves the battalion advanced in the best British style. The 4th R.S.F. and 5th K.O.S.B. presented a splendid spectacle. But casualties came at once. Capts. Howieson (Adjutant) and Gibson and Lieut. Gilmour were wounded almost immediately. Except for the tendency to deviate towards the M.G. fire the attack was a model. The hollow or saddle on the S. side of Outpost Hill once reached, a certain amount of shelter was found and preparations for the assault were made.

There had been two tanks allotted to the 155th. One, as mentioned, stuck in a lateral nullah at the outset and took no further part in the battle, though the crew did. The other managed to keep going, and seems to have been first to storm the lunette, followed by the K.O.S.B., who here incurred more casualties. Lieut. H. W. L. Henery received fatal wounds. Capt. T. Dunn and Lieut. Nicholson were killed almost at the same moment. Good men were at a premium, for the Turk was in fighting mood and had not only bombs and M.G. but Minenwerfer at his disposal and vantage from which to use them. Sergts. Seaton and Beattie were specially useful at this time. The lunette was far from " an end in itself." It was an obstacle till taken and a trap when taken. That is why the time from 10 a.m. till noon was taken up with the sway of attack and counter-attack, through high corn in most places, until the B.G.C. 155th I.B. had to throw in his reserves. Of attacks, those of Lieut. W. B. Campbell and C.S.M. Townsend with him and Major J. C. Kennedy (of the Ayrshire Yeomanry), were all but successful when the leaders fell. Campbell was killed in his attack and Kennedy severely wounded in his.

The lunette was still Turkish when Major Forrest soon after noon left Lees' Hill at the head of two companies of the 4th Battalion, picked up all unattached men in the saddle—a deepish nullah—and led as only a fearless footballer in the prime of life, inspired and inspiring, can.

With irresistible *élan* the Borderers and some 5th R.S.F. followed Forrest up the hill. The garrison fled and the lunette was won. But though it was retained it was at a high price. Forrest was fatally wounded almost at once, and the defects of the place became glaringly evident. There was not enough room. The trenches were too shallow. It was impossible to attack towards Ali el Muntar. Major Crombie of the 5th tried and failed. One head above the parapet, and drum-fire ensued. In the course of the afternoon the remaining companies of the 4th K.O.S.B. were involved as combatants, runners, or carriers of ammunition, or as telephone linesmen. 4th Battalion H.Q. were within 100 yards, and a telephone message was actually received from a point 100 yards from the redoubt.* There was a question of engaging the 157th I.B., but fortunately they were spared needless carnage. 17 April 1917.

The fight ended for the K.O.S.B. in the following way: Towards 6 p.m. Lieut. R. B. Anderson of the 4th was the senior officer in charge of the 70-strong garrison of the lunette. He noticed parties of Turks dangerously far forward between himself and the 4th R.S.F., and wisely decided to evacuate the lunette after seeing to the removal of the wounded. This, of course, could only be managed after dark. It was successfully accomplished, but the gallant young Anderson was shot dead.

That ended the affair of the lunette on Outpost Hill. At one time as many as 400 had been crowded in and in front of it. The garrison were only some 70 strong when it was finally left, and of these 3 officers and 40 O.R. belonged to the 4th Battalion.

On the R. flank, besides the 3 or 4 men of A of the 5th Battalion left with Lieut. Turner, there were a few of B, who had found shelter sufficient to maintain themselves till dark.

On the L. flank the 5th R.S.F. had done their work well, but the cactus groves housed Turks ever ready to dash out, and Lieut. Col. J. R. Simson, D.S.O., a vigilant and efficient C.O., gave this area his personal care. Unfortunately he was mortally wounded—a severe blow to the 5th K.O.S.B., for their H.L.I. ex-regular suited them to perfection.

The painful task of cataloguing the casualties remains. To begin with the 5th Battalion, besides the C.O. and those already mentioned, the following officers were either killed or died of wounds: Capt. A. K. Clark Kennedy, of a well-known Galloway family; Capt. T. Dunn; Capt. W. G. D. Watson; Lieut. S. P. Crombie, a brother of the Major's; Lieut. Scott † (of Lockerbie); C. J. Law, a son of Mr. Bonar Law, the statesman; Geo. C. Macleod of the 9th Battalion; ‡ 2nd Lieuts. R. A. Gibb, who was then vigorously attacking a cactus stronghold, and A. Tweedie. In all 13 officers fell. Eight were wounded, including, in addition to the Second-in-Command (Major Kennedy of Dunure), the Adjutant, Capt. Howieson, and Major Crombie and Lieuts. Gibson and Gilmour, 2/Lieuts. W. Dinwiddie and S. C. Roberts. O.R. casualties amounted in all to 322. That night the battalion mustered 6 officers and 116 O.R. at the bivouac.§

* W.D., *ibid.*.

† "A. R. Scott, Lieut., died of w. 24/4/17" (Official Death Roll, *s.v.* 5th K.O.S.B., p. 224.)

‡ This officer is stated in the Official Death Roll to have been attached to the 1/7th R.W.F. when killed on 19/4/17.

§ Scott Elliot, p. 144.

17 April 1917. It would be impossible to exaggerate the devotion or the skill of Capt. W. T. Gardiner (awarded the M.C. for his courage that day) or the splendid support he received from orderlies and stretcher-bearers.

The 4th Battalion lost "Wattie" Forrest, leader of the storming party, and Second-in-Command; Capt. R. R. M. Lumgair, the popular C.O. of A; 2nd Lieut. J. C. Moore of B; Capt. W. F. Cochrane, C.O. of D, along with Lieut. R. B. Anderson and 2nd Lieut. A. Ainslie; six in all. Nine were wounded—Lieut. Elder * and 2nd Lieuts. J. M. L. Pollok, T. Broomfield, and J. M. Macpherson, *i.e.* the whole of Capt. Lumgair's officers; Capt. T. T. Muir (C.O.) and 2nd Lieuts. R. S. Alexander and W. R. Ovens of B; 2nd Lieuts. J. Dickson and D. Burns of D. C, the reserve company, alone escaped officer casualties.

Of O.R. casualties the feature was the large proportion of wounded to killed and missing—viz. 155 as against 15 and 28 respectively.

The gallant deeds of N.C.O.s and men are to be found in Sorley Brown and Scott Elliot and in Col. Thompson's 52nd Division.

There also may be read in Sorley Brown the balm which the G.O.C. 52nd Division on 24th April poured on the wounds of the brigades involved, and in particular how the "gallantry and determination of the 155th Brigade in its attack on Outpost Hill and the capture and recapture of the redoubt were worthy of the highest traditions of the British Army." The two battalions of R.S.F. suffered in proportion, with a grand total of 500.

Two Floddens for the Lowlands of Scotland within the space of two years!

Fortunately the days of half measures and delegated delegates were numbered. In time would come the single-hearted will to win and the man to do it.

TRENCH WARFARE IN THE ORIENT

The costly † repulse in front of Gaza animated the Turks and correspondingly depressed the British. It was not that the survivors of the disaster failed to show the usual buoyancy of spirits nor made other than the usual grumbles to which soldiers are at all times prone. It was rather an undercurrent of scepticism concerning the direction of the campaign and the utility of their training. They were not sure of themselves. However, they settled down to a second roasting Levant summer and the toil of digging a line from the sea to Apex at Sheikh Abbas, and, when

* For the second time. See p. 245.

† The British losses were about 6,000 and those of the Turks about 2,000.

that was accomplished, to manning it in tours of garrison duty and training behind it when at rest. The sources so often referred to have only one outstanding event—the famous raid by the 5th K.O.S.B. on Sea Post on 11th June 1917. Troops capable of such a brilliant feat had clearly recovered their *moral*. It was a quiet time in the line, casualties were few, and our two units, ably commanded by Lieut.-Cols. Sanders and (after April 1917) A. H. C. Kearsey, D.S.O., of the 10th Hussars respectively, and supervised by their trusted Brigade Commander, soon recovered, and absorbed the excellent drafts sent out. The raid on Sea Post—a strong work on the cliffs overlooking the shores of the Mediterranean—was the fruit of careful planning and practice. The G.O.C.'s interest is testified to by the perfect barrage and by well-timed demonstrations by gunners and infantry elsewhere in the line, to deceive the Turks. It was the first raid on any big scale, although in the wide plain of No Man's Land (often a mile wide) rival patrols hunted one another and scrapped in the dark. In point of time it came in opportunely to avenge a dash by the Turks on a post held by the 5th R.S.F. on the 5th of June, which had resulted in casualties. But its inception was of an earlier date, and reflects great credit on Col. Kearsey's ability and determination to have the raid carried out. He was unquestionably the moving spirit. Air photos had reached the stage when to the instructed eye the structure of field fortifications was revealed as though on a plan to scale. A model of Sea Post was prepared and placed at the correct distance on similar ground to No Man's Land. Movement in accordance with the planned barrage was practised for a week by the storm troops—two parties of 40—and their attendant demolition parties of bombers and axemen, supports, and flank protectors. As part of the drill was to double more than a furlong, it can be seen that the raiders would be in pretty hard condition when *der Tag* came. Gen. Pollok-M'Call's watchful eye and fertile, critical mind were behind the C.O. . He well knew that it would not do to fail.

11 June 1917.

For some days the R.A. fired bursts of concentrated fire on the wire in front of the post. The gaps thus torn were ranged, and the Turks prevented from mending them at night by bursts of fire from M.G. trained on them. As the distance was only a little over 1,000 yards, it is possible that this policy may have contributed to the ample unwired access. But the final bombardment was so intense that it may account for the passages. It took the form of two bursts of two minutes' duration, separated by an interval of two minutes. Directly the second burst ended, Lieuts. Turner and Mackinnon, at the head of the two parties, rushed through the

11 June 1917. gaps and slew or captured all the survivors of the bombardment. They had made a leisurely exit from "Bacon's Ridge" forty minutes before "kick off,"* and were ready for the music to begin. As the guns opened, the raiders rushed to within 200 yards of the post, and were like stones during the two minutes breathing space when no guns fired. It was 9 p.m., and a dark starry night, when the final rush was made. The commander of the raid, Capt. J. B. Penman, followed with the demolition party, and a pretty mess they made of things, and pretty surprises they made for the returning Turk. They took 12 prisoners in shelters. The only two Turks visible to the stormers on entering the fort were beheaded by Pte. W. Fergusson with an axe.†

Stay in the post only lasted fifteen minutes. Here, again, rehearsals in the model enabled everyone to feel at home and do his allotted job in record time. The approaches were blocked. The M.G. gun position was rushed, and a Lewis gun lost at First Gaza was recovered. And now comes the best. There were no casualties. The whistle sounded, the parties collected under their leaders, No Man's Land was recrossed, and a roll-call taken at Bacon's Boil (another name for Bacon's Ridge). Every man answered his name. Capt. Sir R. G. W. Grierson (of Lag), Lieuts. M'George and Burt—the bombing officer and of the 5th A. & S.H. —were the other officers who entered the fort. Of O.R. the C.O. brought to notice, besides the executioner, the following other specially dashing men: Sergts. Sudron, R. Wilson, and P. Brown, and Pte. R. M'Rae. The withdrawal was directed by Capt. Penman, and he and Lieuts. Mackinnon, Turner, and Burt were mentioned by the C.O., and the two former were awarded the M.C.. Pte. A. Paul of the bombers and Pte. J. Dickson of the reserve were awarded the M.M..

Demonstrations by the 5th R.S.F. (not unfortunately without casualties), and by the 5th H.L.I. as far away as Outpost Hill front, helped materially to distract the Turks and draw their fire.

It was a brilliant affair, and is a suitable preparation for the next chapter.

Meanwhile it was not so much what the Borderers and their comrades were doing from day to day in the monotonous rotation of duties and relaxation as what was going on elsewhere that affected their future. The same spring that saw the determination of the British Government to have Jerusalem at least by Christmas

* I use this term without levity, for the teams were recalled by a "No side" whistle (see Scott Elliot).

† Vouched for by Lieut. Mackinnon and recorded in the W.D..

saw the arrival of Gen. Falkenhayn in Turkey and the birth of Yilderim—that promised flashing blade that would regain Baghdad and conquer Egypt for the Crescent. Yilderim was the full muster of the entire Turkish forces round about Aleppo, with more than 6,000 German troops attached for special services, and staffed by more than 60 German officers. But Falkenhayn found his task far from plain sailing. Enver and Djemal, the Turkish leaders, were by no means tools in his hand. Both had wills and ideas of their own, and the latter did not necessarily coincide with German plans. For instance, Djemal, who commanded the Syria-Palestine force, wanted more troops and less German interference. Enver was eager to march on Baghdad. Falkenhayn wished to concentrate the whole might of Yilderim against the British, anticipate their coming offensive, and annihilate them. Autumn 1917.

But by the time that he had got his way and the slow-moving Turks were being organized into the Seventh Army and collecting in Hebron, it was too late.

The British effort was stupendous during the summer and autumn of 1917. Qantara harboured great ocean steamers and was the base of operations. The water-pipe had been pushed on so hard that at Shellal, some 15 miles E. of Rafah, a dam contained 500,000 gallons of water, which could be loaded on camels at the rate of 2,000 *fanatis* per hour. There were guns and shells in abundance. There is nothing like personality. Allenby could get what he wanted out of the Home Government and his fighting force. His cheery presence was an inspiration to all ranks. His aeroplanes dominated the situation, and he was free to prepare in secrecy for the encircling sweep, as a consequence of which Gaza fell into British hands like a ripe peach. Besides his superiority in the air, he had an overwhelming advantage both in quality and quantity in mounted troops. He had about 17,000 sabres as against 2,800 at the outside. He had seven infantry divisions, and considerable numerical superiority in this arm also. He was therefore able to put into operation a sweeping movement directed first against Beersheba in the manner that had nearly succeeded at First Gaza—on a grand scale—and commit himself to no more serious engagement at Gaza than one to put himself in a better position to assault, if necessary, and to deceive the Turks as to the place where the real weight of his attack would fall.

These larger operations are outside this story. In a word, the Desert Army Corps under Lieut.-Gen. Chauvel, and the XX. Corps under Lieut.-Gen. Chetwode, consisting of the 10th, 53rd, 60th, and 74th Divisions, took Beersheba on 31st October.

1917. Meanwhile an amphibious bombardment of 218 pieces had been pouring shells into the fortifications of Gaza since 27th October. On the night of 1/2nd November an attack with limited objectives began. These objectives extended from the sea at Sheikh Hasan, N.W. of Gaza, to " Umbrella Hill," S.W. of the town and about 500 yards from the British front trenches. The attack was done in two widely separated phases. At 11 p.m. the 156th I.B. of the 52nd Division attacked Umbrella Hill. The main task was entrusted to the 7th Cameronians, who stormed the hill in half an hour. Then followed a pause of more than three hours, and then the main attack between Umbrella Hill and the sea was delivered at 3 a.m. on 2nd November by Major-Gen. Hare's 54th Division, which took an ample revenge for the terrible losses at Second Gaza in April 1917. At a cost of 350 killed, 350 missing, and 2,000 wounded the Turkish flank was turned on the sea side; 1,000 Turks were buried and 650 taken prisoners. But more than that, an extra division was diverted to Gaza and away from the place where it was most needed. The bombardment then resumed, and the positions were consolidated.

Meanwhile water difficulties had retarded the development of the success at Beersheba until 6th November, when Hareira and Sheria were captured, after some very stiff fighting, both in repelling counter-attacks and in pushing home the attack. It was then considered ripe for the assault of Ali el Muntar, and in the small hours of the 7th, one after another, Outpost Hill, Middlesex Hill, and Ali el Muntar fell into British hands. The Turks had bolted. The barrier in the path to Jerusalem was down. Speed and hustle were now the prime needs. The 52nd Division never entered Gaza. They were now the vanguard of pursuit, and among them were the 4th and 5th K.O.S.B..

CHAPTER III

THE PURSUIT

UP to this time the K.O.S.B. had been mainly spectators of the change that was being wrought in their lives. They had indeed cut lanes in the wire by day,* to enable the assaulting troops of the 54th to pass through and deploy for the attack. Otherwise they were subjected to the fire of the Turkish guns, but thanks to loose shooting or good work on the trenches only two men were wounded. But the passive rôle was soon to end. The news of the enemy's retreat on the 6th soon got round, and all were ready for the order to advance. Nov. 1917.

On 7th November 1917 both battalions (the 5th acting as brigade advanced guard) † left Sheikh Ajlin and marched without incident along the coast past Gaza (and Sea Post !) until they reached the Wadi el Hesi, 9 miles off. One can imagine a certain difficulty in starting off in the broiling heat ‡ immediately after dinner, heavy laden in full marching order, carrying 200 rounds of ammunition, and wearing steel helmets.

But they were hardened to their task, and despite the bad going over the sand reached their destination before nightfall and got touch with the leading brigade, the 157th I.B., who were on the N. bank of the river in places and still on the S. in others.

On the 8th the march was resumed, but on this occasion the way was contested and a fight ensued. The strength of the resistance lay in a N. and S. running ridge 3 miles long—Sausage Ridge—between the Wadi and the village of Burberah, and while this obstruction was to be attacked from the S. end by the 157th I.B., the 155th, and in the forefront the 5th K.O.S.B., were to move parallel to it, and then wheel and attack the northern half of the western face.

It was a ticklish operation for the 155th. The 157th were somewhat scattered, some occupying the sandhills nearer the sea,

* Scott Elliot, p. 157. † Col. Kearsey's Orders in War Diary.
‡ The Khamsin was blowing. Scott Elliot, p. 159 ; Thompson, p. 374.

8 Nov. 1917. and particularly that mound called Ras Abu Ameireh. "Sausage Ridge" commanded the road and railway from Gaza to the N. It was nearly 300 feet above sea-level, and was strongly held and entrenched. Moreover, the 156th I.B., after their successful share in the Battle of Gaza, were only in a position to leave Sheikh Ajlin on the morning of the 8th, and help could only be expected from them late in the day. It was a large undertaking for two brigades. It might easily come about that while trying to turn the Turkish R. wing the British L. flank might be rolled up from the sea side, and the hunters become the hunted. It was, however, deemed essential that the Turks should not be given time to organize a permanent stand, and the K.O.S.B. entered on the following operation.

The 5th Battalion pushed forward across the Wadi, passed through the 5th H.L.I. on Ras Abu Ameireh, and expelled some snipers from the higher sandhills beyond. Between them and the sea were toiling the 5th and 4th R.S.F., making a wide circle so as to reach a point to the N. of the 5th K.O.S.B.. In reserve followed most of the 4th K.O.S.B., but a company * was retained by the Brigadier for special emergency. The 5th had plenty of time in which to take in their task, which was to assault Sausage Ridge from the W. in line with the R.S.F., who were wheeling round upon the K.O.S.B. as their pivot. All the preliminaries were successful, though the 5th K.O.S.B. had incurred 19 casualties, and the battle proper opened at 12.30 p.m.. The region had never been accurately mapped, and it was something of a surprise that the distance from the jumping-off place in the sandhills to Sausage was about 4,000 yards, and, where the 155th were engaged, consisted of coverless sand, offering a perfect field of fire.† The Turks were well supplied with guns. The British guns were not yet forward, and the task of crossing a hollow more than two miles wide in full view and attacking a hill stronghold was no easy one. Casualties came early. 2nd Lieut. G. M. Mackinnon was killed and Capt. O. P. Oliver of Jedburgh and 2nd Lieut. E. P. Dickie (a brother of W. Dickie who was killed with the 1st Battalion on 1st July 1916) were wounded. But the whole line of the brigade went steadily on, thanks, at a critical juncture, to an adroit change of direction, to circumvent a strong point, directed by Lieut.-Col. J. B. Cook, O.C. 5th R.S.F..‡ The very glacis was reached on the outskirts of Burberah when heavy losses began to be incurred, and it was at the very moment when the

* C Company. Sorley Brown, p. 105.
† Scott Elliot, p. 160.
‡ Buchan, *R.S.F.*, p. 402.

4th K.O.S.B. were being brought into the line that the peril, which Gen. Pollok-M'Call had foreseen, became imminent. Askalon of the Philistines, on the coast 4 miles to the N., sent forth a strong force of infantry, estimated at two battalions, who opened fire on the flanks and rear of the Fusiliers and Borderers. All hope of storming Sausage Ridge had to be abandoned, and a faceabout and a withdrawal begun. Credit is again given to Col. Cook for timely appreciation of the right course. Then followed a defensive action until nightfall, when it died down, and was not renewed. O.R. casualties totalled, for the 5th, 12 killed, 80 wounded, and 7 missing. The 4th had only one casualty but it was a costly one, Lieut. and A/Q.M. G. J. Brown.* † 9 Nov. 1917.

The weary 155th awoke next morning (9th November) to find that a miracle had happened. The Turks had fled. The 6th H.L.I. had captured Sausage Ridge from the S. by a brilliant *coup de main* at night, the success of which was not a little due to the timely arrival of the 156th I.B., which enabled the last unit of the 157th to be employed, and to the shaking the Turks got from valiant and repeated, if unsuccessful, assaults by the 5th H.L.I. and the 5th A. & S.H.. If ever there was an instance of team-work and the value of sustained effort in apparently purposeless attempts, it is the battle of Wadi Hesi. Apparent failure the whole way along the line, and then, at last, the success of the forlorn hope !

" The enterprise of the 52nd had precluded any hope of organizing a stand on the Wadi Hesi, and the next natural defence, the Nahr Sukhereir, was 15 miles farther N.. The only rearguards were dispersed in exhaustion." ‡

The reward of the 157th I.B. consisted in being hurried off next morning to exploit the capture (by a tiny force of Yeomanry) of Askalon and continuing the pursuit to Esdud (Ashdod of the Philistines). The stiff fighting they encountered is outwith this tale, which continues with the 155th resting on the 9th, and to some extent on the 10th, where they were. Presumably they picked up the packs, which had been dumped for the battle.

Once more the 5th K.O.S.B. supplied the brigade advanced guard on the 11th on the march to El Mejdel (half-way to Esdud). On the 12th both battalions marched in pouring rain and muggy heat to Esdud, halted there and dumped packs. But they did not pass the night there, but resumed the march after a rest of four hours. After 8 miles' march in the dark by compass, corrected by careful pacing

* Sorley Brown, p. 105.

† Fuller accounts of this action will be found in Thompson's *52nd Division*, and in Scott Elliot.

‡ Wavell, p. 149.

13 Nov. 1917. and maintenance of contact between units, the 5th K.O.S.B. were able to throw out their outposts about 2 a.m. on the 13th. Their second combat was at hand.

The Turks had now to think seriously about Jerusalem and their southern railway communications. They had still some 20,000 troops wherewith to contest invasion of the bare, open, cactus-covered foothills, dotted with knolls and villages. That their line had the cardinal defect of being parallel to their communications had been " forced on them largely by the hard marching and fighting of the 52nd Division in support of the mounted troops." * But behind them were the rugged inhospitable mountains of Judea, and now or never was the time to stand. It may be pointed out that any delay in following up the Wadi Hesi was due to the difficulty of water, which indeed was the only brake to the chariots and horsemen and camels of Allenby, now 30 miles and more from rail-head.

Another interest attaching to the action of El Mughar is that it represents the beginning of the great wheel E. upon Junction Station, where the railway from Turkey forks E. to Jerusalem and S. towards Gaza and to Beersheba. Not only the XXI. Corps (Bulfin), in which the K.O.S.B. were, but mounted troops on R. and L. were taking part in it. The infantry other than the 52nd Division was the 75th Division, a mixed one of territorial and Indian troops.

And further to stimulate effort, the G.O.C. (Hill) sent a message informing all ranks that the C.-in-C. intended to seize the Jaffa-Jerusalem railway and exhorting them to superhuman efforts.

A glorious sun thawed the chilled limbs of the Borderers as they came off stand-to and fell to their preparations and their breakfasts. There were no enemy in sight, but thanks to good guiding,† good marching, and good discipline, they were found to be where they were meant to be—within easy reach of a crest from which their objective would be visible. They were N.W. of Bethshit and nearly S. of Yebnak, about 2,500 yards S. of El Mughar. The R.S.F. on the R. were to take Katra, the K.O.S.B., to the N. or L., El Mughar. The only cover on the plain was what the beds of the Wadi Jamus (a small stream) and three smaller tributaries might possess. This time the 4th Battalion under Lieut.-Col. Dashwood-Tandy were in front and the 5th, inclined to the L., were in support. But as the attack developed both battalions fought side by side in the most exciting fray in which either was ever engaged. For from the moment the 4th started off to the attack in artillery formation at 7.45 a.m. until the close of the fighting late in the afternoon suspense and effort marked every moment, and almost every minute reflected

* Wavell, p. 153.

† By Lieut. Ramsay of the 5th R.S.F..

the lessons of training actualized in real war. When the hostile shrapnel threatened the compact little columns descending from the high ground, these, as it were automatically, broke off into smaller formations dotted symmetrically over the plain, steadily advancing and ready at a signal to manœuvre into line, so that the whole battalion would advance in eight waves. The 4th were still a mile and a half from the objective when heavy M.G. fire, in addition to gun-fire, necessitated this deployment about 10.30 a.m., and soon after the 5th had to supplement the 4th on the N. side with three companies. By this time the Wadi Jamus was reached. On went the skirmishers by the aid of practised "fire and movement" by alternate rushes.* By the time the front line was still about a quarter of a mile from the village, prodigies of valour had been performed and casualties were numerous. Capt. Allan of D specially mentions Sergt. George A. Craig, a native of Eyemouth, of the Lewis gun section, who fell in the action, and Capt. A. P. Nimmo who was fatally wounded † in the final storm after continuing on duty despite an earlier finger wound, besides Lieuts. Burns, Ross, Wilson, and J. Wood, the last-named of whom was killed in the cactus zone. Owing to the hardness of the rocky soil the entrenching tool was nearly useless.

By 2 p.m. the last company of the 5th joined the 4th—this time on the R..‡ It had been in reserve in the Wadi Jamus. §

Soon things began to stick, and as it was a case of everything or nothing—because behind El Mughar the ground fell away and was flat for 6 miles to Junction Station, whereas if it defied capture it could be worked up into another Gaza—General Pollok-M'Call took the strong step of calling for cavalry assistance, ordering all H.Q. troops into the line and taking his place there in the forefront of the battle, in the very heart of the Borderers, determined to show them the mettle of those who have worn the red hackle.|| Gen. Hill arranged for the 6th Mounted Brigade, composed of the Bucks and Dorset Yeomanry, to charge the Turkish R., and this was to be the signal for a storm by the infantry all along the line. Every available gun was turned on the Turkish position. Every Turkish gun thundered defiance. Those who looked to the L. could see the ordered

* Sorley Brown, p. 108, quoting from Capt. Allan, O.C. D of the 4th Battalion.

† He died on 17th November 1917 (Official Death Roll).

‡ The 5th's War Diary says that 3 companies went forward to the left to assist the attack on the N. side of the position.. Sorley Brown, on p. 106, says: "The battalion was reinforced *on the right* by the 1/5th K.O.S.B.".

§ 5th War Diary.

|| Brig.-Gen. Pollok-M'Call had served in Egypt and South Africa in his regiment, the Black Watch.

13 Nov. 1917. lines of the cavalry sweeping over the plain. So could the Turks, and as they intentionally or involuntarily directed their fire on the charging yeomen, Gen. Pollok-M'Call "snatched up a rifle and bayonet, shouted to the Borderers to follow him, and dashed out into the open. Here, there, and everywhere the Borderers, shouting and cheering, jumped out, and then ensued a wild but steady advance in lines across the open for the gardens of Mughar." *

While the Borderers dislodged the enemy from his nasty nooks and hurled him through the village and out into the open behind, the cavalry rounded off their fine work by heading off great numbers so that more than 1,000 prisoners were taken. As the storming of Katrah took place almost simultaneously, the Turks fled to Junction Station or away to the N., and though rearguards held off the British for one night, Allenby's object was attained on the 14th. The station fell once and for all into our hands. The Turks' forces were split in two. One of his sources of supply was cut off and his last hope of standing on the plain shattered. One field-gun and many M.G. were taken. Masses of rifles and ammunition were salved. But the cost of the victory must be reckoned. The 4th lost in killed, besides 2nd Lieut. J. Wood, Capt. J. M. Watson (the Adjutant), 2nd Lieut. L. D. Robertson, and, besides A/Sergt. Craig, 29 O.R.. The roll of wounded officers amounted to 10, *i.e.* besides Capt. A. P. Nimmo, who died of wounds, Capt. A. Fairgrieve, O.C.A, Capt. J. S. Allan, O.C. D, Lieut. G. D. Sempill, and 2nd Lieuts. R. Bell, H. W. Harvie, B. D. Leslie, H. M. Ross, and R. Graham. One man was missing and 138 O.R. were wounded.

The 5th Battalion lost 2nd Lieut. J. Kerr and 2nd Lieuts. S. Robertson and G. H. Dickie, and O.R. casualties were 20 killed and 110 wounded.

It is right that record should be made of the estimate put on this exploit by those in authority. In his despatch of 16th December 1917 General Allenby wrote: "This Katrah–El Mughar line forms a very strong position, and it was here that the enemy made his most determined resistance against the turning movement directed against his right flank. The capture of this position by the 52nd (Lowland) Division, assisted by a most dashing charge of mounted troops, who galloped across the plain under heavy fire and turned the position from the north, was a very fine feat of arms." He sent a congratulatory message at the time, which is referred to in a letter

* Thompson, p. 420. The full and valuable account of this battle, including of course the storming of Katrah by the R.S.F., should be read by all. It is based on the official documents and is up to the level throughout of the spirited passage quoted.

of Gen. Hill to Brig.-Gen. Pollok-M'Call. Lieut.-Gen. Sir E. S. Bulfin, Corps Commander, XXI. Corps, was equally congratulatory. 13 Nov. 1917.

Major-Gen. J. Hill wrote to the Brigadier expressing his appreciation and admiration of the final charge and capture of 1,200 prisoners, 1 field-gun and 20 M.G. after the strenuous times from the 11-mile march on an abnormally hot day over heavy sand, a day-long fight next day, and two more days' long marching.

Brig.-Gen. Pollok-M'Call issued an order, which emphasized a triumph rare in civilized war won by a weaker force against a stronger force, well armed, holding a position of great strength, and exhorted to hold on to the last. The determined heroism of the 155th had achieved the capture of a front 4,700 yards wide.

It was truly a great day for the South of Scotland, and none the less for the timely moral and physical support of the yeomen of England.

That night both battalions were on outpost duty N. of El Mughar. On the 14th both moved to Katrah and remained there till the 18th.

CHAPTER IV

THE MOUNTAINS OF JUDEA

Nov. 1917. — SINCE they left the trenches facing Gaza the K.O.S.B. had covered some 70 miles * and fought two severe actions in just over a week. They earned the five days' rest, which was only vouchsafed them because of transport difficulties. Lack of water saved the Turks from annihilation.† When they did move on the 19th November, it was due to haste. Allenby was eager to make a dash for Jerusalem and take it by cutting the northward road communications and compelling surrender without the need for fighting near the Holy City. Bulfin's XXI. Corps was directed against the mountains, and the 52nd Division, still on the L. wing, entered upon perhaps the most strenuous ten days of its whole career. "The west side of the Judean range consists of a series of spurs running E. and W. and separated from one another by narrow valleys. These spurs are steep, bare, and strong for the most part and in places precipitous," ‡ and the wadis which wind between them are strewn with great boulders.§ Moreover, the weather had broken and there was "miry clay" at the bottom of the ravines and intense cold on the wind-swept uplands, on which for military precaution's sake the nights had usually to be passed. There was one metalled road secured by the capture of Junction Station and Ramleh (and, it may be added, Jaffa), which led to Jerusalem. Astride it went the 75th Division. The 52nd were on more classic but more uneasy ground, when they took the high road *via* Lydda and the Beth-horons towards Nebi Samwil (Mizpah). Only Biblical students can get the full feel of this part of the campaign, and not one of the talented writers studied for this story can, so to speak, keep his pen off Scriptural expressions and allusions.||

* "The 52nd (Lowland) Division had covered 69 miles in that period" (*i.e.* from 7th to 16th inclusive). Despatch of 16/12/1917.

† Wavell, *Palestine Campaigns*, p. 156.

‡ Despatch *cit. supra* (official edition, vol. viii. p. 110)

§ Wavell, *op. cit.*, pp. 159 and 160.

|| Even the War Diary (of the 5th) abounds in these.

The so-called Roman road from Ludd to Beit Likia is a track unsuited to man or horse or camel, and is like that in Mignon's song on which " the mule seeks his way in cloud," of course utterly unsuited to wheeled traffic—even half a limber—and destructive to shoe leather. It was a terrain for infantry and donkey or pony transport, all but inaccessible to guns. That a few guns sometimes with quadruple teams were brought forward was in part due to the energetic road-making of the 155th Brigade. Into this inhospitable zone—only 20 miles wide, but what a 20 miles !—we now bring the K.O.S.B.. They were dressed (the only possible costume for the Gaza campaign) in drill khaki shorts, and they had neither overcoats nor blankets, because fighting was expected. This light garb was unsuited to the sudden change to the chilly hills. 23 Nov. 1917. —

In the evening of 18th November the Borderers marched 13 miles W. to Ramleh and once more dumped their precious packs. Early next morning, after a pouring wet night, they were off (the 5th K.O.S.B. leading) *via* Annabeh, where the 4th stayed the night, to Berfilya on the track from Jaffa to Jerusalem. Thereafter the stages were Beit Likia (6 miles) and Beit Izza (5 miles), reached on 21st and 22nd respectively. There had been another deluge during the night 20th/21st and the men were drenched, and cold, and badly shod, and had to have recourse to their iron ration. Yet there were no stragglers and no grumblers. They seem to have divined that the shortest way to reach safety and comfort was to beat the Turks. Consequently they were in good fettle when ordered on the 24th to attack the formidable fortress of El Jib.

The situation was that in the wake of the Yeomanry, the spear-head of the advance was now the 75th Division, which on the 21st reached a mosque-crowned height and ridge 2,800 feet above sea-level, Nebi Samwil, 3 miles from the coveted road N. from Jerusalem and only 4½ miles from and in sight of the city. " Here in the driving mist and rain the enemy suddenly developed a new power of resistance. On the 22nd he violently attacked at Nebi Samwil and he forced back the Yeomanry at Beitunia (2½ miles N. of El Jib). The 156th I.B. of the 52nd Division were sent to relieve the 75th, and presently the whole division was engaged on the ridge." *

On the 23rd the K.O.S.B. with the rest of the Brigade moved past the monastery of El Kubeibeh, the 5th to Beit Izza on the heights, and the 4th to the Wadi Amir just N.E. of Biddu. The latter had bad luck in meeting a barrage near El Kubeibeh, with the result that 2 O.R. were killed and 18 wounded.

Thanks to the gallantry of the 157th in advancing on and the

* Buchan, *Royal Scots Fusiliers*, p. 405.

24 Nov. 1917. 156th in defending Nebi Samwil, there was still a chance of forcing the fortress of El Jib, a rocky eminence 2,000 yards N. of Nebi Samwil, capped with a village and cactus gardens. Between it and Nebi Samwil was the Wadi Amir, and it presented a steep, rocky, southern face. If it could be stormed and a passage forced 3 miles E. to Er Ram just beyond the Jerusalem-Nablus (Shechem) road, the Turks might abandon Jerusalem. In any event the best security of Nebi Samwil (the key of the whole British position) was the possession of El Jib (" Gibeon "). Any advance beyond El Jib would be the task of the Reserve Brigade, the 157th.

The 155th attacked El Jib with the 5th R.S.F. on the R. and 5th K.O.S.B., supported by the 4th K.O.S.B., on the L.. To the local commanders the chances appeared none too good. The Brigade was badly under strength owing to casualties. There was open ground to cross before a final climb. The Turks had ample artillery and fresh troops. The artillery support of the 155th consisted of four 4·5 howitzers, six field-guns, and a battery of mountain-guns.* The flank was sketchily covered by Yeomanry, and the 5th K.O.S.B. in taking the only possible line of attack—namely, to attack El Jib from the N. by a wheel pivoting on a walled garden about 400 yards from the village—were widening the nose of the British salient.

The attack was launched at noon on 24th November. In ten minutes Lieut.-Col. Kearsey's invaluable services were lost to the 52nd Division and the 5th K.O.S.B. for good, as he was then severely wounded. Capt. R. Mathieson, who had acted as adjutant from Gaza onwards, was also a casualty. As soon as cover was lost, casualties came swiftly. The distance to the objective has been estimated at 2,500 yards,† and apart from the heavy shelling, there was heavy enfilade fire from the L. flank. Four-fifths of this had been covered by 4 p.m. and the walled garden occupied, but further advance was a stark impossibility. Gen. Pollok-M'Call would have been prepared to repeat the tactics, which won Sausage Ridge, and try cold steel on the Turks in the dark, but fortunately Corps called off any further attempts.

The 5th R.S.F. on the R. had made similar progress—400 yards from El Jib,‡ but found a similar barrier. They too had lost their trusted commander, Lieut.-Col. Cook, a grievous loss. The 5th K.O.S.B., besides the two mentioned, were without Capts. M'George, Gibson, and Penman, and 2nd Lieuts. Millar and Kay. Added to

* Scott Elliot, p. 192.
† War Diary, 5th Battalion.
‡ Buchan, *R.S.F.*, p. 405.

these come O.R. casualties, 7 killed, 64 wounded, and 9 missing, which means much to the assaulting power of a depleted unit. The 4th lost 2nd Lieut. A. N. Wilson and 2 O.R. killed, and 20 wounded. 25–30 Nov. 1917.

After dark, at 7.15 p.m., the K.O.S.B. were withdrawn on relief by the 157th I.B., and when daylight dawned were W. of El Kubeibeh enjoying a short rest, having salved "all the wounded, nearly all the dead, as well as all stores and equipment." *

STOPPING A GAP

" There was particularly hard fighting between El Beit and Beit Ur El Foka, but the Yeomanry and Scottish troops successfully resisted all attacks and inflicted severe losses on the enemy " (Official Despatch).

The faces of the K.O.S.B. were now turned seaward. They were making for the scene of their final exploit in Palestine. But they were not done with the Judean hills yet. Mention has been made of the thinness of the mounted flank screen, who held posts from Beit Dukka to Beit ur el Tahta (Lower Beth-horon). The Turks were able to spare some 3,000 Yilderim troops and a number of guns for an assault on the British flank from the N. on a front extending from Beit ur el Foka (Upper Beth-horon) to Shilta opposite the R. of the 54th Division (Hare). But between Shilta and Lower Beth-horon there was a gap, in the centre of which was Suffa. A mile S. of Shilta was El Burj, nearly a mile S. of which was Bir Main. The Turks headed in force for the gap and prompt measures had to be taken by Gen. Hill to stop it. The 155th I.B. were then at Beit Sira, a mile E. of Bir Main and nearly 2 miles S.S.W. of Suffa. Lieut.-Col. Dashwood Tandy led the 4th K.O.S.B. to attack Suffa at 9 a.m.. On their left were the 5th R.S.F. under Major Paton and A and B of the 5th K.O.S.B.. That battalion did not function as a unit but provided, in addition to the loaned companies, a Brigade Reserve. That reserve was soon called on, being sent to Khurbet Hellabi in front of the Mounted Division H.Q. to reinforce the Yeomanry, and (later in the fight) D and part of C being with the 5th H.L.I. (Col. Morrison). There are therefore three fronts to consider. The 4th Battalion came almost immediately under M.G. fire and sustained casualties. Before 10 a.m. they were to the extent of three companies in extended order. The War Diary indicates that they never advanced more than 300 yards N. of Beit Sira, but the historian of the 52nd Division tells us that they drove the Turks off a ridge, beyond which owing to the nature of the

* Scott Elliot, p. 194.

25–30 Nov. 1917. — country no advance was possible. This position they held all day in the face of vigorous attacks till they handed over to the reinforcing 156th I.B. troops in the shape of the 8th S.R. about 5 p.m., after which they side-slipped R. and prolonged the L. of the line, then occupied by the 7th R.S.. 2nd Lieut. Mercer was killed, Major Locke wounded, and there were 27 O.R. casualties in the course of the day's fighting. They do not seem to have been counter-attacked, for the next two days only brought two casualties, and on 1st December they moved out of the battle zone to Amwas. The counter-attacks were most felt in the El Burj area.

The party with the 5th R.S.F. were at first in reserve and marched first W. for a mile and a half, then wheeled, using the cover of a wood, in the direction of Suffa, leaving El Burj on the L. hand. Attacking after 11 a.m. they made good a ridge at a cost of only 3 O.R. wounded, and retained it until withdrawn to a specially chosen line of defence based on El Burj under cover of darkness. This position was vigorously attacked on the 29th, but the enemy was repulsed at the cost of Capt. M'Creath, mortally wounded, and three O.R. wounded. That night they were relieved by Australian Light Horse and bivouacked at Beit Sira.

The remaining party had the longest dose of the battle. When D reached the line it found itself between the Lincolnshire (L.) and E. Riding Yeomanries. From the fact that only one casualty occurred, we may infer that no serious assault was made on them before the two night attacks at midnight and at 3 a.m. (on the 29th) respectively, both of which were repelled.

Relief by the 5th H.L.I. did not end matters, as D and half of C were once more sent to the line from Lower Beth-horon, to which they had withdrawn to relieve the Lincolnshire Yeomanry on the L. of the 5th H.L.I.. It was on this occasion that 2nd Lieut. Woodhead won the M.C. for a dashing rush across the open to the H.L.I. post at "Two Tree," the Lewis guns of which were out of action. The Turks attacked vigorously at 6 a.m. on the 30th, and it was of vital importance that the little fort should be used to the utmost. He and his team (of D) not only got going with their own guns, but put one of the H.L.I. guns to rights and used it. That steadfast battalion was thus helped in completely beating off the Turks before 7 a.m..

It was well for the K.O.S.B., who were playing the man in a manner not unworthy of St. Andrew's Day and of the 1st Battalion at Cambrai that very day, that they had had time when at El Kubeibeh to be furnished with emergency rations, to be reorganized by Major Crombie into companies after the confusion of El Jib, and, above all, to secure a proper complement of Lewis guns. These guns proved invaluable to a defence, necessarily based on sangars and not on connected fire trenches, and caused severe losses to the brave Turkish stormers. 1 Dec 1917.

Thanks in part to the valour of the Borderers, the flank held, the XXI. Corps were accorded their overdue relief, the XX. Corps took up the good work, and in less than a fortnight Gen. Allenby made his state entrance into Jerusalem, to the immense if short-lived uplift of hearts at home and to the enhancement of British prestige abroad.

The 5th K.O.S.B. were relieved by the Munster Fusiliers of the 10th Division and toiled with aching feet and weary limbs 8 miles by the Wadi-el-Haddad to Amwas, where we left the 4th Battalion. Next day the whole brigade marched through Ramleh to a point 8 miles N.W. of it. That was the occasion on which two men had to get along without boots on a broiling hot, dusty track. However, with emergence from the hills, better times came. Winter clothing was doled out, canteen stuffs were available, magnificent oranges were an issue of diet and were as balm in Gilead to men sick of bully. Not that they were out of the line for long, for, when not in reserve at Ibrak, S.E. of Jaffa, they were in the line S. of the Auja under their new C.O., Lieut.-Col. R. N. Coulson of the 8th Cameronians. Messages of congratulation poured in on them from the C.-in-C., from Gen. Chetwode, commanding the relieving corps, and from their Brigadier, who promulgated the following :—

"At the close of a period, the Brigadier wishes to express to all units and all ranks his admiration of all they have done. In heat, cold, during toilsome marches, in stiff fights—they have fought and died and conquered and never been defeated. No single prisoner from the Brigade has fallen into the hands of the enemy; not one single Lewis gun has been lost. The officers have led dauntlessly, the men have followed with a determination, a stubbornness, and contempt for danger which has earned the respect of all who have witnessed it, not excluding the enemy. . . ."

The campaign from 7th November to 1st December must ever rank as one of the greatest military glories of the King's Own Scottish Borderers and of the men of the Borders, Dumfries, and Galloway.

But space compels a hasty jump to the epilogue of the 52nd's Palestine achievements.

CHAPTER V

THE CROSSING OF THE AUJA

France and the Parting

Dec. 1917. — THE ancient city of Jaffa or Joppa is the natural seaport of Jerusalem. But as long as the Turks had their guns close up to the N. bank of the River Auja, Jaffa, which was only three and a half miles from the nearest point of the river, was liable to be shelled and the landing of stores and the construction of the railway to Ludd impeded. The operation to be briefly recounted was undertaken for the purpose of securing elbow-room. Brevity is justified by the existence of several excellent accounts in the fullest detail and based on the study of official records. Wavell, Thompson, Scott Elliot, and the writers of the 5th H.L.I. in the works so often referred to have done full justice to one of the most brilliant surprises effected by British arms in the war. There was at one time the intention of having a full-dress corps affair with intense preliminary bombardment but, of course, without any element of surprise. There were conferrings between Gens. Bulfin and Hill (G.O.C. 52nd), and in the end the 52nd received orders to force the passage of the river without artillery support and rush the Turkish trenches without firing a shot and using only the bayonet. An assault of that kind could only be carried out in the dark, and the keeping of direction and silence made the highest possible demands upon the discipline of the division, as upon the brigade commanders and the entire divisional staff.

The Auja, a perennial stream, enters the Mediterranean with the usual bar at the mouth, about three and a half miles N. of Jaffa. At the bar its depth varied from 2½ to 5 feet, according to the seasons. Above the bar it was uniformly deep and unfordable. Its banks were low and swampy. On the left bank the ground was black cotton-soil, except right at the coast. The right bank consisted of a series of sandy ridges, two of which were prominent and were strongly held. That nearest the coast (1½ mile) and about 4½ miles from Jaffa was Sheikh Muannis; the one farther inland (3 miles from the sea) was Khurbet Hadrah, about 700 yards N. of a stone bridge over the river, in a state of semi-destruction. The river takes a very winding course after leaving the foothills. In a straight line the stone bridge is 3½ miles from the shore, and the line would pass through the hamlet of Sheikh Muannis. The Turkish line crossed the Auja somewhat above the stone bridge, and swung S. over "Bald Hill" and in front of the fine orange groves of Mulebbis. Half a mile in a straight line S.S.W. of the stone bridge there is a sharp pothook bend in the river. The only other likely crossing besides the stone bridge was a mill dam, also partly destroyed, at Jerisheh, 700 yards W. of the pothook. But neither of these accesses appealed to Gen. Hill. He resolved to send the 157th I.B., all but one battalion, to cross the bar, the 156th and one battalion of the 157th to a point 600 yards inland, where the river runs from E. to W., to cross there by pontoon bridges, and the 155th to cross at the loop by similar means. It will at once be seen what an immense amount of work for the R.E. these two crossings meant, and what deft-footed carriers would have to abound, and what practice was needed for getting on and off (or in and out of) the pontoon bridges or pontoons. The objectives were simple; the orders were short. The H.L.I. were to advance up the coast, their particular battalion, which crossed with the 156th, protecting them on their R. flank. The 156th were to assault Sheikh Muannis. The 155th at the pothook were to account for Khurbet Hadrah. Much would obviously depend on the weather. Fine weather would simplify the crossing, but, if too still, might make surprise more difficult to obtain. In point of fact the weather was awful. There was rain on 5th, 6th, 7th, 8th, 9th, followed by a spell of fine sunny weather. Then on the 18th the rain began again; on 19th December it became stormy; there were heavy showers all day on the 20th. The river was in spate, but the G.O.C. was undeterred. To come to events—at 11 p.m.—(an eleventh-hour postponement of half an hour, very creditable to Gen. Leggett for asking for it and to signals for passing the news round) on 20th December the guns opened a slow bombardment to which the Turks were accustomed. It was zero hour. But even before then there had been much activity. From their hiding-places in the orange groves, near the pothook, pontoon frames had been dragged by the 4th K.O.S.B.—the reserve battalion of the 155th I.B. They were capable of being joined together to form a bridge. There were costly carpets from the villas of the wealthy Jaffa German colony to deaden sound as the troops stepped across. However, the whole of the assaulting troops at the point were ferried across the swollen river, as the bridge could not be got ready in time. Captain Muir of the 5th K.O.S.B. took two companies, B and D, as a covering party, over at 10.30 p.m., and formed a bridgehead at the extremities

20–21 Dec. 1917. of the pothook. At 1 a.m. on the 21st the 4th and 5th R.S.F. began to cross, and about 3 a.m. passed through Capt. Muir's men, some of whom ferried back for a special purpose. The Fusiliers did many a good day's work in the war, but never a better one than when they stormed Khurbet Hadrah and all the objectives beyond, silencing machine-guns and compelling the surrender of a battalion commander, two more officers, and 120 prisoners. The vigil of Muir and Lieut. Scott, his subaltern, for four hours and more must have been eerie work with a foe in front and a flood behind.

Two more parties of 5th K.O.S.B. have to be considered. There was a demonstration party under 2nd Lieut. Richardson, consisting of a platoon of C, who fired with machine-gun and rapid rifle-fire some distance E. of and above the stone bridge. They were under orders to cease fire at 5 a.m., in case they hit our own men. They handled the situation flawlessly.

The most sensational episode was the dashing capture of the stone bridge by Lieut. MacBryde (of Whithorn). It was the final act in a careful study of the bridge and its surroundings—very creditable to him and his C.O.. After a whirlwind Stokes bombardment with two guns, he and Sergt. T. Seaton and 60 men of A rushed the bridge and engaged the Turks in one of the most furious hand-to-hand encounters in the campaign. Seaton's dash in rushing machine-guns was the decisive stroke. The *élan* of the Borderers carried them past the Turkish garrison. Turning on them, the Borderers drove them towards the river, and, as the Turks would not surrender, into it. Thirty of the enemy perished in this way by drowning; 15 were bayoneted; 20 were taken prisoners. For this feat MacBryde won the M.C., and Sergt. Seaton, who had done so well at Second Gaza, the D.C.M..

Such was the part played by the Borderers. They "carried," they formed the covering party, they stormed a nasty stronghold on the flank, and diverted the attention of the enemy from the real *locus* of attack. The famous crossing at the bar by the H.L.I. through water up to the necks of the shorter men was a tribute to two reconnaissances by swimming carried out by Lieut.-Col. James Anderson of the 6th H.L.I.. In "fours," arms linked and steadied between two fixed ropes, the Highlanders forded the water "an guaillibh a cheile," * and took all their objectives. In the middle the 156th crossed partly by pontoons and partly by the pontoon bridge, not easily put together, and successfully stormed Sheikh Muannis. Along the whole of the divisional front there was not a scintilla of failure anywhere.

* *I.e.* "shoulder to shoulder."

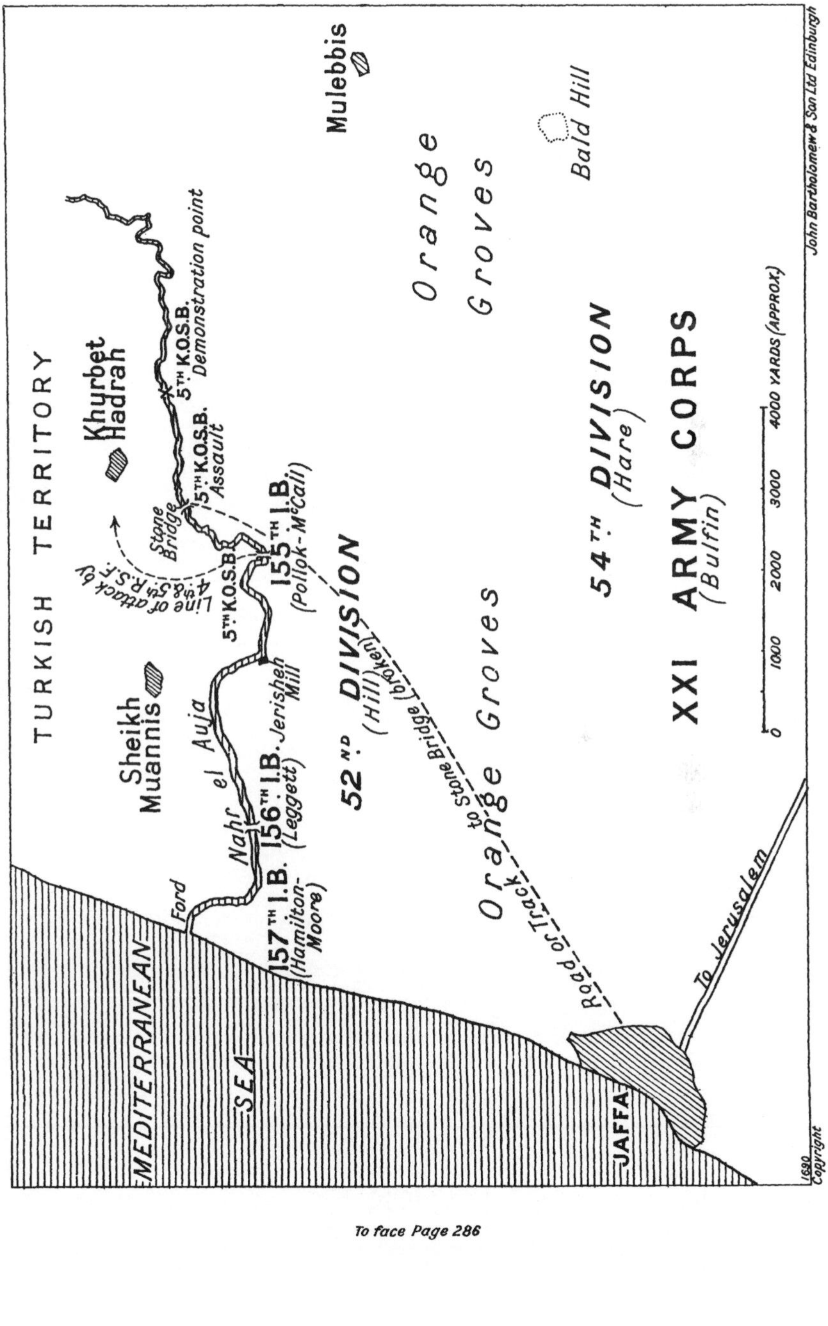

THE CROSSING OF THE AUJA

TURKISH TERRITORY
MEDITERRANEAN
SEA
JAFFA
Ford
Nahr el Auja
Sheikh Muannis
Khurbet Hadrah
Line of attack by 4th & 5th R.S.F.
Stone Bridge
5th K.O.S.B.
5th K.O.S.B. Assault
5th K.O.S.B. Demonstration point
157th I.B. (Hamilton-Moore)
156th I.B. (Leggett)
Jerisheh Mill
155th I.B. (Pollok-McCall)
52nd DIVISION (Hill)
Road or Track to Stone Bridge (broken)
Orange Groves
Orange Groves
Mulebbis
Bald Hill
54th DIVISION (Hare)
XXI ARMY CORPS (Bulfin)
To Jerusalem
0 1000 2000 3000 4000 YARDS (APPROX.)
1690 Copyright
John Bartholomew & Son Ltd Edinburgh

To face Page 286

On the 21st the 4th Battalion helped the R.E. to finish the two light bridges at the pothook and reinforced the R.S.F. in Khurbet Hadrah, being subjected to considerable shelling from the Bald Hill area. But when the 54th Division successfully assaulted Bald Hill on the 22nd December, the enemy abandoned the Mulebbis orange-groves, and towards the coast his resistance crumbled. On the 22nd the 155th advanced in artillery formation as a brigade taking their objectives in scheduled time. On the day after a wet Christmas the 4th K.O.S.B. reached Sheikh Balutah, their northern limit in Palestine. By this time a line was stabilized from Arsuf on the coast, 10 miles from Jaffa running S.E., and crossing the Auja 9 miles from Jaffa, which accordingly was secure. The enterprise had been crowned with complete success; and if, as Gen. Hill wished, there had been cavalry to exploit the situation, there might have been serious strategic consequences for the isolated Turkish Eighth Army facing Allenby's L. wing. The losses had been small. The 5th K.O.S.B. had only 1 man killed and 5 wounded. It must be remembered that in weathering out thunder-showers and standing or wading or, as 5th Battalion H.Q. had to do, sitting in water or liquid mud, the climate of the plain was as different from that of the Valley of Ajalon and Mizpah as is that of Dumfries from that of the top of Queensberry.

21 Dec. 1917.

In his New Year Message * Gen. Hill (henceforth " John Auja " to the men) expresses the opinion that the passage of that 35 yards wide river, reached through bogs, on a night which only became fine when least desired, was the hardest operation he had called on the 52nd to undertake. He also paid a tribute to the magnificent barrage put up by the divisional artillery (" the best ever put up by Scottish artillery "), and to the R.E..†

The crossing of the Auja has not yet had the fame it merits, but it can confidently be asserted that that fame will come and will endure. Col. Wavell terms the capture of over 300 prisoners and the killing of many more Turks at a cost of only 100 divisional casualties as " a brilliant operation, a fitting climax to the many achievements in Sinai and Palestine of this fine division, which was shortly to leave for France."

" The successful crossing of the Nahr el Auja reflects great credit on the 52nd (Lowland) Division. It involved considerable preparation, the details of which were thought out with care and precision. . . . The fact that the enemy were taken by surprise and that all resistance was overcome with the bayonet without a shot being fired

* Scott Elliot quotes it *in extenso*, pp. 217–219.

† The C.R.E. at this time was Lieut.-Col. L. Fortescue Wells.

1918. bears testimony to the discipline of this division." * But the historian of the division uses the most telling phrase of all when he writes: "Finally, by sheer efficiency and wonderful stealth, it had seized the passage of the Auja." Neither space nor intrinsic interest calls for more than a farewell to the Holy Land. The Borderers dug posts, did sentry go, and patrolled the front in rather cold weather. They caught colds in their billets in Sarona—a change from the bivouacs—fed well, rested and generally smartened up, and absorbed ample reinforcements. In due course the summons came from France, where divisional, brigade, and battalion reputations might be lost in as many hours as they had taken months or years to grow, where warfare was bound to present novelties and where the "oldest inhabitants" had had far too much to do in their own sphere to have much knowledge of or interest in newcomers.

On 1st April 1918 the Borderers left Sarona. On the 4th they entrained at Ludd. By 10 a.m. on the 5th they were back on the Suez Canal at Qantara. On the 6th they parted company, the 4th sailing on the *Malwa* and the 5th on the *Kaiser-i-Hind*. Both vessels arrived at Marseilles on the 17th, and by methods by which we are now familiar were ejected from French trains at our old friend Noyelles-sur-Mer, near Abbeville, on the 22nd. The 52nd Division were therefore too late for the defensive fighting in which the 1st and (latterly) 2nd and (possibly most effectively of all) the 6th and 7/8th Battalions had participated. In fact, the brother battalions of so many engagements had to part before they were actively involved in offensive warfare.

A week at Forest Montiers (5th) and Favières (4th), near the sea, saw training started. The 5th had the treat of a *rencontre* in the Forêt de Crécy with their new C.-in-C. and his chief-of-staff, their old and well-loved commander on Gallipoli and at Romani, General Lawrence. The C.-in-C. (and their future Col.), Sir D. Haig, made favourable comments, as well he might, on the appearance of these bronzed veterans of long marches and severe privations. He was not ignorant of their past.

At the end of the month the Borderers trained from Rue (on the Boulogne line) to Aire, in the Hazebrouck region, and billeted, the 4th in the barracks and the 5th in good billets in Wittes, 2 miles N. of Aire. The insistence on gas drill with a brand-new outfit of box respirators must have been an eye-opener for the newcomers.

On 7th May the Borderers moved to the front, but no longer under their beloved "Jock Pollok." He had gone home on leave

* Allenby's Despatch of 18th September 1918, written, be it observed, *longo intervallo*.

5TH K.O.S.B. OFFICERS, SURAFEND, PALESTINE FRONT, 2ND APRIL 1918.

May–June 1918.

after the Auja, having commanded from 14th August 1915 to 11th January 1918; but his health did not admit of his return to the 155th. With deference to his distinguished successors, the mention of the 155th I.B. will call up one name only—Brig.-Gen. Pollok-M'Call. If he had returned, it would only have increased the "home sickness" of the 5th K.O.S.B. at having to leave the brigade. Always respected and loved, ever since El Mughar the General had such a hold that the men would have gone anywhere and done anything for him. Gen. Pollok-M'Call had been succeeded by Brig.-Gen. P. S. Allan, D.S.O., and it was he who trained the brigade in the N. and took them to the Vimy front. But he was succeeded on 19th May by Brig.-Gen. J. Forbes Robertson, who took the 155th to their first western combat. He had just won the V.C. for long-sustained and invaluable gallantry in the dark days of the Lys, when the 1st K.O.S.B. were overwhelmed. He inspired confidence and liking from the first.

On 7th May the Borderers took train to Marœuil (N.W. of Arras), and marched to Neuville-St. Vaast, below the Vimy Ridge, and on the following day the 5th Battalion took over a sector at Arleux from the 7th Gordons and 7th B.W. of the famous 51st (Highland) Division, after traversing a distance of 6 miles, and the 4th one from the 6th B.W.. Thus there met for the first time since they were embodied the representatives of the two Territorial divisions of Scotland after such exploits as have fixed the numerals for Scottish establishment till this very day. They met on classic ground, for the Vimy Ridge "held" in those terrible days of desperate battle in March and April 1918.

The sector was wet and the trenches needed hard work.

After a rest in camp at Mont St. Éloy the 5th Battalion returned to a sector in front of the village of Vimy and experienced the horrors of mustard gas, which accounts for a sick total for the month of 128, which was rather a set-off against 70 recovered personnel from Egypt.

On 28th June, when the 2nd Battalion were doing great things on the Lys, the parting came. The 5th K.O.S.B., the 8th Cameronians, and the 5th A. & S.H. departed in buses for Flanders, and the Second Army (Plumer), and the battalions must henceforth be treated separately. The 5th took with them the blessings of the G.O.C. of the 155th I.B. and of Sir A. Hunter-Weston, who commanded the VIII. Corps, in which they were on 28th June 1918.

CHAPTER VI

THE 4TH K.O.S.B. ON THE WESTERN FRONT

July–Aug. 1918. — THE only incident worthy of remark in the remainder of the time spent in the Vimy-Oppy sector was the complete repulse of a strong German raiding-party following a box barrage at a cost to the battalion of 8 men wounded, the much-valued Sergt. Coonie taken prisoner, and a Lewis gun captured. The enemy left 2 prisoners and 1 officer and 4 O.R. dead. This is the incident which Lieut.-Col. Thompson has, for once, narrated inaccurately, because his version reads that the officer and 4 O.R. killed were Borderers, and that the 2 prisoners were Borderers. The War Diary is, however, clear beyond a doubt, and the official death roll discloses no 4th Battalion officer killed on 6th or 7th August 1918. The 4th K.O.S.B. (B) lads more than held their own.

Although the tide of battle had been ebbing and flowing all the time the 52nd were in France, they had not yet been drawn into the battle. Foch had struck on the Marne on 18th July, and before the end of the month the 5th and 7/8th K.O.S.B. were fighting under Gen. Mangin. The "hundred days" had begun with the battle of Amiens on Ludendorff's *Der schwarze Tag*, the 8th of August. It had been followed by the battle of Albert on the 21st, in which the 2nd Battalion participated. The Somme was aflame. But the 52nd were still out of the line, though moving towards their final battlefield by easy stages, passing behind Arras through such halts (to select those of our battalion) as Caucourt (10 miles N.W. of Arras), Habarq (7 miles W. of Arras), Gouy-en-Artois and Brétencourt on the Crinchon, 5 miles S.W. of Arras. In the direction of Cambrai they faced their future battlefield. And what a battlefield! Their campaign falls into two divisions: the first in the VI. Corps under Haldane at Hénin-sur-Cojeul, at the close of the Battle of Albert, and the second under Fergusson in the XVII. Corps in the battle of the Drocourt–Quéant Switch, associated, to the eternal glory of both combatants, with the effort to win or retain the ruins of Moeuvres.

Sept. 1918.

HÉNIN HILL AND QUÉANT

In dealing with the storming of the Hindenburg Line completeness is out of the question. "The tale of that great achievement can here only be sketched. The record of battalions moves for the most part in the mist: their story is of tactical successes, which may play only a minute part in the major purpose. Rarely, indeed, do they appear like the 2nd Worcesters at First Ypres in the very centre of the stage, when the work of a small unit becomes the key to the strategical fortunes of an army." These words, written by Mr. John Buchan in connection with the two R.S.F. battalions of the same I.B. as that in which the 4th K.O.S.B. fought, I make bold to adopt and apply not only to the 26th August but to Bullecourt, Moeuvres, and Faubourg-de-Paris (Cambrai). It would take years of personal catechism of survivors and an intensive study of every record connected with not only the 52nd but with such divisions as the 3rd, 56th, 57th, 63rd, and the Canadian Corps, and in the end there would probably be no wood for trees. The Hindenburg system was such a labyrinth of deep trenches and birdcage of wire entanglements, new and old, in use and deserted, that the mind finds itself in "wand'ring mazes lost" when it attempts analysis or a time-table or a comparison of orders with results. The true interest of the magic months that freed the world lies in the vast scale on which the blows were dealt and with their generalship and staff work. Our full regimental strength—six battalions in all, and mostly depleted at that—seems a trifle in comparison with the Allied and American millions and dense lines of guns and mortars. Three of them were within a few miles of one another in a corner of Flanders; two were between the Arras-Cambrai road and the Somme-Cambrai battlefields. The remaining one (7/8th) was exploring the German side of the Loos battlefield.

When it comes to the individual man or unit—something personal to the reader—the main interest is, What was he or it doing all that time? Where were they? What sort of battle were they in? How did they fare, and were many gallant lives sacrificed?

Reverting to the 4th K.O.S.B., some such idea may have influenced the diarist and the historian of the battalion to write very brief accounts of the fighting on the 26th. On that day, just after the 52nd had been transferred to the XVII. Corps * from the VI., the two R.S.F. battalions captured Hénin-sur-Cojeul and broke into

* Thompson, p. 525. His account of the whole battle from the 22nd to the 28th from 52nd Divisional point of view is most lucid (chap. xxix.).

Sept. 1918. — the Hindenburg Line, and secured their objectives. Behind them into the din of their first French fight the 4th K.O.S.B. advanced under Lieut.-Col. Dashwood-Tandy in artillery formation. From the shelter of trenches in a sunk road in the captured line at 3 p.m. they proceeded to bomb their way in an entirely new direction from the E.N.E. course hitherto taken, namely, S.E. along the Hindenburg system. This took them at first into the valley of the Cojeul, but the river was dry and easily crossed. Fair and square in front of the Borderers rose the slopes of Hénin Hill, a N. and S. running ridge, rounded, but almost too mild in its curves to be described as a mound. Up this hill the Borderers could be seen moving in extended order in the open. It was not heavily garrisoned, and had the nine tanks allotted to the attack been forthcoming the crest might have been won. As it was, the position reached was just short of the top but in touch with the Canadians on the left. The following day was spent mopping up, while the 157th (H.L.I.) I.B. captured the whole of Hénin Hill by magnificent valour but at terrible cost, and on the 28th, on relief by the 170th I.B., the battalion withdrew to Mercatel and finished the month there. The tour had not been costly, although 2nd Lieut. Walker, attached from the R.S.F., was killed. When they returned to the line in the Bullecourt sector, about 3 miles S.E. of their last position, in freshly conquered territory, they fared worse. From now onwards their lot was hard.

They left Lieut.-Col. Dashwood-Tandy at Mercatel. He was summoned home on 3rd September, and he did not return. His leadership had been long, inspiring, and successful. It was something that his successor, Major P. L. P. Laing, who had served with him in the Palestine campaign, and had led C as a company commander at the storming of El Mughar, was available for the fighting on 1st September.

The unsightly remains of Bullecourt lay within the Hindenburg Line. This was the day preceding the surprise stroke of Gens. Horne and Byng (First and Third Armies) against that auxiliary of the Hindenburg Line, namely, the northward-running trench system, called by the enemy the "Wotan Stellung" and by us the Drocourt–Quéant Switch, which had its root in the Hindenburg Line at Quéant, 2 miles S.E. of Bullecourt, and crossing the Cojeul and the Scarpe joined on to the Lens defences at Drocourt. Bullecourt had been a strong place with hiding-holes, underground ways, and concrete emplacements, and, when the Borderers relieved the London Scottish of the 56th (London) Division (on the night of 31st August/1st September) they found that their title was disputed.

However, with the help of the R.E. and their comrades the 4th R.S.F., they bombed the entire place clear of lurkers, reduced it into possession, and were able to go forward in the evening with their rear secure. Sept. 1918.

At 5.55 p.m., under cover of an ample barrage, the Borderers advanced along the front system of the Hindenburg Line between the 3rd (R.) and 57th Divisions. Brig.-Gen. J. Forbes Robertson, V.C., had put the 4th K.O.S.B. on the R. and the 4th R.S.F. on the L.. Behind were the 5th R.S.F., and very useful they were to prove. The first objective, a trench (Tank Avenue), seems to have been reached with comparatively little opposition. But in the further advance after 6.30 casualties were incurred through M.G. fire from the R., where there was a gap owing to a hold-up of the 3rd Division through fire from Noreuil. This gap was eventually filled up by a company of R.S.F., and the position at darkness represented an advance *en échelon*, for the L. of the Brigade had progressed in sympathy with the capture of Riencourt-les-Cagnicourt by the 57th Division. The K.O.S.B. had found it impossible to get beyond the first objective,* so they proceeded to consolidate it. The chief worry, when night came on, apart from the risk of counter-attack (which did not in any serious sense materialize), was the shower of tear- and the still more dreaded mustard-gas. The action had been particularly costly in officers. Just before the start 2nd Lieut. J. Brown was wounded, and died, and in the fight Lieut. E. C. R. Hamilton-Johnston of the 2nd (attached 4th) Battalion was killed, as was 2nd Lieut. M. Nettleship, who had joined in April in Egypt; 2nd Lieuts. F. G. M. Grey, J. Pollock, G. Manby, J. Bryson, Burrell, and M. Cassidy (Cassidy and Grey being of the H.L.I.) were wounded. Of O.R. 24 were killed, 2 missing, and 104 wounded. After this shattering blow the battalion was reorganized on a two-company basis—X and Y.

The Borderers remained where they were on the first day of the Battle of Drocourt–Quéant, and on the day thereafter—*i.e.* on 3rd September—penetrated behind the victorious troops as far as Quéant, salving five anti-tank rifles *en route*. Their course still lay along the Hindenburg front system. This ended the first round, so to speak, in France. They then became Brigade Reserve on 4th and retired through recently conquered villages—Noreuil, Longatte, and Écoust—to the St. Léger area, where they cleaned up, rested, attended church parade on 8th September, and received, on 9th, Lieut.-Col. E. C. Hill Whitson as their penultimate C.O., under whom they reorganized on a four-company basis. Five days'

* 600 yards from starting place according to Thompson, p. 536.

Sept. 1918. — training followed, and on the 15th they returned to the scene of the second round—Moeuvres, 4 miles E. of Quéant, a village on the little Agache, covering the *dry* part of the Canal du Nord, where the enemy had resolved to stand with the full might of his available forces. But before resuming the story the results of the battle concluded may be summed up. Gen. Sir Henry Horne, using the Canadian and XVII. Corps—six divisions in all—had smashed through some of the strongest positions in France between Étaing, near the Sensée, and Noreuil. The Germans saw Cambrai (only 8 miles from Moeuvres) threatened, and Cambrai was a rail and road nodal point, vital to any sort of stand. Hurled across the Somme in record time by the amazing energy of the Fourth Army (Rawlinson), and the valour of the fighting men typified by the Australians, whose storming of Mont St. Quentin * (the key to Péronne) is one of the wonders of the war, the enemy was uneasily contemplating a stand on the bit of the Hindenburg Line still intact lying W. and S.W. of Cambrai, if the advanced protective line failed to hold, as seemed likely. In these circumstances the unexpected loss of the Drocourt-Quéant Switch involved a rapid retirement to the line of the Canal du Nord, which was full of water from the Sensée until about 3 miles N. of Moeuvres, whence it was dry, and therefore more vulnerable up to a point S. of Moeuvres. No German counter-attack on the lines of that of 30th November 1917 was to be expected. Troops could only arrive at such time and in such numbers as to adopt a defensive attitude.

It was therefore a tremendous feat that had been performed, and this is what Sir Douglas Haig has said about the 52nd Division.† After narrating the capture of Monchy, Wancourt, Guémappe, on the S. of the Scarpe on the 28th August and the complete victory of the northern wing by the Canadians, and 4th Division in taking their share of the switch on 2nd December, he goes on: "On the R. the attack of the XVII. Corps . . . directed its main force at the triangle of fortifications marking the junction of the Hindenburg and Drocourt-Quéant lines N.W. of the village of Quéant. There was stern fighting in the network of trenches both N. and S. of Quéant, in which neighbourhood the 52nd (Lowland) Division performed distinguished service and by the progress they made greatly assisted our advance farther N.." The new arrivals at the Western Theatre received such warm encomia that Sir Charles Fergusson, G.O.C. XVII. Corps, warned them that reputations can be lost as easily as won.‡

* 31st August 1918. † *Official Despatches*, vol. x. p. 99.
‡ *History of 5th H.L.I.*.

MOEUVRES

Moeuvres was situated in the heart of the Hindenburg system. Three-quarters of a mile due W. a small wood, Tadpole Copse, was cleft by the front trenches, which after rounding Quéant curved more to the E., embracing Pronville. N. of both these villages ran the Hindenburg support line, a switch from N. of Quéant past the front of Inchy, right through Moeuvres and E. across the canal about 800 yards E. of the village. The Hindenburg Line turned S. of Moeuvres, and covered the canal, till it crossed it N. of Havrincourt and entered the territory we dealt with in connection with the 2nd Battalion's final fighting. Moeuvres was definitely in British hands when the Borderers relieved the 2/5th K.O. Lancs.. Sept. 1918.

They marched from St. Léger in column of route, and it was only on entering Tadpole Copse that the foul gas-zone drove them to don masks. Thus protected they entered the village and distributed themselves in small posts in it, but mostly on the far side towards the canal. Then followed a trying time. On the next day, the 16th, they were vigorously shelled and had losses, by night there were tentative hostile feelers, and on the 17th towards evening the enemy laid down a well-staged barrage and attacked with vigour and with a certain success against the K.O.S.B. posts on the L.. Three officers, Capt. Harvie and 2nd Lieuts. Dunning and Dickson, were wounded, and a position in rear had to be taken up under Capt. Sempill. This was the occasion when "Hunter's Post" in the H.L.I. sector, slightly N., was left high and dry and held out for ninety-six hours.* The 18th was a racket of mutual bombardments, and that night the Borderers were relieved by men of both R.S.F. and were in support until the 19th/20th, when they became battle reserve and carriers for the R.S.F.. In the former capacity one small party reached the canal but found no position in which to stand.

Moeuvres was still ours when the 4th K.O.S.B. were relieved by troops of the 156th I.B. and retired to rest in reserve behind Inchy, in former German deep dugouts. It took all the resolution of the 156th to beat off another furious attack on the S.E. of Moeuvres, delivered by the Prussian Guards with great dash. But they did it, and the final fighting, for which the K.O.S.B. came in on returning to the line on 23/24th September, was of the scrambling order; agitating rumours of posts lost and regained elsewhere, occasional peeps of enemy in force on the far side of the canal, and all this to

* *The 5th H.L.I.*. This magnificent act of stamina won Sergt. Hunter the V.C. and six men the D.C.M..

Sept.–Oct. 1918.

the accompaniment of shelling and T.M. fire as well. The 26th was the last day and witnessed the repulse of a bombing attack at 1 p.m., and that night the K.O.S.B. were relieved by troops of the 63rd (Naval) Division and marked time, so to speak, in readiness to join the attack, which was once more resumed, until they found themselves on the 30th September in Graincourt, 3 miles nearer Cambrai on the other side of the canal, and got ready for their last pitched battle. Had they shared in the thrilling storm of the canal and the wonderful co-operation of their sister brigades with the Guards Division and the 63rd—the old R.N.D. of Gallipoli—there would be less of that feeling of the "Flowers of the Forest," which the entrance and exit of this fine unit always excites.*

FAUBOURG DE PARIS

To the music of shells and air bombs but without casualties the K.O.S.B. marched from Graincourt straight for Cambrai. Passing Cantaing and crossing the Scheldt Canal, which 1st Battalion men knew so well in 1917, they paused a mile and a half from the high-lying, double-row of houses on the outskirts of Cambrai and on the road to Masnières known as Faubourg de Paris, on the slopes to the W. of which was a strong M.G. position. The Germans fought with the courage of despair. Those who have followed the story of the 1st Battalion will remember that a few days previously the break up of the Flanders front had begun on 28th September. On the very next day the Fourth Army assault on the Hindenburg Line was launched on its irresistible career. The obliteration of the St. Mihiel salient near Metz on 12th September had been followed by a terrific further Franco-American onslaught, aimed at the valley of the Meuse at Mézières. The retreat was carried out under cover of just such rearguard actions as that in which our Borderers took part. The Germans were stubborn, they had well-placed guns and M.G.s, their aeroplanes were active, and it was impossible for the British artillery to know of every target. Had time not been of the essence, there might have been a pause for a full-dress affair. But pressure had to be applied at once.

The two Fusilier Battalions once more led the 155th I.B. in an attack begun on 1st October over open ground. A reserve company of K.O.S.B. (A, under Lieut. G. Fair) was called on early on the 2nd to carry a M.G. post which had helped to wreck the gallant efforts of the R.S.F.. In the glimmering of the morning a heavy

* The final phase of the Moeuvres fighting can be read in the R.S. and H.L.I. Histories, and in that of the 52nd, 63rd, and Guards Divisions.

barrage broke up the party. Fair, a 4th Battalion officer, was killed. That disposed of one already weak company, and the remnant had to lie out all day, without communication with H.Q. being possible.

Oct. 1918.

The final act in the drama was a night attack on 3/4th October on the Faubourg by two companies, B and D. A young regular, 2nd Lieut. H. A. Common, who had joined in Egypt in April 1918, was in command of B, forming the first wave. As soon as dusk fell, tapes were laid down for the starting line. The attack was launched at 11.50 p.m. and was a total failure. 2nd Lieuts. Common, D. Scott, T. Caldwell (another regular), and W. L. Kirkwood (4th Battalion) were all killed; 2nd Lieut. Hirst was wounded. The casualties to O.R. in these two repulses are not given in the War Diary, and the indefatigable Col. Thompson failed to discover them. Those of the R.S.F. are an indication that they were very severe. But this last gallant sacrifice was not in vain. It nailed German men and guns to the spot, while elsewhere Allied victory and advance were secured. In a few days Cambrai was abandoned and the Germans were hurled back on the line of the Selle.

CONCLUSION

What was left of the 4th Borderers were relieved on the night of the 4/5th October 1918 by the 6th H.L.I.. They rested three days in Cantaing. One wonders if anyone looked at Marcoing and Welsh Ridge.—probably not! Their halting-places can be traced on the map, Boursies on the Bapaume road and Vraucourt, N.N.E. of Bapaume. So far on foot! Thence by rail they travelled to Ligny, E. of St. Pol, and thence on foot to Ambrines, where they remained until the 19th. That evening, from a station with the sinister sounding name of Tinques, the 4th K.O.S.B. entrained upon that triumphal march which took them across the Lens battlefield to the neighbourhood of Mons. Bully Grenay was at the back of the Loos front. There they alighted, and when they billeted in Liévin they were still on ground hallowed by memories of 1915. They entered the old zone of German occupation when they passed through Lens to Montigny-en-Gohelle (one night) and Cité de la Basse Noyelle (three nights). Thence on 24th to Rache, about 15 miles. There they were made useful on the roads, and trained, when not wanted for fatigues, until the 28th.

On that day they marched 6 miles to the important railway junction of Orchies, and on another 4 miles to Landas. There they remained till 5th November, and, one hopes, did not train too hard. Valenciennes had fallen on the 2nd. It was *sauve qui peut* for the

Armistice.

once insolent and masterful invader. On the 5th the march was resumed to Rumégies, 4 or 5 miles N.E. of Landas and close to the Belgian frontier. Still in France the battalion proceeded E. by somewhat twisted roads over 10 miles to L'Écarlate. On 10th November the 4th K.O.S.B. added another country to Turkey, Egypt, Sinai, Palestine, and France by crossing at Bonsecours into Belgium, 4 miles N. of Condé, and continuing 8 miles or so E. to Sirault.

Col. Hill Whitson had left in October. Major P. L. P. Laing, a true son of the Borders, was in command when the great news came. They were then at Herchies, not far E. of Sirault and exactly 6 miles almost due N. of Lock 4, where Borderers first taught the Germans the meaning of the national motto—*Nemo me impune lacessit.*

CHAPTER VII

THE FIFTH BATTALION

Final Phase

Part I.—*Beugneux*

The 5th K.O.S.B. fought only their last battle of all under Sir Claud Jacob's command in the II. Corps, in which the 1st and 6th Battalions did such excellent work in the autumn of 1918. But they were always in Plumer's Second Army, *e.g.* in the XIX. Corps commanded by Sir H. F. Watts, and later in the X. Corps commanded by Lieut.-Gen. Sir R. B. Stephens. All that they did in June was to train and initiate the numerous new recruits to hard marching. The uneventful eighteen days in Flanders, either in the Proven (near " Pop.") or St. Omer areas (at Cornette on the W. side), are adequately chronicled by Scott Elliot. Interest awakes when the battalion was suddenly ordered S. and detrained on the morning of 18th July at Senlis, near the forest of fashionable Chantilly, and began to be moved about like a chess-piece. They were part of the reserve of Gen. Mangin's Tenth Army. Fortunately they had a rest during most of the 20th at Feigneux, near our old friend Crépy-en-Valois, where the 2nd Battalion had fought a rearguard action in 1914, because a severe strain lay before them. Rain came on towards evening and continued all night, while the 5th K.O.S.B. marched in the fullest of full marching-order with 200 rounds of ammunition per man to Soucy, 10 miles E. in a straight line, by a route reckoned at about 16 miles. It was an acid test, and it is interesting to note that, whereas many of the newcomers fell out, the veterans of Palestine maintained their record of lasting out the march. A shrewd military observer who saw much of the 52nd (Lowland) Division in the autumn campaign of 1918 was struck by the contrast between the two elements—the veterans and the conscripts. The former were a bit rough to the first glance. The swiftly trained lads were smart and saluted like automata. But place them in the column, at the bivouac, on the field of battle, and July 1918.

July 1918. it was the Palestinians who took charge and on whom reliance was placed. The 103rd I.B. was, of course, a transplanted fraction of one of the most homogeneous divisions that took part in the war, and the remark applies to it and to the Cameronians, A. & S. Highlanders, and K.O.S.B., of which it was composed.

In the course of the 21st the rain cleared off, and the mud of the track through the state forest of de Retz, which they had traversed at night, was to some extent removed. On the 22nd the battalion neared the field of strife by a 9-mile march to Villers-Helon *via* shattered Longpont—while the 101st and 102nd I.B.s attacked on the Tigny-Contremin front and suffered close on 1,000 casualties on the 23rd, when their French neighbours on either hand fared no better. The 103rd, in Corps reserve, was sent to the junction of five roads just W. of Tigny, there to pass four uneventful days subjected to shelling which was, fortunately, not very productive of casualties, although Capt. and Adjutant R. D. Craig, who had shared in the exploits and sufferings of the Sinai and Palestine campaigns, was wounded in the leg and eventually lost it. Such a valuable officer could ill be spared. On the 27th the K.O.S.B. moved to Bois de Bœuf, W. of St. Rémy Blanzy, and on the 28th Col. Coulson made his reconnaissance for an attack on the 29th.

This was not the first engagement of the regiment in the battle of the Soissonnais and Ourcq. On the 26th, in the immediately adjoining French Corps, the 15th Division, and in it the 7/8th K.O.S.B., took Buzancy, some 8 miles to the N.. Of that in due course!

Just a word about the situation. Completely surprising the Germans, Gen. Mangin on 18th July struck at the western face of the huge and crowded salient formed by the last of Ludendorff's thrusts, begun on the 15th July. He drove the Germans back about 5 miles on a front the width of which (over 20 miles) made him feel uneasy about his numbers, especially when the Germans hurled in division after division and stiffened the resistance. At the moment when the 5th K.O.S.B. were ready to join in, the plan of operations, which the G.O.C. 34th Division adopted from the French, was something like this: While the XX. A.C. took Tigny, Villemontoire, and Taux and turned the wood lying N. of Hartennes-et-Taux, the R. of the XXX. Corps (Gen. Penet) was to turn the block of woodland, termed Bois du Plessier and Bois de St. Jean, E. of Contremin, and force him off the dominating heights of Beugneux Ridge.

Although the country between the Aisne and the Vesle and the Ourcq is well wooded and fertile (the crops were high and thick where the 5th K.O.S.B. advanced), it is on the whole high-lying downland, divided by somewhat jig-saw puzzle-like valleys. The village of Beugneux—a more solidly-built hamlet than those of Picardy or Artois—lies on the front or western slope of a plateau over 600 feet above sea-level. It lies a mile E. of Grand Rozoy (in a valley), and both villages are E. of the great road from Soissons to Chateau-Thierry.

25 July 1918.

The shifting of the scene S. a few miles and the ultimate choice of date for the 103rd I.B. to attack was the result of events affecting the Franco-American forces as a whole. To mention one striking event, Fère-en-Tardenois, an important road junction and railway station about 6 miles due E. of Oulchy-le-Château and less distant from the bold ridge called Butte de Chalmont, was captured on the 28th. The enemy was losing his grip. Pushed back from the W., he was now eaten into on his L. flank. Gen. Mangin felt the time had come to strike towards Beugneux, and thus the 5th K.O.S.B. came into the battle. But whether the Germans meant to withdraw in the end or not, there was plenty fight left in them. It took two sharp engagements to win the ridge, and in both of these our unit took part. The first, on 25th July, was something of a disappointment ; the second, on Minden day, a magnificent success. The battalion went into battle well up to strength. On the evening of the 28th they marched S.E. to Oulchy-la-Ville, and then were conducted by French guides of the 38th Division (*i.e.* the one relieved) N.E. towards Bois de Baillette and Beugneux. It was, of course, pitch dark, and it was not surprising, though most disconcerting for Lieut.-Col. Coulson, that two of his companies and the first line transport were lost for a while. But in the end they turned up in the nick of time and were in position before zero—4.10 a.m. on the 29th.

The 34th Division were attacking between the (French) Corps on the R. and the 25th (French) division on the L. . The attacking brigades were the 101st on the L. and the 103rd on the R. . The 102nd within the cover of the Bois de Baillette was in reserve. The brigade order of battle was K.O.S.B. on L. and 8th Cameronians on R. . The 5th A. & S.H. (who very nearly had to be thrown in at the start to replace the missing Borderers) were in brigade reserve, Brig.-Gen. J. G. Chaplin (himself a Cameronian) having his H.Q. at the S.W. angle of the wood.

The barrage was liberal. Besides the divisional artillery under Brig.-Gen. Walthall, there were two regiments of French artillery. Hugging the barrage in dense mist, all the companies (*i.e.* the reserve company as well, as the result of the slight confusion and

25 July 1918. haste) went off into the unknown, cut off from C.O. and Brigade Report Point by a shell-swept zone, in which neither runner could live nor wire remain uncut. The advance was considerable. The Paris defence trench running S. from Grand Rozoy was taken, and it was a mile in advance of the jumping-off place near the great road. There is a wood between Beugneux and Grand Rozoy. The Borderers fought their way through it, and reached a point N.W. of the village, to which they hung on for four hours, till a combination of German M.G. fire and French " shorts " compelled a retreat to the Paris defences, where the night was spent and the remnants counted—some 330. The French on the L. similarly took Grand Rozoy, but had to retire owing to shelling. The 5th A. & S.H. passed through the leading brigades under cover of darkness and took up an outpost line 500 yards or so ahead. If resistance had been stubborn, there was at least no sign of a counter-offensive. The Franco-British artillery strongly discouraged any such attempt, and the next two days were passed by the troops in consolidation and by the staffs in the preparation of plans for the 1st of August. This time the attack was to succeed, *coûte que coûte.*

Up to the 29th casualties had been light. One officer had been killed and 1 wounded ; O.R. casualties were 1 killed and 13 wounded. Between noon on 28th and midnight 31st July, 7 officers were casualties, of whom 2—2nd Lieuts. S. Robertson (3rd Battalion) and A. R. Johnston (5th H.L.I.)—were killed. Of O.R. 17 were killed, 27 missing, and 214 wounded. The effect of these losses was the reorganization of the companies on a two-platoon basis.

The battle of 1st August was a combined effort of the XI. and XXX. (French) Corps. Thirty tanks were employed on the latter's front. No less than 108 field-guns and 32 howitzers were allotted to the 34th's front of two brigades, once more the 103rd on the R. and 101st on the L. .* The K.O.S.B. were on the R., next the French. On their L. were the A. & S.H., and the 8th S.R. were in reserve. The K.O.S.B. attacked with three companies in line and one in reserve. Their objective was slightly to the R. of their last, for they were to turn Beugneux from the S., while the 101st I.B. turned it from the N. . The jumping-off place was slightly in advance of the outpost line gained on the 29/30th July.

MINDEN DAY

From midnight onwards the " heavies " roared. From 4.15 a.m. to 4.45 the fire became intenser. Thereupon the field guns laid down

* Col. Shakespear, *The Thirty-fourth Division* (London, Witherby, 1921), from which much information has been obtained.

a perfect carpet of shells, and officers and men looked at their watches and pulled themselves together for zero—4.49 a.m..* There was a thick mist, and the troops had to grope behind officers, who directed by compasses. Two minutes later H.Q. also moved forward. The barrage was timed to mark time for three minutes, and then to bound forward 100 metres. The two battalions, together hardly amounting to one at full strength, advanced with determination. Twenty prisoners were taken in a trench, which might have given trouble: the wood to the S. of the village was taken, thanks to a platoon under 2nd Lieut. Graham, which silenced a M.G. and became advanced battalion H.Q.; and the front line, absorbing the reserve company, passed outside Beugneux, swung somewhat to the N., and made for the high ground behind the village. For a time contact with the French and the Argylls was lost, but it was soon regained. The latter had lost their C.O., Col. Barlow, and nearly all their officers; but a remnant attached themselves to the K.O.S.B., and with true belligerent spirit joined in the capture of 2 officers, 48 men, and several M.G., and secured touch with the 101st I.B. troops on their L..

1 Aug. 1918.

But one can imagine the query—What about Beugneux itself? The answer is that the reserve battalion, the 8th S.R., could be trusted to deal extra faithfully with the foe in mopping up. They had not forgotten the 29th of July, on which they had suffered severely. No record of trouble from the village is to be found. One company of the Cameronians was borrowed by the K.O.S.B. to strengthen their R. flank. It was not yet 7.30 a.m. when the crest was reached, the "beyond" became visible, and the encouraging spectacle of the French advancing on both flanks enjoyed. There it was deemed advisable to dig in and consolidate, as the 101st on their immediate L. were unable to progress. Eventually, under cover of a fresh barrage, a further advance was made about 7 p.m., and a new line was consolidated under cover of darkness.

Minden Day had been well spent. The Germans decamped that night. Next day the French, to the intense interest and admiration of the Borderers, passed through and continued the pursuit. On the 3rd Gen. Nicholson presented the decorations conferred by Gen. Mangin. The gallant C.O. received the Croix de Guerre (*citation d'Armée*), as did 2nd Lieut. W. F. Richardson. Corp. Kevan won the Croix de Guerre (*citation du corps d'Armée*), and Pte. O'Haire (of Castle Douglas), who, alas, fell in October, received

* In Brigade Orders zero was given as 5 a.m., but Col. Coulson's account in the W.D. gives the various times with a circumstantiality that admits no doubt.

Aug. 1918. the Médaille Militaire and Croix de Guerre (*citation d'Armée*). Not that this list was complete. On the 8th, when the battalion was back in Flanders, the following additional awards were publicly presented—the Croix de Guerre (of the 1st Class), 2nd Lieut. G. W. Dunn, M.C., and Sergt. J. A. Cain; and (of the 2nd Class) to Capt. MacLay, 2nd Lieut. French (whose spirited account of the battle is given *in extenso* by Scott Elliot), 2nd Lieut. W. Graham (wounded), Sergt. Strange, and Corpl. Grant. But the whole battalion had done so well that the decorated represented the undecorated.

Gen. Mangin's tribute was of the warmest. He wrote of the Beugneux plateau being the dominating height, and he attributed to the 34th's conquest of it the 7 miles retreat which the invader was compelled to beat, although his orders had been to hold it at all costs. Nor was Gen. Penet (G.O.C. XXX. A.C.) less appreciative in his tribute to the strenuous exertions of staff and soldiers, their response to every call of the higher command, and he assured the 34th that it had played a very great part in the success won.*

The victory was far from bloodless; 2nd Lieuts. W. Robinson (of the 3rd) and G. G. Carmichael, a newcomer from Coldstream (of the 4th), were killed. Two subalterns were wounded; of O.R. 25 were killed, 24 were missing, and 112 wounded. On 9th August, after the return of 62 O.R. from hospital or home, the battalion contained only 491 O.R., though 31 officers were on the strength.

The K.O.S.B. and other depleted units of the 34th were hurried out of the French area to make way for fresh troops. They parted from the fine countryside of the Soissonnais with regrets that they were leaving it for the nasty, shop-soiled flats of Flanders just when the fighting seemed to be taking on that open character that reminded them of Palestine.

The French were business-like in the transport of troops, as will be seen in the story of the 7/8th, and as all who remember the part played by the Paris taxis in the First Battle of the Marne in 1914 will recall. On 4th August buses were waiting for the battalion at convenient cross-roads reached by marching, and by evening all except the transport were billeted in Dammartin-en-Goële, 10 miles S.E. of Senlis, on the other side of the huge forest which stretches from Chantilly to Ermenonville. Two days' rest in the quaint little town crowning a bold and narrow ridge, waiting for the transport, must have been a boon. About midday on the 6th they marched to St. Mard station, and after a day and a night in the train were deposited in Wormhoudt in the Second Army area. They were about to enter on the final phase of their service in the war.

* Both of these messages given in full by Scott Elliot

PART II.—*Flanders*

The situation in Flanders still remained the same as it had been after the German offensive had spent itself in the capture of Mount Kemmel and the fierce lunge at Merris and Hazebrouck. Although things were moving with a vengeance in Picardy, and the 8th of August, a day of rest for the 5th K.O.S.B., but one of enormous effort and success on the Somme, initiated a never-ceasing offensive, our Territorials entered the front on the R. of the Belgians no farther from Ypres than Potijze. Ypres was out of bounds as a death-trap, and the prohibition was thankfully respected. Aug.-Sept. 1918.

It was quiet, and Lieut.-Col. Coulson was able to depart on well-earned leave when relief was completed. His coolness and resource and leadership had been a tower of strength to the battalion. The fate of a German raid shows that it was not only British troops who felt the sting of their own artillery. The raiders, who expected to find Americans at Potijze (in which surmise they were not far out), were dispersed by their own barrage. One prisoner was taken. Otherwise the tour was without incident, and helped to break in the likely looking, smart lads of eighteen years of age, who didn't care for marching, who invaded the battalion to the number of 247. With an officer strength of 40, including 5 newly commissioned subalterns from Sandhurst, the 5th K.O.S.B. began to feel a little strange; but as Scott Elliot has pointed out—and he knows through questioning the old hands—it was amazing how quickly the lads took on the tone of the battalion. On final relief from the Ypres sector on 29th August the 5th stood by at Zevecoten, just N. of the "mountains," ready to expel the Germans from Mount Kemmel. This they were not called on to do. "On the night of the 29/30th August, impelled alike by the pressure exerted without remission by our troops on the spot and by the urgency of events elsewhere, the enemy commenced an extensive retirement on the whole of the Lys front." * Bailleul was thus recovered, and, as the War Diary tells us, our battalion found itself in pouring rain on the W. slopes of Mount Kemmel in support of the 8th S.R. ensconced there. The Germans had gone, and the 5th K.O.S.B. found that their immediate activities had brought them on foul but famous soil, on which the 2nd Battalion had toiled and shivered in 1914-15. How familiar it sounds to read of Neuve Église still in the hands of the enemy on 1st September and to find mention of the Lindenhoek Road and the Messines Ridge. Such was the

* Official Despatch.

28 Sept. 1918. region in which the 34th Division was trying to find touch with the retreating foe.* The broken weather enabled the unsavoury spot to show its true character, and made a considerable mess of the new recruits and their new clothes.

THE 28th OF SEPTEMBER

The experience of the 5th K.O.S.B. during the concluding days of August had been most instructive. It was their good fortune to be taken out of the front zone on 10th September and spend ten days in training N.W. of St. Omer at Hellebrouck, on the outskirts of the Forêt d'Éperlecques. Time was dedicated chiefly to platoon and company training, for the work before the Borderers was expected to call for initiative on the part of every officer and every N.C.O. and man. A conference, attended *inter alios* by Foch and Haig, had been held on 9th September at Cassel. His Majesty the King of the Belgians, in supreme command "of the Belgian Army,† some French divisions, and all the artillery and a certain number of divisions of the Second British Army," had resolved to win back his country. The offensive was to be opened on the 28th of September at 5.30 a.m.; and if, in contradistinction to the 9th and 29th Divisions, the 34th was only engaged in a "minor enterprise," ‡ the fighting, by which the Germans were driven off the famous Wytschaete Ridge, brought out the fine fighting qualities of our battalion. The C.O. (Lieut.-Col. Coulson was back again) reconnoitred the ground, but it cannot have been his unaided brain that put out orders for the attack, amounting to eight long pages of type, as preserved in the War Diary. The subalterns must have been supermen to master and carry in their heads such detailed and complicated directions. No doubt the kind of warfare expected did not admit of the precision of orders directed to the capture and consolidation of a definite objective. They ran on these lines. It was expected that the enemy would retire; troops were instructed to be on the look-out for signs of retirement. General lines were marked on the map as places to be occupied if the enemy retired by day. If not, then without preliminary bombardment the barrage would fall and the infantry advance simultaneously at zero on J day in successive small parties, all of which received elaborate instructions regarding use of flares

* Col. Shakespear describes these operations in some detail, as does Scott Elliot. Owing to necessity of mentioning other units and of going into detail, the events are of battalion and divisional rather than regimental interest. Casualties were light.

† Despatch, dated 21st December 1918.

‡ *Ibid.*

and S.O.S. signals, aeroplane contact, and a great many "dos and don'ts." The chief danger lay in undestroyed M.G. and blockhouses. 28 Sept. 1918.

The 5th K.O.S.B. seem to have reached Abeele on the Franco-Belgian frontier, and to have marched E. parallel to the "mountains," past Dickebusch to a line of shell-holes S. of Voormezeele, E. of the Bollartbeek and facing S.E. towards the Wytschaete Ridge. The 14th Division (14th A. & S.H.) were on their L. and the 5th A. & S.H. on their R.. Still as mice by day, but always working and patrolling at night, they passed two days. On the night of 23/24th September the line was advanced. It was on that evening that 2nd Lieut. Cairns began the excellent work done by him in this operation. He won the M.C. by beating off three attacks of German *Stosstruppen.*

These new posts were further improved on the two succeeding nights. But on the night of the 27th/28th those E. of a certain point were withdrawn on the L. front to give freer play to the barrage.

For once the night of the 27/28th was fine and the 28th remained so until late.

Punctually at 5.25 a.m. down crashed the barrage; and Cairns, out on the L. with 2nd Lieut. Hyslop at his heels, followed hard on it into a strong place called Piccadilly Farm, a few hundred yards off, and took 1 officer and 38 O.R. prisoners and 2 M.G. just as the 14th A. & S.H. on the R. of the 14th Division joined the party.

The Borderers then took up a position on the ridge slightly S.E. of the Farm, on the Ypres-Messines Road. Further on the R. 2nd Lieut. Wallbank established a platoon at the N.E. edge of Quarante wood, and later on patrols from the reinforcing companies penetrated and eventually crossed that dreaded covert known to contain trenches and probably M.G.. So far things were going well; but so long as the wreckage of Grand Bois to the S. and Louwaege Farm to the E. were in enemy hands, it was impracticable to progress beyond Bois Quarante. There was also the long-range barrage of M.G. firing from Dome House on the junction of the "Damm Strasse" and the St. Éloi-Oosttaverne road and the adjacent "Zero" Farm and "In Den Jaeger" Cabaret. Thanks to very efficient counter-fire by our M.G., Borderers and Highlanders stormed not only Louwaege Farm but also Zero and Dome.

Unfortunately someone had used the S.O.S.; and the faithful gunners, who from the heights of Kemmel were working by sight and not by faith, made it hot for both places, as requested, and drove out the British garrison from Dome House with 7 casualties. The whole brigade front then steadied on the line, more or less, of the prescribed first objective. It was found possible to reoccupy Dome House at 4 a.m. on the 29th, for the simple reason that the Germans had had

28–29 Sept. 1918. — enough and had gone. On both flanks of the 103rd I.B. excellent work had been done by converging advances. The path across the Ypres-Comines Canal was clear. Wytschaete itself fell at 6.30 a.m. on 29th September. This day of daylight fighting, patrol work produced, in addition to splendid team work, individual acts of gallantry. Sergt. Lewis M'Guffie,* of the town of Wigtown, performed the most outstanding feats, and immortalized himself and his regiment by his valour. He began early at the storming of Piccadilly Farm, where he had to take charge of a platoon in consequence of officer casualties, and was responsible for the capture of several dugouts and more than a dozen prisoners. But it was after the men of D, under Cairns, had taken up their position on the road S.E. of Piccadilly that M'Guffie, with complete disregard of personal safety, rushed out single-handed and cowed a German escort into restoring a party of British prisoners. Later on in the day he performed Skinner's feat of firing rifle grenades into the front entrance of a blockhouse. This splendid hero fell on 14th October, and never knew that he had won the V.C..

But the same spirit animated all ranks on a creditable day. Let us hope it buoyed them up through the appalling weather that followed, when they passed shelterless nights (except for bits of iron sheeting and some waterproof sheets) between the ridge and the canal.

The new Quartermaster, Capt. Wynne, was indefatigable in getting up hot meals in special cold-proof vessels and—rum. The first twelve days of October, after relief behind the fighting troops, were spent in the back of the old German front, sometimes on one side of the Ménin road and sometimes on the other, in ground sacred through the gallantry of the "Old Contemptibles." The time was spent in working or training.

On the 13th a move forward was made under a new commander. Col. Coulson went home on leave and returned no more. He was universally popular and much regretted. Major G. R. S. Patterson, M.C., of the H.L.I., succeeded him. A fine specimen of the New Armies' officer, he won further distinction in the engagement now to be described.

Gheluwé

The fearful traffic difficulties had slowed up the pursuit, and the Germans were standing W. of Ménin. But on 14th King Albert launched his forces in the six-day Battle of Courtrai in which seven British divisions took part. The British sector lay between St. Pieter, on the road from Ménin to Roulers, and the Lys at Comines.

* His photograph will be found *ante*, facing p. 108.

The 5th K.O.S.B. had been in the XIX. Corps during the Battle of Ypres. Now they were in the northern half of the X., the southernmost of the three corps engaged. On the R. of the 34th Division was the 30th—also in the X. Corps, commanded by Lieut.-Gen. Stephens, a former G.O.C. of the 5th Division, in which the 2nd K.O.S.B. served. On the L. of the 34th was the 41st Division of the XIX. Corps (Sir H. Watts). To the 41st succeeded the 35th (also in the XIX.), and then came our old friends the 36th (Ulster), the 29th, and the 9th of the II. Corps (Jacob), the two last named containing the 1st and 6th K.O.S.B. respectively. While the 1st Battalion had a comparatively smooth passage through Ledeghem and the 6th Battalion were in Divisional Reserve, the 5th Battalion had a tactical task on the 14th October that taxed its mettle to the full. In co-operation with the 8th S.R., Gheluwé, 2 miles from Ménin, on the road to Ypres, was captured. The riflemen worked past the S. side with three companies, and the Borderers did the same on the N. side. The spare company of each unit was to enter the shelled village from the flanks and mop it up. Zero was at 5.35 a.m., and the barrage opened three minutes earlier. There was thick mist. The enemy had lavished all manner of shells, including gas and smoke, and one stray shell had killed Pte. O'Haire, one of the heroes of Beugneux, and wounded Capt. Gilmour, O.C. C, and A/Sergt. Welsh. These were the depressing preliminaries of the assault. There were, however, compensations. There was no rain; later in the day, about 8 a.m., the sun dispersed the mist. But while it lasted it was possible (and it was successfully accomplished), by the aid of compasses, to advance with enough coherence to exploit a surprise, intensified by a liberal spraying of the village with smoke. The three skirting companies went steadily forward and reached their first objective 600 or 700 yards beyond Gheluwé. C, the company for the village, entered it not from the N. but *via* ditches lining the road from Ypres. But if it was a surprise to the Scotsmen to see the sudden loom of the houses it was much more of a surprise for the Germans. Capt. J. W. T. Dickie's men went for the garrison with a vigour and ferocity worthy of Sea Post. Many M.G. were taken along with prisoners, who gave no trouble, and soon Dickie was able to think about what was going on in front. With sound tactical instinct he took advantage of a path leading E. from the village, and, as the mist rose, he and his men found themselves in sight of the second and final objective, Uniform Farm, about half a mile away. But they were exposed, and not a moment was to be lost. A rush to an old trench and a scramble along ditches landed them among elements of the leading companies of the battalion; but there was a gap on the R., as the Cameronians were

14 Oct. 1918.

14 Oct. 1918. — not yet forward. Uniform Farm with field-guns firing point-blank and a M.G. was barring farther advance. It had been taken by 2nd Lieut. J. Hood, but, as he had too few men to hold it, it had been abandoned to and reoccupied by the enemy. Another company commander was lost to the battalion, Capt. W. S. Brown being killed by fire from the farm. It was seen that the best defence was to attack; so, while Major Patterson reconnoitred the situation on the exposed R. flank to good purpose, C, under Capt. Dickie and 2nd Lieut. J. J. Munro (who fell in the 5th's last battle at Anseghem), and Sergt. Gallagher, who won the D.C.M. by the most spirited dash (modestly told in Scott Elliot's book), tactical skill and—bluff, stormed the fort and held it till the reserve battalion of the brigade, the 5th A. & S.H., came up, passed through them and on to the final scheduled objective. It was a great day, and Dickie fairly won his M.C.. The G.O.C., Gen. Nicholson, congratulated the Borderers on a splendid performance, and the B.G.C. 103rd I.B. (R.I. Rawson, who succeeded Brig.-Gen. Chaplin on 30th August) said he couldn't express his pleasure.

The casualties incurred on the 14th are not given in the War Diary, but as those of the battalion from 1st October up to and inclusive of the 31st are 3 officers killed, 6 wounded, and those of O.R. are 32 killed and 154 wounded, while those at Anseghem on the 31st are stated to have been 15 O.R. killed and 48 wounded, it may be inferred that those on the 14th (the only other important engagement during the month) were round about 15 O.R. killed and 100 wounded. Capt. Brown was the only officer killed, but on 13th 2nd Lieut. J. A. Kirk had fallen. He was a pre-war territorial, residing in Maxwelltown, Dumfries. He served on Gallipoli as a sergeant, was granted a commission, and was only 24 when he was killed, having joined at the age of 19—a Borderer of whom the regiment may well be proud. There were also wounded on 13th October 2nd Lieuts. Bairnsfather, severely, and F. R. Corrie.*

ANSEGHEM

We are now nearing the end of the war service of the 5th K.O.S.B. Their last battle was fought 16 miles nearer Germany than Ménin, which soon fell, thanks, *inter alia*, to the capture of Gheluwé and Uniform Farm. Apparently there was a large supply of spare Lieut.-Cols.. The successful Major Patterson did not long remain

* Scott Elliot, in his Appendix, says he was wounded at Beugneux, which is possibly a mistake. If so, he must have recovered. My authority is the War Diary: Entry 13th October 1918.

C.O.. On the 17th Lieut.-Col. F. S. Courtenay Hood took command. 31 Oct. 1918.
The battalion was still in the neighbourhood of Gheluwé, and on 17th was on the ruined railway in the N. outskirts of Ménin. On the 19th, to the unwonted strains of their band and the still more unwonted plaudits of emancipated Belgians, the Borderers marched to Lauwe, 3½ miles E. of Ménin, and remained there till the 24th. The period till the battle was occupied by mysterious and uninteresting little changes of position, and the Diary bristles with "co-ordinates." Fortunately for the reader I have not the particular sheet of the squared map, and can merely tell him that the 5th K.O.S.B. kept well S. of Courtrai at first, *e.g.* they were at Rolleghem, then they swung N. through such euphoniously named hamlets as Staceghem and Spriete, to Voschenhoek, just S. of the Courtrai-Brussels railway. There they felt symptoms of hostile resistance. On the 29th the 5th K.O.S.B., reinforced by one company of A. & S.H., with their L. on the railway and their R. on the hamlet of Kleineberg, on a front about 1,000 yards long, took over the outpost line from the 101st I.B. of their own division. The 8th S.R. were their neighbours on the L.. Behind both were 5th A. & S.H.. Outside the 5th K.O.S.B. was the 31st * and beyond the Cameronians was the 41st (French) Division. They were about three-quarters of a mile W. of Anseghem, behind which was the commanding hill called Bosschkant, N. of Gyselbrechteghem. Bosschkant was calculated to give trouble. It was full of guns and had observation.

On 31st October 1918, in co-operation with ten French tanks and under the shelter of a three-minute per 100 yards barrage, the 5th Battalion K.O.S.B. stormed through the German posts despite vigorous resistance, and were only brought to a halt by the difficulties in which their French comrades found themselves. They mopped up many prisoners, but a large number of Germans bolted to the high ground. The Borderers got as far as the railway station which serves Anseghem and Gyselbrechteghem, and is equidistant from both, having fought their way nearly 3,000 yards and having contributed to the discouragement of the enemy, so that that night he could not be found by patrols, and next day he was a day's march nearer home. The 63 casualties mentioned, and the loss of 2nd Lieut. J. J. Munro (in command of a company in this his last fight) killed and Capt. W. Macdonald wounded, were not out of the way, though saddening, when one thinks how near the end the war was. Had the ground been more suitable for tanks, the Germans would have suffered a crushing defeat. It was a great day for the 34th Division. The G.O.C. 41st French Division thanked Gen. Nicholson

* Both the 31st and 34th Divisions were in the II. Corps.

Armistice.

warmly, and Gen. Plumer complimented the Division.* A compliment from such a trusted army commander counted for much.

The 5th K.O.S.B. were relieved on 1st November in the evening, and moved backwards by easy stages, finishing up at Halluin on the Lys, close to Ménin. There they heard the glad news, and, like the 4th Battalion, manifested their delight with shouts, music, and high jinks and eventually extorted a speech from the G.O.C.. We shall not stay longer with them in Belgium nor follow them into Germany. Are their doings not faithfully chronicled by Scott Elliot ? The war was over. They had begun it well on the 12th of July. They finished it well near classic Oudenarde ; and in between, true to their ancestry and traditions, they had been making history, which will ever live in the hearts of Britons and particularly those who sojourn in the lovely lands of Dumfries and Galloway.

* *The 34th Division*, p. 293.

BOOK IV

THE SIXTH BATTALION

CHAPTER I

BIRTH

"YOUR KING AND COUNTRY NEED YOU

A CALL TO ARMS

AN addition of 100,000 men to His Majesty's Regular Army is immediately necessary in the present grave National Emergency. 1914.

Lord Kitchener is confident that this appeal will be at once responded to by all those who have the safety of our Empire at heart.

TERMS OF SERVICE

General Service for a period of three years or until the war is concluded.

Age of enlistment between 19 and 30.

HOW TO JOIN

Full information can be obtained at any Post Office in the Kingdom or at any Military Depot.

GOD SAVE THE KING." *

These stirring words were the first-fruits of Lord Kitchener's appointment on 6th August 1914 to be Secretary of State for War. They were posted in public places and inserted in newspapers, and the response was immediate and embarrassingly generous. In Scotland, as in England, the youth of the country felt the call of the blood, and a goodly number found their way into the "New Armies," with two units of which the remainder of this war story will be concerned—the 9th, or senior division, and the 15th, both of them Scottish in name and character, and with an initial and fairly well-maintained predominance in junior officers and rank and file of Scottish birth and blood.

On 5th August 1914 the House of Commons authorized the addition of 500,000 men to the Regular Army. It was a departure from

* Text is printed in *Official History of the War: Military Operations, France and Belgium*, 1914. vol. ii. p. 497.

1914. the scheme of 1908, but, as has been already pointed out, that has nothing to do with the K.O.S.B..* The form of the gigantic effort bears the name and stamp of Kitchener. "K.1," or the "First Hundred Thousand," are the affectionate bynames for the six divisions from 9 to 14. By some happy accident, Scottish divisions headed K.1 and its rapidly formed successor K.2. To the older generation K.1 is associated with the brilliant articles which appeared in *Blackwood* under the title of *The First Hundred Thousand*. Elderly "dugouts" could be seen chuckling over the hitherto unsuspected comic side of orderly-room, lectures, handling of arms, musketry, and parades. People who would have been bored to death in normal circumstances with barrack-room yarns waited with avidity for "The Junior Subaltern's" next, much as early Victorians pined for the next Dickens instalment.† And the best of it is that the particular division described was the 9th, in which the 6th K.O.S.B. served throughout the war.

The historian of the 9th Division was a Borderer—Major John Ewing, M.C..

For two years of its eventful life another Borderer, Col. P. A. V. Stewart, of a warlike Galloway stock, was G.S.O.1, 9th Division. One may rest confident that the scholarly work published by John Murray in 1921 not only fits the facts of the 9th's fate and fortune into their true setting in the western theatre, but does full justice to the part played by the K.O.S.B.. A historian of the K.O.S.B. who ignored Ewing's labours at Audit House, and his patient analysis of the War Diary (some of which he had written up himself), his intimate personal knowledge of the events and places, and, above all, the fact that he was chosen as pre-eminently the right man to write the war story of his regiment, would be shutting out wisdom at one entrance. The writer having read and re-read both Ewing's book and the War Diary,‡ as well as the fourth volume of the *Official History* and other standard works, unhesitatingly and gratefully adopts much of what that book contains.

This section involves sad reading. The appalling slaughter that was dealt out to the Borderers at Loos, in the Somme battle, at Arras, in the Salient, in the classic rearguard action in the second Somme battle of March 1918, and, as if that were not enough, in the Lys battle immediately thereafter, are literally harrowing. But in the course of events there was evolved a military instrument

* In the opening of the book dealing with the 4th and 5th K.O.S.B..

† When the *alias* was stripped off, the author turned out to be "Ian Hay," whose influence for good on Home and American opinion overshadows very solid service in the trenches.

‡ Of the 28th I.B., as well as that of the battalion.

capable of doing what was humanly possible *—a typical and triumphant refutation and silencer of Sir Henry Wilson's scepticism regarding the fighting value of the New Armies.† The 9th Division, and the 6th K.O.S.B. as an integral part of it, vindicated the prescience of Lord Kitchener. The "Old Regulars" died with 1914,‡ but bequeathed their spirit not only to the reinforcements of the 1st and 2nd battalions, or it might be more of the historic regiments, but to those of the new volunteer armies, so that in the Somme in 1916 it was universally admitted that equality between old and new reigned. The 9th Division ranked as second to none, but it had to face a terrible ordeal and undergo something like a rebirth to attain that stature. 1914. —

The formation of the K. battalions of the K.O.S.B. is described by Capts. Goss and Reay in *A Border Battalion*.§ Recruits, who were not accepted if they were serving Territorials, were sent to the depot at Berwick-on-Tweed, and in due course sent in batches to a sort of collecting station at Bordon.|| As there were five battalions already in existence the K.1 battalion became the 6th. Duly attested recruits and rejoined veterans brought the full number for a fighting unit; and early in September our battalion, ready-made in man power, but nothing else, started on the business of learning to be soldiers from teachers, some of whom knew not much more than they did about the kind of things that awaited them in France, but did know how to make soldiers and officers. Such officers of the K.O.S.B. as Major A. E. Burnett and Capts. H. V. C. Turnbull and J. S. Keith were towers of strength to the 6th. Major N. C. Sparling of the Indian Army, with his great experience in the training of troops, was an invaluable acquisition. Where there is a will there is a way, and the discomforts and shortages were faced along with a strenuous dedication to drill and military duties. Wretched accommodation, unsuitable clothing and boots, lack of rifles, monotonous and unappetizing food, were borne with the philosophy due to a strange longing for the front, which when once gratified never returned. Once more must be mentioned the obsession that the war would soon be over, presumably on the theory that the Allies were going to win. For there was certainly nothing

* Lord Plumer's Introduction to Ewing's *9th Division*.

† See an article by Sir Andrew M'Phail in the *Quarterly Review*, which no one interested in plain men and soldiers from Haig to "Jock or Thomas Atkins," as opposed to the super-clever, should fail to read.

‡ Buchan, *Great War*, vol. i. p. 370.

§ Edin. 1920. T. N. Foulis.

|| *From Bordon to Loos* gives a good description of an 18-hour journey from Berwick to Bordon with a typical crowd of 300 recruits in stuffy, overcrowded carriages.

1915. — pessimistic about the song, "When we've wound up the Watch on the Rhine," which was a favourite at sing-songs. Looking around the little Scotland of Bordon the K.O.S.B. could see plenty duplicates of themselves, just as garishly or shabbily garbed in mufti, just as ignorant and just as keen. Recruits continued to pour in. One company was at one time 600 strong, and the battalion contained double its proper strength. The superfluous were, later on, formed into the 7th and 8th Battalions. Whether by accident or design, the result of the transference was that the Scottish element in the 6th greatly predominated, and that the Battle of Loos was a national blow to Scotland, not unlike the 12th of July or Second Gaza. In a short time the mysterious words division and brigade came into use, and the Borderers discovered that there was one greater than their C.O., Lieut.-Col. H. D. N. Maclean, D.S.O., in the shape of Brig.-Gen. S. W. Scrase-Dickens, who wore "red tabs," "crossed swords," and a "brass hat," and that the brigadier-general in command of the 28th I.B. in turn owned allegiance to a divisional commander, Major-Gen. C. J. Mackenzie, C.B.. It may be noted that the G.O.C. was soon succeeded by Sir Charles Fergusson, who had shared the perils of Le Cateau with the 2nd K.O.S.B., and that his reign lasted for six very important months from October to March, by which time the 9th Division was a very different formation from the holiday crowd of August 1914. It was all to the good to have an experienced fighting general, who was destined to be a corps commander from March 1915 to the end of the war, and again and again to control the destinies of Borderers; who added to the discipline of a Guardsman the understanding of his fellow Scots. Brigaded with the K.O.S.B. were the 9th S.R. and the 10th and 11th H.L.I.. There was a Highland Brigade, the 26th, consisting of the 8th Black Watch, 7th Seaforths, 8th Gordons, and 5th Camerons.

The 27th I.B., then commanded by Brig.-Gen. W. Scott Moncrieff, who fell on the Gallipoli Peninsula on 28th June 1915, consisted of the 11th and 12th R.S., the 6th R.S.F., and the 10th A. & S.H., the last being the unit which supplied the fun for the readers of *Blackwood*.

Space forbids mention of the other elements that make up a division.

Coming to the battalion itself, the C.O. was Major H. D. N. Maclean, D.S.O., Major W. J. S. Hosley was Second-in-Command, Capt. J. S. Keith was Adjutant. The company officers will be mentioned later on.

The winter rolled on. K.2 filled up. K.3 was started, and was squeezed into any corners capable of military occupation, and was officered by more antique or intractable material and manned by less physically attractive recruits, who were turned out to be shunted about by cock-sure undergraduates or well-meaning middle-aged aspirants to military fame. And all the time the Special Reserve battalions were raking in the natural successors of the real regulars in the shape of ex-school boys, patriotic men from out in the great world, and former officers who had never thought of redonning a doublet. Among S.R. units the 3rd K.O.S.B. stood high as the provider of officer material of high standard. K.3 K.O.S.B. did not cross the seas. It became a feeder—the 9th Battalion. We shall come to K.2 in the next Book. To return to the 6th, they left Bordon in the middle of March, and trained as a divisional unit at Bramshott, which was a pleasant change from the drilling and digging at Bordon. By this time nearly all of the regular officers, except the C.O., the Second-in-Command, and the Adjutants, had been withdrawn from the 6th, principally to reinforce the 2nd Battalion. But they had done their work, and the writer of *From Bordon to Loos* may be pardoned the boast, "We eventually developed into one of the finest battalions ever raised." Continuity of type was secured, and it endured for the war. *Esprit de corps* was created, and it boded well for the growth of divisional and brigade *esprit de corps*, which necessarily are the growth of dangers and sufferings shared in the course of campaigning. The time was ripe for the best troops that Britain could send out. It was the Germans, rather than the Allies, who had the Merry Christmas and the Happy New Year. Berlin had not been reached. In fact, the situation was not encouraging. Ypres and a small holding in W. Flanders constituted all that was left of free Belgium. France could claim the recovery of Notre Dame de Lorette, but not Vimy Ridge nor the Lens coalfield. The 2nd K.O.S.B. story shows the straits in which the B.E.F. were put to man a sector Lilliputian as compared with that of the French. The 29th Division were wanted elsewhere. Their gallantry was soon to ring in British ears. At last in May word of a move came. Surely the new lot could do what the Special Reserve drafts and the "Terriers" had proved they could do! On the 10th His Majesty King George V. sent the following message to the 9th Division:— 1915.

OFFICERS, NON-COMMISSIONED OFFICERS, AND MEN OF THE NINTH (SCOTTISH) DIVISION

You are about to join your comrades at the Front in bringing to a successful end this relentless war of more than nine months'

1915. duration. Your prompt patriotic answer to the Nation's call to arms will never be forgotten. The keen exertions of all ranks during the period of training have brought you to a state of efficiency not unworthy of my Regular Army. I am confident that in the field you will nobly uphold the traditions of the fine regiments whose names you bear. Ever since your enrolment I have closely watched the growth and steady progress of all units. I shall continue to follow with interest the fortunes of your division. In bidding you farewell, I pray God may bless you in all your undertakings.

CHAPTER II

LOOS

THE 6th Battalion were then at Bramshott. It was early in May, Southern England's loveliest month, when the orders came, and the transport, brand new in harness and horses alike, found its way to Southampton on the 11th, *en route* for Havre, while the infantry on the following day crossed *via* Folkestone and Boulogne. Capt. J. S. Keith had been sent in advance to act as Divisional Entraining Officer and Lieut. Franklin acted as Adjutant *pro tem.*. The combined parties mustered something over 950 O.R. under 29 officers when they foregathered at Pont de Briques Station, on the outskirts of Boulogne, on the morning of the 13th of May, and went by train to St. Omer, which was then G.H.Q., and remained so till March 1916, when it retired to the " remote centrality " * of Montreuil-sur-mer. The 6th K.O.S.B. did not have opportunities of showing the grandees how smartly they could salute or of exploring the very real charms of that most Catholic of towns, but marched at once to billets in the neighbouring village of Tatinghem, where they rested and took stock of their pleasant surroundings. On the 16th they set out for the Armentières sector, passing one night at the foot of the extraordinary hill-town of Cassel, where the great Foch for some years could visit his own monument.† On the following day the march was continued by the road that skirts " the mountains "—*Mont des Cats and his confrères*—and the 6th took up residence for a season in Outtersteene, a suburb of Merris, and about 3 miles S.W. of Bailleul, which was to be the scene of desperate fighting in 1918. May 1915.

The initiation of officers began at once. The C.O. and the Coy. Commanders visited a battalion of the Royal Welsh Fusiliers in trenches near Armentières, and on the 22nd the battalion was distributed among various units of the 6th Division for a two days' tour, which brought the first casualties—5 O.R. wounded and the unexplained disappearance of a lance-corporal. The rest of the

* *Blue Guides N.E. France* (Muirhead and Monmarche), p. 41.

† The Generalissimo died in March 1929.

June–July 1915. month passed uneventfully at Outtersteene, except for the inspection on the 29th by no less a personage than Sir John French, C.-in-C..

In June the weather became hotter, and a move on the 5th by a 16-mile march from Outtersteene to Bourecq, just W. of Lillers (so often a place of passage for British troops), was trying. A week at Bourecq was followed by a short march E. to Robecq on the 14th. Here a prolonged and seemingly featureless stay was made till the 28th, when the battalion marched a short trek along the Aire road to Guarbecque, and thence on the 30th to Locon, close to the canalized Lawe, in the Lys plain, between 3 and 4 miles N.N.E. of Béthune and on the edge of the cockpit of 1914 and 1915, which extends from Givenchy on the S. through Neuve Chapelle to Bois Grenier. The last combats had been the sanguinary failure to take the Aubers Ridge in May 1915, so poignantly told in the 4th volume of the *Official History*, and the stalemate at Festubert. At Locon the 6th Battalion were about 3 miles from the front, and it was in this sector that they entered their first firing trench.

Diarists vary. Some are communicative, even discursive, others are laconic. The 6th K.O.S.B. possessed one of the latter kind. One would not gather from a succession of entries about troops remaining in billets and a record of (on the whole) delightful weather, that the period from landing to taking over the line had been in fact one of intensive training, especially in throwing bombs. Apart from the keenness of officers and men from the C.O. to the latest reinforcements, Brig.-Gen. Scrase-Dickens was a Spartan in habit and a glutton for work. The 9th Division was the first of the new divisions in number, the first to land in France,* the first in the trenches, and among the first in battle. Such standard as was attainable by civilians of goodwill and physique in ten months of arduous toil was theirs.

As the 9th did not fight in the Festubert zone it is unnecessary to dwell on the two months spent in that sector. It was a stiff apprenticeship, for the Germans had the advantage of the ground and an overwhelming superiority in artillery, mortars, and hand grenades. The 28th I.B. was the last to reach the front, and the K.O.S.B. relieved the 8th Gordons on the 7th of July. From and including that date there was a steady, though slight, drain due to casualties. This tour lasted a week in the fire trench and a week in reserve trenches, succeeded by ten days at Pont d'Hinges, on the La Bassée Canal, slightly farther W. than Locon.

The same routine was begun with the 1st of August ; the same

* First arrivals on 9th May.

dribbling losses and the same fine weather were experienced. The War Diary records an officer fatal casualty on 2nd August. This was Capt. H. J. F. Newbould, killed while on observation-post duty. Already the 6th had absorbed 100 men in drafts of 50. Relieved on the 17/18th by troops of the 7th Division they withdrew to rest at Le Cornet Bourdois, near their former training ground round Lillers. These initiatory tours in the trenches taught the 6th Battalion the priceless value of a competent and thoughtful Q.M.. Never once did Lieut. W. H. S. Staple fail to do the utmost possible at all times. The sad thing is, that no sooner had the enthusiasts of K.1 got to know him than they were nearly all killed. Later comers are left to sing his praises.

Aug. 1915.

September brought cold, wet weather and a side-slip S., for on 31st August the last billets before entering the line were at Verquin, 2 miles S. of Béthune, and the sector was that in which the 2nd K.O.S.B. had fought so nobly in 1914. The seven-day tour was marked by more officer casualties—Lieut. Graham and 2nd Lieut. Milne Home—and was succeeded by three days in the N.W. suburbs of Béthune. They were at last on the field of battle so eagerly dreamed of and awaited. Before the month was out it was all over, and the mangled remains were being nursed into some semblance of a military organism.

Although the 6th's participation in the battle of Loos admits of nothing but brief, blunt words, whereas that of the sister battalions in the 15th Division has more incident and duration, it seems better here to give the minimum of introduction to that puzzling operation.

Although the British C.-in-C. was in theory independent of the French C.-in-C., in practice great deference was inevitably paid to the wishes of Gen. Joffre and his famous lieutenant in the N.—Foch. Sir John French had been inclined to assert himself at first; but, as Sir Frederick Maurice maintains in an article in the *Edinburgh Review*, January 1929, the Prime Minister, Mr Asquith, instructed him to fall in with the French view in any vital matter. In the present instance there was a cleavage of opinion. Sir John had no objection to an autumn offensive in principle, though he would have preferred to await the following spring and use more fully trained men and unstinted munitions. But he knew that the Allies were in a considerable majority, owing to the large force employed by the Central Powers against Russia; and the clamant call to free French soil from the invader made the strongest possible appeal to any chivalrous ally, especially one who could not deny the charge of utter unpreparedness for the kind of war which had come about. What he objected to and what the Commander of

Sept. 1915. the First Army, Gen. Haig, still more strongly criticized was the particular rôle assigned to the British in the proposed autumn offensive. From June onwards there were comings and goings and conferences and exchanges of views which ended in the collapse of Sir John's resistance.

The Germans had been checked in their mighty inrush in 1914 in such a way that while one-third of their line ran from the sea at Nieuport, due S. (allowing for bends) to Montdidier, there was an even longer line nearly E. and W. between the Oise and the Meuse, the districts of the Aisne, Champagne, Argonne, and Verdun. The plan of the generalissimo, as Joffre was styled both officially and unofficially, was to strike hard in Champagne northwards as the main effort, while a minor but substantial converging attack was to be pressed eastwards towards Douai and Valenciennes from a front between Arras and La Bassée of 17 miles. The larger subdivision of this latter task was entrusted to Foch, and consisted in the storming of the Vimy Ridge, which previous attacks had failed to wrest from the invader. The British were to support this attack by one between the canal, which runs E. and W. between Béthune and La Bassée and the northern outskirts of the mining town of Lens, *i.e.* almost 5 miles wide, and was to include the capture of a village called Loos, which has given the name to the series of operations which, started by a big bombardment on 21st September, died down on 15th October. This is not the place to discuss the merits or demerits of the plan nor to outline the structure of the battle in any detail except in the sector of the 9th Division and the 6th K.O.S.B.. Whereas the 7th and 8th's battles were in the S. area of the IV. Corps (Rawlinson) among the chalk undulations of the foothills of the Artois plateau,* the 6th Battalion in the I. Corps (Gough) were opposite Auchy-lez-La Bassée in the grimy plain with only a battalion of H.L.I. and the 2nd Division between them and the canal.

Looking back on it in the light of subsequent experience we may marvel at the sanguine notion that the expenditure of a lavish, but impoverishing, gun-fire in a four days' preliminary bombardment, combined with the use of gas in its experimental stages at the hour of assault, would result in the breaching of the Germans' two systems of field fortifications—the gaining of the open country and a triumphant reunion with equally victorious French troops, somewhere between Valenciennes and Maubeuge, which would have vast strategic consequences. "Our objective was explained to

* See description earlier in the account of the 2nd Battalion's doings on the Vimy Ridge in 1917. *Ante*, Book I. chap. viii.

us. The town-hall clocks of Haisnes and Douvrin were to be our guiding marks." * Haisnes was to be taken quickly and therefore easily. Yet it was 3,000 yards away, and some formidable obstacles lay between it and the K.O.S.B.. There was talk of gas, but not much about the Hohenzollern Redoubt—" a great thorn sticking out and bristling with M.G." . † The redoubt proper was the tip of a huge arrowhead projecting 600 yards in front of the general run of the German front line. There was a good field of fire in every direction. From it there ran N. some 500 yards of trench called " Little Willie," which ended in the main line. " Big Willie " ran E. from the S. end of the redoubt to the main line, which, between its junctions with Big and Little Willie, was about 1,100 yards long. No Man's Land was usually well over 500 yards wide, but the Hohenzollern Redoubt was about 250 yards from the British front line.

Sept. 1915.

The 6th K.O.S.B., in order to reach Haisnes, had to cross as nasty a bit of ground as any on the battlefield, and it was the choice of ground by the French for the British to attack over that originally excited the opposition of Generals French and Haig. The miners' houses, in rows called *corons*, the slagheaps, the railways and roads were calculated to provide a ghoulish type of village warfare, in which direction would tend to be lost and congestion at one place and gaps at another would result. British opinion favoured an attack N. of the canal; but the French insisted that the difficulties were not insuperable and that Lens would be " pinched " and abandoned by the Germans in consequence of the lateral advance on the Vimy and Loos fronts.

But the first and main difficulty was to get across No Man's Land. As usual, the Germans had the advantage of the ground, and the wire opposite the 6th K.O.S.B. was invisible. The general direction of the attack was N.E., the 6th K.O.S.B. having their L. astride the road from Vermelles to Auchy, on which there was a strong point—" Mad Point "—at a point in Madagascar Trench, which ran from Railway Work in 2nd Division territory some 600 yards S.E. to the junction with Little Willie. The continuation of the main line was called Fosse Trench for about half its length and Dump Trench nearer Big Willie. Fosse 8 and the Dump were enormous heaps of spoil or bings, and played a part in the story of the 26th I.B. but not in that of the 28th. The K.O.S.B.'s R. was directed against the N. end of Little Willie; the centre faced the re-entrant line between Mad Point and Little Willie. The larger and S. portion of Little Willie, including a projecting fortlet called

* *From Bordon to Loos.* † *Ibid.*

25 Sept. 1915. Strong Point, which projected to within 200 yards of the British line, was the objective of the 5th Camerons, who with the 7th Seaforths were responsible for the capture of the Hohenzollern Redoubt.

From Vendin-lez-Béthune the battalion entered the reserve line in front of Annequin on the 11th of September and on the 14th occupied a sector slightly N. of that occupied for the battle. On the 17th they side-slipped S. to their ultimate sector. On the 20/21st they returned to Annequin, and at 7 a.m. on the 21st the bombardment of the German line began. The fine weather of the earlier part of September showed signs of breaking when the battalion took over from the 11th H.L.I.. That evening the wind was still favourable for a gas attack.

The 10th H.L.I. were on the L. of the K.O.S.B. and the 11th H.L.I. and the 9th S.R. were in reserve.

By the evening the march up by platoons had resulted in A and B being in front to open up the attack and C and D in the support line behind them. Various duties were assigned. There were bombers, stretcher-bearers, signallers, runners, and riflemen. The time before an attack is always depressing, but when the time draws near a " tot " of rum does wonders. Zero was still a secret. It was not until the small hours that definite word came that the gas would be discharged at 5.50 a.m. and that the infantry would attack at 6.30 a.m.. The guns also opened with full force at 5.50, and the delayed but expected German barrage fell on the British front and communication trenches. A few minutes elapsed and the battalion was *minus* a C.O. and an Adjutant—Col. Maclean (almost immediately) and Capt. Keith, who assumed command, a little later, being both wounded and *hors de combat.* But what they could have done had they got forward is hard to say—except get killed.

The wind was falling and becoming fitful. All the men wore gas masks. A and B disappeared into a motley fog, and the supporting companies took their places in the front line. As the air did not clear and no news came from the front nor orders from behind, C and D and the gallant Major Hosley, the Second-in-Command, went over the top and into the jaws of death. They were met by terrific gusts of M.G. fire, and dropped like ninepins. *From Bordon to Loos* gives a vivid picture of the horrors of wounds, manglings, convulsions due to gas, and the stunning effect of the German barrage and the terrific shock of a disabling wound. Yet such was the effect of discipline that a few of the second wave joined the first in front of the German line only to find uncut wire and a covered ditch filled with

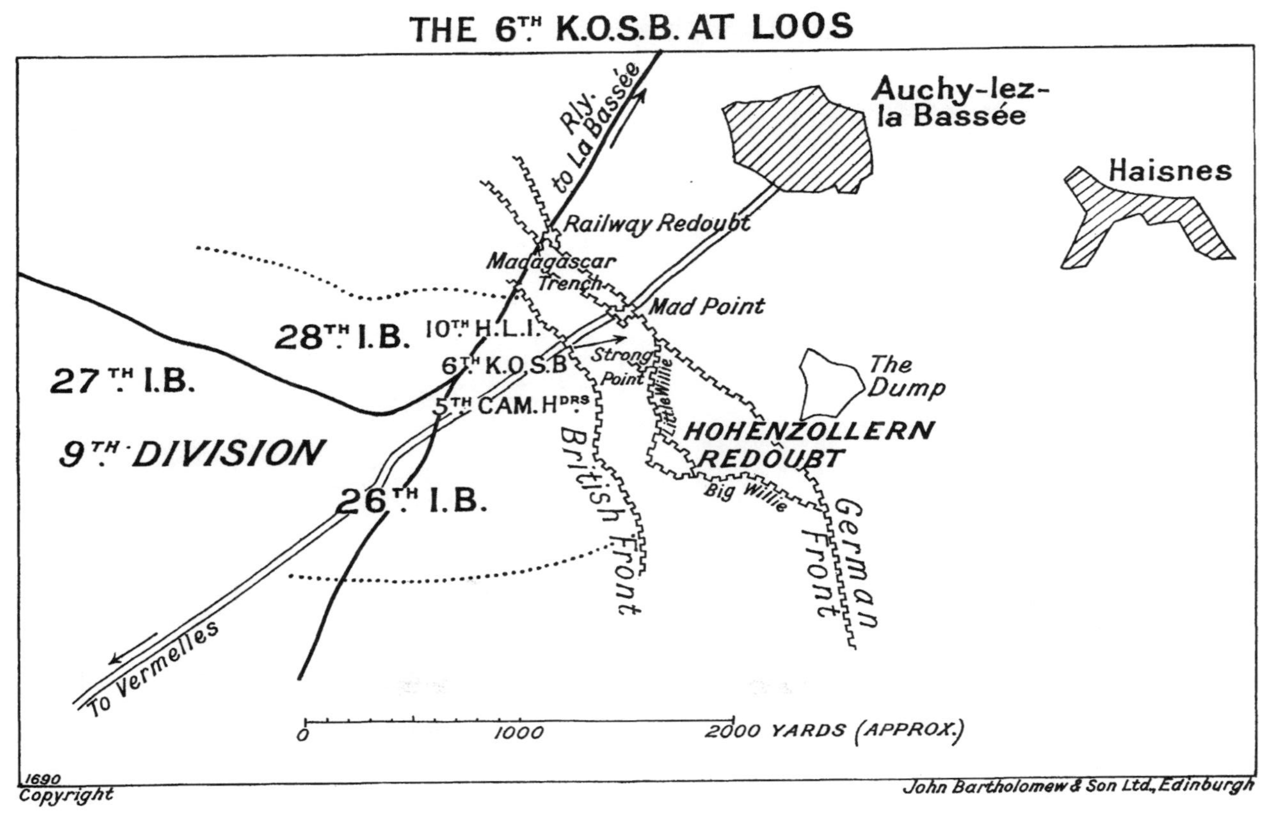

THE 6TH K.O.S.B. AT LOOS
Auchy-lez-la Bassée
Haisnes
Rly. to La Bassée
Railway Redoubt
Madagascar
Trench
Mad Point
28TH I.B.
10TH H.L.I.
6TH K.O.S.B
5TH CAM. HDRS.
27TH I.B.
9TH DIVISION
26TH I.B.
Strong Point
Little Willie
The Dump
HOHENZOLLERN REDOUBT
Big Willie
British Front
German Front
To Vermelles
0
1000
2000 YARDS (APPROX.)
1690
Copyright
John Bartholomew & Son Ltd., Edinburgh

To face Page 326

barbed wire. Farther advance was a sheer impossibility. There was nothing to be done but to get back to the old front line. No unwounded officers returned and only a sorry remnant of a splendid band of warriors. The killed and missing amounted to 358. 272 were wounded or gassed. Two-thirds of the N.C.O.s and men were casualties. 11 officers were killed and 8 were wounded. Among the killed were Majors Hosley, N. C. Sparling (O.C. B), and R. E. W. Maxwell (O.C. D); Capts. D. H. Brown (A) and F. C. Cobb (O.C. C); Lieuts. G. C. Jackson (A), W. H. Franklin and N. H. Greener (both C), and J. V. H. Marsters (D); 2nd Lieuts. W. Skinner (B) and E. Stocker (B). Not a single officer escaped unscathed. Besides Col. Maclean and Capt. Keith, the following were wounded: Capts. A. C. Campbell (O.C. A), R .H. Dodds (B), and Waller (D); Lieuts. Evans, Franklin (C), and Swanston (D). It was all over in a few minutes. The wonderful product of months of zeal, energy, and patriotism was "knocked out" without opportunity of doing more than set an example to posterity by their bravery. "He was the finest and grandest old man in the regiment, and we were justly proud of him," wrote Lieut. Waller of Pipe-Major Robert Mackenzie, a man of over 60 years of age, who played the men over the parapet until shot in both legs. He died of these wounds, having well deserved the V.C.. Waller himself owed his life to the devotion of his servant, who assisted him to crawl back—in from two to three hours—to the British line. R.S.M. Mackay was wounded while doing splendid work, and another invaluable man was lost in Sergt. Scott of the Signals. C.Q.M.S. Canning was throughout of the greatest use. The stricken remnant were employed as an attached company of the 11th H.L.I. in clearing the trenches of dead and wounded. Over that painful, long-drawn-out labour and anguish in the congested firing and communication trenches a veil is drawn. On that day the M.O., Lieut. W. N. Watson, won golden opinions not only for his handling of the wounded but for leadership in extricating the leaderless troops from their predicament. He took over from Capt. Keith, when he was taken away wounded. Lieut. R. P. Hills, a recent arrival to the 6th, had been detailed for liaison duty with the 26th I.B., and thus missed the fatal attack. He found himself next morning the senior officer, and was sent to command the battalion during the trying period of four days. On the evening of the 29th the 6th K.O.S.B. left—for good—the Béthune coalfield, which proved the grave of so many Borderers in 1914 and 1915, and rested in billets at Béthune.

25 Sept. 1915.

The course of the battle of Loos, so far as affecting Scottish Borderers, will be followed in dealing with the 7th and 8th. It is

Sept. 1915. — enough to say that, despite the most stubborn heroism of the 2nd, 9th, and 7th Divisions, the whole of the I. Corps (Gough) attack was a failure. No ground had been gained in the end of the day. The corps commander sent a consolatory message to the 9th Division, couched in most appreciative and laudatory terms.

PIPE-MAJOR ROBERT MACKENZIE.

CHAPTER III

BETWEEN LOOS AND SOMME

THE 6th K.O.S.B. were spared further stay in the dismal and dangerous Loos area. But they made the acquaintance of the Ypres salient in the Zillebeke sector N. of Hill 60, and a less attractive spot in which to pass a first Flanders winter can hardly be imagined. The trouble was that there was no pleasant hinterland to resort to after the actual duty in the trenches. Huts at Dickebusch compared very unfavourably with the back areas of the Arras and Somme fronts or even with Lens, and could not hold a candle to Le Bizet and other villages in the " Plugstreet " region. Winter 1915–16.

After relief on 29th September the relics of the battalion reached Béthune by march and bus, and billeted there until 2nd October, when they trained (minus transport, sent ahead on 1st October by road) to Abeele *via* Hazebrouck, and encamped at Busseboom. When they moved to Dickebusch on the 5th they numbered 17 officers and 302 O.R.. There they remained till 16th October, when they relieved the 2nd London Regiment in the line in unsatisfactory trenches, shallow and ill equipped with cover. The tall 2nd Lieut. W. J. MacCombie, originally of the 9th, was sniped immediately and received his first wound. A daily toll of casualties ensued until the 24th, when the battalion were relieved by the 10th H.L.I., and retired to huts and bad weather at Dickebusch. The outstanding event was the inspection on 27th October by H.M. King George V. of various bodies of the V. Corps, among them one under Major C. E. Andrews of the 11th H.L.I., then O.C. 6th K.O.S.B., Lieut. R. P. Hills, and 20 O.R. who provided a 6th K.O.S.B. quota to the representative company of the 28th I.B. (in which they still were).

On the evening of 1st November the battalion returned to the trenches over 430 strong, and spent a less wearing time than before. The weather was bad at the start, but improved. When in support they were in dugouts in the Ypres-Comines Railway embankment. And so life dragged on. Zillebeke trenches, support dugouts, Dickebusch huts, all these succeeded one another with a monotony

1916. worthy of the garrison life of their eighteenth century predecessors on the rock of Gibraltar * or in front of Namur, though the care taken by the authorities in 1915 enabled the life to be borne much more philosophically than in the bad old times. Besides, the men were fighting for their lives and their homes in a just cause.

After an even shorter command than that of Major Andrews, Major Forbes, also of the 11th H.L.I., was succeeded in the command of the 6th K.O.S.B. by A/Lieut.-Col. J. C. W. Connell, of whom we read in the story of the 2nd and will read of as in command of the 7th Battalion for a short spell after Loos. Lieut.-Col. Connell commanded from 15th December 1915 until after the creditable action in October 1916 in front of the Butte de Warlencourt. He was therefore largely responsible for the training of the battalion for the Somme fighting. Between 4th December, the date of his appointment, and his arrival on 15th, Major H. A. Fulton of the 9th S.R. was in command. The conclusion of the northern tour was marked by a sporadic but stiffish hostile bombardment on 19th December, which wounded 3 men, and by persistent shelling during relief on the 20th, which wounded 2nd Lieuts. Janes and Lee-Barber and 5 O.R., before relief by troops of the 50th Division was completed and the march to Vlamertinghe well under way.

A change for the better was in store. A short train journey in the dark made the W. circuit of " the mountains," and when day broke on 21st December the 6th found themselves (after a short tramp from the train to billets) close to Strazeele, between Hazebrouck and Bailleul, and within reach of baths at Caestre. They finished the year about 500 strong in that short and rare haven of bliss after a long spell of trenches—G.H.Q. Reserve.

1916, therefore, opened quietly, and it was not till the end of the month that the battalion moved forward to La Crèche, between Bailleul and Armentières, feeling they were now due for a spell of trench life once more. A short march took them to Le Bizet, where civilians still remained, just N. of Armentières. Eventually on 5th February the 6th K.O.S.B. took over from the 11th H.L.I. a quiet sector on the Franco-Belgian frontier near Le Touquet, and about 2 miles S.E. of Bois de Ploegsteert (" Plugstreet "). The death of an officer on the very next day, while looking through glasses over the top, was a sharp warning that the Germans were not to be trifled with. The tour passed off quietly. February 1916 was surprisingly genial; and to round off the first visit to the new sector a concert, given under

* The 25th Foot, then styled Middleton's, arrived at Gibraltar on 27th March 1730. See three articles by the Hon. Sir John Fortescue on 17th, 19th, and 20th August 1929, in *The Times*.

the auspices of Miss Lena Ashwell, was held at Le Bizet on the 14th. The wind was watched anxiously, but though several "easterly" winds are recorded none of them seem to have tempted the apostles of Kultur to proselytize by projections of poison gas, though there was one false alarm.

There are indications that the trenches needed and received attention. "The rebuilding of the trenches is being steadily pushed on," runs one entry. One feels rather sorry for a German observer whose *modus operandi* was discovered. A trap was laid to induce him to show himself at his O.P., and the sharp-shooters of the 6th waited their chance and duly "downed" him on 5th March. On the 13th Capt. C. H. V. Crichton-Browne of the 3rd and Capt. A. Innes-Browne from the 9th arrived. The latter, who had come to join up all the way from S. Africa, stuck closely to the 6th Battalion, and having S. African experience behind him rose to be Second-in-Command and to be a tower of strength. The former was soon wounded, being hit in the shoulder and lung on 10th April. On 23rd April Pte. W. Wilson earned the M.M. (bestowed 10th May) for gallantry in bringing in 2nd Lieut. Binning, then fatally wounded in No Man's Land. On the 24th a former A/R.S.M. E. Canning returned with a commission as a 2nd Lieut.. Unfortunately he fell on 6th July at Bernafay Wood.

The feature of May was the arrival of the S. African Brigade and the contraction of the Scottish units to two brigades—the 26th (or Highland) and the 27th (or Lowland). From this time on the 6th are associated with the 11th and 12th Royal Scots and, until the reduction in brigade strength to three battalions, the 9th S.R..

Towards the end of May another period began. The battalion ceased the routine of in-and-out in the Le Touquet sector, and on 28th May withdrew to La Crèche and on 30th to Doulieu, both in the heart of the historic Lys battlefield of April 1918. On 1st June the move was continued. On the march near Vieux Berquin the battalion marched past the Second Army Commander, Gen. Plumer, and continued S. of the Forêt de Nieppe to Witterness and (on 2nd) Reclinghem on the Upper Lys, just W. of Bomy. Here intensive field-training was practised for a fortnight before entraining at Lillers for Longueau, E. of Amiens.

On the 15th they were marching to Corbie. On the 18th they were at Bray, supplying working parties for digging assembly trenches. During the huge bombardment they were in huts in Bois des Célestines, and from the 27th in "Grovetown," near Albert. They were keen and eager for battle on the 30th June 1916.

CHAPTER IV

THE SOMME

July 1916. — THE services rendered by the 6th K.O.S.B. in the terrible battle of the Somme fall into two distinct epochs—that of the early development of the success won by the Allies N. of the Somme between Moulin de Fargny and La Boisselle in July; and that of the methodical, unremitting pressure on the enemy by that time ousted from the dominating ridge between Courcelette and Combles, already described. The former subdivides into two distinct episodes, each eternally bound up with a wood—that of Bernafay Wood and that of Delville Wood. The latter has, as a rule, the more sinister associations for British hearts; but in the case of the 6th K.O.S.B. by far the heavier losses were incurred in and near Bernafay Wood, where so many fought their first and last fight. As the result of the two phases the battalion, like every other unit of the 9th Division, was completely exhausted. The second epoch in October is summed up in one place-name—the Butte de Warlencourt—and two monosyllables—bog and slime.

THE CAPTURE OF BERNAFAY WOOD

Perhaps the most conspicuous British success on Saturday, 1st July 1916, was the capture of the village of Montauban, some 1,200 yards from the nearest British trench, by the 30th Division of the XIII. Corps (Sir W. Congreve, V.C.), in which the 9th Division also served, and of the pulverized Briqueterie half a mile to the S.E. of the village and a quarter of a mile S. of Bernafay Wood, an asymmetrical copse, mostly about 500 yards wide but tapering at the N. end and about 1,000 yards long. On the 1st of July it was well timbered and thickly undergrown. On 2nd July the gains at Montauban and the Briqueterie were maintained in the face of strenuous counter-attacks, but no British advance was attempted there, although the capture of Fricourt and its wood marked a tactical success on the L.. On these two days, as part of a reserve division, the 6th K.O.S.B. acted as carriers for the 18th Division of the same corps at Pommiers Redoubt (between Mametz and Montauban), at which the 2nd Battalion used to gaze a year gone by. On 2nd July they relieved the 18th Manchesters, 90th I.B., in the E. perimeter of Montauban. On the 3rd, at 7 p.m., orders came that they were to attack Bernafay Wood, and in two hours they did attack it as R. battalion in co-operation with the 12th R.S. and in considerable depth, having a frontage of only one company. Lieut.-Col. Connell describes his men as being then " in splendid condition and very keen." * They were under a C.O. whose entire thoughts centred round them. They respected Brig.-Gen. Scrase-Dickens profoundly, and, as for the G.O.C.—Lieut.-Gen. Furse—he stood for the Division; and the Division, even more than at Loos, was "it" to every unit, Highland or Lowland. " General Furse made the 9th Division, and " the 9th Division made General Furse," is a sentence quoted by Ewing † as an *on dit* of a much later date, but his personality had already told. He was not actually directing the movements of the 27th I.B. that evening. The brigade was under the orders of the G.O.C. 30th Division.‡

3 July 1916.

No picture from inside of the way in which the wood was taken has come to hand. As it was taken completely by 11.30 p.m.§ at a cost of five casualties,|| after a bombardment of ten minutes,¶ it must have been more of an exciting nocturnal mystery (through inevitable confusion) than a nightmare to those engaged. In fact, there was not much resistance.** Some of the R.S. operated on the W. flank outside the wood.†† The K.O.S.B. claim 11 prisoners and 2 M.G..‡‡

The wood was taken. But then, as the lectures and handbooks had dinned into ears and eyes often receptive but not always transmitting to the brain, there is always a counter-attack to be expected on these occasions. Of course, every man was consolidating. That was a standing order. Yet, one wonders, if these lads quite expected such an early acknowledgment that they had been victors so far, but must now pay the price. Down dropped the counter-barrage at 11 p.m., and shells rained all night. It went on, while the Borderers dug for their lives, all the 4th intensely, all the 5th, 6th, and 7th. The men had to be withdrawn more and more into the wood.§§ Battalion H.Q. had to be changed twice,

* War Diary.
† *9th Division*, p. 171.
‡ *Ibid.*, p. 97; 27th I.B.W.D..
§ 27th I.B.W.D..
|| Battalion W.D..
¶ Ewing, *op. cit.*, p. 98.
** *Ibid.*.
†† *E.g.* at Triangle Post (Ewing, p. 98).
‡‡ Brig.-Gen. W. D. Croft's *Three Years* (p. 53) calls it "a very neat little night show with complete success."
§§ 27th I.B.W.D..

July 1916.

and Lieut.-Col. Connell eventually, after narrow escapes, found shelter in a deep dugout, once German, inside the wood. On the 8th, *minus* C, sent back 2,500 yards to Talus Boisé (*i.e.* "wooded bank"), the battalion watched troops of the 30th Division pass through Bernafay Wood and attack, about 7.15 a.m., a similar copse, lying to the E., shaped like an Indian club, called Bois de Trônes. The 6th had been at work the night before, clearing away wire from in front of the wood.

They themselves received unwanted attention from enemy guns, although their only offence on this occasion had been to lend a few Lewis gunners and snipers to their English comrades. Otherwise they had kept quiet.

That evening B and C and H.Q. were relieved, but the two remaining companies stayed with the 2nd S. African Regiment until the following night, when they too were relieved. Then came the roll-call of present and absent.

Exact data as at the end of June are not in the War Diary, but the strength entered at the end of May indicates that on July 3rd the battalion mustered something between 700 and 800. On the 9th, when casualties were counted for the six days spent in Bernafay Wood, they amounted to 16 officers and 300 O.R. .* On the 3rd 2nd Lieuts. R. R. MacBryan and J. C. Wilson (slightly) were wounded; on the 4th 2nd Lieuts. E. Canning,† H. S. Soulsby, and Lieut. J. H. T. Graham were killed, and 2nd Lieuts. S. Rae, T. N. Graham, and Roche wounded, the last two being shell-shocked; on the 5th Capt. L. M. Sandison and 2nd Lieuts. J. J. Poustie, H. M. Hillier, T. Holdstock, and C. H. Gavin (shell-shock) were wounded; on the 6th Lieut. and Adjutant W. Wright was killed (R.S.M. Britton being wounded), 2nd Lieuts. Smith and A. C. Philps suffering from shell-shock; on the 7th the acting Adjutant, 2nd Lieut. J. Watt, demitted office on being wounded on a day on which there were 40 O.R. casualties; on the 8th 2nd Lieut. F. A. J. Ellicott,‡ a close friend of Capt. A. D. Young-Herries, was killed, and 70 O.R. were casualties, but Smith and Philps, with the elasticity of youth, were soon back at duty.

This gruesome stroke had to be taken passively. Unable to hit back, the battalion lost half its fighting strength and more than that in leadership. An adjutant had to be borrowed from the Royal Scots in the shape of Capt. Turner during the three days' rest and reorganizing in Billon Wood, behind Carnoy, once a Battalion H.Q. of the 2nd Battalion in the quiet days of 1915.

* War Diary. † The Official Death Roll gives the date as 6th July.
‡ Official Death Roll.

DELVILLE WOOD

The grand attack on Longueval and the Bazentins on 14th August was the first entry of the 9th Division, as such, into the battle of the Somme. On that tremendous day the 6th K.O.S.B. acted as carriers of water, bombs, S.A.A. and R.E. stores under heavy fire to their own 27th I.B., which on the R. of the 3rd Division and L. of the 26th I.B. attacked, on a front W. of Bernafay Wood, across Caterpillar Valley, objectives from three-quarters of a mile to a mile off—and uphill. Of these the most important was Longueval. The first trenches to be taken were still from 300 to 500 yards * off, after a most creditable night advance of more than 1,000 yards had been made. 14 Aug. 1916.

The brigades thus proved that they were well disciplined.† When daylight came they proved that their discipline had also made fighters of them, for by 8 a.m. they had won half the village of Longueval and by 4 p.m. the whole of it, barring two strong points.‡ The battle of Bazentin was a great day for British arms.§ The 15th and 16th July were spent by the 6th K.O.S.B. in the same way as the 14th, *i.e.* carrying while the fight raged round the orchards of Longueval and that vast cemetery of British and Germans—Delville Wood,|| which lies close up against Longueval, on the N.E. side. Indeed, some houses attacked by Borderers were in the wood.¶ But on the 17th they were called on, in conjunction with the 11th R.S. operating on their L., to take a hand. The task assigned to them savoured of a forlorn hope. Things had not gone so well since the 14th. Delville Wood was not entered on that day, nor was Waterlot Farm, on the road towards Guillemont, taken ; worse still, the strong points, which alone held out in Longueval on the 14th, still baffled repeated attempts. It was unlikely that the R.S. and K.O.S.B. would fare better. The M.G. posts required to be obliterated. But higher command was insistent, and at 2 a.m., after an unobserved bombardment of an hour and a half,** the K.O.S.B. advanced in the dark, but were soon cut to pieces, and lost two most promising officers in A/Capt. W. J. MacCombie and 2nd Lieut. W. J. Dunn, both of the 9th Battalion, and 2nd Lieut.

* Official Despatch, vol. vii. p. 13.

† Compare the crossing of the Auja by night in the preceding Book.

‡ Official Despatch, vol. vii. p. 14.

§ The gains of the 14th are described in the 2nd Battalion's story.

|| Delville Wood is symbolic of the terrible fighting in July, August, and September, the effect of which on the future course of the war has yet to be fully appraised.

¶ W.D..

** Ewing, pp. 128 and 129.

Late Aug. 1916. A. C. Philps, who had pluckily returned from his gassing. The first named, in particular, by his powerful physique and stamina, and by his leadership and equable temper, had made a place for himself in the 6th just as he had done in the 9th. Deservedly popular with all ranks he was much missed.

It was a small remnant that collected at Talus Boisé that evening. But they were not yet done with Longueval. To repeat an expression used earlier, oranges were squeezed dry in the Somme.* On the night of the 18/19th the 6th K.O.S.B. were ordered back to the firing-line in Clarges St. and Pall Mall, and to close support in Sloane St., all of them alleys or roads in Longueval. No sooner had they got there than a heavy bombardment began, and by the time they were relieved on the night of 19/20th they had suffered the loss of 6 officers and 120 O.R. killed and wounded, leaving only about 100 O.R. and 3 officers to form one exiguous company in place of a battalion. The following from the War Diary speaks for itself. A, under Lieut. Brewitt, consisted of 1 officer, 1 N.C.O. and 20 men ; B, under 2nd Lieut. C. B. Tweedie, M.C.,† consisted of 1 officer and 50 O.R. ; C, under 2nd Lieut. J. H. Tiltman, who remained on duty though wounded, consisted of 1 officer and 6 men ; D consisted of 30 O.R. . A few more stragglers from other units turned up, but the battalion was a skeleton, even more of a skeleton than after Loos. The losses of the rest of the division are in keeping, viz. 314 officers and 7,303 O.R. .‡ The praise of Gen. Rawlinson and their own G.O.C. were nobly earned, and the 9th left the Somme with an enhanced reputation. The following officers were wounded : 2nd Lieuts. J .F. Irving, W. N. Cave-Allen, J. A. Darling, R. S. Smith, J. A. M'Kenzie, and J. Guild.

The 6th Battalion did not return to the Somme till after the first week of October. They recuperated in the way now so familiar to readers of this story. Entraining at Méricourt l'Abbé on the evening of 23rd July, they detrained at Hangest, on the L. bank of the Somme between Amiens and Abbeville, and marched to Coquerel, near Pont-Rémy. Next day they took train at Pont-Rémy for Diéval, between St. Pol and Bruay. There training was begun in fine weather, and was even more elaborately conducted at Beugin, a little farther S., and the following items find mention

* The disproportionately large number of wounded in the Somme, as in other theatres of the Great War, far exceeding the modern 3 as against the more usual 5 w. to 1 k., is due to policy. It was thought that comparatively light wounded men would recover quicker if evacuated than if they stayed on in the trenches.

† D. of w. received at Arras as a Capt. on 17th April 1917 (Official Death Roll).

‡ Ewing.

—throwing hand-grenades, bayonet practice, gas-mask drill, and the steady drill of the square. There was instruction by the C.O. in wood-fighting.* The days of the rifle-range practices and fire and movement were yet to come. The training was designed to suit limited objectives. The next stage of recuperation in France was usually a period in a quiet sector, and the particular one allotted to the 6th was the Carency sector, on the N. end of the Vimy Ridge. Here tunnelling operations, involving "mining fatigues" were continuously carried on by both sides and formed a subject of speculation and even of apprehension. But nothing happened. By the end of August the battalion mustered 20 officers and 465 O.R..

Sept.–Oct. 1916.

Relieved by S. Africans on 6th September, the 6th K.O.S.B. withdrew about 5 miles W. to Estrée-Cauchie, and resumed training when not working under direction of R.E.. Their M.O. Capt. Liley was decorated on 14th September with the M.C. for gallantry at the recent fighting.

Substantial drafts added about 250 O.R. to the strength, and junior officers from various units were attached.

The second tour in the line was in the Berthonval sector, farther S. towards Mont St. Éloi. The 8th Black Watch was the unit relieved. The tour lasted only five days in trenches; and Camblain-l'Abbé and Villers Brulin, just N. of the St. Pol–Arras road, were stages on the march to Beaufort in the Arras rest area on 28th September.

On 5th October the march Sommewards began by a creditable 12 miles march to Barly, N.W. of Doullens, where the whole of the 6th was spent. On the 7th it poured with rain; and they had to wait from 9 a.m. till 1.30 p.m. for buses, which eventually dropped them within a march of Mirvaux, N. of the Amiens-Albert road, reached at 10.30 p.m. A trying beginning of a trying time.

On the 8th a slow, much obstructed but well-endured march brought them to Laviéville near Hénencourt, a little W. of Albert, in the château of which were the H.Q. of the III. Corps (Pulteney), in which they now were along with the 15th (Scottish), the 47th (London), and other divisions. Next day conquered territory was occupied. Mametz Wood was now the area of the brigade in divisional reserve. It was a cheerless scene for Major A. R. Innes-Browne, just returned off leave, to go to ground and discuss the situation with the C.O., while the men made the best of their shelters. But there was so much to do for all ranks that nobody was too

* For one of the raciest descriptions of how wood-fighting should be organized and put into execution, see *Three Years with the 9th Division*, by Brig.-Gen. W. D. Croft, London, 1919. John Murray, pp. 135–139.

Oct. 1916. particular. Mametz Wood was their abode until the 19th, and the time was spent in the usual back-area way—cleaning up filth and burying stray corpses, drawing " battle stores," working on road and rail for R.E., and touching up the technique of homicide. On the evening of the 18th orders came to relieve the 4th S. Africans in front of the Butte, and with the orders, for the first time for several days, came the rain. But before we take the 6th into the cheerless zone of battle we must see what was going on and what was expected.

THE BUTTE DE WARLENCOURT

The progress of the Battle of the Somme, from our regimental point of view, is marked by the attacks of the 2nd Battalion near High Wood in July, and near Guillemont at the beginning of September. There then followed on 15th September the capture of Martinpuich by the 15th Division, in which, as we shall see, the 7/8th K.O.S.B. distinguished themselves. In the close of September the 2nd K.O.S.B. were at the capture of Morval—a great day. By the end of September the culminating ridge between Albert and Bapaume had been entirely conquered, and the enemy had been followed down the various ridges and hollows that run N.E. or N. off the ridge, until he stiffened his resistance at this or that strong point, when he would be attacked and pressed and harassed day and night till he yielded or made good his position. In this way Flers, Lesbœufs, Gueudecourt, Le Sars, and Eaucourt-L'Abbaye had been captured by the time the 6th K.O.S.B. returned to the Somme to the appalling conditions which were described in connection with the 1st Battalion. Eaucourt fell to the 47th London Division on 3rd October and Le Sars on the 7th. Le Sars is on the great road from Albert to Bapaume, which falls all the way through the village and past it, until a stream is crossed, and then rises slightly. On the slope of a swell of ground to the R. one suddenly sees the Butte de Warlencourt, white and bald, and domed like a beehive. It is difficult to believe it is not natural; but a few yards to the N. of it is the quarry out of which it was dug and deposited on its present site in ancient times. It has enough elevation, some 100 feet of height, to command, even over the rising ground to the S. and S.E. of it, wide views towards Martinpuich, Delville Wood, Ginchy, and has a foreground towards Eaucourt like a glacis (and the weather saw to it that it was a glacis). It was honeycombed with deep dugouts and M.G. emplacements impervious to shell fire, and was one of the strongest *fortins* of the Somme.

By the time the 9th Division took over the front, trenches of a kind had been dug N. of Eaucourt and faced the Butte, which was 700 yards to the N. Between the British front trenches and Le Sars was a small isolated mound—the Pimple. The nearest post to the front trenches was the Nose, at the junction of two German trenches Snag and Tail, the former parallel to the British line, the latter running in the direction between the Butte and Le Sars. 18 Oct. 1916.

On 9th October the 9th Division relieved the 47th in this sector, and made a hurried attack on the Butte, which failed to reach Snag across 250 yards of No Man's Land. It was not that the Highlanders or S. Africans fell below the highest standards. It was because the artillery was not properly "shot in" (there were complaints about shorts), and the storm of fire from M.G. showed that few of them had been silenced. On the 14th the Pimple was occupied by S. Africans and held against assaults.

On the 18th a second attempt was made by the 26th and S. African Brigades, not on the Butte, which plainly could not be swallowed in one bite, but on Snag and Tail. A section of Snag was carried with great dash by the 5th Camerons, and barricaded on both sides and eventually connected with the old front line. But the Nose defied all assaults. Apart from the skill and bravery of the German garrison the weather was against the attackers. A huge downpour of rain fell. "All firmness had been soaked out of the ground, which became a sea of pewter-grey ooze." * There was a second attack on the 18th, but when the K.O.S.B. arrived in the line they found that the sway of battle had left things much as they were after the first assault. There had been a savage counter-attack with Flammenwerfer early on the 19th. But the position was that Snag was ours and the Nose was German and the Butte well out of reach. This was ascertained by Col. Connell on the way up and intimated to Brigade H.Q..

The 6th K.O.S.B. left Mametz Wood about 10 a.m. on 18th October in column of platoons at 100 yards interval between each. By noon they reached High Wood, and waited there dismally for orders, which they received about 2.30 p.m.. They were to take over from the 1st S. Africans opposite the Nose, but the first thing was to get there. Brevet Major John Ewing, M.C., was then serving with the 6th as a subaltern, and the account in his *9th Division* † has obviously been based on a thorough study of the War Diary as well as personal experience.

"The relief will never be forgotten by any officer or man of the Ninth who took part in it. In the forenoon, under a soaking rain,

* Ewing, p. 160. † *Ibid.*, pp. 163 and 164.

18–20 Oct. 1916. — the 27th Brigade marched first to High Wood, and even there a man sank up to his ankles in mud. . . . The trial came on as soon as the communication trenches were entered. . . . Men struggled along waist-deep in mud. Darkness had fallen when they reached the trenches near Eaucourt L'Abbaye, and an intense hostile barrage added to the horror. . . . Unspeakable was the fate of any man who was wounded that night; he sank below the mire, and the men in the rear pressed on all unconscious that the welcome firmness, which momentarily sustained them, was the body of a comrade. Progress could only be made with the greatest exertion; a yard seemed a mile. Every now and then the men had to halt for a brief space, resting their elbows on the sides of the trench to prevent their whole bodies from being engulfed in the mud.

"It was not surprising that the relief was not completed till 6 a.m. on the 20th October."

They were conducted by guides who lost their way in the darkness, with the result that the companies were somewhat mixed up. Men were often dug out of the mud, and the last only got clear at 7 a.m..* The K.O.S.B. were thankful they did not wear the kilt. It was worse for those who had weight to carry. One Lewis gunner, when extricated by tug-of-war, was found to have both his ankles broken. The work of stretcher-bearers beggars the imagination.

In the course of this terrible progress from the evil to the worse 2nd Lieut. F. Montgomery was killed by shell-fire either on 19th, as in the Official Death Roll, or on 20th, as he was entering the trenches.†

What happened to the Borderers happened to the 12th Royal Scots on their R.. Neither unit was fit to undertake an operation at daybreak. Fortunately their C.O.'s message had borne fruit, and the K.O.S.B. had until 4 p.m. in which to ease the sense of fatigue and take in their unsavoury surroundings.

At 4 p.m., under cover of a creeping barrage, one company (D) started to bomb along Snag towards the Nose, while another (B) stood by, ready to attack across the open if the bombers failed. If the open attack were made, the Butte was to be heavily bombarded to protect these skirmishers.‡ A third company (A) was alert in the Pimple ready to rush the Nose. The remaining company was under the C.O.. The task allotted to A was the C.O.'s own idea, and it proved the success of the day. For when the German M.G. were

* Similar conditions prevailed near Le Transloy later on, a man being pulled out of his boots (gum boots) just before dawn (*The Story of the 29th Division*, p. 86).

† War Diary.

‡ 27th I.B.W.D..

occupied with the attacks from the E. a platoon dashed across from the W. under 2nd Lieut. Johnson and took the Nose. The garrison were for a time withdrawn, apparently after dark; but as soon as the C.O. heard this unwelcome news he at once ordered A to retake the Nose and D to join up from Snag. This was duly done; but meantime Gen. Dickens, informed of the loss of the Nose but not of its recovery, sent up a company of 11th Royal Scots which formed a timely reinforcement and worked up Tail to a barricade, and posts were occupied in front of the Nose and Snag. The allotted task was done. "Thus on the night of the 20th all the objectives of the attack of the 18th were secured." *

20–22 Oct. 1916. —

The cost was not so severe in battle casualties. Lieut. D. S. Porteous was killed and 2nd Lieuts. T. Archer (afterwards killed in Flanders on 24th April 1918) and W. A. Durward (afterwards M.C., killed in action on 17th October 1918) were wounded. There is an entry for 22nd October, which indicates that the total O.R. casualties, originally estimated at about 200 for the tour, were 22 killed, 135 wounded, 50 missing, and 12 sick. Many were killed and wounded by heavy shelling from 3.30 a.m. to 5.30 a.m.. The men are described as being very tired but cheerful, despite the mud and the stench from the corpse-littered battlefield.

Relieved by the 11th Royal Scots, the 6th K.O.S.B. toiled back in the evening of the 21/22nd to the support or Flers line.

Large parties saw to the recovery and evacuation of the wounded. It was something that on the 20th and 21st and 22nd the weather was bright and cold. But on the 23rd the weather broke again. The improvement in the ground was nullified; men and officers began to feel the strain and to look forward with apprehension to an impending attack.

But to their unfeigned relief the 27th I.B. was being taken out of the line. On the 24th the Borderers returned to Mametz Wood. Thence by easy stages Bécourt (tents), Franvillers in III. Corps back area, and Mirvaux once more to Talmas. Here on the morning of 29th October they left the Somme and bussed to Croisette, 5 miles S.W. of St. Pol.

The strain of this second spell of the Somme proved too much for the health of Lieut.-Col. J. C. W. Connell, D.S.O.. He was invalided home, and never again commanded the 6th K.O.S.B.. He took with him the good wishes of all ranks and the knowledge that he and his men had, in spite of daunting physical difficulties, scored a tactical success and rubbed in a fair share of that "attrition" which eventually banished the Germans to the Hindenburg

* Ewing, *op. cit.*, p. 166.

Oct. 1916–17. — Line and kept them there on the defensive till the spring of 1918.

And what of the Butte de Warlencourt? It was never taken until the general withdrawal, but in January 1917 the 8/10th Gordons, commanded by Lieut.-Col. J. G. Thom, D.S.O., raided it with a thoroughness that can have hardly left any of the garrison in life, or whole, and yielded 17 prisoners.* This exploit was the talk of the III. Corps and Fourth Army for days.

* See Stewart and Buchan, 15*th Division* (Blackwood), pp. 102 and 103.

CHAPTER V

THE BATTLE OF ARRAS

BEFORE the 6th were again in action certain changes in the higher command took place. The G.O.C., Sir W. T. Furse, K.C.B., who had remade the 9th after Loos, became Master General of the Ordnance in December 1916, and was succeeded by the popular Sir H. T. ("Tim") Lukin, K.C.B., hitherto in command of the S. African Brigade. Brig.-Gen. Scrase Dickens was promoted to command the 37th Division. His abilities and devotion deserved better luck than was meted out to the 27th I.B. at Loos and on the Somme. He was succeeded by one of the knightly figures of the war, Brig.-Gen. F. A. Maxwell, V.C., C.S.I., D.S.O., who was an inspiration and an example to his brigade at Arras and in the gloom of Passchendaele, where he gave up his life. Brig.-Gen. J. Kennedy, C.M.G., D.S.O. (A. & S.H.), commanded the 26th I.B., and Brig.-Gen. F. S. Dawson, C.M.G., D.S.O., succeeded the new G.O.C. in the S. African Brigade. 1916–17. —

Lieut.-Col. P. A. V. Stewart (a Borderer) was still G.S.O.1 and Brig.-Gen. H. H. Tudor was still C.R.A.. For nearly a month the 9th Division were out of the line near St. Pol, and when they took over the sector guarding Arras on the N.E. they entered as quiet a sector as there was in the British zone. There was a calm, which only their own fighting spirit disturbed. It was the nearest thing to going into winter quarters in the good old style of Cæsar or Marlborough, which befell any Borderer unit. As a rule, in the Great War, Sunday was as Monday, and winter as summer.

Major Innes-Browne had a short reign at Croisette and at Neuville-au-Cornet, 5 miles E. across the St. Pol–Doullens road. On 18th November he handed over to Brevet Major G. B. F. Smyth, D.S.O., R.E., a one-armed Irish warrior of dauntless courage and one of the outstanding figures in this battalion of Borderers during most of the remainder of the war.* On 20th November the 6th found

* He was afterwards waylaid and murdered by a gang of Irish assassins in Cork in 1920. See Ewing, p. 209.

Spring 1917. itself back in Beaufort, which they had left in June 1916. They were nearing Arras, and on the 21st they slept in the old-world, lifeless, once Spanish capital of Artois for the first time.

Training had not been violently carried out in the country. Rest and recreation were the clamant needs. In the town, where the remainder of the month was spent, there were daily fatigues, while officers visited the front, which they were soon to take over. After a flying visit to Beaufort and a return *via* Dainville the 6th entered brigade reserve area in the St. Nicholas district on the night of 2nd December, and on 10th relieved the 12th R.S. in the Roclincourt sector, which the 2nd Battalion had held in 1915-16.

At this stage in the regimental story it is unnecessary to treat the pre-battle period in detail. The main point was the development of training as sketched in the 1st Battalion's story. What Gens. de Lisle and Lucas and Col. Welch were doing in the 29th in the spring of 1917 was being done by Gens. Lukin and Maxwell and Lieut.-Col. Smyth in the 9th. Back to the rifle, back to Field Service Regulations, but expounded and demonstrated and carried on not only in back areas but in any dead ground near the front. By these means the drafts, *e.g.* one of 167 on 14th December 1916, and young officers were made ready for the 9th of April. But more was wanted. As soon as the G.O.C. had got his trenches up to standard, and, as befitted a R.E., no one insisted on a higher standard than Col. Smyth, that mode of life began, in which raids prevailed and the fighting spirit was instilled. For instance, on 11th January 1917, C secured identification of a particular German infantry regiment by capturing 3 prisoners in a raid under 2nd Lieut. T. M. Reid (who fell on 5th May 1917) at the cost of 2nd Lieut. J. M'Laren (died of wounds) and 1 O.R. killed and 1 wounded.

Such being the life, it remains to express it in terms of topography and chronology. In December, from 2nd to 10th were spent in Brigade Reserve; from 11th to 18th in the front line; from 19th to 24th in Arras in Division Reserve; thereafter in the front line till the 30th. The battalion finished the year in Brigade Reserve.

On 5th January 1917 the K.O.S.B. returned to the line and were relieved after the raid and were at Arras till the 19th. The immediately following tour caused 9 O.R. casualties, and 2nd Lieut. R. B. M'Connell was killed on 22nd January.* The month was finished in brigade reserve. February passed similarly, until on 23rd the 6th K.O.S.B. left Arras for Étrun (23rd) and Pénin (24th). There the mornings were given over to training and, incidentally, to dexterity

* Official Death Roll.

in whipping on and off the new box respirator. Games were played in the afternoons. But the bulk of the time out was spent in Ostreville, 3 miles N.E. of St. Pol, and on the training-ground near at hand at Monchy Breton, which made a nice day's outing. They were in Allenby's Third Army and in Sir Charles Fergusson's XVII. Corps. April 1917.

Brig.-Gen. Maxwell must have been pleased, for after the entry "training completed" the War Diary records that rarity—a Brigade holiday! When the 6th K.O.S.B. returned to Arras and the front, everything was changed. The whole place was humming with activity. The very sewers of the town had been cleaned out and lit up, and troops could rest or shelter or assemble there and in the famous "*caves*" or quarry-workings, in complete security.

The battle of Arras has now to be fitted into its place in the campaigns of the Great War.

The battle with its brilliant opening and its ineffective continuation was the result of deference to the wishes of the Ally on whose soil the British were principally engaged. The C.-in-C. had planned the capture of the Vimy Ridge as the prelude to a vast effort to free the coast of Flanders (and incidentally ease the situation at sea caused by submarine bases existing on the Belgian coast), and obtain elbow-room and vision by a thrust in the dry season of spring and early summer at Messines, Wytschaete, and the amphitheatre which we associate with Hill 60, Klein Zillebeke, Gheluvelt, Broodseinde, Passchendaele, Westroosebeke, and Houthulst Wood. This was a long-cherished scheme of Sir Douglas Haig, but it had to be abandoned on the removal of Joffre, who favoured it, and the appointment of Gen. Nivelle to command the French forces. Nivelle had prepared a short way to finish the war by storming the heights between the Oise and Rheims. The rôle to be played by the British was to take over a good stretch of line hitherto held by the French and to attack not only the Vimy Ridge but to advance astride the Scarpe towards the still uncompleted Drocourt-Quéant Switch. What was to happen after the first assault and its exploitation would depend on the success attending the French effort.

That effort failed in the main, the French troops were dangerously affected thereby, and the British had to keep the battle going and finally embark on the Flanders adventure months too late. For the fighting troops at Arras it meant the usual sequence of initial spurt, big captures, small losses, and successful consolidation, followed by more hurried local operations at considerable cost and negligible results, as the Germans threw reserves into such strongholds as Greenland Hill, Rœux, Infantry Hill near Monchy, and Guémappe.

9 April 1917. In following the 6th K.O.S.B. on 9th April 1917 it will not be necessary to treat of matters outside the 27th I.B. except to a slight extent. The 9th Division was to advance on the R. of the XVII. Corps with its R. resting on the Scarpe and its inundations. On the other side of the river, and advancing in a parallel direction, was the 15th Scottish Division in the VI. Corps (Haldane). Both service battalions of the K.O.S.B., therefore, were in the thick of that amazing thrust which between the 9th and 13th April flung the Germans back from the outskirts of Arras for a distance of 4 miles, with a heavy loss of prisoners and guns.

By a strange accident more Scottish units were congregated into one small theatre than at any one time or place during the war. John Buchan gives the total as 38 battalions. On the L. of the K.O.S.B. were the 16th R.S. of the 34th Division, beyond which was the 51st (Highland) Division, while on their R. were the 12th R.S. of their own brigade.

There was no element of surprise. The colossal collection of guns and howitzers began wire-cutting and shelling the communications of the enemy for three weeks prior to *der Tag*—Easter Monday. "Das Geburtstagskind" * has himself told us that by 6th April he had definitely localized the Arras front as the danger zone, and had countermanded a German offensive submitted to him by the Sixth Army, and approved of by him for the improvement of the Souchez front. Fortunately for us the divisions withdrawn to form a reserve for counter-attacking purposes did not reach the Scarpe valley in time.† The bombardment began a second stage of intensification on the 5th April. The final vehemence excelled anything seen or heard so far in the war. "On the 9th, after not a long but an uncommonly strong artillery preparation, a vehement thrust, headed by tanks, smote the army on both sides of the Scarpe." ‡

The 6th, under Lieut.-Col. Smyth, left their close billets in Arras on the very day of battle. Headed by C, the entire battalion (less dumped personnel) threaded their way through St. Nicholas and communication trenches with names since forgotten, not only to the firing trench but beyond to a pair of craters in No Man's Land, known as Claude and Clarence.§ While arranging themselves in their prescribed positions casualties were caused by "shorts"

* General Ludendorff (the birthday child) was born on 9th April 1865.

† *Kriegserinnerungen*, p. 332.

‡ Ludendorff, *op. cit.*, pp. 332–333.

§ For the characteristics of the three craters, "Cuthbert," "Clarence," and "Claude," see *The Fifth Division*, p. 103, quoted in connection with the 2nd Battalion (*ante*, p. 74).

from the divisional field-guns firing smoke. Ewing says "some," the War Diary says "severe," but no figure is given. The time was drawing near. The battalion was in good heart. They knew that the 2-in. mortars had smashed the wire in front of the first trenches. The task before them was the familiar one of following a barrage, taking a stated objective, and then being leapfrogged. They knew that two tanks were heading the brigade (not that the 9th Division were ever materially assisted by tanks, as things happened), and that the 11th R.S. (two companies of which had come up with them in the long *queue* from Arras to the front) were supporting them along with three sections of the brigade M.G. company. Special sections were told off to mop up.

9 April 1917.

The gigantic barrage fell sharp at 5.30 a.m., and the 6th K.O.S.B. in the long line followed its pillar of fire and smoke. In little over half an hour they had reached their objective, some 800 yards E. of their point of start—a trench called Obermayer, just beyond which they pulled up in a sunk road, where they took prisoners in numbers and let the 11th R.S. carry on the good work by taking the railway (Arras–Lens), which was the second objective, or Blue Line. There was a risk in not adhering to the assigned objective; mopping up was of such importance in these full-dress attacks. However, little harm resulted. But they kept a good look-out, and C showed an initiative which might well have been copied in the less happy engagement in May. For when the 16th R.S. were on the L. seen to be held up by a M.G. post, C settled that post by advancing and bringing flanking fire to bear on it. The 16th were then able to proceed.

Brig.-Gen. Maxwell moved his H.Q. forward to Obermayer about 9.30 a.m. and took stock of his troops. He decided that the 11th R.S. and the 9th S.R. were least tired and best suited for the assault of the third objective. Telling the 4th Division to have their troops in readiness to go through, he sent the 27th men forward soon after noon, and the third objective fell and 50 prisoners were taken.

Not that the Borderers were idle. While B, extended and in close support, was practically part of Croft's force (the 11th R.S.), the remaining three companies followed in artillery formation within a quarter of a mile. One of these, A, had the honour of filling another interdivisional gap and of advancing to the successful storm of a fortified house, with an excellent view of and into Arras, called Point du Jour. Ewing, then adjutant, tells us that the Borderers "devoured the lunch" of the M.G. team. This admirable bit of liaison work, involving true initiative, was most

9 April 1917.

gratifying to those who had trained the battalion, to Col. Smyth and Gen. Maxwell and the G.O.C., who always preached co-operation.*

The Brown Line was ours; and at 3 p.m. the 4th Division, despite a long march from the back of the front, took the Green Line in great style well within the German third line system, including the " Hyderabad Redoubt," while the men of the 9th saw to their arms, salved the battlefield, buried their fallen comrades, and counted their losses.

Two officers were killed and 12 were wounded.† The figures for O.R. are not given, but they do not seem to have been out of the way. The division took 51 officers, 2,086 O.R., and 17 guns, as well as M.G. and T.M.. It was a great day, due to a great barrage, and casualties would have been less had the troops followed it with less impetuosity.‡

The next two days were spent consolidating on the line of the railway, and on the 12th the 6th K.O.S.B. were lucky enough to escape the evening attack on Greenland Hill on 12th April, which crippled the remaining units of the 27th I.B.. Two companies of Borderers helped to collect and carry back the wounded.

On the 14th the division was withdrawn, and gradually found its way to the Hermaville area, W. of Arras, the K.O.S.B. being at Laresset (4 miles) and Pénin (10 miles) W. of Arras. There they marched, trained, this time adding rifle " grenades " and " physical jerks," and played games until their return to the trenches, relieving the 13th K.R.R. near Gavrelle on 29th April.

As they were due for the next brigade attack they were withdrawn to Obermayer, the first objective of the 9th April, and waited for orders.

On 3rd May at 3.45 a.m., to the tune of a crashing barrage and the illumination of German fireworks, they entered upon a disastrous day. They were hustled into a night attack (for it was dark, though fine) on the unreconnoitred western slopes of Greenland Hill, and

* The 11th Royal Scots had seen the Germans fleeing from the fort. There was the wire pretty well intact! But some panic, due perhaps to one of Gen. Tudor (the C.R.A.'s) best smoke barrages suggestive of gas, had seized the Germans, and R.S. and K.O.S.B. raced for the Point du Jour. Lieut.-Col., afterwards Brig.-Gen., Croft tells the tale as he knew it in the 11th; but, as he says nothing about " lunch " or " breakfast " (the word used by Gen. Maxwell in his Report), the 11th R.S. must have been outpaced or less lucky than the Borderers. (See Croft, *Three Years*, p. 116.)

† W.D.. 2nd Lieut. A. S. Birrell seems to have been one of those who fell in this fight. Official Death Roll, p. 101: (6th Battalion) Birrell, Andrew Smith, 2nd Lieut. (T.F.), killed in action, 9/4/17.

‡ Gen. Maxwell ascertained this from the position of the bodies (27th I.B.W.D.).

when dawn came there was no trace of three companies of the K.O.S.B.. The enemy were not taken by surprise.* Soon after the wounding of Lieut.-Col. Smyth at 5.50† a message came back to Brigade H.Q. from the K.O.S.B. to the effect that neither the 9th S.R. on their R., who started slightly behind them, and for whom they (the K.O.S.B.) were to wait five minutes, nor the 31st Division troops on their L., were forward. What seems to have happened is that the 6th K.O.S.B., according to instructions, penetrated farther and farther into German territory, until the latter, biting in from the flanks, got between them and the British line. An advance on a big scale in the dark was beyond the skill of officers and men in the absence of drill-like practice for days in advance. Their training was far from complete, in spite of the entry "training complete," and the 14 officer casualties of the 9th April put the clock back. It was ever thus all through the war with all units of infantry. They were invariably depleted at the moment when the individuals composing them had acquired cohesion and mobility. 3 May 1917.

But to return to the K.O.S.B., despite the most valiant efforts of a platoon of D, the reserve company, under Lieut. R. B. Campbell (of the 5th Battalion), to advance half-right and form a defensive flank connecting the existing line with those in the void, and despite a barrage laid down at the request of Gen. Maxwell on the interposed Germans, followed by a gallant effort on the part of 150 men of the 12th R.S., only a dribble of some 50 K.O.S.B. ever returned through the zone of fire under cover of darkness.‡ To everyone's grief Lieut. Campbell was among the slain.

The account of the battle as a whole can be read at length in Major Ewing's *9th Division*, who has evidently had many sources of accurate information, besides and including the brigade and battalion diaries, which the writer has read. The M.O., Capt. Liley, was wonderful. The C.O., as we have seen, was hit (for the fourth time) in the shoulder. He had with his usual disregard for safety, when duty called, exposed himself in the endeavour to clear up the situation. Tiltman was again wounded, and so were Lieuts. I. D. Scott and C. W. Brown (O.C.D.) the last named mortally.§ The following were reported missing, and have since been registered as killed in action—2nd Lieut. T. M. Reid, Lieut. D. M'Laren, Lieut. J. A. Laurie, Lieut. J. R. Little, and Lieut. G. Reid. The

* Note by Capt. C. B. Anderson, then of D.

† 27th I.B.W.D..

‡ *Ibid.*

§ (6th Battalion) Brown, Charles William, 2nd Lieut. (T.F.), died of wounds, 23/5/17.—Official Death Roll.

May–June 1917. — following officers were missing—Samson, Scott, Lushington, Nelson, and Greenaway. O.R. casualties amounted to 403. Of these 51 were killed, 152 wounded, and 200 were missing. It was a real bad day for the British Army * and for the 6th K.O.S.B., but it is comforting to read, "The Borderers did their job, which was what one would have expected of them; but few, very few, out of these two companies who did their wheel and reached their objective ever got back. I think they were the only men who did reach their objective on the whole British front." † The remnants of the battalion, commanded within about an hour of Smyth's wound by Major Innes-Browne,‡ worked in brigade reserve along with odds and ends of S. Africans and Highlanders under the same officer, being attached to the 17th and 12th Divisions on and after the 10th May until the 14th, when they marched to Arras, and, helped by buses as far as St. Michel, billeted at Grand Camp just E. of St. Pol. There they remained till the 22nd, when they route-marched E. 7 miles to billets in Frévillers in the Artois plateau.

The tour in early June near Fampoux was not without wastage. 2nd Lieut. M. Anderson was killed on the 11th by a sniper.§ This was most unfortunate, as that afternoon the battalion was relieved and actually slept that night at Frévillers, 15 miles N.W. of Arras. Capt. Johnson, M.C., and 2nd Lieut. D. L. Keir were wounded, and besides 11 killed and 5 missing. O.R. casualties amounted to 78 wounded. But of these at least 9 were incurred in the later part of the month through experimenting with rifle grenades. The battalion was unable to do more than carry and furnish wiring parties and covering fire in the neat little operation on 5th June, by which an improvement was effected in the front line by the 27th I.B. and 34th Division.‖ From the 11th inclusive to the end of the month the 6th trained at Frévillers.

* Ewing, p. 212; Croft, p. 123.

† Croft (O.C. 11th R.S.), p. 123.

‡ It was like Smyth that he wouldn't be removed till Innes-Browne came and that in the interim he gave cool, lucid orders (C. B. Anderson).

§ W.D..

‖ See Ewing, *9th Division*; and Shakespear, *34th Division*.

CHAPTER VI

THE THIRD BATTLE OF YPRES

IN the second half of 1917 the 6th K.O.S.B. was only engaged in two major operations, one in September and the other in October, and both were steps in the painful climb towards the ridge which will for ever be associated with one word—Passchendaele. It is comforting to reflect that for the 9th Division the stay in the salient was sandwiched in between two periods as refreshing and as instructive as fell to the lot of any division during the war. And both periods bore fruit. The *élan* and precision shown on the 20th September were rivalled by the pluck and endurance shown on the terrible 12th of October. And the sea breezes of Malo-les-Bains, the eastern suburb of Dunkirk, followed by the alert sojourn in the Cambrai battle area braced the division for, perhaps, the greatest of all its achievements, the rearguard actions of March 1918, and, so far as the survivors of that period of *Sturm und Drang* are concerned, for the stone walling on the Lys in the second week of April. July 1917.

On 2nd July 1917 the battalion moved S. 5 miles across the Arras–St. Pol road to Izel-lez-Hameau, and were delighted to find good beds with mattresses in the "*granges*" or barns which were to be their dormitories for more than three weeks. Plenty work and plenty play, proper Sabbaths with services and rest, baths, concerts, and sports. The training under Maxwell in wood-fighting and grenade-firing was most realistic, but any wounds caused were slight. On the 13th Major A. C. Campbell joined up and resumed his distinguished career in the 27th I.B., which ended in his death from wounds when doing most gallant work in the 11th R.S..

But at last the moment to part from Artois came. On 29th July, after 47 days far from shell or din, the battalion marched 8 miles still farther S. to Saulty near which it entrained for no less famous a place than Bapaume. Even the transport used the railway, which cannot be termed a swift mode of conveyance, as the troops were

Aug. 1917. four hours on the train. Yet as the crow flies, Bapaume is only 16 miles from Saulty. By the time buses had picked them up at Bapaume after a tea interval and deposited them at Bertincourt, 5 miles E. of Bapaume and 3 miles W. of the enormous but despoiled wood of Havrincourt (the best of the timber of which was in the Hindenburg Line by this time), all ranks were weary with fourteen hours and more in pelting rain. Next day an easy march took them to Dessart Wood, near Gouzeaucourt, in brigade reserve.

Minden Day was uneventful, and for that matter the whole month in the Hermies sector N. of the canal in its E. to W. bend between that village and Ruyalcourt.

On 9th August the original C.O., Lieut.-Col. H. D. N. Maclean, took over from Major Innes-Browne and with him reported Capt. Bird and Lieuts. G. E. Main,* Kennedy, and Douglas. The battalion were thus well N. of the scene of their future exploits on the line Gouzeaucourt–Nurlu–Combles–Méaulte, and their patrols, working-parties, reliefs, and training when in divisional reserve at Bertincourt have only significance as furthering their efficiency in Flanders. The Germans sat quietly behind their forest belts of barbed wire snug and secure in their up-to-date fortress serenely oblivious of the coming shock on 20th November 1917. It was a peaceful time. What chiefly shocked our troops was the ghastly look of the systematically destroyed country, which obtruded itself on eyes feasted with the greenery and blossoms of Artois. It was just as much of a surprise, but opposite in effect, as that one when they had come out of the line in May and found the country they had left in bare, wintry nakedness an ocular feast of colour and life. Then they had burst into song with glee, now grief and rage were blended. The sight was not calculated to make the Jocks think gently of the enemy they never spoke of as Germans.† It seems as if all the Germans did not approve of Ludendorff's order by any means. But it was carried out and the stigma sticks.

On 25/26th August the battalion left the line and withdrew to Bertincourt, from which they proceeded on 29th, on relief by 10th R.I.F., partly by road and partly by light railway, to Courcelles-le-Comte, about 6 a.m. N.W. of Bapaume in the Gommecourt salient, out of which Gough's Fifth Army's well-directed pressure had compelled the enemy to retire in March 1917. Here they stayed putting on the final polish for what they well knew would prove a grim business until 12th September, when they marched back to Bapaume in full

* Killed in action, 12th October 1917.—Official Death Roll.

† Vivid descriptions of the desolate region will be found in Ewing and Croft couched in widely different but equally effective language.

view of the Butte de Warlencourt and the historic ridge behind it and took train for Proven. This was the 9th Division's first visit to Belgian Flanders since that awful post-Loos winter, but not their last. But patience! one more visit and their path to the Mülheim Bridge over the Rhine will be clear. On 15th September they moved to the Brandhoek area, and on 16th marched to South Camp just outside Ypres, where they made them ready for battle on 17th, 18th, and 19th. That night, in the usual pelt of rain and for the most part in single file along duckboards, they marched up to the line with a view to fighting at dawn next day. Sept. 1917.

Part I.

The Battle of Ménin Road.

In our regimental story it is the case that in the Third Battle of Ypres the last were first. In the first phase, usually called the battle of Pilckem, 31st July–2nd August (stopped by rain), the 7/8th K.O.S.B. figured, as we shall see, in the XIX. Corps of the Fifth Army. In the battle of Langemarck, 16th–18th August—the second round—the 1st K.O.S.B. (as well as the 7/8th) took part, as we have read. In the third round, *i.e.* in the five-day battle, to gain the ridge cut by the Ypres–Ménin road, which opened on 20th September, the 6th Battalion hold the stage. The battle of Polygon Wood (26th September–3rd October) and Broodseinde (4th October) recall the 2nd Battalion's ordeal opposite Polderhoek Château and the 1st Battalion's share of the battle of Poelcapelle. With the first battle of Passchendaele on 12th October we shall have immediate concern. The second and last battle of Passchendaele concludes K.O.S.B. participation, when the 2nd Battalion wrestled with the mud in those first two weeks of November.

The battle was staged and mounted on an imposing scale. Eighteen divisions were ear-marked for it. The front was 8 miles long between the canal on the S. to the Staden railway on the N.. The front curved like a fan. Just about the middle were the 9th Division extended on a front of nearly a mile on the Frezenberg ridge (or rather swelling) facing E.N.E. and the ruined hamlet of Zevenkote on the L. front, while on the R. the more important and more remote Zonnebeke lay behind the objectives. The R. sector was that in which the 6th K.O.S.B. fought. The scene was an indescribable universe of death—brown and pitted with shell-holes holding water, and how heavily laden infantry were to cross the inundations of the choked Hanebeek and take objectives at distances varying from

20 Sept. 1917. 900 to 1,200 yards off was indeed a problem. But it is wonderful what can be done by stout fellows well led and supported by gun-fire of astonishing efficiency, considering the difficulties of ground and counter-shelling.

We left the K.O.S.B. on the boards in the rain. When they reached the point of assembly and were marshalled along the tapes * they relieved troops of the 42nd Division and found on their R. men of the 5th Australian I.B. to whom the Second-in-Command (Innes-Browne) had been allotted as liaison officer with admirable results. On their L. were the 9th S.R., and beyond them again the S. African Brigade. The R. company, C, under Capt. Bird, had as their first objective to cross Hanebeek Wood. To aid them in this task they not only had their many weeks' training in wood-fighting but, thanks to a device of Brig.-Gen. Tudor's in manipulating the barrage, D on their L. would be able, after advancing, to detach a force to the R. and take the wood from the rear. As events turned out, C did make a short halt on the edge of the wood, and did owe it to D that 50 prisoners and 4 M.G. were taken with the wood when they advanced.† A supported C and B supported D. At zero—5.40 a.m.—the barrage fell and the troops started. The rain had gone off but there was mist. Hugging the barrage, C entered the wood, and thanks to it and to the co-operation of D took the wood and the first objective in scheduled time, reorganized and waited for the second bound to the final objective—Zonnebeke Redoubt. It was creditable liaison in plan and execution. Brig.-Gen. Croft had gone away temporarily on promotion and Sir John Campbell (of Ardnamurchan, probably as sound a regimental officer as there was serving in the division), then in command of the 11th R.S., lent Col. Maclean (whose Battle H.Q. had been in a crater *in advance* of the jumping-off place) a company, as A in supporting C had caught the hostile barrage and suffered considerable casualties. Thus reinforced, the line went forward soon after 7 a.m., and barring a single M.G., faithfully dealt with by the Borderers, the final objective was taken and a line of shell-holes joined up and consolidated under direction of that most intrepid of men, Gen. Maxwell. Was he too brave ? The very next day as he was going round the new line with the Brigade Major he was sniped near the railway and killed, and the 9th Division and the British Army had to get along without him. There is no getting away from the cloud of witnesses. He was quite unique in the combination of

* The tapes had only just been laid, but the ground had been already "strung." String, of course, did not show up in the daytime as tape would have done.—27th I.B.W.D..

† *Ibid.*

technical mastery of his profession and fearlessness with the power to draw willing response by the charm and nobility of his personality. The Borderers yielded to none in their devotion to and admiration of this splendid Paladin, and the force of his example and the sagas of his doings influenced them in the dark days ahead. Oct. 1917.

The 21st witnessed reciprocal "hates," but no counter-attack was delivered. When the 1st Northumberland Fusiliers relieved the 6th K.O.S.B. on the 22/23rd they took over a line on which work had been fairly continuously put in. By the 24th the battalion were in Winnezeele N.E. of Cassel. They had not got off unscathed, but no officers had been killed. The casualties were: 8 officers w., and of O.R. 26 k., 200 w., and 27 m..

Five officers and 315 O.R. made a substantial reinforcement for the battalion, but the task ahead of the new arrivals was formidable, namely, to get to a point of assembly in the dark, to keep up with the barrage over the universal swamp, to keep direction on a thinly manned front, to keep their rifles in a fit state for firing, to avoid drowning in the treacherous craters, and to keep their wits at all in such a hell on earth.

It had not forgotten to rain since their last visit to the front. The Battle of Poelcapelle which opened on 9th October was fought when the craters were brimming, and on the 11th it rained cats and dogs and kept on raining "steadily throughout the whole of the following day." *

Part II.

The First Battle of Passchendaele, 12th October 1917.

The direction of the Poelcapelle fighting had been N.E. towards Houthulst Forest and parallel to the Ypres–Staden railway. That of the battle of 12th October was slightly more E., directed against the culminating ridge between Westroosebeke and Passchendaele villages, the churches of which used to be landmarks in 1916 from the Wieltje area.

The scene of action for the K.O.S.B. was the valley on the L. bank of the Lekkerboterbeek then in spate about a kilometre S. of Poelcapelle. The exact objectives of the attack, timed for 5.25 a.m. (normal time), will be found elsewhere.† The K.O.S.B. had the dubious advantage of being in brigade reserve in the supporting brigade, and events did not shape so as to interest them in what might have been. It was the Highlanders' turn to lead; the Lowlanders

* Official Despatch. † Ewing, p. 239.

12 Oct. 1917. were to follow, and the S. Africans were in reserve. The front of attack was nearly a mile long.

To reach the ground there were two routes and two only, the Mouse Trap Track on the S. and the Alberta on the N.. It was along the latter slippery bridge of boards that Major Innes-Browne and his men toiled in the inky blackness of a torrential downpour in the small hours of the 12th.

Their progress had been gradual. They had exchanged Winnezeele for Rubrouck (sometime before 1st October),* which was nearer D.H.Q. which were at Arneke near Cassel. This rest camp was left on the 8th, and Dirty Bucket Corner, N.W. of Vlamertinghe, reached by train. Two comfortless days in camps best forgotten, and one better one in the canal bank brought them to Irish Farm, exactly one mile N. of the N. end of the ramparts of Ypres. By the time they boarded the Alberta track they had already come 3,500 yards since breaking camp at 3 a.m., and they still had 3,000 yards to go to get to Winchester Farm and form up along an almost obliterated road on the ridge beyond the Stroombeek, a confluent of the Lekkerboterbeek, from which they were to be ready to exploit any success won by the 26th I.B.. But there never was any sign of success. The 18th Division on the L. of the 26th I.B. could do no more than any combatant did with the better known inundations on the Belgian coast or in the valleys of the Scarpe, Ancre, or Somme. They could not swim and fight. They could only drown or stay where they were. Many of the 26th I.B. were drowned in a gallant attempt to cross the Lekkerboterbeek. Nor were the New Zealanders able to make progress on the R.. The Black Watch had made ground, and in consequence disappeared for good.† Sir Douglas Haig wrote: "Our attack launched at 5.25 a.m. between the Ypres–Roulers railway and Houthulst Forest made progress along the spurs and higher ground, but the valleys of the streams which run westward from the main ridge were found to be impassable." "The advance . . . was cancelled." One tactical incident marks the entry of the K.O.S.B. into the confused combat. One company joined with the 11th R.S. and the original attackers, the 10th A. & S.H., in smothering one of the most destructive pill-box garrisons that ever exploited the von Armin system of elastic defence. The garrison were accused of having hoisted the white flag.‡ and it is more surprising that 5 unwounded prisoners were taken than that 31 were killed, when the 4 deadly M.G. were finally

* The move is not recorded in the W.D..
† Croft, *Three Years with the 9th*, p. 161.
‡ Ewing, p. 241.

captured. The line was then found to be overcrowded and the K.O.S.B. were wisely withdrawn to the Winchester position, where they reorganized and consolidated, leaving the 11th R.S. to hold the line. The Highlanders' remnant, who had had forty-eight hours of the front before the fight began, withdrew. The state of the ground was such that the enemy made no counter-attacks. The K.O.S.B. do not even record extra shelling on the 13th. Thankfully they handed over on the 13/14th to the S. Africans and tried to come to life in tents at Irish Farm with the aid of hot tea and food and foot-slapping. Shells expelled them to damp dugouts in the canal bank. Farther off they did not go, for they were due to relieve the S. Africans on the 20/21st. Oct. 1917.

The losses on the 12th were heavy considering that, strictly speaking, no attack was made. Gas, H.E., bullets, drowning account for 196 casualties—15 k., 154 w., 27 m. (probably drowned). The number of wounded, even allowing for walking cases, raises a picture of the herculean labours of stretcher-bearers, medical orderlies and their splendid officers, and the ministrations of chaplains, in the rain, in the filth, and general hideousness. The following officers fell—Lieut. G. E. Main and 2nd Lieuts. H. M'Gilliwie, A. Carmichael, W. G. Pringle, and G. A. Adamson. 2nd Lieuts. I. G. M'C. Nicol, J. Rutherford, and H. Kennedy were wounded. So also were Capt. J. A. Liley, a devoted and resourceful M.O. for many months, and Lieut. R. H. Pringle, K.O.S.B., a veteran of Gallipoli and a member of the last party of Borderers to leave the front trenches there, who after an apprenticeship to staff work in the 29th Division had joined the 27th I.B. as staff captain before the Battle of Arras.

The physical strain proved too much for Col. Maclean's constitution. It was a young man's war, and zealous veterans often ended their careers in hospital. The gallant colonel was evacuated sick on the 19th, and on the 24th Lieut.-Col. Smyth, R.E., returned just after the Borderers had helped the 18th Division in a successful attack on the 22nd by a display which drew heavy fire and caused 10 casualties, including 2nd Lieut. R. T. Taylor killed. He found them at Irish Farm, and took them *via* Wormhoudt to Uxem, near Dunkirk, where marvellous good news came on the 28th. They were to go to the seaside. Church parade was short that Sunday, and before night the 6th K.O.S.B. were billeted in that cheery suburb—Malo-les-Bains—for a delectable fortnight, most beneficial to lungs and feet and souls. We islanders, especially Scots and North-country folk, must have our taste of the sea every year for a season. It was indeed a glorious change, and by the time they

Nov. 1917–March 1918. — had been told all the nice things that generals too grand to have familiar names thought about their services in the salient, they felt ready for Fritz at any moment, and in the meantime to face a long route march from the Flanders coast to woody Fressin in the Pas de Calais, 4 miles N. of Hesdin.

Sir Ivor Maxse, G.O.C. XVIII. Corps, wrote to Gen. Lukin a letter quoted in full in the War Diary, in which the following is found. "Our failure to capture the objective of the 12th was in no way due to the 9th Division. Indeed, on that day the division played a splendid part, and in spite of the awful mud, carried on the attack in the most gallant manner. They went where they were told to go, and they could not have done more. I am extremely sorry such a splendid division should no longer be in this Corps."

The 6th celebrated St. Andrew's Day at Fressin. They had marched *via* Bergues, which is inside a Vauban fortification, passed Cassel on the W., and on S.W. by Heuringhem and Verchocq (the latter passed by the 1st Battalion a few days later in much more inclement weather when they trekked N. from Cambrai). How long they were meant to stay out is not known. They were resting at Verchocq when the Cambrai battle opened, and when things looked bad on 2nd December after the great German counter-attack they were hurried off to Hesdin on the Canche on foot, and thence direct by rail to Péronne, and without delay sent on to a camp at Haut-Allaines on the following day. By the 6th they relieved the 3rd Cavalry Division in the Gauche Wood sector near Gouzeaucourt. It was hallowed ground. The Guards and tanks, cavalry, and odds and ends had counter-attacked, and not only checked but hurled the Germans out of Gouzeaucourt.* The fight was over, but much remained to be done to make the line secure. It was the very job for which Brig.-Gen. W. B. Croft (late O.C. 11th R.S.) was cut out. He was now in command of the 27th Brigade.

"We burowed into that chalk like beavers." † Every Borderer in the Lowland Brigade, as the Brigadier preferred to call it, will endorse the truth of that sentence. Sunk roads gave scope for tunnelling shell-proof galleries.

The events that have to be chronicled in March are so important that space compels a cursory glance at the intervening period. For one thing, the division was in the Corbie area for the whole of February. December and part of January were marked by great cold, and, when it suddenly ended, the defects of chalk were strikingly

* See Col. Headlam, *Guards Division*, and Buchan, *History of the Great War*.

† Croft, p. 173.

shown. The trenches simply collapsed into an amorphous, glutinous mud-pie, and the line was held in pockets till drier weather hardened up the soil.* Unlike the Highlanders, the 27th I.B. were not involved at any time in actual fighting. But a bomb, soon after their arrival, wounded no fewer than 4 subalterns, Lieut. I. D. Scott, and 2nd Lieuts. E. I. Martin, J. Johnstone, and J. Henderson, besides causing 9 O.R. casualties.† March 1918.

On returning to the front area the K.O.S.B. were never in their former trenches. They worked at Gurlu Wood and trained at Sorel-le-Grand for the first three weeks, during the last of which they became involved in one of the most famous rearguard battles of the whole war.

* Both Ewing and Croft describe the incident at length.

† The worst bomb of all caused 51 casualties to the 11th Royal Scots at Ypres on 17th September 1917. See Ewing, p. 231.

CHAPTER VII

THE SECOND BATTLE OF THE SOMME

March 1918. — THE *débâcle* on the British front in the last ten days of March 1918 presented a very different aspect to those serving in France from what it presented to the workers or waiters on the Home Front. On this side of the Channel consternation amounting to panic was rife. Angry complaints against Government and generals were heard, along with demands for heads on chargers.* Even the troops came in for criticism from "arm-chairs." The shock of surprise permeated the outlook.

In France the whole episode was regarded from a prosaic, matter-of-fact point of view. The German thrust was bound to come. The point was, where the attack would be made and in what force. G.H.Q. rightly localized the *locus* and took all possible steps to meet the impending assault in mass.

Taking a leaf out of the German book, the plan of defence adopted in the areas of the Third and Fifth Armies, was to hold a front outpost line by means of fortlets at intervals. Behind that was to be the main fighting zone, and behind that a third reserve line, to which reinforcements could be brought in case of need. With feverish energy gangs of polyglot labourers worked at yet farther back defences.

But the weather and the sheer force of numbers made these plans idle. Several weeks of dry, windy days and nights made the going good for the German *Aufmarsch.* The low, clinging, morning mist on 21st March 1918 enabled the Germans to "infiltrate" the outpost line in a way which they totally failed to accomplish in front of Arras in clear weather. To stout troops with M.G. the more the assailants the better the target.

Once through the outpost line the Germans overwhelmed great sections of the thinly held, gas-drenched battle zone, and the good-

* That of Gen. Gough commanding the Fifth Army, with particularly little justice.

going carried them on till the impetus of the particular unit gave out. Their mode of progression has been often described—by no one better than John Buchan: "It was the system of shock-troops carried to its extreme conclusion. . . . The assault was made by picked troops, in open order, or rather in small clusters, carrying light trench-mortars and many machine-guns, with the field batteries close behind them in support. The actual method of attack . . . may best be set forth by the analogy of a hand, the fingers of which are shod with steel, pushing its way into a soft substance. The picked troops at the fingers' ends made gaps through which others poured, till each section of the defence found itself outflanked and encircled." Behind the assaulting units the supporting divisions were echeloned. They were to pass through, and, to use James Pigg's phrase, "keep the tambourine a-rowlin'." Out into the void they were to press, relying on heavy iron rations and what they could pick up at British canteens and supply dumps. And to what extent they succeeded is evidenced by the change effected in the front line between 21st and 27th (incl.) March 1918. They had advanced *ex adverso* of St. Quentin nearly 30 miles. Such old back haunts as Sailly-Laurette on the Somme were now German. Farther N., Albert had gone, and with it nearly all the classic battle-field of 1916. Farther S., Montdidier was lost, and there was a nasty fluidity about the situation there, which eventuated in a 10-mile farther push towards and within 3 miles of the Paris railway and only about 8 miles S.E. of Amiens itself. By the 5th of April the loss of territory suffered by the Allies amounted to 1,050 square miles. The following figures explain the alarming result. The Germans had 64 divisions ready for the attack—a force larger than the entire British Army in France and Belgium. Forty of these were launched against the Fifth Army (Sir Hubert Gough); 24 attacked the Third Army (Sir Julian Byng), which had 19 divisions. It was like a migration, and it was heralded by a short but unprecedented whirlwind barrage from guns ranged side by side, one per hundred metres.* The troops of the Fifth Army, which were extended on a preposterously long line from Gouzeaucourt in the Cambrai battlefield of 1917 to the R. Oise at Barisis, something like 42 miles, consisted of only 14 infantry and 3 cavalry divisions, and disintegrated considerably. An eye-witness, who with all the authority of red tabs and a major's crown, and the "right way with him" (as befitted a veteran and a regular), rallied the numerous stragglers, told the writer that there was no panic.

* See the "Epic of the 9th Division," by Walter Shaw Sparrow, *National Review*, 1920, vol. lxxv. p. 234.

March 1918. Things had got out of gear, and it was no use going forward or staying still; so they were just walking quietly back. But they were quite eager to fight, if supplied with leaders and orders. Indeed, in all these fateful days, what turned the scale was whether this or that division, brigade, or battalion, or M.G. company, preserved military cohesion.

Anyone can realize that the Germans did not march through in procession. The vast hordes were by no means manned with *Sturmtruppen* throughout. Here and there they encountered stubborn resistance, only ended through need to conform to the general retrograde movement. It was the good fortune of the only representatives of the old "25th" in this "Battle of St. Quentin" to be in the 9th Division, then under Major-Gen. H. H. Tudor, to be in the 27th I.B. under Brig.-Gen. W. D. Croft, to have that incarnation of the fighting spirit, Smyth, as their C.O., and —may we say it?—to be themselves, using the term to include their comrades in brigade and division alike. The 9th Division was well up to strength for these times—something over 12,000 in all, was rested, had trained, and knew that much was expected of it. It was in the VII. Corps, commanded by a V.C.—Lieut.-Gen. Congreve.

The fascinating story of how the 9th Division remained unbroken, dealing out shrewd blows, when necessary, fighting to the end; of how and why from 5 p.m. on the opening day of battle their N. as well as their S. flanks were menaced; of the Thermopylæ of the South Africans; of the far-flung "Odyssey" of Kennedy's Highlanders in the effort to keep touch with the 47th Division and the Third Army, is not for these pages. In this battalion story we are in a fairly well-defined compartment—a series of rearguard actions directed by brigade, and of ordered, plugging marches by night, to repeat the process of a stand, until relief by Australians on the Ancre after six days of fighting and seven of tension. Just enough of others' doings to explain those of the 6th K.O.S.B., and no more!

The battle of Cambrai left a marked salient called after the famous village of Flesquières.* The line nearest Flesquières faced N. and the true blunted tip faced N.E. between Ribemont and our old friend Marcoing. By the time the bend S. reached Gouzeaucourt it faced a little S. of E.. This was the sector entrusted to the extreme division of the VII. Corps and Fifth Army, the 9th. On their L. were the 47th Division of V. Corps and Third Army; on

* The 51st (Highland) Division suffered heavily there on 20th November 1917 in the Battle of Cambrai.

their R. the 21st Division. The Gouzeaucourt sector (N.) of the second-brigade front was held by the 26th I.B., the Gauche Wood sector (S.) was held by the S. Africans. Its N. strong-point was Quentin Redoubt, near Gen. de Lisle's old H.Q. in the Cambrai battle. Chapel Hill, to the S. of Gauche Wood, would have rounded off the sector nicely, but it was held by the 21st Division. Our Lowlanders were with their B.G.C. (Gen. Croft) at Sorel-le-Grand, 3½ miles from the front line; and T/Major-Gen. Tudor, in the absence of Major-Gen. C. A. Blacklock (who succeeded Gen. Lukin, K.C.B., in March as G.O.C., 9th Division), was at Nurlu on a high hill 8,000 yards from the front zone. Lieut.-Col. T. C. Mudie had replaced Lieut.-Col. P. A. V. Stewart (K.O.S.B.), so long the mainstay of the 9th, as G.S.O.1.. **21 Mar. 1918.**

Let us join Winston Churchill, himself an old 9th man and a friend of Tudor's, at Nurlu on the 21st March 1918. It was known that the attack would come next morning. Trench raids of the previous evening had revealed no less than eight enemy battalions on a single half mile of the front.* There was no surprise about the time or general direction of the attack. The surprise consisted in its weight and power. "The 'Michael' must be regarded without exception as the greatest onslaught in the history of the world."† Mr. Churchill was on a mission and could not remain; but he carried away two impressions: one was material—of the incredible fury of the bombardment, which included a rather inaccurate H.V. gun aimed at D.H.Q.—the noxiousness of the gas, and the thick fog. The other was spiritual—of Tudor, as "an iron peg hammered into the frozen ground, immovable." ‡ If he had been in Sorel he would have seen the K.O.S.B. playing football,§ and his belief would have been intensified. Lest we forget to insert it in its proper place, let us add: "And, indeed, it so proved. The 9th Division held not only its battle but its forward zone at the junction of the Third and Fifth Armies against every assault, and only retired when ordered to do so in consequence of the general movement of the line." ||

Let that be the text upon which to hang the events. It was not quite accurate to say the forward zone was held *in toto*. Gauche

* *World Crisis*, 1916–1918, Part II, p. 410.

† *Ibid.*, p. 412. "Michael" or "Michel" (pronounced as in broad Scots) was the name given by the Germans. It personified all they believed themselves to be (except when expounding ruthlessness)—a sort of unsophisticated, rustic John Bull, not over "gleg at the uptak," but full of the milk of human kindness.

‡ *Ibid.*

§ 6th K.O.S.B.W.D..

|| *Ibid.*

23 Mar. 1918. Wood had to be given up by the small garrison of 40 S. Africans. But they dug in on the W. side between the wood and the railway, and it proved a *damnosa hereditas* to the Germans, to succeed them in the wood, thanks to our gunners and riflemen. In substance, therefore, the line held. The Highlanders were not seriously molested, and by far the worst news came at 5 p.m.. At the junction of the IV. and V. Corps a breach had been made in the front system near the Arras–Cambrai road at Doignies. The 9th were urged at once to withdraw to their battle zone and abandon the forward zone. There had been trouble farther S.; but the S. Africans, assisted by the 11th R.S. under Major A. C. Campbell, K.O.S.B., had secured Chapel Crossing and recovered Chapel Hill.

Friday, 22nd March, lit up to show the same pair of brigades ensconced in the so-called "Yellow" and "Brown" lines of the *battle* or second zone of defence. The 12th R.S., the 6th K.O.S.B. (24 officers and nearly 900 men), with the 9th Seaforths (pioneers) were in divisional reserve, the 12th R.S. being at Fins and the others at Sorel.

At 9 a.m. heavy fighting broke out. The 21st Division seemed to be "getting it hot"; the flank opened up, and the S. Africans took up a position from Revelon Farm along the ridge towards Gouzeaucourt. But even here a stand could not be made. The general situation called for a farther retirement to the Green or final organized system of defence. Thus the reserve was not used to counter-attack, and the 6th K.O.S.B. came into the fight by sideslipping S. towards Liéramont and holding the high ground between it and Sorel in echelon of companies to the R., until the S. Africans completed their retirement. "That flank-guard was skilfully handled by S—— of the one arm, as one knew perfectly well he would." *

Everybody, therefore, was in the Green line by the morning of the 23rd (Saturday), and the K.O.S.B. sector ran from and including Nurlu to and excluding Épinette Wood and directly covered Moislains (D.H.Q., 2 miles due W.) on the Tortille and Canal du Nord.

It was then that troubles developed on both wings: that on the N. separating the Highlanders from our brigade for several days, that on the S. affecting the Borderers directly. At 7 a.m., from their elevated position they could see the Germans successfully attacking their neighbours on the R. in Épinette Wood and beyond. A dashing counter-attack by some of the S. African remnant † prevented

* Croft, p. 184. He is referring to Lieut.-Col. Smyth.

† They had lost 900 O.R. in the two days preceding. Croft, p. 186 (Sparrow, article cited).

an envelopment; and the K.O.S.B., fighting every inch of the way, withdrew in a series of bounds on the principles of fire and movement down the W. slope to the canal, crossed it, and passed through Moislains and up to the heights N.W. of the village. From the original position down to the canal is more than 2 miles. The control of this difficult, hotly contested manœuvre was in the capable hands of Lieut.-Col. Smyth, and Capt. Cockburn, O.C. A (rearguard company), specially distinguished himself. Extrication took many hours; but the Borderers were neither rolled up nor rolled over, and A, well covered in its turn, passed through the remainder, to comparative peace, at the S., tail-like end of St. Pierre Vaast Wood.

23–24 March 1918.

But it was of short duration. As darkness came on the Germans pressed on in hordes and forced the three companies back on to A and Battalion H.Q.. It was then that the fertile mind of Smyth bethought him to make a reconnaissance in force with A and B northwards between the Bois St. Pierre Vaast and the Bois des Vaux. In the dark Germans were found *en masse* and fired on with M.G. with good effect as they debouched from the B. des V.. But once more the C.O. was wounded—for the 5th time—(but even that didn't finish him, and he was back in May), and Cockburn withdrew these two companies and with all that was left of the battalion took up a position S. * of Rancourt.

The next morning, Sunday, 24th March, brought fresh attacks and another daylight retirement, in the course of which Combles was occupied and abandoned, and Guillemont followed suit. It was open warfare with a vengeance, and the K.O.S.B. put in some good shooting in co-operation with the artillery. There were targets *gu leoir*; the gaunt wilderness was seething with "Feldgrauen." If ammunition held, all would be well. But what about the R. flank? And where were the S. Africans? Dead mostly, and the wounded and exhausted survivors in captivity after winning eternal renown.† To them the K.O.S.B. owe it that they were able to fall back on the Somme on their R. at Maricourt. Their S.W. line of retreat had ended without their being trapped between the Germans moving W. from the Gouzeaucourt-Épehy front of the Flesquières salient and then pressing S.S.W. from Doignies on Péronne. Like a bird out of the snare of the fowler they had escaped. Let us hope their next Psalm was the Old 124th, and that they did justice to it. Nobody grudged the German aviators their prowess and intrepidity. But

* The Battalion W.D. says E.. I have followed the Division Report.

† J. Buchan has also written an admirable *History of the South Africans in the Great War*.

25–28 March 1918. — you will never get Britishers to think it a legitimate *ruse de guerre* to dress up German aeroplanes in British colours.*

A lull now followed. The K.O.S.B., being human, were growing weary. On the 25th they were withdrawn to Talus Boisé and ultimately to Étinehem, also familiar. Then a fresh scare led to their doing a night march N. across the front with flank-guards out on the R. to cover the crossings of the Ancre; and on the 26th the 6th K.O.S.B. held a position in reserve on the Albert–Dernancourt road. If Moses had his Joshua, so the 6th Borderers had an Innes-Browne to lead, when Smyth was *hors de combat*. On the 27th the enemy made his last attack on this part of the front at 10 a.m.. He found the K.O.S.B. in readiness on the Albert–Amiens railway (just S. of Albert), as the War Diary tells us, in order of companies (from S. to N.) C, A, B, D.. He attacked after a prelude of artillery, including howitzer, field-guns, and T.M.. The Borderers attending to their own job repulsed the massed attacks with great slaughter, profoundly unconscious, until it was all over, that there had been trouble on both flanks. It was a great finish.

That night the 6th were relieved by Australians and slept the sleep of exhaustion in Hénencourt Wood, near the château which had been III. Corps H.Q. in the battle of the Somme. But the morning (28th) brought gas, and it made the wood uncomfortable, so they packed up and marched to the pipes to Querrieu (Fourth Army H.Q. in the Somme) to billets. The 9th made an orderly contrast to numerous stragglers passed *en route*.

The retreat of the 9th Division is one of those masterpieces of tactical skill, made possible by the valour of the troops, which will ever be the study of soldiers. The spirit of sacrifice is typified by the S. Africans, the spirit of enterprise and aggression by the Highlanders, the spirit of dour resistance by the Lowlanders. While we give credit to Gens. O. von Below and von der Marwitz for their impressive exploitation of their tremendous engine of offence, we may cherish a still warmer spark of admiration for the G.O.C. 9th Division, H. H. Tudor, whose improvized plans did so much to deprive the "Michael" offensive of strategic consequences. The Kaiser is reported to have said that, had other divisions fought as well as the 9th Division, he would have had no more troops to go on with. The C.-in-C. made special mention of the 9th.

Casualties, although not on the devastating and revolting scale of a miscarried positional action of a few minutes, were severe. Although 2nd Lieuts. A. G. Hutton-Balfour and C. A. P. Wallace,†

* Croft, p. 190. 9th Division (Official) Narrative of Operations, 21–27/3/18.
† Official Death Roll. Both on 22/3/18.

both of the 3rd Battalion, were the only officers killed in the battalion,* 10 were wounded and 1 was missing. Of O.R. 26 were killed, 177 were wounded, and 189 were missing. The loss represents 44 per cent. of the strength as at 21st March 1918. March 1918.

* The gallant Major A. C. Campbell, D.S.O., was hit on the 27th March when in command of 11th R.S., and died of wounds on 3rd April (Official Death Roll). "An incomparable leader whom we could ill spare" (Croft, p. 203).

CHAPTER VIII

A FIGHT TO A FINISH IN FLANDERS

PART I

Backs to the Wall

April 1918. — IT was a mere nothing of a march on 29th March from Querrieu to Coisy. On the 30th the battalion did nothing. On 31st an easy route march took them to Canaples, where they slept their last night in Picardy, bound up with the memories of Bernafay Wood, Longueval and Delville Wood, the Butte de Warlencourt, and the Long Trek.

On 1st April they entrained at Candas, and on the following day alighted at Abeele, just N. of " the mountains," and marched 7 miles to La Clytte, no nicer abode than it had been when the 2nd Battalion were there in 1917, but a shade drier. On the next day the meagre War Diary notes : " Went into line at Hill 60 " (grave of brave Borderers in 1915), and, for the following eleven days, " in line at Hill 60." Behind this contribution to history (the remaining entries for the month being equally informative but not always accurate) lurks a drama, second only to the Long Trek in thrills. The reader will have been saying to himself, that a division which survived the Somme in March and went to Flanders in April was leaving the frying-pan for the fire. He will remember what happened to the 1st Battalion in the Lys on the 11th and what chaos the 2nd found S. of the Forêt de Nieppe on the 12th. His thoughts will instantly fly N. to the Passchendaele salient, he will wonder what happened up there when the Germans followed up the " Michael " assault with the " Georgette " and rammed at Hazebrouck and the channel ports. A word, therefore, about the situation : The Somme offensive had spent itself by 4th April. It was no doubt a " dazzling feat of arms * and will ever be so regarded in the world's history. Strategically we did not gain, what might have been hoped on 23rd, 24th, and 25th." †

* " Glänzende Waffentat " (Ludendorff's *Erinnerungen*, p. 482).

† *Ibid.*

10 April 1918.

Then came the critical battle of Arras, which ended in the repulse of the Germans on the 28th and the retention of the Vimy Ridge.* But the enemy had far from used up his reserves, and on 9th April he thrust once more on the Lys. Estaires, Armentières, Merville, and Messines Ridge were gone before the 12th, and that very night the withdrawal from the dear-won Passchendaele Ridge was begun. It is in this atmosphere of defeat and instability that the 9th Division and 6th K.O.S.B. entered the northern arena.

They were in the IX. Corps (Hamilton-Gordon) of Plumer's Second Army, and they relieved the 1st Australian Division in the forward slope (facing Zandvoorde and S.E.) of that ridge that had proved such a bane to our tenure of Hill 60 in April to May 1915. The K.O.S.B. sector is easily found. The visitor to Hill 60 † has only to take the high road to Zandvoorde past Klein Zillebeke and pause at the bottom of the hollow between the Wytschaete-Ghéluvelt-Passchendaele Ridge and the hummock on which Zandvoorde stands. He is between two scrubby woods—Belgian Wood on S. and Bulgar Wood on N.. The canal from Ypres to Comines is about a mile to the S.W.. It was here the 6th K.O.S.B. held the line—a series of pill-box outposts, of which Brig.-Gen. Croft thoroughly disapproved, with entrances facing the wrong way and therefore apt to be death-traps, and a supporting trench line higher up on the ridge. On their R. were the 11th R.S. beyond the canal and in front of what once was Hollebeke. The divisional sector was unpleasantly long—some 4,000 yards—when an extra bit had been taken over from the 19th Division ‡ on the 9/10th April. Battalion H.Q. were at Hill 60 in tunnelled dugouts, and when not holding the line the battalion sheltered there.

On the morning of the 10th the enemy began shelling the divisional front. After 1 p.m. he assaulted the divisional front on both sides of the canal. He had never forgotten or forgiven the loss of the Messines Ridge in 1917, and Mont Kemmel had been a thorn in his flesh since 1914. If he could storm the mountains, the Ypres salient and the entire maritime plain E. and N. of St. Omer would have to be abandoned.

It was a tricky situation for the 6th K.O.S.B., full of new recruits §—fine stuff, but young and inexperienced. However, to their credit, they did not lose more than two posts, which were recaptured

* See part dealing with 7/8th Battalion.

† Hill 60 is painfully popular. There is an ample supply of beer, cigarettes, and picture postcards to be had at a price.

‡ Praised along with the 9th for valour in the March retreat by Sir D. Haig.

§ The April reinforcements totalled no less than 518 O.R. (27th I.B.W.D.).

10–16 April 1918. — at night * with the aid of the gunners and M.G. Companies and took heavy toll of the assailants. The attack never became serious against their main line. But a grievous loss befell them. Their acting C.O., the *fidus Achates* of their absent C.O., and himself a splendid soldier, was killed at Hill 60 along with his A/Adjutant, 2nd Lieut. T. R. Stoney.† And danger threatened from the S.. The 11th R.S. (under Lieut.-Col. Sir J. Campbell) had more trouble with the outposts, all of which were overwhelmed but held their ground on the main line. The peril lay in an outflanking movement which threatened the important back area between the R.S. and the canal represented by the ruins of the late King Leopold's White Château, its grounds and stables (all in ruins, of course). The timely arrival of two companies of the 12th R.S., of the 9th (Pioneers) Seaforths, and finally of the 7th Seaforths, A/Lieut.-Col. (afterwards Brevet Lieut.-Col.) the Hon. D. Bruce, restored the situation. Attacked at dawn on the 11th in the sunk Dammstrasse the 7th Seaforths accounted for many of the enemy.

All the same, Capt. Cockburn, now in command, was ordered to abandon his posts and to treat the main line as the outpost line and hold the reserve line as his main line. A similar adjustment was made farther S.. But that night, 11/12th, 2nd Lieut. T. Archer (afterwards killed in action on the 25th) showed the offensive spirit by taking a patrol to "Potsdam Farm," one of the old posts, and bringing back an officer and one man as prisoners. A similar raid against the Hessian posts, 300 yards or so S.W. of Potsdam, led by 2nd Lieut. J. P. Stark, found the enemy alert. Stark was badly wounded, and died in Germany on 3rd September 1918.‡

This line held until events elsewhere forced a withdrawal on the 15/16th April to the back line. This was quietly carried out in spite of the nearness of the enemy, and it was matter of favourable comment that the Borderer patrols went out as usual.§ The K.O.S.B. on 16th occupied a line from the Bluff, a spoil heap on the N. bank of the canal 1,000 yards S.W. of Hill 60, up to and including that famous mound. It was, needless to say, a favourite target; but the Australians had put their heads as well as their hearts into their spade work, and left on the surface an innocent blankness on which the observer could spot no special mark at which to aim, and the heavy shelling at random did little damage to human life. As for

* Croft, p. 215.

† (6) Innes-Browne, Ambrose Robin, C.M.G., D.S.O., T/Major, A/Lieut.-Col., killed in action 10/4/18 (Official Death Roll; T. R. Stoney, Lieut., killed in action 10/4/18.

‡ 27th I.B.W.D. and Official Death Roll.

§ 27th I.B. Report of 4th May 1918.

the "hill," it had long ago lost its looks and had no beauty to spoil. 16 April 1918.

This was the day (16th) on which Wytschaete fell.* So the steadiness of the 9th Division was the more appreciated. The "backs to the wall" call had been made, and this was their response. The K.O.S.B. stuck it out till relieved on 19/20th, and the only mishap—a lost post—was made good and a prisoner taken. The relievers were troops of the 7th Division, and the K.O.S.B. retired to Dickebusch, then to Ouderdom † N. of La Clytte, and on 22nd forward to the brigade reserve line known as "Vierstraat" (after the village on the Ypres–Neuve Église road) on the spur running from Mont Kemmel to Vierstraat. It was on 25th April that Prince Rupprecht and his Bavarians made the tremendous effort against Mont Kemmel, Kemmel village, and Spanbroekmolen on the Wytschaete Ridge, which seemed to be the *coup de grâce* to the Allies and in reality was the effort in which the Germans shot their bolt.‡

They had had to fight hard to work their way out of the Lys Valley. The stories of the 34th and 29th Divisions (the 88th Brigade, of which was attached to Gen. Nicholson) give an idea of the determined resistance put up in the battle of Bailleul. But Bailleul fell on the 15th April, and with the capture of Wytschaete the scene was staged for the crowning mercy.

"Following upon a very violent bombardment at about 5 a.m. the enemy attacked the French (reinforcements from Foch's reserve) and British positions (from Bailleul to the Ypres–Comines Canal) with nine divisions, of which five were fresh and one other had been but lightly engaged. . . . At that date the British right flank lay on the Messines–Kemmel road at a point about half-way between Kemmel and Wytschaete. . . . The weight of the attack in the British sector fell on the 9th Division and attached troops of the 49th Division. . . ." §

The front of the division was not satisfactory. In fact, a British counter-attack was in contemplation for the 26th. The Germans, by possession of Wytschaete, Madeslede Farm, 400 yards W. of it, and Spanbroekmolen, could make things wretchedly uncomfortable for troops in the lower, overlooked line—La Gache Farm, Petit

* How nearly it was recovered by superb fighting on the part of 7th Seaforths, with aid of a smoke barrage, can be read in Ewing at p. 305, and Croft at p. 220.

† When at Ouderdom, 2nd Lieut. Archer and 50 O.R. had the honour of parading for inspection by M. Clémenceau (27th I.B.W.D.). The famous statesman and patriot died in November 1929.

‡ Ludendorff, *op. cit.*, p. 489.

§ Sir D. Haig's despatch.

25 April 1918. Bois, Somer Farm, and so on to Dammstrasse. But the German attack on the 25th afforded a different solution. At 4 a.m. the K.O.S.B., in support at Vierstraat and in brigade reserve at Beaver Corner, 900 yards N. of Kemmel village, an outpost in front of the last, La Clytte or "Cheapside," system of defence to which Brig.-Gen. Croft attached much importance, heard the thunder of the guns. At 7 a.m., although the 12th R.S. reported their line at La Gache intact, they became painfully conscious that something was wrong in the French sector on the R. of that battalion. It was only too true. Kemmel Hill and village were stormed, and the Germans poured through the gap. The 12th R.S. were surrounded and massacred at leisure. The two forward companies of K.O.S.B., fighting often back to back, were killed or captured, but not till they had taken heavy toll of the enemy. Battalion H.Q. were rushed, and Major H. S. Wilkie, the C.O., and Lieut. Archibald, A/Adjutant, were seen to fall. All seemed lost. But there were still A and C, all that was left of the 6th K.O.S.B., under Capt. R. B. Cundle, now C.O.. These retired upon the Cheapside line, to which reinforcements were hurried to strengthen the 9th K.O.Y.L.I. of the 21st Division, then in occupation. Two companies of the 11th R.S. were hurriedly flung in. The 8th B.W. came up from Ouderdom, and there were welcome "outsiders" besides. The gap was stopped. But the K.O.S.B. were not content with passivity. Capt. Cundle organized a counter-attack. Thanks largely to the remarkable dash of Lieut. G. Ainslie (who died of wounds received in the August fighting), and of 2nd Lieut. C. G. Capey, only eight days at the front, on his first visit, who stalked and "bagged" a nasty M.G. with two parties, each six strong, this well-planned raid took 58 prisoners. For this feat the two officers were awarded the M.C.. The Black Watch went one better, for they took 67 prisoners in a similar way. The conquerors of Kemmel were not all heroes.

That night the Borderers were relieved and withdrew to trenches near Ouderdom. On the 26/27th they went to Poperinghe, and on 28th to Watou, on the French frontier W. of "Pop".. They had experienced a terrible ordeal at the end of five weeks' almost continuous fighting. They had 21 officers and 413 O.R. casualties during April. Besides Innes-Browne, Stark, and Stoney, Lieuts. H. L. Armstrong and C. Gardiner of the 4th Battalion, and N. I. Bryce Smith and T. A. Archer, were killed on the 25th. Besides Wilkie and Archibald, Capt. J. Findlay, 2nd Lieuts. G. Penman, Livingstone, Farquharson, and J. P. Hodges * were reported wounded and missing. Capt. Cundle was wounded, but remained at his post. Also

* In point of fact he was k. in a. on 25th in this battle (Official Death Roll).

wounded were 2nd Lieuts. D. Murray, P. Ormiston, H. Fraser, and D. M'Phedran. T. C. Lamb was gassed.* Of the O.R. more than half were missing, representing the surrounded companies B and D. 25 April 1918.

By the end of the month the Flanders offensive died down. The Ypres salient was flattened out and the town was almost in the front line. But the main range of the mountains still held. Mont Rouge and Mont Noir remained intact, and the line ran through Locre between those heights and Mont Kemmel S. westwards in front of Strazeele and the Forêt de Nieppe. The grit, determination, and power of resistance of the 9th Division in April 1918 have received such praises that to repeat them here is needless. Foch, Haig, and all the intermediate commanders testified their admiration.† Perhaps the following from Sir D. Haig to " Winston " strikes the most intimate note. " I hear your old division, under Tudor, has been doing wonders." ‡

Part II

The Lull before the Storm

From the tower of St. Bertin's church in St. Omer one can see miles of country N. of conspicuous Cassel. With a little imagination and a map one can trace the 6th K.O.S.B. moving by easy stages in May, " stepping westward " from Watou through the flats, to get their turn of the real country, with hills and dales and woods S.W. of St. Omer. The names of the stages are becoming familiar—Herzeele, Winnezeele, Wormhoudt, and Zeggers Cappel. Pantgat is new, about 9 miles N.N.E. of St. Omer. There, on the 5th, there was a brigade church parade, but the Diary says nothing about the 124th Psalm. Two days at Buyscheure, N. of the marshes in close view of St. Omer, were followed by a route march of 19 miles through the ancient town and on *via* Wizernes to a camp N. of Lumbres. Here a profitable fortnight was spent, and musketry figured largely in the training programme. Brig.-Gen. Croft, in his racy narrative, tells us that hedge-fighting was practised from the point of view of offence and defence as a preliminary for the Meteren sector. On the 24th the battalion moved (presumably by train) to Hondeghem (to be their abode for some time when " out "), just N. of Hazebrouck, where they camped. On the last day of the month they relieved the 7th Seaforths on the front opposite Meteren, within 3 miles of Bailleul. May 1918.

* Casualties from 27th I.B.W.D..

† See Ewing, pp. 314–316. Croft, p. 228.

‡ *World Crisis*, vol. ii. p. 438.

June–August 1918.

On 1st June Lieut-.Col. Smyth was welcomed back, succeeding Lieut.-Col. J. Colchester Wemyss. On the N. towered "the mountains," Mont des Cats being specially prominent. Behind was Flêtre with its thick-walled, safe château for the supports. The country was covered with standing corn in fields intersected by thick hedges. As compared with recent times it was quiet on the whole, for in spite of alarms of a fresh German push, apparently well founded, to judge by the growth of huge dumps, nothing was done on a large scale.

The colonel was full of his usual go. The corps commander, Gen. de Lisle, was restless energy in person; so, no doubt, were the youthful troops who replaced the wastage of April. Raids were the order of the day, but the first raid, led by 2nd Lieuts. Alexander and Martin, on the night 2/3rd June was not a success, being caught in a hostile barrage and resulting in 15 casualties. On the following night the battalion withdrew to work on the support-line defences, and on 11/12th was back at Hondeghem.

On the 22nd a very neat bit of cutting out under Lieut. Caven, as the result of good scouting by Sergt. G. Smith and Pte. W. Wilson, secured 3 prisoners without the enemy knowing anything about it. The K.O.S.B. took no more part than to be ready at Flêtre, when the Highlanders took the pulverized site of Meteren on 19th July. But the boys * showed they were of the right kind when they beat off a raiding party in the early hours of the 25th, taking 2 prisoners, and another stronger raid early the next morning. A scrap on the 31st between rival scouts resulted in 8 casualties, but the Borderers claimed to have killed many Germans in hand-to-hand fighting.

Minden Day was spent quietly at Flêtre, but August 1918 is a month to be remembered in the first place for the inspection † of the battalion by H.M. King George V. at La Bréarde near Hazebrouck, and for the action on 18th August at Hoegenacker Mill, in conjunction with the 1st Battalion, the 9th and 29th Divisions fighting side by side. The purpose and setting of that success have already been treated in the 1st Battalion story. It was Gen. Cayley's opinion that the 9th carried out their share of the operation brilliantly.‡ Nothing had been left to chance. Even the trenches were camouflaged § with grey sacking stuff stretched on poles, with

* The expression "boy scouts" would have been no misnomer. They had to do a great deal of patrolling.

† 2nd Lieut. Capey has still preserved the holograph orders written out by Col. Smyth. The number of clean suits available did not exceed fifty.

‡ *The Story of the 29th Division*, p. 200.

§ 2nd Lieut. Capey made his copy of the elaborate corps instructions available.

[*Imperial War Museum Photograph. Copyright reserved.*

6TH K.O.S.B., 9TH DIVISION, MARCHING PAST H.M. THE KING, NEAR LA BREARDE, 6TH AUGUST 1918.

a black stripe down the centre and sprinkled with earth at the edges to make the trenches of assembly look empty from the air. The barrage after a somewhat ragged start was a perfect "Tudor" smoke and H.E. specimen, and if the enemy had not returned such a vigorous counterblast casualties would have been fewer. It was a de Lisle touch that the men were to count ten after the barrage opened and then go forward. As it was, the 6th K.O.S.B., although far from free from the fault of bunching and straggling and losing direction, and at one time having to be recalled to enable the final objective to be bombarded, took the assigned objectives, were duly leapfrogged by the senior battalion, and dug in on the ground won. Late that night touch was secured with the 1st Battalion, who had gone on and taken Outtersteene. Another feature was surprise, secured (1) by the absence of a preliminary barrage, and (2) by the selection of an hour—11 a.m.—most unusual for an attack. The L. flank was guarded by a scatter of M.G. bullets, "a wall of steel," * over the area from which a hostile counter-attack might come, and by the 9th S.R. (which with the 2nd R.S.F. and the remnant of the S. Africans formed the 28th I.B., from which the 9th S.R. were on loan), who formed a defensive flank, as the gap between the advancing 9th and the stationary French widened. The reconstructed 12th R.S. † carried for the two battalions of assault, the 6th K.O.S.B. on R. and the 11th R.S. on the L.. The only sign of a hold-up was the recall mentioned above near Terrapin Farm, the S. limit of the attack. At the start when the counter-barrage was troublesome early in the day a German M.G. was very active, but a favourite device of Gen. Croft's silenced it. A Lewis gunner, name unknown, rushed it, firing his gun from the hip.

18 Aug. 1918.

All the tactical objectives were gained. Both the divisions were virtually "through." But they rested content with what they had secured by the success of the plan, viz. a ridge giving observation of miles of German defences. The K.O.S.B. took at least 100 of the 297 prisoners taken by the division, along with *materiel* to correspond. The cost was 7 officers and 168 O.R. casualties (25 k., 4 m., 139 w.), of the former 2nd Lieuts. C. M. Gall ‡ and E. I. Martin ‡ were killed; Capt. G. Ainslie, M.C., received wounds of which he died on 21st August; 2nd Lieut. C. G. Capey, M.C., was wounded along with 2nd Lieuts. Urquhart, Penman, and Sinclair.

The 9th Division were relieved on 25th August, and the 6th

* Croft, *op. cit.*, p. 244.
† They had been annihilated at Kemmel.
‡ Official Death Roll.

28 Sept. 1918. K.O.S.B., who had been relieved in part by 12th R.S. and in part by 1st K.O.S.B., withdrew to Meteren, then to Hondeghem, and finally trained to a remote camp in the Racquinghem area, between Aire and St. Omer, called Pont d'Asquin, where they were reviewed by Gen. Tudor on 27th, and finally settled down at Campagne hard by. It was then that the brave S. Africans said farewell, and were replaced by the Royal Newfoundland Regiment, a unit * with a fine record.

Part III

The Finish

Hoegenacker Mill had revealed certain defects in the tactical standard of the 9th at this stage. The time spent at Campagne was devoted to the elimination of these, so far as not interfered with by the weather, which had begun to break. The move E. began by a route march to Lederzeele, N. of St. Omer, near Rubrouck on September 12th. Next day the battalion settled down for a week at Zeggers Cappel. On the 20th they trained to "Pop.," near which they camped till the eve of the last Battle of Ypres, fought under the supreme command of the King of the Belgians, in Plumer's Second Army and Jacob's II. Corps.

On the opening day—the 28th—the K.O.S.B. were in the reserve brigade and were the reserve battalion in it. It was a dreadful day of rain when they detrained at Ypres and ploughed along as best they could in the direction of Bécelaere (*i.e.* due E.) in the wake and turmoil of the fight.

They could get no farther than the Butte de Polygone, a little N. of horrible Polderhoek, that day on which the 29th Division on the R. of the 9th took Ghéluvelt, and the Belgians on the L. made good the Broodseinde Ridge S. of Passchendaele. The 9th therefore devoted the afternoon to the capture of Bécelaere on the E. edge of the historic plateau between Broodseinde and Ghéluvelt. The R.S. battalions of the 27th I.B. took the village after stiff fighting.

On the 29th, soaked to the skin, the division resumed the advance, and two companies (C and D) of our battalion, pushed into the line by Col. Smyth, helped to prevent the Germans from rallying on the wired position known as Flanderen Stellung and to capture and mop up Dadizeele, 3 miles E. of Bécelaere. Nearly 10 miles in two days was a novelty in the salient. And this in spite of paucity of roads and almost indescribable congestion of traffic. Off the roads—we know what that was like. On the 30th, a pouring wet day, the

* See *The Story of the 29th Division.*

9th had to mark time, as it was ahead of its neighbours—the Belgians and the 36th (Ulster) Division who had replaced the 29th. 28 Sept. 1918.

It was probably in this sense that Col. Smyth described the 28/29th as "great days." It was not that the 6th K.O.S.B. were walking through hosts of Germans. It was that the great move had begun—a new world was opening up.

On 1st October he commanded his last action as C.O. of the 6th K.O.S.B. And through no fault of his it was what he called a "dud show." Confronting the Royal Scots and Borderers was the (inhabited) village of Lédeghem beyond the Roulers–Ménin road and just behind a light railway. The K.O.S.B. were on the R. and the 12th R.S. on the L.. Orders for the attack came late on the 30th September.

At 5.30 a.m. the attack began under a smoke barrage, but the K.O.S.B. came at once under heavy M.G. fire from a height S. of Dadizeele labelled Hill 41. The Ulstermen had at one time secured it on the 29th but had been driven off. Two farms and an undetected position on the railway were particularly pestiferous. To meet this A and C were sent down the railway to try and storm the hill, but heavy fire stopped all progress. At this moment the enemy were seen—about a battalion strong—gathering for a counter-attack. Smyth made swift and suitable arrangements for meeting this, but a sudden, fierce attack by the 1st R.I.F., once of the 29th now of the 36th, was delivered on Hill 41, which distracted the enemy's attention, enabling the Borderers to make their hitherto exposed R. flank secure and recover some lost ground. But advance was out of the question that day, and the failure of the K.O.S.B. reacted on the R.S., who had splendidly carried Lédeghem but were forced out of it by the second of two powerful counter-attacks. Lédeghem was eventually taken by the 29th Division on the 14th.* With co-ordination and co-operation it would have fallen on the 1st. But it is easy to be wise after the event.

The K.O.S.B. were taken out of the line to Dadizeele, where they parted from one of the best C.O.s who commanded any unit of the regiment in the war. Capt. J. W. Thompson who had served under Smyth in 1917 (in sending a letter from Smyth to himself as characteristic of the man) wrote to Major Ewing "I take it, no story of the 6th would be complete without him."

No doubt a soldier of his calibre would find greater scope in a brigade (he was appointed B.G.C. 93rd I.B.), but when he wrote on 22nd October his heart was still with his Borderers. Here is a sentence showing what that five wound-stripe soldier liked in the

* *The Story of the 29th Division*, pp. 211 and 212.

Oct. 1918. way of comrades. " C.S.M. Craig rolled up again after an adventurous career. He came out to France as a corporal marked ' B '. He was posted to a B battalion of the H.L.I. and refused to go. Eventually he was reclassified as ' A ' and posted to the 7th. He jumped off the train and came to us, and when I last saw him he was a sergeant in charge of No. 13 platoon."

Smyth had only one arm, but he knew how to use it, and his murderers were well advised to sneak up to him in overpowering strength and catch him unawares. As long as the 6th K.O.S.B. lives in men's memories it will be associated with this great gentleman and warrior.

To attempt to follow the story of the vast *débâcle* of the Germans would mean to lose sight of the 6th K.O.S.B.. It is enough to fix our eyes on Cuerne just N. of Courtrai on the L. bank and Harlebeke on the other bank of the Lys.

On the 14th October the battalion bussed from " Pop." to Keiberg on the Roulers–Ménin road, and the following evening entered Cuerne and occupied an outpost line E. of it.

On the night of the 16/17th the 6th K.O.S.B. crossed the Lys by R.E. bridges and successfully attacked the Courtrai–Harlebeke road at 8 p.m.. Harlebeke itself was too hard a nut to crack, and by Gen. Croft's orders Lieut.-Col. R. F. Ker, once a subaltern in the 9th, who had won his way by sheer ability to command, at the early age of 23, the very battalion in which he had seen all his service at the front, formed a bridgehead, which was held with three companies (C being sent back after suffering in an attempt to surround Harlebeke) until relieved in due course by the 2nd Hants of the 88th I.B. early on the 18th. A counter-attack, in which, unfortunately, 2nd Lieut. J. A. Dowens * was killed and Lieut. Dunne and 2nd Lieut. Mayall were wounded, was beaten off during the night. At 5 a.m. on the 17th dismounted cavalrymen of the German 7th Cavalry Division made a more formidable attack. The centre company of the bridgehead, B, was broken and its gallant leader, Capt. A. Durward, M.C., killed, but the flanking companies, A and D, charged with the bayonet, " a weapon to which the Borderers were addicted," † B quickly rallied, and the enemy was repulsed, leaving 30 slain. Capt. White, O.C. D (of the H.L.I.‡), in the opinion of all greatly distinguished himself in this charge. To make assurance doubly sure two companies of 12th Royal Scots crossed the river under fire. On reading *Three Years with the 9th Division* and the War Diary I am left with the feeling that the situation was not nearly

* Of the 4th Batt. (Official Death Roll).

† Croft, *op. cit.*, p. 276. ‡ Col. Smyth's letter of 22/10/18.

so perilous as it was described in *The Story of the 29th Division*.* Arrangements had been made for supporting fire of all arms, and aeroplanes dropped not bombs but nice things like food and unexploded ammunition and cheery messages. Some Royal Scots actually carried ammunition over dry, above their heads. When the battalion came out they were singing, as well they might, adds Brig.-Gen. Croft in the Bde. War Diary.

Oct.–Nov. 1918.

On " relief," not " extrication," these Borderers hovered about the back of the front at Heule, Laaga Cappel, and Cappel St. Catherine, till on 20th the Lys was peacefully crossed and on 21st they billeted in Vichte *en route* for the Scheldt, which, however, they only crossed peacefully later on. A neat little operation on the 22nd—the day on which Smyth wrote his letter to Thompson—ended the fighting of the 6th K.O.S.B..

The 9th Division were between the 29th (on the R.) and the 36th Divisions. The plan of attack, timed for 9 a.m., was as follows: The brigade, from assembly point 1,500 yards W. of Vichte, were to advance under cover of smoke till the Railway Station marked the proximity of the village. They were then to deploy and advance supported by a barrage for 500 yards, when the 11th R.S. were to assault a height called Hill 50, half-way to Ingoyghem, a village 3 miles from the Scheldt. Courtrai was by this time 4 or 5 miles behind. The K.O.S.B. were then to go through and attack Ingoyghem. In part the attack came off as planned. The 11th R.S. did take Vichte and the K.O.S.B. saw to its being mopped up. But on continuing the advance the R.S. were held up by M.G. fire from " Klijtberg " and Hill 50, and could not reach the latter. That the K.O.S.B. did storm it was due to the effective co-operation of a battery of that wonderful brigade, Col. MacLean's 50th R.F.A.. Ker led his men up the hill and threw out feelers towards Ingoyghem. But that village and Ooteghem were strongly held. The Brigadier called off the assault and the 6th K.O.S.B. fired no more shots in anger and sheathed their bayonets except for ceremonial. The casualties for October are severe. Besides those mentioned, 2nd Lieut. J. Wedderburn Maxwell of the 3rd Battalion was killed on the 1st at Lédeghem.† The list of wounded in the 27th I.B. Diary does not give the dates when the wounds were received. The Battalion War Diary is curiously uncommunicative. The wounded were Capts. Chapman ‡ and H. P. Whitworth ; Lieuts. S. E. Simson and

* Pages 215–216. Ewing seems to incline to the view it was too risky, and he was Adjutant, but his C.O., Col. Ker, remains convinced that his position was secure, and that great advantage would have come of developing the situation before the enemy rallied.

† Official Death Roll.

‡ O.C. D Company. Lieut.-Col. Smyth's letter of 22/10/18.

Dec. 1918. C. W. Boyd; 2nd Lieuts. C. Hawthorn, D.C.M., M.M., J. Wyper, A. Scotland, W. R. S. M'Millan, R. Hamilton, W. Whyte (stayed on duty), and T. Blair. The O.R. casualties are thus made up: 34 k.; 230 w.; 75 m..

In less than a month they and their comrades had covered 26 miles of hard-fought territory. The Flanders fighting has less spectacular features than the great drive in more spacious France. But it was the real thing. It hammered the enemy into the spirit of surrender. Little more remains to be told. The noble King of the Belgians and his Queen reviewed the 9th Division on the 5th of November at Hulste * aerodrome near Harlebeke, and said many kind and gracious things about the division.

The news of the Armistice on the 11th was felt most profoundly. A thanksgiving service was conducted by the chaplain, Capt. the Rev. R. G. M'Connochie, M.A., C.F..

After reorganizing in the Cuerne area, the 6th Battalion began moving towards Germany in the middle of November. Five officers and 20 O.R. attended the formal entry of King Albert into Brussels, where they received an ecstatic welcome.

On 4th December the frontier was crossed at 9.45 a.m. at Cornelimünster. On the 10th they reached Cologne *via* Düren and Modrath. On the 13th December 1918 the 9th Division, including the 6th K.O.S.B., saluted Sir Charles Fergusson, the successful divisional commander of the 5th Division at Le Cateau, the successful corps commander of the XVII. A.C., and now governor of Cologne, a Scot of the Scots, as they marched in pelting rain but with jaunty step to the strain of the pipes over the Mülheim Boat Bridge to Wald in the bridgehead. The 1st Battalion were crossing the Hohenzollern Bridge just about the same time. It was a Red Letter Day in the history of the regiment, a fitting moment for saying farewell to a battalion that had all through those years of dedication, preparation, struggle, anguish, reverse, and success, been worthy of the parent regiment, the land in which that regiment was raised, and the Empire which it helped to save.

* The 7/8th Battalion was also present.

BOOK V

THE SEVENTH AND EIGHTH BATTALIONS

AND

THE SEVENTH/EIGHTH BATTALION

CHAPTER I

PREPARATION

THE eager response to Lord Kitchener's appeal led to a miscalculation as to the number of battalions that K.O.S.B. resources could maintain at strength in a war of duration. It might have been better if the 8th had been the Reserve Battalion, with a sufficient complement of men to secure more commodious surroundings and a readier ear than the exiguous 9th ever succeeded in getting. Only one instead of two battalions would have been bled white at Loos, and the training standard of drafts might have been at a higher level. As it was, the 7th and 8th Battalions were like one large battalion. A stranger could not tell them apart, nor separate the flocks of Padres Symington (Presbyterian) or Forbes (Episcopal Church in Scotland) into their " 7th " or " 8th " component parts. They were twins, coming into being on 12th September 1914, when the establishment of the 6th Battalion was complete. They shared the same quarters at Bordon, they went through the same transformation process from civilians into soldiers. Each was commanded by Borderer officers of distinction and character, in the persons of Lieut.-Col. G. de W. Verner (7th) and Lieut.-Col. T. B. Sellar (8th). Both shared in the crumbs that fell from the K.1 tables, those D.P. rifles, antiquated tunics and headgear, then real rifles and real uniforms. They cannot be separated, either when inspected by H.M. King George, while still in mufti shortly after formation, or by Lord Kitchener and M. Clémenceau in a drenching snowstorm in uniforms of divers hues. So long as they maintained separate existences they were in the same brigade, the 46th of the 15th (Scottish) Division, formed as soon as the 9th was complete. In the same brigade were the 10th Cameronians and the 12th H.L.I.. 1914–15.

The experiences of the 46th I.B. in England do not differ to any extent in character from those of the 27th. One day was like another, and the work was unceasing and strenuous.

On 20th February, while the 44th (Highland) and 45th I.B. moved with D.H.Q. to Salisbury Plain, the K.O.S.B. battalions

1915. and the 10th S.R. moved with Brigade H.Q. (Brig.-Gen. A. G. Duff of the Black Watch commanding) to Winchester, the 12th H.L.I. being at Romsey. Life in billets is infinitely pleasanter but somewhat more distracting than life in huts or tents or barracks. It was a necessity in France. In England during the long training it was apt to result in soft feet and soft bodies. At any rate, in spring, when the division moved to Marlborough, the 46th found the change to Parkhouse Camp, Bulford, on Salisbury Plain near Stonehenge, both abrupt and beneficial. Soon rifles were forthcoming, and real bayonets and even real machine-guns, and a consciousness of division as well as of brigade and battalion began to dawn. Although rather less than half * the men came from Scotland, all were proud of belonging to a Scottish division. A sufficiency of pipes was soon forthcoming through the generosity of officers, and the men began to feel and to look like the soldiers they proved themselves to be.

A final spell at Chiseldon, just S. of Swindon, finished the training, and they were inspected by His Majesty once more on Sidbury Hill, between Perham Down and Tidworth, on 21st June 1915. There were no unfits, and the only people who missed that inspiring event were those on final home leave. Yes! it was now known that the 15th (Scottish) Division was soon to sail for the Western Front, where, as they well knew, the 9th (Scottish) Division had been for some time.

On 4th July orders reached the 7th to mobilize for embarkation. On 8th July, according to both diaries, the move southward began. It was during the period just preceding the 8th that bands of very displeased looking young men in the garb of 2nd Lieuts. used to arrive at the gaunt camp at Stobs, to which the 9th (Reserve) Battalion K.O.S.B. had moved from Dorchester in June. These were the K.O.S.B. officers supernumerary to establishment, who had hitherto been trained in the 15th Division, but were not yet (they thought never) to go to France. They little knew what was in store for them in the post-Loos battles. Meanwhile, it may be admitted that their lot was not too attractive at Stobs. The 9th had supplied at least one draft to the Mediterranean, and, although recruits were still coming in, there were far too few men for the numerous officers. The additional supernumeraries of the 7th and 8th were, along with others of other units, in a similar plight,

* This is the conclusion drawn from an analysis of the Death Roll. The 7th were just about half-and-half of Scottish and non-Scottish birth. The 8th were well over a half non-Scottish—about 3 to 2. After amalgamation the proportion is the other way, 3 Scottish to 2 non-Scottish, much the same as the regulars.

isolated and drilled by themselves. Had more advanced instruction been available, it would have been less damping. Meanwhile the selected ones entrained at Chiseldon for Folkestone and Southampton. The transport of both battalions and two companies of the 8th went by the latter route and sailed to Havre. The majority sailed in the *Invicta* to Boulogne and camped at Ostrohove. It was like the 6th Battalion's experience over again. The whole battalion joined up as one at Pont-de-Briques, and spent their first night in billets at Zutkerque, just S. of Audruicq Station, on the railway between Calais and St. Omer. July 1915.

It is at this moment that the personnel and strength become of interest. Both battalions were well up to strength, *i.e.* with over 900 rank and file. The officers were as follows: Lieut.-Col. Verner * was C.O. of the 7th, and Major G. S. D. Forbes, C.M.G., D.S.O., was Second-in-Command, the other majors being B. J. B. Coulson and T. A. Glenny.* The four captains are headed by M. F. B. Dennis, one of the finest officers of the New Armies, and include F. R. Hutt,* P. Newton,* and T. Blackburn; Lieuts. J. B. Waters, P. L. Lethbridge,* Adjutant J. D. Denniston, C. B. Bird, and A. K. Gilmour; 2nd Lieuts. J. M. Sellar,* T. A. Stewart, J. Frew, J. Seafield-Grant, J. Scott,* J. W. Jarvis, * W. Haddon,* J. R. Milne, T. K. Newbigging, J. L. S. Allan,* F. M. C. Tod,* M. W. Duirs,* W. G. Kerr, A. S. M. Tuck, M. C. de B. Young,* and C. H. M. Horne,† transport officer. The Q.M. was Lieut. F. Hopkins. The chaplain (Pres.) was Capt. the Rev. T. S. Symington, M.A., C.F..

The 8th Battalion War Diary was started and maintained by Lieut.-Col. T. B. Sellar at a standard of completeness and interest which is without a rival among K.O.S.B. diaries. That excellent little book, *A Border Battalion*, privately printed by T. N. Foulis, is manifestly the result of a close study of the 7th, 8th, and 7/8th diaries. Not that the short 7th Diary is not good too. It is that the 8th is super-excellent. The officers are arranged in the 8th by companies, and every warrant officer and N.C.O. is named. Meantime they are given in order of rank. Besides the C.O. there were Major G. M. Hannay, Second-in-Command, and Major H. M. Forster;* Capts. J. S. M'Arthur, Adjutant H. T. Cruickshank * (of the 1st Battalion), H. P. Hart, S. S. Lang, H. H. Smith,† J. P. Larkin, and W. W. Home; Lieuts. C. H. Crawshaw,‡ J. R. Lear-

* Killed at Loos or died of wounds in consequence.

† Killed in action as temporary Capt. 27th January 1916.

‡ Who distinguished himself as C.O. and Second-in-Command of the 1st Battalion in 1918.

July–Aug. 1915. — month, A. F. C. Hartley, C. W. Stump, W. Thomson, P. M. Ross, P. C. Drummond,* V. N. Surtees (M.G. officer), H. F. Brigstocke (transport officer), and J. Goss, the Q.M.; 2nd Lieuts. W. G. Douglas, I. Ardill,* W. G. Herbertson,* C. K. Thursby-Pelham, J. D. Brown, H. G. Mitchell, S. G. M'Clelland,* and J. S. Wyper. The Rev. E. A. Forbes, M.A., was chaplain (Epis.), and Lieut. S. Jackson, R.A.M.C., was M.O..

By the 17th July both battalions were in Allouagne, S.W. of Béthune, and there they remained till 3rd August. They had stayed at Zutkerque from the 12th to the 15th, and had marched in two days to Allouagne halting at Arques just S.E. of St. Omer, St. Hilaire (8th), and Lambres (7th), just S. of Aire—places familiar once to many sojourning or passing Borderers. They experienced the usual dust and new-boot trouble. Once at Allouagne a new stage began. They were only 14 miles from the trenches. The boom of the guns was distinctly audible. Parties visited the front for attachment, just as the 6th had done. The first casualty showed that German shells were no respecters of persons. Major Forbes was mortally wounded on 21st—a serious handicap for the 7th. The issue of gas helmets was another reminder that the business on which they were engaged was serious. Their original Brig.-Gen. Duff was replaced late in July by Brig.-Gen. T. G. Matheson of the Coldstream Guards, who commanded the 46th I.B. at Loos and the Somme. He inspected the 7th and 8th K.O.S.B. on 30th July at the neighbouring village of Lozinghem. The training during July does not seem to have been of an ambitious nature—physical drill, gas-helmet drill, route marches, saluting, bayonet exercise. With Mazingarbe reached on 3rd August a farther stage began. The Borderers were within reach of the front line in one march. After fatigues, not so heavy as nasty, the 7th entered the S. Maroc sector and the 8th the N. Maroc sector on 10th August 1915. They were just S. of the sector held by them for the battle. The troops relieved were the 47th (London) Division—one of the *élite* of the territorial divisions. The 15th Division formed the R. of General Rawlinson's IV. Corps in Sir D. Haig's First Army and beyond them on the R. were the French. On the L. were the 1st Division. It was a cheerless mining district—bleak country in the foothills of the great bluff of Artois, studded over with pithead machinery, chimneys, slagheaps (*crassiers*), and with those grimy little cottages (*corons*) that seem to go with this branch of industry in all but a few favoured localities in the world. The ground is by no means flat; there are folds and pockets characteristic of chalk formations. In one of these latter the village of Loos was situated

* Killed at Loos or died of wounds in consequence.

Sept. 1915.

But neither in August nor in the battle of 25th September were Borderers exactly opposite Loos, nor was it entered except by wanderers or stragglers in retreat. The actual village belongs to the 44th I.B.'s story. On this, their first visit, the Borderers confronted the "Double Crassier," of which much can be read in connection with the 47th Division. The first tour was one of hard work on trenches. No serious casualties occurred; and on relief on 14th August by the 7th K.O.S.B., the 8th withdrew to Les Brebis, returning to the line on the 16th, in relief of the 10th S.R. in a slightly different sector, for a six-day tour, which was more productive of casualties. Loos was a quiet sector, but far from dead. There was sniping and occasional gusts of shrapnel. After relief by the 7th, the 8th went out of the line to Les Brebis on 22nd August, and thereafter, on 25th, both battalions marched to divisional reserve area at Fouquereuil (8th) and Labeuvrière (7th), 2 miles S.W. of Béthune. Here throwing of the cricket-ball bomb was practised and instruction was given to parties of bombers at Noeux-les-Mines. Machine-gunners were also polished up by instruction at Wisques, 4 miles S.W. of St. Omer. Parties of officers and N.C.O.s were sent to visit the new sector labelled "X," of which more anon.

On 2nd September the 8th Battalion returned to Saulchoy Farm, between Noyelles and Mazingarbe, and worked hard under the R.E. on communication trenches and handling stores till the night of the 7th, when they relieved the 6th Cameron Highlanders in the sector from which the 7th ultimately attacked, battalion H.Q. being in "Quality Street," about one mile from the front line and just S. of the Béthune–Lens road.

September had been, so far, a broken month, and much rain fell; indeed, on the 25th the advance was sensibly retarded by the sticky chalk-soil balling on the feet, and there was much to do in the way of cleaning and strengthening the trenches. A few casualties occurred, more than made good by a draft of 20 men. On 12th September the battalion was relieved by the 11th A. & S.H. and bivouacked in Noeux-les-Mines, and on 13th returned to Labeuvrière to train and prepare for the coming battle. The 7th meantime, as became the battalion of assault, had stayed on at Labeuvrière until 7th September, and never went farther forward, or back for that matter, than Mazingarbe and Philosophe, the latter being situated on the Béthune–Lens road, a few yards S.E. of its junction with that from Grenay. It also trained and prepared as well as circumstances admitted of, and entered the assembly trenches late on the evening of 24th September 1915. The 8th left Labeuvrière on the morning of the 22nd and marched to Mazingarbe (D.H.Q.), where the neces-

Sept. 1915. sary extras were issued, such as hedging-gloves and wire-cutters, sandbags, marking-flags, and picks and shovels (for four platoons of the 8th were to have some heavy digging to do in joining up the captured German trench with the old British line). They moved forward by different routes in small parties to a rendezvous just in front of Philosophe. With them were their cookers. They were not to fight on empty stomachs if Col. T. B. Sellar and Q.M. Goss could by any human means prevent it. The night was, as the Scots say, a bit " saft," but at least it was not the deluge of the night before.

CHAPTER II

THE BATTLE OF LOOS

THE general course of the Battle of Loos is known to everybody who has taken an interest in the war. It has been frequently and well described. The worry and ultimate disappointment concerning the gas projection; the solid achievement of the Londoners between Loos and Lens; the surge of the Highlanders through Loos; the short breather and then the leisurely sweep up to and into the Redoubt on Hill 70's N.W. edge, then the drive over the summit and the excusable but unfortunate loss of direction which landed Highlanders and Lowlanders and Londoners in a very pit of destruction at Cité St. Laurent instead of Cité St. Auguste; the heroic fight for Hill 70, in which Lieut. Johnson, R.E., won his V.C.; the attempt at retirement; the rows of dead, mostly kilted, facing the foe; the inevitable failure of the 21st Division, tired and hungry and raw; the gradual settling down to the front that waited till October 1918 for change—these are probably the best-known incidents in the 1915 campaign, and can be studied in many books.* From the point of view of the K.O.S.B. the cardinal points are: (i) Puits 14 *bis*, a minor pithead just W. of the Lens–La Bassée road, just a mile (and a " bittock ") N. of the German defences of Cité St. Laurent and half a mile N. of the Redoubt on Hill 70, and no less than a mile and three-quarters E. of the British trenches, where the 15th and 1st Divisions joined one another; (ii) the L. flank, facing N.E. in consequence of the inability of the 2nd Brigade to make headway for a long time, and the welcome support of the 6th Camerons; (iii) the magnetic attraction of Hill 70 on the R. for, often, officerless men. 25 Sept. 1915.

The morning of Saturday, 25th September 1915, brought a heavy ground mist. The rain had ceased, but the trenches were slippery. At 5.50 a.m. the final bombardment fell on the German front and support lines. Then followed forty minutes of gas and smoke

* The *Official History*, 1915 (vol. ii.), is a marvel of compression and detail. The chapter on the attack of the 15th Division is a model of lucidity. The Loos section occupies 291 pages.

25 Sept. 1915. projection from cylinders in alternate bursts of twelve and eight minutes respectively. At 6.30 a.m. the British infantry from the La Bassée Canal to the suburbs of Lens went over the top.*

The 7th K.O.S.B. were under command of Lieut.-Col. Verner, who had been sick but had returned on 9th September. On their R. were the 10th S.R. and beyond that the 44th I.B., under a Borderer Brig.-Gen., namely, M. G. Wilkinson, and on their L. two companies of the 12th H.L.I.. Beyond these H.L.I. were the 2nd Brigade of the 1st Division. In support were the remainder of the 12th H.L.I., under Lieut.-Col. Purvis, and the 8th K.O.S.B. at Philosophe, under Lieut.-Col. Sellar.

Brig.-Gen. Matheson had his H.Q. 600 yards behind the front line in a work called Loos Road Keep, just S. of the Vermelles-Loos road. The Reserve Brigade, the 45th, had H.Q. at Philosophe.

The 7th went over the top. In itself it meant a physical as well as a moral effort. Half smothered in their smoke helmets they had to scramble over the 250 yards of fire trench in which they were crowded, get through the gaps cut in the wire, and spread out to something over 400 yards of frontage—and this, heavy laden (though minus packs) and with rifles with fixed bayonets. The advance against the strong-point called Loos Road Redoubt, across about 200 yards † of No Man's Land, was made in column of platoons of two companies, A and B. C followed A in similar formation and D followed B. Fifty yards interval was prescribed between each wave; but, by the time the first wave had penetrated the German fire trench, the interval had been reduced to a few yards.

As can be imagined, things did not go like clockwork. Men were affected by gas. It was Hobson's choice—to be half choked for want of air, or wholly choked in the attempt to get it. The impetus forward might have been lost, had not a sound fallen on the ears of these anxious and embarrassed neophytes to war which pointed the path and steeled the will. It was the skirl of the pipes of D. Laidlaw,‡ who, with a complete *sang froid*, strutted about on the parapet playing the "Blue Bonnets." He kept on playing till he was wounded, and won the first V.C. awarded to a Scottish Borderer in the Great War. By that time the attack was under way and for a few steps under control. But before the German trenches were stormed many officers were dead or *hors de combat*. Two sweeps of two unsilenced M.G. did the business. This rebuff could not stop the determined

* The French did not attack the Vimy Ridge till 12.45 p.m. (*Official History*).

† Thanks to Russian saps (which the 8th toiled to convert into a communication trench). *Official History*, p. 194.

‡ His photograph will be found facing p. 198.

Borderers, who pressed on and took the trench, thanks to good wire-cutting by the R.A., despite continued casualties from rifle and artillery fire. The heartbreak is that after 1,000 yards * advance from the original front things became quiet, and the 7th K.O.S.B. found a new weird and empty world, in which they and their supports the 12th H.L.I. could make progress, if they took the right direction. But by that time only 3 officers were left, and patrols sent out to L. could not get into touch with the 2nd Brigade.† Undeterred they pressed on. The fact that Major T. Glenny was still to the fore explained leadership and direction up to a point. At 9.15 a.m. he sent back the message : " Have reached 300 yards S. of Puits 14 *bis*. Going strong. Have halted for another blow, as our artillery are firing a bit short. Shall push on again immediately." ‡ In other words, he was facing Châlet Wood, and on or just short of the road from La Bassée to Lens, *i.e.* on high ground N. of Hill 70, and had taken the fifth objective and was within half a mile of the German second system covering Cité St. Auguste. The pithead was conspicuous, and Glenny cannot have mistaken his direction. 25 Sept. 1915.

But all had not kept the straight path. An estimated 100 Borderers were attracted to the 44th I.B., as the 10th S.R. had been. Major Glenny was reported missing, but subsequently found to have been killed.§ His death, at a moment when things required re-formation and redirection, was a culminating misfortune. It seems clear that in the end the 7th K.O.S.B. swung to the R. in sympathy with the general movement, crossed Hill 70, and then came in for casualties by flanking fire from Cité St. Laurent, which ultimately drove their remnant to the W. slopes of Hill 70, where, beneath the redoubt on the N.W. crest recaptured by the Germans, they dug in with a motley crew of 44th and 46th I.B., and held their ground till relieved on the 26/27th.

Two of the three points made at the outset have now been dealt with, namely, Puits 14 *bis* and Hill 70. The third—the L. flank—involves the story of the 8th Battalion, but not to the extent which was needed. For the 8th went considerably astray and joined the big crowd, where they were least wanted.

Presumably because the lines of advance of the 15th and 1st Divisions tended to converge, the task of the 12th H.L.I., two companies under Capt. Torrance, was to clean up the German front line by bombing between the 7th K.O.S.B. and 1st Northants (of 1st

* Estimate in 7th's W.D..

† What insuperable difficulties the 1st Northants and other units had to contend with will be found in the *Official History* at pp. 210–211.

‡ *Ibid.* Footnote on p. 197.

§ Official Death Roll.

25 Sept. 1915. Division) sectors. It cost them 9 out of 10 officers to get across No Man's Land! Thereafter they were to join the rest of Col. Purvis's force, and follow in support of the 7th K.O.S.B., while the 8th K.O.S.B. came up from Philosophe behind them.

The 7th K.O.S.B. were thus the L. of the 15th Division, and it was most important to protect that flank which was advancing more and more into the air. That duty devolved upon the 12th H.L.I. (who carried it out) and the 8th K.O.S.B. minus the 4 platoons digging and carrying and receiving their first lessons in the gentle art of "mopping up" through the experience of being sniped, long after the first line had disappeared into the beyond, and having a dozen or so casualties.

When Lieut.-Col. Sellar arrived at the front line he found no trace of the 12th H.L.I. nor of C nor A. Of A it may be at once stated that it had been obliged to leave the R. "Up" trench, as it was blocked with wounded and had diverged too much to the R. after clambering out on to the open and reforming. Capt. H. P. Hart was soon wounded; and Capt. H. H. Smith, of whom Col. Sellar had the highest opinion, was killed on Hill 70, as was Lieut. Drummond. One company therefore, A, was not available for the L. flank. C also seems to have crossed the front line in what had been 10th S.R. territory and to have joined the majority on Hill 70. There was only half D and all B in hand. These were sent forward to follow the H.L.I., and seem to have been more successful in steering an easterly course towards the big road and Puits 14 *bis*. Capt. Cruickshank, O.C. B, must have been in the right region, for when last seen he had just sent a patrol into Bois Hugo, due E. of Puits 14 *bis*. He disappeared on a solitary reconnaissance, and is registered as killed in action on 25th September 1915. The results of the years of study of the same sources of information as those available to the writer, and no doubt many more besides, are epitomized in Map 10 of the *Official History*, which marks 8th K.O.S.B. troops (i) in northern Loos; (ii) heading past the Redoubt on Hill 70; and (iii) in their proper place between Châlet Wood and Bois Hugo.

The main story of the flank belongs to the 12th H.L.I., 6th Cameron Highlanders under Lieut.-Col. Douglas-Hamilton, and the 1st Division, who by pluck and luck eventually in the afternoon overpowered the Germans and pressed forwards towards Chalk Pit Wood.

Capt. S. S. Lang, O.C. D, was wounded near the Lens road, and thus every company commander was disposed of, as Major H. M. Forster, O.C. C, was wounded mortally early in the day and died three days later.* It was fortunate that the Germans held the

* Official Death Roll.

THE BATTLE OF LOOS

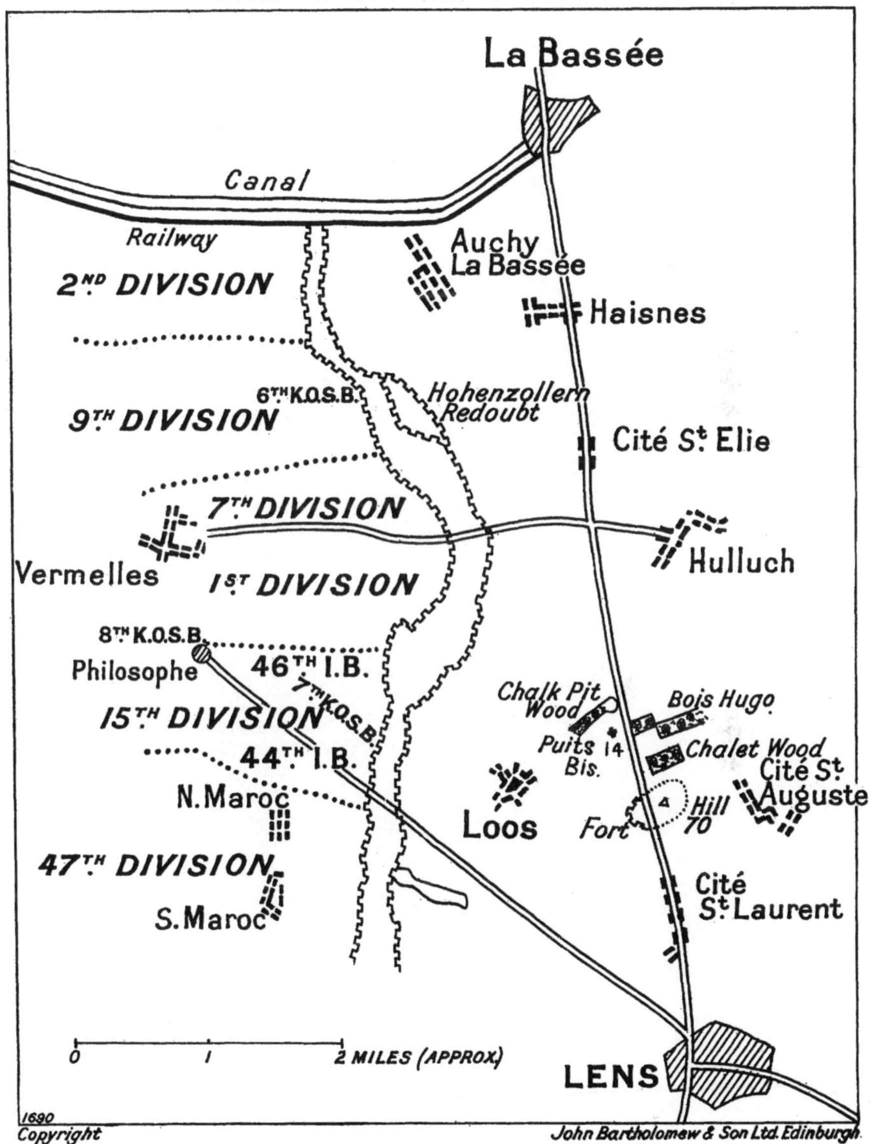
La Bassée
Canal
Railway
2ND DIVISION
Auchy
La Bassée
Haisnes
6TH K.O.S.B.
Hohenzollern
Redoubt
9TH DIVISION
Cité St Elie
7TH DIVISION
Hulluch
Vermelles
1ST DIVISION
8TH K.O.S.B.
Philosophe
46TH I.B.
7TH K.O.S.B.
15TH DIVISION
Chalk Pit
Wood
Bois Hugo
Puits 14
Bis.
Chalet Wood
44TH I.B.
Cité St
Auguste
N. Maroc
Loos
Fort
Hill
70
47TH DIVISION
Cité
St Laurent
S. Maroc
0
1
2 MILES (APPROX)
LENS
1690
Copyright
John Bartholomew & Son Ltd. Edinburgh.

To face Page 392

sector from Hill 70 lightly, and that reinforcements were not available to cut in between the 1st and 15th Divisions. By night the bolt of the K.O.S.B. offensive, as indeed of the whole 46th I.B., was shot. They remained on the defensive till the night of the 26/27th, when they were withdrawn. The circumstances of the subsequent failure of other troops to exploit the divisional success and to relieve the division belong to the general history of the battle. As far as the K.O.S.B. are concerned they finished their share that night. 25 Sept. 1915.

The losses were deplorable, and of course the 7th fared worst. They had 611 casualties out of 950 O.R.. The 8th had 379 out of much the same strength. The 7th had 20 officer casualties and the 8th 14. No indication has reached the writer as to the circumstances of Col. Verner's mortal wound nor of Capt. and Adj. Lethbridge's death. The gallant C.O. lived on until 10th October. The debt that the nation owes to veterans like Verner and Sellar, who trained and inspired " the new model "—on the lines of the old—ought never to be forgotten. Besides Major Glenny, Capts. Hutt and Newton, Lieuts. Sellar, Jarvis, and Scott, and 2nd Lieuts. Scott, Allan, Duirs, Tod, Haddon, and Young were killed or died of wounds. Capt. T. Blackburn was wounded and taken prisoner. Capt. Dennis was wounded. The future C.O. gave a taste of the qualities that made him such a splendid leader. An officer of the brigade recently told the writer how Dennis managed on at least one occasion to slip away forward from the First-Aid Post to get back to his men at the front, and how he was always spoiling for a fight. Also wounded were Lieuts. Denniston, A. K. Gilmour,* J. Frew, and 2nd Lieuts. A. S. M. Tuck and W. G. Kerr. *A Border Battalion* pays a warm tribute of gratitude to Capt. O. Day (R.A.M.C.) for his devotion to the wounded in Quality Street.

The 14 officer casualties of the 8th were the following, besides those mentioned above: 2nd Lieut. W. G. Herbertson (B), 2nd Lieut. I. R. Ardill (reserve M.G. officer), and 2nd Lieut. M'Clelland (C) killed. Besides Capts. Hart, Home, and Lang, 2nd Lieuts. C. K. Thursby-Pelham (B), P. M. Ross (D), and H. G. Mitchell (C) were wounded. The two last named were taken prisoners. As Col. Sellar put it in the Diary, only one officer of those who went forward with the companies returned unscathed—Lieut. Crawshaw—and he probably owed his life and certainly his health to Capt. Hart, who found him badly gassed and had the forethought to place him where the wind could get at him on the parados of a trench.

* A. K. Gilmour, a lad of great promise, fell in the 15th Division's first participation in the battle of the Somme on 16th August 1916 (Official Death Roll).

Sept. 1915. The casualties of the two leading brigades of the 15th Division are appalling. Out of a division casualty total of 228 officers and 6,000 O.R. the 44th I.B. suffered casualties of 69 officers and 2,387 O.R.. Those of the 46th are nearly as bad in men and worse in officers, viz.: 72 officers and 2,280 O.R.. The 45th (Brig.-Gen. F. E. Wallerston) was spared the initial holocaust, and the figures are over 60 officers and about 1,430 O.R..*

The 9th and 15th Divisions amply justified the War Minister's plan for the creation of a New Army, just as the Territorials justified the Haldane scheme. But the instant fame and recognition won and the tributes paid to their valour from the C.-in-C. downwards (there is a very beautiful one by a future G.O.C. 15th Division—Maj.-Gen. Thuillier—given in the *History of the 15th (Scottish) Division*, at p. 49), including the pride expressed by Major-Gen. Sir F. M'Cracken, the 15th's own G.O.C., never can remove the feeling that the Loos salient was not worth the sacrifices from Double Crassier to the canal, and that there was a waste of life. The French attacks on the Vimy Ridge were at no time so successful as to affect the fortunes of the British attack. The attack in Champagne had a certain measure of tactical, but no strategic, success. There was, therefore, no reunion nor likelihood of one at Douai or Valenciennes, as had been so optimistically planned.

* The figures for the 44th and 46th I.B. are the sum of those revised battalion casualties given in brackets as the result of the most recent investigations on p. 339 of the *Official History*. The very careful and elaborate analysis of Lieut.-Col. John Stewart in the *15th Division*, Appendix G, gives a slightly different result.

CHAPTER III

BETWEEN LOOS AND SOMME

MAJOR J. C. W. CONNELL arrived on 27th October at Mazingarbe and took over the command of the 7th K.O.S.B.. By the 29th both battalions were billeted in Haillicourt, about 6 miles W. of Mazingarbe, still in the Béthune–Lens coalfield, from which the 15th Division never emerged till they entered the Somme in August 1916. They, so to speak, sat rather than stood by. The squaring of accounts in the Loos salient was still going on. The arrival of the French to take over the defence of Loos and Hill 70 enabled the 15th to have a real rest week at and near Lillers. Leave home for six clear days was freely granted, and a regular rota started. It was during the stay there that the news of Col. Verner's death arrived. Oct. 1915.

On 11th October both battalions returned to Noeux-les-Mines area, and from now on to the time when they were taken out into Corps Reserve they had their fair share, turn about with one another and other units, of garrisoning, cleaning, draining, revetting, and digging dugouts in the trenches in the "Quarries" sector, *i.e.* just S. of the Hohenzollern Redoubt and of the scene of the 6th Battalion's suffering on 25th September. Vermelles was the nodal point, and owing to the observation possessed by the enemy from Hohenzollern Redoubt and the Dump, 2½ miles of communication trench had to be dug, and was an additional burden to maintain. Brigades took over the front system in spells of from twelve to fourteen days and withdrew to Divisional Reserve for from six to eight days. At this stage in a Regimental History it is impossible to sustain an interest in the everyday doings of trench warfare. The 7th and 8th were treading the path of experience trod by the 2nd Battalion in the autumn and winter of 1914–15. Whether the 9th or the 15th Division had the most uncomfortable existence in the winter of 1915–16 would probably be decided in favour of the 9th. But what admits of no doubt is that the 15th had as dangerous and costly a sector to hold as any on the Western Front. The German

1915–16. guns knew the range of the trenches to a nicety. The support line had been the German front line. The snipers were well placed and skilful. They were alleged to be supplied with stereoscopic sights superior to anything in use in the British army. If ever a situation eased the advent of those heavy hideosities, the iron helmets (" tin hats "), it was one in which the daily toll often grew to alarming proportions. Without any big battle the 15th Division had nearly 4,000 casualties between April 1916 and July 1916.* The fatigues when out of the line were large and heavy. Sometimes one battalion would be asked for 300 men and more at a time.

The men, we are told, often returned to the front with alacrity to escape from these fatigues at which they (somewhat unreasonably) chafed. Lieut.-Col. Connell, as he became, was translated to the 6th in December 1915 as we have seen. His successor was Lieut.-Col. B. J. B. Coulson. About the same time Lieut. and Q.M. G. A. Lord, who as Q.M. had been the backbone of the 9th Battalion, where he was universally liked, took over from Lieut. Hopkins—sick.

On 1st November Capt. J. R. G. Garbutt, R.A.M.C., M.O. of the 8th Battalion, was killed by shell-fire. By a slip on the part of Col. Stewart he is entered as killed at Loos with the 7th Battalion (see *15th Division*, p. 367), but the Official Death Roll confirms the War Diary. A special entry of keen regret is entered by the C.O. on 12th.

When out of the line the Borderers sojourned in such villages as Labourse and Gosnay towards Béthune or Burbure and Raimbert nearer Lillers. Béthune was to K.2 what Bailleul had been to the Regulars in the previous winter, a place of refreshment and pleasure, only too rarely visited. But Béthune was a much grander affair than Bailleul. Ian Hay has eulogized it in the *First Hundred Thousand*.

It so happened that, though on St. Andrew's Day the Borderers were in the line, they managed to spend Christmas and New Year in Corps Reserve at Burbure.

Borderers are apt to associate the " Kaiser's Birthday " with the brilliant *coup de main* of the 87th I.B. on 27th January 1917. But the 7th Battalion have sombre thoughts of 1916 when a terrific imperial hate was indulged in. It was in pre-raid days (*i.e.* of systematic, mutual raiding), but something big was expected and the troops in readiness to repel the attack could not help coming in the way of a hail of projectiles, as the result of which Capt. C. H. M. Horne and 2nd Lieut. T. M. Miller were killed and 2nd Lieut. J. B. Penfold died on the following day. No attack materialized.

* *15th Division*, p. 76.

2nd Lieut. Thompson of the 8th was buried by a shell and had to be invalided. At this time the Borderers were in the Loos sector in the Hill 70 sector with Mazingarbe as their background. There are very few allusions to trench feet in the Diaries of the time, but Col. Sellar never relaxed his vigilance nor his exhortations to take care of the feet. The weather was the usual wintry-spring type. In March there was a considerable amount of snow, and the men had as much as they could do to keep dry. Apparently the smartness of the Presbyterian parade party at Noeux on Sunday 19th March 1916 did not come up to the standard expected by the Corps Commander.* But as the C.O. noted, more in sorrow than in anger, bright buttons and unstained garments are hard to find on men who have no equipment (and that " by order ") with which to clean the former and have no change of raiment, but just what they stand up in when they man the firing trench.

11 May 1916.

The most exciting incident was the affair of the " Kink," just S. of the Hohenzollern Redoubt, a sharp angle in the front line trench due S. of Fosse No. 8. This occurred after a second spell in Corps Reserve from 24th March to 24th April, and was the grand finale of an epoch of tunnelling and mining and general above-ground frightfulness with Minenwerfer and snipers that made the Kink—well !—generally disliked. Early on 11th May a stiff barrage was laid along the division front. It rose and fell during the day. Nearing 6 p.m. it took the character of a box barrage, and at 6 p.m. an attack was launched straight for the Kink and penetrated it, the 12th Royal Scots being stunned with the volume of the fire and *minus* their entire H.Q. personnel through a shell-burst. The counter-attacks made at the time were only partially and very slightly successful. The Kink was flattened out.

Three days later, on 14th May, Col. Sellar received orders to recover the Kink that night. That officer made excellent dispositions for assembling the storming party (composed of men of A and C) and launching it at the first objective a short *boyau* numbered " 99," connecting what had once been the British firing-line with its support line. The attack was aimed parallel to the line of the British front trenches, and the jumping-off place (B.98) was the next *boyau* S. of and almost parallel to " B.99." A British barrage, feeble compared with the German one of 11th May, played for half an hour on the wire covering B.99 and the trenches on each side of it. But though Capt. Crawshaw, as might be expected of him, led with heroism and took his four wounds un-

* The 15th were transferred to the I. Corps (Sir H. de la P. Gough) on 2nd March (*15th Division*, p. 63).

May–July 1916.

flinching, and was well backed up by 2nd Lieuts. W. W. Henderson and R. Clark, and although Major Hart gave good support with A, the assault ended in failure and heavy casualties. Fortunately for the participants there were eye-witnesses and the failure brought not curses but congratulations. What happened is, no doubt, what Col. Sellar all along expected. No sooner had the *boyau* been taken than the German fire concentrated on it and made it completely untenable. At the risk of being instantly shot, the writer would class this as another instance where the man (or staff) *not* on the spot exaggerate the importance of some little local feature. The Kink changed ownership once more and reverted to its German name, and yet we did not instantly lose the war. The athletic and promising Clark was dead after a noble charge; so was 2nd Lieut. K. M. Hamilton. Major Hart and 2nd Lieut. J. Cragg were wounded; 83 O.R. casualties were suffered. The only consolations were that the fighting spirit was there, unimpaired, enhanced, and the thought—it micht ha' been waur.*

To the 7th and 8th K.O.S.B. the 19th of May brought *de facto* amalgamation. It had proved impossible to rebuild the two battalions to their original strength. Col. Sellar was given formal command of the new 7/8th Battalion on 28th May, and Major Frederick (as he signs himself) Dennis, who had commanded the 7th for two months, became Second-in-Command. The companies and officers and W.O.s and N.C.O.s were sorted out and the surplus was sent to the base on 30th May.

The same causes had thinned out the ranks of the 9th Division which ceased to have a Scottish 3rd Brigade but had a S. African one instead. Two amalgamated H.L.I. battalions, now the 10/11th, joined the 10th S.R., the 12th H.L.I., and 7/8th K.O.S.B. in the 46th Brigade, thereby exchanging the 9th for the 15th Division.

Tours in the Hohenzollern and Hulluch sectors call for little comment. The atmosphere of the approaching push affected both combatants. Mining activity accounts for most of the entries in the Diary.

The events of 1st July put an end to all rumours. It was known that the attack astride the Somme had had enough success to indicate exploitation with all available forces. The 15th Division had been confined to the coalfield and its outskirts for a year and were sick to death of the place. They looked forward almost eagerly to the day when they would start Somme-wards. That day came for the 7/8th K.O.S.B. on 21st July when they left their billets at the Orphanage in Béthune and marched 6½ miles to Marles-les-Mines.

* The gist of the W.D. account is contained in *A Border Battalion.*

On the 22nd, as 3rd unit of the brigade, they marched 12 miles to Heuchin (*i.e.* due W.), where they paused for three days, profitably spent in practice-marches in artillery formation, in field-firing at an impromptu range (Heuchin lies in a valley with steepish sides and a nice burn for washing feet in) and in drinking in the C.O.'s wise counsel regarding discipline—a favourite topic of their G.O.C., Major-Gen. F. W. N. M'Cracken, C.B., D.S.O., ever since 22nd March 1915—and their feet, if they wished to do credit to the regiment and division. July–Aug. 1916.

On 26th July the march was resumed, this time in a S. direction, St. Pol being cleared on its W. side, and Écoivres being reached after a march of 13 miles. On 27th, for the second time in succession next after Brigade H.Q. and handicapped by blistered feet due to the heat of the day before, the battalion marched 8 miles across the Canche to Villers L'Hôpital and next day to Candas in Fourth Army territory, crossing the Authie and passing through the Bernaville district, so soothing to Somme sufferers. Here a welcome rest was taken and fired feet treated. There was a real swimming bath with accessories (good old R.E. when not Pharaoh's task-masters !) and glorious long bathes the men had on Saturday 29th July and Sunday after church parade. On 31st July the battalion moved before the heat of the day 7 miles still farther S. to Flesselles (12 miles N. of Amiens) and practised (Mills) bombing hard for three days at the Army School there, while boots were attended to. It was boots and not neglect nor poor spirit that caused much suffering and a few falls out every day on the trek. When a bus turned up for the lame ducks * no one would admit his inability to pile on packs and equipment including, in the case of bombers, bombs, and struggle forward. On 4th August, up betimes, a march of one and a half hours took the battalion on the next stage to the battle, to Molliens-au-Bois. A similar matutinal march brought them to Franvillers within sound of the roar of the unceasing traffic on the Amiens–Albert highway.

This ferment was something quite new to *these* Borderers and made them feel that they were fairly in the neck of the bottle. Church parade on Sunday 6th August, followed by a short march and a bathe in the Ancre, finished the preparation. Next day they were in the trenches and sustained 3 casualties. The 15th Division and the 7/8th K.O.S.B. among its units entered the Somme as fit as any troops in France, and the march up was taken in their stride.

* Expression used in W.D..

CHAPTER IV

THE SOMME

Aug. 1916. — THE 7/8th K.O.S.B. were the fourth and last battalion of the regiment to take part in the longest and hardest fought of the battles of the war. On 1st July the 1st Battalion met a fate similar to that of the 6th opposite Little Willie and had departed to Ypres. The 6th had fought in the battles of Albert, Bazentin, and Delville Wood in July and were now out of the line. The 2nd had attacked the High Wood—Longueval ridge, towards the end of July. It was now the turn of the 7/8th to maintain the example of steadiness and gallantry set them by their predecessors.

They were not partakers of any major offensive for more than a month. Leaving Franvillers at 6 a.m. on the 7th the battalion followed the big road, and on nearing Albert opened the spaces between the companies. Turning off for Bécourt just E. of Albert they were there met and guided in a direction N.E., *i.e.* parallel to the Albert–Bapaume road, which meant that they were heading straight for Martinpuich between Pozières (L.) on the big road and Bazentin-le-Petit (R.). Since Bécourt they had moved by platoons, but on reaching the *boyaux* they filed up and joined the advanced party in a trench extending along the summit plateau of the great ridge from Courcelette to Combles, from a point about 500 yards N. of and on the road from Bazentin-le- Petit to Martinpuich (which is situated on the reverse slope) to a point on the track from Contalmaison across the ridge to Martinpuich.

It was on the extreme R. of this sector that casualties chiefly occurred. The very next day, *i.e.* on night 8/9th August, 2nd Lieut. J. B. Walmsley, a " gallant young officer," was killed on patrol, and a party working on a sap suffered to the extent of 3 killed and no fewer than 30 O.R. wounded. On 9th the drain continued, and " another splendid officer," 2nd Lieut. J. H. Lawrie, fell, and 7 O.R. were killed and 28 wounded. Relief from the actual front did not mean safety in the Somme fighting. When the battalion handed over to the 10th S.R. and, after a day's rest, were turned on to carrying work in the battle of 12th August, they suffered appreciably. 2nd Lieut. J. M. Ure—a quiet officer from the 9th Battalion, of mature years and imperturbable nerve, and greatly esteemed by all—was wounded mortally * on 12th and there were 19 O.R. casualties. On the succeeding wet days of 13th and 14th things were quieter, but on 15th the death of Capt. A. K. Gilmour, when in charge of a working party, brought fresh gloom. He had just come back to duty from a course at Fourth Army School in which he had distinguished himself, and bade fair to have a brilliant career before him, for he was young and keen and stout hearted as well as intellectually gifted and was already C.O. of B. The 16th brought increased losses, and on 17th the heavy shelling incidental to a German counter-attack brought heavy casualties to all ranks. A/R.S.M. G. Readman, ear-marked for a commission and at the time acting as an officer in A, was killed on 17th, and later in the day Capt. A. R. Brown, who, after eleven months as a company commander, might claim to be a veteran, also fell, while assisting a wounded comrade towards the aid-post. 2nd Lieut. J. M. M'Alpin, who afterwards fell at Arras on 11th April 1917,† was wounded in the neck on the same day, and O.R. casualties, which amounted to 35 killed or died of wounds, 159 wounded, and 27 missing, necessitated the temporary amalgamation of C and D on the following day, 18th. On that, the last, day of this first visit to the great charnel-house, two officers, 2nd Lieuts. C. K. Thursby-Pelham and G. T. Mitchell were buried by shell-fire and evacuated, and Lieut. G. A. Fraser was badly wounded.

Altogether in this battle of Switch Line and Intermediate Trench ‡ the 7/8th K.O.S.B., although only engaged in a secondary degree, suffered severely, especially in trained officers, and were thankful to be relieved on 18/19th by the 10th S.R. from the front, and by the 6th Cameron Highlanders from support on the 19th and withdraw to a camp outside Albert on the Amiens road and rest and clean up and absorb such officers and O.R. as were forthcoming. Sniping, signalling, musketry, mask-drill, and the pull-together routine associated with the square were the order of the day.

On 29th August the 1st Black Watch were relieved in the support area and on 31st the 10th S.R. were relieved in the front trenches. The battalion then had only 11 officers, were short of N.C.O.s, and the drafts were far from trained. It was perhaps, therefore, just as well that no serious tactical effort was required

* He died of wounds, 16/8/16 (Official Death Roll).

† Official Death Roll.

‡ See *History of the 15th Division*, pp. 81–87.

15 Sept. 1916. — of them before they passed out into Divisional Reserve on 4th September and practised for the attack on the 15th September. Such work as they had consisted in supporting the unsuccessful efforts of the 1st Division to take an obstinate corner of High Wood still in German hands by Lewis gun support from a trench W. of High Wood's W. angle. Another unsuccessful German counter-attack delivered on 3rd September brought copious shelling, during the course of which Lieut J. S. Wyper received mortal wounds,* of which he died on 8th September 1916.

Relieved in the front system on the 4/5th, the 7/8th K.O.S.B. withdrew to Divisional Reserve at "Scots Redoubt" in the old German support line, and in so far as not interfered with by the necessity for supplying working parties and of absorbing reinforcements, practised the attack for an impending operation of some magnitude.

Martinpuich.

It will be remembered that at an early stage of the Somme battle the exploitation of the line of least resistance had led to a bulge or salient at the junction of the Franco-British forces, while such strongholds as High Wood, Delville Wood, Guillemont, and Ginchy delayed advance in the more western parts of the new ground broken. It was in the eastern area that the 2nd Battalion suffered so terribly at Falfemont Farm on 3rd September. While the 15th Division were toiling away at minor but bitterly contested operations or were hanging on to their captures, preparations were being made for a series of assaults against the eastern strongholds. Guillemont was stormed on 3rd and Falfemont was surrounded on 5th, while Ginchy at last fell to the British on 9th September. Meantime the British line in the Martinpuich sector was pushed over the crest, and though the northern part of High Wood had not yet been won and it cost the 47th Division (the 15th's neighbours at Loos) many lives to clear it on the 15th, Longueval and Delville Wood were ghastly memories but definitely ours, and from various coigns of vantage the features of the downslopes towards the Butte de Warlencourt and Bapaume (to select two of the more conspicuous) were exposed to the interested scrutiny of artillery and other observers. Such was the situation when the C.-in-C. decided to follow up a subsidiary operation on the 14th by the 11th Division of the Fifth Army, then at grips with the S. Ancre German defences associated with Thiépval, by a grand attack on the 15th from and including Courcelette (an objective of the Canadian Corps in the Fifth Army)

* Official Death Roll.

to a point short of Combles. Our concern in this story is confined to the L. of the Fourth Army front, where the 15th Division confronted the village of Martinpuich, which in the ephemeral but expressive slang of the period was their exclusive "pigeon," the 50th Division boundary on the R. and the 2nd Canadian Division boundary on the L. both excluding any part of Martinpuich. The objective as at first defined was the southern part of the village, the first ruined houses of which were about 600 yards from the jumping-off place. Just before the battle, and too late for practice, orders were issued that if the attack were successful the whole village should be captured. The 46th I.B.'s movements were specially complicated by a late-hour modification of the movements of the 7/8th K.O.S.B., whose first wave had to wheel three-quarters L. with half their force and man and make good a sunk road on the flank towards the Canadians. But they had first to advance 500 yards towards the village, as the 10/11th H.L.I. écheloned slightly behind on the L. were attending to the nearer portions of the sunk road. This initial advance meant the capture of the 1st German ("Bottom") trench. Thereafter subsequent waves were (*a*) to consolidate and hold "Bottom" and (*b*) to develop the sunk road position by a three-quarters R. wheel (*i.e.* back into the straight) which would land them, it was hoped, in a trench inside the village called Factory Line and bring them in touch with the 10th S.R. on their R.. These "extraordinary manœuvres," as Col. Sellar terms them (and the reader may be reminded that this was the first occasion on which a creeping, or rather leaping, barrage was employed in the war), were probably only achieved by the fact that though the orders came late they were in time to enable the manœuvre to be practised three times on the 14th before the battalion left Scots Redoubt for the front at 7 p.m..* As the War Diary account is so faithfully, almost literally, followed in the battalion history, *A Border Battalion*, it is unnecessary to treat this successful operation other than with broad touches.

15 Sept. 1916.

Fitted with all the panoply of the period, including smoke bombs and a pick or a shovel (like a choice of dishes on a *table-d'hôte* card), but not *both* per man, the battalion moved up by platoons to the shell-holes which had to shelter the farthest forward detachment, and trenches for those behind. "Liver" † and "Bacon," as these

* *The History of the 15th Division*, p. 89, says there was no practice. Probably there was no brigade practice, but Col. Sellar is quite explicit in the War Diary.

† Liver Trench did not exist. The counter-bombardment had flattened it. Bacon was recognisable as a trench, and the third and fourth waves waited there.

15 Sept. 1916. were called, will have special significance for those Borderers who survived that day, and their descendants. A breakfast worthy of such an appetizing name could not be expected in the flesh on 15th September 1916, but the men had a crust and a good draught of hot tea, and at 6.20 a.m.—zero—they preceded the brand-new and on this occasion not very impressive tanks in the direction of Martinpuich. It was, for once, a fine day, that Friday, and things went well. The enemy seemed to be surprised. Three officers and 60 O.R. were taken in "Bottom" before 6.45 and the difficult manœuvre with its double wheel or wriggle was accomplished, so that all three objectives were in occupation by 7.35 a.m.—*i.e.* sunk road and Factory Line, as well as the first objective. Beyond excellent work by strong patrols under 2nd Lieut. E. O. Rodger (who only joined on 18th August) which secured a haul of 13 prisoners, 6 of whom were officers (so that 9 in all were taken by K.O.S.B.), and reported the village clear of enemy, nothing further in the way of offensive operations was undertaken until the afternoon, when, in accordance with orders, posts were pushed out and established N. of Martinpuich, representing an advance of 1,400 yards from Bacon Trench, and 5 enemy trenches captured. Three M.G. were handed over to the 46th I.B. before the battalion retired on relief by the 9th York & Lancs. to a support position called Shelter Trench. It was a great day, and thanks to Capt. Parker, R.A.M.C., the wounded were swiftly removed. The C.O. was at the front, Major Dennis, perforce, behind, and Capt. J. P. Larkin admirably did the duties of Second-in-Command.

The cost has to be considered. Nine officers and 280 O.R. were casualties. The younger lads were sufferers. 2nd Lieut. G. Snowie, who on 3rd September had shared the dugout with Wyper and not been hurt, met his fate. 2nd Lieuts. M. M. M'Farquhar and C. R. Murray,* both of the 9th, were also killed, and 2nd Lieut. C. C. Mahood died on 16th and 2nd Lieut. R. M. Middlemass on 28th September of wounds received on the 15th. 2nd Lieut. T. A. Skinner was wounded, but his day was not yet.† 2nd Lieuts. J. C. Wilson, R. R. Harkus, and C. M. Holme were wounded. Twelve officers only were fit for duty at the end of the day. The figures in *A Border Battalion* (p. 104)—viz. 68 officer casualties since arriving in Fourth Army area—are plainly wrong. The War Diary puts them

* The Official Death Roll gives the date of this officer's death as "18/9/16." The W.D. is ambiguous. He may have fallen in the aftermath of the battle.

† "2nd Lieut. T. A. Skinner (Tp.) died of wounds 10/8/17" (Official Death Roll). After his wound on 25th September he returned to duty on 9th November 1916.

at 34 (including 6 sick), and those of O.R. at 886, a heavy enough total in any event. Relieved on the night 17/18th September, the battalion found its way to division rest area *via* Laviéville to Béhencourt nearer Amiens than Albert, and just N. of the main road. Here the inevitable difficulties of reconstruction were enhanced by the intrusion of a band of unsuitable dwarfs called Bantams, and mitigated by proper drafts from Scotland, as far as these escaped English units.* The jumble, however, must have saved someone a lot of trouble. Winter 1916–17.

"A better conceived and better executed operation (than the capture of Martinpuich) it would be difficult to find. Artillery, engineers, and infantry worked together in a manner little short of marvellous; losses were not excessive, and a serious blow had been dealt to the enemy." † At both stages of the battle contact had been maintained between H.L.I. and Borderers, and Borderers and Cameronians, and between Cameronians and 45th Brigade troops. There is no question that the 15th Division won an instant reputation as a *corps d'élite* as the result of the capture of Martinpuich.

The Fourth Army undertook no operations of magnitude during the remainder of the winter. The Reserve, or Fifth Army, in the battles of the Ancre Heights and the Ancre in October and November, which culminated in the capture of Beaumont Hamel by the 51st Division, did the bulk of the fighting, and the only advances made in the area occupied by the 15th Division were made by other divisions, *e.g.* the capture of Eaucourt L'Abbaye by the 47th and Le Sars by the 23rd. The 7/8th K.O.S.B., therefore, were engaged in precisely the same sort of existence and duty as the 1st K.O.S.B. and the 6th (apart from that unit's affair opposite the Butte). First and foremost in their lives bulked the weather, wet and stormy till the iron frost of January 1917. Then came the state of the ground consequent on the weather. Men cowered in grouplets in shell holes, isolated all day and on tenterhooks all night when on sentry duty in the front. They could only get back or forward by a physical exertion which exhausted, without any improving effect on any muscles useful in marching or fighting. It was easy to lose the the way, to fall into awful green craters, to stick in the mud, even to drown. The camps became begrimed. They were comfortless and chilly, and some dugouts were preferable to them. There were endless fatigues on the muddy roads, often in pelting rain. Washing facilities were inadequate, and many of all ranks became lousy.

* Col. Sellar has some caustic remarks under date 30/9/16. Besides Borderers, Royal Scots and Lanarkshire Yeomanry were acceptable.

† *History of 15th Division*, p. 93.

Oct.- Nov. 1916. The 15th Division's experience only presented such variations from the universal experience of the Somme as lay in the exposed, upland terrain held, and in the way things were run. There is little to record save the duration of tours and rests and such outstanding events as the temporary loss of the C.O.. The scene of action varied little, extending from N. of the Albert–Bapaume road to a point opposite the Butte de Warlencourt. If any Jocks were to be seen about Contalmaison or Bazentin-le-Petit they were pretty sure to be 15th men, and a very fine looking set they were, both officers and men, obviously making the best of things, like Sam Weller in the rain.

Analysing the movements of the 7/8th K.O.S.B. after the battle of Flers (to give the fight on 15th September its official name), the remainder of the month was spent at Béhencourt in all-round and specialist training. On the 30th the battalion marched 11 miles to billets in Albert, and stayed there for ten days continuing their training. On the 9th, when the division relieved the 23rd Division (their previous relievers on 19th September) in the Le Sars sector, the battalion went forward to Scots Redoubt, *i.e.* in the old German support line, and occupied dugouts there, training and working on the roads, till on 15/16th October they relieved the 6/7th R.S.F. of the 45th I.B. in recently taken trenches in and W. of the N.W. edge of Le Sars. Naturally in " Chalk Pit " Trench and its neighbours there was much to do to make things safer. Dryness was unattainable as it poured on 16/17th. Stays in the front were short, as the season turned towards winter, and the 10/11th H.L.I. were welcomed on 17/18th in heavy rain. The support line was comfortless. Cooking was out of the question. But stay there was brief, and on 18/19th they withdrew to reserve brigade area to a chilly canvas camp—Lozenge Wood—and cleaned it and themselves as best they could. Fatigues followed till the second tour in the front, when the battalion relieved the 6th Cameron Highlanders by 9.30 p.m. on 28th October. The trenches were in places hip-deep in sticky mud. The two days in the front were marked by the wounding of Lieut.-Col. T. B. Sellar with shrapnel, necessitating his evacuation, much to his annoyance. But as he returned in time for Arras, it was probably just as well for him and the battalion that he missed the physical strain of eleven weeks of Somme winter. Major Dennis took over command in the interim, except when Capt. Larkin acted for him while he was home on leave in January, or on courses at G.H.Q., and also for six days early in November, when Dennis was with the 12th H.L.I.. Most of the time when the division was out (having been relieved by the 48th Division on 3rd November) the 7/8th K.O.S.B. were at Millencourt, between Albert and III. Corps H.Q. (which was close to the worst of all camps—Hénencourt Wood *) at Hénencourt, and trained strenuously. The future regimental colonel, the C.-in-C., Sir Douglas Haig, inspected the battalion at 2 p.m. on 19th November, and expressed his satisfaction at the appearance of the troops, who paraded ready for a march. On 13th November the battalion moved farther W. to a camp near D.H.Q. at Baisieux, but were glad to be quit of the filthy spot and get satisfactory billets at Havernas and Wargnies, W. of the Amiens–Doullens road. The 14-miles march was done in full marching kit. The stay was profitable. They were near Army H.Q. (Querrieu) and advanced G.H.Q. (Beauquesne), and the number of courses for all ranks from the C.O. downwards is impressive. By the end of the month (they had moved back to Warloy near D.H.Q. on the 27th) a much refreshed battalion, they celebrated St. Andrew's Night, and made ready for a return to the serious but unpleasant duty of garrisoning the British front. Considering the prodigal expenditure in certain lines, it seems hard that a fuel shortage should be such a constant complaint. However, one knows that nothing is more flagrantly wasted by the thoughtless than fuel.

1917.
—

From 1st to 14th December the battalion was in Bécourt Camp just E. of Albert. On the latter date, fitted out with "gum boots" and two days' rations, the battalion toiled up to the front, now more than 7 miles off, and by 8.30 p.m. relieved the 7th Worcesters in the Le Sars sector in fortified shell-holes reached by duckboard tracks. The division completed the relief of the 48th on the 16th, and remained there till 3rd February 1917. It was much colder, and that scourge of winter campaigning, trench feet, began to appear. Casualties ran from 3 to 4 a day. Three days in the line were succeeded by six in support and three in reserve. Then followed three in the line, after relief of the 9th B.W., in which no casualties occurred, then two days camp, and then back to the line, where the New Year was somewhat unsociably brought in.

The middle of January 1917 brought a great change—intense cold and hard frost. The first half was marked by the unfortunate shooting of Capt. H. F. Brigstocke by a sentry when he was returning off patrol with a prisoner and an orderly at a point some way off his original exit. A valuable officer was thus lost to the battalion.

Lieut.-Col. Sellar returned on the 20th, when the battalion was in Scots Redoubt. His main concern was with feet; in fact, if one may use the expression, he was a "whaler" for feet, because he

* Entry in W.D., 6th November 1916.

Feb. 1917. — favoured the application of hot whale-oil in preference to camphor powder. The frost saw this battalion of Borderers out of the Somme for ever, for it was still ringing when the 15th Division were relieved by the 2nd Australian Division on 3rd February, and departed for the VI. Corps (Haldane) of the Third Army (Allenby) and Arras. The 7/8th K.O.S.B. were out of the line on 29/30th January when Lieut.-Col. Thom's 8/10th Gordons brought off the historic raid on the Butte de Warlencourt,* so that 15th September stands out unrivalled in their Somme memories, and the first answer to any questioner asking what the 7/8th Borderers did would be: "They took Martinpuich."

February opened with three days at Albert and nine at Warloy. Then the march N. began. Beauval was reached on 13th February; Hem, near Doullens, on 14th; Rebreuve, 6 miles N. of Doullens, on the 15th; and Izel-lez-Hameau, 10 miles W. of Arras, on the 16th. There a pause was made for rest, cleaning up, and a military bracing-up. On 22nd February, showing due respect for shells and gas at the Baudimont gate, the 7/8th K.O.S.B. were the third battalion of the regiment to set foot in Arras of the "*boves*" † and sewers and easily reached trenches. In this region the battalion were destined to be severely tested in offensive and defensive warfare in successive years.

* See *History of 15th Division*, pp. 103–111.

† Underground chambers. The 2nd Battalion had been there in 1915 and the 6th had just preceded the 7/8th from the Somme.

CHAPTER V

ARRAS

1917

THE 7/8th K.O.S.B. took active part (1) in the first three days of the battle in the sector immediately S. of the Scarpe and on the N.W. approaches to Monchy; and (2) in the severe fight from 23rd to 25th April, both inclusive, round Guémappe, between Monchy and the Cojeul. In short, the battalion fought in the opening stages of both the First and Second Battles of the Scarpe, and was spared the later and less edifying combats in May and June. As they were in the reserve brigade on the 9th and 23rd they do not figure so prominently as they did at Martinpuich. But their record is one of which the regiment may well be proud. The battle of Arras has already been staged in connection with the 6th Battalion. The 9th and 15th Scottish Divisions were separated by the Scarpe, and were to move parallel to one another to the three consecutive objectives—the Black, the Blue, and the Brown Lines. The 15th Division were on the S. or R. bank of the river. The capture of the Black Line meant the clearing of the suburban hamlet of Blangy. The capture of the Blue Line involved the capture of the strongly fortified triangle of railway embankment formed by the bifurcation of the lines Arras–Lens and Arras–Douai, half a mile E. of the British front, and the connecting switch 500 yards farther E.; while the capture of the Brown Line, the allotted task of the Brigade of Reserve, *i.e.* the 46th I.B., in which these Borderers were, involved the capture of Feuchy Redoubt and village and the occupation of the strong double-trench back line of the Germans known as Himalaya Trench, more than 2 miles from the British front, and running due S. in front of the prominent Orange Hill to the Arras–Cambrai road just E. of Feuchy Chapel, and so on out of our ken. On the capture of this stronghold the allotted task of the 37th Division, who were to follow hard after the 46th I.B., was to pass over the N. slopes of Orange Hill and capture Monchy.

April 1917.

Having ascertained that the 7/8th K.O.S.B. were dedicated to

March–April 1917.

a leapfrogging advance to a limited objective in the later stages of a full-dress battle, we can now resume the narrative. The initial stay in the trenches was not long, and was in the main quiet. The principal incident was a successful raid of the 11th Middlesex on 26th February, which brought 5 casualties to the Borderers through retaliatory fire. On the 28th a morning relief by 10/11th H.L.I. brought the 7/8th Borderers back into Arras and its subterranean life. On 2nd March a move was made to a camp near Duisans (D.H.Q.), and preliminary training for the " push " began, physical fitness being a special aim. A draft of 114 had to be put into the mould. On the 9th the battalion marched about 8 miles to Ambrines, where the tactical side of the training was emphasized. On the 15th there was a brigade exercise, and again on the 17th, when the G.O.C. himself (M'Cracken) was present. The Brig.-Gen. was still T. G. Matheson, but he did not command the 46th at Arras, as on 18th March he was promoted to command the 20th (Light) Division. He was succeeded by Brig.-Gen. E. A. Fagan of the Indian Army. Brig.-Gen. Matheson expressed his satisfaction with the battalion, who by vigorous cheers showed their appreciation of him. Relations between Brigade H.Q. and the battalion were always harmonious.

The period from 19th to 23rd was spent in the line. Patrols carefully examined and reported on the state of the enemy's wire. There were some big working parties to find when they returned to Arras on 23rd. H. P. Hart, who had been wounded at Loos and now had the rank of Major, returned along with Capt. T. K. Newbigging, M.C. . The battalion returned to the line on 29th and came out on 31st March for the last time before fighting. Thereafter six days were spent at Duisans ; and then in the evening of 6th April, in wet weather, the battalion marched into Arras and went to ground till the great day. Col. Sellar was in command, and Major Hart was Second-in-Command. Major Dennis had been unwell, but on his strenuous representations he had been let out of hospital and appointed on the 8th to serve with the 12th Division as liaison officer.[1] That division was attacking on the R. of the 15th.

All through the unprecedented bombardment they lay snugly underground. " Games, etc., were provided during sojourn there " is an entry for the 7th (Saturday), but we are left to speculate what they were. Easter is usually associated with an escape from the confinement of winter in towns to the air and sun and skies of the country in spring. One remembers Faust's stroll with Wagner on an Easter morning. But here things were reversed.

At 6 a.m. on Easter Monday, 9th April 1917, the 7/8th Battalion left the Grande Place cellars for the underway (once a sewer) and emerged at 7 a.m., and made their way, in the face of sleet and an icy blast, at first in and across trenches, then over No Man's Land, then across the German front and support trenches, then over the open to the point of assembly at the remains of a plantation called Fred's Wood, in the black or first objective. The move was taken in a leisurely fashion. There was plenty of time before they would be needed. They were in position soon after 9 a.m., and heard how the 44th on the R. of the division and the 45th on the L. or river sector in front of themselves had stormed—not without heavy losses at Blangy—the first system. No further move could be made till Railway Triangle fell, and it was not till after 12.30 p.m. that its capture was announced. Then at last came the moment for the Borderers to be up and doing. A was on the R., C in the middle, D on the L., and B in reserve. The awful work of the British guns was realized when Feuchy Redoubt (*alias* Intermediate position) was found not to exist as a fortress. In fact, the principal impediments were one nasty group of riflemen at a bridge, on the Arras–Douai Railway, who were silenced by a dashing rush by 2nd Lieut. Strachan and Corp. West, who with only 4 men captured 17 Germans, and a certain number of "shorts" from our own guns. After this had been stopped through brigade, progress was made, and by 4 p.m. Feuchy was mopped up and left behind, and by 5 p.m. the Brown Line was reached and consolidated and patrols sent out, *e.g.* to Orange Hill and towards Monchy. Apparently at this point they were "through," and there were neither earthworks, nor wire, nor men to stop them. Ultimately a line was established fully 500 yards ahead of the original objective, and the *triste* chill of the approaching night was mitigated by the calorific of labour and the moral uplift of a signal victory. The 37th Division went through farther on the R. at about 6.30 p.m.,* but none are recorded as passing through the 7/8th K.O.S.B. before 3.30 a.m. on the 10th. Mention is made of a cavalry patrol of 120. The losses were not heavy—5 officers and 120 O.R., and the number of guns captured is surprisingly large—16. One of the officers wounded was the invaluable Capt. Parker, the M.O.; and the only officer killed was 2nd Lieut. G. Sutherland,† of the 4th Battalion, which supplied excellent reinforcements to this battalion from time to time.

9 April 1917.

The next day brought no change to the battalion, as the 12th Division had found part of the Brown Line, Himalaya Trench, un-

* *History of the* 15*th Division*, p. 121.

† Official Death Roll, *History of the* 15*th Division*, Appendix I. p. 371.

11 April 1917. destroyed, and so far impregnable. But on the 11th a somewhat hurriedly improvised attack was ordered. In the story of the 1st Battalion the importance of Monchy has been stressed from the point of view of retention. The happenings on the 11th stress the original difficulties in the way of conquering that dominating hilltop, crowned by a fortified village full of deep dugouts and supplies and Bavarians.

The 37th Division were to capture Monchy itself, while the 15th were to push on to the E. between Monchy and the Scarpe. It was a tough task. Apart from frontal opposition, posts in Roeux on the other side of the Scarpe could sweep the exposed northern slopes of Orange Hill and fire into the Happy Valley, which ran from it to the Scarpe. The coping-stone of discouragement was supplied by an abominable snowstorm from the E..

The K.O.S.B. advance was not to be made from the forward zone. They had first to fall back on the Brown line and then go forward in the wake of the 10/11th H.L.I.. Brig.-Gen. Fagan had no easy task.

The attack had to be launched at 5 a.m., and the K.O.S.B. had only an hour and ten minutes in which to unstiffen their scarcely rested limbs and *reculer pour mieux sauter*. In point of fact, the leading companies were not those originally detailed when the forward movement began. Can a more cheerless opening to a day of carnage be imagined than when D on the R. and C on the L., in those squat columns known as artillery formation. faced the blast, while the shivering leaders spelled out the course for their little flocks with a luminous compass? The H.L.I. were in front, and the whole force moved at 5 a.m.. There was no artillery support. A loss of direction must be admitted. The R. company, D, had no business to find itself in Monchy. Yet they were reported as actually " going through " the village. They were the first Scottish Borderers to enter that place of contention. The aberration was seen from Battalion H.Q., and strenuous efforts were made to correct direction more to the N.. It is utterly unimportant to mark the spot where the advance ended. But the statement that the K.O.S.B. pushed S. and E. of Monchy towards Boiry-Notre Dame * is inconsistent with Col. Sellar's co-ordinates, which place the line ultimately dug in as N. and N.W. of Monchy. It is also less consonant with the retirement, on relief by the 10th W. Yorks, to Railway Triangle—a simple and natural enough move if the battalion were N.W. of Monchy.

The main point is that the 46th I.B. and our Borderers, under

* *History of the 15th Division*, p. 124.

conditions hideously adverse, had helped the 37th Division and some cavalry units to take Monchy. The whole thing was over by 7 a.m., and the rest of the day was spent in preparation to resist counter-attacks which never eventuated. But German shells rained around. The sufferings of the numerous wounded, some of whom were unable to brush the snow off their faces (*A Border Battalion*, p. 148) before they could be collected, must have been great. Casualties were considerable. Col. Stewart has put the K.O.S.B. Arras casualties, *i.e.* including 23rd March to 15th April, at just under 450 in O.R..* Two hundred of these, *i.e.* about double of those on the 9th, were inflicted on 11th April. Second Lieuts. J. M. M'Alpin and G. G. Lang were killed, and 2nd Lieut. J. Jarvie died on 17th as the result of wounds received on 11th April. In all, from 9th to 11th April, 7 officers (subalterns) were wounded in addition to the M.O.. But perhaps the severest loss was that of A/R.S.M. J. A. Munro (of Golspie), M.C., who received on 9th the wounds of which he died on 12th, "after carrying away Pte. Morrison, who had been wounded." † The M.C. was a posthumous award.

April 1917.

After a halt at Railway Triangle the battalion returned to Arras by day and were joined in billets there by the 10 per cent. left behind, as usual. Congratulations poured in and were read out by the C.O. on parade. The senders included Sir D. Haig, Sir E. Allenby, Sir A. Haldane, and the G.O.C. 15th Division. After cleaning up, bathing, and noting requirements, the battalion went to huts near Duisans on 14th, and stayed there till 19th April, when they returned to Arras and made ready for their coming attack on 23rd April in a sector farther S. than before, between the 29th (L.) and 50th Divisions, S. of Monchy, and facing Guémappe between the Cambrai road and the Cojeul, then (unlike the early September days in 1918, when the 4th Battalion walked dry-shod across it) holding water.

Once more the 44th I.B. were to be on the R., and Guémappe was their very first and very formidable objective. The 45th on their L. were to advance along the slope E., in sympathy with both the 44th and 88th Brigades.‡ The 46th I.B. were in reserve, and the 7/8th K.O.S.B. were its reserve battalion.

Major Dennis returned from hospital on 20th and Col. Sellar was compelled to enter it on 21st. The former handled his watching brief admirably. The battalion, although up early and ready to

* See *History of the 15th Division*, Appendix I., *cit. supra*.

† *A Border Battalion*, p. 148.

‡ As we know, the 1st Battalion K.O.S.B. were beyond the 88th on the top of the Monchy plateau.

23 April 1917. move, took no combative part in the battle of 23rd April until quite late in the day. They began the day near Tilloy and finished it between Guémappe and La Bergère on the Cambrai road. The proximate cause of their partial entry into the battle was the capture by the 10/11th H.L.I. of a portion of the second objective, half a mile due E. of La Bergère. This feat having been done by the H.L.I. *alone,* in consequence of countermanding orders not arriving in time, there was a gap which Major Dennis filled by sending C forward to a trench known as "String," where they remained until the following evening, when they were caught up by the advance of the rest of the battalion. Eighty men of B also did good work carrying ammunition and water to the front line. Casualties were few, and the thrills and throes of the Guémappe fighting must be read elsewhere.*

On the 24th there was no aggression on either side until the afternoon. But it was made known that the 46th I.B. would again be attacking and that the 7/8th K.O.S.B. would be in support of the 12th H.L.I., who had replaced the depleted 10/11th H.L.I. under cover of darkness, in an attack on not only the Blue but the Red or final objective. As the attack was to be by daylight and the 7/8th K.O.S.B. were half a mile behind the jumping-off place, their initial advance promised to be a ticklish operation. As a matter of fact, platoons were dribbled up one after the other at intervals of not less than five minutes, so that between 1 p.m. and 3 p.m. the whole three companies were got to the jumping-off line. At 4 p.m. the attack was launched; and the K.O.S.B., being nearly as much behind the H.L.I. as the distance already covered, and having shells chiefly to fear, at this stage adopted artillery formation and got rapidly clear of a position which came in for heavy shelling. The attack did not progress well. The Blue Line (second objective) was indeed taken; but the 10th S.R. on the R. of the 12th H.L.I. could not take the stronghold called Cavalry Farm, which commanded the field of advance for the H.L.I. and their K.O.S.B. supports. Consequently the latter, soon after passing String trench and absorbing their loaned company C, dug in in support of the H.L.I. in touch with the 29th, represented by the 1st K.O.S.B.† then in support. At one time there was a gap on the L. of the 12th H.L.I.; but Major Dennis sent 12 Lewis guns and a couple of platoons to fill it, and they made good in shell-holes.‡

* Notably in the *History of the 15th Division.*

† W.D. of 7/8th, corroborated by that of 1st Battalion.

‡ There is a slip in *A Border Battalion,* p. 150. Red should read Blue. The Red Line was never near being taken.

The support line was continuous and well sited, being inconspicuous and having an ample field of fire. The night passed quietly and rations reached the front. From the point of view of a C.O. it was a long and trying day and casualties of about 150 were the inevitable result of a fire-swept battle zone. Before morning the battalion was relieved by 45th Brigade troops, and was back at Le Fosse on the big road behind the original starting-point of the day. There Col. Sellar was welcomed on 26th April, but alas, not for long. For the 7/8th K.O.S.B. the fight was over. Nothing serious happened on the 25th, 26th, or 27th, and a return to Arras was made on relief of the division on the night 27/28th April. 2nd Lieut. W. A. Howard was killed on the 24th, and 4 officers were wounded—Major Dennis,* Lieut. W. Thomson, 2nd Lieuts. P. Reay and N. D. Kennedy. It is not an easy battle to picture; but, from darkness on the 23rd morning to the night of the 25th, din and death reigned around. The author of *A Border Battalion* paints the contrast, when the 7/8th K.O.S.B. reached Duisans on the 28th, and the climatic contrast (long overdue and therefore the more violent) already noted in these pages, with all the vividness of one who had been through it. A glorious, warm Sunday of rest was the prelude to a peaceful and profitable three months of summer, most of it spent far from the field of strife, preparatory to two savage bouts in that salient, which the 4th Battalion alone of the regiment failed to know to their bitter cost. This stage of the pilgrimage slipped pleasantly past. At Duisans there was a cleaning up and the usual shake-down to formal military life. Then on 7th May they marched about 7 miles S.W. to Fosseux, where they remained till 21st May, when they moved *via* Sus-St. Léger (one night) and Bonnières (about 7 miles W. of Sus-St. Léger) to Willencourt, just W. of Auxi-le-Château on the Authie—a river deep enough for a good swim. Here real halcyon days were enjoyed from 23rd May to 16th June. But the 7/8th K.O.S.B. had parted with their beloved C.O..

April–May 1917.

The Somme, with its nasty arm wound, and Arras, following on the strain of 1914, and the shock of Loos, had proved too much for Col. Sellar. He truly shortened his life by many years in his zeal for his country and regiment when he came forward at the outbreak and shouldered a heavy burden for a man of his years. He was proud of the battalion, and always spoke with enthusiasm of the officers and men who served under him. With a feeling of relief all ranks learned that as he had to go he was to be succeeded

* *History of the 15th Division*, Appendix I. (not mentioned in Battalion W.D.).

June–July 1917.

not by a stranger but by Major Dennis, and that Major Hart was Second-in-Command. These appointments took effect as and from 27th May, and Dennis became an acting Lieut.-Col. on 1st June. Nevertheless, the parting with Lieut.-Col. Sellar was a wrench. His power to influence as well as instruct, and his unflagging zeal in attending to the interests of his battalion, were great qualities. His keenness on cleanliness of body and dress, and sound feet, and on good food and comforts, were known and appreciated. Sellar's services were valued, as his C.M.G. and D.S.O. and Italian Order "Cavalier of St. Maurice and St. Lazarus" testify.

Although Major-Gen. M'Cracken superintended the training of the 15th Division he did not command it in Flanders. He was promoted to command the XIII. Corps, and his departure was much regretted. It was not till they got to know Major-Gen. Thuillier, C.B., C.M.G., R.E., that the K.O.S.B., like other units, realized that sometimes there are as good fish in the sea as ever came out of it. This parting came on 17th June, just after the G.O.C. had inspected the battalion and seen them engaged in field-work, and had expressed his satisfaction. The life led by this battalion was much the same as that led by the 29th Division in the Bernaville area. These were indeed good times; and even when the train wafted them in leisurely fashion from Frévent to Hopoutre it introduced the 7/8th to the salient at its best, if it had a best, and fate had still a spell of training in the Rubrouck area in store for the 7/8th.

Want of training, one of the suggested causes of the somewhat disappointing results of the battle of Pilckem (31st July–2nd August 1917), cannot be alleged against the 15th Division or the 7/8th K.O.S.B.. The very assembling of the elements of the assaulting brigades other than the two battalions actually holding the division's line, in the dark and at the last moment, is proof positive of a discipline and a training of the highest order, fruits of an assiduously practised programme extending over weeks. By the time the K.O.S.B. reached their bivouacs near Ypres before the battle there was hardly a feature of training, as mentioned in histories or diaries, that they had not studied. The rifle, its bayonet, Lewis guns, the box respirator, bandages and field dressings were put to their various uses. The men were drilled, could march, patrol, lay wire, advance through woods, co-operate with tanks and contact air craft, and take part in brigade exercises. There were courses for specialists, lectures on minor tactics. Signalling and message-sending were not forgotten. The whole work rested on healthy recreation. Sports, cross-country running, shooting competitions gave scope for inter-platoon rivalry. There was, of course, a divisional horse show, and the pipers gave the final cachet to the military life. That the 7/8th K.O.S.B. were not backward in their studies is proved by the special praise given by the C.-in-C. himself to 2nd Lieut. J. Weir (who was awarded the M.C. for gallantry in October) for a masterly field practice demonstration on 15th June with a platoon line composed of picked men of the K.O.S.B. specially called for by the Corps Commander.

June–July 1917.

The 46th I.B. were first in the line, relieving troops of the 55th Division astride the Ménin road between the Ypres-Roulers railway and Warwick Farm, where the 1st Battalion K.O.S.B. had been in 1916. On alighting at Hopoutre at noon on 17th June the 7/8th marched to Toronto Camp, between "Pop." and Vlamertinghe and destined to be very familiar, and after a rest on the 18th relieved the 5th S. Lancs. Regiment in brigade support in and S.E. of Ypres, and worked for the all-important tunnellers. On the 20/21st they took over the front rather S. of their attack position, with their R. on the railway. Working parties still continued to be supplied, and after a slight readjustment the line was held by a rotation of company reliefs within the battalion until relieved by the 10th S.R. on 25/26th June. They then returned to Toronto and another camp and worked for the R.A. of the XIX. Corps (Sir H. E. Watts) in which they then were. On 1st July the battalion marched from Toronto to Watou, where some of the men had a chance of cheering H.M. King George V., and, after a week there, to Broxeele about 6 miles N. of St. Omer near Rubrouck where the final polish for the assault was applied. The march back began on 21st July, stages being Winnezeele (13 miles) and Watou (8½). After three days of camp life, during which respirator technique was perfected, the 7/8th in fighting kit took the track round the S. side of Ypres, and at a cost of 15 casualties, incurred during a block in a communication trench caused by the presence of trespassers, took over the front from the 10th S.R..

There they stayed till the attack, and so did not share in the intricate movements by which the bulk of the 15th Division were brought into battle positions.*

* *History of the 15th Division*, pp. 155, 159–161.

CHAPTER VI

THE BATTLE OF PILCKEM

31st July–2nd August

31 July 1917. As these Borderers advanced at zero at the outset of the belated 1917 Flanders campaign, a word of introduction may be pardoned. The weight of the allied effort was under direction of Gen. Gough, and consisted of 4 army corps of the Fifth Army. The army's front of attack was over 7 miles wide, and was flanked on the N. by the French and on the S. by Plumer's Second Army, the 41st Division of which was to contribute a minor operation. The general direction was to the E., but in a fanning, centrifugal fashion, to widen the cramping prison bars of the existing salient. Farthest to the N. and next the French was Lord Cavan's XIV. Corps, next the XIV. came the XVIII. (Maxse). Then came our XIX., and beyond the XIX. the II. (Jacob). The 15th Division was between the 8th Division of the II. Corps and the 55th of the XIX.. The 15th's front was three-quarters of a mile broad, and its R. rested on the Roulers railway and included it, the direction of advance being parallel thereto. There were two elaborate systems of trenches to be overcome, the front containing Verlorenhoek and the rear containing Frezenberg, the latter being protected by a work crammed with M.G. known as the Frezenberg Redoubt. With the capture of these two systems the first phase ended. The 44th I.B. with the 8/10 Gordons next the railway and the 9th B.W. next the K.O.S.B. were the R. brigade of assault. On the L. of the K.O.S.B. were the 10/11th H.L.I., both in the 46th I.B., the L. brigade of assault. The Borderers were right opposite Frezenberg, distant seven furlongs, and the H.L.I., extending to Warwick Farm, confronted Verlorenhoek. Two miles behind Frezenberg was Zonnebeke. The battlefield was only too well-found in pill-boxes, and success depended on the efficiency of the preliminary bombardment and of the creeping barrage on the day of battle. If the first phase was successful, the 45th I.B. was to pass through the 44th and 46th and attack the

green or final objective, "a system of trenches and concrete defensive points some 1,500 yards farther back." * 31 July 1917.

For twelve days prior to the 31st a heavy and continuous bombardment played on the German trenches and strong points, and counter-battery groups, of which the XIX. Corps had two, attended to the German retaliatory fire.

The 7/8th K.O.S.B. were in position in front of their wire by 1.30 a.m. and ready for the assault at 3.50 a.m. on 31st July 1917. They advanced in four waves. A company of 10th S.R. was sandwiched in to mop up. The barrage was excellent. The Blue Line behind the front hostile system was reached without serious opposition, but with a certain loss of direction to the R. and consequent bunching and intermixing. Frezenberg Redoubt was alive and vocal, and speedy re-formation was needed, in order to put a stop to its attentions. It was just here that 2nd Lieut. F. G. Causley (late of the Coldstream Guards) proved himself invaluable, as did 2nd Lieut. A. M'Call of the 4th Battalion who was mortally wounded later in the day, and received a posthumous M.C. after his death on 23rd August 1917.† By this time the acting Second-in-Command, Capt. H. W. Sutherland, afterwards C.O. and D.S.O., and the remaining company and platoon commanders were casualties.‡ Once reorganized, the battalion resumed the advance until fire from the redoubt stopped all direct advance. 2nd Lieut. Causley's last service was to find the flank route by which the redoubt was ultimately turned. But after executing his wheel he and 2nd Lieut. R. H. Conochie of the 4th Battalion, also a company commander, were killed by M.G. fire while charging the emplacement of the redoubt. However, 2nd Lieut. E. M. S. Houston rushed the place and kept it. Meanwhile the S. end of the redoubt yielded to the combined efforts of Borderers and Royal Highlanders using rifle grenades and aided by Stokes mortars and, last but not least, by tanks. So their practice in the training area had not been wasted! It was then about 8 a.m. and the 1,300 yards of ground gained had taken over four hours to win. A battle is a slower thing than people are apt to suppose. The barrage had moved on and was therefore of no use, and the advance to the Black Line had to be made by rushes with aid of covering rifle-fire. At 9 a.m. the battalion dug in at a ruin called Frost Farm 200 yards E. of Frezenberg, after sending 160 prisoners to the rear or using them as stretcher-bearers. Battalion H.Q. were brought forward to the old German front system at "Iberia Reserve." While consolidation was proceeding, the

* *History of the 15th Division*, p. 156.
† Official Death Roll. ‡ W.D..

1 Aug. 1917. 45th I.B. passed through to exploit the capture of the Black Line by advancing to the final objective. Mopping-up had not become such a fine art as later, and both the 6th Camerons and the 7/8th K.O.S.B. suffered from a M.G. and snipers. No counter-attacks materialized and the battalion remained where they were all night and next day. Early on 1st August rain, which had begun intermittently in the afternoon of the 31st, fell so heavily that much of the work of the 31st was undone. Having once begun, the rain kept on all the time the battalion were in the line. It was evident from the appearance of occasional stragglers on both days from the front that the 45th I.B. had had and were having a hard time of it. But that they had made good was proved by the 42nd Division troops, who relieved that brigade, passing through the K.O.S.B. position at 10 p.m. on 1st August, and the news at 3.35 a.m. on 2nd August that the line in front was taken over. The battalion accordingly retired as far as a line between Potijze and Hell Fire Corner, and stayed there during the hours of daylight. After dark they entered by the Ménin Gate, traversed Ypres, and embussed on the W. side for Oudezeele near Winnezeele, drenched to the skin.

In the battle of Pilckem the 7/8th K.O.S.B. had taken their objective and had dug a support line behind that taken by the 45th I.B. and 1,500 yards in front of the old British line, but at a terrible cost. Besides those mentioned, 2nd Lieuts. W. H. Allan * and Bryson † were killed and 2nd Lieut. T. A. Skinner was wounded, and died in consequence on 10th August 1917.‡ Ten officers were wounded. The War Diary and 15th Division figures are practically the same for O.R.. The latter are given as being revised figures. They amount to 38 killed, 240 wounded, and 19 missing. At the then strength of the battalion it was estimated by Col. Dennis that 45 per cent. of the strength were casualties by the time Frezenberg Redoubt was taken. *A Border Battalion* records the grief of the C.O. and Major Hart as the name of one valued man after another was intimated a casualty. Not a single company commander was left, for among the wounded was Capt. A. B. Lawson. If ever hell was let loose it was on 31st July. How men kept sane is a wonder. If any imagine that the K.O.S.B. were the only sufferers, they have only to read the *History of the Royal Scots Fusiliers* or

* Official Death Roll. His initials are given A. H. Allan in the Appendix I. of *History of the 15th Division*.

† Appendix cited. His name and initials have been sought in vain in the Official Death Roll, in which an Alexander B., who belonged to the 5th K.O.S.B., is entered " d. of w." 25/6/1917.

‡ Official Death Roll, in which " d. of w." should replace " K. in a."

that of the 15th Division or of the Guards Division to realize that it was the same everywhere. All things considered, the 7/8th got their third Ypres over, not painlessly but quickly. One more short visit and they were back at the Scarpe before it was too cold to enjoy a swim. Aug. 1917.

The vileness of some of the back area camps stands out in contrast to the many perfections of B.E.F. organizations. The posts, comforts, rations, clothing, transport, and canteens were marvels. But the heroes of Frezenberg found cold comfort in the tents at Oudezeele.*

On 2nd August 1917 Brig.-Gen. D. R. Sladen, C.M.G., D.S.O., K.O.S.B., who had commanded the 2nd Battalion in many a fight, succeeded Brig.-Gen. Fagan † in command of the 46th Brigade, and remained there till February 1918. On 9th Gen. Thuillier, G.O.C. 15th Division, conveyed the thanks of Gens. Gough and Watts to the battalion for their work in the recent battle. It is interesting to note that 2nd Lieut. E. Gillespie (a promising subaltern of the 9th in " 14–15 ") was now in command of C with acting rank and badges of captain. 100 per cent. New Army men were coming to the fore.‡ There were only 30 O.R. excluded (as new arrivals) from the G.O.C.'s benediction. So it is plain that a weak battalion both in numbers and in quality of reinforcement marched to Abeele station on 15th August and trained for Ypres. By the 17th the 7/8th K.O.S.B. were back in the line with H.Q. in their conquest, the redoubt, and the companies pretty much in their old Black Line between the Zonnebeke road and Frost Farm. It was evident that little progress had been made since they were last there. The front consisted of isolated posts situated in exposed terrain. The relief took a long time through failure on the part of guides. Casualties were constant, and one shell on 19th August killed 2nd Lieut. W. M. Douglas, then commanding B, and wounded 2 other officers § and several O.R.. The shelling was so fierce that rations could not be conveyed to the front during darkness. It is the one of the rare cases the writer has met with (though it must have been common) where iron rations were used " by order." A long and tedious relief

* For details see *A Border Battalion*, p. 179.

† He was gassed on 29th, and the 46th I.B. was commanded by Lieut.-Col. K. G. Buchanan (of the Seaforth Highlanders) in the big battle.

‡ Far the most remarkable in the 15th was Lieut.-Col. G. L. Wilson, D.S.O., M.C., who died in Belgium at the early age of 24. He had enlisted in 1914 (see *History of the 15th Division*, p. 281). But Lieut.-Col. R. F. Ker, D.S.O., affords another instance of the triumph of youth in the 6th Battalion, K.O.S.B. and 9th Division (see Book IV. last chapter).

§ One of these, 2nd Lieut. J. Black, died the same day (Official Death Roll). J. Black's name the writer owes to *A Border Battalion*.

Aug.–Sept. 1917.

on 20/21st August by the 13th R.S. (K.O.S.B. guides sometimes failed like their neighbours), and the K.O.S.B. tried to sleep in a bivouac camp W. of Ypres and tune up for a speedy return to the front.

On 26th August the move forward was made, and in the moist and insecure old German front trenches the battalion remained till 28/29th when they took over from the 8th Seaforths about 1,000 yards N.N.E. of their last battlefield, *i.e.* in front of Pommern Redoubt. B.H.Q. were at Square Farm, a grandiose pill-box of immense solidity, capable of turning (as it did) direct hits except of the heaviest of shells.

The operation in which they were engaged was perhaps the least interesting of any to be recorded. The battle of Langemarck in which the 1st Battalion fought was finished by 18th August. The battle of the Ménin road did not open till 20th September. Between these dates minor attacks were shattered against Armin's concrete fortlets and prompt, devastating barrages. While the 46th were still W. of Ypres, the 44th and 45th I.B. had fought in an attack on 22nd August that makes sad reading.*

When the 7/8th K.O.S.B. went up on the 26th a fresh attack was planned for the 27th and they were in 44th Brigade Reserve under the orders of Brig.-Gen. F. J. Marshall. They were not called on that day, but their cover was insufficient, and as the result of a direct hit on A's H.Q. all of that Company's officers—the O.C., Lieut. G. O. D. Watson, and 2nd Lieuts. J. Rae and J. D. Scott were wounded, and Lieut. Royce and 2nd Lieut. R. R. Douglas had to be borrowed from elsewhere to help to fill the vacancies. The latter, mentioned as a revolver expert and a valuable officer, was badly wounded on the following day and died on the 30th.† On the 28/29th the battalion once more relieved the 8th Seaforths, and on the following night, after an adjustment of the line, became part of the 46th once more. The 30th was also spent in the front, until relief by troops of the 42nd Division completed at 1.40 a.m. on the 31st. O.R. casualties for the tour amounted to 26. The decorations awarded on 1st September related to the battle of Pilckem (31st July–2nd August). Lieut.-Col. Dennis had a bar to his D.S.O.. Lieut. C .K. Thursby-Pelham received the M.C., as did 2nd Lieuts. J. F. Irving, A. B. Dickson, and H. K. M'Kee. A/C.S.M. R. Douglas and Pte .J. A. M'Vinnie won the D.C.M.. Such an honour for a " full private " marks signal services in that most important of posts, battalion runner.

Thus ended inconspicuously the 7/8th's experience of the justly dreaded salient. As we are finishing with that abomination of

* *History of the 15th Division*, pp. 178–186. † Official Death Roll.

desolation, let us place the battalions in order of suffering. The 2nd must have pride of place: 1914; Lindenhoek, Hill 60, and Pilckem Ridge in 1915; and the concentrated horror of twice assailing Polderhoek in 1917. But the 1st Battalion had more of it, and the months in early 1918 at its climatic worst exclude other competitors for second place within the regiment for sheer stationary discomfort. The 6th Battalion did not find the Frezenberg sector improved in October 1917, and the First Battle of Passchendaele on 12th October outdid even 22nd August in misery. The 7/8th come in fourth but well ahead of the 5th, although even *their* lot in 1918 was no bed of roses.

1917.

CHAPTER VII

AT ARRAS ON GUARD AND ON TRIAL

1917. REINFORCED by 3 officers and 400 O.R. the 7/8th K.O.S.B. moved by train from Bavinchove station, near Cassel on the S.W. side, to Aubigny for familiar Duisans. There on the 4th September, when the rebound of the changes made them cheerful, almost hilarious, they received the famous " Will ye no come back again ? " message from Gen. Gough, their late army commander. The K.O.S.B. War Diary is not the one that records the comment " No —— fear ! " but it is unlikely that the sentiments of the battalion would differ. The Fifth Army was not popular during Third Ypres.*

The remainder of 1917 passed off uneventfully in the front won in the spring fighting. There was an urban instead of a rural background. Men who preferred mining villages to agricultural hamlets would prefer Arras to the best of the villages W. of it. Taking it all in all, it was the best time enjoyed by any Borderer unit. Not that there were not incessant fatigues, so many as somewhat to hamper training when the battalion was out, as well as equally incessant toil in the trenches when in. But the sector was quiet, and such aggression as there was was British. The 7/8th were once more in Sir C. Fergusson's XVII. Corps, and the divisional line was on both sides of the Scarpe from Monchy to the railway beyond Roeux. Pelves, on the R. or S. bank, was in German hands, and as their front was 600 yards farther W. than the British front on the N. bank, No Man's Land was considerably larger than usual. Like many of the French rivers, such as the Somme and the Ancre, the Scarpe meandered through water-meadows dotted and lined with water-loving trees and lesser vegetation, and here and there swelled out into lagoons. It was navigable, and quite a fair amount of use was made of it, including the conveyance of working parties. In this part of the line the front consisted of isolated posts which, unlike the ordinary trenches connected by *boyaux* with the rear, could only be relieved in the dark. The front line was about 4 miles E. of Arras

* The whole of p. 187 of *History of the 15th Division* repays perusal.

and embraced the conquests of the spring read of in the stories of the 1917–18.
1st, 6th, and 7/8th Battalions. Thus, for example, the first night (6/7th September) this Battalion slept E. of Arras on leaving Duisans, was at " Fred's Wood." * The 15th Division were taking over from the 4th and the K.O.S.B. relieved the 2nd Essex. Then began the steady routine, which re-made division and battalion to be strong in the hour of need. Eight days in the front, eight days in brigade reserve, eight days in divisional reserve in a camp or actually in Arras. The battalion History gives many touches besides the moves and daily items in the War Diary. Men attached to the New Zealand tunnellers lived a delightful subterranean existence. The 15th had a capital troupe—" the Jocks " ; barbers were available, baths easily procured. For those with cash anything from oysters to regalias were on sale. Civilian life had sprouted up again in Arras and a shell was an event. It was when in divisional reserve that training was ordered, the rifle playing an increased part.† The battalion, like all units, were sorry to part in October with Major-Gen. Thuillier,‡ and he to part with them. He prophesied fame for them, and the sequel will show whether his confidence was merited. The last G.O.C. of the 15th Division was Major.-Gen. H. L. Reed, V.C. (and many other decorations), an artilleryman with a varied and interesting career.§ These changes recall the arrival of Major R. D. Whigham on 27th Sept. He had been at the Landing and in the early Gallipoli battles. What with Brig.-Gen. Sladen at 46th B.H.Q. and (in December) Capt. T. K. Newbigging, M.C., as his Brigade Major the regiment were well represented in high places. St. Andrew's Day, so critical for the 1st Battalion, was passed quietly enough in the front line as was the last day of 1917 and New Year's Day 1918. On that day at dusk they were relieved by the 2nd Scots Guards, and returned to Arras, making use of a light railway which now plied between Arras and Fampoux.

A photograph given in the battalion History shows Col. Dennis in the centre of a group of stalwarts—a very even-looking lot in one sense, though in another the lofty Lieut. W. R. Gaskell (who had good service in the 1st Battalion behind him) broke the line. The photograph (which, alas, hasn't got the names) was probably taken during the training in Corps Reserve at Hermaville a few miles W. of Arras. The officers may be taken as a symbol for the N.C.O.s and men serving with them. It was a good battalion in a good division.

* See *ante*, p. 411.

† The rifle helped greatly to save Arras (*History of the 15th Division*, p. 214).

‡ He was appointed to an important post in the Ministry of Munitions.

§ *History of the 15th Division*, p. 190.

Spring 1918.

Training in a broken, austere January was a rather comfortless, cheerless beginning to 1918, in its earlier phases a gloomy year indeed. It would have been much worse if the " comforts " had not arrived, profoundly appreciated. Another ray of joy was the news of Col. Sellar's C.M.G..* His health had been drunk on " anticipated Christmas Day " (16th December) between the loyal toast and " absent friends," so no reminder was needed of him and his services. All were genuinely delighted with the news.

Neither before nor after New Year were the sectors always the same. At one time the battalion lay astride the Scarpe, but it was mostly S. of the river, and it was there that the shock was borne in March. The return was broken by a week in Arras when Major A. E. Burnett rejoined. By this time the three-battalion plan for watering brigades had been adopted. Both H.L.I. battalions disappeared, and their place was taken by the 9th Black Watch. Brig.-Gen. Sladen had been succeeded by Brig.-Gen. A. F. Lumsden of the Royal Scots. The 46th I.B. therefore consisted of Borderers, Cameronians, and Black Watch. It occupied the Pelves or L. sector of the division next the 45th holding the Monchy or middle sector, while the 44th extended to and beyond the Cambrai road. Beyond one K.O.S.B. raid, in which the enemy were too alert, and in which 2nd-Lieut. M'Quade was wounded, some neighbouring raids, and numerous " stands to " February and March were devoid of incident till the great German attack on 21st March or rather (for this battalion) 28th March. The battalion were at Tilloy from the 16th to the 22nd, and when they went forward on 21/22nd they took up a position on the N.E. slopes of Orange Hill. Even if it is chronologically an unsuitable moment to mention it, it may be stated that they knew before the storm broke that the safety of Arras was in the hands of them and their division. They were in what their C.C. called a post of honour, and he said : " I am glad it is in the hands of a Scottish Division who, I know, will never let the enemy pass." †

It will be remembered that the great German offensive opened with the battle of St. Quentin, spread to the Somme–Ancre area and, by the time the battle of Rozières was dying down, Amiens was to all appearances as good as gone. The nature of that fighting was dealt with in the last Book. On the 28th the final stage of the first phase of the offensive began. A determined effort was made to storm Arras and part of the Vimy Ridge. If a deep break through

* The W.D. records for same date an award of the D.C.M. to Sergt. J. Carmichael, the " Signalling " instructor.

† Message sent on 26th by Sir Charles Fergusson.

were made at Arras the whole Vimy Ridge would fall. If the battle of Arras 1918 had been lost, the consequences would have been disastrous. The new unity of command under Foch would have had no opportunity of justifying its adoption. Considering the damage done a few days later in the battles of the Lys * after the repulse of the Germans in Artois, the ruin that would have resulted from their success there can hardly be exaggerated. March 1918.

The first local signs of the expected attack were felt on 21st March when the battalion was still at Tilloy, and consisted of a four hours' shoot of the lightly held front and the noise of a much bigger bombardment farther S.. No attack eventuated on the 15th's front and the 22nd was quiet there, but on 23rd the retirement of troops beyond the 3rd Division (on R. of 15th) compelled a sympathetic retirement on the part of the 3rd and 15th Divisions, which was carried out silently and "according to plan" to a line just E. of Orange Hill. The commanding Monchy and its plateau were thus handed over, but the Germans' advance was delayed by a series of rearguard actions after dawn on the 23rd. These cost them, massed as they were in groups, considerable casualties, and more were suffered in the process of digging a new line between the Monchy *massif* and Orange Hill, on which the 15th Division were going to make their stand in trenches known as Minorca, Corsica, and (in the K.O.S.B. sector) Jerusalem. Although the 3rd Division was attacked on the 24th they held † their ground, and as no attacks were made on the 15th's front no change took place. The next three days passed quietly; on one of them a draft of 86 was absorbed in the battle-line, and on the 28th the Germans at last launched their expected attack.

At this time the K.O.S.B. were on the L. of their brigade and division with the 9th B.W. on their R. and a unit of the 4th Division on their L.. The barrage started at 3 a.m., roared and shrieked like legions of demons let loose for two and a half hours, and then, with the moral and substantial support of the dreaded Flammenwerfer and a flotilla of sniping aeroplanes, the enemy's infantry came over. But fortunately for the K.O.S.B. the weight alike of projectiles and men was directed against the line farther S. than where they were. The first time mentioned in the War Diary is 8.10 a.m. as the moment when a S.O.S. signal was observed on the R.. It was gradually discovered that there was a gap on the immediate R. in consequence of a retirement of the 9th B.W., small by comparison with that

* See Book II. chap. vi.

† The 8th Seaforths and the 44th I.B. T.M.B. did fine work on their left flank (*History of the 15th Division*, p. 204).

28 Mar. 1918. farther S.. Col. Dennis was able to form a defensive flank with the aid of a company of 10th S.R.* and so contact was maintained with the B.W.. At what o'clock the two attacks recorded as having taken place on the battalion front were delivered is not quite clear, possibly about 9 a.m.. But they were both beaten off by B and C, the companies in the line, with rifle grenades and Lewis guns. Although a raw drizzle came on later in the day, the morning atmosphere was clear. For once the weather was kind to the British. Massed formation was generally used by the Germans and the gunners and infantrymen had splendid targets, though the former, as was natural in a defensive battle, were firing at long range. The plan of the Third Army (Gen. Byng) was to fight a stubborn rearguard action to the Army Line in front of Tilloy and along Observation Ridge, *i.e.* about 2 miles E. of Arras, nearly two miles behind the K.O.S.B. and stand to the last there. Their motto was, so to speak, to be that of the heroes of Verdun: "Ils ne passeront pas."

Up till about 11 a.m. the K.O.S.B. had held their original position. It was then found that their L. flank towards the river was denuded of troops, and the last company in reserve, A, in a trench called Invergordon, advanced in echelon to form the usual defensive flank, but at noon, probably owing to events farther S.,† the 46th I.B. were recalled and the K.O.S.B. began a slow, steady retirement which landed them in the Army Line on Observation Hill about 3 p.m.. Details are unfortunately lacking. Contact with the enemy must have been lost, because when, for tactical reasons, the K.O.S.B. were sent forward again to form an outpost line as much as 500 yards ahead of the Army Line, they scattered in the dusk a somewhat apprehensive screen of the enemy. The most tiring part of a tiring day was when the shell-holes selected were being dug into some sort of semblance of trenches. That concluded the German *offensive* against the 7/8th K.O.S.B. and the 15th Division—one day—as against the Borderers' offensives at Loos, the Somme, Arras, and Ypres, Soissonnais, and the final advance. If the Borderers had found the Germans tough defenders, they certainly proved themselves such on the only occasion when they were tried. The battalion History rings true, when it says that they were surprised at having to go back, because they had the situation well in hand and were confident in themselves. As it was, they were not

* *History of the 15th Division*, p. 210, and *A Border Battalion*, p. 210. Probably D in support in Cromarty Trench was used too (W.D. entry for 22/3/18).

† The *History of the 15th Division* disclosed a much more violent battle waged by the 44th and 45th Brigades.

tried, as they had been and were, alas, destined to be. 2nd Lieut. N. P. Laird was the only officer to fall and 10 O.R. were killed, one man being wounded and missing. 28 Mar. 1918.

Lieut A. E. Forbes-Dennis * and 2nd-Lieut. G. Jackson * and 36 O.R. were wounded and, according to the W.D., 39 missing. The bulk of the missing must have returned, as Col. Stewart's figures show 92 wounded and only 2 missing. Sir Charles Fergusson's message has a note of thankfulness and allayed anxiety about it. " I knew you could be relied on to stick it out to the end. Well done! There are fresh troops in support of you now, but I want the honour of holding Arras to be yours alone."† The K.O.S.B. accordingly spent the next ten days pretty much where they were at the end of the battle, shelled but otherwise unmolested. On the night of the 7/8th April they withdrew, on relief by 10th S.R., to caves near the suburb of St. Sauveur and within reach of baths. The caves produced a crop of sickness, and being in brigade reserve meant plenty of fatigues. So a return to the front line in Battery Valley on the 12/13th was not so unwelcome, especially as a real relief was bound to come soon. It began on 14th and finished at a former haunt, Agnez-lez-Duisans, on 15th April. A week resting and cleaning up was succeeded by a short visit to Arras, when the effects of the last terrible offensive against the British on the Lys and in Flanders, of which the 1st, 2nd, and 6th Battalions had experience, were felt in the shape of a sudden migration by bus to Burbure near Lillers on 24th April. There they remained in uncertainty as to the next move until 3rd May, when, partly by road (to Pernes and from Maroeuil stations) and partly by rail, they returned to Arras, and on 4th took over the line from Canadian troops astride the Scarpe. In spite of rumours no more German attacks were delivered, and the battalion tackled the fatigues of brigade reserve undepleted. The next tour in the line was saddened by the death of the C.O., the " splendid and gallant " Lieut.-Col. Frederick Dennis, due to a stray shell.‡ A moving account of his funeral is given in *A Border Battalion*. To Gen. Reed's well-chosen epithets above, the word " beloved " can safely be added. Dennis was exactly the right man to follow Sellar, and his handling of the situation on 28th March seems to have been flawless. Letters of sympathy came from Col. Sellar and Brig.-Gen. Fagan. Fortunately there was still one of the old lot available in the shape of

* *A Border Battalion*, p. 217.

† Quoted in *History of the 15th Division*, p. 213.

‡ Curiously enough, Brig.-Gen. Lumsden was the victim of casual shelling. He was killed, greatly regretted, on 24th June 1918. He was succeeded by Brig.-Gen. V. M. Fortune, the Black Watch.

May–July 1918.

Lieut.-Col. H. P. Hart, D.S.O., who took over command (from Major Burnett, commander in the interim) on 26th May. He had held command of the 7/8th R.S.F. when a pioneer battalion in the 59th Division and had been badly wounded near Bullecourt in the March fighting.* The back area during the last Arras sojourn was the N. suburbs of the city, to which we were introduced early in the 2nd Battalion story. The life in and out was so normal, and the Scarpe valley so familiar, that although it was not till 12th July that the 7/8th K.O.S.B. said farewell to the front, we may conclude by a reference to (rather than an account of) Capt. Paton's successful raid, which yielded 6 prisoners and a M.G. on the night of 24/25th June and earned warm commendation from the XVII. C.C. and the G.O.C.. Careful preparations brought the party undetected to the taped assembly-point. A model box barrage covered the advance. The German wire was poor and the three actual raiding parties rushed the trench, the L. party securing a M.G. and 6 prisoners, and the R. party 8 prisoners (afterwards killed by their own shells on the way over). The ground was formerly British, and one of the objectives, a big cave, was identified by the centre party and treated to a R.E. charge of explosive. At least 24 of the enemy were killed, one of them being shot with a revolver by 2nd-Lieut. Haining. Unfortunately 2nd-Lieut. I. Dryborough was fatally wounded,† and died almost at once. He belonged to the 1st Battalion and was attached to the 7/8th. The other casualties amounted to 16 O.R. and two officers wounded besides Dryborough.

* Buchan, *R.S.F.*, p. 416.

† On his way back (*A Border Battalion*, p. 230). The same source has preserved the name of Bugler Dodds, killed while sounding the "Come to the Cook-house Door" for the recall.

CHAPTER VIII

WITH THE FRENCH

WE have now reached the last major engagement of the regiment to be recorded in these pages. It was, of course, far from being the last chronologically, but it was the last of the junior battalion. It is bound up with the recovery of the initiative by the Allies on the failure of the last despairing thrust of the Germans on 15th July towards Paris. On the 18th July Foch launched the first of the counter-offensives, which resulted in the defeat of the Germans between Château-Thierry and Soissons. He stipulated for a reserve of British divisions. Thus it came about that the 15th Division was hurried, within a matter of hours rather than days of escape, from a long, wearying spell of the front, into an unknown battlefield, there to co-operate with strangers and to some extent with a strange tongue. The 7/8th K.O.S.B. must have been loth to tear themselves away from Gauchin-légal in the extreme N.W. corner of XVII. Corps territory on the sunny slopes of the Artois plateau, S. of the fine Bois d'Olhain, and pack up and march to the railway (the nearest point was about 5 miles off) in pouring rain. Warning came on 15th July. One hopes there was time for all to bathe at Estrée-Cauchie before an early start for Savy Station on the 16th. Thunder and lightning were suitable preliminaries for what was to come.

July–Aug. 1918.

On 17th July, just a day before the 5th Battalion arrived at Senlis, the 7/8th Battalion detrained at Pont St. Maxence, where the 2nd Battalion had entrained from the Aisne in 1914. A short march N., and they settled down three companies in Les Ageux and one company at St. Martin Longeau. The Oise was near enough to the former to be a blessing in the heat.

Early on the 19th the battalion took a roundabout course for the front by marching W. to Cinqueux. There a flotilla of buses took them over dusty, crowded roads all round the country, as it seemed, until in the end they were deposited at Hautefontaine, well to the E. of the Forêt de Compiègne. All next day they lay

July–Aug. 1918. — quiet and moved up by night to the St. Pierre Aigle area, and felt the proximity of battle. And well they might, for they were only 7 miles W. of Buzancy (still in German hands), and the width of the French indentation was 20 miles—so there was a certain amount of noise. They were within 8 miles of Soissons and 6 of the Aisne, on the N. tip of the Forêt Dominiale de Retz. Northwards lay the bare, cultivated tableland of the Soissonnais, which stretched E. for 4 miles before being furrowed or scooped into between Chaudun and Buzancy. Like the 5th Battalion, the 7/8th were in General Mangin's Tenth Army. The particular A.C. in which the 7/8th were was the XX. (Gen. Berdoulat).

The Second Battle of the Marne stands second in interest only to the First Battle of the Marne, and invites an exhaustive study. In both battles the attacked became the attacker with dramatic suddenness, and the consequences were momentous. The first won from the very jaws of annihilation the right to fight, and the second won an initiative which was never lost till victory was won. In both cases the fascinating inquiry arises—How was it done? A regimental historian can only accept the facts as they happened, and only lift the veil of mystery from a tiny corner of the field by recounting what his particular unit did or endured. He can tell of ground gained or lost or held, and the circumstances will reveal the *moral*, which is such a mighty factor in war. The achievements of the 7/8th K.O.S.B. in the Second Marne consist of no long advance, no stronghold captured. Their contribution was a vigorous offensive, a dourness in taking punishment, a readiness to resume the offensive with reduced numbers, so that in the end what was impossible for themselves was appreciably more possible for others.

The 15th Division relieved the 1st American Division in the Berzy-le-Sec front with orders to continue the advance. Corps orders came late to D.H.Q., and naturally more time was required to bring them through to B.H.Q. and on to Col. Hart, so he did not get his orders out till 11.30 p.m.. It had been known, however, that the battalion would be fighting somewhere on that front, and the move forward—it was *open warfare*—began at 6 p.m..

It has been indicated that between Chaudun and Buzancy the ground is broken. While the high ground continues N.E. to Berzy-le-Sec before tipping over into the Crise Valley, and extends for a long way S.E. by Charantigny and Villemontoire, due E. of Chaudun, a small chine enclosing Chazelle leads to the valley in which the Soissons–Paris railway runs from Vierzy to the Crise at Noyant. As advanced Battalion H.Q. were to be one kilometre E. of the junction of the little road from Chazelle and the railway, the K.O.S.B. had to leave the big plateau, drop into the valley, cross the marshy ground at the bottom, and ascend the heights, which face Buzancy across another valley running N. from Villemontoire. The front line was on the plateau, and getting there was very difficult owing to darkness and unfamiliarity. Still, K.O.S.B. on right, and Cameronians on left, were in position when the Franco-American-British barrage fell at 4.10 a.m. on 23rd July 1918. The 10th S.R. faced Rozières, and the K.O.S.B. faced the open country between Rozières * and Buzancy. Buzancy was the objective of the 87th (French) Division. At 4.55 the attack was launched, but something had gone wrong with the barrage. M.G. fire was immediately experienced, and the K.O.S.B. progressed only 200 yards at the outside, and nobody else got quite so far. The 87th Division could not advance at all, nor could the 69th (French) Division beyond the 45th Brigade. The K.O.S.B. formed a defensive flank with the French by borrowing a company from the 10th S.R.. In that stagnation there were many rumours of fresh efforts, but they came to nothing. When Col. Hart was badly hit, in the late afternoon, it must have seemed as though it was all up with the battalion. They had already suffered grievous casualties to gain their few yards. Lieut. V. T. Cowley and 2nd Lieuts, John Sloan and A. B. White (both of the 5th Battalion), and 2nd Lieut. James Wyper were all killed. Besides the C.O. the following were wounded: Capts. Taylor and Paton, Lieut. M. Fenwick, Intelligence Officer (and of great use in locating and placing the men in the jumping-off position), 2nd Lieuts. Macaulay, Lidster and Honeymoon. Of the 309 O.R. casualties, 32 were killed and 214 wounded. The vast majority of the 63 O.R. missing were killed.

23 July 1918.

Five officers alone were left. Fortunately Capt. J. Weir, M.C., the Adjutant, was one of these, and he carried on as C.O. till Major F. L. Hamilton was sent up on the 24th from details to take over command.

Relief of the (Dandy) 9th R.S. (now in the 46th I.B. in place of the depleted 9th B.W.) took place in the small hours of the 24th, and the battalion retired to dead ground near Chazelle, and, after the brigade was relieved, to trenches N.E. of Chaudun, a kilometre farther W. to a defensive position. Two days of showers did not add to the cheerfulness of things.

When next the K.O.S.B. took part with the 10 per cent. personnel and the officers who had stood down, they were farther S., *i.e.* S. of Villemontoire. Things admitted of more deliberate handling,

* Not to be confused with Rozières-en-Santerre of the battle, which is 18 miles E.S.E. of Amiens.

1 Aug. 1918. — and the relief on 28th July of the 72 Inf. Regt. of the 87th (French) Division went very smoothly, thanks to the efficiency of the guiding and smoothness of the arrangements. The K.O.S.B. were unaffected by the famous attack of the 44th and 45th I.B. on 28th July upon Buzancy—the capture of the stronghold and the ultimate retirement in consequence of other units' failure.* They just held the line for the remainder of the month, and, like the 5th Battalion, wound up their career with the French by a pitched battle on Minden Day. But whereas the 5th got back at the enemy, the 7/8th were treated to a repetition of the 23rd July. They were only 260 strong when the fight opened; and M.G. playing from derelict tanks stifled a morning and an afternoon attack, although pressed with determination, as the deaths of 2nd Lieuts. Macmillan, Shannan, and A. J. Lewis (of the 1st Battalion),† and the decimation of its ranks testify. Their sacrifices were not unavailing. As we remember, in the Beugneux district a great victory was won, and after 1st August the whole German force was in retreat. No unit suffered more than the 7/8th K.O.S.B.. Consequently the French Army Commander's General Order may be inserted with legitimate pride.‡

X^E^ ARMÉE,
ETAT-MAJOR, *Au Q.G.A., le* 5 *Août* 1918.
3e *Bureau.*

ORDRE GÉNÉRAL No. 343

OFFICIERS, SOUS-OFFICIERS ET SOLDATS DES 15^E^ ET 34^E^ DIVISIONS BRITANNIQUES

Vous êtes entrés dans la bataille à son moment le plus rude. L'ennemi vaincu une première fois, ramenait contre nous ses meilleures divisions, en nombre plus considérable que les nôtres.

Vous avez continué à avancer pied à pied, malgré sa résistance acharnée, et vous avez gardé le terrain conquis malgré ses violentes contre-attaques.

Puis dans la journée du 1er Août, vous avez enlevé, côte à côte avec vos comrades Français, la crête qui domine toute la contrée entre L'AISNE et L'OURCQ, et que ses défenseurs avaient l'ordre de tenir coûte que coûte.

* See *History of the 15th Division*, p. 244. † *Ibid.*, p. 250.

‡ The rustic monument erected by the piety of the late General Gassoins, with the warm-blooded inscription about the noble Thistle of Scotland ever flourishing amid the Roses of France, still stood in 1928 in a field cultivated up to the very base. But the lettering was becoming blurred. It is to be hoped the appropriate British Authority has acquired, or will acquire, the monument and a right of access.

Avant échoué dans sa tentative pour la reprendre avec ses dernières réserves, l'ennemi dut battre en retraite, poursuivi, bousculé, pendant 12 kilomètres. Aug. 1918.

Tous, Anglais et Ecossais, jeunes soldats et vétérans des FLANDRES ou de PALESTINE, vous avez montré les magnifiques qualités de votre race, le courage et l'imperturbable ténacité.

Vous avez fait l'admiration de vos compagnons d'armes. Votre pays sera fier de vous, car vos chefs et vous avez eu une large part dans la victoire que nous venons de remporter sur les barbares ennemis des peuples libres.

Je suis heureux d'avoir combattu à votre tête et je vous remercie.

The following awards indicate satisfaction in high quarters in both British and French Armies. A bar to the M.C. was bestowed on Capt. Weir, M.C., and the M.C. on Capt. A. B. Paton (of the raid), and Lieut. P. Reay. L./Corp. D. M'Clure and Pte. W. Montgomery won a second bar to their M.M., and 11 M.M.s were conferred. But the French had been even quicker. Major F. L. Hamilton, M.C., received the Croix de Chevalier of the Légion d'Honneur. The Croix de Guerre (avec palmes) was awarded to 2nd Lieut. W. D. Jamie, Sergt. Smart, M.M., and L./Sergt. J. Ralston. Six Croix de Guerre and two Médailles Militaires complete the list.

CHAPTER IX

FROM LOOS TO VICTORY

Aug.–Sept. 1918.

RELIEVED by French troops on 3rd August, the Borderers gradually returned on their tracks till on the 6th the train took them from Pont St. Maxence to Tinques, 4 miles from their billets at Gouy-en-Ternois, in the Arras rest area. After ten days they were once more in the line in the Cambrai road sector, which was quiet enough, till the 23rd, when, on relief by a Canadian unit, they went to Arras and slept their last war night there. Their destination was the Loos front, and they were in the line between Puits 14 *bis* and Hill 70 by the 27th. One night had been spent at Château-de-la-Haie, N.N.W. of Arras, and two at Hersin, at the northern fort of the bluff of Artois, and a few miles W. of Loos.

There were still some who remembered 1915. They would approve of the structural alterations, such as a long tunnel between Loos and the front, which greatly facilitated reliefs. The quiet of the time, which contrasted so markedly with the contemporaneous turmoil on the Somme and the stir beginning in W. Flanders, was broken on 18th September by a daylight reconnaissance in force by A and B, assisted by moppers to the number of two platoons from the remaining companies. If a two-company front represented unusual width, half a mile represented unusual depth. The plan was well practised with tapes at Mazingarbe, and the raid, as it is called, has been described by the divisional historians as a success. But it was so only by comparison with less successful ones. The tangible results were some papers establishing the regiment and division of one dead man, and the information that the front system was in poor repair and unoccupied, and that the main defence was in that "Hulluch" trench on the reserve line, which was the final objective of the raid. No prisoners were taken, and our casualties were heavy in proportion to the estimated number of 25 Germans killed (at least 11 by preliminary gun-fire), namely, Capt. H. L. Deans, the leader of the expedition, and Lieuts. J. J.

Gracie, M.C.,* and G. B. Hopkins,* all killed, the last officers to be killed in this unit, 3 more wounded, viz. Lieut. Tod,* and 2nd Lieuts. Irvine and Pritchard, twice hit, and 64 O.R. casualties. Gracie had only been with the 7/8th for about a month. They could not be expected to know what they had lost. But the 1st Battalion K.O.S.B. and all his old friends did, and the news came with a sense of real and lasting loss. He was a son of the regiment, and his future lay there. He was one of those who pulled his full weight in the Great War. Oct 1918.

The details of the raid are somewhat confusingly reported. The battalion History has reduced it to readable dimensions. It started at 4 p.m., and trouble began as the final objective was neared, the trench being only reached in one or two places. The Germans were full of fight, and many acts of bravery and dash were performed on both sides. Capt. Deans fell early. Capt. M'Kee, M.C., won a bar for his gallantry in throwing bombs into the objective trench. 2nd Lieuts. Mellalieu and Groine and L./Corps. Muirhead and Pickard, as well as Ptes. Reid † and (notably) Morrison,† are specially mentioned. Pte. Blackwood was a most gallant and indefatigable dresser of the wounded. If it was of the nature of a repulse, the enterprise reflected the greatest credit on the veterans of the Marne and the youths who had since joined.

The Germans remained obstinately undislodged until the beginning of October. On the 2nd, in consequence of a prisoner's statement, the Borderers, then in the sector fronting Hulluch, pushed out patrols through the *terra ignota* with its nasty possibilities in booby-traps and other surprises. About a mile E.N.E. of Hulluch Wingles had been prominent for three tall towers which had defied destruction for four years. The Borderers saw the last of these fall as they followed their patrols eastwards to the next stopping-place dictated by the defensive position taken up by the enemy behind the Haute Deule Canal. In the course of these operations 5 O.R. were killed (the last) and 10 were wounded. Capt. G. A. Whyte, M.C., had the distinction of being the last officer to be wounded. By that time it was the 5th of October, and the K.O.S.B. were relieved and returned from near Pont-à-Vendin to old Mazingarbe, eventually coming forward to Loos on the 10th—Loos without an enemy at hand! When the battalion returned to the line on 13th October it was commanded by Lieut.-Col. H. W.

* Official Death Roll. These officers' names are given by *A Border Battalion*, p. 263. The W.D. does not mention them.

† Both awarded D.C.M.. There were also 2 M.C.s and 8 M.M.s awarded (*A Border Battalion*).

Oct.–Nov. 1918. — Sutherland, D.S.O., Capt. Patrick, M.C., was Second-in-Command (*vice* Major Hamilton on leave), and Capt. P. Reay was Adjutant. On negotiating a difficult relief of troops of the 75th I.B., it was found that the canal still had to be crossed. However, the Germans found they had more pressing calls elsewhere. On the 15th, cheered by a " light barrage," * the K.O.S.B. crossed by improvised bridges to find that the bird had flown, and the last stage of the war opened—the pursuit.

Every night saw a new lodging. Leaving Pont-a-Vendin on the 17th, Épinoy was reached on the 17th ; La Neuville on the 18th ; Capelle on the 19th. On the 20th the frontier was crossed, and they were in Belgium approaching the canalized Scheldt S. of Tournai. The first pause was made at Wcz Welvain. This canal was a much more serious impediment than the Haute Deule. It merited and received great respect. On the 29th the battalion was relieved and retired to Lecuelle and trained and drilled.

The first eight days of November passed in this quiet fashion. On the 9th the battalion (under orders of the B.G.C. 44th I.B.) advanced to Vezon. Their line of march lay over classic soil. They passed close to the village of Fontenoy, where the 25th of Foot had so nobly fought in 1745 against the French under Saxe.† On the 10th they were distributed between Vieux Leuze and Ervaux. On Armistice Day they were at Maffles, on the far side of the Blaton Canal. That happy night, with the nightmare off their chests, the 7/8th K.O.S.B. lay thus : H.Q. in the Château de Maffles ; A in Tongres St. Martin ; B in Mévergnies ; C at Brugelette ; D in Arbre —all villages close to Ath, of the proud but gloomy memories.

A modern Sterne might write of the 25th on the 11th November 1918 : " You should have seen what a prodigious regiment we had in Flanders." The 4th K.O.S.B. were at Herchies, 8 miles N. of Mons. Six miles N. were the 7/8th Battalion. The senior battalion was at Celles, N. of Tournai ; the 5th were at Halluin ; and the 6th were at Hulste, N. of Courtrai. A goodly company ! The 2nd Battalion finished the war in the splendid isolation in which the war was begun, not so very far away, on the outskirts of Flanders. Not one of these six battalions had let down the honour of the regiment. The fame of the youngest will rest for all time bound up with the great names—Loos, Martinpuich, Arras (1917), Frezenberg, Arras (1918), Buzancy.

* W.D..

† There is an account of this bloody battle in Buchan's *Scots Fusiliers*, in which is quoted a noble passage from Sir John Fortescue's *History of the British Army*.

The 7/8th Battalion never invaded Germany. There was a review by the C.-in-C. of the triple Allied force, H.M. the King of the Belgians, at Ormeignies on 7th December. At it were the Prince of Wales and the Duke of York (then Prince Albert). On 27th January the commander of the corps in which they then were, Sir R. Butler, presented colours to the 7/8th K.O.S.B. on the hallowed field of Waterloo. The rest is told elsewhere. The Service battalions ceased to exist save in memory. There they will live on as the personification of patriotism. From the toils and discomforts of the home-training, through the toils, miseries, and perils of those terrible three years, they won through to Victory. 1919.

BOOK VI

"*THEY ALSO SERVED*"

CHAPTER I

THE TENTH BATTALION

THE need for economy in man-power led to the formation of garrison battalions in 1918. On 10th June the 9th (Garrison) Battalion was formed at Étaples under command of Lieut.-Col. M. Archer-Shee, D.S.O., of the 19th Hussars. It was composed of men thought not quite fit for the strain to which first-line troops were put, and graded suggestively as B1 and B2. They were far from being "crocks," for 800 strong they were able to march in full marching order from Watten Station (6 miles) to Buysscheure without anyone falling out. The battalion was composed of drafts collected at hazard or local convenience from labour companies. There does not seem to have been any reason why the 9th (Garrison) Battalion should on 16th June have received the new name of 10th Battalion, the King's Own Scottish Borderers. The Death Roll of the rank and file—19 in all—discloses only 2 private soldiers who had enlisted in the K.O.S.B.. The remainder had served in other units without any particular regard to Scotland. What is true of the part is probably true of the whole. But the 10th Battalion got through the last five months of the war with credit to itself and the regiment, and a few words will suffice to tell the tale. It was in the 120th I.B. of the 40th Division (Major-Gen. J. Ponsonby, C.B., at that time) of the XV. Corps (de Lisle). The training started from the very beginning. There was square drill and physical drill, anti-gas drill and route marching. They were fit enough to play games.

1918.
—

On 23rd June a move was made to La Belle Hôtesse and a B1 standard definitely adopted. Forty rejects went back to labour companies.

Early in July the 120th I.B. was inspected by that experienced soldier H.R.H. The Duke of Connaught, and the satisfaction which he expressed at the appearance of the brigade was most encouraging to men about to occupy a section of line known as West Hazebrouck. Here the men were instructed in trench duties and discipline. On the 8th they were subjected to a more rigorous inspection by Major-

1918. Gen. Sir Wm. Peyton, C.B., who saw them at work on the training-ground and on the range. And on it went, the machine—now well-nigh perfected—turning out soldiers in record time. Great heed was given to musketry and to signalling and handling of messenger pigeons, and the M.O. gave lectures and demonstrations, including the bearing of stretchers.

The garrison battalions were not there for ornament. After the XV. Corps had dealt the shrewd blows at Meteren and the Hoegenacker Ridge described previously, the 48th Division and the 10th K.O.S.B. on it took part in the offensive. On 28th August the 10th K.O.S.B. relieved troops of the 92nd I.B. near La Becque, and on the 23rd delivered a vigorous but not wholly successful attack at a cost of 23 casualties (3 fatal). These were slightly supplemented before relief through gas- and other shells. At the end of the month the battalion withdrew to Eeckhout Casteel and spent the first eleven days of September there, returning to the line at the "Nieppe Switch," near Armentières, and patrolling vigorously. On the 23/24th they were relieved and went into reserve.

October opened quietly enough still near Armentières but on 12th things got going and the 10th K.O.S.B., leapfrogging a battalion of Cameron Highlanders, advanced and took about 800 yards of a trench—Incarnate Trench—and on relief by the Camerons withdrew from the battlefield, and, as far as offensive operations were concerned, from the Great War.

CHAPTER II

THE THIRD BATTALION

It is impossible to write a short notice of the achievements of the 3rd Battalion K.O.S.B. without a note of sadness. To all intents and purposes it has been disbanded Its Scottish Borderer Militia colours, gifted in 1877, now hang in Greyfriars Church, Dumfries. The current Army List discloses one solitary officer's name beneath the heading, 3rd Battalion—an honoured one it is true, but alone—that of Col. Archibald Hume of Auchendolly in the Stewartry.* Such existence as it enjoys is shadowy and unsubstantial. That the Service battalions should come to an end as soon as their task was over was inevitable. That the Special Reserve should be wiped out at the end of four years' solid success is one of the puzzles. The omission of Parliament to thank the Special Reserve is a mere instance of human frailty. It forgot. But the abolition of the Special Reserve was an act as deliberate as that creating it, but with greater consequences. For whereas the Act of 1907, in so far as it created a Special Reserve, was merely adapting the already existing, historic Militia, that of 1920 in disbanding the Special Reserve wiped out the Militia. This characteristically English institution, with its quaint, arresting title " the Constitutional Force," needs no defence here. It took firm, if slow-growing, root in Scotland at the close of the eighteenth century, when the dread of invasion was rife. For 110 years, from and including 1798 to 1907, the regiment which became the 3rd Battalion K.O.S.B., whether called Fourth Regiment of North British Militia, or Seventieth Regiment of Militia, or the 81st Regiment of Militia, or the Dumfries Militia or, after 1864, the Scottish Borderers Militia, worthily upheld the standards of the service. The story is fully and interestingly told by the late Dr. R. W. Weir, D.D., of Greyfriars, Dumfries, for so long chaplain to the regiment. Charles, 4th Duke of Buccleuch, was an early and most capable colonel. His own and his family influence were perhaps the most important factors in the creation of the regiment. His brother-in-law, Charles (Douglas), 5th Marquis of Queensberry, succeeded him

1798.
—

* On the death of Sir George Walker, Col. Hume succeeded him as Hon. Col. of the Battalion. He had previously succeeded him in the command.

1854. as colonel, and received a compliment on the efficiency of the regiment from Major-Gen. Sir Sidney Beckwith in 1825. During most of the long period of disembodiment, between 1825 and the Crimean War, John, 6th Marquis of Queensberry, was colonel of the regiment in succession to his brother. As John Douglas of Lockerbie he had acted as second to his kinsman, Sir Alexander Boswell of Auchinleck, in the famous Fife duel, when Boswell was fatally shot by James Stuart of Dunearn in 1822 near Auchtertool.

A new epoch begins with the year 1854—that of Lieut.-Col. John M'Murdo, son of Lieut.-Col. A. M'Murdo who had commanded the local yeomanry, and Sir George Walker. No reader of Dr. Weir's pages can escape the conviction that the modern Scottish Borderers Militia was largely the work of these two devoted men, and especially Sir George Walker. The experience of the former in the Madras Army and the enthusiasm of the young Capt. Walker, fresh from a training with the Scots Guards, overcame all difficulties. In 1858 the regiment was the most efficient unit in the whole of the Militia, and placed 14th in order of merit in the British Army. It was the absorption of the Stewartry quota of the Galloway Rifles in 1860 that suggested to Col. M'Murdo the idea of changing the name of the regiment. Moreover, nearly all the officers belonged to the nobility and gentry of four Border counties, Berwick, Roxburgh, Dumfries, and Selkirk. In 1864 the change was approved. For the first time Scottish Borderers served as a regimental name and undoubtedly referred to Borderers on the Scottish side of the frontier between England and Scotland. The 25th of Foot or King's Own Borderers had, as explained, no connection with the "Borders." What the Royal namer had in his head may have been a part of the Highland line between, say, Sheriffmuir and Killiecrankie. It was a happy accident that a word of somewhat obscure meaning came in 1887 to win a definite local significance.

Outstanding events were the acquisition of Kingholm Merse on the L. bank of the Nith between Dumfries and Carlaverock in 1870, and the presentation of the Regimental Colours—the gift of the ladies of the district—by Louisa, Countess of Dalkeith (afterwards Duchess of Buccleuch), in 1877. These colours were not long in use, because affiliation to the Royal Scots Fusiliers in 1881 necessitated fresh colours, which no sooner arrived (somewhat late in the day) than they were superseded by the affiliation of the regiment to the King's Own Scottish Borderers in 1887, which entailed yet another set of colours, beautifully reproduced opposite p. 90 of Dr. Weir's History.* But the 1877 colours remained a treasured possession of

* These are now preserved in the National War Memorial at Edinburgh.

the regiment until, on 30th June 1929, they were handed over to the kirk-session of Greyfriars, Dumfries. The officers of the colour party consisted of Lieut.-Col. John M'Kie, C.B.E., D.S.O., of Bargaly, who had actually received the identical colour, he handed over in 1929, from the hands of Lady Dalkeith in 1877, more than half a century before, and Major Sir James Bruce Wilkie Dalyell, Baronet, of the Binns, who joined in 1887 and served in S. Africa and in the Great War. 1914. —

Once it had become bone and flesh of the K.O.S.B. the regiment maintained its reputation as a unit of high efficiency in tactics and in marksmanship, and put the coping-stone on the years of training and tradition by the voluntary campaign in S. Africa under Lieut.-Col. J. K. Maxwell-Witham of Kirkconnell with Capt. F. J. Carruthers of the 1st Battalion (now of Dormont) as Adjutant. The S. African War came very soon after the retirement of Col. Hume in 1898 after a successful command of five years.

He was immediately asked to become honorary colonel of the regiment, and in that capacity his name continues to represent the officers of the 3rd Battalion K.O.S.B..

The S. African War story is told elsewhere. But it left its stamp on the 3rd K.O.S.B., on officers, N.C.O.s, and men. The atmosphere of the Verne in 1914 was military and professional. The multitudinous majors with medals, the weather-beaten warrant officers and N.C.O.s strode the barracks as men used to war, and the S. African medals became familiar. The parades—all day visible here or there—the court-martial proceedings, the model mess arrangements, the bearing and style of all ranks, proclaimed the soldier on active service. But when the Great War broke out the militia regiments were not allowed to volunteer. They had become Special Reserve in the interval between the two wars, and their function was to fill the gaps in the regular battalions, while occupying positions suitable for defending the shores of the country against invasion, the Territorials not being ripe for that, their appropriate task, in sufficient numbers. As the 3rd K.O.S.B. never were called upon to essay the latter duty in operations, the former will suffice for an introduction to the war story. "The personnel of such reinforcements had to be found in various directions : first, among the officers and men of the battalion, who could be spared ; then among the members of other battalions, who had been invalided home and were sufficiently recovered to return to active service ; but, most of all, among the fresh recruits that were continually being raised, and had to be trained and equipped from the foundation. As the war operations extended and increased in intensity, the calls for these

1914. became correspondingly urgent, and taxed to the utmost the energies of the remanent members of the battalion." These words from Dr. Frew's *Memoir of Capt. A. D. Young-Herries** accurately define the duties of a special reserve battalion in time of war. The purpose of this chapter is to sketch how the task was performed, and who directed its performance.

It so happened that when war broke out the 3rd K.O.S.B. had completed their annual training and undergone their annual inspection at the Kingholm. The troops had gone home on 31st July, but war was in the air, and it only took three days after the declaration to reassemble the officers and men of the battalion and to gather in many more—*e.g.* time-expired men.

On 8th August 1914 the regimental colours were handed to the Provost of Dumfries for safe custody by Major W. D. Young-Herries in the absence of Lieut.-Col. H. W. A. F. Crichton-Browne, the C.O.. Early on the following morning, a Sunday, Lieut.-Col. Crichton-Browne and the battalion, some 800 strong, boarded two trains at Dumfries, bound for a far-off station—Verne Citadel Barracks, on the Isle of Portland, that strange excrescence on the Dorset coast. And there but for a short interval, when the main body of the battalion were hurriedly moved to Sunderland, no doubt owing to some scare of invasion (these were the days when imagination "roved without rein"), the battalion remained in the country and atmosphere of Hardy's *Trumpet Major* for eight months. One company was actually quartered at the Red Barracks in Weymouth (Budmouth Regis).

The C.O. had 30 years' service behind him, which included four years with the Bechuanaland Border Police and three years of the S. African War. Major W. D. Young-Herries, who had joined two years later, was Second-in-Command.

Capt. T. P. Wingate of the 2nd Battalion K.O.S.B. was adjutant, and Hon. Major B. E. Parkinson, who had served in the Sudan in 1888, as well as in Chitral, Tirah, and S. Africa, was quartermaster. During this period the Verne was a hive of activity. As we have seen, if drafts were not out in time for Le Cateau or the long retreat, they were welcomed when the advance began in September, and played their part at the Aisne and in the Race to the Sea. From that moment on the 3rd Battalion never failed to send to the 2nd or 1st Battalions reinforcements up to the level of any sent out by any units. There was no shortage of candidates for commissions, and enthusiastic volunteers of all ages from forty or older to striplings thronged the ante-room and drill-grounds of the Great Fort. The

* William Blackwood & Sons, Ltd., Edinburgh and London, 1928.

grim realities of war were brought home by the deaths of such men as Major W. L. C. Allan, a S. African veteran, and Lieut. Ivor MacRae in the cut-throat combats near La Bassée in October 1914. It has been said again and again that the Expeditionary Force could not have held the field for six months if it had not been for the Special Reserve, and it has been calculated that out of the total number of men raised for the entire British forces, *i.e.* Dominion and Colonial as well as Home forces, the Special Reserve supplied just about a quarter of the whole. At one time the 3rd Battalion K.O.S.B. mustered 4,000 men—*i.e.* in 1916 or 1917. More than 40 officers are labelled 3rd Battalion in the Official Death Roll, and this conceals the names of many who are credited to the line or service battalions. 1914.

No one who has ever witnessed the later stages of the formation of a draft, heard the stirring words of C.O. or G.O.C. district when bidding it godspeed, or seen the final march off to the tune of the pipes, under the command of an officer exuding energy, can ever efface the impression. The 3rd Battalion formed a rallying-ground for regular and ex-regular officers out of employment for the moment. A 1914 group of officers outside the mess-house at Kingholm shows Major H. D. N. Maclean, D.S.O., who afterwards trained and led the 6th Battalion, and Capt. G. Hilton, who had been for some time in the Egyptian Army and fought at Hill 60 and the Somme. Major S. Campbell-Johnston, who commanded the battalion at the end of the war and served in France, was an early arrival at the Verne.

The training in the earlier stages was not of a very ambitious standard. What was wanted in those days was a man who would do and could be depended on to do what he was told. Recruits who reached the Special Reserve needed just as intensive and extended initiation into close-order drill and the drill aspects of moving in extended order as the recruits in the humble 9th Battalion. The difference was that instead of being at the mercy of well-meaning novices in the way of officers, the recruits of the 3rd Battalion were taught by N.C.O.s as smart, as experienced, and as kindly as could be found, who worked them into shape in record time.

Col. Crichton-Browne was favoured with the best of adjutants. Besides the experienced Wingate, there was available an ex-regular, Capt. C. P. J. Ovans, as assistant and understudy, who was a worker of inexhaustible energy, directed into the most orderly channels. In their hands, and, after Capt. Wingate had been killed at Hill 60, when Ovans was adjutant, the machine was *omnium consensu* perfected, and things worked smoothly, with the result that the battalion was well reported on consistently throughout the war.

1915–19. The need for feeding the 1st Battalion as well as the 2nd with reinforcements had just emerged, when the station of the battalion was suddenly changed to Edinburgh. Recruiting may have been an influencing factor in the move. Before June 1915 the 3rd K.O.S.B. encamped in the King's Park, Holyrood, thereafter moved to the Marine Gardens, Portobello, with H.Q. and one company in the hideous chocolate factory just W. of the town. When the winter was over, a fresh move was made to huts erected by themselves (K.O.S.B.) in Duddingston Park. There they remained till November 1917. Thus the representatives of the old Edinburgh Regiment spent a longer spell of service in the Edinburgh than in any other area during the war. The remainder of the war was spent in Ireland, first at Templemore, Tipperary, and then at Claremorris, Mayo, and finally at the Curragh.

In the spring of 1919 the 3rd K.O.S.B. returned to Scotland and ended its active days at Lochend Camp, Dunfermline, by becoming the 2nd Battalion. The last officer of the old Militia to command the 3rd K.O.S.B. was Lieut.-Col. W. D. Young-Herries, a life-long son and friend of the Regiment.

Of the 13 lieutenant-colonels who with 3 brigadier-generals composed a deputation, which waited on Mr. Churchill and the Army Council at the War Office in 1920, to urge the inclusion of the Special Reserve as units in any future reserve force, none had a better right to be proud of the record of his battalion than Col. Crichton-Browne. It is some consolation that the title Militia has been restored, and that if and when the 3rd Battalion K.O.S.B. is re-embodied, it will be a unit of that historic force, possibly liable to take the field as it did so well in 1900. But though it suffered and fought piecemeal in other units of the regiment, or it might sometimes be in a different regiment altogether, and though many of the indispensable officers and N.C.O.s never had a chance of seeking distinction other than a sense of duty done, yet the service rendered in shouldering the burden of coast defence, in feeding the forces at the front with the right stamp, and in helping to build up the New Armies, will stand out as the most signal and solid in the whole 120 years' life of the Scottish Borderers Militia.

CHAPTER III

THE NINTH BATTALION

THE volunteer officers and men who were squeezed out of Bordon after the 8th Battalion was complete, and squeezed into a tight corner of the Verne fondly imagined that they would take the field as a unit in due course. That was certainly the conviction of the late Capt. W. P. Donaldson (the adjutant) till 1915 was well begun. The amputation of large drafts, the first of which was mostly drowned on the way to Gallipoli when the trooper on which it was being conveyed was sunk, to the grief of all, soon brought about the realization that the 9th was to be a reserve battalion and fulfil the same functions with less resources and humbler status than the 3rd Battalion. Its records have been unattainable. Many of those who could have supplied data have passed away, like Capt. Brabazon or like Capt. Rattigan, settled at the opposite ends of the earth. It was the daily round, the common task, in that battalion with a vengeance. Life at the Verne was one long drill, punctuated by lectures, attendance at courts-martial, and meals. The hospitality of the 3rd was unbounded. But perhaps Lieut.-Col. C. J. E. A. M'Arthur preferred the more independent existence, which began on the 1st of February 1915, when the 9th flitted into billets in Dorchester—the Casterbridge of Hardy's Wessex. A more delightful station could hardly be imagined, and Borderers and townsfolk seemed to get on well together. The country round afforded many delightful route marches. The next change was somewhat abrupt—to a bleak hillside above Stobs railway station in the middle of June, where it still occasionally froze at night. Stobs will always be associated with a superfluity of officers and messing under difficulties. Hitherto only two officers had gone to the front, and it was somewhat of a case of the last shall be first. Capt. A. C. Hamilton and Lieut. B. Rooney were, however, the only officers really ready at the time. That was in May 1915. In August the stream began to flow. Two senior lieutenants took a large draft to the M.E.F. about the middle of

1914–18.
—

1914–18. the month, and thereafter the flow was continuous until the appalling losses of the 6th and 7th Battalions, and the very serious ones of the 8th drained the supernumeraries to the last man and reduced the establishment of the 9th to the minimum of officers necessary or suitable for home service. After a time the 9th escaped from Stobs, only to harbour at Catterick Bridge, about which one never heard hymns of praise. Most of the war was in the end spent at Kinghorn in Fife. The 9th had quite a character of its own. Unquestionably Capt. G. A. Lord, the imperturbable and efficient quartermaster, had much to do with the comfort and carrying-on of the Battalion in its early days. No subaltern could grouse or sulk in his presence. Never did he miss a chance of securing a good issue, be it Witney blankets or real ammunition, boots or service rifles. In R.S.M. Williamson and Q.M.S. Souttar, as in C.S.M. A. Paul (late of the Royal Scots) and C.S.M. J. Edgar, the C.O. had A1 helpers, while to mention one specially from personal association, C.Q.M.S. W. H. Shillington was a sure stand-by to a company commander in matters of pay, billeting, and all the minutiæ of military life, so bewildering to civilians first confronted with them. The excellent Shillington was thriving in June 1929, and his portrait is in the *Chronicle* of 30th September 1929.

Naturally, N.C.O.s and senior officers were not an export of the 9th Battalion. Reinforcements and subalterns were its main output, and the most impressive tribute to the 9th is the Official Death Roll. The writer has endeavoured throughout to notice the fallen officers' battalions of origin, *e.g.* in the account given of 1st July 1916. Many who find honourable mention belonged to the 9th, *e.g.* Lieut.-Col. Ker, D.S.O. The brisk little martinet of a C.O. and his colossus of an adjutant have both passed away. The friendly little throng of the Verne and Dorchester is long since broken up. The initiation to a military life seems like a dream. Yet it happened, and the 9th has its share, and no mean one, in the struggle to Victory.

CHAPTER IV

WOMAN'S SHARE

THE longer the strain of war the greater the need for *moral*. Much of the burden of Ludendorff's dirge in the last quarter of his *Erinnerungen* is that the civilians at home were losing heart for the war and infecting the troops at the front. In the British Empire the idea of the possibility of defeat was confined to comparatively few, whose activities and passivities are best left to oblivion. The general spirit was magnificent, and found vent in deeds, not in words. The women of the country found scope for every kind of service. But the two which had the most direct effect on the *moral* of the soldier in the field were the supplying of comforts to the soldiers and attention to his affairs at home. A man will fight the better if he feels that he is more than *Kanonenfutter*, that he is remembered as an individual and a brother. The things that touch himself nearest are his corporeal wants—to be fed and clothed. The army and the canteen saw to these in their broad aspects, but a touch of variety in diet or tobacco and an extra "hap" against "cranreuch cauld" make all the difference to those fleeting situations, when sudden and unwanted comes the summons to extra resolution. Still more touching to the soldier is the thought of those he has left behind him. The absent-minded beggar is the exception rather than the rule. Let him feel that his dependents —to use the phrase most in use—will not be forgotten when he is dead, and he throws himself more whole-heartedly into the strange medley of digging, carrying, marching, training, and eventually going over the top, which, with the short intervals of play and leave, constitute his life. But the helplessness of the ordinary taxpayer when confronted with an income-tax form is nothing to the helplessness of a soldier in the ranks, or his kin, to understand how things stand with regard to pension in the event of his death on service. The former can employ an expert, whose fee is well worth what he saves by submitting claims it never would have entered into his own head to make. The latter has neither time nor money nor opportunity to consult. The exigencies of the life around him exhaust every corner of his mind, and leave him fit for the simplest relaxation only, much as a learned judge may solace his long vacation with a glut of railway novels.

To both these needs the ladies connected with the regiment devoted hours of well-directed work, and attained such a measure of success that competent judges have again and again expressed the opinion that no unit of the British Army was better looked after in the way of comforts and " advice " than the King's Own Scottish Borderers.

CENTRAL COMFORTS FUND

Independent of (financially) but affiliated to the Queen Alexandra's Field Force Fund,the K.O.S.B. Central Comforts Fund was founded under the presidency of Lady Woollcombe, wife of the colonel of the regiment, supported by a very strong committee, representative of the officers of the regiment and the regimental district. Their names are printed in full, for they have associations with the tale that has been told, and in a dozen cases at least with bereavement due to the war. Lady Hamilton-Dalrymple, the mother of Lieut. J. R. Hamilton-Dalrymple, and herself the daughter of a V.C., was Hon. Treasurer, and Lady Woollcombe, along with Mrs. A. Lockhart, acted as joint-secretaries.

Committee

Mrs. Amos.
The Lady Nina Balfour.
Mrs. Becher.
Mrs. A. C. Campbell.
The Viscountess Churchill.
Mrs. E. S. D'E. Coke.
Mrs. Crichton-Browne.
Mrs. Dennis.
Mrs. Furber.
Mrs. D. D. Gunn.
Mrs. A. E. Haig.
Mrs. G. M. Hannay.
Mrs. Francis Hawkins.
Lady Jardine of Applegarth.
Lady Buchanan Jardine.
Mrs. Campbell-Johnston.
Miss I. Law.
Mrs. Chandos Leigh.
Mrs. D. A. Macfarlane.
Mrs. E. A. Marrow (now Mrs. L. F. Machin).
Mrs. R. E. W. Maxwell.
Mrs. W. H. S. McAlester.
Mrs. C. J. E. A. M'Arthur.
Mrs. M'Neile.
Mrs. Eric Macdonald.
Mrs. J. B. W. Pennyman.
Mrs. T. B. Sellar.
Mrs. W. D. Sellar.
Mrs. D. R. Sladen.
Mrs. Harold Stanton.
Mrs. Stephenson.
Mrs. C. Wade.
Mrs. A. J. Welch.
Lady Wilkie Dalyell.
Mrs. Youngson.

Donations in kind and cash poured in. The affiliation mentioned enabled articles to be sent out carriage free, and those bought to be bought at wholesale prices, also enabled a draw to be made on the bonded stores of the Q.A.F.F.F. for tobacco. The writer well remembers the delight caused by a comforts distribution in the last days of Gallipoli. Care was taken to send the right things to the right places and to avoid a glut. This was managed by keeping in touch with the C.O.s of the various units. The Committee, with its London centre, would have been helpless, particularly in the clothing side of the comforts, without the loyal and widespread local support of ladies interested in the regiment. The output of articles was prodigious, the response to appeals for subscriptions generous. All through the war consignment after consignment brought joy and contentment to the trenches. What sort of things did they get? Take the food line! In peace time "glass-lemon," raisins, curry, and lemonade powder and condensed milk excite no gluttonous passion, but it was a very different story in Sinai. Chocolate and sweets generally are no staple of a grown man's diet, but soldiers at the front, like mountaineers, soon found the value of both in times of exertion approaching exhaustion. Christmas pudding, vermicelli, soup squares (so priceless as a relish for bread), cocoa, and café au lait eked out the ordinary ration in a luxurious style that paved the way for the woodbine to follow the coffee, and added a zest to life. On the clothing side the following have only to be mentioned to be appreciated—handkerchiefs, towels (by the thousand), candles, boot-laces, mufflers, helmets, gloves and mittens, socks, soap, tooth- and nail-brushes, shirts, and "semmits" (please excuse Scots!), toilet wallets *et id genus omne*. The reports contain expressions of gratitude and satisfaction from the C.O.s of every battalion—*e.g.* Lieut.-Col. Welch on behalf of the 1st, Lieut.-Col. T. B. Sellar for the 7/8th, Brig.-Gen. E. S. D'Ewes Coke for the 2nd, and Lieut.-Col. R. F. Ker, D.S.O., M.C., for the 6th, who, writing at the end of the war after three years' service in that battalion, said: "I do not think any regiment in the Service can have been better provided for than our own." Owing to the namelessness which pervaded the middle of the war it is difficult to identify the C.O. of the 5th or 4th, but it was the same tale, and the Territorials, having their background in the district, were further blest with special battalion sources of comforts. The men wrote how cheering, what a tonic the presents were, and how it eased the task to feel they were in the thoughts of those at home. Consequently in telling the Committee it could look back with satisfaction from 1919 through the years of war, and in emphasizing the gratitude of the saddest of war's victims—the prisoners—Sir Charles

Woollcombe, K.C.B., was putting in a sentence a definite, proved fact.

And thereby hangs a tale. When it became known that the bulk of C Company, 2nd Battalion, commanded by Capt. Macdonald, had been surrounded and taken prisoner at Le Cateau, Capt. Macdonald's wife lost no time in starting a private organisation for sending parcels of food to the prisoners of war of that battalion. Mrs. Macdonald's scheme held the field till the question was taken up regimentally and officially, and the K.O.S.B. P. of W. Fund instituted. Mrs. Macdonald gave the benefit of her experience by becoming Hon. Secretary, Mr. Arthur Young of Garroch becoming Hon. Treasurer, and quite invaluable in that capacity. This is no place in which to discuss the sufficiency of the dietary or the sanitation of German prisoners' camps. It may safely be asserted, however, that many of the K.O.S.B. prisoners would never have returned to their native land but for the regular supply of nourishing food sent from home.

The main committee was stationed in London, but it was considered advisable to have another kindred organisation operating near the depot, and here again the right people were to hand. Lady Dalyell of the Binns and her daughter Miss Norah Dalyell worked untiringly at Castle Hill, Berwick-on-Tweed (the former as President and the latter as Hon. Secretary), packing and despatching parcels of clothing, almost if not quite as necessary for the health of the prisoners as the food.

The gratitude of the prisoners of war was unbounded. After the armistice a host of small subscriptions poured in on the suggestion of Lieut.-Col. A. E. Haig (who, like Lieut.-Col. Stephenson, had had the misfortune to be wounded and captured at Le Cateau), with the result that Mrs. Macdonald is the possessor of a bowl and Lady Dalyell and Miss Dalyell of a salver each, to remind them that no warmer hearts beat than those of the men who suffered so sadly in their effort to keep these shores inviolate and achieve the ultimate victory.

WIDOWS AND ORPHANS ADVISORY COMMITTEE

Under the presidency of Mrs. T. B. Sellar, a wonderful organization came into being at the end of 1915—*i.e.* after the tragedies of Gallipoli and Loos. At first it was confined to the Line and Service battalions, but in a short time the Territorials followed suit. Each battalion had a secretariat, the 1st having the services of Mrs. A. J. Welch, Mrs. Koe, and Mrs. M. A. N. Becher; the 2nd, those of Mrs. J. B. Pennyman; the 6th, Mrs. R. E. W. Maxwell and

Mrs. A. C. Campbell; the 7th, Mrs. Frederick Dennis; and the 8th, Mrs. H. P. Hart. When the 10th (Labour) Battalion was formed, Mrs. Hogg was its secretary. For the 4th, Mrs. R. R. M. Lumgair acted, and for the 5th Mrs. Scott Elliot, wife of the gallant and learned historian of that unit. Not a soldier's name there that cannot be found in the preceding books of this history.

Mrs. Sellar's mastery of the system under which pensions are granted was the mainspring of the activities which extended over the whole field of K.O.S.B. recruitment. The task essayed was of a boldness to stagger more than the faint-hearted—namely, to communicate, after the death of any and every soldier at the front, with his relatives at his last known address, express sympathy, and offer help other than pecuniary aid. Advice as to pensions was specially mentioned, and perhaps the best idea of the activities of the Advisory Committee will be to give a few results. In 1928 no fewer than 88 pensions were obtained for dependents, who would probably have otherwise languished in poverty cursing the country's ingratitude. In 1916 three pensions lost through intemperance were restored on re-establishment of character. In 1916 a decent, respectable mother, very nearly blind, obtained a pension of 3s. 6d. In another instance a mother who had lost three sons in the war and still had one son left at the front had her pension raised from 5s. to 15s., with arrears of £29. The arena for inquiry was enormously extended early in the war by inclusion to pension rights of wives "off the strength," and a little later of "parents wholly or partially supported." As can well be imagined, if completeness were to be attained—and it *was*—official information had to be at the disposal of the Advisory Committee. It was made forthcoming, thanks to an intelligently exercised discretion of the authorities and a patriotic devotion of hard-worked subordinates to the cause. Only by a perusal of the reports can the magnitude of the work and the huge number of cases be realized.

But it must not be imagined that clearing up the pension mess was all that the Advisory Committee accomplished. Tracing lost kit, securing medical advice, obtaining grants from various funds, tracing details of death, rectifying separation allowances, generally looking after the welfare of the widows and orphans, and also of the parents as they grew old and became unable to earn even a partial livelihood. Inquiries revealed an amount of child sickness that was distressing. The reports for 1917, 1918, and 1925 (for the Advisory Committee long survived the war) speak of the efforts made by and through the Advisory Committee to secure treatment and convalescent homes for invalids of all kinds—phthisis, anæmia, paralysis, collitis. These were under the special charge of Mrs. Amos, and the report for 1919 shows 41 cases where something was done—*e.g.* out of the 3rd Battalion grant, ever open to deserving cases, to alleviate suffering and promote cure. In no activity connected with the regiment was *esprit de corps* more *en évidence* than in the work of the ladies connected with the regiment, and their friends and helpers.

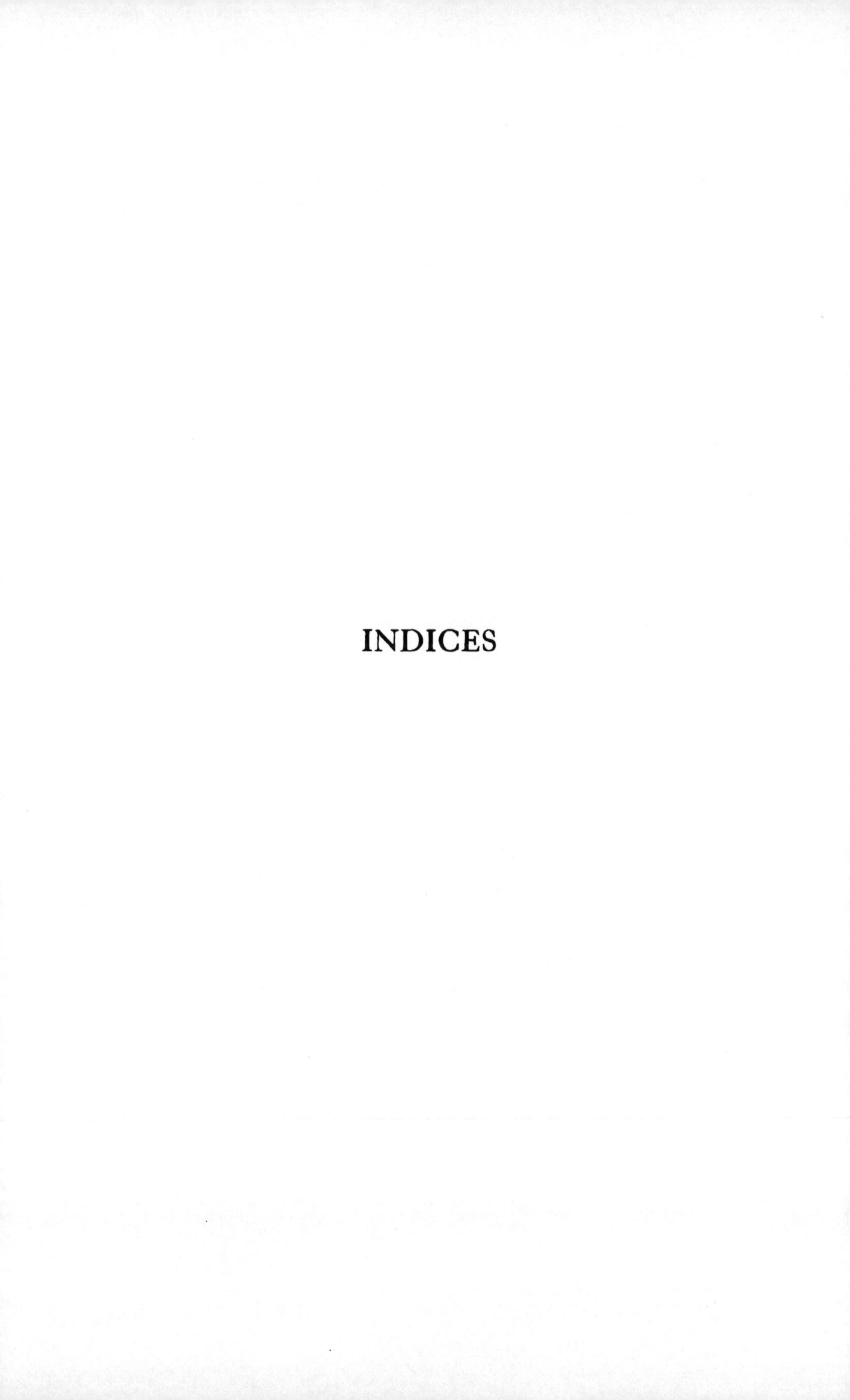

INDICES

NAMES OF PERSONS

* *Official Death Roll*, "k. in a. 2/10/18." This does not appear in the text.

* This initial H. is given as K. in the text by mistake. H. stands for Henry (*Official Death Roll*).

NAMES OF PLACES AND GENERAL INDEX

INDEX TO ARMIES AND LESSER UNITS

(The dates refer to incidents or references in this book.)

PRINTED IN GREAT BRITAIN AT
THE PRESS OF THE PUBLISHERS

Printed in Great Britain
by Amazon.co.uk, Ltd.,
Marston Gate.